Rethinking Corporate Crime

Law in Context

Below is a listing of the more recent publications in the Law in Context Series

Editors: William Twining (University College, London) and
Christopher McCrudden (Lincoln College, Oxford)

Rethinking Corporate Crime

James Gobert
Professor of Law, University of Essex

Maurice Punch
Visiting Professor, Mannhiem Centre, London School of Economics

Butterworths
LexisNexis™

Members of the LexisNexis Group worldwide

United Kingdom	LexisNexis Butterworths Tolley, a Division of Reed Elsevier (UK) Ltd, Halsbury House, 35 Chancery Lane, LONDON, WC2A 1EL, and 4 Hill Street, EDINBURGH EH2 3JZ
Argentina	LexisNexis Argentina, BUENOS AIRES
Australia	LexisNexis Butterworths, CHATSWOOD, New South Wales
Austria	LexisNexis Verlag ARD Orac GmbH & Co KG, VIENNA
Canada	LexisNexis Butterworths, MARKHAM, Ontario
Chile	LexisNexis Chile Ltda, SANTIAGO DE CHILE
Czech Republic	Nakladatelstvi Orac sro, PRAGUE
France	Editions du Juris-Classeur SA, PARIS
Hong Kong	LexisNexis Butterworths, HONG KONG
Hungary	HVG-Orac, BUDAPEST
India	LexisNexis Butterworths, NEW DELHI
Ireland	Butterworths (Ireland) Ltd, DUBLIN
Italy	Giuffrè Editore, MILAN
Malaysia	Malayan Law Journal Sdn Bhd, KUALA LUMPUR
New Zealand	LexisNexis Butterworths, WELLINGTON
Poland	Wydawnictwo Prawnicze LexisNexis, WARSAW
Singapore	LexisNexis Butterworths, SINGAPORE
South Africa	Butterworths SA, DURBAN
Switzerland	Stämpfli Verlag AG, BERNE
USA	LexisNexis, DAYTON, Ohio

A CIP Catalogue record for this book is available from the British Library.

ISBN 0 406 95006 7

Typeset by Doyle & Co, Colchester

Printed and bound by Bookcraft (Bath), Midsomer Norton

Visit Butterworths LexisNexis *direct* at www.butterworths.com

Preface

In *The Devil's Dictionary* (1911), Ambrose Bierce defined a corporation as 'an ingenious device for obtaining individual profit without individual responsibility'. Never has Bierce's wit had more bite, or seemed more apt, than it does today. In transport, technology, pharmaceuticals, financial services and other sectors of the economy, one can find examples of transgressions by companies that have resulted in considerable loss and harm. Bhopal, BCCI, *Herald of Free Enterprise*, Thalidomide and the Ford Pinto have virtually entered the lexicon as synonyms for corporate malfeasance. In the United Kingdom, in the past several years, there have been major train crashes at Southall, Ladbroke Grove, Hatfield and Potters Bar. Despite the damage, the injuries and the loss of life in each of these tragedies, and despite evidence of arguably gross negligence on the part of the relevant company, obtaining a criminal conviction has proved highly elusive. In the financial sector, the City of London has been shaken by an embarrassing number of scandals over the past few decades, including Guinness and Barings; and, more recently, revelations of major corporate fraud in the United States have shown that the deviant practices can extend to the highest levels of the corporation. These new cases have drawn intense media attention and have prompted a spate of legal actions against such well-known companies as Enron, Tyco, Arthur Andersen and Xerox. Combined with previous studies documented in the standard literature, these cases have revived interest in the nature of corporate crime and what can be done to prevent its occurrence.

Ever since Edwin Sutherland coined the phrase 'white-collar crime' over a half century ago, by which term he clearly meant to include corporate crimes, there has been research, public inquiries, lawsuits and media attention on deviance and law-breaking in the corporate world. An ever-mounting body of evidence indicates that companies often deliberately and, sometimes repeatedly, flout the law; that the consequences can be extremely grave (both financially and in terms of loss of life and limb); and that, if caught, the likelihood of a prosecution is remote, the prospects for a conviction, if there is a prosecution, are not promising and the sanctions following the infrequent conviction can be derisory. Nor does the public seem overly bothered. The public's views on most forms of corporate crime stand in stark contrast to their views on 'street' crime, the type of ordinary crimes that tend to form the grist for political debates and media scare stories. Yet, on almost every measure, the effects of corporate crimes are more harmful, more costly, more extensive and more debilitating than those which follow from street crime.

Are crimes that occur in a business context attributable to individuals or organisations? We believe that where a company's goals, systems, ethos or culture contribute to, tolerate or encourage law-breaking, the company should be subject to legal accountability. Corporate criminality inheres in the culpable failure to prevent crimes that could have been averted had the company paid proper attention to, and better managed, risk. But why are successful prosecutions of companies so rare? Does the problem lie at the investigatory stage of the proceedings, or at the trial stage? Does it lie in flawed criminal doctrines, or in procedural and evidentiary rules that are ill-suited to corporate defendants? Is it our understanding of the dynamics and pressures of business and the market place that is deficient? If corporate crime is as widespread – or even endemic – as some critics would have us believe, if the government is less than fully committed to combating it, if the law is not up to the task, and if the public is not much exercised (save for the occasional high-profile disaster), does it follow that large and powerful companies are effectively beyond legal control?

In this study, we, a lawyer and a sociologist-criminologist, have combined our background, experiences and perspectives to take a fresh, inter-disciplinary look at corporate crime. While the landscape for our study is potentially vast (and would include commercial crimes, antitrust and cartel-formation, fraud, environmental offences, occupational health and safety violations, and those activities of 'organised crime' that interlock with corporate crime), we have chosen to give particular emphasis to crimes involving 'corporate violence'. This is both because they reveal the critical role of improper risk management and its potentially disastrous effects, and because these cases have proved peculiarly resistant to legal control. One might well ask why the legal mind has so much trouble perceiving that a company can be guilty of causing death? Why has it proved so difficult in the United Kingdom to convict a company of manslaughter?

At one point, there appeared to be a groundswell for reforming the law in this area. In 1996, the Law Commission recommended a new offence of 'corporate killing', and, in 2000, the Labour government embraced this recommendation in a consultation paper on 'involuntary manslaughter' (Home Office: 2000). Hopes for reform ran high; but in the Queen's speech at the opening of Parliament in November 2002, it soon became clear that, more than six years after the Law Commission had first proposed changing the law, there would be no new legislation in this session of Parliament. Were the legal issues that complex? Was the problem simply the legal profession's traditional resistance to change? Or was the road to reform sabotaged by the political clout of 'big business'? Perhaps the government was led to see the potentially adverse repercussions for the nation's economy – and its own political future – if multinational enterprises were to move their headquarters to a more corporate-friendly environment. Whatever the explanation, the effect is that the difficulties of prosecuting a company in England and Wales for causing death are not going to disappear in the foreseeable future.

In this book we will examine not only issues raised by cases of corporate violence, but also by other forms of corporate misconduct. We plan to draw on law, social science, criminology and management studies, to the extent that they shed light on our analysis. We will also look to the laws and practices of other jurisdictions when that would be helpful, and will try to illustrate our points with real-life examples from well-documented cases. Our goal is to make the topic of corporate crime accessible and comprehensible, not just to lawyers and academicians, but to all persons who find the subject intriguing and who recognise its relevance in contemporary society. We would hope that our efforts will prove of value to legal practitioners, to judges, to legislative and other policymakers, to enforcers and regulators, to professionals in compliance and legal departments of companies, and, of course, to the senior managers of corporate United Kingdom.

Given the rapidly unfolding developments in this field, it might seem that any analysis of corporate crime will be hostage to the next scandal or disaster. We would not disagree, but have tried to surmount the problem by concentrating on developing a *framework* for understanding and analysing corporate wrongdoing. We have entitled our book 'Rethinking Corporate Crime' because we plan to take a fresh look at the topic and offer some, hopefully, innovative solutions to long-standing problems. We begin by examining the causes of corporate crime, looking beyond the conventional view that attributes corporate offences primarily to a desire to enhance profits. This entails looking closely at the organisational and managerial context in which corporate misconduct takes place, and the range of variables that may contribute to decisions, or the failure to take decisions, which lead to criminal offences. We will examine the role of 'criminogenic' environments, systemic failures and ineffective supervision; and shall see how a corporate 'culture' or ethos can contribute to, support and even encourage illegality. In respect to the law, we will critically assess traditional tests which impute liability to companies based on crimes committed by individuals, but will also try to develop a theory of 'organisational fault' that, in our opinion, better captures the essence of corporate criminality. More controversially, we will explore the case for defining corporate crimes without regard to results. We intend also to re-examine evidentiary and procedural rules that seem somehow inappropriate when a company rather than a natural person is in the dock; and we will propose a range of more meaningful sanctions that might be imposed when corporations are convicted of serious offences. Finally, we will scrutinise the problem of 'policing' companies, and explore the feasibility of collective and individual self-regulation, which we believe may offer a more effective approach to corporate crime-prevention than that pursued by traditional regulatory agencies.

The list of individuals who have commented on all or parts of this manuscript is extensive, but would include David Bergman, Michael Clarke, Neil Cohen, Janet Dine, Geoff Gilbert, Carolyn Hamilton, Sheldon Leader, Michael Levi, Vittorio Manes, Sabine Michalowski, Peter Muchlinski and Sir Nigel Rodley. Several of these individuals were also kind enough to provide us with unpublished articles and works in progress, as well as suggestions for further lines of inquiry. To all of these persons, and to others whom we may have inadvertently overlooked, we are indebted. We, of course, bear full responsibility for whatever defects, mistakes and errors remain. Maurice Punch would like to thank Corry, Julio, Maria and George for their support during the writing of this work; and he would like to express his appreciation to his colleagues in RBC Network (Nic van Dijk, Veronique van der Heijden, Tineke Melis, Johan Heilbron and Geert de Vries) for their valuable insights arising from researching issues of 'corporate governance' within the financial services industry. Similarly, James Gobert benefited greatly from discussion with his colleagues in the 'Starship Enterprise' project (Steve Anderman, Janet Dine, Sheldon Leader, David Ong and Bob Watt) on the topic of 'corporate governance' and would also wish to acknowledge their unstinting support. The invaluable research assistance of Emilia

Mugnai was far more than any academic has a right to ask for or expect. Finally, James Gobert is most grateful to the University of Essex and its law department for providing him with research leave to work on this project, and to the Arts and Humanities Research Board for a grant under its Research Leave Scheme, which enabled this book to be brought to fruition.

James Gobert
Maurice Punch
February 2003

Contents

Table of statutes

References in bold indicate the page at which the text of listed provision is set out in part or in full.

List of cases

CHAPTER I

Understanding the nature and causes of corporate crime

A.   WHITE-COLLAR AND CORPORATE CRIME

Corporations break the law; and they get away with it. This was the fundamental insight of Edwin Sutherland (1949), who coined the term 'white-collar crime', over sixty years ago. Whereas criminologists prior to Sutherland had tended to concentrate on young, disadvantaged males as the main perpetrators of crime – and, indeed, continue to do so (Maguire: 1997) – Sutherland recognised that there were well-educated, socially successful business executives in legitimate companies who also broke the law. In the 'Introduction' to their 'White-collar Crime' (1983: ix), Geis and Goff wrote of Sutherland that he:

> ... documented in detail derelictions by corporations, concluding that their 'rap sheets' resembled, at least in length and frequency, those of many professional predators, such as con men and bank robbers, persons who by choice prey upon the public. He focused on such

representative corporate offences as antitrust violations, false advertising, theft of trade secrets and bribery.

Unlike their juvenile and adult counterparts, however, corporate executives and senior managers routinely escaped prosecution and sanction (in particular custodial sanctions) for their offences. Furthermore, they generally did not see themselves as criminals, even when they were consciously aware that they were violating the criminal law.

Although Sutherland referred to 'white-collar criminals', a term which implies individual offenders, he clearly intended to include corporations within this category of offenders:

> Corporations have committed crimes.... These crimes are not discrete and inadvertent violations of technical regulations. They are deliberate and have a consistent unity.... the criminality of the corporations, like that of professional thieves, is persistent: a large proportion of the offenders are *recidivists* (Sutherland:1983: 227; emphasis added).

Similarly, when Braithwaite (1985), the leading modern scholar in the field, later wrote an overview article on white-collar crime, he too soon slipped from individual offences into highlighting corporate wrongdoing.

In essence, the study of corporate crime focuses on individual, collective and organisational wrongdoing in a business setting. The path then leads to an examination of the criminal law in this area, and how it applies and should apply to organisational entities, and on the 'policing' of companies through regulation, investigation, prosecution and sanctioning. (Tonry & Reiss: 1993; Slapper & Tombs: 1999; Shover & Wright: 2001).

Sutherland's lapidary insights continue to underpin much of the research in this area. What has changed significantly since Sutherland's time, however, is society's appreciation of the seriousness and urgency of the problem. Scholars, politicians, policy makers, enlightened managers, NGOs, action groups, the media and concerned segments of the public have become increasingly aware of the power of business and industry and their ability to inflict harm – and often catastrophic harm – on society. In transport, technology, financial services, pharmaceuticals, environmental and waste industries, medical care, the food chain and in other sectors of the economy there have been widely-publicised examples of significant law-breaking leading to considerable loss and injury (including deaths). In Britain, for instance, the *Herald of Free Enterprise*, *Piper Alpha*, the *Marchioness* and the Bristol Royal Infirmary have become virtually synonymous with institutional failures leading to widespread death while the Clapham, Southall, Paddington, Hatfield and Potters Bar crashes are all well-documented rail 'disasters'. Yet in the wake of virtually all of these tragedies lies a trail of failed, or never attempted, prosecutions. In the corporate crime arena, then, one finds not only an increasing awareness of the financial, human and social costs of corporate wrongdoing but also a growing appreciation of the difficulties associated with holding companies legally accountable for their wrongs.

In an age of global capitalism, cybercash, e-commerce and a rapidly shifting industrial infrastructure (with some traditional high-risk technologies being exported to developing countries), there arise new patterns and fresh opportunities for crime amid a backdrop of patchy and inadequate local, national and international controls. On virtually all economic indicators, and on many non-economic indicators as well, corporate crimes can be held to be more damaging to society than so-called 'common' crimes (understood in terms of those crimes recognised in the British Crime Survey or the FBI's Uniform Crime Reports – such as mugging, burglary, car theft and aggravated assault; Maguire 1997: 154). Yet obtaining criminal convictions against both company directors and corporations has proved elusive. Why should this be so?

Part of the problem can be attributed to the inadequacies of the law but the inadequacy of the law may itself reflect our limited understanding of the nature of corporate deviance. Sociologists have explored the causes of corporate crime, but typically their efforts go no further than analysis. Left untranslated into something that has either organisational or legal significance, their insights are unlikely to affect corporate practices. Economists too have addressed themselves to the problem of corporate wrongdoing but they tend to have little sensitivity for the human, cultural and structural causes of corporate crimes. Their market-driven models would limit the role of the State to that of a tardy night watchman. But such a role, while perhaps facilitative of economic growth (but perhaps not), is insufficient to meet society's need for protection from harm.

B.   AN OVERVIEW OF THE LITERATURE

In the past the bulk of the criminological research on corporate crime has been North American in origin, with a small but growing number of contributions from Britain and Australia (and with some recent non-English publications from other countries; eg in the Netherlands, Huisman and Niemeijer: 1998; Huisman: 2001). Sutherland, as noted previously, was the first leading North American academic to draw attention to this area. His groundbreaking speech to the American Sociological Association in 1939 can still be read today with little amendment as a forceful invitation to focus on the crimes of the business world (Sutherland: 1940).

I.   The formative years

Sutherland followed up his speech with published research which examined 70 large corporations and 15 public utilities, and detailed their persistent and illegal practices (the uncut version had to wait nearly 25 years for publication because of legal reticence in naming companies in the first edition; Sutherland: 1949; 1983). He documented that executives acting on behalf of corporations deliberately broke the law, frequently escaping prosecution and sanction, and that those who were exposed for illegal violations rarely suffered the stigma attached to ordinary criminals. He also found that many major companies, some with household names and seemingly of good repute, were frequent and repeat offenders ('recidivists'), and that their criminality could be seen over and over again in 'reports of investigations of land offices, railways, insurance, munitions, banking, public utilities, stock exchanges, the petroleum industry, the real estate industry, receiverships, bankruptcies, and politics' (Sutherland: 1983: 8). Many of these corporate 'offences', however, fell outside the strict contours of the criminal law and were dealt with under regulatory, administrative and civil law provisions. This meant that corporations often escaped the full weight of the criminal law, as well as criminal sanctions and the usual stigma attached to a criminal conviction.

Drawing an analogy with 'benefit of clergy' in the Middle Ages, Sutherland concluded that large corporations received relative immunity from the criminal law by virtue of 'benefit of business' (ibid: 57). Dominating his analysis was a strong sense of injustice that the poor were pursued and punished while wealthy, trusted and respected businessmen – employed by reputable companies – could exploit their privileged positions, status and power to escape the full force of the law (Friedrichs: 1996).

Sutherland had carved out a new terrain for sociological and criminological research, but few took up his challenge to probe the crimes of the powerful. (Exceptions included Hartung: 1950; Clinard: 1952; and Cressey: 1953.) In 1967 Geis published a study of the 'Heavy Electrical Equipment Anti-Trust Cases of 1961' (1967). In these cases, where respectable business executives had conspired to fix prices in their industry, the executives claimed that their offences were committed 'for the company', and that they did not personally profit directly from them. Psychologically, they perceived their behaviour as a 'normal' way of conducting business, and, as a result, were devastated when they were treated like 'ordinary' criminals. Geis's findings were to be replicated in the white-collar crime research that was to follow: corporate executives committed offences 'for the good of their company' and, while their conduct was clearly illegal, it was somehow 'clean-hands' crime conducted in a rational, controlled manner to sustain business operations and profitability. At most, the executives may have been prepared to concede that their actions were illegal, but 'victimless'. While the case studies characterised the executives as amoral calculators – 'economic man' rationally deciding to break the law in response to the fluctuations of the business cycle – the offenders themselves insisted that, because they had not personally benefited and no one was 'harmed', they had done nothing 'criminal'. In this way could they reconcile their actions with their conscience, and emerge with no moral perception of having done anything 'wrong'.

After almost thirty years of little attention to the field, apart from a handful of stalwarts such as Geis, a major impetus was given to the field of 'organisational' crime by the Watergate scandals of the early nineteen seventies. These scandals not only exposed deviance in the highest levels of government (with President Nixon eventually being forced to resign) but also revealed widespread covert and illegal contributions from major corporations to Nixon`s re-election campaign. There followed a period of critical scrutiny of big business in America, with Senator Church's Sub-Committee on Multinationals focusing on the political machinations of American multinationals abroad, including their extensive use of bribery in dealing with foreign officials. (Reisman: 1979: Katz: 1980).

Legislative investigations in turn stimulated greater academic attention to the 'crimes of the powerful' (Krisberg: 1975; Pearce: 1976; Quinney: 1977), with studies of political deviance finding common ground with those of corporate deviance. (Ermann and Lundman: 1978; Johnson and Douglas: 1978; Geis and Stotland: 1980). Many of these mostly American texts, however, turned out to be little more than wide-ranging collections of essays designed for teaching in undergraduate and graduate programmes, probably within a general course on crime. (See Ermann and Lundman: 1996, who have added articles on the Holocaust, the My Lai massacre in Vietnam, and the police beating of Rodney King in Los Angeles to their previous material of 1978 and 1982.) They tended to lack internal coherence while ignoring the problem of corporate crime in other societies, despite the fact that corporate crime was increasingly being recognised as a global phenomenon.

Among the 'survey' studies of corporate crime, perhaps the most ambitious was that of Clinard and Yeager (1980; see also Reiss and Bidermann: 1980), who examined the records of over 500 corporations during a period of two years in relation to violations brought by 24 federal agencies. Based on successful prosecutions only, they established that over 1,500 offences had been proved, that 371 firms had at least one violation and that many of the offenders were 'recidivists'. They also found that often cases proved difficult to investigate and prosecute (Clinard and Yeager: 1980: 6). Their conclusions echoed those of Sutherland before them and served as a powerful reminder of his legacy. Many large American companies broke the law, and did so consciously and at the highest levels of corporate governance, with extremely favourable chances of escaping criminal sanctions. Unfortunately, the data on which Clinard and Yeager based their analysis were collected in the mid-1970s (1975 and 1976) and are now very much out of date. It is unfortunate that no researcher has repeated this type of survey more recently, particularly given the improvement in techniques of data recording, retrieval and analysis.

One can also find quality and depth in a number of published papers first presented at academic symposia (eg, Tonry and Reiss: 1993; Pearce and Snider: 1995). However, almost by definition such disparate collections are apt to be fragmented and diverse. There are also many detailed case studies, particularly with respect to financial and environmental offences committed by companies, but the conceptual analysis in these studies is often thin. Some case studies, written by well-informed, investigative journalists, have proved valuable not only as secondary sources but also in furthering the development of the law. In England and Wales, for example, the probe by the Insight Team of *The Sunday Times* chronicled the background and consequences of the thalidomide scandal (Knightley et al: 1980) and led to Parliament's reform of the law as it related to civil liability for injuries incurred before birth.[1] Unfortunately, because such studies are so case-specific, they have had only marginal effect on the overall development of the law of corporate crime. Many of these studies are now also dated.

The British were slow to take up the challenge of corporate criminality and the academic output has significantly lagged behind that produced by their counterparts in America. Box's early voice in the wilderness – with his indictment of crimes of the powerful exacting more 'physical, economic, political, social and human suffering' than street crimes (1983: 25) – was well-received but generated little in the way of follow-up research. When academics later turned their attention to business crime, they were attracted by the scandals in the City of London to focus on fraud and other financial offences (Levi: 1987 and 2001: Clarke: 1990). More recently, Wells (2001) and Bergman (2000) have helped to shift the focus to 'corporate violence'. Corporate regulation has also come under scrutiny, with the Oxford Centre for Socio-Legal Studies playing a leading role with a range of empirically based case-studies of regulation in action (Hawkins: 1984; Baldwin: 1985; McBarnet and Whelan: 1999). The British pioneer in this area was Carson (1970; 1980), with his research into the enforcement of factory legislation and the functioning of the early Factory Acts. His subsequent work on the North Sea oil and gas industry demonstrated how production pressures can lead to a neglect of safety (with resulting high casualty rates compared to other industries) and how the government's desire to exploit an industry

---

1   See Congenital Disabilities (Civil Liability) Act 1976.

for its own economic benefit can contribute to a culture that is tolerant of regulatory violations (Carson: 1982). Carson's insightful research highlighted the role of the State in corporate deviance and showed how a government could become, whether consciously or inadvertently, a silent witness to, or even an active abettor of, corporate crimes.

In Australia, most of the research initiatives can be traced to John Braithwaite. Working with several different collaborators in Australia as well as in the United States and Britain, Braithwaite has produced both case-studies and theoretical treatises on corporate crime and the dilemmas of regulation. His groundbreaking ideas on shaming and reintegration (1989), particularly as they might apply to convicted corporate executives and companies, have generated considerable debate and discussion in the academic community (see, eg, Levi: 2002). Among academics, Braithwaite is especially noteworthy for the fact that he has himself held posts in several regulatory agencies that have allowed him to put his theories into practice. The application of these theories to companies and corporate executives challenge basic assumptions as to how best to tackle the problem of corporate deviance.

The heavy Anglo-Saxon imbalance in the literature should not be taken to suggest that corporate crimes do not occur in other parts of the world. In countries with no tradition of legal or criminological scholarship, no expertise in investigative reporting, little in the way of government auditing, and perhaps widespread corruption, a great deal is simply not reported or known. Potentially valuable studies may be published in a foreign language, rendering them largely inaccessible to outsiders. In recent years some insight into corporate criminality in the wider world has been provided courtesy of various non-governmental organisations (NGOs) such as Greenpeace, Amnesty International, and Transparency International. Their reports, along with those of the United Nations, have drawn attention to corruption and human rights abuses committed by companies operating abroad, such as Shell in Nigeria (Amnesty International: 1996). On the other hand, relatively little attention has been paid to the relationship between organised crime and legitimate business (but see Ruggiero: 1996) although it is plain that the vast profits from some sectors of organised crime, particularly but not exclusively from drugs, have led to the penetration of the financial services industry by 'dirty' money that needs to be 'laundered' (Savona: 1999). Too often scholars have artificially separated corporate crime from organised crime.

2. New directions in research

It is curious and surprising, given the considerable harm that corporate crime can cause to employees, markets, governments, the environment and the public, that the field has not attracted the same measure of academic interest as other more 'standard' areas of Criminology, Sociology, Socio-legal studies and Law. But recently there have been some major developments that are changing the picture.

One such development is the recognition of a category of offence that might be referred to as 'corporate violence' (Mokhiber: 1988). Starting with the Ford Pinto case in the United States, when defects in the placement of a petrol tank on Pinto cars led to fatal explosions following rear-end collisions and eventually to the prosecution of the company for homicide, there has been an increasing acceptance that companies might be and arguably should be criminally liable for clearly avoidable deaths (Punch: 2000). In the UK the topic of corporate violence has been thrown into the spotlight by a series of what at first were deemed tragic 'accidents', including the *Piper Alpha* explosion, the Clapham train crash, the Hillsborough Stadium disaster, the King's Cross fire, the collision between the *Marchioness* and the *Bowbelle* on the Thames, and the capsize of the *Herald of Free Enterprise* at Zeebrugge. Subsequent inquiries, however, revealed that the deaths that had occurred in these cases were attributable to corporate malfeasance more than to the unlawful actions of individuals. In the past decade, a number of train crashes at Southall, Paddington, Hatfield and Potters Bar each resulted in multiple fatalities. Failed prosecutions, as well as the failure to bring prosecutions, underlined the legal difficulties in prosecuting a company for manslaughter under conventional criminal law doctrines and spurred the search for new and more imaginative approaches to the problem of 'corporate killing' (Gobert: 1994b; Bergman: 2000; Wells: 2001).

Drawing on Marx and others in an attempt to place corporate violence within the political context of a capitalist society, Slapper and Tombs (1999) offer a synthesis of many of these developments. Based on an examination of deaths and injuries in the workplace, the authors conclude that the workplace can be a highly dangerous place for certain groups, that there is a class and gender bias leading to differential victimisation, that competition and cost-cutting can lead to the neglect of safety, and that, far more than is warranted, the criminal justice system fails to take this form of violence seriously in terms of investigation, prosecution and sanctioning. A company whose flawed or defective systems result in the death of workers will probably escape prosecution, but if prosecuted and convicted, is likely to receive a fine that bears scant relation to the gravity of the harm that has occurred. The analysis of Slapper and Tombs leads them to the conclusion that corporate crime is intrinsically related to the 'structural necessities' of corporate capitalism, the primacy of free markets, competition, profit maximisation and managerial authority. In their view companies are 'inherently criminogenic' and 'there are good reasons for accepting that criminality is endemic in business activity within corporate capitalism' (Slapper and Tombs: 1999: 155). Their self-professed 'partisan scholarship' is reminiscent of the moral tone in some of Sutherland's work. While many might not accept all of their suppositions or conclusions, Slapper and Tombs make a valuable contribution to the literature by placing corporate crime within the broader context of economy and politics.

A further dimension of the corporate crime problem was revealed by the accounting frauds in the Enron, Arthur Andersen and WorldCom scandals that were widely reported in the summer of 2002. These cases demonstrated the previously barely conceivable extent of damage to economic and financial interests that could be wrought by corporate fraud. In these cases the life savings and pensions of thousands of innocent employees were destroyed by attempts to conceal the true financial state of the companies involved. What is also interesting about these scandals is the outpouring of political condemnation and the rapid introduction of new legislation that these cases generated. One might compare this rapid response to the lack of urgency demonstrated by the British government in enacting into law a 'corporate killing' offence, first proposed by the Law Commission in 1996, then incorporated into a government consultation paper in

2000, and still, as of February 2003, yet to be included in the Queen's speech. While some might suggest that the response to the financial scandals confirms the Marxist view that economic interests are taken more seriously in capitalist societies than injuries and deaths to workers (a juxtaposition of the normal position in the criminal law where harm to persons is judged to be more serious than harm to property), it may have been the extent rather than the type of damage that was so shocking. Also, the involvement of well-respected corporations, as opposed to 'cowboy' outfits, suggested that no companies were above suspicion and that financial reports issued by even the most highly regarded accounting firms were not to be trusted. But 'trust' is essential to a laissez faire capitalist economy and the downward ripple effects on the American and world stock markets that followed in the wake of these scandals were perhaps inevitable.

Another dimension of corporate fraud that had previously come to light in the Savings and Loan scandals (Calavita and Pontell: 1991 and 1993; Rosoff, Pontell and Tillman: 1998) was the predatory behaviour of some executives who appeared to have set out to plunder their own company (on occasion in collusion with organised crime). There was also an echo in England, where Robert Maxwell raided his companies' pension funds before his death (Greenslade: 1992). In all of these cases, the company itself was the victim of greedy and rapacious owners. If you wanted to rob a bank, it was remarked, it was best to own it (Calavita and Pontell: 1990: 321).

These Anglo-American developments have served not only to demolish the 'victimless crime' image of corporate and white-collar crime, but have also revealed the extent of physical and financial damage that can be perpetrated by companies which encourage, tolerate or engage in illegality. Also exposed as myth has been the stereotype of the white-collar criminal who commits offences for the good of the company (Katz: 1988). It is now clear that not even their own companies are immune from the ravages of corporate executives. And there have definitely been victims – some deprived of their life savings and some of their lives – and an increasing consciousness of harm in contemporary accounts of corporate crime.

3. What have we learned?

Many insights can be gleaned from these accumulated studies of corporate criminality. One obvious reality is that companies are clearly powerful entities, individually and collectively, with substantial financial, legal, political and social clout. In Britain companies employ millions of people, represent billions of pounds of wealth, and contribute enormously to the national economy, not least by the taxes which they pay. While the good 'corporate citizens' may invest substantially in the communities where they are located and visibly support the arts, sport, charities and other good causes, at the other end of the spectrum can be found companies which repeatedly seem to cause property damage, financial loss, serious physical injury and death.

A second insight is that the range of offences committed by companies is much wider than may have previously been imagined. A modern list of corporate offences would include price-fixing, stock market manipulation, insider trading, anti-competitive market manipulations, the formation of illegal cartels, the manufacture of highly dangerous products, the pollution of the environment, transgressions of health and safety rules in the workplace (often leading to death and serious injury), false or misleading advertising, consumer fraud, racial and gender discrimination and other related employment offences, bribery, fiscal offences and industrial espionage. That companies can commit homicide has ceased to be a matter of debate.

The cost of corporate crime is also much greater than previously imagined. Whereas the costs of 'common' crime are put at somewhere between £30-50bn per annum in the UK (including the costs of operating the criminal justice system), the costs of corporate crime have been estimated as 10-35 times higher (Taylor: 1997; Slapper and Tombs: 1999: 67). Of course, these estimates are extremely speculative, as it is difficult to know the full extent of corporate wrongdoing. There are probably far more unreported corporate crimes than unreported common crimes, both because it is less obvious when one has been a victim of a corporate crime and because workers who have been victimised may have strong social and economic reasons for not going to the police. Surveys of companies reveal that they too believe themselves to have been a victim of crimes which they did not report (Johnston: 1992; Ernst & Young: 2000).[2]

Fourth, whereas formerly some commentators drew a qualitative distinction in the type of harm caused by a corporate crime compared to the suffering and trauma of victims of, say, a violent physical or sexual assault, it is now increasingly recognised that companies too can cause considerable pain and suffering, serious injury and even death (Punch: 2000; Bergman: 2000). Awareness of the truth of this proposition has gained strength during the last decade not only in the academic community but also among the general public as well. The public outcry that followed the capsize of the *Herald of Free Enterprise* at Zeebrugge, with the loss of nearly 200 lives, coupled with the government's subsequent failure to secure convictions against the company and its directors, triggered calls for new and tougher legislation. The Law Commission responded by drafting recommendations that included an offence of 'corporate killing'.[3] Four years later, the Labour government, stung by the Southall and Paddington rail crashes, issued a consultation paper containing, as its centrepiece, a modified version of the Commission's draft Bill.[4]

Studies of corporate crime have also revealed how small a role traditional criminal laws play in controlling corporate illegality. Typically, companies are prosecuted for violation of regulatory offences carrying relatively minor monetary penalties that bear little relationship to the harm that may have occurred. Even when a formal criminal prosecution is undertaken, corporate defendants are well-positioned to defend themselves. Large companies are able to hire the best lawyers, secure 'professional' expert witnesses, and engage in delaying tactics that will outlast the political pressure that prompted the government to initiate a prosecution in the first place. Given the difficulties in securing a conviction, the tendency is for the parties to engage in a form of 'plea-bargaining' where the company agrees to try to do better in the future and the government agrees not to prosecute for offences committed in the past.

The lesson seems to be that the criminal justice system, as presently constituted, is simply not a viable forum for tackling corporate wrongdoing. This is hardly surprising given that the criminal law was not developed with companies in mind.

2   Unsurprisingly, these companies are not asked about the crimes they themselves had committed.
3   Law Com No 237 *Legislating the Criminal Code: Involuntary Manslaughter* para 8.37 (1996).
4   Home Office (2000) *Reforming the Law on Involuntary Manslaughter: The Government's Proposals*.

Concepts such as mens rea and actus reus, which make perfectly good sense when applied to individuals, do not translate easily to an inanimate fictional entity such as a corporation. Trying to apply these concepts to companies is a bit like trying to squeeze a square peg into a round hole. In the United States a company whose misconduct is exposed may be able to enter a plea of 'nolo contendere', whereby it indicates that it does not wish to contest the charges but at the same time does not admit that it broke the law (the advantage to the company being that the plea cannot be introduced in evidence in subsequent civil suits by victims of its wrongdoing). The unfortunate consequence of not prosecuting companies for crimes such as aggravated assault or manslaughter, when they have caused serious harm to victims, is that the victims, as well as members of the public, are left with an uneasy sense that 'justice' has not been done (Bergman 2000). Much of the analysis in the subsequent chapters will be directed to the ways in which the law might be reformed so that it can better address the problems of holding companies legally accountable for their offences.

Even should a company be convicted of a crime, finding a suitable punishment is problematic. Companies obviously cannot be sent to jail and the typical sanction following a conviction is, almost by default (or, perhaps more accurately, by virtue of a lack of judicial imagination), a fine. The fine is often a mere slap on the wrist for a large and successful company, and may be viewed by it as a cost of doing business, to be passed on to consumers. While in theory individual directors could be given prison sentences, this rarely happens, for a number of reasons, including the offender's lack of a criminal record, good reputation and standing in the community, and the unlikelihood of re-offending (Doig: 2000: 119). Even when a corporate official is sent to jail, the sentence is usually served in an open prison because s/he is not deemed dangerous or likely to pose a threat of escape. It has been observed that the rich get richer and the poor get prison (Reiman: 1990), but even when the rich get prison, they get a better class of prison, with a more relaxed custodial regime and enhanced opportunities for remission of sentence, than do other offenders.

Finally, research has highlighted the difficulties faced by law enforcement personnel in policing companies. Crimes occurring inside companies typically first come to the attention of internal corporate agents and may be subjected to a 'private justice' system established by the company (Tonry and Reiss: 1993). Offenders found 'guilty' are likely to be disciplined, demoted or dismissed. In a large number of cases the police will not be informed because the company wishes to avoid unfavourable publicity. If a corporate crime independently comes to the attention of the police and they decide to investigate, their efforts may be blocked by the reluctance of employees and officials to co-operate. The police may also be hampered by a lack of training in unravelling the intricacies of corporate wrongdoing. Even specialised units, such as fraud squads, face structural, cultural and inter-institutional problems when investigating business offences (Levi: 1987; Doig, Johnson and Levi: 2000). These problems are exacerbated when the police do not have the technical expertise required (eg, with respect to insider dealing, money laundering or potential crimes in relation to road haulage offences). Small wonder that there is a growing tendency to refer investigations to specialised bodies such as Customs and Excise, Inland Revenue, Health and Safety Executive, Department of Trade and Industry, and the numerous inspectorates, trade associations, self-regulatory 'watchdog' agencies (eg, for the Stock Exchange) and professional bodies.

What is one to make of this accumulated knowledge, and the often mixed signals emanating from government and big business? Some 60 years after Sutherland asserted that companies frequently break the law, and do so with virtually no prospect of prosecution or serious sanction, are we no further on? We believe that we can add to the debate in three main ways that are still poorly represented in the literature. In our view there has to be, first, a more profound analysis as to why companies break the law. Too many authors focus on the consequences of corporate crime from an external, narrowly criminological perspective rather than looking at the internal processes that lead to law-breaking. Second, there needs to be a thorough and critical scrutiny not only of why the law fails to control and deter companies but also of how the law could be reformed to become more effective. And thirdly, the area of corporate policing, with particular focus on the feasibility of allowing companies to engage in self-regulation, merits examination. It is in these three areas that we hope to make a contribution and advance the understanding of the dynamics of corporate crime and how the law can best be used to address the problems arising in this complex area.

C.   BUILDING THE FOUNDATIONS

In using the term 'corporate crime', we mean to refer to criminal offences which are committed by companies and other for-profit organisations[5] and are punished by the State. To some this might seem to be an exercise in reification, attributing to an inanimate, fictional entity – the company – an ability to think and act which is normally associated with human beings. 'How can a flow chart be guilty?' was how Wolf (1985: 273) provocatively put it. Although Peter French (1984) counters that there exist within companies internal decision-making structures that allow one to say that a company has made a decision, what may be easier to agree is that companies can and should be legally liable when culpable decisions and actions by persons employed by or associated with a company result in the commission of a crime, especially when these acts and decisions are done with the intent to benefit the company. Whether or not an organisation can be said to make decisions and take actions, it can be held legally responsible for decisions and actions that are done on its behalf or in its name.

There are several preliminary points worth noting. First, although crimes are defined by the criminal law, in practice many of the criminal offences committed by corporations are violations of 'regulatory' laws. Interestingly, much of the research in this area from Sutherland onwards has tended to examine offences which were not technically criminal and did not lead to prosecution in a criminal court (Tappan: 1947). Sutherland and his followers may well have been guilty of confusing corporate misconduct which

5   In its consultation paper in which it proposes a crime of corporate killing, the government takes the position that the offence should not be limited to companies but should extend to all 'undertakings', a term that would encompass partnerships and other commercial organisations, as well as not-for-profit organisations (Home Office (2000) *Reforming the Law on Involuntary Manslaughter: The Government's Proposals* para 3.2.3). While we would take issue with the government's failure to distinguish more carefully between not-for-profit undertakings and for-profit undertakings (see discussion chapter 3), we would agree that limiting the offence to 'companies' narrowly defined, would be ill-advised. While in the text we will typically refer to companies or corporations, the reader should be aware that we will normally have in mind the broader concept of a for-profit organisation.

they felt *should* be criminal (because similar conduct by a natural person would have resulted in a criminal conviction) and what was actually proscribed by the law.

The above observation does not end the matter, however, for the reasons why corporate misconduct has not been criminalised are themselves illuminating. Powerful corporations have historically wielded considerable influence over the legislative process. A not insignificant amount of corporate time and money is spent in lobbying MPs. More subtly, political parties of all stripes are aware of the critical relationship between corporate campaign contributions and electoral success. An industry may not have to engage in overt lobbying to mould the development of the law; legislators will be aware of and may accede to corporate interests in order not to jeopardise their campaign budgets. Even where corporate pressures do not succeed in preventing criminalisation, they may affect how offences are defined and what sanctions are attached to violations. The large body of regulatory laws, not civil but not criminal in the traditional sense either, may be testimony to this dimension of corporate influence (Abraham: 1995).

To judge the extent of corporate crime by the number of convictions of companies can be grossly misleading. As noted, much corporate misconduct has not been made criminal, not because it is not harmful but because corporate lobbying has been successful at deflecting formal criminalisation. In any event, in the case of non-corporate crimes one would hardly dismiss trials without convictions as evidence that no crime had occurred. Before there can be a conviction, a crime has to be recognised, reported, investigated and prosecuted, and the fact-finder must be convinced of the defendant's guilt 'beyond reasonable doubt'. The outcome of this complex, filtering process is partly determined by the power of the actors involved to determine outcomes (Clinard and Yeager: 1980), and companies can be very powerful actors in the legal arena. They may be able to persuade a prosecutor not to press formal charges, or be able to negotiate their offences out of the criminal justice system.

With respect to non-corporate crimes, victimisation studies reveal that only a fraction of offences are ever reported (Zedner: 1997). Victims may not be aware that they have been victimized, may have little confidence in the police or the criminal justice system, or may fear retaliation if they were to press charges. If a crime is not reported, it is unlikely to be investigated and there will probably never be a prosecution unless the crime independently comes to the attention of the police. This phenomenon is even more likely to occur with respect to corporate crimes. These offences normally take place within the business environment, where, unlike in the case of a burglar caught in a private home, the offenders are legitimately on the premises. That a crime has occurred may not be discovered until long after the event and far from the point of decision-making (Pearce and Tombs: 1998). As a result, victims may not be aware of the cause of their injuries or the identity of their 'assailants'. If they are aware that the policies of their employer were somehow connected with their plight, they may be reluctant to go to the police out of fear of losing their jobs. If the offence first comes to the attention of the company, on the other hand, it may prefer to resolve the matter internally, thus avoiding potentially embarrassing publicity, perhaps by generously compensating victims for their injuries – and thereby ensuring their silence. While one may never be able to identify the full panoply of factors that lead to corporate crimes not coming to the attention of the authorities (Clarke: 1990: 20), it is probably fair to assume that the recorded instances of corporate crime represent the barely visible tip of a large iceberg (Levi: 2001).

Offences for which a company can be held liable may be committed by the company's officers, employees or agents while they are engaged in the company's business. They may also be the product of deliberate decisions, or a culpable failure to take a decision, on the part of persons who have decision-making authority within an organisation. The latter would include, but not be limited to, the CEO, the directors, the company secretary, senior managers and other corporate executives. What is essential to understand with respect to all of these situations is the relationship between organisation, offender and offence. The institutional environment forms the backdrop, the business context provides the setting and the opportunity, corporate reward structures may supply the motivation, and the 'greater good of the company' allows for easy rationalisation of the offence. Organisational structures may permit the offence to be camouflaged under the facade of trust and respectability accorded to a legitimate business (Bologna: 1984; Friedrichs: 1996). Offences may be the product of formal and/or informal corporate goals, standard operating procedures, and the cultural norms and ethos of the corporate organisation.

Although corporate crimes are often assumed to be committed in order to promote the greater good of the company (Kramer: 1984: 18), companies can also be the victims of offences, ranging from embezzlement to petty pilfering, committed by their officers and employees. In other words, a crime can be committed against, as well as on the behalf of, a company (Tonry and Reiss: 1993). Despite this fact, much of the literature has tended to focus on those offences which are aimed at benefiting the company. This focus may reflect a conventional view that deviant behaviour in business is geared to enhancing economic goals and securing profits and/or operational continuity (Shover and Wright: 2001) and a restricted, if not naïve, conception of organisational reality and managerial motives. At the same time, the assumption that corporate crimes are committed to benefit the company begs the question of what constitutes a 'benefit' to a company. A criminal conspiracy aimed at solving a short-term problem, such as the illegal dumping of waste that exceeds the capacity of the firm's facilities to process, may prove highly damaging to the company in the long run and may even lead to its going out of business (Huisman and Niemeijer: 1998).

Putting together a number of the above features, we can arrive at a set of foundational ideas and themes that will be useful in informing our subsequent analysis:

- corporate crimes entail violations of the criminal law to which criminal sanctions are attached;
- corporate crimes may involve the use or abuse of an individual's position of power, influence or trust within an organisation;
- corporate crimes are perpetrated within the legitimate economic order in ostensibly bona fide organisations;
- the corporate form and a business context provide a means both to commit illegal acts and to conceal them;
- the corporate environment provides the opportunity and setting in which crimes can occur;
- illegal acts may be for personal, group or organisational 'gain' (including short-term individual gains and long-term institutional goals related to profitability, continuity, market share, competition, etc);
- the company itself may be the victim of a crime committed by one or more of its employees or officers;

- in some situations companies can and should be held legally accountable for what might ostensibly appear to be a crime of an individual;
- that a company is held criminally liable for an individual's offence should neither require nor preclude a concomitant or separate prosecution of the individual; and
- while both a company and an individual may bear responsibility for a crime arising from the same acts and/or decisions, their relative degree of culpability may differ and the two need not be prosecuted for the same offence or be subjected to the same or comparable sanctions.

In this book we propose to examine the causes of corporate crime (chapter 1), the legal theories that have been employed to hold companies liable for their wrongdoing (chapter 2), possible directions for reforming the law (chapters 3 and 4), the procedures and rules of evidence appropriate when a company is on trial (chapter 6), the sanctions that might be imposed on a company following a conviction (chapter 7), and the investigatory and enforcement mechanisms that have been or might be put into place to combat corporate crime and to police companies (chapters 9 and 10). We also propose to look at the legal responsibility of individuals (chapter 8) and that of parent companies for the crimes of their subsidiaries, with special attention to the case of overseas subsidiaries (chapter 5). Our attempt to assess the potential for the legal regulation and control of corporate crime will be informed by the insights provided by a criminological and organisational understanding of companies. While it is easy to be pessimistic, if not fatalistic, about society's ability to rein in powerful corporations and check corporate criminality, recent initiatives in corporate self-regulation suggest that corporations themselves are increasingly aware of the problem and are trying to reform themselves. The law, we believe, needs to be restructured to support and promote these initiatives.

D.   THE ROOTS OF CORPORATE CRIMINALITY

With regard to the question of why corporate crimes occur, what tends to be missing from traditional analyses is an appreciation of how the 'organisational' dimensions of companies – systems, structures, procedures, managerial style, culture and ethos – contribute to corporate crime. The organisation provides the setting, motive, means, opportunity and rationalisation for criminal and regulatory offences. Furthermore, business relations and organisational politics can involve power struggles, rivalries, rule-bending and even seemingly irrational risk-taking. And, then, behind a veil of ostensible order and coherence can be found poorly run companies, including some which, on occasion, are virtually out of control (Punch: 1996).

Despite the plethora of sociological studies on corporate wrongdoing in a variety of contexts, no all-embracing causal explanation for corporate criminality has emerged. All sorts of companies break the law for all kinds of reasons while others, who are seemingly similarly situated, do not. While it might seem logical that companies in financial difficulties, or which were performing poorly, would be more inclined to violate the law than financially solvent organisations, the correlation appears weak (Jamieson: 1994). Many underperforming companies do not succumb to illegal shortcuts, and perhaps even more significantly, many companies that are prospering also break the law (Snider: 1993: 75). Single variable explanations, such as the pursuit of profit, the pressures of competition, market conditions, or greedy managers, fail to explain why some companies are inclined to criminality while other similarly situated companies are not.

While not proposing to make an exhaustive survey of all possible explanations, we believe that five key variables are worthy of closer examination. First is a constellation of social, economic and cultural factors that may contribute to a climate that is tolerant of corporate law-breaking. Second, different organisational structures may have an impact on whether or not a company engages in rule-bending. Third, it may be useful to consider to what extent corporate crimes are the product of intentional and rational decisions, or whether they are attributable to incompetence, negligence, recklessness or sheer bad luck. This variable will take on particular importance in determining legal accountability. Fourth, what effect does engaging in criminal activity have both on a company and those who make the decisions to turn to illegality? Does it affect the latter's operating style and self-image? And what defence mechanisms and techniques do they, and the company, employ to dissociate themselves from the criminality? A fifth and final consideration is the nature of various industries. Most industries offer some opportunity for illegality; some, however, may be more 'crime-facilitative' than others, and a few may even be described as virtually 'crime-coercive'.

1.   Social, economic and cultural factors

General explanatory factors of corporate crime include the nature of society, economies and industries. Transparency International ranks countries on a 'corruption scale' that reveals clear differences in standards of conduct in government and business. It would be surprising if a national culture that tolerated corruption were not reflected in some way in the level of corporate deviance (Transparency International: 2001). In some countries bribery and 'grease' payments are a long-established custom. It would, goes the argument, be culturally discriminatory to ignore local customs. Indeed, the perception by many multinational enterprises that officials in developing countries are susceptible to bribes may account in part for the increasing trend to shift to these countries the illegal aspects of the company's business (see chapter 5).

It would be a mistake, however, to draw simplistic distinctions between developed and developing/undeveloped, or third-world and first-world, or northern and southern, countries. Carson (1982) documents how the British government, in its rush to develop the North Sea oil industry for its financial benefit, contributed to or actually encouraged a level of unacceptably low compliance with regulatory standards that were arguably rather weak to begin with. His study illustrates how the state of a nation's economy can combine with market forces to produce official tolerance of corporate deviance. The rush to develop new sources of oil seems to have blinded the British government to its obligation to enforce its own safety regulations.

As we have noted, some commentators are inclined to 'structural' explanations of corporate deviance, seeing business crime as an almost inherent feature of a capitalist system. (Slapper and Tombs 1999; Pearce and Tombs: 2000). On the other hand, situational-specific factors appear better to explain some particular instances of corporate criminality. For example, the antitrust violations in the American heavy electrical equipment industry appear to have been the product of a pragmatic and adaptive response to shifting market conditions (Geis and Meir: 1977). In the Pinto case, the Ford motor company was faced with intense foreign competition and a fluid market at a time when it had only one product that it thought would have a major impact on its sales. The financial, but also the psychological, pressure to stand by one's product, with extremely tight production deadlines set by Lee Iaccoca, the then CEO of Ford, may well have influenced the decision not to alter the dangerous placement of the fuel tank after the company had become aware of the defect (Gioia: 1996). These same pressures may help to explain the aggressive, adversarial stance taken by Ford to subsequent court cases in which the company was sued civilly (for injuries sustained after fuel tanks had exploded following a rear-end collision) or criminally prosecuted (Swigert and Farrell: 1980) and to its dealings with government regulators.

Part of the problem in making generalisations about corporate criminality is that while a murder or rape committed a century ago may not differ fundamentally from the most recent reported instance of the offence, the nature of corporate crime seems to be constantly changing. Many of the corporate crimes that society now takes for granted, such as money laundering and insider trading, were not illegal twenty-five years ago. New technologies, and in particular computerisation, have made possible business frauds that could not have been perpetrated until quite recently. What this means is that studies conducted over 25 years ago, while making for interesting reading, are now very much likely to be out of date.

Not only are many of the leading studies dated but also, in retrospect, they can be seen as having been highly contextual. For example, the automobile, oil and pharmaceutical industries have in the past been singled out as chronic law violators. However, this conclusion was based largely on research from the 1970s when these primarily American-based industries were notoriously and aggressively anti-regulation and anti-government. This attitude may well have fostered among corporate executives and managers an ethos of non-compliance with the law (Clinard and Yeager: 1980). To understand the implications, consider the case of an oil company that has invested heavily in exploiting an oil field. If corporate executives regard regulations as an example of bureaucratic harassment by politicians and policy makers who do not understand the industry (Jackall: 1988) and are only out to make a name for themselves, they may have no hesitation in encouraging an operational attitude on the part of their workers to ignore what they see as nit-picking regulatory rules.

It is not difficult, in hindsight, to come up with a host of explanations as to why a company may have violated the law. What is more difficult is to explain why one company breaks the law and another, similarly or even worse placed, does not. We are dealing with highly complex variables that may explain deviance, but there is no reliable evidence on the extent of deviance in any one company in any one industry at any one time. Were those who were exposed as rule-breakers simply unlucky enough to be found out? Might not ostensibly 'clean' companies be closet rule-breakers? Until its collapse, the Enron corporation was regarded as the model of a modern corporate enterprise, winning awards at the same time as its apparent profits soared. When its accounting 'irregularities' were exposed, a revisionist appraisal of its success was inevitable, but how many other 'Enrons' are waiting to happen? Irregularities in smaller companies with relatively uncomplex structures may have a higher chance of being detected than the crimes of multinationals with multiple subsidiaries and layers of bureaucracy. Smaller companies may also lack the political clout to avert or deflect a prosecution.

Two points are of particular relevance in this context and bear repeating. The first is that even where there is strong evidence that certain industries are more conducive to rule-breaking than others (eg real estate, car dealers, waste disposal and construction: Clarke, Smith and McConville: 1993; Leonard and Weber: 1970; Huisman and Niemeijer: 1998), this evidence does not explain why one company in such an industry will violate the law and another will not. The answer may depend on another set of specific and situationally contingent variables, including a company's financial solvency, its market position, the product it wishes to develop and the product's life cycle, the hoped-for return on investment, the perceived opportunities and rewards for deviance, the personalities of the directors and executive officers charged with giving direction to the company, the practices of competitors, the prevailing regulatory climate, and so on. This means that cases have to be located in time and in a setting in order to explain why a particular company took a criminal path while similarly situated others (as far as we know) did not (Braithwaite: 1997). Some companies break some laws some of the time; other companies break some laws all of the time; we hope that few companies break all laws all of the time and as matter of corporate policy; and then there are the companies which enjoy a deserved (or perhaps undeserved, if more were known about their activities?) reputation of being consciously law-abiding.

The second point is that one must be wary of drawing conclusions from data that is out of date, and that out of date data may be only a couple of decades removed. Today's companies have become sophisticated players of the legal game. They have learned that hostility, recalcitrance and resistance can be counterproductive. Instead, the modern company is more likely to at least feign co-operation with regulators and may even seek out their advice while engaging in 'creative compliance' (McBarnett and Whelan: 1999). But the question which must be asked is whether it is all a charade. Have corporate attitudes towards observance of the law really changed; or is what we are witnessing a mere surface gloss designed to conceal even more devious, aberrant and illegal behaviour lurking underneath?

2. The nature and structure of organisations

In order to better understand the nature of corporate crime, it is useful to have an understanding of the nature of organisational life. There is a vast literature on organisations (eg, Reed and Hughes: 1992; Weick: 1979) but we will restrict ourselves to a limited number of observations. First, the analysis of organisations, and particularly of business organisations, may over-emphasise formal structures. Adherence to procedures, coherence in policies and rationality in decision-making sound eminently plausible and yet one finds insider accounts of organisations that portray the irrationality and even chaos of organisational life (Burrell: 1997). 'Loosely coupled systems' may allow parts of what may in effect be a unitary structure to have little idea of what other parts of the system are doing. Within corporations can be found institutional fragmentation and cultural segmentation, rivalries and 'turf wars', and poor communication. One must, therefore, be cautious in attributing too much coherence and 'rationality' to organisational decision-making.

Second, organisations can exert powerful 'pressure cooker' forces on individuals within the organisation, turning them into group actors responsive to institutional demands (Jackall: 1988). In this environment individuals who may be highly moral in their private life may submit to group pressures and concur with amoral or even immoral decisions that they would never have taken with respect to their own affairs. Individual responsibility may give way to an invidious form of 'group think' (Janis: 1972) wherein members of a homogenous and cohesive group will defer to views with which they disagree in order not to alienate a valued colleague, undermine what would otherwise be a unanimous decision, or give the appearance of being 'difficult' (Harvey: 1988).

Third, rationally formulated means can become ends in themselves. Managers often feel that they have to achieve corporate objectives whatever the cost (Gross: 1980: 72; Monahan and Novaco: 1980: 5). In the transport industry, for example, managers will put pressure on employees to break safety rules in order to keep to schedules, a phenomenon that has been noted with respect to airlines, ferries and road transport. This short-term thinking can only be accomplished by blinding oneself to the possible consequences of one's actions. When the *Herald of Free Enterprise* capsized outside of Zeebrugge, the subsequent Report of Court (Dept of Transport: 1987) noted that the ship's master was proceeding too rapidly in leaving the harbour. The master, however, may have been responding, either consciously or subconsciously, to company directives that set as the target arriving not just on schedule, but ahead of schedule (Dept of Transport: 1987; para 11.3). Similarly, in a public inquiry arsing from an El Al plane crash that occurred near Amsterdam in 1992, maintenance employees revealed that their warnings about the unsafe condition of aircraft, some of which they felt were too dangerous to fly, were often overruled by managers who insisted the planes would fly despite these defects in order to maintain schedules (Parliamentary Inquiry Bijlmer Disaster: 1999). This sort of head-in-the-sand behaviour also has been uncovered in technology companies where the pressure to stick to production quotas can lead to an institutional reluctance to heed warnings and to stop services – even in the face of serious and persistent warnings of danger.

The fact that the above factors seem to apply to virtually all business organisations could lead one to the generalisation that organisations are in some sense inherently criminogenic. The generalisation is unhelpful, however, because it does not explain why some companies break the rules and others do not. Also, while the competitiveness, pressure for results, skewed reward systems, antagonism to regulation, etc, that characterise the business world may appear obviously conducive to illegality, one can find similarly stressful forces at work in non-business organisations such as armies, universities, voluntary agencies, charities and churches. As these other contexts have received far less attention compared to the corporate context, we simply do not know the extent to which these comparable or equivalent forces foster deviant solutions to their institutional dilemmas.

3.   Intent, rationality and competence

In examining corporate decision-making with regard to rule-breaking it is valuable to know the extent to which individual decision-makers are in fact behaving 'rationally' and with an awareness of the consequences of their decisions. In criminal law the allocation of blame is generally reserved for those who act intentionally, knowingly or recklessly. At one extreme can be found corporate executives and managers who are aware of what they are doing and have thought through the consequences carefully. Indeed, both companies and corporate executives are often characterised in the literature as rational albeit 'amoral calculators', fully conscious of their conduct ('[T]oday's most widely accepted model of corporate crime portrays the business firm as an amoral, profit-seeking organisation whose actions are motivated wholly by the rational calculation of costs and opportunities.' Kagan and Scholz: 1984: 69). Risk analyses are a routine part of the decision-making calculus with cost-benefit calculations often underpinning the choice among options. But this form of calculation may induce a mind-set causing executives to exaggerate their control over circumstances while, at the same time, distancing themselves from the consequences of their behaviour (Monahan and Novaco: 1980). Thus, the Ford Motor Company decided that settling the occasional lawsuit arising from injuries sustained when the petrol tanks of its ill-designed Pinto exploded would be less costly than altering the design prior to production or later issuing a general recall to reposition the petrol tanks (which Ford was eventually forced to do anyway). More intangible factors can also enter the calculation, such as, in Ford's case, whether its reputation would suffer (with possible long-term loss of sales) if it admitted that its automobile designs were faulty.

On the other hand, as suggested in the previous section, contextual and institutional factors may affect rationality. March and Simon (1958) speak of 'bounded rationality'. What they intend to convey by this concept is the fact that organisations rarely possess total information on a given topic and are forced to make choices on the basis of incomplete data. Few decisions are ever fully rational. It is probably more accurate to conceive of a continuum: while many decisions are rational, others are not 'fully rational' and some veer closer to irrational, with a few at the end of the spectrum which might appear to be pathological or even self-destructive.

In most cases there is an assumption that, however misguided a decision, it is taken within a business paradigm of ensuring continuity, enhancing performance, fixing a short-term problem, generating profits and so on. But there are times when decisions are made that are divorced from any conventional business logic, that appear to be destructive of company interests, and that can scarcely be seen as 'rational'. Towards the end of his career, Robert Maxwell had lost control of his finances to such an extent that he was taking desperate decisions that led to flight and, some believe, his eventual suicide. In the Goodrich Brake scandal engineers produced false figures on an aircraft brake which they knew would be highly dangerous when tested operationally. More difficult to understand is the fact that they must also have known that when the defective brake led to accidents, and even loss of life, their duplicity and falsification would inevitably be discovered. Similarly, in the DC 10 case, McDonnell Douglas took a decision to produce a plane but seemed to blind itself to a product defect with potentially fatal consequences (Eddy, Potter and Page: 1976). Before its collapse, Barings Bank was sending sums of money to Nick Leeson in Singapore for amounts that in some instances exceeded both the bank's assets as well as the limits set by the Bank of England (Barings Report: 1995). That Baring's most senior management were oblivious to the dangers seems in hindsight incredible; and this in a highly reputable bank of long standing.

The implication seems to be that either decision-makers are blind to risk or that they have very selective perceptions of events and their consequences. Coffee (1977: 1103) describes a 'recurring management style' characterised by over-zealousness, an action-orientation, and a 'remarkably low level of risk aversion'. Whatever the explanation, the above examples caution against assuming that all corporate decisions are 'rational'. Decisions can probably be placed on a spectrum of rationality: at one end are those that are well thought out and logically impeccable, while at the opposite end can be found decisions that are impulsive, reckless and irrational. Compounding the problem of analysis is the difficulty of reconstructing what may have gone through the minds of corporate directors asked to approve a criminogenic policy (Reed: 1989). Furthermore, while there tends to be an assumption that board members are highly qualified, they may be lacking in the special expertise necessary to address and resolve a specific type of business problem. In the Barings/Leeson affair, for example, apparently many Barings executives did not understand the nature of 'derivatives' and the 'futures' markets in which Leeson was trading (Rawnsley: 1996). With respect to the collapse of the Enron Corporation, board members later claimed not to have understood the complicated partnership arrangements that they had approved but which concealed the true financial state of the company from shareholders and creditors alike. In neither Barings nor Enron did directors appear to understand their basic fiduciary duties. When decisions are made in specific settings, executives may misread a situation or misinterpret data, make poor judgments, or simply not possess the requisite skills for the task.

What is the link, if any, between poor judgment, moral responsibility and criminal liability? In law, misguided decisions and negligence will usually not lead to criminal liability, but the line between these and objective recklessness, which can, is not always clear. Whether poor judgment constitutes negligence or recklessness may depend on exactly how poor a defendant's judgment has been. We shall look more closely at the law in subsequent chapters, but for the present purposes it may be useful to draw a crude distinction between decisions that no reasonable manager in the same or similar position would have taken and decisions that in retrospect may be seen to have entailed considerable risk, but at the time appeared innocuous. If for no other reason, this distinction may be helpful in allocating blame, both legally and morally. The person who makes choices intending, knowing, or consciously aware that the choice will likely lead to harm, or will engender a high degree of risk to innocent individuals, may be deemed culpable in both a moral and a legal sense.

Over time, and with an increasing number of successes to one's credit, a decision-maker can become impervious to risk. The disastrous consequences that such imperviousness can have are demonstrated by the explosion of the *Challenger* space-shuttle. Vaughan (1996) recounts how NASA, a highly sophisticated and risk-conscious agency with explicit procedures to guarantee safety, gradually and imperceptibly built an unconscious escalation of risk into launch decisions, as each launch, carrying an inherent measure of risk, proved successful. Nobody in NASA seemed to appreciate that the lives of the astronauts might be endangered at the 1986 launch, even though there had been technical debates about safety issues prior to launching (as routinely occurred in respect to all launches). When the shuttle exploded, with the concomitant deaths of seven astronauts, they were no doubt as shocked as anybody (but see Boisjoily, Foster Curtis and Mellican: 1996).

Clearly nobody in NASA expected, wanted, or intended that the *Challenger* explosion should occur. However, the psychology of risk-taking teaches that success in a risky venture can induce a false sense of optimism, or even invincibility, that undermines rationality and encourages further and ever-increasingly dangerous risk-taking. This is why companies that succeed in risky escapades, rather than count themselves fortunate for having avoided a disaster, may go on to even riskier ventures. The distance between executive decision-makers and those endangered by their decisions also may cause the executives to lose sight of the fact that the lives of flesh-and-blood persons are at risk. This loss of perspective may have contributed to the deaths of the space-shuttle astronauts. The rich intricacies and complexities of decision-making within NASA are carefully unravelled by Vaughan, who demonstrates not only that an excellent past safety record is no protection against disaster, but also how past successes can surreptitiously foster a blindness and a latent vulnerability. And of course there is a difference between hindsight and foresight, between how risk is perceived at the moment of decision and how external assessors (in a legal trial, the judge or jury) appraise that risk at a much later point in time and in light of actual events.

4.   Defence mechanisms and techniques of dissociation

When companies violate the law to address a short-term problem and do not get caught, the danger is that law-breaking will become a habit and then a way of doing business. Whether or not this sequence occurs may depend on the psychological effects of law-breaking on those who take the decisions to bend the rules, and the effect these decisions have on their self-identity. Do they become 'criminals'? Do they experience guilt or shame? What defence mechanisms do they, and their company, adopt to dissociate themselves from their crimes?

The typical corporate executive who commits a crime is unlikely to conform to the popular stereotype of the criminal, even conceding the virtually infinite forms of the criminal character. Most 'common' criminals tend to be young, with a strong sense of hedonism and often belonging to a tightly-knit peer group. Common criminals tend to display a predilection for rule-breaking and for challenging authority, and may take pleasure in their outsider role. They often will exhibit a blindness to consequences (McIntosh: 1975). Gottfredson and Hirschi (1990: 90) reason that such individuals, because they lack self-control, will 'tend to be impulsive, insensitive, physical (as opposed to mental), risk-taking, short-sighted, and non-verbal', all of which characteristics contribute to their tendency to engage in criminal and analogous activities. The one 'encouraging' statistic about the criminality of most common criminals, however, is that it tends to decrease with age.

By and large, corporate executives who commit crimes do not share the same motives, behaviour or persona as common criminals. Typically, the corporate executive who commits an offence is, in most respects, a model citizen with no criminal record or any of the stereotypical character traits of the common criminal (Canter and Alison: 2000). He (most corporate executives are male) will be from the upper or middle classes, 'well-socialised' and well-educated (Taylor: 1997), mature and capable of deferring gratification (having had to display personal and emotional control in order to advance in his corporate career). Unlike the common criminal who is an outsider, the corporate executive is pre-eminently an insider who will rarely challenge authority and, if anything, may represent an over-socialised type of 'organisational man' (Whyte: 1956). Also, unlike the common criminal, the corporate executive is likely to commit his offence at a relatively old age. The reason why is that the crimes of corporate executives tend to be opportunistic – specific business opportunities offer options that can lead to instrumental and temporary law-breaking. A senior executive may suddenly find that after many years of service he is presented with an opportunity that could only present itself to a person in his position of authority and only with the specific powers that he can exercise as a senior manager or board-room executive. Thus, in terms of self-identity, roles played, 'career' paths in and out of crime, age at involvement in crime, and so on, the corporate criminal is distinguishable from the (stereotypical) common criminal. The main trait that they will often share in common is a blindness to consequences. Peer groups may also play a significant role in each's offence, as the corporate executive may need the support of colleagues, as well as the corporate form, to perpetrate his offence.

Unlike those common criminals who take pride in their criminal exploits and boast of their toughness, the corporate executive will normally take pains to avoid the stigma of criminality. Either to preserve their self-image or perhaps, more simply, to avoid personal criminal liability, corporate executives will seek to distance themselves from the criminal consequences of their decisions. Senior managers may pressure more junior members of staff to bend rules, but in a way that allows them to dissociate themselves from any offence that might be committed. For example, the senior manager may set overly ambitious targets while leaving the means of achieving the targets to those subordinates who have to meet them. If the latter choose criminal means, the manager can simply state that he did not dictate or intend the methods chosen. Similarly, a compensation system may be established with such attractive rewards for achieving targets that employees will adopt whatever means are necessary, including those which are illegal, to obtain their bonuses. Directors too may take a 'head in the sand' attitude toward wrongdoing that may be committed by employees and staff. Thus, for instance, Barings Bank executives in London discontinued the previous practice of receiving regular reports from Nick Leeson on his trading activities in Singapore. This allowed the directors to later disclaim responsibility for Leeson's illegal activities. At the same time, however, the absence of internal accountability removed one of the constraints that might have prevented Leeson from taking liberties with the law.

Nor do corporate executives who are exposed for having broken the law view themselves as criminals. Rather, they tend to rationalise their behaviour. In the 'Revco Medicaid' case, for instance, Revco was losing money on payments from the State of Ohio related to Medicaid because the State's computer system was rejecting certain forms. In order to regain the money that it was felt was 'owing' to the company, a small group of executives set up a separate department, concealing its purpose from others in the organisation, and systematically falsified forms (Vaughan: 1980). The executives did not see their actions as 'criminal', but more as a means for restoring equilibrium. As a result they were taken aback when prosecuted (in cases such as this the prosecution tends to be brought against individual executives and not their company). Similarly, corporate executives exposed for bribing officials in developing countries tended to rationalise their behaviour by arguing that they were only conforming to local customs and that to do otherwise would have been to impose moralistic western standards on countries that operated under a different set of traditions (Coffee: 1977).

Companies too may engage in, but seek to dissociate themselves from, criminal activity. A common technique is to assign the dangerous or criminogenic aspects of one's business to a subsidiary organisation. This phenomenon can be seen most plainly in the case of multinational enterprises which 'export' the legally dubious dimensions of their business operation to subsidiaries in developing countries where law enforcement is more lax and officials less scrupulous. This particular problem will be examined more closely in chapter 5.

5.   Crime-facilitative and crime-coercive industries

Data seem to suggest that certain industries are more crime prone than others. Explanations will be industry-specific but are usually not difficult to discover. In the pharmaceutical industry, for example, companies face large up-front investment costs in research and testing, a long and sometimes tortuous path before a drug may be licensed and approved for sale, and a considerable wait thereafter for a return on the company's investment. It may take fifteen years from development to market for a drug in the United States, where the Food and Drug Administration (FDA) can be quite demanding in its requirements. As Braithwaite (1984) made clear in his seminal study of the pharmaceutical world, these structural components of the industry can lead to a range of attitudes and behaviour that accept conscious and systemic rule-breaking. A drug company can easily convince itself that it has made a breakthrough that will not only reduce suffering and promote health but also generate vast profits (and perhaps it has), but that excessive regulation is delaying bringing the product to market. In this self-justificatory climate, improper inducements to doctors, undue influencing of research findings, interference with laboratory experiments, and kickbacks and bribes are not only not uncommon but also easily rationalised (Abraham: 1995).

Price-fixing and the formation of cartels were also revealed in Stanley Adams' (1984) insider account of Hoffmann La Roche. That such practices continue across time is revealed by a contemporary case where Hoffmann La Roche was the ring-leader of a cartel consisting of 13 companies whose interactions spanned a nine year period. Eight of the companies were convicted of violations of EU laws and received a record fine of €855m (although the fines were reduced because the companies co-operated, having earlier also come to an agreement in the US courts with regard to offences against American regulations). Five companies escaped prosecution because the offences were beyond the limitation period for prosecution (de Volkskrant, 22 November 2001). Earlier case studies related to Thalidomide, Bendectin, and MER 29 reinforce the picture of an industry that is not unprepared to resort to criminal deviance when necessary (Dowie and Marshall: 1982; Knightley et al: 1980).

Weapons manufacturing provides another example of an industry where huge investments can be tied up in a single product. Sales of weapons to foreign governments may be critical to the survival of companies in the industry. It was therefore not altogether surprising that, when faced with stiff competition from the dominant American arms lobby, some European manufacturers resorted to bribing government officials. Both Dassault and Augusta were revealed as having bribed Belgian politicians with the latter endeavouring to influence their decision on a military helicopter competing with the favoured American product. But, for their part, American companies had adopted disreputable tactics to enter and influence new markets in the 1970s. Indeed, the widespread practice of companies such as

Lockheed and others of bribing foreign officials led in the United States to the passage of the Foreign Corrupt Practices Act 1977 (Reisman: 1979). In these cases structural and cultural features of a highly competitive industry, characterised by 'winner-take all' contracts, may have combined with a constellation of situational-specific factors (such as new markets that elicit corruption from newcomers for entry with influential middlemen demanding 'sweeteners' for officials) that proved irresistibly conducive to law-breaking (Reisman: 1979).

A distinction can be drawn between crime-facilitative and 'crime-coercive' industries, although perhaps it is not so much a distinction as a continuum. Many industries are crime-facilitative in the sense that they offer opportunities for gain by criminal means with low risk of detection. In a crime-coercive industry, on the other hand, companies see themselves as virtually 'forced' into opting for criminality in order to survive. For example, where car manufacturers require their dealers to sell at sharply reduced prices, with low profit margins to the dealers, the dealers may feel they have to make up for their 'lost' profits from sales by billing customers for unnecessary repairs or by selling used cars for cash so that the sales may be concealed from the revenue (Farberman: 1975).

In the construction industry government contracts are often awarded pursuant to a process of public tendering. Firms in the industry are required to submit closed bids to obtain contracts. In order to ensure that all companies get a 'fair' share of the market, companies may enter into collusive arrangements, agreeing covertly to carve up the market by allowing each company to succeed on a particular bid. Such agreements between companies also can be used to hike the price of the 'lowest' bid to a highly profitable level. Even in the absence of collusion, the tendering process can indirectly lead to illegality. Where a company has built in an overly low profit margin in order to secure a bid, it may compensate by employing illegal immigrant labour for which it can avoid paying minimum wages and national insurance. Alternatively, the company may subcontract responsibility for parts of the contract to low-cost, marginal firms with a reputation for unscrupulous and unlawful methods. This stratagem also allows the principal contractor to insulate itself from any subsequent offences (eg in the health, safety, labour or fiscal areas). Finally, the vulnerabilities of the industry – poor weather conditions, failure of subcontractors to deliver components, strikes, unforeseen technical obstacles, accidents, raids by the authorities, and so on – can lead to illegal short-cuts, dangerously poor quality in production and/or the falsification of accounts. In the Netherlands an extensive network comprising some 60 building companies has been exposed for cartel-forming and price-fixing, including illicit prior deals on an 'equitable' distribution of contracts (with compensation agreements among ostensible competitors for those who failed to gain a bid), secret meetings that were never recorded in company and personal diaries, fake billing, the exclusion of competitors, the bribing of officials for inside information, shadow book-keeping (with destruction of some documents) and huge overcharging on some government contracts (leading to Parliamentary Inquiry Construction Industry: 2002).

Sometimes 'straight' companies are infiltrated by criminal elements and turn to criminal activity because of the influence of their new 'partners'. In the case of the Banco Ambrosiano, Roberto Calvi struck deals with the Mafia in order to attain the bank's (and his personal) objectives but wound up colluding in clearly criminal ventures (Gurwin: 1984; Raw: 1992). On a 'passive' level, many financial institutions have unwittingly laundered money for organised crime, and others have colluded in the dubious transactions of dictators and drug-dealers by simply not asking too many questions (Savona: 1999; Levi: 2001). In some situations 'symbiotic' relationships develop between legitimate and illegitimate companies, as, for example, in the garment industry where illegal sweat-shops deliver to respectable clothing firms (Huisman: 2001). Grey markets in cigarettes, alcohol and medical drugs have also sprung up in which legitimate companies end up buying or selling products illicitly (Punch: 1996).

Companies that are consciously set up as 'fronts' for criminal activities are usually not included in corporate crime statistics because they are not seen as bona fide enterprises, but rather as instances where the corporate form is misused as a cover for illegal activity. Sometimes, however, it may not be clear into which category a company falls. At the time of its downfall, the Bank of Credit and Commerce International (BCCI) was the seventh largest bank in the world, providing legitimate banking services for many of its customers. At the same time, however, it was systematically engaged in various illegal practices. It made questionable loans for dubious purposes without pressing for repayment and constructed false accounts through a shadow treasury to cover the increasing volume of suspect transactions. To sustain the illusion of a legitimate enterprise and to conceal its activities from regulators, BCCI illegally acquired as cover a legitimate bank in the United States. Whether the full illegal dimensions of the bank's later operations were envisaged from the outset or whether it found itself caught up in a criminal spiral over which it had increasingly less control and from which it could not escape, is a matter of dispute. Robert Morgenthau, the New York District Attorney who prosecuted BCCI for its illegal takeover of First American Bank, thought the former, declaring that 'BCCI was operated as a corrupt and criminal organisation throughout its nineteen year history'. The Governor of the Bank of England concurred, describing the culture of BCCI as 'criminal' (Kochan and Whittington: 1991: 168). If they were correct, then BCCI was a case of one of the most elaborate fronts of a legitimate business being used for illicit purposes, although few would have described the bank's founders as conventional criminals.

6. Conclusions

We have now examined a number of variables that help to explain corporate crime. While sociological and criminological explanations are not the same as legal judgments on liability, we would maintain that the legal test of corporate criminal liability should be informed by an understanding of why corporate crimes occur. To briefly sum up the major points so far:

- the discussion has been aimed at pointing out the complexity of the issues that can arise in analysing a company's responsibility for criminal behaviour;
- the causes of corporate crime are many: there are general and industry conditions, organisational features, levels of intent, rationality and negligence, and degrees of criminality;
- we do not pose a single variable theory of corporate criminality but argue instead for a multi-causal explanation with contingent, situational factors playing an important role in individual cases;

- we have noted that companies provide the opportunity for crime (and within companies opportunities are not evenly distributed; there are vulnerable segments and segments with low opportunities), the incentive for crimes, the means to commit crimes, and the rationalisation for criminal behaviour; and
- the fact that some companies take decisions, or fail to take decisions, that lead to illegality where others do not demonstrates that crime is neither an inevitable nor an inherent feature of capitalism, and strengthens the case for legal responsibility.

While the corporate environment may provide the setting, opportunity and context for a crime, the role of individual choice cannot and should not be ignored. Just as some companies turn to crime while other similarly situated competitors do not, so too do some corporate employees and executives opt for criminal solutions to seemingly intractable problems while others faced with the identical problems adhere to the legal line. The fact that an individual has made a choice to employ illegal means might suggest prosecuting the individual rather than his/her company. But where individual choices are a foreseeable response to corporate pressures, individual and corporate responsibility become entangled, and a prosecutor must carefully consider whether justice will be best served by bringing charges against the individual perpetrator, the company, both, or neither. Clearly individuals should not be made the scapegoat for corporate failures, but equally clearly companies should not be made the scapegoat for an individual's derelictions. The issue becomes more complicated when the individuals in question are directors and officers with ultimate decision-making authority, subject to the implicit 'paradigms' and world views on how businesses are conducted in the 'real world'.

E.   PARAMETERS AND CASE STUDIES

Drawing on the previous section we now wish to examine a number of cases to establish the 'parameters' of corporate crime. What shape, in terms of participants and social processes, do the real-life cases have? In order to answer these questions a careful consideration of a number of issues is required, including:

- what sort of offence was committed?
- who was involved and at what level in the organisation?
- why did the individuals in question make the choices that they did; what was their motive (recognising that motives can be mixed, and that many explanations are little more than after-the-fact rationalisations)?
- how was the offence committed?
- how far-reaching was the offence?
- what was the nature and extent of the damage?
- who were the victims?
- how serious was the offence in the eyes of society?
- what was the nature of the regulatory environment and did this affect the decision to turn to criminal means?

With these questions in mind, we will now look at four case studies of corporate wrongdoing.

1.   Waste disposal and the TCR case: a magnet for criminals

As noted earlier, there are some crime-facilitative industries in which one can discern a recurring and disproportionate pattern of criminal activity. Persons with a criminal record may be attracted by the opportunities provided by these industries, seeing in them the potential for remunerative illicit business. The waste disposal industry in the Netherlands may be such an industry.

Huisman and Niemeijer (1998) identify some of the features that make the waste disposal industry so attractive to persons with a criminal background. Companies are paid prior to delivery and, as a result, are easily tempted to take on contracts they cannot possibly fulfil. They then will turn to illegal methods for satisfying their obligations. The firms involved are typically small and run by managers with a dominant managerial style but few qualifications. By providing high rewards and/ or by establishing dependency relationships, managers who are averse to regulation and unions are nonetheless able to create a loyal workforce. At the same time these managers will strive to forge good contacts with government officials, employing professional consultants to advise them on how to portray an image of being environmentally friendly in a country where lucrative government subsidies are available for environmental initiatives. Behind this facade the companies will consciously and systematically violate the law.

The 'TCR' case is illustrative. The firm had on its staff a number of managers who had previously been implicated in criminal investigations. Through the aid of powerful lobbyists, the company was able to secure substantial government subsidies, and took on contracts it could never have hoped to fulfil. When it ran into difficulties, it resorted to criminal solutions. For instance, having obtained the contract to clean out ships' tanks in Rotterdam, and having discovered that it could not dispose of the waste without incurring substantial unbudgeted-for costs, it simply dumped a large part of the waste into the Rotterdam Harbour. TCR's actions were not only in breach of its contract but also constituted serious environmental offences. The critical decisions were approved by the company's senior management, consisting of three brothers. The managers were able to convince the relevant regulatory agencies of their good faith by continually involving them in the solution of their problems. Those corporate officers who balked at the regulatory violations were ridiculed at staff meetings while those who colluded in the rule-breaking were rewarded with high salaries and a company car. To hide its crimes, the company engaged in a conscious and manipulative strategy of excuses for non-performance. Last-minute improvements were made as needed to deflect regulators, and double bookkeeping systems with insider codes and special computer programmes were constructed to camouflage the company's illegalities. Data on dangerous products was doctored and fake samples were supplied to the government. Insurance fraud, subsidy fraud, VAT fraud and other fiscal and employment offences were also committed. The 'victims' of the company's numerous offences were the government, the environment and those companies which played by the rules.

Lax government enforcement of regulatory laws also played a role in the TCR case. Despite warnings to officials and politicians of the criminal record of some of the principal managers, the company was able to attract substantial subsidies. However, when the true facts came to light, the same officials and politicians claimed to be outraged. The case also was taken seriously by the prosecuting and judicial authorities. The individual defendants were tried and convicted, and received sentences ranging from three to six years.

The TCR case highlights the significance of context. Although the waste disposal industry itself may have had bona fide pretensions and undoubtedly contained many legitimate companies, it also offered opportunities for quick profits with low risks by unlawful means. As a result, it attracted managers and staff with a criminal background and with a history for dubious ways of doing business. A near monopolistic industry with complex rules, fragmented regulation and lax inspection combined with an 'inverted incentive structure', where payments were made prior to performance, to facilitate what may have been a natural inclination on the part of at least some managers towards illegal solutions to business problems. Private-public partnerships and quasi-collusive arrangements with government agencies exacerbated the difficulties of supervision and decreased the likelihood of exposure (Huisman and Niemeijer: 1998: 61). Virtually never was a licence revoked. The opportunities were so rich, the regulation so weak, and the risk of apprehension so small that companies could almost be said to have been seduced into crime. The circumstances proved irresistible to devious managers who were eager to earn 'quick money' at the expense of depredations to the environment. These managers proved shrewd at manipulating the regulators and were quite impervious to the consequences of their actions.

2. Road transport and the Roy Bowles case: eyes wide shut to danger

In 1998 a lorry travelling on the M25 motorway near London crashed into the rear of another vehicle which in turn jumped the safety railing, hit an oncoming car and caused two deaths. The driver of the lorry worked for Roy Bowles Transport Company. Eyewitnesses claimed that the lorry had been driving erratically before the crash and the suspicion arose of driver exhaustion. The driver confessed to being tired and to speeding, but maintained that his employer had encouraged and rewarded such practices. He produced letters from the company secretary to confirm his assertions.

The company appears to have effectively operated at two levels or with what might be described as a 'split personality'. On the surface it appeared to be a model employer. Its chairman had been awarded an OBE for services to the Road Haulage Association and was chairman of the Ealing local magistrates' court. The company had passed inspections and had received the required 'ISO' certificates of quality. Yet the firm apparently encouraged its drivers to work excessively long hours and to falsify the tachometer readings that recorded their length of time at the wheel. It was self-evident, and especially should have been self-evident to those in the road transport industry, that these practices greatly increased the risk of a serious accident. Thus, while the company was, to the outside world, an exemplary and law-abiding corporate citizen, internally it was engaged in systematic and deliberate rule-breaking that entailed a high risk of injury and death for both its employees and other road users.

The M25 crash presented the Crown Prosecution Service (CPS) with a number of possible options. It could have charged the driver with various traffic offences and/or the company with a number of technical offences related to road transport. However, the police investigation had revealed that the company's drivers, with the encouragement of senior management, routinely spent irresponsibly long hours at the wheel. That the driver's behaviour on the occasion in question was not atypical was confirmed by interviews with other drivers and that the company had encouraged such practices was evidenced in its correspondence. The falsification of tachometers was indisputable. The offences appeared to be continuous over an extended period of time. Although some police forces might have approached the case as a routine road accident with fatalities, the police force concerned took a strong position on road deaths and had the resolve, expertise and will to conduct an in-depth investigation. As a result of this investigation, the decision was made to treat the deaths as culpable homicide. However, instead of charging the company with 'corporate manslaughter', the CPS chose to charge three members of the board and the driver with manslaughter. Two members of the board were convicted and were given suspended sentences (having changed their pleas to guilty during the course of the proceedings). The driver was also convicted but he received a custodial sentence. One director was acquitted.

What prompted the CPS's decision to prosecute the directors of the company and not the company itself? This must to some extent be a matter of speculation but two considerations, one in favour of prosecuting the directors and the other against prosecuting the company, suggest themselves. The first is that, because the company was small, it was relatively simple to trace the connection between directors' decisions and illegal driver practices. Secondly, it appears that the CPS may have been reluctant to prosecute the company because of its past lack of success in corporate manslaughter prosecutions (although what few successes it had achieved had been against small firms). The senior investigating officer believed that there was a determination to obtain a homicide conviction of some sort and that this outcome would have been jeopardised by a decision to pursue the more high-risk strategy of a prosecution of the company for corporate manslaughter.[6]

In the Roy Bowles case seemingly 'respectable' business executives systematically engaged in high risk ventures that endangered lives on a regular basis. One can only guess at the thinking of those involved in this particular case but it appears that the relevant decision-makers managed to dissociate their decisions from their possible consequences. It was as if the executives lived in a segmented world where they were able to filter out non-fitting and uncomfortable data. This defence mechanism enabled them to blind themselves to the consequences of their decisions and the actions of those who worked for them. This segmentation, which in some forms approximates to 'cognitive dissonance', can also be seen in the Thalidomide and Dalkon Shield cases where credible information on the harmful side-effects of corporate products was ignored by the company (Punch: 2000).

The Roy Bowles case, like the TCR case, reveals how various aspects of an industry can induce law-breaking (Clarke: 1990). The road transport industry has many small firms, low profit margins and ineffective regulation. Legal checks of vehicles are sporadic and it is relatively easy to patch up vehicles as necessary to pass inspections. The financial incentives to engage in illegal shortcuts are great. The reality is that the Roy Bowles case was not exceptional – spot checks consistently reveal that road haulage and coach firm drivers do not observe speed limits, doctor tachometers, do not possess legally required papers and operate unsafe

6   Personal communication with the authors.

vehicles. Those responsible for running these companies manage to blind themselves to the dangers and rationalise their decisions. They appear able to compartmentalise their thinking to the extent that they can live with this constant dichotomy. Side by side with a surface normality there exists a submerged reality wherein corporate policies routinely endanger the lives of their own employees, as well as those of innocent others who may become their random victims. In the context of a fragmented industry, with many small and marginal companies, low profit margins and high operating costs, there had developed a willingness, that for some had become a standard way of doing business, wherein risks with respect to maintenance were regularly taken, inspections were passed by temporary and patchwork repairs, and overtired drivers were allowed if not encouraged to remain behind the wheel.

3.   Guinness: a conspiracy of high flyers

Some cases feature executive decision-makers who appear to be in control of events and who take a fully-informed, conscious decision to break the law. Substantive crimes include conspiracies to fix prices or form an illegal cartel, industrial espionage, and the systematic bribing of foreign government officials. The critical decisions may form an instrumental, temporary or cyclical adaptation to business conditions. Crime is often not so much a generalised way of doing business, as it was in the waste disposal and road haulage industries, but rather a response to a unique combination of events, circumstances and commercial opportunities.

Often the key decisions are taken at the highest levels of a company, and the criminal schemes are sophisticated in their conception and implementation. In some instances they constitute concealed strategies for either the company's survival or expansion. As these cases often involve a conspiracy of corporate executives who need to camouflage their activities, the conspiracy may be confined to a small number of people or may be carefully covered by a temporary structure kept apart from normal business activities. All of these features figured prominently in the Guinness case.

The case arose against the backdrop of a spate of hostile takeovers in London in the 1980s. The takeovers were stimulated by financial deregulation and were patterned after the aggressive tactics developed in American markets. Ernest Saunders, the CEO of Guinness, a leading drinks company, made a decision to acquire the Distillers Company. The decision was nominally prompted by a desire to see Guinness grow so that it itself would not fall prey to a hostile takeover, but Saunders' personal ambition may also have entered into the equation. Complicating the acquisition was the fact that there was a rival bid for Distillers from the Argyll Group. In order to enhance the prospects of the Guinness bid being accepted, Saunders and several powerful business associates set out to misrepresent the value of the Guinness offer. They did this by embarking on an illegal share-support scheme which involved artificially driving up the value of Guinness shares in the stock market, thereby making the Guinness offer appear more attractive to Distillers shareholders than it was in reality.

When the share support scheme came to light, it led to a series of investigations and trials. In the first of these trials in 1990, Saunders, who was seen as the ringleader, was convicted and sentenced to five years' imprisonment. At the sentencing hearing the judge was scathing in his condemnation of the conspirators. He spoke of the corruption of public and commercial life, of an attack on the integrity of the market, and of the need for a deterrent sentence ('the sentence I pass must send a clear message that persons who seek commercial advantage by acting dishonestly can expect little mercy from the courts'; *The Times* 29 August 1990).

Although the judge, and portions of the media, regarded the offences as extremely damaging to the reputation of the City of London and undermining of its integrity, not all commentators were prepared to be as critical. Some were of the opinion that the behaviour of the defendants was not significantly different from that of other so-called 'corporate raiders', who were held in high esteem in the business community for their daring and acumen. It later emerged that the Serious Fraud Office, which prosecuted the case, was aware of other similar schemes which they had not disclosed to the defendants. Had they done so, it would have bolstered the defendants' claim that their actions were, if not 'business as usual', at least not self-evidently illegal.

One of the more intriguing features of the Guinness case is how the company managed to escape not only prosecution, but also any form of public censure. Although only a handful of individuals were involved in the conspiracy, they were at the highest level of the company. Other members of the board of directors, however, were kept in the dark. This allowed these directors, as well as the company itself, to portray Saunders and his co-conspirators as mavericks who were not acting in the best interests of the company. The company reinforced this claimed separation by subsequently dismissing Saunders and severing its ties with the other defendants.

To a sceptic, these efforts to dissociate the company from the conspiracy might seem somewhat disingenuous. Had the takeover bid succeeded, few questions would likely have been asked about the methods employed, and Saunders and his colleagues would probably have been hailed as the saviours of the company. Furthermore, without the corporate setting, and the camouflage it provided against regulatory scrutiny, the crime probably could not have been committed. Nor were the other directors lacking in clues that should have raised a suspicion about what was going on. The board was asked to approve and did approve significant outlays of funds that were needed to underwrite the share support scheme. One may genuinely wonder why so few questions were asked about where the authorised expenditures were being directed. While the company's role may have been more passive than active, it could be faulted for not more carefully superintending the activities of its officers. It seemed rather as if the board preferred to keep a buffer zone between itself and Saunders and his associates, thereby allowing it to disown them when their illegality was exposed.

The Guinness case can also be placed in a cultural and economic context. The deregulation of financial services had fostered a new spirit of entrepreneurial activities and corporate expansion, and had given rise to a culture of 'moral ambivalence and the primacy of financial gain' (Doig: 2000: 99). New more combative rules of the takeover 'game' were evolving, and in this context Saunders and his colleagues no doubt saw themselves as aggressive innovators rather than corporate criminals. Unfortunately for them, both the law and the courts thought otherwise.

4. The Southall rail crash: human error and systemic failure in a world of deregulation

Although rarely does a company consciously set out to cause death, often managerial decisions and board approved policies form the backdrop against which deaths can nevertheless occur. Corporate pressures to maximize profits can lead to the downgrading of safety as a priority. In those industries with a potential harm factor for employees, consumers and others – transport, pharmaceuticals, chemicals, food, etc – this downgrading can lead to the creation of serious risks. While we saw in the Roy Bowles case an illustration of managers blinding themselves to consequences that must have been apparent to them given their closeness to operations, the same phenomenon can occur in companies where senior management is far removed from day-to-day, on-line practices, and where there is a lengthy chain between strategic decisions and operational risks. Companies which are ostensibly risk averse and safety conscious may, in certain circumstances, find themselves on a 'slippery slope' of unconscious risk-taking whereby small, incremental steps that lead to successful performance imperceptibly foster an increasing margin of risk – as we saw in the case of the *Challenger* space shuttle accident.

The Southall rail crash serves to illuminate the type of unintended and unforeseen disaster that can result. The crash occurred on the Swansea to Paddington run when an express train of Great Western Railways (GWR) passed through two warning lights and a red light and collided with a commuter train at Southall. Seven passengers died and many more were injured. At the time of the crash the driver was packing his bags in preparation for his journey home (Uff Report: 2000). While the crash might seem like a clear-cut case of driver error, the situation was complicated by the fact that installed on the train in question were both the Automatic Warning System (AWS), which would have alerted the driver that a warning signal had been passed but would have required his intervention to bring the train to a stop, and a pilot version of the Automatic Train Protection (ATP) system, which would automatically have stopped the train after it had gone through a red light. Neither system was in operation at the front of the train on the return run from Swansea. The AWS was operational at what was now the rear of the train but, to have been of benefit to the driver, the train would have had to have been turned around. As this would have caused a delay, a decision was taken at operational management level not to turn the train around. For his part, the driver had never driven without AWS. Nor was there a second person in the driver's cab, which would have been the better practice and would also have helped to avert the disaster. Stripped of both human and technological backup, the driver's error was, while not inevitable, clearly not unforeseeable. Charges of manslaughter were brought against both the driver and the rail company, but the charges against the company were dismissed on technical legal grounds[7] (the failure of the prosecution to show the involvement of persons who could be said to be 'identified' with the company) and those against the driver were dropped thereafter by the CPS.

The immediate cause of the accident may have been a combination of driver error and systemic failures, but the disaster can also be placed in a political context. From being a nationalised industry, the railways under Margaret Thatcher's Conservative government went to a privatised structure of competing companies with some 25 separate firms running services, three rolling-stock companies, and one company – Railtrack – being responsible for the track and its maintenance. In all about 100 different companies were involved in the management of the railways (Jack: 2001: 51). There was a lack of co-ordination among companies, and most seemed to be out

---

7   See *A-G's Reference (No 2 of 1999)* [2000] QB 796.

for short-term profits. In the balance, issues of safety received relatively low priority. While representatives of the industry would doubtless maintain that safety was a high priority, several post-Southall crashes, as well as evidence presented to the House of Commons Select Committee on Transport and hearings of inquiries into the Clapham, Southall, Hatfield and Ladbroke Grove crashes would all seem to belie their claims.

Strategic decisions at various levels contributed to the Southall crash. Within the industry could be discerned a general resistance to adopt the more advanced ATP system, which is in use on many continental trains and required in some European states, largely because of its cost. The government, which had just divested itself of the railways, was reluctant to make a financial contribution to the development of the ATP, or to share the costs of its implementation. Nor did it appear to wish to impose this financial burden on the recently privatised companies. At an operational level the decision was made not to turn the train around at Swansea. Unlike the industry and government decisions, however, the decision not to turn the train around would not have entailed undue expense but only delay. The decision can be seen as symptomatic of the relative emphasis given by the company and the industry to safety compared to the adherence to schedules. The government may have also contributed to this prioritising by threatening with fines those companies which chronically failed to keep to schedule, while not taking vigorous action against companies which had poor safety records. While it could be argued that the train should not have been allowed to depart with a safety system that did not fully comply with technical specifications, the relevant regulations were worded to allow for exceptions. This was one more factor in the chain leading to this 'avoidable accident'.

Assuming, for the sake of argument, that the immediate cause of the Southall crash was driver error, did the contributory decisions of management amount to recklessness or gross negligence to the extent that the relevant executives and the company – neither of which 'intended' to cause death – could be prosecuted for manslaughter? Following an investigation by the British Transport Police the decision was made to prosecute both the driver and GWR, but not individual members of the board. This decision might seem anomalous in light of the 'identification' test of corporate criminal liability that was then in force, under which a company is criminally liable for manslaughter only if a person who was part of its directing mind is guilty of manslaughter, but the decision was deliberately and consciously taken with a view to presenting the courts with the opportunity to adopt a more embracing view of corporate criminal liability. In the event, however, the prosecution's theory was rejected, although the company was fined £1.5m after having admitted to breaches of health and safety regulations.

The prosecution team believed that the blame for the Southall crash could be found in the grossly negligent practices of the company, and in particular its cavalier attitude to issues of safety, but the Court of Appeal was not prepared to accept this conceptualisation of fault as a substitute for satisfaction of the 'identification' test of corporate criminal liability. Nor was it prepared to adopt it as a new test of liability. While it might have been argued that the decisions of intermediate management at Swansea were responsible for the crash, this option was not pursued, no doubt because these managers lacked sufficient overall decision-making authority within GWR to satisfy the identification test. The driver clearly made a tragic error of judgment but if he alone had been convicted then he might have been seen as a sacrificial lamb.

The Southall crash, unfortunately, was not an isolated incident. Over a fifteen year period, the rail industry had been dogged by a series of highly publicised fatal 'accidents' from Clapham in 1987 to Potters Bar in 2002. Although the decision not to install ATP doubtless cost lives, it can be placed in the broader context of an industry characterised by poor service, high prices and a dubious history of track maintenance (Jack: 2001). What is less clear is whether the critical decision-makers, from operational managers to corporate executives to boardroom directors, had considered the possibility or likelihood of such crashes. Or did they accept the occasional crash as a business inevitability that could never be totally eliminated? Were the dangers simply too remote to have been clearly perceived?

Unlike in the Roy Bowles case, where the decision-makers were not far removed from the practices of the firm's drivers, the board of directors of rail companies such as GWR are less likely to have first-hand knowledge of on-line flash points. Furthermore, the characteristics of the decision-makers in the two cases were quite different. In the Roy Bowles case, the decision-makers were intimately familiar with the nature of the transport industry. The so-called 'new breed' of railway executives, on the other hand, could boast extensive experience in finance, property, hotels and retail services, but their knowledge of engineering may have been deficient and they were lacking in experience in running a railroad. This inexperience was compounded by corporate structures which elongated the links in the chain from boardroom to 'scene of the crime'.

The impression, reinforced by the public inquiries referred to previously, is that rule-breaking in the rail industry is not only widespread but also of long-standing. Despite repeated promises by the rail companies to pay more attention to safety, dangerous practices have been allowed to persist. Much maintenance work is subcontracted and firms are under pressure to perform with penalty clauses for delays. There have even been reports of intimidation of safety officers who had recommended delays because such delays would have affected workers' income (Jack: 2001: 60-61; Cullen Report: 1990). As in the Guinness case, blame may also be attributed, to a certain but indeterminate extent, to the climate of the times and, more particularly, to the effects of deregulation, privatisation and competition. These forces had served to generate fragmentation in the industry, an emphasis on short-term profits, reliance on antiquated rolling-stock, a lack of co-ordination on safety issues, a neglect of maintenance, and a new breed of corporate executives who understood business management but not the rail industry. A subtle shift in the authority for decision-making had occurred from engineers to persons of diverse backgrounds more versed in property and commercial dealing, and the culture of the industry had been indelibly altered. Although the Health and Safety Executive had a special section for the railways, its regulators had not shown themselves to be capable of preventing major accidents.

The analysis of the Southall crash illustrates the difficulties of untangling the many threads of responsibility when a corporate disaster occurs. Liability may rest with individuals (ranging from on-line workers to operational management to boardroom executives), operating systems, regulatory bodies and oversight institutions appointed by the government, and even the prevailing culture and ethos. Usually it will be easier to prosecute individuals than companies, and certainly much easier to prosecute either of these than something as ephemeral and intangible as a culture or ethos.

F.   PREVIEW: CORPORATE CRIME AND THE LAW

To understand corporate crime entails looking at a range of offences and contexts from the relatively benign to the pathological, while meaningful reform of the law will require proposals anchored in an understanding of the criminological and organisational dimensions of companies. We have seen that not all companies in an industry break the law and that corporate crime is not an historical inevitability. This strengthens the case for prosecuting those companies who do choose to break the law. They had a choice, and, like human offenders, should be held accountable when they exercise their power of choice in a criminal way. Further underpinning the case for criminal sanctions is a recognition that companies are capable of changing their behaviour. Corporations can be deterred by the prospect of criminal sanctions and can be reformed in response to an appropriate court order.

Given a company's capacity to reform itself and to go from being a law-breaker to being a compliant corporate citizen, how can a generalised strategy be devised for effecting such change? One of the more promising developments in recent years has been an apparent willingness on the part of companies, led by many of the major corporations in the United States, to establish corporate compliance departments designed to prevent wrongdoing, promote observance of the law and ferret out illegal violations when they occur. Companies are also formulating codes of conduct and organising ethical and fraud-consciousness training sessions. However, some would argue that this 'ethical revolution' is a temporary luxury linked to expanding markets and buoyant profits that would evaporate if profits sagged or companies faced poor results. Others see the new ethical codes as formalistic evidentiary markers that could be introduced at a trial to demonstrate the company's seeming good faith. The cynics will not be surprised to learn that none of these measures have prevented a number of self-proclaimed 'clean' companies from being exposed for their failures to comply with their own rules and public promises (eg the Prudential Insurance Company and 'mis-selling' of pensions; *Guardian*, 17 November 1997). What the ethical revolution does highlight, however, is a potential, which needs to be harnessed, for internal systems for controlling corporate wrongdoing.

How these self-regulatory initiatives can be fitted into a state's legal system is one of the main themes that we will be exploring in this book. Before widespread self-regulation can be contemplated, the law needs to be strengthened so that companies have an incentive to regulate themselves. Where the law is weak, the chances of prosecution slight, and the sanctions following a conviction feeble, companies may choose to adopt illegal but profitable strategies and absorb the occasional fine as a cost of doing business (Gobert 1998; Braithwaite: 1985: 7). It is clearly imperative, however, that any economic advantage to violating the law be removed and that companies come to see that it is in their self-interest to obey the law.

We start from the premise that companies are corporate citizens, with all the responsibilities of citizenship. The issuance of a charter, or, in more modern times, a certificate of incorporation is, for a company, the analogue of a grant of citizenship to a natural person. Companies can also receive licenses to engage in activities denied to ordinary citizens and those companies to which a license is not granted. As the quid pro quo, companies arguably incur various obligations, including the obligation to obey the law and to foster obedience to the law by their staff and officers. However, experience has taught that many companies do not take these obligations seriously, and that when they do not, the criminal justice system has encountered considerable difficulty in holding them to account. Legal violations frequently occur in the course of a company's business and can result in substantial harm, harm which if caused under comparable circumstances by a human offender would lead to a criminal prosecution, a term of imprisonment, and the social condemnation and stigma that accompanies a conviction. Why do not the same consequences flow from a company's violations of the law and why does the criminal justice system encounter such difficulties in holding companies legally accountable for their wrongdoing?

There are a number of possible explanations. These range from a psychological failure to perceive corporate crimes as 'real' crime; to inadequate investigatory mechanisms for detecting when a corporate offence has occurred; to a legal test of liability which fails to recognise the nature of modern corporate decision-making; to rules of evidence and trial procedures which were designed with individuals in mind and may be ill-suited to the trial of a company; and to a scheme of sanctions and penalties that typically amounts to little more than a slap on the wrist of the offender. Each of these failings interrelates with and compounds the others. The bottom line is that the criminal justice system, as presently constituted, fails to deter, detect or meaningfully punish corporate wrongdoing.

Until fairly recently, neither the government nor the public seemed to view corporate crime as being a serious problem, and they still may not see it being as serious a problem as more common forms of crime such as burglary or theft. The government's reluctance to take corporate crime seriously may be borne of self-serving motives. Profitable, albeit law-breaking, companies pay taxes, reduce unemployment and contribute to the international reputation of the state – as well as to the funding of political parties. It is simply not in the government's interest to put such companies out of business. Even the threat of a possible prosecution may prompt a decision to relocate in a more corporate-friendly environment, or stifle the innovation required to compete in a global economy. The message is conveyed and reinforced by business executives turned politicians, and by ex-politicians turned business executives. There is often an incestuous interchange between political and managerial elites, with former executives winding up with ministerial posts and former ministers being appointed as non-executive directors at a range of companies (Useem: 1984).

Equally understandable perhaps is the public's lack of concern over corporate crime. Street crime is more visible, more immediate, and more threatening than is corporate crime. The public does not fear corporate crime as it does street crime. There is a sense of personal violation when one's home is burgled or one's possessions stolen. There is a palpable fear when one is confronted by a violent hooligan or knife-wielding robber. But how many passengers fear, or are even aware, that they are being transported by a train equipped with a faulty or inoperative warning system or a ferry that is defectively designed and subject to capsize? Consequently, there is not the same public outcry to 'do something' about 'crime in the suites' as there is about 'crime in the streets' (Punch: 2000). Indeed, particularly with respect to offences against the revenue, the public is often prepared to collude with wrongdoers. Thus, consumers may be willing to pay in cash in exchange for a lower price, well appreciating that the contractor may be seeking to evade paying VAT. Similarly, purchasers are willing to buy goods in a grey market, their desire for a bargain overcoming whatever reservations they might have that they are handling stolen goods and thereby abetting thieves.

The moral ambivalence that permeates this area (Nelken: 1997) can be seen in a highly-publicised case from the Netherlands. A well-known family firm, which ran a chain of hotels and motorway restaurants, was prosecuted for tax fraud. The offences had been deliberate and persistent (the family also had a tendency to build motels without proper planning permission and licences), the sums were large (on the order of £70m), and the defendants had displayed an aggressive recalcitrance when dealing with the authorities. They publicly belittled the regulators, compared their methods to those of the Nazi occupiers in the war, blamed the trade unions for betraying them (and argued for their abolition), and posed as socially conscious employers espousing essential 'Dutch' values of industry and thrift. They were, in particular, scathing about the pettiness and irrelevance of rules which were a meddlesome brake on healthy and 'honest' enterprise. On the other hand, the defendants provided much sought-after local employment as well as excellent value to customers. After they were convicted and given prison sentences, there was widespread public outrage that these industrious entrepreneurs should be treated as criminals, even though the amounts involved were astronomical in relation to most conventional crimes (a feature which attracted high sentences: Helmer: 1997). Interestingly, on appeal the sentences were reduced to terms of community service (Huisman and Niemeijer: 1998).

The same moral ambivalence is discernible in Britain, and extends to judges as well as the public. After Terry Ramsden of Glen International pleaded guilty to a fraud amounting to £90m, the sentencing judge observed that the defendant had built up 'an honest, impressive and phenomenally successful business' of which he could justifiably be proud. The judge continued that Ramsden's character stood him in good stead and that, while offences of the sort he had committed would normally warrant a sentence of imprisonment, a suspended sentence in his case would satisfy the demands of justice. In another case a financial services company collapsed with some £34m in debts. The Serious Fraud Office mounted a substantial investigation, planning to bring 42 charges, but in the event the defendant was allowed to plead to one charge and was sentenced to 180 hours of community service (Doig: 2000: 119-120).

Public and judicial ambivalence toward corporate criminality fit comfortably with the government's desire not to ruffle the feathers of its tax-paying corporate citizens. Yet the risks that such organisations create by their illegality can cause harm that far exceeds that which could be wrought by the most dangerous of human offenders. The largest industrial accident ever, at Bhopal in India, may have killed as many as 5,000 people and injured over 2,000,000. Although criminal negligence was suspected, the disaster did not lead to a prosecution and conviction, as criminal proceedings were halted following a settlement between Union Carbide and the Indian government (Shrivastava: 1987; Fortun: 2001).

If a government were committed to curbing corporate crime, it would as a preliminary matter have to allocate the resources to detect offences. In England, however, the responsibility for enforcing most of the criminal laws that control corporate activity is entrusted to regulatory authorities or inspectorates rather than to the police. As part of the 'deregulatory' movement, successive governments have also decreased the funds allotted to these agencies. Furthermore, they are often understaffed. The experience of the Serious Fraud Office, which is neither underfunded nor understaffed, demonstrates that even under the best of circumstances, it is not easy to bring a corporate offender to heel. Business dealings are complex, and the proof of a criminal violation may lie buried in corporate archives and computer data that require years to sift through and make sense of (assuming they have not already been 'cleansed' or shredded). Financial transactions designed to conceal money laundering, for example, may involve the transfer of funds around the world several times over in the space of minutes, yet following the money trail may take years of painstaking work. For an underfunded and understaffed agency, which may receive at best lukewarm support from the government, the problems are acute.

Bringing a criminal prosecution against a corporate wrongdoer can be problematic as well. As we shall discuss in greater detail in the following chapters, a large part of the difficulty lies in devising a test of liability that is suitable for companies. Traditional legal doctrines were developed with respect to human offenders. In superimposing these doctrines on to corporate defendants, the courts have had to locate the corporate mind for purposes of assessing mens rea. For the English judges the company's mind was to be found in the mind of one of its directors, officers and senior managers, persons who could be 'identified' with the company for legal purposes. But even a rudimentary understanding of how corporate decisions are made would indicate the futility of this approach. In a company, ideas that may originate with an individual will be reviewed by working parties, committees, senior managers, vice-presidents in charge of whatever phase of the company's operation is involved, CEOs and, ultimately, a board of directors. The final product may bear little resemblance to the originator's conception. Where responsibility is so diffused, it makes little sense to strive to link decisions with particular individuals.

Tests of corporate criminality that impute human fault to companies are unsatisfying all around. For the company they are unsatisfying because, as an institutional entity, it may not have behaved in a blameworthy manner. The crime may have been in direct contravention of corporate policy, and the company may have tried its best to prevent its commission. In some instances the company may find itself the victim of the crime, yet at the same time be legally liable for its occurrence. For the prosecution, the link between corporate criminal liability and individual criminal liability is unsatisfying for, while it may be obvious that a crime has been committed, it may be impossible to trace responsibility for that harm to a particular individual because of the diffused nature of corporate decision-making. In the final analysis the linkage of corporate fault to human fault is unsatisfying because corporate fault is not the same as human fault, just as the body corporate is distinct from the individuals who are its directors, officers and employees. The goals of a company cannot automatically be equated with the goals of any one person or combination of persons, nor can one derive the goals of the company by adding together potentially conflicting individual goals. A company has its own distinctive goals, its own distinctive culture, and its own distinctive personality. It is an independent organic entity, and, as such, should be responsible in its own right, directly and not derivatively, for the criminal consequences that arise out of the way that its business is conducted. This is not to preclude prosecutions of individuals when they have committed an offence, but rather to recognise that, in addition to the prosecution of individuals, the company must shoulder its share of the legal blame to the extent that it bears responsibility for an offence. When that responsibility dwarfs that of the individual actor, then a prosecution of the company alone may be warranted.

What is needed is a theory of criminal liability that captures the distinctive nature of corporate fault. We start from the insight that a significant proportion of corporate offences are, in fact, crimes of omission rather than commission. Typically, the company's fault will lie in its failure to have put into place protective mechanisms that would have prevented harm from occurring. It is for this failure that the company bears responsibility for the harm. Recognising that corporate crimes are more often crimes of omission than commission reinforces the poverty of derivative theories of corporate liability that attribute the offences of individuals to a company. While it may be feasible to link wrongful acts to particular actors, it is often impossible to determine who should have done something that was not done. The obligation to put into place systems that would avert crime is *collective* and the failure to do so is a reflection of the way that the company has chosen to conduct its business.

Once a viable legal theory of criminal liability is established, courts need to consider the rules of evidence and criminal procedure that should govern the trial of a corporate defendant. Little thought has been given to these issues and judges have generally taken the path of least resistance and adhered to the same rules and procedures as when a human defendant is in the dock. The burden is on the Crown to prove the company's guilt 'beyond reasonable doubt'. But is the analogy to human defendants persuasive? In the trial of a natural person, the defendant's liberty is at stake for a conviction can lead to imprisonment. It is generally agreed that, given this potential loss of liberty, courts should bend over backwards to avoid erroneous convictions; hence the aphorism that it is better that ten guilty defendants go free than that an innocent defendant go to jail. In contrast, when a company is on trial, it is not facing imprisonment if convicted. The most likely penalty that will follow a conviction is a fine (although we shall argue in chapter 7 for a more encompassing and imaginative approach to sanctions). Although a fine goes to the State and not to the victims, it is in nature more akin to the damages awarded in a civil suit than it is to traditional criminal punishments. In a civil case a plaintiff has the burden of establishing his/her claim by a 'balance of probabilities'. While a civil standard of proof in the criminal trial of a company may be a bridge too far, a lesser standard than 'beyond reasonable doubt' may be warranted because of the fact that the company's 'liberty' is not at stake. Similarly, rules of evidence that traditionally have been applied to a criminal trial of a natural person may merit re-thinking in the context of the trial of a company. The analogy to a civil proceeding is arguably far stronger than to a criminal prosecution, even if the company's wrong is nominally titled a 'crime'. It is not the same type of crime that we think of when we contemplate murders, rapes and burglaries.

Finally, there is the issue of sanctions following a conviction. To the company's way of thinking, this may be a more important issue than that of guilt. When it deliberates policies that may take it down a path that can lead to its criminal prosecution, a company may be the epitome of the rational cost-benefit calculator. It is concerned with consequential, not moral, reasons for obeying the law. What it wants to know is what will happen to it if it violates the law. If the company's analysts see that it is in the company's financial interest to obey the law, the company will do so; if the analysts think it is not, the company will not. In this economic calculus, the fine imposed for a violation of the criminal law may become simply another entry on the corporate ledger sheet. The company's maximum exposure is readily determinable, being bounded by the highest penalty permitted by the relevant statute and the jurisdictional authority of the court in which a prosecution is most likely to be brought. The fine can thus be internalised as a cost of production and passed on to the consumer.

The task of constructing a viable regime of corporate sanctions, like the task of constructing a viable theory of corporate liability, has been hampered by the anthropomorphic tendency to equate companies that violate the law with individuals who violate the law. Because companies cannot be imprisoned, monetary sanctions have become the penalty of default. Since the days when felons were hanged, the law of sentencing with respect to human offenders has evolved significantly, and innovative penalties, including community service and, more recently, electronic tagging, have been developed. No comparable evolution in the field of corporate sanctions, however, can be discerned. In chapter 7 we propose to look more closely at what punishments might be imposed on companies that are convicted of criminal offences in light of the theoretical justifications of punishment.

These, then, will be the themes and ideas that we will be enlarging upon in the ensuing chapters. Our goal is to add a fresh, up-to-date perspective – drawing strongly from sociology/criminology and the criminal law – to the existing literature. Sociology and criminology are wide-ranging disciplines that explore human behaviour in all its richness and variety. They can help us to understand why those in business – from workers to directors – behave in the way that they do. It is a complex issue, and sociologists and criminologists tend to favour multi-factored rather than unitary explanations. Looking at behaviour through legal lenses is quite a different exercise, as the criminal justice system is an instrument for narrowing issues, clarifying whether or not offences have occurred, and determining to whom fault should be attributed.

In this introductory chapter we have drawn on sociological, criminological and legal sources, and from these have derived a number of key insights that will inform our subsequent analysis: that the corporate form can both create the opportunity for crime while camouflaging those crimes that are committed; that corporate offences may in some cases inure to a company's benefit and in other cases harm the company; that the motivations of corporate actors can be multiple and varied; that investigation and prosecution often involve intricate processes of definition that can be affected by a company's power to bargain in both the political and legal arena; and that many executives who are engaged in criminal practices do not see themselves as criminals, or their behaviour in terms of being criminal. We do not subscribe to the view that there is a single all-encompassing explanation for corporate crime, but rather see the causes of corporate criminality as many and diverse, with roots in the contingent and contextual dilemmas faced by executives within corporations. Our primary focus is not on individual or 'white-collar' crimes, but rather on the role that the *organisation* plays in an individual's offence. But perspectives can vary with one's vantage point. To an outside observer the business environment 'produces' deviance by creating the opportunities, means, incentives and rationalisation for criminal activity, while to those on the inside illegal responses to the stresses of the business world may be perceived as technical violations or even as standard, even if covert, procedures representing 'business as usual'.

While not denying that there are white-collar criminals whose offences are motivated by the same types of impulses that drive ordinary criminals, many corporate executives who opt for criminal solutions to business problems may be seen in a different light: not as morally reprehensible deviants, but as social actors responding to the pressures created by a corporate environment where contingent choices have to be made which may or may not conform with the law. At the same time, it would be clearly erroneous to assert that the corporate environment somehow deprives business executives of free will. They are able to choose criminal or non-criminal solutions to their problems, and the removal of potential criminal liability might well tempt some to yield to the criminal options, which would obviously not be in society's interest. These conflicting perspectives of the white-collar criminal complicate the allocation of legal responsibility between individuals and their companies. That we choose to focus primarily, but not exclusively, on the legal responsibility of the latter is because the company's responsibility, while not ignored (see Fisse and Braithwaite: 1993; Slapper and Tombs: 1999; Bergman: 2000; Wells: 2001) has tended to receive less attention and analysis than the liability of individuals.

The foundation for our analysis rests on our view of the company as an organic entity that has a responsibility as a corporate citizen to obey the law and to promote law-abiding behaviour by its employees and officers. Our analysis will be situated primarily within an English law context – not for parochial reasons, but because the problems encountered in England have resonance for corporate crime throughout the world. While the analysis in this chapter of why companies commit crimes has been based in significant part on an empirical examination of case histories, we propose in future chapters to strike out on a more normative path, particularly in regard to the analysis of legal issues. In a new century with a relatively new government in Britain promising a new regulatory climate, it is appropriate to go beyond the often dated material and limited perspectives of much of the standard literature and case law. Our aim is to provide new insights on the nature and causes of corporate crime, on the weaknesses of the law and how they might be overcome, and on the problems of policing companies. In light of the growing recognition of the seriously deleterious effects of corporate crime, and the increasing awareness of society's inability to cope with the problem, we hope that our analyses and proposals will stimulate the thinking of legislators, lawyers, judges, businessmen and women, academics and all concerned citizens.

CHAPTER 2

Corporate criminality I: Imputed liability

A. INTRODUCTION

In chapter 1 we saw that behind a crime that occurs in a business context may lie a multiplicity of causes. Human error may combine with misguided policies and ill-advised decisions against the backdrop of a corporate culture or ethos wherein compliance with the law is given low priority. The source of that culture may be traceable to a political climate wherein regulatory controls had been weakened as a result of a prevailing philosophy of deregulation. Yet when deaths, serious injuries, financial losses and other significant damage occurs and a criminal prosecution is brought, it is most likely to be brought against the individual whose acts form the most immediate link to the harm. Perhaps this is understandable. The fault of the individual – be it the train driver who, by his own admission, was packing his bags and paying insufficient attention to the signals on the line at the moment of the Southall crash; or the assistant bosun of the *Herald of Free Enterprise* who was asleep and failed to close the bow doors – is readily apparent. The responsibility of the managers, officers and directors of a company, and, even more so, that of the company itself, may be shrouded in obscurity and ambiguity. A prosecutor may be disinclined to take the time and effort required to work up a complex case against a large and powerful company that has the will and the financial resources to mount a vigorous defence to a criminal prosecution. Political pressures may also be brought to bear against the prosecution of companies by politicians of all stripes who are reluctant to be branded as 'anti-business', or by government officials who do not wish the government's role in the offence to be too closely probed.

None the less, prosecutors should not blind themselves to the role that companies can play in the criminal offences of their staff and officers. As we have observed, the corporate environment may provide the opportunity, the incentive, the setting, the means and a ready rationalisation for an employee's offence. If the ultimate goal is the elimination or at least a reduction in the number of business-related crimes, the company is in the best position to prevent the offence. It can screen applicants for jobs and hire only those whom it judges to be competent and responsible. It can instruct its workforce on how it wishes the company's business to be carried out, and establish whatever rules, regulations and operating procedures it deems to be appropriate and necessary. It can back these up with what amounts to a private justice system, in which it may discipline, demote and perhaps ultimately dismiss those who fail to meet the company's standards. As illustrated by the Southall case which we discussed in chapter 1, it is now often feasible to introduce technological safeguards to protect against human error. A company can also appoint supervisors and compliance officers to monitor its workforce and uncover any breaches of its policies.

That a company's control over its business operation is both sweeping and potentially omnipresent is indisputable. The question, however, is whether a company that does not exercise such powers of control or fails to superintend the actions of its employees, agents and officers should be *criminally* liable if a crime is committed by one of these individuals. And if a company does make a good faith and reasonable effort to exercise such control but a crime is nevertheless committed, should this preclude the possibility of a prosecution? Or is there a case to be made for corporate criminal liability regardless of the good faith efforts of the company to prevent the crime? Is there something about the corporate context that warrants a departure from the general principle of criminal law that, absent a showing of complicity, one defendant is not ordinarily liable for the crime of another?

A company's connection to a criminal offence committed by one of its employees may run the gamut from 'passive acquiescence', where the company could have prevented the offence but did not, to 'active encouragement', where the company's structures, policies, practices, rewards, procedures, ethos or culture seem almost to have precipitated or promoted the offence. Few companies would be so crass as to order an employee to commit a crime, but often a company will set unrealistic goals that seem to be attainable only by cutting legal corners (a frequent complaint/ excuse of employees who are caught offending). At the same time the company may convey the impression, either explicitly or implicitly, that it is not terribly concerned with the means by which its goals are realised. Financial rewards and promotions may await those who meet assigned targets; demotion and redundancy may be the fate of those who do not. Incentives and bonuses, as well as psychological pressuring, may cause employees to cross an ethical and legal divide. Tight deadlines, fostered by a 'time is money' mentality, may exacerbate the pressure to adopt illegal methods for attaining hard-to-achieve objectives. In an environment where ends take priority over means, and profits over principles, where phrases such as 'by hook or by crook' may be uttered without the trace of a smile, undue pressures may be felt by employees to ignore the proscriptions of the law. Appeals to the corporate mission can erode an employee's sense of personal responsibility, with right and wrong in danger of becoming equated with the achievement of organisational goals. At the same time, these goals offer a ready and seductive rationalisation for any illegality. In this way are criminal offences instigated, encouraged, fostered and facilitated by the corporate environment.

There are a number of possible positions that a criminal justice system might stake out with respect to a company's criminal liability for offences committed by persons who are employed by it or are empowered to act for it. First, the law might take the position that crimes are committed only by human beings who can commit proscribed acts with a wrongful mental state, and not by inanimate, fictional entities which lack both body and mind. This is the view of the so-called 'methodological individualists', and is reflected in the laws of those countries, including many in continental Europe, where a company may be guilty of an administrative offence, but not a traditional crime. While the picture is rapidly changing, Belgium, Germany, Sweden, Spain and Switzerland, among others, took this position as of the year 2001.

We shall examine the question of whether a company is capable of committing a crime first, as, unless one accepts the validity of this proposition, there is little point in proceeding to a lengthy disquisition on the appropriate test of corporate criminal liability. A related but perhaps less dogmatic position would concede that companies are capable of committing crimes, and therefore should potentially be subject to criminal liability, but that criminal prosecutions should be resorted to only as a last resort. For those who hold this position, the criminal law is a crude and inefficient way to control corporate misconduct, a bit like using a sledgehammer to crack a nut. They see civil law suits, or regulatory actions which do not involve the courts (such as revocation of a license or right to trade) as superior ways of securing compliance with the law. While we plan to examine the viability of civil suits as a means of deterring corporate misconduct in this chapter, we shall defer to chapter 9 the discussion of regulatory controls.

A second and contrary view holds that the most effective way to induce a company to take measures to prevent criminal activity by its personnel is to hold the company liable for all crimes committed by those who represent the company or are engaged in carrying out its business. In the United States federal courts and in most American state courts, a company can be held criminally responsible for an offence committed by an employee, agent or officer of the company who at the time is pursuing the company's business with an intent to benefit the company. There are exceptions to this rule, but American judges seem on the whole disinclined to exonerate corporate defendants. The converse inclination can be discerned among the English judges, who seem to search for reasons *not* to hold companies legally responsible for crimes committed by their staff or workforce. A more limited form of liability prevails in England, with companies being held responsible only for the offences of persons who can be said to be 'identified' with the company, a category comprised primarily of the company's directors, executive officers and senior managers. After briefly examining the history of corporate criminal liability, we shall critically examine the American and English approaches, each of which has advantages but both of which have shortcomings.

The main shortcoming of theories of vicarious, derivative or imputed liability (the terminology may differ but the idea is the same – the company is responsible for a crime committed by an individual) is that they fail to identify what exactly it is that a company has done wrong to warrant the offence of a natural person being attributed to it. Without a convincing rationale for corporate liability in such circumstances, companies will be hard pressed to know what they need to do to avoid liability. Arguably, like natural persons, companies should not be subject to criminal sanctions unless it can be shown that they have been in some sense blameworthy. The principle of *nulle poene sine culpa* (no punishment without fault) is deeply engrained in the criminal law, and should be departed from only if the aims of the criminal justice system cannot otherwise be achieved.

Keeping faith with the *nulla poena* principle suggests a third possible approach to corporate criminality, which would be to limit liability to cases where it could be proved that the company had been at fault in inciting, encouraging, aiding, abetting, facilitating, counselling, rewarding or in some other way significantly contributing to an offence committed by a person working for, or connected in a significant way with, the company. The company's liability would be akin to that of an accessory. Conceiving of corporate criminality in terms of accessorial liability arguably offers a more coherent rationale for imposing criminal penalties on companies than simply invoking the phrase 'vicarious liability', which often is little more than another way of stating a conclusion – that a company is criminally liable – without providing a reason for that conclusion.

This chapter will focus on criminal liability that is imputed or attributed to companies for offences committed by natural persons. This is the traditional approach taken in most countries where companies are subject to criminal liability, including both Britain and the United States. In the next chapter we shall consider an altogether different approach premised on the recognition that business-orientated crimes often are a function not only of individual deviancy but also of a failure on the part of a company to guard against criminologically significant risk. Companies arguably have, or should have, a legal duty to devise and implement systems that would prevent criminal offences by their staff and officers, to monitor closely those individuals whom they have placed in a position to commit a crime or cause harm, and to foster a corporate culture where illegality is simply not acceptable. In this new approach to corporate criminal liability, a company's crime would consist of its culpable failure to prevent offences of its personnel from occurring. The link between that offence and the accessorial offences discussed in the present chapter is that in both instances liability is grounded in a showing of corporate fault. In chapter 4 we will extend the discussion even further and ask whether, if such fault can be shown, criminal liability should be dependent on the occurrence of overt harm.

Our goal in this inquiry is not to provide an exhaustive catalogue of the crimes that companies can commit but to establish a framework for analysing corporate criminality. To achieve this goal it is necessary to identify the principles and policies that should govern a regime of corporate criminal liability. The present law of corporate crime in England and Wales has, in our opinion, rightly been criticised; but before reform can be contemplated, it is necessary to flesh out and understand the principles which should control the analysis. Any effort to develop these principles must be guided by an understanding of the reasons why corporate crimes occur. We have attempted to identify some of the main reasons in the preceding chapter. They are many and varied, with some companies deliberately flouting the law, others doing so through incompetence, inadvertence or negligence, and still others blind to the possibility of the harm that can result until after it has occurred. If the criminal law is effectively to prevent and deter corporate crime, it needs to take account of the various scenarios, and devise methods of dealing with each of the variations.

B. COMPANIES AND THE CRIMINAL LAW

Behind the question of the appropriate test of corporate criminal liability lies an assumption that companies are fit subjects for the criminal law and that criminal prosecutions of companies are both necessary and desirable. These are not self-evident propositions. To the extent that criminal liability is founded on notions of moral blameworthiness, it is not clear how an artificial, impersonal fictional entity such as a company can be said to be 'morally' blameworthy. The idea of corporate criminal liability also fits uneasily with the traditional legal concepts of mens rea (guilty mind) and actus reus (wrongful act), which would need to be modified or adapted in order to be applied to companies. How does a company act and where is its mind to be located? Whether the strains that would be placed on criminal law doctrine are warranted by the benefit of being able to hold companies criminally accountable will depend to some extent on whether one believes that criminal liability is needed to prevent corporate misconduct. Many 'law and economics' theorists would argue that market forces and civil liability offer a more effective and efficient means of control.

1. Are companies fit subjects for the criminal law?

Who should be held criminally liable when a crime occurs in the course of a company's business operation: the person or persons whose acts are the direct cause of the resulting harm or the company itself, without whose existence the opportunity for the offence might never have arisen? In a stimulating article, Wolf (1985) advances the argument that companies should *not* be subject to the criminal law. She begins by drawing a distinction between an organic and an atomic view of an organisation. The 'atomist' position is based on the philosophy of 'methodological individualism', which attributes social and economic phenomena to human agency and to human agency alone (Sullivan: 1996). For the methodological individualist, praising or blaming a company for outcomes is a nonsense which rests on a misconception of the nature of a company. Praiseworthy corporate outcomes are the product of human decisions and acts, and it is the persons who formulated and implemented the relevant policies who deserve whatever credit is due. By the same token, these persons should be the ones held accountable when their decisions and actions result in a violation of the law.

Wolf is not content to rest her case against corporate criminal liability solely on an atomic conception of companies, however. Wolf's argument against imposing criminal liability (as opposed to civil liability, to which she is not opposed) on companies is premised not only on her view of the nature of a company but also on her view of the nature of criminal law. Her argument proceeds along syllogistic lines:
(a) criminal liability entails moral blameworthiness;
(b) moral blameworthiness requires an emotional capacity to appreciate the harmfulness of one's actions;
(c) a company lacks emotional capacity; therefore
(d) a company is not a moral agent; therefore
(e) a company should not be subject to criminal liability.

One might take issue with each of these propositions. The first step in the argument links criminal liability to moral blameworthiness. Although undoubtedly there is a moral dimension to the criminal law, Wolf seems to blind herself to the law's other functions. Moral blameworthiness is not the criminal justice system's sole concern, and perhaps not even its primary concern. Of more critical importance, particularly in the corporate context, may be the prevention of social harm and the deterrence of conduct likely to lead to such harm – regardless of whether the conduct in question can be characterised as immoral. What constitutes immorality is itself often contentious, but, this issue aside, some criminal offences fall into a category known as *malum prohibitum*. This category embraces acts and omissions that are wrong not because of their allegedly immoral nature, but simply because the legislature has decided to enforce a social prohibition through criminal sanctions. There is, for example, nothing inherently moral or immoral in driving on the left, as opposed to the right, hand side of the road; but the law of countries where automobiles are in common use typically will specify on which side of the road one should drive and will make it a *criminal* offence to drive on the opposite side. That two countries such as the United Kingdom and the United States may disagree as to the side of the road on which one should drive only serves to reinforce the essentially amoral nature of the issue.

From the questionable assertion that criminal liability entails moral blame-worthiness, Wolf proceeds to the even more questionable assertion that moral blameworthiness requires an *emotional capacity* to appreciate the moral turpitude of one's actions. Wolf supports this proposition by invoking the example of the sociopath. Sociopaths are intellectually capable of understanding the consequences of their acts, but lack the capacity for empathising with their victims. As a result, they do not experience guilt or remorse when their victims suffer. Because sociopaths lack emotional capacity, it follows for Wolf that they lack moral responsibility. And because of the link that she posits between moral responsibility and criminal liability, she concludes that a sociopath should not be held responsible for what would otherwise be a criminal offence.

The example of the sociopath is a curious one because, as an empirical proposition, there are few, if any, criminal justice systems that would fail to convict the sociopath who kills, rapes or commits a comparably heinous crime. Indeed, the sociopath's lack of emotional sensitivity would seem to strengthen, rather than weaken, the case for criminal sanctions. Without the normal constraints of conscience that inhibit wrongdoing, the constraints of the law and prison are all the more needed to counteract the dangerous propensities of the sociopath. Sociopaths need to be restrained, and society needs to be protected against them. Commitment to a mental institution may not be an option because, although sociopaths are without doubt dangerous, sociopathy or psychopathy may not constitute a recognised category of mental illness (unless one wished to posit that it was a mental illness per se).

Wolf argues that sociopaths, because they lack moral responsibility, should not be subject to criminal sanction. But is there any principle of law that supports her position? Are sociopaths in some sense insane and not responsible for their acts? Under *McNaghten*, which forms the basis of the law of insanity in England and many American states, a defendant, in order to establish a defence of insanity, must prove that 'at the time of the committing of the act, [he] was labouring under such a defect of reason, from disease of the mind, as not to know the nature and quality of the act he was doing; or, if he did know it, that he did not know he was doing what was wrong'.[1] It is hard to see how a sociopath could satisfy this test. Sociopaths, although perhaps insensitive to the suffering of their victims, are able to think rationally about what they are doing. Even assuming that their lack of empathy with their victims could be characterised as a defect of 'reason', it would not have as its source a *disease of the mind*, unless, again, one were prepared to accept sociopathy per se as a disease of the mind. Finally, there is no evidence that sociopaths are incapable of appreciating the nature and quality of their actions or that they are 'wrong' in the required legal sense of that term. Although there is a so-called 'irresistible impulse' extension of *McNaghten*, recognised in some American jurisdictions (although not in England), that would allow a defence to persons who are able to appreciate the wrongfulness of their conduct but who are unable to refrain from engaging in that conduct, there is no reason to believe that sociopaths are not able to control their actions. It seems more the case that they simply choose not to do so. Thus even this highly contentious branch of *McNaghten* (some maintain that there is no such thing as an irresistible impulse when a policeman is at one's elbow) would not necessarily avail the sociopath of an insanity defence.

Because the third step in Wolf's argument, that a company lacks emotional capacity, is dependent for its relevance on her view that emotional capacity is critical to moral blameworthiness and, hence, criminal liability; and because, as we have seen, that position is not supported by legal authority, it is tempting to dismiss her statement that companies lack emotional capacity as irrelevant. In fact, her position seems not so much irrelevant as perverse. In the general scheme of the criminal law, those whose crimes are rationally conceived and executed are generally deemed more culpable than those whose crimes are attributable to emotion: the criminal justice system takes a sterner view of the cold-blooded murderer than it does of the person who kills in the heat of passion. Corporate decisions are more likely to be dictated by a cost-benefit analysis than an emotional impulse. Often they are taken by committee or are the result of a consultative exercise, with the ultimate approval residing in a board of directors. The fact that many minds will have considered a policy reduces the chance that it will be the product of emotion. Wolf's analysis errs in equating the capacity for feeling guilty with legal guilt. Although morality is generally considered a virtue, Wolf is apparently prepared to reward a company's *amorality* by exempting it from criminal sanction.

The merits of Wolf's analysis aside, it would be imprudent to ignore the question that she raises. What is it in the nature of a company that justifies holding it criminally accountable? For that matter, what qualities are there in a sociopath that justify holding the sociopath responsible for a criminal offence? The answer to both questions is the same. What companies share with sociopaths is not an emotional *incapacity* but a *rational and physical capacity*. Both a sociopath and a company, in terms of the collective decision-making taken on behalf of the company, have the rational capacity to understand that their actions will cause injury to innocent victims, and the physical capacity to refrain from engaging in those actions. It is these two features, taken together, which differentiate both companies and sociopaths from those whom the law does not hold responsible for their actions. The argument to the contrary is not only ill-conceived but positively dangerous. It would allow both

---

1   *R v McNaughten* (1843) 1 Car & Kir 130n, sub nom *M'Naghten's Case* (1843) 10 Cl & Fin 200.

sociopaths and companies to disclaim responsibility for the harm they have caused and would deny the state the deterrent of criminal sanctions to prevent the commission of future harm by the offender and others similarly situated.

To be contrasted with an 'atomic' model of companies is an 'organic' model. The latter views a company as a holistic entity with an identity that is not reducible to the company's officers, directors, managers or employees. This view of a company, it might initially be observed, may be more consonant with how ordinary people think about companies. When ordinary people refer to IBM, BT and Esso, for example, they do so without having in mind any particular individual or individuals. There are exceptions, of course – one may identify Microsoft with Bill Gates and Virgin with Richard Branson – but even then there is an awareness that far more people than these high-profile executives are involved in the company's decision-making processes. In a horizontally structured company, many individuals may be invested with limited decision-making authority. Even in a more vertically structured, 'command and control' model of a company, autocratic power is rare; there may well be dominating individuals, such as Robert Maxwell when at the Mirror Group, but they still typically function with a board and with legal and fiscal advisors if only to provide the legal camouflage for their personal hegemony. Trying to link a harm-producing policy to a particular individual in a complex, diversified company is often little more than an exercise in finding a sacrificial lamb. The organic model of companies thus not only conforms to the layperson's perception of companies, but also to the power structures of the large modern corporation. A final point in favour of the organic model is that it helps to explain the ongoing nature of a company. Corporate officers may retire, the board of directors may be expanded or contracted, and employees may be made redundant, but what persists throughout these metamorphoses of the company is the company itself.

Organic theory comports with the adage that the whole can be greater than the sum of its parts. When many individuals join together on a project, the outcome will be different, and usually better, than if each person had worked separately and the various contributions had been added together. There is a synergy that occurs when individuals meet, talk face to face, and are able to share thoughts and challenge each other's thinking. A chance or offhand remark by one member of a group may spark a breakthrough insight by another or a different way of looking at a problem. Potential stumbling blocks are more readily identified when many minds apply themselves to the task. The outcome of this dynamic process may not accord with any individual's conception of the final solution as of the outset. But to whom, then, should this outcome be attributed? It seems more accurate to attribute it to the group as a whole rather than to a number of named individual members of the group. So too with respect to corporate decision-making.[2]

The reason for what some may see as a somewhat lengthy diversion into the atomic-organic debate is that it makes little sense to proceed to a discussion of the appropriate test of corporate criminal liability before the case has been made that

---

2   Of course, the opposite effect can occur, with an intimidating member of a group stifling potentially valuable contributions by others that would have found expression if each member of the group had worked independently. Even in the absence of intimidation, a group may go along with an idea which holds no particular appeal to anybody because each member of the group is under the mistaken impression that the idea appeals to the others. Nobody speaks against the idea for fear of alienating colleagues (see Harvey: 1988).

companies *should* be subject to criminal liability. Wolf's analysis of the issue arguably got off on the wrong foot in its implicit assumption that the criminal justice system had to choose between an atomic theory of organisations, with individual responsibility, and an organic theory, with collective responsibility borne by the corporate entity. Individual and corporate criminal liability are best viewed as offering complementary rather than competing approaches to the control of corporate crime. An individual should not be the scapegoat for a crime committed by a company but by the same token a company should not be the scapegoat for the crime of an individual.

Whether in a given case criminal charges should be brought against an individual, a company, both or neither, will depend on the facts and circumstances of the case. If, for instance, an agent of a company manages to evade corporate controls that are reasonably designed to prevent crime and that are rigorously enforced, it would arguably be unfair to hold the company responsible for the agent's offence. The agent alone should be prosecuted. In contrast, where a company has endorsed or encouraged illegality, or where it has forced its employees to work in clearly crime-conducive conditions, it may well make sense to prosecute the company and not the unfortunate worker who might almost be considered a victim of circumstances. That said, it would be imprudent to give workers the impression that they can commit crimes with impunity; the possibility of personal criminal liability may need to be maintained if only to strengthen employee resolve to resist corporate pressures to resort to illegal methods. But it is precisely such corporate pressures that warrant holding the company criminally accountable.

2. Is corporate criminal liability needed?

Assuming that companies are subject to the criminal law, there remains the pragmatic question of whether corporate misconduct is best dealt with through criminal prosecutions and sanctions or through some other means. Many free-market economists would argue that the government should take a hands-off approach to corporate matters generally. They maintain that whatever regulation is needed can most effectively be brought to bear through market forces. They would also support the somewhat more contentious proposition that if companies cause harm, the most economically efficient response will be a civil suit for damages brought by the injured parties. The government is obviously spared the costs of litigation, which are borne by the plaintiffs, and the lower threshold for an adverse judgment – guilt in a criminal trial must be proved 'beyond reasonable doubt', while proof by a 'balance of probabilities' will suffice for a civil judgment – should in theory increase the deterrent force of the law. Another advantage to civil suits is that the damages awarded are more likely to bear a closer relationship to the loss suffered than will a criminal fine. Unless specifically designed to provide compensation or restitution, a fine might far exceed the amount of the loss, or fall far short of what it would cost to remedy it.

It is interesting that economists opposed to prosecutions of companies for criminal acts committed by their employees have no objection to civil suits against the company for injuries caused by those acts. To the contrary, as we have noted, they see civil suits as the appropriate response to corporate malfeasance. The injured party will receive compensation, and the damages awarded will be commensurate to the harm caused. The company will virtually always be in a better financial position to bear the loss than the employee who might be more directly responsible for causing the injuries. Many employees are in effect 'judgment-proof', meaning that there is little point in suing them for they lack the financial wherewithal to pay off a substantial judgment. In contrast, their company will usually be in a position to absorb a damage award as a cost of doing business, perhaps with the back-up of a contingency fund for mishaps and disasters, or can protect itself against the risk of an exorbitant damage award through the purchase of insurance. Some companies will be able to pass on damage awards to their customers in the form of price hikes.

There is also a logical argument for holding companies civilly liable. The company will be responsible for hiring, training and supervising the employee who caused the injury. For the company not to compensate the victim would in effect allow it to profit from its employee's tort. It is because of such considerations, coupled with the obvious social utility of providing compensation to injured victims, that the courts have developed the doctrine of *respondeat superior*. Under this doctrine, an employer is civilly liable to those injured by the torts of their employees if at the time the employee was engaged in carrying out the company's business.

But are civil suits against companies, designed to seek out a 'deep pocket' from which to obtain compensation for injured victims, also capable of *deterring* corporate criminality? Economists argue that, to avoid expensive damage claims, companies will take steps to prevent behaviour that can lead to civil liability. These steps will include putting into place systems that, at the same time that they deter tortious acts, will also serve to prevent crimes. This analysis, however, is immediately called into question, at least from a purely economic point of view, where the cost of preventing harm exceeds the damages likely to be awarded in a civil lawsuit. A real-life illustration of the type of cost-benefit balancing that can take place occurred with respect to the Pinto scandal, where the Ford Motor Company may have decided that it would be less expensive to pay damages to victims than to pay the costs of recalling all vehicles whose petrol tank would need to be relocated to reduce the danger of an explosion following a rear end collision. Similarly, a company might well not see it to be in its economic interest to spend millions of pounds on safety equipment to avert accidents likely to cost it only thousands of pounds in damages. As insurance can be purchased to cover potentially ruinous damages, the 'true' cost to companies of damage awards from tort suits consists of their insurance premiums. It might be noted in this regard that it is usually held to be against public policy to allow potential criminal defendants to obtain insurance to cover criminal sanctions.

There are further difficulties with relying on civil suits to deter corporate crime. First, there must be a plaintiff who is able and willing to bring a lawsuit. When the drug Thalidomide was marketed with inadequate regard for the risks posed to pregnant women, many children were subsequently born deformed. It was questionable, however, under the law in force at the time, whether the children had 'standing' to sue for injuries that they had incurred in the womb. In other cases, such as when a petrol station deliberately sets the gauges of its pumps to provide only 98% of a litre of petrol yet charges customers for a full litre, with the result that each customer overpays a few pence per litre, the overall gain to the offender may be enormous but the loss to any particular customer may be so small that it hardly warrants the trouble of bringing a lawsuit. And that is assuming that a customer is even aware of having been cheated. Then there are the cases where victims are aware that they have suffered a loss but do not know who to sue for damages. Landowners, for example, may well appreciate that the river which runs through their property has become polluted but may not know which of many factories which may have dumped their waste into the river is the cause of the pollution and may lack the money to conduct a proper investigation. In all of these examples, moreover, there are identifiable victims who have suffered loss, who would have standing to pursue and an interest in pursuing their legal remedies. In some cases of corporate wrongdoing there will be no victims. If a company fails to install legally required safety equipment in a factory but no worker is injured, or a shipping company allows unseaworthy vessels to take to sea but its ships manage to stay afloat, then there are no victims to bring a civil lawsuit (although actions by regulatory authorities remain available).

'Law and economics' analysts tend to assume that the purpose of imposing criminal sanctions on a company is to deter criminal activity, and that civil damages are as, if not more, effective to achieve such deterrence than a criminal fine. Without qualification, both assumptions are questionable. With respect to the first assumption, that the purpose of imposing criminal sanctions on a company is to deter criminal activity, while undoubtedly the state may seek to deter corporate criminality through criminal sanctions, it may also want to be in a position where it can order a company to reform the way that it carries on its business. This is not possible following a civil judgment. Also, a civil damage award will usually be limited to the harm suffered by the plaintiff. The judgment cannot take into account, as can a criminal sentence, the fact that the defendant is a chronic recidivist. Nor can the civil judgment require a corporate tortfeasor to make reparation to the state for the harm that has been caused to it by the company, which is one of the objectives to be achieved in criminal sentencing. While punitive damages, designed to both punish and deter, may be available in a civil suit, there is no guarantee that they will be awarded. In any event, if a company judges that the compensatory and punitive damages that it might ultimately have to pay are less than the profits to be made from its illegal way of doing business, it may not be deterred from its chosen course.

With respect to the assumption that civil liability can be as effective a deterrent to corporate misconduct as a criminal prosecution, what the 'law and economics' analysts tend to underestimate is the stigma, censure and damage to a company's reputation that can follow a criminal conviction. A company's good name may be its most important asset. Just as law-abiding citizens may shun individuals convicted of a heinous offence, they may also shun a company's products because they do not wish to do business with a 'criminal' company. Because a criminal conviction has a greater potential to damage a company's reputation than does a civil judgment, the threat of a prosecution may have a greater effect on corporate behaviour than the threat of a civil lawsuit. If a company's reputation is threatened by a civil suit, the company can always choose to settle with the potential plaintiffs, if necessary on unduly generous terms, in order to avoid the public's ever learning of its alleged misconduct. The settlement will, moreover, typically contain a stipulation that the company does not admit to fault, which is acceptable to litigants because their goal is to recover damages, and which will appeal to the company because it is then under no legal obligation to alter its practices. In the absence of a court judgment, a company can legitimately claim that its way of doing business has not been held to be illegal.

In a criminal prosecution there may be little incentive for a public prosecutor to negotiate with a company charged with a serious offence. If the prosecution is willing to accept a plea, the company will still have to plead guilty in open court. The plea will then become a matter of public record and may be reported in the press or media. In addition to the resulting stigma, the conviction can also have adverse financial consequences beyond the fine that may be imposed by the court as a sentence. If consumers choose not to do business with the 'disgraced' corporate offender, the lost revenues might far exceed the fine, or, indeed, any damages that might have been awarded in civil litigation. Moreover, the deterrent effect of a criminal conviction should in theory extend beyond the company prosecuted to other similarly situated companies. A civil judgment, on the other hand, may only cause other companies to increase the amount of their insurance coverage.

This analysis leads to the conclusion that civil suits are not an adequate substitute for criminal prosecutions. However, as in the debate between individual and corporate liability, there is no reason why the law must make an either-or choice; the civil and criminal justice systems are complementary, not in competition. Civil suits are needed to provide compensation to injured victims, while criminal prosecutions are needed to vindicate public interests. The aim of a prosecution may be to inform the public of the offender's wrongdoing, to punish the offender, to deter similarly situated companies, and to allow for a variety of sanctions (see chapter 7) that may not be available following a civil judgment. Whereas the injured victim can choose whether or not to file a civil suit, and may abandon the suit when offered sufficient monetary incentives, it is the responsibility of a public official to initiate a prosecution, and that official can persevere with the prosecution regardless of the inducements to discontinue.

In fact, criminal and civil liability do not exhaust the avenues available to hold companies legally accountable for the harms that they cause. In modern Britain, the most common form of accountability occurs when a company is found to have committed a 'regulatory' offence. The relevant statutes (typified by those governing health and safety) are usually drafted with companies specifically in mind. They have a quasi-criminal character to them, but differ from traditional common law crimes (eg, rape, murder, theft) in their definitional elements, in the sanctions that will be imposed following a conviction, and, most significantly, in the mechanisms through which they are enforced. The topic is complex and we shall defer its examination until chapter 9, where we will address it within the context of how to 'police' companies.

C. CORPORATE CRIMINAL LIABILITY: THE FORMATIVE STAGES

Oliver Wendell Holmes (1897) advised law students that if they wished to understand the law, they needed to examine its historical roots. Laws often are more the product of history than logic. The development of the law of corporate criminal liability serves to illustrate the point.

In the embryonic stages of the industrial revolution it was understandable that the government would not wish to bring criminal prosecutions that might stifle industrial development and damage corporations that were struggling to survive. As these corporations become more firmly established, however, one might have thought that such considerations would carry less weight. Yet the reluctance to prosecute companies persisted. In the Criminal Law Act 1827, s 14, Parliament had laid the foundation for potential prosecutions by declaring that the word 'person' in a criminal statute would include corporations unless a contrary legislative intent appeared; but it was one thing to say that companies could be subject to criminal liability, and quite another actually to apply the criminal law to companies.

When the English judges turned their minds to the question of whether a company could commit a criminal offence, they naturally looked to the applicability of existing criminal laws, principles and doctrines. These, however, had been developed in cases involving natural persons. How to apply such distinctly human concepts as actus reus and mens rea to an inanimate legal fiction was bound to tax the judicial imagination, and, in retrospect, the judges might have been better advised to have accepted from the outset that fresh doctrines were going to be needed that took account of the unique characteristics of organisational entities. The judges appeared to lose sight of the fact that they had fashioned the concepts of actus reus and mens rea to facilitate legal analysis, and that where they did not facilitate the analysis, they were not obliged to follow them. Concepts that a court constructs under its common law powers can be torn down by virtue of those same powers, and should be when there are sound and valid reasons for doing so. As companies, which lack a body and mind, are clearly distinguishable from natural persons, there was no reason why the concepts of actus reus and mens rea had to be applied in the same way to them as they did to natural persons, or indeed at all. Had the courts not been consumed with fitting corporate square pegs into the round holes of existing criminal law dogma, the law of corporate criminality might have developed in a less strained fashion.

In England the earliest prosecutions of organisational entities were brought against municipalities that had failed to comply with a statutory duty owed to the public. Criminal prosecutions were held to be needed to enforce these duties. Because the actus reus of these mostly nuisance offences consisted of an omission on the part of the municipality, the courts did not have to address the issue of how a legal fiction might perform a positive act. And because liability was strict, there being no mens rea element to satisfy, the issue of where to locate the municipality's mind did not arise. When the public functions of municipalities were taken over by commercial enterprises, it was relatively straightforward to transfer to these enterprises the legal obligations, backed up by potential criminal sanctions that went with them. With the principle of corporate criminal liability thus established, liability was soon extended from public nuisance offences to all offences not requiring criminal intent.

The next major extension to the law of corporate crime occurred in *R v Great North of England Rly Co*,[3] where the court held that a corporation could be criminally liable for acts and not just omissions. There was merit in abolishing this distinction between 'nonfeasance' and 'misfeasance', because a statutory offence drafted in terms of nonfeasance (the failure to do something in a satisfactory manner) can just as easily be drafted in terms of misfeasance (doing something in an unsatisfactory manner). The semantic distinction was simply not meaningful. With the demise of the nonfeasance-misfeasance distinction, however, the question of how a company could be said to 'act' could no longer be avoided. The answer given by Lord Denman in the *Great North of England Rly* case was to attribute to the company the acts of its

3   (1846) 115 ER 1294, 9 QB 315.

employees. However, Lord Denman qualified his position by questioning whether a corporation could ever be guilty of a crime involving immorality, as these 'derive their character from the corrupted mind of the person committing them'.[4] The question of whether and how a company might be said to possess a mens rea remained for a future day.

Lord Denman's test of vicarious corporate criminal liability found its roots in the tort doctrine of *respondeat superior*. While attributing the torts of employees to employers may have been designed principally to facilitate the recovery of damages from a defendant possessing the ability to pay, policy considerations suggested that the doctrine also had relevance to criminal cases. A legal counterweight was needed to the economic pressure on companies to maximise profits at all costs, and to encourage corporate employers to exercise the maximum care in the selection, training, and supervision of its personnel. The imposition of vicarious liability also avoided awkward problems for the prosecution in cases where it was reasonable to expect, but difficult to prove, that an employee had acted at the behest of the employer. Often the pressures placed on workers to commit an illegal act are subtle and may take the form of incentives or rewards for specified results rather than direct commands to violate the law.

In the United States, the transference of the civil doctrine of *respondeat superior* into the criminal law appeared to the judges natural and uncontroversial. In *New York Central & Hudson River Railroad Co v United States*,[5] the US Supreme Court stated:

> Applying the principle [of *respondeat superior*] governing civil liability, we go only a step farther in holding that the act of the agent, while exercising the authority delegated to him ..., may be controlled, in the interest of public policy, by imputing his act to his employer and imposing penalties upon the corporation for which he is acting in the premises.[6]

In fact, the transplantation of *respondeat superior* from its home in civil law to criminal law may not have been as straightforward as the Supreme Court implied. In civil law, as we have seen, the doctrine was needed to provide compensation to injured victims because the person most directly responsible for causing the injury may well have been 'judgment-proof'. But the fact that the responsible individual was judgment-proof should have no bearing on a criminal prosecution. What social purpose, then, was to be achieved by holding the employer criminally liable? The point is not that this question is unanswerable, but rather it merits closer attention than was given to it by the Supreme Court.

D.   VICARIOUS CORPORATE CRIMINAL LIABILITY

In the US federal courts, and in most American state courts, a company can be held liable for a crime of an individual who at the time was engaged in the company's

---

4   (1846) 115 ER 1294 at 1298.
5   212 US 481 (1909).
6   212 US 481 (1909) at 494.

business with intent to benefit the company.[7] The individual's status within the organisation is irrelevant. The seminal decision was that of the Supreme Court in *New York Central & Hudson River Railroad Co v United States*.[8] In this case an assistant traffic manager of a railroad had granted illegal rebates to preferred customers in violation of the Elkins Act. Section 1 of the Elkins Act stipulated that the acts of a carrier's officers, agents and employees could be attributed to the carrier. The defendant argued that this section was unconstitutional because it punished the company not for its own wrongful acts, but for the acts of its employees. The defendant also argued that its stockholders were being deprived of their property without due process of law, as guaranteed under the US Constitution. The Supreme Court rejected both arguments, and held that a company's criminal liability could be premised on the acts, omissions and failures of persons acting within the scope of their employment.

Although *New York Central* presented an issue of statutory construction, the policy implications of the case never seemed far from the minds of the Supreme Court Justices. The case arose at a time when businesses were becoming increasingly powerful. Without the threat of criminal liability, there was little incentive for companies to curb illegal but profitable practices that might be putting the safety of innocent persons at risk. Nor was there any motivation to rein in employees who broke the law while attempting to increase corporate profits. For reasons discussed previously, civil liability did not provide a sufficient disincentive to corporate criminal behaviour, and the threat of a prosecution was thought to be needed in order to strengthen the deterrent force of the law. If companies perceived that they could be criminally liable for the illegal actions of their employees and agents, as well as civilly liable for the damages caused by these actions, the combined effect should be enough to stimulate the company to control its workforce.

In one sense, the doctrine of vicarious liability imposed on companies a 'private policing' role, enlisting them in the prevention of crime by their employees. Presumably, if a company discovered that an employee was acting illegally, it would take corrective measures to remedy the situation in order to avoid its own prosecution. If the prosecution were to be limited to the individual at fault, the company would have no incentive to discourage the individual's actions, particularly if they were beneficial to the company. Why would the company care? – most employees, even senior managers, are replaceable. Consider the situation from the point of view of the employee who is simply carrying out company policies – if the employee obeys an order of a superior to commit an act that has criminal implications, the employee exposes himself/herself to a criminal prosecution; if the employee disobeys the order, s/he might be disciplined for insubordination.

Although the Supreme Court in *New York Central* was able to discern an intent on the part of Congress to impose criminal liability on companies, in subsequent cases the policy justifications for vicarious liability came to be relied upon more than legislative intent. The principle of vicarious liability was extended to most public welfare offences. Liability was not restricted to acts that the company had ordered or authorised, but was applied also to acts that the company had ratified or even simply

---

7   See *United States v Bank of New England* 821 F 2d 844 (1st Cir) *cert denied* 484 US 943 (1987); *Egan v United States*, 137 F 2d 369 (8th Cir) *cert denied* 320 US 788 (1943).

8   212 US 481 (1909).

tolerated.[9] The class of persons whose acts could lead to the company's criminal liability encompassed directors, officers, managers, white- and blue-collar workers, and independent contractors, the latter to prevent companies from contracting out the criminogenic aspects of their business operation.[10]

There are limitations to a company's vicarious liability. One limitation is that the agent whose offence is sought to be imputed to the company must have been acting within the scope of his/her employment. This is a fact-specific inquiry, but what constitutes 'scope of employment' has been liberally construed. It is sufficient to show that the agent's act was in some way related to the employee's actual or apparent authority. Actual authority exists where the corporation specifically authorised the employee's actions. Apparent authority is a more subtle concept but may be found where a third party reasonably believes that an agent possessed the authority to act on behalf of a company based on the agent's position in the company, the responsibility entrusted to the agent on previous occasions or the circumstances surrounding the agent's past conduct.[11] Once actual or apparent authority is established, liability will not be defeated by the fact that the employee's actions had been explicitly forbidden or were against company policy.[12]

A second limitation on vicarious corporate criminal liability is that the employee's crime has to have been committed with intent to benefit the company. This requirement can be satisfied even though the employee's primary objective is personal gain.[13] Courts recognise that benefit to an employee often can be indirect. For example, the salesman who fraudulently misleads customers may not divert the illegal profits to a personal bank account, being content to accept the commissions, bonuses, promotions and other rewards which flow from a high volume of sales. But as the company also benefits, in that it retains the profits of the fraudulent sales, it is plausible to argue that the company has a stake in the crime, and, more importantly, no interest in preventing it. On the other hand, American courts have also held that the fact that a company has received no actual benefit from the commission of an offence does not preclude its prosecution for the offence, as long as the offender acted with intent to benefit the company.[14]

While developing a framework for analysing corporate actus reus did not pose significant conceptual difficulties for the courts – how else but through employees, agents and officers could a company act? – developing a theory of corporate mens rea was to prove more challenging. While there is no problem in saying that a company's acts consist of the sum of all of the acts of all the persons who work for or are connected with the company, a similar aggregation of all of the mental states of the company's personnel would leave the company with a jumble of conflicting thoughts and states of mind. This would give rise to the question of whether the

---

9 See eg *Continental Baking Co v United States* 281 F 2d 137 (6th Cir 1960); *Steere Tank Lines Inc v United States* 330 F2d 719 (5th Cir 1963).
10 See *United States v Parfait Powder Co* 163 F 2d 1008 (7th Cir 1947).
11 See *United States v American Radiator and Standard Sanitary Corpn* 433 F 2d 174 (3rd Cir 1970).
12 See *United States v Twentieth Century Fox Film Corpn* 882 F 2d 656 (2d Cir 1989); *United States v Hilton Hotels Corpn* 467 F 2d 1000 (9th Cir 1972) *cert denied*, 409 US 1125 (1973).
13 See eg *United States v Automated Medical Laboratories Inc* 770 F 2d 399 (4th Cir 1985).
14 See *United States v Carter* 311 F 2d 934 (6th Cir) *cert denied* 373 US 915 (1963); *Old Monastery Co v United States* 147 F 2d 905 (4th Cir) *cert denied* 326 US 734 (1945).

mental states of some individuals – and, if so, which ones – might count more than the mental states of others in determining the company's state of mind.

Although aggregating the mental states of diverse individuals in order to arrive at the mental state of a company may not generally advance the analysis of corporate mens rea, there is one class of case where there is a strong argument in favour of such aggregation. It is where the issue is what a company 'knows', which may be crucial when, for example, a statute proscribes 'knowingly' causing a result. There is no conceptual difficulty, and much to be gained, from equating the knowledge of the company with the sum of what is known by all who work for the company in relation to the matter in issue. The American courts have in fact accepted the logic of this position.[15] The topic of aggregated fault is more usefully examined in the context of a general discussion of organisational fault, however, and we shall therefore postpone it until the next chapter.

One way of avoiding the issue of how to determine a company's state of mind is to make the issue irrelevant. Where a statute imposes 'strict liability', proof of actus reus and actus reus alone is sufficient to warrant a conviction, and the prosecution does not have to prove mens rea of any sort. Strict liability statutes are problematic, however, because they operate without regard for fault, and can therefore penalise companies which have made a good faith, reasonable, or even exemplary, effort to prevent criminal activity. None the less, beginning in the late nineteenth century, strict liability statutes began to proliferate in America. The judiciary also contributed to the development of a regime of corporate strict liability by construing statutes that imposed vicarious liability to also impose strict liability.[16] This, of course, does not follow as a matter of logic – a legislature can impose one without the other.

The issue of whether a company acted knowingly can be avoided under the 'wilful blindness' doctrine. This doctrine will be invoked when a corporate agent has reason to suspect that a crime may have been committed, but refrains from investigating the matter further in order to avoid confirming his/her suspicions.[17]

A third approach to corporate mens rea would be to impute to a company the mental state of the person who committed the actus reus of the offence. If a company can be attributed the acts of an agent, why cannot it also be attributed the state of mind of that agent? The analogy is suspect, however, because it ignores the fact that while a company may have the power to control the actions of its employees, it lacks a comparable ability to control what goes through its employees' minds.

Although there is a body of federal criminal law in the United States, the overwhelming majority of criminal prosecutions are brought in state courts for violations of state criminal laws. Each state legislature can and has enacted its own body of criminal statutes. It should not be surprising that different States have opted to take different approaches to corporate criminality. Even where two States have enacted an identically worded statute, comparisons must be drawn with caution because the statutes may be interpreted differently by each state's Supreme Court (which has ultimate responsibility for interpreting state law). None the less, virtually

15 See eg *United States v Bank of New England* 821 F 2d 844 (1st Cir) *cert denied* 484 US 943 (1987).
16 See eg *State v Anderson* 127 La 1041, 54 So 344 (1911).
17 See *United States v Mapelli* 971 F 2d 284 (9th Cir 1992).

all states accept the principle of vicarious liability for the purpose of attributing the acts of a company's personnel to the company.

When it comes to mens rea, on the other hand, the thinking among states is more diversified. Many state legislatures have patterned their law of corporate criminality on that proposed by the American Law Institute in its Model Penal Code.[18] The Code envisages three distinct forms of corporate liability – for regulatory offences, for failures to discharge duties imposed by law, and for penal law violations. With respect to the first two categories, the Code would permit strict liability unless a contrary legislative intent plainly appeared, and vicarious liability, but with a due diligence defence, whenever corporate liability was intended by a legislature. The most marked departure from the developing federal law was with respect to the third category of penal law violations. Whereas the federal law allows the acts of a wide range of individuals to be imputed to the company, the Code would significantly narrow the range of relevant actors. Specifically, Section 2.07(1) of the Code provides in relevant part:

> A corporation may be convicted of an offence if...
> (c) The commission of the offence was authorised, requested, commanded, performed, or recklessly tolerated by the board of directors or by a high managerial agent acting in behalf of the corporation within the scope of his office or employment.

We do not propose to analyse the concept of 'high managerial agent' further for, as will be seen, it is remarkably similar to the concept of persons who can be 'identified' with the company, which forms the backbone to corporate criminal liability in England. It is to the English model, therefore, that we now turn.

E.   THE 'IDENTIFICATION' DOCTRINE

Whereas the American courts did not hesitate in embracing a doctrine of vicarious corporate criminal liability that had its roots in English jurisprudence, their judicial counterparts in England remained sceptical. The English judges yielded to the force of vicarious liability only reluctantly, in cases of nuisance and criminal libel where a historical tradition had been established, and in cases where there appeared a clear intent on the part of Parliament that a company should be subject to criminal sanctions and vicarious liability seemed the obvious path for realising this objective. The nature of the inquiry was set out in *Mousell Bros v London and North-Western Rly*,[19] where the manager of a company had misdescribed the goods being carried by the company's lorry in order to avoid the payment of tolls. The question was whether the company should be liable for the manager's offence, and the court stated that the answer depended on Parliament's intent in enacting the statute. In order to ascertain Parliament's intent, the court looked to the wording of the statute, the nature of the duty imposed, the person who would be expected to perform that duty, and the purpose to be achieved.

18 American Law Institute, Model Penal Code, s 2.07 (1962).
19 [1917] 2 KB 836.

The road to a general law of corporate criminal liability based on imputed criminality was not charted in England until the 1940s. That decade saw three notable decisions on this point. In the first of these cases, *DPP v Kent and Sussex Contractors Ltd*,[20] the company was alleged to have furnished false information in order to obtain petrol coupons in violation of defence regulations then in force. The critical issue was whether it was possible to attribute to the company the state of mind of the corporate official who had submitted the misleading documents. The Divisional Court reasoned that, as a company could only speak or act through those empowered to speak or act in its behalf, the state of mind of those individuals could be imputed to the company. Thus, if the defendant's officers had an intent to deceive, then the company too could be attributed with an intent to deceive. The decision is significant for it demonstrates how a mens rea can be ascribed to a company.

In the second case, *R v ICR Haulage Ltd*,[21] the managing director of a company was charged, along with nine other persons, with conspiracy to defraud. The company was also charged with the same offence. Again, the critical issue was mens rea. Stable J, delivering the judgment of the Court of Criminal Appeal, stated that in order to establish a company's guilt of a crime involving mens rea, the intention, knowledge or belief of a company's officers could be attributed to the company. Although the previous cases had for the most part involved statutory violations, while the offence charged against ICR Haulage was a common law crime, the court ruled that this distinction did not make a difference. The court did accept, however, that a company could not be charged with crimes, such as bigamy or perjury, which could only be committed by human offenders, as well as crimes, such as murder, where the company could not be subjected to the penalty specified in the law. These, however, were the exceptions. Stable J opined that the law of corporate criminality was undergoing a process of transformation in which what had formerly been a general rule of non-liability was being converted to a general rule of liability.

In *Moore v Bresler Ltd*,[22] the third of the 1940's cases, the secretary of a company, along with a sales manager at one of its branches, had sold the company's goods for private gain and with the clear intent to defraud the company. In order to conceal their illegal sales, the two had submitted false documents to the revenue relating to the purchase tax on the items sold. Both the individuals in question and the company were charged with violating the Finance (No 2) Act 1940. The company argued that not only were the individuals not acting as its agents or with its authority, but that that, indeed, the individuals had committed a fraud against the company. However, the Divisional Court held that the critical issue was whether the individuals were acting within their authority, and not whether they were acting in furtherance of or contrary to the company's best interests. If they were acting within their authority, their acts were the acts of the company, and their deceit could be imputed to the company. That the two officers may also have been committing a crime against their own company was irrelevant as to the company's liability for deceiving the tax authorities.

The proposition that vicarious corporate criminal liability will be found where intended by Parliament is relatively non-controversial in a legal system which adheres

20 [1944] KB 146.
21 [1944] KB 551.
22 [1944] 2 All ER 515.

to the principle of Parliamentary sovereignty. However, the English courts seemed inclined to slip from this non-contentious proposition into its more dubious converse – that vicarious liability will not be found unless specifically intended by Parliament. An often-cited authority is *Seaboard Offshore Ltd v Secretary of State for Transport.*[23]

In *Seaboard,* a ship's engine had broken down three times within the space of a twenty-four hour period while the ship was at sea. The chief engineer, whose job it was to inspect the engine, had failed to board the vessel until approximately three hours before it was to embark, when expert opinion held that a minimum of three days was required for an engineer to acquaint himself with the ship's mechanical operation. The company was convicted of violating that section of the Merchant Shipping Act 1988 which required the owner of a ship to 'take all reasonable steps to secure that the ship [was] operated in a safe manner'. The House of Lords held that the company could be liable only if the owner of the ship or the manager of the company responsible for the ship had failed personally to fulfil the statutory duty. The company would not be liable if a subordinate employee, such as the engineer, was responsible for the violation. According to Lord Keith:

> Of particular relevance in this context are the concluding words of section 31(4), referring to the taking of all such steps as are reasonable for *him* (my emphasis) to take, i.e., the owner, charterer or manager. The steps to be taken are to be such as will secure that the ship is operated in a safe manner. That conveys to me the idea of laying down a safe manner of operating the ship by those involved in the actual operation of it and taking appropriate measures to bring it about that such safe manner is adhered to.[24]

Lord Keith's analysis would suggest, and certainly would not rule out, that a successful prosecution might have been founded on the company's failure to promulgate adequate guidelines to prevent a mishap such as had occurred. If the company in *Seaboard* was to be faulted, it was for not having in place clear policies that would have prevented the ship from proceeding to sea before those responsible for its safety, including the chief engineer, had sufficient time to satisfy themselves that the ship was seaworthy. However, this argument had not been presented to the magistrates in the first instance, and the House of Lords was not minded to entertain it on appeal.

Although one might be tempted to dismiss *Seaboard* as a case where a narrowly drafted statute had combined with an ill-conceived theory of liability to produce an unsatisfactory result, the House of Lords opinion may reflect a deeper judicial antipathy to vicarious liability. This antipathy is grounded in a mixture of theory and pragmatism. On a pragmatic level, the judges are sensitive to the formidable burden that would be placed on companies if they were required to supervise, at their legal peril, potentially thousands of employees working at countless different sites. Vicarious corporate criminal liability can also present problems of proof to prosecutors. Before a company can be held liable for the crime of an employee, a prosecutor has to show that a person whose acts and mental state can be imputed to the company has committed an offence. While it often is clear that a criminal wrong has occurred, it is not always equally clear who is to blame. Taking *Seaboard* as an

---

23 [1994] 1 WLR 541.
24 [1994] 1 WLR 541 at 545.

example, was the violation of the Merchant Shipping Act really the fault of the chief engineer, who failed to arrive in sufficient time to familiarise himself with the ship's operation; or the ship's master, who gave the order to embark before the engineer had completed a thorough inspection; or the board of directors, who had failed to provide adequate guidance as to what checks needed to be carried out before the company's ships could embark? Might some design fault in the ship's engine have contributed to the problem? It is often the case that no single cause of an illegal result may be clearly identifiable. Different individuals within a corporate network may bear varying degrees of responsibility and fault may be diffused throughout the company. In such cases it may make more sense to attribute the offence to the corporate body as a whole rather than to try to unravel the myriad strands of individual fault. Yet a theory of vicarious liability requires identification of a human offender whose offence can be imputed to the company.

The practical problems of supervising a large workforce can be overcome, for the expense of monitoring can usually be passed on to consumers of the company's products. Harder to circumvent are the principled objections to vicarious liability. As an a priori matter, it is desirable that criminal convictions be based on a showing of blameworthiness. The Latin maxim *nulla poene sine culpa* (no punishment without fault) expresses the idea that only defendants whose culpability has been demonstrated should be subject to criminal sanctions. The principle of just deserts likewise conveys the idea that convicted defendants are punished because they deserve to be punished, which again implies fault. Vicarious liability, however, can penalise companies which have not been at fault and which have not behaved in a blameworthy manner. A company that may have taken not only reasonable but exemplary steps to avert criminal offences would still, under vicarious liability, be liable if a maverick employee were to manage to evade its system of controls and commit a crime. It would seem perverse to punish a company for the crime of such an employee when the actions of far more of the company's personnel had been directed to thwarting criminal activity, where the criminal acts were forbidden by corporate policy, and where the overwhelming majority of the company's workforce had conducted itself in a legally scrupulous manner; but under vicarious liability such considerations would be irrelevant. Criminal liability in such circumstances hardly seems a fair reflection on how the company conducts its business.

We have discussed the development of the law of corporate criminality in England and the three 1940s cases which demonstrated how mens rea could be attributed to a company. Building on this foundation, the English judges devised their own distinctive model of corporate criminal liability. The leading modern authority is the decision of the House of Lords in *Tesco Supermarkets Ltd v Nattrass*.[25] The case involved a branch manager at one store in a national chain of supermarkets who had allowed items to be put on display for sale at a price which did not conform to that which had been advertised. Charged with violating the Trade Descriptions Act 1968, the company relied on section 24(1) of the Act, which provided that a company would not be liable if it could show that it had taken 'all reasonable precautions' and had exercised 'due diligence' to avoid the default of 'another person'. The specific issue in the case was whether the branch manager was 'another person' for purposes of the Act. The argument, accepted by the House of Lords, was that 'the

25 [1972] AC 153.

company' was comprised of a group of senior individuals of which the branch manager was not a part. This group consisted of the controlling officers and directors of the company, persons who could be said to represent 'the directing mind and will' of the company.

The holding in *Nattrass* was potentially quite narrow and need not have extended beyond the statute at issue. However, the decision has come to stand for the broader proposition that a company is criminally liable only for offences committed by those individuals who are 'identified' with the company. According to Lord Reid in *Nattrass*, these persons are not the alter ego of the company but rather, for all intents and purposes, *are* the company, in whose minds can be found the mind of the company. The reasoning rests on a crude distinction between persons who can be described as the 'brains' of a company, and ordinary workers, who are said to be its 'hands'. As stated by Lord Denning in *H L Bolton Co Ltd v T J Graham & Sons Ltd*:[26]

> A company may in many ways be likened to a human body. It has a brain and nerve centre which controls what it does. It also has hands which hold the tools and act in accordance with directions from the centre. Some of the people in the company are mere servants and agents who are nothing more than hands to do the work and cannot be said to represent the mind or will. Others are directors and managers who represent the directing mind and will of the company and control what it does. The state of mind of those managers is the state of mind of the company and is treated by the law as such.[27]

Under *Nattrass* a company will be criminally liable when a person who can be said to be 'identified' with the company commits a crime, orders that a crime be committed, or delegates his/her authority to another person who commits a crime. Although criminal liability might thus appear to be fairly sweeping, the law's broom sweeps in places where there is likely to be little dirt. The identification doctrine propounds a test of corporate liability that works best in cases where it is needed least and works worst in cases where it is needed most (Gobert: 1994a). In small companies, the directors and officers are likely to take a hands-on approach to the company's affairs and be actively involved in the company's activities, including its illegal activities. Indeed, the rare convictions of companies for manslaughter have involved precisely this 'one-man band' type of operation, where the corporate structure is uncomplicated, the person in charge is readily identifiable, all policy decisions are made by that person, and the trail of responsibility is easily traced.[28] However, in such cases, the prosecution can and usually will be brought against the person in charge. If s/he is convicted, there is little to be gained by prosecuting the company. It is unlikely to continue in business if its main and often only officer is sent to jail. In contrast, the senior officers in a large company are unlikely to be actively involved in the day-to-day operations of the company. Should a criminal offence occur, they will be far removed from it. The prospect of personal criminal liability will be remote and the 'identification' doctrine will frustrate efforts to impose corporate liability.

Despite the distinctive nomenclature, the 'identification' test of corporate criminality can readily be seen as a species of vicarious liability. It is, to be sure, a restrictive species in that, unlike in the United States, few persons associated with

26 [1957] 1 QB 159.
27 [1957] 1 QB 159 at 172.
28 The first of these was *R v Kite* (1994, unreported).

the company will possess the requisite status to cause the company's being held liable for their crimes. None the less, when this occurs, the prosecution will undeniably be based on principles of vicarious liability – the acts and mental state of natural persons will be imputed to the corporate enterprise, and the company's liability will be derivative rather than direct.[29]

A recent proposal of the health and safety commission (2001) that would require companies to appoint a health and safety director highlights the convoluted path that needs to be taken if a criminal conviction of a company is to be secured. From a legal perspective the effect of the proposal would be to allow the company's failure to attend to safety to be attributed to the health and safety director (who might as well be given the title of 'vice-president in charge of going to jail'; see Braithwaite: 1985: 7) and then derivatively imputed to the company. This roundabout way of finding a company criminally responsible for maintaining an unsafe working environment is necessitated by the constraints of the identification doctrine.

The 'identification' test of corporate criminality opens a Pandora's box of questions, not the least of which is how to identify those individuals deserving of 'identification' status. Metaphors referring to 'hands/brains', 'nerve centres', and 'directing mind and will' are ultimately unhelpful. One would be hard pressed to find a job description that used any such terminology. In *Nattrass*, Lord Reid offered, as examples of persons who could be identified with a company, the company's board of directors, its managing director and 'perhaps other superior officers of the company who carry out functions of management and speak and act for the company'. Viscount Dilhorne proposed a functional approach that would have limited 'identification' status to persons who were 'not responsible to another person in the company' for the manner in which they discharged their duties.[30] Few persons other than a company's CEO and its directors would qualify under such a stringent standard. Lord Diplock took a still different tack, suggesting that the answer was to be found in the company's constitution and articles of association.[31] A similar approach would be for a court to examine documents submitted to the state that identified the company's officers either by name or by position held.

None of the above approaches will necessarily capture the 'realpolitik' of decision-making within a company. A pliant board of directors may be little more than a 'rubber stamp', and a CEO with a high profile may be a mere figurehead. Junior executives may wield far more power behind the scenes than their job title would imply. Perhaps there may be external others – funding authorities, consultants, informal advisors, and even friends and lovers – who exert dominant influence over those in power. The Company Directors Disqualification Act 1986, s 22(5) specifically recognises a category of 'shadow directors' who may have no formal links to a company, but it is far from clear how they would fit within the *Nattrass* test. In any event, the time and effort required to determine whether a particular individual has the requisite 'identification' status may well prove a distraction at trial. In *R v British Steel Plc*[32] Steyn LJ (as he then was) referred to a 20 day trial in which three-quarters

---

29 But in *Nattrass*, Lord Diplock purports to draw a distinction between direct corporate liability and vicarious corporate liability.
30 *Tesco Supermarkets Ltd v Nattrass* [1972] AC 153 at 187.
31 [1972] AC 153 at 199.
32 [1995] ICR 586.

of the time was taken up in determining whether various individuals were part of senior management for purposes of being 'identified' with the company.

Arguably, the crux of the matter is not an individual's title or job description but rather the decision-making power of the individual within the organisation. But how much power must one have before one acquires 'identification' status? In *Nattrass* the House of Lords seemed almost to be looking for total power – 'his mind is the mind of the company' – but, except in the smallest of companies, this is an unrealistic standard. In non-hierarchical or horizontally structured companies, decision-making authority is very likely to be shared, with many individuals enjoying significant authority but only with respect to the limited sphere of the company's operation for which they have responsibility (Vice-president in charge of *X*). Even in more hierarchical and vertically structured companies, few individuals, up to and including a company's CEO, will wield absolute authority. Where a firm has numerous branches, as did Tesco in the *Nattrass* case, it is naïve to expect a handful of executives located at a central headquarters to be able to keep tabs on what is happening on a daily basis at all of the company's branch stores. To operate under such a centrally controlled system would leave the company poorly placed to respond to local problems, not to mention crises, that might arise and might ultimately lead to corporate paralysis. Day-to-day decisions perforce have to be entrusted to local management. Yet this discretion, because it relates to the *implementation* of policy rather than its *formulation,* is, according to the test of *Nattrass*, insufficient to bring a local manager within the 'identification' test. *Nattrass* thus seems to convert a business inevitability into a legal defence (Gobert: 1994a).

In *Nattrass* the House of Lords did accept that a company could be liable for a crime committed by a person to whom decision-making authority had been delegated. The delegation, however, had to come from a corporate officer with 'identification' status, which of course brings the inquiry full-circle, except that in the process it becomes more complicated. Even if granted by a person with 'identification' status, will the delegation have to be total in order to transfer that status?[33] If partial delegation will suffice to transfer 'identification' status, just *how much* authority has to be transferred? By simply reserving an ultimate veto power over any authority delegated, can a board of directors insulate the company from criminal liability? The answers to these questions are by no means obvious, and the English judges have approached the issue of delegation cautiously.

A case in point is *R v Redfern and Dunlop Ltd (Aircraft Division)*,[34] where the European sales manager of Dunlop, who was four steps down the reporting ladder from the chief executive, was held not to possess sufficient standing within the organisation to be deemed part of its controlling mind. On the issue of delegation, the Court of Appeal questioned whether the sales manager had been delegated the authority to sell military equipment to a proscribed regime in violation of a legal embargo. However, to ask the rhetorical question whether a company's ruling hierarchy would delegate the authority to commit a crime is to invite a perfunctory negative answer. Did the court really expect to find a direct order from a board of directors to commit the offence? Delegated authority is often of a general nature,

---

33 See *R v Winson* [1969] 1 QB 371 (partial delegation insufficient to impute knowledge to a licensee).
34 [1993] Crim LR 43.

with aims and goals identified but with considerable discretion being left to the presumably trustworthy person to whom authority has been delegated. Furthermore, the court in *Redfern* seems to have ignored the company's responsibility for placing the sales manager in a position where he could commit the crimes in question, for providing him the leeway to do so, and for failing adequately to monitor his transactions. Given that the profits from the illegal sales presumably inured to the benefit of the company, it was incumbent on it to ensure that the sales manager was not garnering these profits illegally. The possibility that limiting criminal liability to the sales manager might make him the scapegoat for illegal corporate policies did not seem to bother the court, which appeared to be fixated on the 'level of management and control' of the sales manager within the company rather than on the company's role in the offence.

It might be argued that the source of a criminogenic corporate policy is not as important as the fact that the policy has been approved or ratified by persons who constitute 'the directing mind and will' of the company. If this consideration were to be accepted as critical, a company would be liable for harms resulting from a criminogenic policy or practice approved by a board of directors regardless of the level of staff with whom the culpable policy or practice originated. The negative implications are troubling, however, and may help to explain why prosecutors have been reluctant to charge companies with serious criminal offences. Under the 'identification' doctrine, a corporate enterprise is criminally liable because a person 'identified' with the enterprise has committed a crime. But if this is true, then so too must be the converse: if a company is guilty of a crime, then there must be some person 'identified' with the company who is also guilty of that crime. But is it fair to subject corporate directors to criminal sanctions because they may have deferred to the expertise of managers within the company who proposed a policy that had unforeseen and unanticipated criminal implications? If the policy leads to a death, should the directors be charged with manslaughter? If such serious criminal liability were to be based on so thin a reed, the effect might be to deter qualified candidates from accepting a position on a company's board of directors. The alternative of a corporate board's disengaging itself from policy reviews is equally unpalatable, as this is the antithesis of the oversight function that a board is supposed to be performing.

It is not clear, however, that a conviction of an executive officer or director must precede or accompany the conviction of a company under the 'identification' doctrine. No doubt proof of some executive's guilt would have to be established at the company's trial, but the executive may not have to be formally charged. Of course, such proof would inevitably stain the individual's reputation. Awkward questions might also arise as to why the executive was not being personally prosecuted for actions that brought about the prosecution of the company. Some would see in the failure to prosecute a director or corporate executive another example of the favourable treatment accorded to the rich and powerful within the criminal justice system.

The practical utility of the 'identification' test is limited if for no other reason than that the number of persons within a large company who will possess the required level of decision-making authority will inevitably be a very small percentage of those associated with the company. By restricting a company's liability to crimes committed by a handful of individuals, the English judges lose many of the advantages of the American version of vicarious liability. First, there will be lost the pressure that the law can exert on companies to monitor their workforce. Indeed, the pressure in England will be precisely in the opposite direction – the seeming way to avoid corporate criminal liability is for directors and officers to place a barrier between themselves and knowledge of the criminal actions of the workforce. Their company cannot be held liable for what they do not know. Also lost will be the practical utility of the American approach. It is relatively straightforward to ascertain who is an employee or agent of a company; it is far more difficult to determine who wields sufficient decision-making authority to be 'identified' with the company. As internal decision-making structures will vary from company to company, legal precedents also will not be of much value. And what should a court make of a co-operative in which all persons who work for the co-operative are accorded an equal vote in management decisions? It might seem that in such a case the co-operative would be liable for the acts of any of its workers. If so, this would reduce the 'identification' test to the virtual equivalent of the American version of vicarious liability. Regardless of its theoretical merits, it would seem that it would be folly from a criminal law perspective for an organisation to structure itself in a co-operative form.

Several cases in the 1990s suggested that a reaction against the 'identification' test was beginning to set in among the English judges, and three in particular highlighted this trend. In the first, *Tesco Stores Ltd v Brent London Borough Council*,[35] a sales clerk had sold an '18' video to an under-aged customer. The issue was whether the employer should be charged with the knowledge and information of the clerk. Relying on *Nattrass*, the company argued that the only knowledge that mattered was that of the persons who constituted the company's 'directing mind and will'. The court disagreed. *Nattrass* was distinguished on the basis of differences in statutory language, but arguably the more powerful point made by the court was that, if the 'identification' doctrine were to be applied, it would defeat the objectives of the statute. In a large company it would be virtually impossible to find corporate officers who were personally aware of the age of each and every video purchaser. For the statute not to be rendered nugatory, the 'knowledge and information' referred to had logically to be that of the person who sold the film to the purchaser.

In *R v British Steel Plc*,[36] a workman was killed after a steel platform collapsed on the job site. The supervisor of the project was an engineer employed by British Steel. Prosecuted for violating the Health and Safety at Work etc Act 1974, s 3(1), the company argued first, that the engineer had conducted himself in an appropriate manner, but that, even if this were found not to be the case, he was not part of the company's 'directing mind and will'. The Court of Appeal rejected both contentions. It construed the statute to impose an absolute prohibition and held that the 'identification' doctrine was inapplicable. The purposive interpretation of the statute echoed that in *Brent London Borough Council*. To quote Steyn LJ (as he then was):

'[I]t would drive a juggernaut through the legislative scheme if corporate employers could avoid criminal liability where the potentially harmful event is committed by someone who is not the directing mind of the company.'[37]

35 [1993] 2 All ER 718.
36 [1995] ICR 586.
37 [1995] ICR 586 at 593.

Displaying a sensitivity to the policy implications of his decision, Steyn LJ stressed the desirability of promoting 'a culture of guarding against the risks to health and safety by virtue of hazardous industrial operations'.

A revisionist perspective of 'identification' was offered by Lord Hoffmann in the Privy Council's decision in *Meridian Global Funds Management Asia Ltd v Securities Commission*.[38] The issue in the case was whether the corporate defendant had violated the New Zealand Securities Amendment Act 1988 when its Hong Kong investment managers had failed to comply with the Act's notification requirements. In addressing this issue, Lord Hoffmann interpreted the identification doctrine as a sub-part of a broader rule of attribution. For an employee's acts or knowledge to count as that of a company, the employee had to have the authority to act as he did. Whether or not he possessed such authority was to be determined by examining the company's 'primary rules of attribution'. These could be found in a company's constitution and articles of association, or be imposed by principles of company law. Also of relevance to the inquiry were general rules of attribution contained in, for example, principles of agency. Finally, Lord Hoffmann recognised that in some instances a court might have to fashion 'special rules' of attribution in order to prevent frustration of the purpose of the statute at issue. In the latter situation the critical question would be whether the statute was intended to apply to companies, and, if so, whose acts, knowledge or state of mind were to count as the acts, knowledge or state of mind of the company under the statute. Such questions were to be answered by resort to principles of statutory construction. In short, while the 'identification' doctrine *might* be relevant in some cases, a court need not confine its inquiry to this issue and should consider all applicable rules of attribution.

Commentators saw in Lord Hoffmann's location of the identification doctrine within a broader rule of attribution the seeds of an expanded scope of corporate criminal liability. This prospect, however, was rejected by the Court of Appeal in *A-G's Reference (No 2 of 1999)*,[39] at least in respect of common law crimes. As previously discussed, the case arose out of the Southall train crash. Great Western Railway was charged, along with its driver, with gross negligence manslaughter. The prosecution sought to circumvent the identification doctrine by arguing that if it could be shown that the company had been grossly negligent, it should not be necessary to prove any specific officer's gross negligence. The company's alleged gross negligence consisted of permitting its train to operate without either the Automatic Warning System (AWS) or the Automatic Train Protection (ATP) system, both of which were installed on the train but neither of which was functioning at the time. As a result, the driver had no technological back-up when his attention lapsed and he failed to observe two warning signals and a stop signal.

The trial judge dismissed the manslaughter charges against Great Western and the Court of Appeal affirmed. The Court of Appeal reasoned that no evidence had been presented that a specific corporate officer had behaved in a grossly negligent manner, and that this absence of proof defeated application of the 'identification' doctrine. However, the court failed to explain why 'identification' was the proper test of the company's liability. The court was referred to *Meridian*, although it is not

---

38 [1995] 3 All ER 918.
39 [2000] QB 796.

clear how *Meridian* would have advanced the prosecution's thesis that a company should be guilty of corporate manslaughter if its operation, viewed holistically with respect to the offence, has been grossly negligent. That issue became moot, however, when the Court of Appeal rejected Lord Hoffmann's account of 'identification'. The court distinguished *Meridian* as involving a statutory offence, while manslaughter was a common law crime. While the point is technically correct, the Privy Council had before it in *Meridian* a statutory scheme that it needed to interpret in order to resolve the case at hand and any broader pronouncement on its part would have been obiter. It hardly follows from this general constraint on judicial decision-making that the 'identification' doctrine should control the analysis of corporate liability for common law crimes. The Privy Council's decision in *Meridian* simply did not speak to this issue. The Court of Appeal's conclusion that it was only through the 'identification' doctrine that a company's liability for a common law crime could be established seemed to ignore the fact that the doctrine itself was developed primarily in cases involving statutory offences.[40] One might submit that the absence of a statutory definition of manslaughter, far from wedding a court to the 'identification' doctrine, should have freed it to exercise its historic power to develop the common law.

The decision in *Attorney-General's Reference* highlights one of the major drawbacks of the 'identification' test of corporate criminal liability. It encourages companies to structure internal lines of communication so that knowledge of the criminogenic aspects of the company's operation do not reach those at the top. In this way the directors of a company seemingly can insulate the company from criminal liability. But an approach dictated by a desire to reduce a company's exposure to criminal liability may none the less lead to incompetent management decisions. The dangers are illustrated by the demise of Barings Bank. The bank's troubles were precipitated by the unauthorised and reckless financial dealings of its head trader in Singapore, Nick Leeson. Leeson's dealings and the steps he took to cover them up were not discovered in part because Barings management in London discontinued the practice of requiring regular reports from Leeson. As long as Leeson's dealings appeared to be highly profitable, Barings management did not wish to know how he managed to generate such profits in an area of trading that should have been generating slow but steady gains. Management also continued to honour Leeson's repeated requests for additional funds without closely questioning why these funds were needed. Warning signals were thus repeatedly ignored (Barings Report: 1995). This policy of benign neglect may have served to limit the company's exposure to criminal liability – if it turned out Leeson had acted illegally, he could be sacrificed to the criminal courts, as in fact happened. The lesson to be drawn, however, is that a company can wind up paying a very dear, even if not a criminal, price for such shoddy management practices. Barings wound up being bankrupted by Leeson's recklessness.

---

40 Eg, *Nattrass*. However, in *P&O European Ferries (Dover) Ltd* (1991) 93 Cr App Rep 72 (Central Criminal Court), the court held the identification principle applicable in a case where the company was charged with manslaughter.

F. RETHINKING THE BASIS OF IMPUTED CORPORATE CRIMINAL LIABILITY: THE COMPANY AS ACCESSORY

The criticisms raised by the English judges against vicarious corporate criminal liability had undoubted merit. Their concerns, it will be recalled, were basically twofold. The first was the practical problem of requiring a company to oversee the operations of potentially thousands of employees. This fear may have been a bit exaggerated, for no court would have expected directors personally to supervise each and every corporate employee, and a more liberal conception of delegation would have alleviated any potential unfairness. The more telling criticism of vicarious liability, however, was that it would allow criminal sanctions to be imposed on a company that had taken reasonable or even exemplary steps to prevent its staff and personnel from committing criminal offences. Criminal liability without fault is inherently troubling, and even more so when liability is vicarious.

While the English judges may have put their finger on the weakness of vicarious liability, their alternative of limiting a company's liability to offences committed by persons who represented the company's 'directing mind and will' or were 'identified' with it may have been a cure that was worse than the disease. At least judged by the number of convictions for serious offences, the 'identification' test has proved to be, as an empirical matter, an ineffective tool for holding companies to legal account for serious misconduct. Despite numerous public inquiries that have found deaths to be attributable to the equivalent of corporate gross negligence,[41] rarely has a company been prosecuted, and even more rarely has a company been convicted, of manslaughter. Because there are so few convictions, the deterrent force of the law inevitably will be weakened.

While the 'identification' doctrine may have addressed the unfairness of forcing a company to supervise potentially thousands of employees, it failed to answer the question of why a company that had taken reasonable steps to prevent wrongdoing should be held liable when one of its directors, officers or senior managers managed to evade the controls in place and commit a criminal offence. Under the 'identification' doctrine, and under the American version of vicarious corporate liability as well, a company's efforts to avert criminal activity by others – no matter how well-conceived, no matter how well-intentioned, and no matter how generally effective – are in the final analysis irrelevant. The way to address the issue of principle, and perhaps also the objections of the English judges that the American approach to vicarious liability is too broad, would be to require a showing of fault as a prerequisite to a company's conviction. But in what way can a company be said to be at fault when a crime has been committed by one of its employees, agents or officers?

Under English law one who intentionally aids, abets, counsels or procures another to commit a crime can be held liable as an accessory to the crime.[42] An accessory may be tried for the same offence as the principal (the person who perpetrates the actus reus of the offence with the legally required mens rea), and will be subject to the same sanctions if convicted. If no substantive offence is committed by the principal, the defendant may still be guilty of incitement. There would appear to be

---

41 See eg Dept of Transport (1987) The Merchant Shipping Act *mv Herald of Free Enterprise*: Report of Court No 8074; also report of Lord Cullen (Cullen: 2002) on the causes of the crash at Ladbroke Grove.

42 Accessories and Abettors Act 1861, s 8.

no reason why a company could not be found to be an accessory to an offence committed by one of its agents. A company's policies, practices or culture may encourage, facilitate, aid, abet, or even reward illegality.

It would fall to the courts to determine what amounts to a sufficient contribution by a company to an offence by a natural person to warrant conviction as an accessory. The company's role is likely to be more subtle than is the case when a natural person is charged as an accessory. When, for example, a natural person pays a principal to commit a crime, the payment will be strong evidence of encouragement; the 'payment' from a corporate defendant may take the form of a bonus or promotion for results achieved, the legal significance of which may be more ambiguous. The natural person who is an accessory, furthermore, will usually have to make clear to the principal what illegal action is expected, but a company may not have to say anything to its employees, trusting to the employees to draw the intended inference, while leaving itself in a position to argue that any offence was the employee's own idea. To give a concrete example, consider the case of a transport company. It does not need to order its lorry drivers to break the speed laws if it compensates them on the basis of the mileage they log. Either way, the drivers will be more likely to speed than if they were paid a weekly wage and worked defined hours. If an innocent individual is then killed as a result of a driver's excessive speed, the company will doubtless disclaim any responsibility for the death, arguing that it did not instruct its drivers to break the law. Indeed, it may have told them the precise opposite. But to accept such a disclaimer is to ignore the role of corporate policies in encouraging dangerous driving.

The lorry company in the above example would undoubtedly, and probably truthfully, argue that it did not intend that anybody be killed or injured. While the English law of complicity requires that an accessory have *intended* to provide assistance to the principal, 'intent' in this context does not require that the accessory subscribe to or endorse the criminal aims of the principal. A leading authority is *National Coal Board v Gamble,*[43] where a weighbridge operator employed by the coal board issued a ticket to a lorry driver that allowed him to take his vehicle on to the road despite the fact that the load exceeded the maximum permissible weight. The operator had no vested interest in whether the driver committed an offence and went so far as to warn him that he would be violating the law. None the less, the Coal Board was convicted of being an accessory to the lorry driver's offence. On appeal, Devlin J stated that knowledge that one's acts would assist the commission of an offence constituted prima facie evidence of an intent to assist. The reasoning in *Gamble* was subsequently approved by the House of Lords in *DPP for Northern Ireland v Lynch,*[44] where the driver of a getaway car for a terrorist gang was convicted of being an accessory to the murder by gang members of a police officer. Their Lordships stated that a conviction for being an accessory could be based on the provision of assistance, with knowledge of the circumstances of the offence, and that it was not necessary to show that the accessory approved of the principal's illegal aims.[45]

---

43 [1959] 1 QB 11.
44 [1975] AC 653.
45 There are cases to the contrary, however, that suggest that liability as an accessory will not lie unless there is an intent to promote the principal's criminal objectives. See, eg *Gillick v West Norfolk and Wisbech Area Health Authority* [1986] AC 112.

What kinds of actions or omissions might warrant prosecuting a company for being an accessory to a criminal offence? The role that a company might play in a crime committed by a person who represents, works for or is empowered to act for the company can run the gamut from passive to active, and from inconsequential to indispensable. The involvement might take the form of:

- selecting or hiring the offender;
- failing to properly train the offender;
- providing the opportunity for the offence or placing the offender in a position to commit the offence;
- providing the tools or instruments without which the offence could not have been committed;
- failing to supervise or monitor the offender;
- tolerating or turning a blind eye to past known instances of illegality; or
- creating a compensation or reward system that encouraged illegality.

A failure on the part of a company to identify the relevant risks and take effective countermeasures with respect to any of these areas may support a charge that a company is liable as an accessory to an individual's crime.

The hiring stage might seem a remote place to begin but the nature of some jobs demands that one exercise a high degree of care in filling the position. In England, in the summer of 2002, a widely publicised murder of two children, allegedly by a school caretaker, triggered demands for more rigorous vetting of teachers and other school employees who had regular contact with children. A private firm had primary responsibility for the required background checks, but it found itself overwhelmed by the task and unable to fulfil its remit completely by the start of the school year. In the event the government was forced to retreat from its commitment that no person who had not been thoroughly vetted would be allowed to teach in the classroom. But what if the company had lied and said it had completed the requisite background checks, or decided to run haphazard and superficial checks in order to meet its deadline? And what if this had led to the hiring of a teacher with a history of paedophilia, who subsequently abused a child? Why should the company not be prosecuted as an accessory to the teacher's offence? Evidence of 'aiding and abetting' might include the failure to conduct an effective check of an available sex offender register, or ignoring credible information that had been communicated to it regarding the history of one of the applicants. Of course, if the company received no such information, and if it checked the relevant register but the applicant's name did not appear on it, and if there were no 'red flags' to otherwise have put it on notice of an applicant's sexual proclivities, then the company would have a strong argument that it had not been at fault.

The paedophile example involves a situation where a company was under a contractual duty to weed out unsuitable job applicants. If special skills are required to perform a job properly, then a company might similarly be deemed at fault for not screening applicants to determine if they have the requisite skills. Compounding any deficiency in the selection of employees may be a failure to provide proper training. It is the company's responsibility to train its personnel as to how to perform the tasks they will be required to undertake. Inadequate training, by itself or in conjunction with faulty hiring procedures, will support the case for holding a company liable as an accessory to a crime which would have been averted had the employee been properly trained. At a minimum, a company should alert its employees to whatever risks are inherent in the assignments they are to carry out, and instruct them on ways to avoid or minimise these risks. What further training is required will depend on the specific tasks to be performed and the risks involved. If a job involves a high level of danger to the employee or others if not properly executed, then training commensurate with the degree of danger will be required. Training may be especially critical when a company places a dangerous instrument at the disposal of an employee. Dangerous instruments are not limited to firearms or comparable weapons. In *Rubie v Faulkner*[46] the court held that a driving instructor had the duty to ensure that a learner under his tutelage drove safely and carefully, and could be liable as an accessory when the learner did not. In the hands of a learner driver, a car is a dangerous weapon. So too is a lorry or a forklift entrusted to a worker untrained or inexperienced in their use.

A company has both the power to control and the right to control the acts of its employees while they are engaged in the company's business. Wilson (1998: 588) would go one step further, arguing that the right of control becomes a duty to control in three situations:

1. where the secondary party has ownership or control of property used by the principal;
2. where the secondary party stands in the relationship of employer and the principal is an employee or independent contractor;
3. where the secondary party has ownership or control of premises used by the principal.

All three situations have clear applicability in the corporate context. A company will typically own or control the property, equipment and tools used by its workforce. The relationship of a corporate enterprise with those who work for it or represent it will almost always be one of employer-employee or that of independent contractor paid by the company. Wilson argues that in these situations the failure to satisfy a duty of control constitutes unlawful encouragement or assistance.

Should the mere fact that a company places an employee in a position where the employee might commit a criminal offence be considered relevant in determining whether a company should be held liable as an accessory to the offence? There may be some situations where it would be clearly reckless to entrust a particular task to an employee with an unsuitable background. It would be folly to put a person with a history of child abuse in charge of a day care centre for children. Where the temptation to criminal activity is highly foreseeable, as when a poorly paid employee is entrusted with large sums of money, a company may be at fault in not adequately supervising or monitoring the employee. A company may exacerbate an already potentially perilous situation by the basis on which it compensates its workers. We discussed previously how paying lorry drivers on the basis of the mileage that they log could cause drivers to ignore speed limits or persevere in their routes despite being overtired. Similarly, compensating sales staff on a commission basis with liberal opportunities to earn bonuses may encourage salesmen to engage in fraud to bolster their sales. In various forms of piece-work involving dangerous machinery, where salaries are directly linked to output, the failure to monitor employees may also constitute reckless behaviour on the part of the company. Having created a dangerous situation, it becomes incumbent upon the company to defuse the danger,

46 [1940] 1 KB 571. See also *Du Cros v Lambourne* [1907] 1 KB 40.

and a failure to do so may render the company liable as an accessory to a subsequent offence.

The creation or tolerance of a corporate culture in which profitable criminal activity is deemed acceptable presents one of the strongest cases for holding companies liable as accessories to the crimes of their workforce. Such a culture or ethos should arguably override factors that would otherwise count in a company's favour. The corporate defendant may have hired competent staff, provided adequate training and forbade criminal conduct, but all this may be overshadowed by a showing that the company fostered an ethos where illegality was deemed acceptable if it led to greater profits. To extol, promote or pay generous bonuses to staff whose results are well-known to be the product of illegal shortcuts sends a clear message to the company's workforce as to where its priorities lie.

Capturing in a statute the elusive nature of this type of corporate fault is not easy but a commendable attempt to do so can be found in the Australian Criminal Code. Among the bases for attributing criminal responsibility to a company that the Code recognises is 'that a corporate culture existed within the body corporate that directed, encouraged, tolerated or led to non-compliance with [the applicable law]'.[47] This subsection holds companies responsible for allowing a criminogenic corporate culture to persist. The following subsection goes further, imposing on companies an affirmative duty to establish a non-criminogenic culture. Under the latter subsection, liability can be founded on the fact 'that the body corporate failed to create and maintain a corporate culture that required compliance with [the applicable law]'.[48] The Act defines a corporate culture in terms of 'an attitude, policy, rule, course of conduct or practice existing within the body corporate generally or in the part of the body corporate in which the relevant activities take place'.[49]

The recognition of a criminogenic corporate culture or ethos is a dynamic development in the law's war against corporate criminality. Where a company has put into place workplace structures, practices and procedures that are conducive to criminal activity, or has allowed a criminogenic culture or ethos to be created or to persist, then the company should be liable as an accessory to offences committed by its workforce. The fact that the company may have published mission statements opposed to illegality or instructed its personnel to obey the law should not automatically defeat liability. Such 'social defences' will be betrayed as mere rhetoric and window-dressing by the company's failure to take steps to prevent criminal activity. On the other hand, if a company does make a good faith, reasonable and appropriate effort to monitor its workforce and to defuse the potential for crime, it should be entitled to a defence of 'due diligence'. Consistent with the emphasis that we believe should be placed on fault, due diligence negates fault. The defence of due diligence will be explored more fully in chapters 3 and 6.

The English courts are not insensitive to the accessorial role that a company can play in an employee's crime, as evidenced by the decision of the Court of Appeal in *R v Robert Millar (Contractors) Ltd and Robert Millar*.[50] In this case, a lorry driver was convicted of causing death by dangerous driving when a defective tyre on the

---

47 Criminal Code Act 1995, s 12.3(1)(c).
48 Criminal Code Act 1995, s 12.3(1)(d).
49 Criminal Code Act 1995, s 12(6).
50 [1970] 2 QB 54.

heavily-weighted lorry and trailer that he was driving at the time burst and the lorry crashed into a car, killing its six occupants. The driver knew of the defective state of the tyre, as did the managing director of the company (the driver having complained to him of it on more than one occasion). The company was charged with counselling and procuring the driver's offence. The Court of Appeal upheld the company's conviction, reasoning that the company, through its managing director, was aware of the serious risks to other road-users that were posed. The fact that the deaths were not intended, and may not have been foreseen, did not affect the company's liability.

There is another aspect of the case, in addition to the conviction of the company as an accessory, which is worthy of note. At the sentencing hearing, the driver was dealt with rather leniently by the judge, receiving only a modest fine and a disqualification. By all accounts, the company was given a comparatively more severe sentence. The Court of Appeal agreed that the heavier sentence to the company was justified because it bore the primary responsibility for the deaths. Such apportionment of blame in corporate crime cases is often not inaccurate. A company is almost invariably better placed to rectify criminogenic and dangerous conditions than are its personnel. Employees may be afraid to protest for fear that they will be retaliated against or lose their jobs. In any event, an employee may be powerless if the corporate employer chooses to ignore his/her complaint, as did the company in the *Robert Millar* case. In law an accessory may be more culpable than a principal and incur a more severe penalty as a consequence. This apparent juxtaposition, infrequently found by the courts, may be particularly appropriate in cases involving both corporate and employee fault.

G. CONCLUSIONS

The value of conceptualising corporate criminal liability in terms of complicity is that liability is based on fault, the specific nature of which must be made clear. Under the present law of both England and the United States a company may be criminally liable even though it has done nothing to bring about the offence of an individual. Indeed, it may be liable even though it has taken exemplary steps to prevent the individual's offence. Criminal liability, with its attendant denunciation, stigma and sanctions, should not rest on a blameless foundation. A civil judgment against the company may have social utility in that it provides compensation to an innocent victim who has suffered injury at the hands of one of the company's employees, but criminal liability should require a showing of fault on the part of the company. The fault involved in being an accessory satisfies the need for such a showing.

Unfortunately, accessorial liability is unlikely to prove a panacea for holding companies to criminal account for a variety of reasons. First, there may be no individual who has committed an offence to which the corporate enterprise can be made an accessory. The case of the Clapham rail crash may serve to illustrate the point. The Hidden Report (1989) found that the immediate cause of the crash was faulty wiring by a British Rail technician. The technician's 'error' was not an isolated incident, but rather represented standard operating procedure as he understood it. He had never been reprimanded nor received any indication that his approach to his job was unsafe, even though it was in fact in violation of British Rail policies. A secondary cause of the accident identified in the Hidden Report was the failure of the technician's supervisor to check the wiring as was also required by company policy. The technician, however, testified that he could not recall such a supervisory check ever having been made. Nor had either the technician or the supervisor ever received a copy of the relevant policies. A further fact which came to light during the course of the inquiry was that in the thirteen weeks before the accident, almost a third of the local British Rail workforce had worked every day of the week and over another third, thirteen days out of a possible fourteen. The technician who made the fatal mistake had worked every day but one over a three month period. A failure properly to train and supervise its workforce, along with an ethos that seemed to prize unstinting devotion to work over safety – and in which long hours were generously compensated – combined to bring about fatal results.

But who might have been charged with manslaughter with respect to the victims who died in the Clapham crash? Neither the technician nor the engineer had an intent to kill or cause serious bodily injury, and neither's behaviour could be described as grossly negligent. The absence of any reprimand or criticism seemed to imply that there was nothing improper in the way they carried out their respective jobs. Nor was there anything in the circumstances to have put them on notice of the possible disaster that was about to occur. If blame were to be meted out, the lion's share would seem to belong to British Rail, which had failed to instruct the technician and his supervisor in their job responsibilities, and even failed to supply them with copies of its own policies and procedures. The monitoring system that the company had put into place was inadequate to reveal the dangers or to prevent the harm. The company could further be faulted for tolerating or encouraging a working schedule that ignored the self-evident truth that tired workers are accident-prone workers.

Despite its poorly conceived mode of operation, the basis on which British Rail could have been charged with manslaughter is by no means obvious. The 'identification' test would not be met because of a lack of evidence that anybody sufficiently senior in the corporate hierarchy to be 'identified' with the company was aware of the workers' misfeasance or the risks that had been created. The technician was clearly the 'hands' of British Rail and his supervisor was no more its 'brains' than was the branch manager of Tesco in the *Nattrass* case. Even under the more expansive American version of vicarious liability, it is doubtful that either the technician or his supervisor was guilty of a crime that could be imputed to the company. If so, would being able to charge British Rail as an accessory be of any advantage? Without a showing that the technician or his supervisor had committed a criminal offence, there would be no crime to which the company's fault, which consisted of its arguably gross mismanagement of risk, could be attached so as to render it liable as an accessory. What is needed to overcome the hurdle is a fresh approach that would allow a company's own organisational fault to form the basis of a criminal prosecution.

Attempting to impose accessorial liability on companies may founder for a different reason. If the English courts were to persist in adhering to the 'identification' doctrine, it would be necessary to show that the person who incited, encouraged, facilitated or contributed to the employee's offence had sufficient status within the organisation to be 'identified' with it. This was not a problem in *R v Robert Millar (Contractors) Ltd and Robert Millar*, discussed previously, for the managing director was aware of the defective tyre that rendered the driver guilty of causing death by dangerous driving. The managing director's awareness could be imputed to the company for he had sufficient status within the company to satisfy the 'identification' test. In contrast, in *A-G's Reference (No 2 of 1999)*,[51] the case of the Southall train crash, manslaughter charges against Great Western Railway were dismissed as there had been no showing that a person 'identified' with the company was aware of the fact that the technological warning systems on the train were inoperative. Whatever gross negligence the driver of the train may have been guilty of could not be imputed to the company because the driver was not part of the company's decision-making hierarchy. Again, a concept of organisational fault would be needed to hold the company criminally liable. Although arguments to this effect were rejected by the court in the case, it was on the basis of existing precedent and not on the basis of their merit. As we shall see in the next chapter, the UK government has come around to this way of thinking about corporate fault in its proposals for an offence of corporate killing.

We have identified a spectrum of possible complicit actions and inactions by companies, ranging from passive acquiescence of illegal shortcuts to active encouragement of illegality through misguided practices, policies and cultures, or, indeed, direct orders, that might warrant charging a company as an accessory to a crime committed by one of its employees. At the passive end of the spectrum, the company's involvement may frequently appear to be innocuous. For example, the mere fact that a company assigns an employee to a job where there is the potential for criminal activity may not seem sufficiently culpable to warrant holding the company liable as an accessory to a crime committed by the employee. However, if added to that fact, the company has failed to think about, devise and implement systems to prevent the criminologically significant risks posed, or has failed to monitor the employee's actions, and is known to generally ignore illegal actions by its workforce, then the case that the company has been blameless becomes more and more tenuous. But to capture this added dimension of accessorial liability, a theory of organisational fault is needed, and it is therefore to this topic that we turn our attention in the following chapter.

51 [2000] QB 796.

CHAPTER 3

Corporate criminality II: Organisational fault

A.   THE PICTURE SO FAR

In chapter 2 we saw that the English judges were slow to accept the principle of corporate criminal liability for traditional penal offences (as opposed to regulatory offences), and that when they finally did so, they opted for a legal test that restricted a company's liability to offences committed by persons who could be said to be 'identified' with the company. As a practical matter, this meant that a company could only be prosecuted for offences committed by a handful of persons in positions of high authority, such as the company's directors, executive officers and senior managers. In terms of breadth, this test compared unfavourably with the approach taken in the United States, where a company could be 'vicariously' liable for an offence committed by any of its personnel, including front-line workers and independent contractors, if done in the course of their employment and with intent to benefit the company. In contrast, proof of an intent to benefit the company was not essential to a successful prosecution of a company in England; it was sufficient that the official whose crime was sought to be imputed to the company had the authority to act as s/he did.[1]

---

1   See *Moore v Bresler Ltd* [1944] 2 All ER 515.

While differences thus existed between the English and American tests of corporate criminal liability, the philosophical and overarching common element was that in both countries companies incurred liability derivatively for offences committed by natural persons. The offence of the natural person was attributed or imputed to the company. Derivative liability, however, can be unsatisfactory for victims and companies alike. For victims and their families seeking explanations, the role of the company may not be revealed at trial, for it is sufficient for the prosecutor to show that an individual has committed an offence and that the individual is a person for whose acts the company bears responsibility. For companies, vicarious liability can be frustrating as well, for they may be convicted of an offence even though they may have tried their utmost to prevent the offence and the offence was in direct contravention of corporate policy. To convict and punish a company under such circumstances would seem to conflict with the well-established criminal law principle of *nulla poena sine culpa* (no punishment without fault), as well as the sentencing principle of 'just deserts'.

To avoid potential unfairness, we proposed in the preceding chapter that a company should only be criminally liable when it could be shown to have been at fault in inciting, encouraging, aiding, abetting, facilitating, counselling, rewarding or in some other way significantly contributing to the employee's or officer's offence; in other words, when a company could be characterised as an accessory to the individual's offence. The gain in fairness, however, might be offset by a loss in deterrence if convictions proved, as they likely would, more difficult to secure. Old stumbling blocks, albeit in a somewhat new guise, would also remain. The commission of a crime by an individual would still have to be proved, not for the purpose of vicariously attributing it to a company, but to establish an offence to which the company could be linked as an accessory. In any event, if the English judges persisted in adhering to an 'identification' test of corporate criminal liability, analysing a company's liability in terms of complicity would offer little advantage. Before an accessorial offence could be imputed to the company, the prosecution would still have to show that a person of sufficient status in the decision-making hierarchy of the company to be identified with it had committed an act that would render him/her liable as an accessory. As is presently the case, the company might well be able to avoid liability by insulating its directors and officers from knowledge of the legally dubious actions of its personnel. And yet it is arguably this very act of insulation that constitutes the fault that warrants holding a company criminally liable in the first place.

The fundamental problem with imputed liability is that it does not capture the company's role in offences committed by its personnel. Holding companies liable as accessories, while an improvement in that it would identify the nature of the fault that justifies the imposition of criminal sanctions, by itself will not solve the problem. In the modern company, results, be they for good or evil, are typically the product of many interdependent decisions, actions and inactions. A potentially criminogenic policy that originates with an individual may be reviewed by a working party or a committee, then by senior management, perhaps by the CEO, and in some cases by the board of directors before it becomes official company policy. The persons responsible for formulating the policy will not be the same persons whose approval is needed to bring the policy into force or the persons who will be assigned the task of implementing the policy. But who, then, should be charged when the policy leads to a criminal offence?

If the Crown were to prosecute all who were associated in any manner with the policy, liability might be spread too thinly, with the link to personal responsibility becoming attenuated if not lost. If the prosecution were confined to the person with whom the plan originated or the worker who performed the harm-causing act, it might seem an exercise in finding a scapegoat. If the prosecution were brought against the directors of the company, on the theory that they should bear ultimate responsibility for all aspects of the company's business affairs (and, perhaps more specifically, for having approved the criminogenic policy), this too could result in unfairness as the directors would had not have been directly involved in either the conception or execution of the policy. Sometimes, moreover, critical information will be withheld from directors by management because disclosure would damage the reputation of a division of the company or specific individuals (although one might argue that directors have an affirmative obligation to find out what is going on in *their* company). In any event, imposing legal liability on directors might succeed only in deterring highly qualified individuals from taking on corporate directorships.

The equating of corporate and individual fault can yield a misleading and sometimes incomplete picture of why corporate crimes occur. What is missing from the picture is the role that the company's structures, policies, practices, procedures, ethos and culture play in the commission of the offence. In many instances legally cognisable harm that occurs in a corporate setting is the result not so much of acts of misguided or deviant individuals but of corporate ways of doing business that have failed adequately to address the risk of criminality. Often the source of illegal acts and criminogenic policies can be found in a culture or ethos that is tolerant or even encouraging of anything that is profitable. This culture or ethos may have been put in place by persons who are no longer active in the company's management (which is not to absolve those who perpetuate the culture), and workplace practices may have evolved over time. It is not uncommon, moreover, for corporate decision-makers to subordinate individual ambitions to the greater good of the company. What emerges from this 'mind-set' are policies and practices that do not necessarily reflect the views of any one person or persons in the company but which are more accurately described as those of the company. Bucy (1991) maintains that companies can have their own distinctive 'personality' that is unrelated to and independent of any particular individuals within the company.

If a company's structures, policies, practices, procedures, ethos or culture promote, facilitate or tolerate criminal activity, then the company must share in the blame for any offences that result. Responsibility may be distributed among policy-makers and policy implementers. It extends to those who lack the foresight to anticipate the potential for illegality and who fail to formulate, implement and enforce systems that would prevent such illegality. Where liability is so diffused, however, it makes little sense to try to single out individual wrongdoers. It is the organisation that is at fault. The *collective* nature of corporate criminality is best captured within a legal regime where it is companies that are prosecuted and, if convicted, punished. Such a regime stands in stark contrast to the prevailing tests of corporate criminality which attempt to impute the offence of an individual to a company.

Simply stated, companies should bear responsibility for consequences that follow from the way that they have organised their business operation. When these consequences are criminal, then the company should be subject to criminal liability. What is currently lacking is a theory of 'organisational fault' that captures the company's role in a criminal offence committed ostensibly by one of its personnel. It might be observed that the distinction between individual and organisational fault parallels the distinction between an atomic and organic view of companies that we examined in the previous chapter; but whereas the distinction then was presented to examine the case that only individuals and not companies should be subject to criminal prosecution, the debate has now moved on, and the distinction is relevant to determining the proper test of corporate criminal liability. Whereas traditional tests of liability have been premised on imputing crimes of individuals to their companies, we believe that a company, as a collective entity, should be subject to criminal liability and that liability should be based on the company's organisational fault. Organisational fault inheres when a company has organised its business in such a way that persons and property are exposed to criminal victimisation or the unreasonable risk of harm, when the company has failed to devise and put into place systems for avoiding criminological risk, when its monitoring and supervision of those whom it has put in a position to commit an offence or cause harm is inadequate, and when the corporate ethos or culture is such as to tolerate or encourage criminal offences.

The criminological risks against which a company must guard will vary depending on the nature of the company's business: in production and manufacturing, for example, the main risk may be to the health and safety of workers; in transport, to road-users and pedestrians; and, in financial services, to the economic interests of the public, as well as those of the company's shareholders and employees. Different subdivisions of a company, moreover, may be involved in different types of activities, with each posing a different type of risk. The company's responsibility will be to address each of these risks individually. Whatever the nature of the risk, organisational fault inheres in the company's culpable failure to take appropriate steps to prevent criminal harm that could have been averted had proper attention been paid to the task.

What is needed is a fundamental reconceptualisation of the nature of corporate criminality – away from theories of vicarious, derivative and imputed liability, where corporate liability is indirect and linked to the crime of an individual, to a theory of organisational fault, where a company's liability is direct and based on its own blameworthiness. This reconceptualisation is not intended to deny individual culpability. Often corporate and human fault are linked, but they should be linked not, as is presently the case under the vicarious liability test and the 'identification' doctrine, in a purely formal sense, but in a logical and relational sense. A prosecution of an employee does not and should not preclude the prosecution of the company for failing to prevent the offence of the employee. In some cases prosecution of both company and individual may be warranted; in others organisational fault may have been so overwhelming that the individual wrongdoer will emerge as little more than a pawn in the game. In such cases, it might be appropriate that the company alone be prosecuted. But the basic point is that where a company is at fault, it should be liable in its own right, regardless of whether or not there is also a natural person who can be prosecuted for a separate offence. Finally, it should be noted that the offences for which company and individual will be subject to liability might not necessarily be the same. While the individual's culpability might be for a substantive offence, the company's might be for the culpable failure to prevent the substantive offence.

B.   AGGREGATED FAULT

When boards of inquiry have looked into the causes of a disaster, often they have discovered a web of interrelated errors. Misguided policies, inappropriate actions or inactions, and failures of supervision can combine to bring about tragic consequences. Remove one of these links from the chain and the tragedy might not have occurred. This is perhaps unsurprising, for many everyday events defy simple causal explanations. What is surprising is that the judicial analysis of corporate criminal liability has been so resistant to this common sense truth.

The Department of Transport Report (1987) into the capsize of the *Herald of Free Enterprise* provides an instructive case study. The *Herald* capsized outside of Zeebrugge after water entered through its open bow doors and destabilised the ferry. As a result, nearly 200 passengers and crew lost their lives. The report into the causes of the capsize unearthed a catalogue of errors. The assistant bosun, whose duty it was to close the bow doors, was asleep when he should have been at his station. The Chief Officer, whose job description included ensuring that the bow doors had been closed, failed to carry out this safety check. The master of the *Herald*, who had overall responsibility for the ship and its passengers, assumed that the bow doors were closed because he received no information to suggest otherwise. In addition, the ferry may have been leaving the harbour at too rapid a speed, in part spurred by pressures from management for its ferries to arrive at their destination not only on time but ahead of schedule. The company's management was faulted for failing to give clear directions to ferry staff and for not establishing a foolproof system that would have prevented the ship from sailing with its bow doors open.

Had the assistant bosun not been asleep when he should have been attending to the bow doors, had the Chief Officer satisfied himself that the bow doors were shut, or had the master insisted on first-hand assurance that the bow doors were closed, the Herald might never have capsized. By the same token, had management been more safety conscious and had they heeded the recommendation of ships' masters for warning lights on the bridge that would have alerted them when the bow doors remained open, the tragedy might also have been avoided. In such circumstances, where fault is so widespread, is there any point in trying to attach blame to one specific individual? The catalogue of errors that led to the capsize was summed up in the report on the incident prepared by Sheen J for the Department of Transport (1987): 'From top to bottom the body corporate was infected with the disease of sloppiness.'[2] Given the *systemic* failures, the fact that individuals may have been confused about their duties or have acted irresponsibly, was perhaps not surprising. Systemic failures, however, are arguably more properly attributed to an organisation as a whole than to specific individuals.

The capsize of the *Herald* was noteworthy in that it was one of the infrequent instances where a criminal prosecution for manslaughter was brought against a company (as well as against several members of the crew and directors of the company). After hearing evidence, however, Turner J dismissed the charges against the directors because the Crown had failed to prove that the directors, who could be

---

2   Department of Transport, Report of Court (1987), para 14.1.

'identified' with the company, had been reckless[3] in not being aware of the dangers associated with open bow sailings. Under the prevailing 'identification' test of corporate liability, it followed that the charges against the company also had to be dismissed. While members of the crew may have been aware of the dangers, these employees did not play a sufficient part in the formulation of corporate policy to satisfy the 'identification' test, and so the company's liability could not be built on their fault. While members of the crew could still have been prosecuted for their own role in causing the capsize (as a matter of logic, the criminal recklessness of the employees was independent of the criminal recklessness of the company), the prosecution in fact decided to drop the charges against these defendants.[4]

While in law there can be more than one cause of a death, in practice prosecutions tend to be brought against the person or persons whose acts form the closest temporal, spatial and causal link to the death. Legal doctrine promotes this tunnel vision by allowing a defendant accused of homicide to defend on the ground that the interventions of some other person broke the chain of causation between the defendant's wrongful act or omission and the death. But, not atypically, many actions and inactions combine to produce a proscribed result. In the case of the *Herald*, as we have observed, the resulting deaths would not have occurred if the assistant bosun had closed the ferry's bow doors, if the Chief Officer had properly carried out his supervisory responsibilities, or if the ship's captain had insisted on a first-hand report that the bow doors were closed. The short-sightedness of senior managers and directors in not properly attending to issues of safety also played a major role in the tragedy. This is not atypical. When a crime occurs in a business setting, often it is the result of a breakdown in more than one sphere of a company's operation. Rather than setting off the various failings of different individuals against one another in an attempt to determine who should be held liable for legal purposes, it would seem to make more sense to add the various failings together in order to build up a complete picture of the company's role in the affair.

This is what an 'aggregation' model of corporate liability attempts to do. It would allow the acts, omissions and mental states of more than one person within an organisation to be combined in order to determine the organisation's actus reus and mens rea. As noted in the preceding chapter, federal judges in the United States have accepted aggregated fault as a proper basis of liability for crimes whose mens rea is knowledge. In *United States v Bank of New England*,[5] for instance, the bank was prosecuted for a violation of the Currency Transaction Reporting Act. The bank had compartmentalised its operation, with different individuals being assigned different responsibilities with respect to the reporting requirements of the Act. The critical issue in the case was 'what did the bank know?' The court held that the bank's knowledge consisted of the sum of what was known by its employees: '[I]f employee A knows one facet of the currency reporting requirement, and B knows another facet of it, and C a third facet of it, the bank knows them all.'[6]

3   At the time of the case, recklessness was the mens rea of involuntary manslaughter. Subsequently the courts decided that gross negligence offered a more appropriate benchmark for determining when a defendant should be convicted of this offence.

4   One might speculate that the prosecution felt that to pursue the prosecution of the crew when the case against the company and its senior officers had been dismissed would make sacrificial lambs of underlings who had been forced to carry out the misguided policies of management.

5   821 F 2d 844 (1st Cir) *cert denied* 484 US 943 (1987).

6   821 F 2d 844 at 855.

In *United States v Bank of New England* aggregation was used to establish a company's knowledge. In that case no single individual knew all of the relevant facts which made up the company's knowledge. Each saw a part of the puzzle. It was only when each individual's piece of the puzzle was added to that of the others that a complete picture was able to emerge. Aggregation, however, can also be used to better explain the situation where only one person in an organisation is aware of a danger. If the knowledge of the company consists of the sum of the knowledge of each of its staff, then the knowledge of any one person is also the knowledge of the company. When the 'identification' doctrine is invoked, this result is reached by equating an officer of the company with the company. Aggregation thus provides a sounder conceptual basis for attributing the knowledge of a corporate official to the company. The company has 'knowledge' in the same way as a quiz team knows the answer to a question whenever any of the members of the team has knowledge of the correct answer (Gobert: 1994a).

A theory of aggregation arguably better captures the nature of corporate fault than a theory which imputes to the company the crime of a particular individual. There are times when, as a result of employee negligence, victims are seriously injured. Negligence, however, is generally not deemed sufficient to warrant imposing criminal liability on an individual and therefore also insufficient, even under the American test of vicarious liability, to hold a company liable for the agent's acts. However, for a company to encourage or tolerate widespread *negligence* by its employees may constitute *gross negligence* on its part. To apply this thinking to the P&O case might have led to the dismissal of charges against crew members, if it were found that they had only been ordinarily negligent as opposed to grossly negligent, while allowing the continuation of the case against the company on the theory that it had been grossly negligent in tolerating negligent practices by its employees.

What many find troubling about aggregation is that the total seems to exceed the sum of its parts. How can several non-culpable states (ie, negligence) be added together to yield a culpable state (ie, gross negligence)? The answer lies in recognising that the acts and knowledge of various individuals are not being looked to for the purpose of assessing the guilt of those individuals, but rather for the purpose of capturing the nature of the company's knowledge and fault. Under a test of aggregation, unlike under a test of vicarious liability, the conviction of a company for a criminal offence does not carry the implication that any or all of its workers were guilty of any offence.

This reasoning has failed to persuade the English judges, however. The leading opinion is that of Bingham J (as he then was) in *R v HM Coroner for East Kent, ex p Spooner*.[7] The case involved a review of the inquest jury that had returned a verdict of unlawful killing with respect to the deaths arising from the capsize of the *Herald of Free Enterprise*. Although allowing the prosecution against the company to proceed, Bingham J was sceptical about basing corporate liability on aggregated failures:

> Whether the defendant is a company or a personal defendant, the ingredients of manslaughter must be established by proving the necessary *mens rea* and *actus reus* of manslaughter against it or him by evidence properly to be relied on against it or him. A case against a personal defendant cannot be fortified by evidence against another defendant. The case

7   (1989) 88 Cr App Rep 10.

against a company can only be made by evidence properly addressed to showing guilt on the part of the company as such.[8]

Bingham J's starting point that a 'case against a personal defendant cannot be fortified by evidence against another defendant' is undoubtedly correct. Guilt against an individual is by definition personal, and rightly so, for the defendant on trial will suffer any sanction that follows from a conviction. It would be unjust to convict a natural person on the basis of the guilt of another natural person in the absence of a showing of a conspiracy or complicity. But this is to misconceive the nature of aggregation in the corporate context. The idea is not to allow a company to be convicted on the basis of proof of the guilt of one of the company's employees (that would be a straightforward application of the American version of vicarious liability), but rather to allow the fact-finder to be able accurately to assess the full nature of the company's fault. Further, unlike in the scenario visualised by Bingham J, any sanctions imposed as a result of a conviction of the company would be visited on the company and not on the specific individuals whose acts and mental states were aggregated to determine the company's fault.

If a theory of aggregated fault were to be accepted in England, the courts would have to consider the question of whose acts and whose mental states should be aggregated. This question would take us back to the division between an American model of vicarious liability and the English 'identification' variant. Should only the acts and mental states of persons who can be deemed to be part of the company's 'directing mind and will' be subject to aggregation or should aggregation extend to all employees regardless of rank? Aggregating acts of only persons 'identified' with the company makes little sense for reasons already discussed with respect to the 'identification' doctrine itself. In a large company, directors, officers and other senior officials who can be 'identified' with the company are unlikely to take a hands-on approach to carrying out the day-to-day activities of the company. If their offences are to be attributed to their company, the basis is typically going to be for criminal policies that they have ordered to be implemented, rather than for harm-causing acts they have actually perpetrated. These acts will be performed by ordinary workers who will not qualify as the 'brains' of the company. The value to be gained in adding these acts to the executive orders is to get a clearer picture of the criminogenic dimensions of the policies adopted.

Aggregating the *knowledge* only of persons who can be said to be 'identified' with the company makes even less sense. While a company may find it difficult to control the actions of all of its employees, it is in a position to inform itself of the knowledge of those employees. The company has the ability to establish channels of communication whereby dangers of which its workforce is aware can be brought to the attention of those with the authority to order changes. The law should be framed in such a way as to encourage the opening of such lines of communication. If it is not, then a board of directors could insulate its company from criminal liability by isolating senior management from ordinary employees and the dangers of which the latter are aware. In the manslaughter prosecution of P & O, however, this analysis was stood on its head. One of the reasons cited by Turner J in dismissing the prosecution against the company was the fact that there had been no showing that

8   (1989) 88 Cr App Rep 10 at 16-17.

its senior management was aware or ought to have been aware of the risks of a ferry sailing with its bow doors open. It might be recalled, however, that the masters of the company's ferries had been sufficiently aware of the danger and sufficiently concerned with the risk that they had recommended that warning lights be fitted on the bridge to indicate when a ferry's bow doors remained open. These proposals were not seriously considered by the company's directors. This fact, in a rather perverse way, was used to strengthen the directors' argument that they were not aware of the risks of open bow sailings. To the contrary, such ignorance was evidence of the company's culpability. A company, as we shall argue, has a responsibility to make itself aware of the dangers involved in its operation, and to take reasonable and appropriate steps to eliminate the dangers. The knowledge of the ships' masters should therefore have been attributed to the company. Instead, the court converted a mens rea bordering on 'wilful blindness' into an affirmative defence, and rewarded culpable ignorance in a situation where it should have been structuring the law to encourage knowledge (Gobert: 1994a).

C. ORGANISATIONAL FAULT

Although aggregation arguably captures the interdependent nature of corporate fault better than theories of vicarious liability and identification, it nonetheless shares some of the weaknesses of these other approaches. It too depends on a showing of human error. A prosecutor will still need to identify individuals whose acts and mental states can, albeit cumulatively, be attributed to the company. These individuals will need to be identified and will be stigmatised even if they are not convicted. Aggregation might also lead to the conviction of a company that has taken reasonable steps to prevent criminal activity from occurring, but the danger here is probably less than where a test of vicarious liability or identification prevails. When one employee or officer commits an offence, it may well be an isolated aberration. It is far more difficult to dismiss as aberrational a large number of wrongful acts by various employees in a company. There is, in such circumstances, a strong inference either that the company has failed to monitor its personnel effectively or that it tolerates a culture of negligence.

If a theory of aggregation is not accepted, where might a court locate the fault that warrants holding a corporate enterprise criminally liable? Our thesis is that organisational fault inheres in a company's culpable failure to prevent business-related crimes that could have been averted had proper attention been paid to the risk of criminality. Under this analysis, a company's gross negligence would be found not in the gross negligence of any of its employees, or even in the aggregated negligence of all of its employees, but rather in the company's failure to prevent its employees from behaving in a negligent or illegal manner. The company's criminal liability would be premised on its failure to prevent a criminal offence rather than on the particular offence that might be committed by one of its employees, officers or staff. Penalties would not necessarily track those for the substantive offence, although some overlap might be appropriate where organisational fault rendered the company liable as an accessory to the individual's offence.

Corporate liability based on organisational fault is intended to supplement rather than to displace existing theories of corporate criminal liability. It is not designed to displace the identification doctrine or preclude vicarious liability, accessorial liability, or liability based on aggregated fault if these alternatives offer a better way of understanding the company's role in a particular case. Organisational fault would simply become another weapon in the prosecutor's arsenal to combat corporate crime. However, we believe that often it will prove to be a more useful and more accurate weapon because it better captures the nature of corporate wrongdoing.

I.   Mens rea

The vehicle traditionally used by the law to capture culpability, as well as to measure the degree of culpability, is mens rea. We have already examined the problems in attributing to a company so distinctly human a concept as mens rea. There is, therefore, a case to be made for rejecting traditional notions of mens rea and starting afresh. However, before setting off in this direction, it is desirable that we satisfy ourselves that traditional mens rea formulae are wanting. In fact, there may be some useful ideas which can be borrowed from the existing law and profitably transposed to corporate entities.

The varieties of mens rea that have been recognised in the law comprise a spectrum that includes intention, knowledge, recklessness (with branches of subjective and objective recklessness), gross negligence, negligence and, at the extreme end of the spectrum, strict liability. Of these, the concepts of knowledge (in the form of wilful blindness), objective recklessness, gross negligence and ordinary negligence may have particular relevance to our inquiry.

a   Intention

Can companies be said to have an intent of their own, rather than having an intent based on imputing the intent of individuals to them? One might initially observe that crediting an inanimate entity with 'intent' is not a linguistic concept with which the law is unfamiliar. Courts often refer to legislative intent, well aware that a legislature, per se, has no mind of its own, and that not every member of a legislature who votes for a particular bill may have the same understanding of its meaning and scope. A minority of the legislature may have opposed the bill, but their intent may count as little to the judicial analysis as it did to whether or not the bill was passed. According to Dworkin (1986), the reason for attributing a collective state of mind to a legislature is because it provides a framework within which to discover the aims that a statute was designed to achieve, thus allowing the statute to be interpreted in its most plausible and sensible light.

Legislative intent can be gleaned from the words of a statute and from its legislative history, but where might corporate intent be found? The Australian Criminal Code, examined in the preceding chapter, would infer intent from a company's 'culture'. The corporate policies, standing orders, regulations and institutionalised practices that make up a company's culture serve as evidence of the company's aims and intent. These are authoritative because they are the product of decision-making processes established by the company and recognised as legitimate within the company.

French (1984) also seizes on the importance of a company's decision-making processes as a basis of inferring intentionality. What French terms a Corporation's

Internal Decision (CID) structure has three components: an organisational flowchart that clarifies the rank and responsibilities of persons within the organisation, procedural rules that govern how decisions are to be arrived at, and policies that articulate the company's basic principles, goals and beliefs. This CID structure represents for French the mind of the company at work: 'when the corporate act is consistent with an instantation or an implementation of established corporate policy, then it is proper to describe it as having been done for corporate reasons, as having been caused by a corporate desire coupled with a corporate belief and so, in other words, as corporate intentional' (French: 1984: 44). No doubt in the twenty-first century, computer-generated models will increasingly be used to formulate corporate policies. If so, these policies may not reflect the preferences of any of the individuals who are nominally responsible for them or even those of the persons who programmed the computers.

Although one can thus conceive of ways that a concept of 'intentionality' might be attributed to a company, it is not exactly clear how this breakthrough advances matters. In criminal law, the term 'intent' is generally used not to refer to an act that was intended (in law the concept of an intentional act is subsumed within the idea of a voluntary *actus reus*) but rather to a *purpose* to achieve a proscribed end. Accordingly, the courts speak of an intent to kill, an intent to cause serious injury, an intent to cause criminal damage, and so on. It would be odd to find corporate policies espousing the achievement of such ends. To the contrary, corporate policies and mission statements can be expected to proclaim the company's opposition to all forms of illegality. These statements may be cosmetic, but it is none the less fair to say that it would be rare to find a corporate policy that was adopted with an intent to cause death or injury. Corporate decisions are more normally directed to the achievement of business objectives. Operational choices may be intentional, as opposed to accidental or inadvertent, but in the absence of a criminal purpose this dimension of intentionality will not be enough on which to charge the company with a crime whose mens rea is intent.

The realm of *purposeful* results need not exhaust the ambit of intention, however. In England, an intent to kill may be found where death is a virtually certain consequence of a defendant's acts and the actor is aware that it is a virtually certain consequence.[9] In its Draft Criminal Code for England and Wales (1989), the Law Commission similarly took the position that a defendant acts 'intentionally' when s/he seeks 'either to bring [a result] about or [is] *aware that [the result] will occur in the ordinary course of events*' (emphasis added). Applying this test to companies, one can envisage situations where it could be argued that a company is aware that harmful results will almost certainly follow from its intentional decisions. If a manufacturer knows of the dangers of asbestosis yet persists in exposing its workforce to asbestos, it is surely aware that serious injury, if not death, is virtually certain to occur. But where would a court draw the line? An automobile manufacturer may know that, as an empirical fact, a certain percentage of its cars will be involved in fatal accidents. It does not follow, however, that the company 'intends' to cause loss of life; no doubt the company hopes that very few of its cars will be involved in any crashes, let alone fatal ones.

---

9   See *R v Woollin* [1999] AC 82; *R v Nedrick* [1986] 1 WLR 1025.

b. Knowledge

Like intent, knowledge would appear to be a distinctly human concept. What does it mean to say that company has knowledge of a fact or circumstance? Wherein lies a company's knowledge? If it can be found within an individual or individuals, we must ask further whose knowledge should count as that of the company? We have seen that an aggregation theory of knowledge would attribute to a company the cumulative knowledge of all of its staff, but advocates of the 'identification' doctrine might prefer that aggregated knowledge be limited to the knowledge of those who comprised the company's 'directing mind and will'. What if workers choose not to alert their company to situations of danger of which they are aware (perhaps because they fear internal repercussions from being classified as a 'whistleblower')? Should the workers' knowledge in these circumstances still count as that of the company? Difficult questions, not dissimilar from those arising with respect to intent, would need to be answered.

There is, however, a second string to 'knowledge' that does not exist in relation to 'intent'. For the purposes of legal analysis, the courts have been prepared to equate what they refer to as a state of 'wilful blindness' with knowledge. In *Westminster City Council v Croyalgrange Ltd* Lord Bridge explained:

> [I]t is always open to the tribunal of fact, when knowledge on the part of a defendant is required to be proved, to base a finding of knowledge on evidence that the defendant had deliberately shut his eyes to the obvious or refrained from inquiry because he suspected the truth but did not want to have his suspicion confirmed.[10]

The idea of wilful blindness has a strong resonance in the corporate context. Companies have the resources to analyse the risks in a proposed course of action and to develop ways of avoiding or minimising these risks. Even if the company lacks the staff with the requisite expertise, it can employ qualified consultants to advise it. Front-line workers may have a first-hand awareness of dangers in the company's operation, which can be tapped through the use of 'suggestion boxes' (advantageous because they allow employees who fear retaliation for 'whistleblowing' to remain anonymous). While *knowledge* of risk might be present at various levels of a company's workforce, *wilful blindness* can be attributed to those in positions of high authority without actual knowledge if they fail to seek out what their employees know. An employee may not be able to demand an audience with an executive officer or the board of directors to warn of the dangers of which the worker is aware, but the directors and officers are able to ascertain the views of the company's workforce.

In analysing the case for a crime of 'corporate killing', the Law Commission (1996) decided against imposing a requirement that the risk of the potential for death had to have been obvious to the company charged with corporate killing or that the company had to have been capable of appreciating the risk. It explained its position by stating that it had been persuaded that, because of the metaphysical nature of a company, it would be fruitless to speak in terms of a risk being obvious to it. This analysis overlooked the capacity of a company to acquire knowledge by availing itself of the input of its workforce or through the employment of consultants.

10 [1986] 2 All ER 353 at 359.

Because of this capacity, there is nothing inapt in saying that the company has the capacity to evaluate risk. Indeed, a company arguably has a far better capacity to evaluate risk than does the ordinary individual. For a company to fail to do so may render the company, for purposes of the law, 'wilfully blind'.

c.   Recklessness

There are two strains of recklessness recognised in English law: subjective recklessness and objective recklessness. Subjective, or '*Cunningham*'[11] (after the name of the case most often associated with it) recklessness occurs where a defendant is aware of the consequences inherent in a course of conduct yet persists in conscious disregard of the risks or ambivalent as to whether they will eventuate. The defendant does not desire that any harm should result – if s/he did, an intent to cause harm would be present. Subjective recklessness differs from knowledge primarily as a matter of degree. Both the defendant who acts knowingly and the defendant who is subjectively reckless are consciously aware that a course of action has identifiable risks attached to it. The defendant with knowledge, however, has a more certain appreciation of what will transpire if s/he proceeds along the chosen path than the defendant who simply ignores the risk of danger.

Objective or '*Caldwell*'[12] (again, after the name of the case where the concept was first articulated) recklessness does not reject criminal liability based on a subjective awareness of risk. Rather, it extends liability to cases where the risk involved in a course of action would be obvious to a 'reasonable person' even if it was not obvious to the particular defendant. The failure of the defendant to direct his/her thoughts to the possibility of such a risk constitutes the recklessness. As the benchmark against which the defendant is judged is a reasonable person, objective recklessness has two evidentiary advantages over subjective recklessness: first, the fact-finder does not have to ascertain what was going through a defendant's mind at a particular moment in time – the fact-finder only has to consider what would have been going through the mind of a reasonable person; and second, the fact-finder does not have to determine whether a defendant's denial of an awareness of risk is credible, as the unawareness of risk would be irrelevant if a reasonable person would have recognised the risk.

The merit of a standard of subjective recklessness in a corporate context is questionable. When a natural person is charged with a criminal offence, society may be reluctant to subject the defendant to punishment unless it can be shown that s/he has behaved in a morally blameworthy manner. Society satisfies itself that a defendant is morally blameworthy by a finding that the defendant either knew, or was aware of but ignored, the fact that injury or harm would follow from a chosen course of action. At the very least, one can say that in such circumstances the defendant has displayed a callous attitude to potential victims (Duff: 1990). The justification for corporate criminal liability, on the other hand, has less to do with moral blameworthiness and more to do with the need to deter corporate deviance that can lead to criminal harm. Further, if a subjective standard of recklessness were to be applied to a company, it would have to be asked whose 'awareness of risk'

11 *R v Cunningham* [1957] 2 All ER 412.
12 *R v Caldwell* [1982] AC 341.

counted as that of the company, which could again re-raise all the difficulties associated with an identification test of liability. A failure of a company to make itself aware is a different matter but in that case the company can be said to be wilfully blind. A comparable concept to wilful blindness, however, does not exist with respect to subjective recklessness for it requires a conscious awareness, as opposed to an unawareness, of risk. Indeed, wilful blindness seems more akin to objective recklessness.

The *Caldwell* test of objective recklessness has been the subject of heavy academic criticism. Perhaps the most telling of these criticisms is that, because the test of objective recklessness measures a defendant against the standard of a 'reasonable person', it can work an injustice when a defendant does not possess the competency of a reasonable person. The danger is that a defendant whose only fault was not to be sufficiently intelligent or astute to appreciate a danger will be convicted of a criminal offence that implies moral culpability. The decision in *Elliot v C*[13] is often cited to illustrate the point. A subnormal, 14-year-old schoolgirl had set fire to a shed. In affirming her conviction of arson, the Divisional Court held that, as the risk of fire would have been obvious to a reasonable person, the defendant's failure to appreciate it was objectively reckless. Goff LJ (as he then was) concurred in the judgment, but was troubled by the fact that it was possible, if not probable, that the defendant lacked the same appreciation of the risk of fire that a reasonable person would have had.

While the result in *Elliot v C* may be disquieting, the risk that an objective standard of recklessness would work a comparable injustice in the field of corporate criminality is one that need not concern the courts. A natural person, born with subnormal intelligence, may not be able to improve his/her comprehension of risk. On the other hand, as the comprehension of risk within a company is collective, it is extremely unlikely that all of a company's personnel (at least in a fair-sized company) will be incompetent. Even if this were the case, the company is able to employ consultants to address whatever pockets of ignorance might exist with respect to the risks posed by a proposed course of action. It is this feature of companies – their ability to raise their own level of competence to a standard of 'reasonableness' that might be set by the law – that makes objective recklessness a particularly attractive test of liability in the corporate context.

Under the *Caldwell* test of objective recklessness as originally conceived, if a defendant creates a risk that would be obvious to an ordinary prudent individual and does so without giving thought to the possibility of the resulting harm, the defendant can be said to be reckless.[14] This test would need to be modified in the corporate context. The corporate defendant's awareness of risk should be measured not against that of a 'reasonable person', but against that of a *similarly situated, reasonable company*. The dangers involved in operating, say, a chemical or nuclear plant, may not be obvious to a reasonable company in the garment business, but they should be obvious to a company involved in the very same industry.

There is a danger, however, in employing a test of objective recklessness that measures a corporate defendant's conduct against that of similarly situated companies. The possibility cannot be discounted that all companies in an industry are reckless.

13 [1983] 1 WLR 939.
14 *R v Caldwell* [1982] AC 341 at 354.

In the prosecution of P & O, Turner J drew on the testimony of executives of other ferry companies, to the effect that they were not aware of the dangers of capsize associated with open-bow sailings, to find that P & O officials had not been reckless. Turner J apparently did not consider the alternative hypothesis that this self-serving testimony only demonstrated that other companies conducted their business operation in as reckless a manner as did P & O. Nor can collusion be ruled out, for if each company in an industry is to be held to a legal standard created by the others, it would be to the obvious advantage of all to lower the bar as far as possible. Yet society's interest lies in the opposite direction – to raise standards of safety as high as possible.

It is submitted that the critical question should be not what risks would be appreciated by other similarly situated companies, but *what society has the right reasonably to expect from a company in the way of risk appreciation.* Utilisation of such a standard would result in a higher threshold of objective recklessness being applied to companies than is applied to individuals. This more demanding standard, however, would not be inappropriate. Companies differ from natural persons in that, unlike natural persons, they are not limited by their own abilities. As we have argued, even if the directors of a company are not themselves competent to identify and assess risk – although one could argue that it is reckless for a company not to include on its board of directors at least one member who is knowledgeable of the risks associated with each sphere of the company's business – the company is able to employ experts who are. Unlike in the case of a natural person, moreover, whose decision to act may be made without opportunity for proper reflection, a company can delay implementing a potentially criminogenic or dangerous policy until such time as it has fully studied the potential ramifications. In some industries such reflection and scrutiny is legally mandated, as in the pharmaceutical industry, where the results of laboratory tests, animal trials, and sometimes human trials may need to be submitted to and approved by a government agency before a drug can be sold to the public.

d. Gross negligence

In England, gross negligence has replaced recklessness as the mens rea of manslaughter. The leading authority is *R v Adomako*,[15] where an anaesthetist failed to notice that the oxygen supply to his patient had become disconnected. The patient died, and the anaesthetist was charged with manslaughter. His conviction was affirmed by the House of Lords, which held that the proper test of manslaughter in these circumstances was that of gross negligence. The House identified five elements that needed to be proved: (1) a duty of care to the victim; (2) a breach of that duty; (3) that the defendant's actions created a risk of death; (4) that the defendant behaved so badly that his conduct could be said to amount to gross negligence; and (5) that the defendant's breach of duty caused the death of the victim. The Adomako test is phrased in objective terms, and any lingering doubts as to whether the test was intended to be 'objective' (as opposed to being 'subjective' and requiring proof of mens rea) were laid to rest in *A-G's Reference (No 2 of 1999).*[16]

15 [1995] 1 AC 171.
16 [2000] QB 796. See also *R v DPP, ex p Jones* [2000] IRLR 373.

The applicability of the five-part test of *Adomako* to a company is not difficult to envisage and, indeed, one could see how it could be modified to provide a generic test with respect to *all* crimes that a company might be capable of committing. Companies owe a 'duty of care' to their employees to provide a safe place to work, to their customers to supply non-defective and non-dangerous products, and to their shareholders and investors not to take foolhardy risks with their moneys. This of course does not exhaust the range of duties that a company might owe, but it does illustrate the potential for finding that a duty exists to prevent harm. If the company breaches that duty (step 2 in *Adomako*), and does so in a way that can be said to amount to gross negligence (step 4), and causes legally cognisable harm as a result (step 5), then there would seem to be no reason why the rationale of *Adomako* should not apply.

One reason why the House of Lords in *Adomako* preferred gross negligence to recklessness was because of the confusion that had developed among courts regarding the proper test of recklessness in the context of homicide, and, in particular whether objective recklessness was an appropriate standard of liability when manslaughter was charged. The conviction of a natural person, who possibly acted either in ignorance or due to a lack of intelligence, may, as has been argued, be unjust, especially for a crime carrying as great a stigma as manslaughter. That danger does not disappear when gross negligence is substituted for objective recklessness but is to some extent ameliorated by the requirement that the defendant's negligence be shown to have been *gross*. The use of the term *gross* serves to signify that a *high degree of deviation from the norm* will need to be proved, and probably not just that which might be induced by a lack of sophistication or intelligence, to warrant conviction for manslaughter. It is arguably the degree of deviation from the norm which serves to distinguish gross negligence from objective recklessness.

We have already suggested that it would not be inappropriate to apply an objective recklessness test to companies in assessing corporate fault. If that were to be accepted, it would follow, a fortiori, that a company would also be liable if it were to be shown that the company had behaved in what is arguably a more culpable manner; ie with gross negligence. Whether the more rigorous gross negligence standard or the less demanding objective recklessness standard is appropriate for measuring corporate fault is a question on which reasonable minds might differ. From a policy perspective, if the goal is to spur companies to a higher standard of diligence in guarding against risk, then the lower threshold of objective recklessness may be desirable. On the other hand, this lower threshold might lead to liability being too readily imposed, and induce in companies an undesirable degree of caution. It may not be in society's interest to stifle entrepreneurs. Nor may it be in society's interest to insist on the elimination of all risks, however remote, if it would burden companies so much that they were driven out of business. If this were to happen, the ironic effect might in some cases be to cause the workers whose safety was being protected to lose their jobs. The more demanding gross negligent standard would seem to allow innovation and experimentation, while still providing a measure of protection to potential victims.

In practice, the distinction between gross negligence and objective recklessness may not be that great. Under both tests, a company has a responsibility to guard against criminologically significant risks to which it would be unreasonable to expose potential victims. To determine whether a risk is unreasonable requires a balancing of the social utility of the corporate activity in question against the likelihood of harm, and the type, extent and magnitude of harm that would follow *if* a particular risk were to eventuate. For example, if the harm that would follow from a rear-end collision of an automobile equipped with a flimsy bumper guard was simply greater damage to the car, then it might not be unreasonable for the manufacturer to install such bumpers on its cars in order to reduce the cost of the car to its customers. On the other hand, if foreseeable personal injury would follow, then a stronger case can be made that the manufacturer had been negligent or even reckless. Gross negligence may be argued if the risk that was ignored involved not injury but virtually certain loss of life. Some risks are so great that the highest degree of care is called for. Even if the likelihood of the malfunction of an airplane's engine were judged to be extremely low, the risks posed by a mid-air malfunction would be so catastrophic that the strictest standard of care would be warranted.

Risk is often a part of any business venture, and can rarely be completely eliminated. The courts are aware of this and all that is demanded is that companies act reasonably with due regard to risk. At some point the probability of a risk is so negligible that, in light of the social utility of a business, it becomes acceptable. Otherwise, manufacturers of automobiles, aware that some of their cars will inevitably be involved in a fatal accident, could only escape criminal liability by building the equivalent of a heavily armoured tank. Airline companies might be forced out of business altogether (there is a saying in the industry to the effect that one can build a perfectly safe plane, except that it would not be able to fly). Safety may be a paramount consideration, but it cannot eclipse all other considerations. Even those most exposed to the risk would in the abstract be likely to agree. Few consumers would opt for an automobile that was 100% crash-proof if its top speed was 20mph and it cost twice as much as the competition.

e. Negligence and strict liability

So far we have suggested that wilful blindness, gross negligence and objective recklessness may be suitable standards of fault to apply to companies. These standards are objective, and it is not necessary to impute to the company the state of mind of a natural person or persons. All that remains to be considered is whether the less rigorous objective standard of negligence might be applied, or, indeed, whether there is a case to be made for ignoring mens rea altogether and holding companies strictly liable for their harm-causing conduct.

It is obvious that the problems that have arisen with respect to the analysis of corporate mens rea would be eliminated if mens rea were to be eliminated from the definition of corporate offences; in other words, if liability were to be 'strict'. Where liability is strict, it does not matter if a company's violation is intentional, knowing, reckless or even negligent. Nor are the reasons for the violation relevant (unless they are relevant to a defence). All that matters is that the company failed to meet the standard set by the law.

A statute which does not have a mens rea element on its face may be construed to impose strict liability when its application is limited to a particular industry or profession. Companies which choose to enter a field can be presumed to be aware of the rules (including rules of strict liability) which will apply to them and to have consented to these rules. Courts are also more inclined to construe a statute to impose strict liability where the statute touches on risks to public health and safety, which demand a very high duty of care. All of these factors were present in *Pharmaceutical Society of Great Britain v Storkwain*,[17] where the defendants were convicted of having sold medicines to customers who had presented forged prescriptions. There was no evidence that the defendants had acted dishonestly, deceitfully, recklessly, negligently or in any other way improperly, but the critical role of pharmacists as the main line of defence against illicit drugs, the risk to public health which would ensue should such drugs enter the public domain, and the fact that the statute was aimed at those in a narrowly delineated profession, combined to support the case for construing the relevant statute to impose strict liability.

None the less, objections to strict liability can be raised similar to those raised against vicarious liability. The most serious of these objections is that a company can be convicted of a strict liability offence even though it has taken reasonable or even extraordinary steps to prevent the offence from occurring. Keeping faith with the principle of *nulla poena sine culpa* would require that fault should have to be shown before criminal liability could be imposed. If strict liability statutes did in fact induce companies to be more careful, a utilitarian case could be made for their passage, but if a company is already exercising a high degree of care, it is not clear what more it can do.[18] To the contrary, such statutes could prove counter-productive – if companies perceived that their best efforts to prevent crime would not affect their criminal liability, they could decide that high expenditures to this end were not warranted. Given the costs of monitoring and supervising a large workforce, a company might well conclude that it is financially better off paying the occasional fine, or hoping that its offences are not detected.

To avoid the potential unfairness of strict liability, while evoking the high degree of diligence that many believe is necessary in a business context, it would be advantageous to employ a 'negligence' standard of liability in criminal cases involving companies. Normally, negligence is the test of civil liability, where the primary objective is to compensate victims. It is infrequently used in criminal cases, perhaps because individuals who are 'only' negligent are generally not seen as deserving of the moral condemnation and stigma of a criminal conviction. Often the negligent actor has simply failed to think about the possibility of risk. Sometimes s/he may lack the education or intelligence to appreciate risks that would have been obvious to a 'reasonable person'. These criticisms of negligence may sound familiar, for, as we have already seen, similar objections have been raised against objective recklessness as a legal test of criminal liability, which is no coincidence, as critics of objective recklessness would maintain that it surreptitiously imports a negligence standard into the criminal law.

Regardless of the merit of using negligence as a test of criminal liability for individuals, the case for holding companies to a standard of negligence is more compelling. Companies cannot credibly claim to be ignorant of risks, or what needs to be done to avoid them, as they can overcome any ignorance that might exist within their ranks by seeking the advice of expert consultants. The failure to do so itself may be argued to constitute negligence on the company's part. Further, by better training its employees on how to carry out their tasks, a company can reduce the opportunities for negligence by its workforce. The company can also appoint

17 [1985] 3 All ER 4.
18 A point made by Lord Reid in *Tesco Supermarkets Ltd v Nattrass* [1972] AC 153 at 174. See also the Canadian decision in *R v City of Sault Ste Marie* (1978) 85 DLR (3d) 161.

supervisors and compliance officers to monitor its workforce and in some instances can make use of technology (eg CCTV cameras) to detect worker negligence. Employees who are identified as performing in an irresponsible manner can be re-assigned or dismissed.

For a company to fail to try to curb negligence by its employees suggests a corporate ethos or culture that is tolerant of risk and callous to the dangers posed to potential victims. Such a culture poses a particularly grave threat in the corporate context because of the potentially large number of victims who may be exposed to harm as a result of negligent behaviour by the company's workforce. If, for example, a company that turns a blind eye to negligence by its employees has a workforce of ten thousand, it would mean that up to ten thousand persons might be going about their jobs in a potentially dangerous manner. The number of victims exposed to risk would be 10,000 times greater than when a single individual was comparably negligent. The likelihood of actual harm occurring, recognising that often one can be negligent but lucky in that no adverse consequences ensue, would be correspondingly increased. While civil judgments may be adequate for compensating the injured victims of this negligence, a more robust response may be required to induce the company to change its culture and the attitude it takes to the negligence of its personnel. Imposing criminal sanctions on companies who tolerate employee negligence would demonstrate the seriousness with which the law views this problem.

Ashworth (1999: 199) asserts that negligence is a defensible basis of criminal liability when three conditions are present: the harm is great, the risk is obvious and the defendant has the capacity to take precautions to avoid the harm but fails to do so. The applicability of Ashworth's criteria to companies is patent. The potential harm when a company allows its business to be conducted in a careless manner will of course depend on the nature of the company's business and the nature of the risk associated with its activities and products, but clearly the risk of harm can be enormous. Indeed, in the case of a large company involved in hazardous activities, the risk may not just be 'enormous' but catastrophic (as was witnessed at Bhopal). As to 'obviousness', risks that might not be obvious to an ordinary person may be argued to be 'obvious' to a company, as long as it would not be unreasonable to expect the company to employ expert consultants to identify the risks. Similarly, a company has the 'capacity' to seek advice regarding how to avoid risk, and the financial resources to underwrite the costs of any preventative measures that may be necessary.

On the other hand, there are disadvantages to a negligence standard of corporate criminal liability. Especially in the hands of a zealous prosecutor, this less demanding standard would expose companies to costly prosecutions. The danger is compounded if there is to be a jury trial (see chapter 6 for a discussion of the appropriateness of jury trial in corporate cases) because of the risk that jurors may be affected by an anti-business bias. Even if a corporate defendant is acquitted, its reputation may be tarnished. In fact, the damage may occur long before trial – the accountancy firm Arthur Andersen lost many of its clients following its indictment for obstruction of justice in the Enron affair and, even before the testimony of the first witness in the case was heard, was struggling to remain viable. Adoption of a negligence standard of criminal liability would also erode the distinctions between civil and criminal law. Psychologically, the importation of a negligence standard of liability into the criminal law could cause both members of the public and corporate executives to equate corporate crimes with civil torts. Criminal laws which adopt a civil standard of liability are less likely to be considered 'true crimes', with the consequence that the censure, stigma and damage to reputation that normally attaches to a criminal conviction will not materialise.

Considering the thin line that may separate objective recklessness from negligence in practice, it might be preferable to adhere to the more censorious sounding standard of objective recklessness. On the other hand, if priority were to be given to allowing law enforcement personnel to intervene to address and neutralise crime-conducive corporate practices and policies before they can lead to damage and harm, then a negligence standard of fault would be desirable. In the next chapter we shall pursue this theme with respect to offences of endangerment.

2. Actus reus

We have argued that corporate criminality should be based on the culpable failure of a company to assess and manage risk, and to monitor effectively and supervise those whom it has placed in a position to cause physical or economic harm, or commit crimes. As is apparent from this summary, corporate liability will usually be grounded in an omission – the company's failure to organise its business or superintend its workforce so that innocent victims do not fall prey to crimes the opportunity for which has effectively been created by the company. However, under orthodox principles of English law, criminal liability for an omission will lie only when there is a legal duty to act; there is no general duty to protect others from harm. From where, then, might such a legal duty arise with respect to companies? There are several possibilities worth considering.

The English courts have found a 'legal' duty to act when a person creates a situation of peril and fails to take the appropriate steps to defuse the peril. In the leading case of *R v Miller*,[19] the House of Lords upheld the arson conviction of a vagrant whose burning cigarette had caused a fire in the house in which he was squatting. Although the fire had started when the vagrant was asleep (and thus could not have any mens rea), this fact did not defeat the defendant's liability. According to Lord Diplock, the defendant's actus reus consisted of his *failure* to make an effort to extinguish the fire after he became aware of its existence. It was at that point that a legal duty arose to take steps to avert or at least minimise the potential for damage that the defendant had created. Similarly, it could be argued that a company incurs a legal duty to prevent harm when it has created risks by the way that it conducts its business.

The discussion of the Clapham Junction rail crash from the preceding chapter might be recalled. In that case, faulty wiring by a British Rail technician combined with a failure by the technician's supervisor to check the wiring to create a dangerous situation that led to a fatal crash. The company's role in the affair consisted of its failure properly to train and supervise the technician, as well as its failure effectively to communicate its safety regulations to the technician or his supervisor, neither of whom had received a copy of the relevant policies. It also consisted of the corporate

19 [1983] 2 AC 161.

practice of encouraging, or at least not discouraging, staff from working extremely long hours (the technician responsible for the faulty wiring had worked every day but one over a three month period). The company appeared oblivious to the common-sense truth that tired workers are accident-prone workers. While obviously the company did not wish a crash to occur, its workplace policies and practices did nothing to decrease, and may have done much to increase, the likelihood of such an occurrence (Field and Jorg: 1991).

In *Miller*, the vagrant who failed to extinguish the fire was held liable for his inaction after he became aware of a danger. With respect to the Clapham Junction crash, British Rail's fault arguably lay in its failure to discover the dangerous state of its rails. But is there a legal duty also to discover such dangers? In *R v Stone and Dobinson*[20] the defendants were convicted of manslaughter for failing to provide care for an anorexic relative whom they had taken into their home. The Court of Appeal held that the defendants had, in effect, isolated the victim, preventing her from receiving assistance from others. The defendants, neither of whom were particularly competent, apparently were faulted for not having appreciated the seriousness of the victim's condition, for it was because they did not perceive the danger that they failed to obtain the necessary medical treatment. However, having assumed a legal duty of care, the defendants incurred an obligation (that they would not otherwise have been under) to carry out their responsibilities in a non-grossly negligent manner.

These precedents can be applied to British Rail's role in the Clapham Junction crash. As in *Miller*, British Rail had allowed a situation of danger to be created. As in *Stone and Dobinson*, potential victims were effectively isolated, unable as a practical matter to avoid the risk to which the company had exposed them (Gobert: 1994a). Passengers cannot be expected to inspect the railway lines or to satisfy themselves that they are in proper working order and are therefore dependent on whoever is responsible for the safety of the tracks. Indeed, by statute British Rail was legally responsible for passenger safety.[21] At a minimum the company should have provided proper training for its staff, adequate monitoring to discover potentially dangerous situations, and a working environment that was conducive to safety. British Rail should have satisfied itself that its safety policies were being implemented properly.

Another possible basis for finding a duty on the part of companies to prevent criminal offences by their staff was identified by the Law Commission (1996) in the consultation paper in which it advanced a proposal for a crime of corporate killing. The Commission analogised an employer's duty to prevent an unlawful killing to the employer's duty to ensure the safe management and organisation of its business.[22] To fulfil the latter duty, an employer has an obligation to employ competent staff, to utilise appropriate and properly functioning equipment, and to provide a safe system of work.[23] The provision of a safe system of work in turn envisages the proper organisation of the work to be done and the way it is to be carried out, the giving of

---

20 [1977] QB 354.
21 See Railways Act 1993.
22 See Law Com Report, para. 8.10.
23 Law Com Report, para 8.12.

adequate instructions (especially to inexperienced workers), the ordering and sequencing of tasks, the taking of appropriate safety precautions, the accurate determination of the number of persons required to do a particular job, the delineation of the role of each worker, the correct calculation of the time required for each worker to perform his/her tasks, and any special notices, warnings or instructions required under the circumstances.[24] While the Commission limited its analysis to a company's duty to prevent an unlawful killing, the body of precedent on which it drew would support a more extensive duty on the part of companies to prevent all types of serious workplace injuries, and not just deaths, an extension justified by the fact that the line between death and serious injury is often a matter of chance.

In order to discharge its legal duty to prevent illegality, a company would need, first, to identify areas of risk and the types of crimes likely to be committed by its personnel. These will vary depending on the business in which the company is engaged, and the part of the company's sphere of operation that is at issue. Risks to workers' health and safety may be posed by the company's production processes, risks to members of the public by its property and delivery systems, and risks to property interests by the techniques adopted by its sales force. With respect to each type of risk the company needs to devise and put into place systems that will identify, detect and prevent the relevant risk from materialising. Codes of conduct need to be established for employees, and rules and regulations put into place. Training of staff is indispensable, although the form that the training will take will depend on the staff member's responsibilities. Systems of supervision and monitoring will also be essential, but again the specifics will vary with the particular company and the nature of its business. This leeway is appropriate. Considerations of autonomy argue in favour of allowing a company to set up systems of training and monitoring that are appropriate to it, although companies in a particular trade or industry may, through trade associations, prefer to adopt an industry-wide set of standards and regulations. Regardless of the nature of the company's business, it has an obligation to create and support an ethos or culture that is opposed to illegality (Bucy: 1991).

As a practical matter, capturing the nature of a company's ethos or culture is rarely going to be straightforward. Corporate mission statements are unlikely to be of help, as these can be expected, somewhat ritualistically and even perfunctorily, to assert the company's opposition to illegal behaviour by employees and officers. This means that a fact-finder will have to look carefully at corporate practices and policies to see whether or not they are conducive to illegality. Constant pressure to maximise profits, with few questions asked about the means used to achieve ends, can induce a culture that is tolerant of rule-bending and unlawful shortcuts, as can a bonus/reward system based solely on results. Bucy (1991) suggests other circumstantial evidence from which the fact-finder can discern a company's ethos. These include the company's reaction to prior offences (are violators disciplined or demoted or is their status in the company unaffected or even enhanced?); the company's efforts to educate its employees about the requirements of the law (are there regular briefings of employees or newsletters explaining changes in legal regulations?); the mechanisms in place for auditing employee conduct (are unannounced audits a regular or infrequent occurrence, and are they taken seriously by both auditors and employees?); the basis on which the

24 Law Com Report, para 8.17.

company provides compensation (are there rewards for a good safety record and compliance with ethical standards?); whether channels of communication facilitate the reporting of legal infractions within the organisation (are employees rewarded for bringing violations to light or chastised for not being a team player?); and whether the company indemnifies the expenses of personnel who are criminally prosecuted for company-related offences (are their legal costs paid for by the company and are they reimbursed for any resulting fine?). The United States Sentencing guidelines (discussed in chapter 7) lay particular emphasis on the establishment of effective compliance departments and the self-reporting of offences before they are discovered by the relevant authorities. Fisse and Braithwaite (1993) deem significant the company's reaction to disclosure of criminal activity – are remedial steps promptly taken or does the company prevaricate and contest liability? This list of factors could be expanded but an exhaustive list would be impossible to compile for what will take on importance in a given case will depend on the circumstances of the case and the nature of the company's business.

D.   A DEFENCE OF DUE DILIGENCE

As we have noted, the traditional vehicle for capturing fault for the purposes of the criminal law is the concept of mens rea. The presence of mens rea serves to identify those defendants who have acted in a blameworthy manner, and the various types of mens rea (intent, knowledge, recklessness, etc) allow the criminal justice system to differentiate among degrees of blameworthiness. A defendant who acts intentionally to cause harm generally is deemed to be more blameworthy than one who acts recklessly, and the latter is usually deemed to be more blameworthy than the defendant who is merely negligent. The degrees of blameworthiness are in turn reflected in the sanctions for each type of offence.

The concept of mens rea was developed largely in cases involving natural persons, and little thought was given to how meaningful the concept might be if applied to companies. It is obvious, however, that a company is not a natural person and does not have a 'mind' of its own. This poses a problem, as we have seen, where fault is defined in subjective terms. Where liability is based on an *objective* standard of fault, on the other hand, all that is required is a showing that a defendant has failed to conform to the standard that the law has set for it. An objective test can as readily be applied to companies as to natural persons. It is for this reason that we concluded that wilful blindness, objective recklessness, gross negligence and even ordinary negligence may all be suitable measures of a company's fault, depending on the harm which the legislature wishes to avert. Once the prosecution has made a prima facie case of fault, however, the company should be able to defend on the ground that it has conducted its business operation with 'due diligence'. Due diligence is the antithesis of fault. If a company can show that it had taken appropriate and reasonable steps to avoid the harm that had occurred, it should be able to escape criminal sanction.

We have encountered the concept of due diligence previously. In *Tesco Supermarkets Ltd v Nattrass*,[25] best known for the House of Lords' articulation of

25 [1972] AC 153.

the 'identification' doctrine, the defendant Tesco argued that the offence of which it had been charged was committed by 'another person' within the meaning of the statute and that it had conducted its business operation with 'due diligence', which was recognised as a defence under the controlling statute. Other examples of this defence can be found in statutory law, including the Weights and Measures Act 1985,[26] the Trade Descriptions Act 1968,[27] and the Sale of Food (Weights and Measures) Act 1926.[28] These statutes usually form part of a larger regulatory scheme and are limited in their application. What we have in mind, on the other hand, is an across-the-board due diligence defence which would exonerate a corporate defendant where the company has made a good faith, reasonable effort to identify and prevent the occurrence of the crime in question. Most defences (as opposed to offences) are developed by the courts under their common law powers, and there would seem no reason why the development of a general due diligence defence could not follow this course.

Where a criminal defendant has raised and introduced some evidence of a defence, the burden of persuading the trier of fact that the defence is lacking in merit usually will rest with the prosecution.[29] The prosecution will have to meet its burden by proof 'beyond reasonable doubt'. However, there are some affirmative defences, such as insanity, where the burden of proof is on the defendant. Statutes which create a due diligence defence often also switch the burden of proof of due diligence to the defendant. Where the burden of proving a defence is placed on the defendant, however, the defendant will only be required to establish the defence by proof that meets a 'balance of probabilities' standard. In other words, the defendant will have to convince the trier of fact that the defence is more likely than not to be valid. This can be seen as a compromise between requiring the prosecution to rebut a defence by proof 'beyond reasonable doubt' and requiring the defendant to establish the defence by proof 'beyond reasonable doubt'. The latter burden is arguably too onerous for a defendant who has been involuntarily brought into criminal court by the state, but placing the burden of rebuttal on the prosecution would put it in the invidious position of having to disprove a defence where virtually all of the relevant evidence may be in the hands of the defendant. The question of which side the burden of proof should be allocated with respect to due diligence, and by what standard of proof, will be examined in depth in chapter 6, but here it might be observed that it will generally be easier for a company to show what it has done to avert illegality than for the prosecution to prove what it has not done. The relevant documents and memoranda will lie within the company's files, and its directors, executive officers and senior managers will be able to testify as to what steps the company has taken to prevent the commission of the crime.

How might a company go about proving its due diligence? We might begin by indicating what should not suffice. It should not be enough for a company to show that its operation conformed to the generally prevalent standard in the industry. Although compliance with an industry standard may be evidence of due diligence, the possibility cannot be ignored that all companies in an industry conduct their

---

26 Section 34.
27 Section 24(1).
28 Section 12(5).
29 See *Woolmington v DPP* [1935] AC 462.

affairs in a legally culpable manner. A corporate defendant should have to establish that it has conducted its own business with due diligence. If a corporate defendant claims to have been unaware of a risk, it should also have to show that it was not unreasonable for it to have been unaware of the risk. Nor should the obligation of establishing due diligence be satisfied by introduction of policy or mission statements that express the company's opposition to law-breaking. Such pro forma statements are often cosmetic and designed to bolster the company's public image. The retention of profits engendered by employees' illegality without questioning the source of the profits might be prima facie evidence that the company's professed opposition to illegality was mere window-dressing. Even where an employee has acted for personal gain and contrary to the company's interest, where it might seem unfair or even perverse to hold the company liable for the employee's crime, the company might be at fault for failing to put into place adequate systems that would have prevented the crime.

The specific content of due diligence will inevitably depend on the nature of a company's business and the facts and circumstances of the case. The likelihood of harm and the extent of harm, were the risk which had been created by the company to eventuate, will need to be balanced against the social utility of the activity in question, the practicability and cost of eliminating risk, and what the company had done to avert the danger. Trains, ferries, lorries and automobiles cannot ever be made risk-free. Factory machinery may be inherently dangerous. But the dangerous can be replaced by the less dangerous. Where before-the-fact mechanisms to prevent harm are not feasible, due diligence may require systems which will set in motion procedures for identifying when harm has occurred and for minimising the scale of the harm. How a company deals with a real situation of risk may be a better indicator of its corporate culture, and its attitude to the law, than any perfunctory pronouncements in a mission statement.

A potentially complicating factor in the analysis of due diligence is that value judgments will inevitably enter into the determination of what diligence is due and what might reasonably be expected of a company under the circumstances of a case. Judges who believe in a laissez faire, free market economy may be prepared to place more of a burden on consumers and workers to protect themselves than judges who believe that safety is a paramount consideration. To allow Parliament to set the content of due diligence will mean that the relevant debates will take place in the rarefied atmosphere of the Houses of Parliament. If the debate takes place in the abstract, the potential for harm may not be clearly perceived or be minimised; if it takes place in the wake of a highly publicised disaster, it is all too easy to overstate the likelihood of results which may in fact have been statistically extremely unlikely. A delicate and objective balancing is called for, and whether it is done by Parliament or by the judiciary is not as critical as the need for the potential for death and serious injury to be realistically weighed in the formulation of the appropriate test of due diligence.

E.   LEGISLATIVE MODELS

We have examined the case for constructing a regime of corporate criminal liability based on organisational fault largely in the abstract, and it is fair to ask what shape such a scheme might take in practice. In this section we shall examine two legislative examples of the type of approach that we have in mind. The first, as of the writing of this book still only in draft form, is the proposal contained in the UK government's consultation paper (2000) for a crime of corporate killing. Because this proposal marks such a dramatic break from conventional English thinking on corporate crime, and because organisational fault is central to the offence, it merits examination despite its uncertain future. The problem with the proposal is that it addresses one small aspect of a much larger problem. While undoubtedly corporate killings represent corporate crime in its most destructive form, they are far from commonplace within the full range of corporate crimes. Without extrapolation, the government's proposals do not provide the basis for a general theory of corporate criminality.

Our second example is an Italian law enacted in 2001. It addresses economic and financial crimes committed by companies and other organisations with or without legal personality. Because of its focus on crimes against property interests, it provides a suitable complement to the UK government's proposals, which are directed to crimes of corporate violence against the person which result in death. The Italian statute is noteworthy in that it demonstrates how a vicarious model of corporate criminality can co-exist with a model based on organisational fault and how the content of due diligence may vary with the standard of substantive fault.

I.   An offence of corporate killing

The background leading to the UK government's proposal for a crime of corporate killing sheds light on the interplay between events and legal reform. The public consternation regarding the role of the ferry company P&O in the deaths that resulted when the *Herald of Free Enterprise* capsized led to the company's prosecution for manslaughter. As an initial matter, the court had to determine whether a company could be prosecuted for manslaughter. Turner J, having reviewed the caselaw and precedents from other jurisdictions, concluded that 'where a company, through the controlling mind of one of its agents, does an act which fulfils the prerequisites of the crime of manslaughter, it is properly indictable for the crime of manslaughter'.[30] While thus accepting the theoretical possibility of convicting a company of manslaughter, Turner J adhered to an 'identification' test of corporate liability that significantly diminished the practical prospects of a conviction. In fact, the judge wound up dismissing the manslaughter charges against P&O because there was insufficient evidence that any corporate official had behaved recklessly (as required under the then prevailing standard of 'reckless' manslaughter). He reached this conclusion on the basis that the risk of deaths resulting from a ferry's sailing with its bow doors open would not have been 'obvious' to a reasonably prudent person in the position of the defendant's directors and executive officers. This conclusion stood in stark contrast to that of Sheen J in his report for the Department of Transport (1987) that, 'from top to bottom the body corporate was infected with the disease of sloppiness'.[31]

---

30 *R v P&O European Ferries (Dover) Ltd* (1991) 93 Crim App R 72.
31 Department of Transport, Report of Court (1987), para 14.1.

The storm of criticism that followed the dismissal of charges against P&O may have induced the Law Commission (1996) to re-examine corporate manslaughter as part of its review of the law of involuntary manslaughter. Rejecting both vicarious liability and identification as the proper tests of corporate criminal liability (although it did not preclude liability under the identification doctrine), and viewing aggregated fault as little more than a gloss on identification, the Commission proposed a stand-alone offence of 'corporate killing'. Under its proposal, a company would be guilty of corporate killing when its conduct fell far below what could reasonably have been expected of it in the circumstances and that conduct was one of the causes of a death.[32]

Following its publication in 1996, the Commission's report lay fallow for almost four years. There then occurred, within a relatively short space of time, three major train crashes – at Southall, Ladbroke Grove and Hatfield – which heightened the public's sensitivity to the potentially calamitous consequences of corporate misconduct. All three crashes involved extensive damage and significant loss of life. In each case the possibility of prosecuting the corporate entity for manslaughter was mooted and, with respect to the Southall crash, a prosecution was in fact brought against Great Western for its responsibility in the deaths of seven passengers (see chapter 1). The theory of the prosecution was that Great Western had been grossly negligent in allowing its train to operate without either the Automatic Warning System (AWS), which would have alerted the driver when he went through a cautionary signal light, or the Automatic Train Protection (ATP), which would have automatically brought the train to a halt in such circumstances, both of which were installed on the train but neither of which was operative at the time of the crash. The prosecution's argument continued that, if it were accepted that these failures constituted gross negligence on the company's part, it should not have to prove that any senior official in the company was guilty of manslaughter, as required by the identification doctrine. However, in *A-G's Reference (No 2 of 1999)*,[33] the Court of Appeal rejected the prosecution's argument and held that the identification test provided the only basis in English law on which a company could be convicted of a common law crime. As there was no evidence that a director, executive officer or even a senior manager of the company was aware of the fact that neither the AWS or ATP systems were operative on the train in question, there was no individual who could be said to be identified with the company who was guilty of gross negligence, and the prosecution against the company had to fail. The driver's palpable negligence could not be imputed to the company, as he clearly was not part of the company's 'directing mind' for purposes of the identification test.

The political, media and public criticism that followed in the wake of the decision spurred the government to bring forward a consultation paper that in effect resurrected the Law Commission's proposal for an offence of corporate killing. Under the government's version of the offence, an 'undertaking' (the term was deliberately chosen because it was more encompassing than company)[34] would be guilty of a corporate killing if 'a management failure by the company [was] the cause or one of

---

32 Law Com Report No 237 *Legislating the Criminal Code: Involuntary Manslaughter* Pt VIII (1996).

33 [2000] QB 796.

34 Home Office (2000) *Reforming the Law on Involuntary Manslaughter: The Government's Proposals* paras 3.2.3-3.2.6.

the causes of a person's death'; and 'that failure [constituted] conduct falling far below what [could] reasonably be expected of the company in the circumstances'. Echoing the Law Commission, the government explained that 'there is a management failure by a company if the way in which its activities are managed or organised fails to ensure the health and safety of persons employed in or affected by those activities; and such a failure may be regarded as a cause of a person's death notwithstanding that the immediate cause is the act or omission of an individual'. [35]

The proposed offence of *corporate* killing – the term, of course, is a misnomer given the government's declaration that the offence should apply to all undertakings – is noteworthy in several respects. First, it would change the test of manslaughter as the law applied to companies. Second, it would require a reconsideration of whether deaths attributable to dangerous working practices are to be treated as cases of corporate killing rather than simply violations of health and safety law. Third, it would ground a company's liability in organisational rather than individual fault, and, more specifically, in the way that the company manages risk. Finally, it would adopt a more 'realist' and meaningful approach to issues of causation in homicide than had previously been taken by the courts. When there is a management failure to ensure the health and safety of persons employed in or affected by that business, and when that management failure is *one of the causes* of a death, then the company can be charged with corporate killing.

We have examined previously the concept of aggregated fault, and it might be thought that the concept of 'management failure' constituted an attempt to breathe new life into aggregation. A not implausible construction would be that a 'management failure' consisted of the aggregated or collective failings of those persons who can be characterised as a company's managers. However, although 'management' might include a wider range of individuals than those who could be characterised as somehow being 'identified' with the company, corporate liability would remain derivative, still requiring proof of fault on the part of natural persons – the company's managers. Trial courts would still have to determine which individuals within an organisation were part of the corporate defendant's management team for purposes of attributing their criminal failures to the company.

A concept of 'management failure' consisting of the acts and omissions of a company's managers, however, does not appear to be what either the Law Commission or the government had in mind. Rather, the term 'management' is used to refer to the management of the company's affairs, and not the actions or inactions of persons who can be classified as managers. According to the Law Commission:

> For the purpose of the corporate offence and by contrast with the present law…there would be no need to identify the controlling officers of the company. The question would be whether there had been a management failure, rather than, as at present, whether there was blameworthy conduct on the part of any individual or group of individuals which should be attributed to the company. [36]

The proposed corporate killing offence on its face does not seem to contain a mens rea element. However, the language that speaks of 'falling far below what [could] reasonably be expected of the company in the circumstances' might be

35 Law Com Report, draft Bill cll 1 and 2.
36 Law Com Report, para 8.20.

interpreted to require a showing of objective recklessness or perhaps even gross negligence. A somewhat similar standard can be found in the Road Traffic Act 1991, where dangerous driving is defined as driving that 'falls far below what could be expected of a competent and careful driver'. The Road Traffic Act formulation takes as its benchmark a 'competent and careful' driver. In contrast, the proposed corporate killing offence refers to 'what can reasonably be expected of the company under the circumstances'. If it were to be determined that the appropriate yardstick for measuring what could reasonably be expected of the company under the circumstances was what was done by other similarly situated companies, then the possibility would exist that a defendant corporation in a corporate killing prosecution could be judged by what other companies, which were themselves not competent and careful in conducting their business, were doing. By looking to the practices of similarly situated undertakings (and this assumes that there are similarly situated undertakings; some companies (eg Railtrack) may enjoy a virtually monopolistic position), the corporate killing offence could unwittingly encourage gross negligence on an industry-wide scale.[37] But the encouragement of such ignorance is clearly not in the public interest and we have already suggested that, rather than asking what can reasonably be expected of a company in the circumstances, the courts would be better advised to ask what society has a right reasonably to expect of a company in the circumstances. The expectations of those in the industry may be of evidentiary relevance, but they should not be determinative of the issue.

But is it any easier to ascertain what society has the right reasonably to expect of a company in a particular industry? When the House of Lords in *Adomako* was faced with a comparable problem of standard-setting with respect to what constituted *gross* negligence, it chose to leave the question of what constituted gross negligence to the jury. The problem with that solution in a corporate context is that many jurors may be subconsciously (or consciously) biased against large, impersonal companies because of past personal experiences unrelated to the facts of the case, and this bias may skew their assessment of the defendant's fault. As the jurors' natural sympathies are more likely to lie with the deceased worker and his family than with the corporate defendant, and as they may also be aware that their verdict could have ramifications for a subsequent civil suit (regardless of whether the issue is specifically mentioned), they may well improperly convict. Even if they strived to be fair, jurors unfamiliar with an industry could none the less experience considerable difficulty in determining what it was reasonable to expect of a company in the industry. Such a determination would likely tax even experts in the field. It would seem that the problem of what it would be reasonable to expect from companies would have to be articulated by Parliament, or through the promulgation of codes of good practice by regulatory agencies.

Another somewhat mystifying aspect of the government's corporate killing proposal relates to what is meant by the cryptic phrase 'in the circumstances'. Exactly what circumstances would it be appropriate for a fact-finder to take into account? The Law Commission referred to 'such matters as the likelihood and possible extent of the harm arising from the way in which the company conducted its operations [as compared to] the social utility of its activities and the cost and practicability of taking steps to eliminate or reduce the risk of death or serious personal injury'.[38] Is

---

37 The Law Commission was prepared to accept that trade and industry practice might be a relevant consideration. See Law Com Report para 8.7.

38 Law Com Report para 8.6.

the implication in the reference to 'cost and practicability' meant to suggest that a company's unprofitability might excuse its failure to install basic safety protections for its workforce? In *R v Howe & Son (Engineers) Ltd*,[39] the Court of Appeal firmly rejected such thinking in a case where a health and safety violation had resulted in a worker's death. The court's position seems sound – unprofitable companies should not be able to behave in a grossly negligent manner and then excuse their gross negligence by their inability to turn a profit.

On the other hand, one can conceive of instances where financial considerations might be relevant. In contrast to the recommendations of the Law Commission, the government would extend the reach of the corporate killing offence from companies, strictly defined, to all 'undertakings'.[40] In some ways this is a welcome development, for artificial distinctions based on whether a 'for-profit' enterprise takes the legal form of a company, partnership or unincorporated association should not be determinative of its criminal liability. But what about undertakings that are not 'for-profit'? The term 'undertaking' is a broad umbrella that would also cover, by the government's own examples, hospital trusts and schools. These 'undertakings' are subject to budgetary constraints that are often beyond their control. Should an underfunded school or hospital, which decided to allocate its limited funds to the education of students or the treatment of patients respectively, be liable for a death attributable to its failure to render safe its physical premises? Perhaps this is an example of financial 'circumstances' that should be taken into account.

Of all of the departures from criminal law orthodoxy contained in the proposed corporate killing offence, perhaps the most path-breaking relates to its approach to causation. In the context of corporate killings, the act or omission most directly linked to a victim's death, in a time/space framework, will usually be that of a front-line employee. Although *in theory* the criminal law is prepared to accept the possibility of more than one cause of death, *in practice* prosecutions typically are brought against the person whose acts form the closest temporal and spatial link to the resulting death. A defendant accused of having 'caused' a particular result may defend on the ground that the acts of some other person broke the chain of causation between the defendant's acts and the resulting death. Thus, when prosecuted for an offence whose actus reus has been perpetrated by an employee, a company on trial could argue that the employee's acts superseded whatever 'but for' cause could be attributed to the company.

There is something intuitively unsettling about the use of this break-in-the-chain argument in the corporate killing context. To allow, for example, the arguable gross negligence of the driver of the Great Western train to excuse the company for depriving him of the technological back-up that would have avoided the crash, would seem to make the driver the scapegoat for the company's systemic and operational failures. Such a perception was apparently shared by the prosecution, which dropped the charges against the driver following the trial court's dismissal of the manslaughter counts against Great Western. Similarly, all charges against the crew of the *Herald of Free Enterprise* were dismissed following Turner J's ruling that P&O could not be held guilty of manslaughter.

The test of causation in the corporate killing offence would allow the Crown to prosecute an enterprise without being defeated by an argument based on a break in

39 [1999] 2 All ER 249.
40 See Home Office (2002) *Reforming the Law of Involuntary Manslaughter: the Governments's Proposals* para 3.2.3, etc.

the chain of causation. The rationale for accepting legal causation that might appear remote in space and time to the fatal event was provided by the Law Commission:

> [I]f a company chooses to organise its operations as if all its employees were paragons of efficiency and prudence, and they are not, the company is at fault; if an employee then displays human fallibility, and death results, the company cannot be permitted to deny responsibility for the death on the ground that the employee was to blame. The company's fault lies in its failure to anticipate the foreseeable negligence of its employee, and any consequence of such negligence should therefore be treated as a consequence of the company's fault.[41]

Accepting the force of this analysis, the government echoes the Law Commission in proposing that an undertaking should be subject to conviction for corporate killing when its management failure can be regarded 'as a cause of a person's death notwithstanding that the immediate cause is the act or omission of an individual'.[42]

The proposed offence of corporate killing severs the anthropomorphic link between corporate fault and human fault and for that reason alone constitutes a major advance in the conceptualisation of corporate crime. Organisational fault has displaced individual fault as the basis of liability. However, the phrasing used to express fault – conduct falling far below what [could] reasonably be expected of the company in the circumstances – may be too vague to provide fair notice to companies of what they must do to avoid liability or guidance to the fact-finder as to when a conviction is warranted. Moreover, the proposal is obviously limited in its scope. As drafted, it would not apply to Crown bodies, or to corporate killings committed by a foreign subsidiary of an English parent company (the latter issue is examined in chapter 5). The extent to which individuals within a company could be secondary parties to the corporate offence is left for future resolution. The major weakness in the proposal, however, is the obvious one – it applies only to homicides. Although a more general model of corporate criminality could be fashioned around the concept of organisational fault contained in the proposal, the government makes no attempt to do so, apparently satisfied to have responded to what had become a politically sensitive issue.

2.   Lessons from Italy

A more embracing, yet at the same time complementary (because it addresses financial offences rather than crimes against the person) model of corporate criminality than that contained in the government's corporate killing proposals can be found in an Italian decree enacted in 2001.[43] The decree embodies a generic model of criminal liability that can be applied to companies and other organisational entities whether or not they have 'legal personality'. The purpose of the decree was to bring Italian

---

41 Law Com Report para 8.37.
42 Law Com Report para 8.39.
43 DLgs (Legislative Decree) of 8 June 2001 n 231 (Decreto Legislativo 'Disciplina della responsibilita amministrativa delle persone giuridiche, delle società e delle associazioni anche prive di personalità giuridica'). The decree and its implications are examined in Gobert and Mugnai (2002), on which the analysis which follows is drawn.

law into compliance with European Conventions and Protocols that required member states to enact laws that would hold companies and other legal persons liable for a range of offences, including bribery of foreign officials in international business transactions,[44] the protection of European community financial interests[45] and the combating of corruption by officials.[46]

Under the Italian Constitution (Article 27), 'criminal responsibility is individual'.[47] Only natural persons can be held liable for a criminal offence. To circumvent this restriction, the statute describes the corporate liability envisaged as 'administrative'. However, the fact that companies will be responsible for criminal and not just administrative offences, the fact that cases will be heard by criminal courts rather than administrative tribunals, and the fact that criminal rather than administrative procedures will be followed in a trial, all suggest that the contemplated liability is in reality more criminal than administrative in nature.

The Italian statute applies both to bodies that have legal personality, such as companies, and those that do not have legal personality (Article 1). However, unlike the English proposal for an offence of corporate killing, it would not apply to public bodies or companies that are not-for-profit. Thus, public schools, public universities and public hospitals are excluded from the coverage of the statute as are local government bodies such as municipalities, councils, and regional and municipal assemblies. This seems like a sensible improvement for public and quasi-public bodies are dependent on the government for their funding in a way that private companies obviously are not. Moreover, these public and quasi-public bodies do not have the flexibility of a for-profit company, which, for example, can raise the prices of its products in order to finance the development of systems designed to promote safety or protect against illegality.

Another sensible improvement over the English corporate killing proposal is that a company which has its headquarters in Italy can be prosecuted in Italy for an offence committed by one of its overseas subsidiaries if criminal proceedings have not been initiated in the host state of the subsidiary. This provision arguably better accords with the needs of a modern global economy for a more expansive view of jurisdiction than that provided by traditional doctrines of territoriality and will

---

44 OECD Convention on combating bribery of foreign public officials in International Business Transactions, Paris 17 December 1997.
45 Convention drawn up on the basis of the Treaty on European Union, Article K.3 on the protection of the European Communities' financial interests. OJ C316 27.11.95 pp 49-57.
   Protocol drawn up on the basis of Treaty on European Union, Article K.3 to the Convention on the protection of the European Communities' financial interests – Statements made by Member States on the adoption of the Act drawing up the Protocol. OJ C313 23.10.96 pp 2-10.
   Protocol drawn up on the basis of Treaty on European Union, Article K.3 on the interpretation, by way of preliminary rulings, by the Court of Justice of the European Communities of the Convention on the protection of the European Communities' financial interests – Declaration concerning the simultaneous adoption of the Convention on the protection of the European Communities' financial interests and the Protocol on the interpretation by way of preliminary rulings, by the Court of Justice of the European Communities, of that Convention – Declaration made pursuant to Article 2. Official Journal C151 20.05.97 pp 2-14.
46 Convention drawn up on the basis of of the Treaty on European Union, Article K.3(2)(c) on the fight against corruption involving officials of the European Communities or officials of Member States of the European Union. OJ C195 25.06.97 pp 2-11.
47 Italian Constitution, Article 27(1).

allow the Italian courts to deal with multinational enterprises that might seek to avoid criminal liability by locating the criminogenic aspects of their business in subsidiaries in countries which have a reputation for allowing considerable legal leeway to multinationals.

The statute that was initially enacted covered only a small number of crimes involving corruption, theft and fraud *against the state*.[48] This limitation was imposed largely for practical reasons. The legislature was of the opinion that introducing so radical a departure from traditional modes of criminal liability to too wide a range of crimes would have created major problems of adjustment for many companies. It was therefore decided that it would be preferable to restrict liability to a relatively few offences at the outset, with a view to expanding the relevant offences after companies had gained experience in setting up the types of systems of control and supervision envisaged in the legislation. In March 2002 the Italian government redeemed this pledge by enacting another legislative decree that extended the scope of liability from property crimes against the state to similar crimes where the victim was a private party.[49]

The statute creates two types of corporate liability. The first, presumed in the case of a crime committed by the 'head' of a company, is a form of vicarious liability, not dissimilar to that which is found under the 'identification' doctrine. The second, and more radical, form of liability is based on the negligence of a corporate body in not considering the possibility of an offence which has occurred and in not having in place mechanisms to avert its commission. This second form of liability is grounded in organisational fault. Both forms of liability can be rebutted by a showing of due diligence, but what is required to establish due diligence varies with the particular form of liability.

The core provisions of the statute are contained in Articles 5-8. Article 5 sets out the 'objective element' of the crime: an underlying offence committed by a member of staff of the corporate body. Articles 6 and 7 address the 'subjective' element – the intent, negligence or, more generally speaking, the 'blameworthiness' of the company with respect to the crime.

Article 5 distinguishes between liability from acts of a 'head', director or manager of a company and liability for offences committed by the company's subordinate staff. In referring to the former category, the legislature decided not to provide an exhaustive list of all the relevant positions of command, preferring instead to give a more general definition that could be adapted on a case-by-case basis to the individual circumstances of the corporate defendant. Thus, under Article 5(1)(a) it would be possible to hold a company liable for offences committed by a stockholder who holds a majority of the shares of the company and who, although not having an official directing role, none the less has influence over corporate policies. Article 5,

---

48 The more recent version of the statute, not yet published at the time of writing, will include Article 25 bis and Article 25 ter that will allow liability of legal persons also for crimes not committed against the state. See n 48 below and accompanying text.

49 This statute has not been published at the time of writing. Said statute was enacted following the directions given in a previous statute that required the government to discipline the responsibility of companies and commercial undertakings: Legge Delega of 3 October 2001 n 366. Previously, DLgs 231/2001 had been expanded to include the responsibility of companies guilty of counterfeiting currency by Law of 23 November 2001 n 409, article 52-quinquies.

para 1(b) enables the company to be held responsible for crimes committed by a subordinate member of staff (someone who is not in a decision-making position) when the offence stems from corporate policy or structural negligence on the part of the company. A link to individual fault is retained for an underlying human offence must be proved, although under Article 8 it is not necessary to identify the actual perpetrator of the offence or to demonstrate that s/he could actually be convicted if charged.[50]

Whether a company's criminal liability is based on an offence committed by the head of the company or a subordinate member of staff, the requirement of a mental element on the part of the company has to be satisfied. Attaching liability to companies on the basis of a straightforward theory of vicarious liability was rejected by the Italian legislature as being contrary to the *nulla poena sine culpa* principle. Accordingly, the prosecution will have to show that the offence constituted an expression of corporate policy or that it stemmed from structural negligence within the company. Whether liability is premised on the acts of an officer or an ordinary employee, however, the purpose of the actor has to have been to benefit the company or advance its interest.

The innovative element in the Italian statute is the concept of 'structural negligence'. It is in structural negligence that can be located the 'blame' that warrants attaching criminal liability to a company. However, what constitutes structural negligence will vary depending on whether the crime is committed by the head or director of the company, on the one hand, or a subordinate member of staff, on the other. In either case, however, the company needs to have established guidelines and control systems that take into account the risk of the offence being committed. If it has not, then it will be found to be 'structurally negligent'. The control system, moreover, needs to be detailed and tailored to specific risks. It is not enough that the company has set up a generic control system.

Article 6 addresses the type of control system that has to be established with respect to heads and persons in positions of authority within the company. According to Article 6, the company will not be liable if it proves that a control system aimed at preventing an offence of the kind committed had been set up and was running efficiently prior to the occurrence of the offence. This entails proving that:

- the directing board had enacted and effectively applied, before the offence was committed, organisational and managerial schemes appropriate for the prevention of offences of the kind that was committed;
- the supervision and updating of the schemes had been allocated to a body with autonomous powers of initiating controls;
- the offender had deliberately managed to evade the organisational and managerial controls in place;
- there had not been a lack of supervision by the body listed under (b).[51]

Furthermore, Article 6, para 2 requires that the envisaged schemes have to respond to certain criteria relating to the amount of delegated powers and the risk of commission of offences. Specifically, a qualifying scheme should:

- single out the various spheres of activities in which crimes might be committed;

---

50 Article 8, para 1 DLgs 231/2001.
51 Article 6, para 1 DLgs 231/2001.

- foresee specific protocols directed at programming the taking and implementing of decisions of the company regarding the crimes that have to be prevented;
- find ways of managing the financial resources of the company that would prevent the commission of crimes;
- create duties/obligations to inform the supervising body on the implementation and functioning of the schemes;
- introduce an appropriate disciplinary system to sanction violators.[52]

One might question the need for an 'artificial' form of intent or negligence to be created in order to attach liability to a company in a situation in which the offence has been committed by someone who is a representative of the company, and whose 'will' and 'intent' are presumably the expression of the 'will or intent' of the company itself. However, the statute takes account of companies organised in more complex, horizontal ways where decision-making powers are distributed among various persons. Under Article 5 of the statute a company can be held liable for offences committed by a head of an independent sub-unit or subsidiary.[53] In a horizontally structured company, however, attributing liability to the company on the basis of the decisions of a person with limited but independent discretion, without taking into account the possibly contrary positions of other managers, may seem unfair. To combat any potential unfairness, the company is allowed a defence of due diligence under Article 6.

The onus of proving a control system sufficient to defeat liability rests on the company. With respect to heads, directors and managers, Article 6 reverses the usual allocation of the burden of proof, providing that 'the company will not be liable if *it proves*' (emphasis added) that an efficient and suitable control system has been put in place.[54] The presumption is that if a crime has been committed by a head or similar such person, then the company is liable because normally the head would be representing the company and there would be a coincidence of 'intent' between the head and the company. If the presumption is inaccurate, then it is up to the company to prove that to be the case.

Under Article 6 a defendant company will have to prove that it had created guidelines suitable to prevent crimes like the one that had occurred and that those guidelines were efficiently in place before the crime was committed. It will further have to prove that there had been effective control and supervision of the guidelines (usually through an independent body internal to the company), and that the head of the company who committed the offence did so with an intent to evade the existing control system. These requirements provide guidance to companies as to the 'procedures' or 'structures' that need to be put into place, and how to go about achieving that end. First, a company needs to identify the areas of activity in which there is a risk of offences being committed. The nature of the risk may be different in different spheres of the company's operation, and the company needs to address each of these variations. Second, the company has to establish guidelines by which the managing staff will have to abide when making decisions for the companies (for example, guidelines and procedures on funding from public grants), including guidelines regarding the expenditure of financial resources that are aimed at reducing the risk of criminal

---

52 Article 6, para 2 DLgs 231/2001.
53 Article 5, para 1(a) DLgs 231/2001.
54 Article 6, para 1 DLgs 231/2001.

activities (for example guidelines on how payments should be made and on the transparency of transactions). Finally, there is an obligation to keep the control body fully informed on the activities and the management of the company.

The nature of the due diligence defence is quite different in the case of crimes committed by subordinate employees. Most significantly, Article 7 does not reverse the ordinary burden of proof. The prosecution will have to prove the requisite degree of negligence on the part of the company. If it had been difficult for the Italian legislature to envisage absolute vicarious liability of a company for offences committed by one of its heads, it would have been harder still to hold the company responsible for the criminal acts of its subordinate members of staff without running foul of the *nulla poena sine culpa* principle. As in the case involving a head of the company, the key to the company's liability is proof of 'structural negligence'. This negligence will be found where the company has failed to set up an effective system of control and supervision over its employees. If the company introduces evidence that it has a system of supervision in place, the burden of proof will shift back to the prosecution to show that the system was ineffective to prevent the kind of crime that had occurred. However, the necessary components of such a system need not be as rigorous as those that have to be shown in the case where a crime is committed by a head of the company. Article 7 only requires periodic review of the system and appropriate changes when experience or research reveals flaws in the system or where alterations to the structure or the activities of the company have occurred. There still must be an appropriate disciplinary system.[55]

There are many advantages to the Italian approach to corporate criminal liability that has been described. First, the linkage of corporate liability to a showing of negligence (the 'structural negligence' of not having set up a system responding to the statute) preserves the element of fault and addresses the theoretical, constitutional and policy objections to liability that is strict. Second, the law provides fair notice to companies of the types of control systems that they must put into place to avoid criminal liability. In this context it might be recalled that one of the objections to the UK government's corporate killing proposal was that the level of generality in the proposed test of liability failed to give proper guidance to companies as to what was expected of them. The greater detail provided by the Italian statute also gives more meaningful guidance to legal fact-finders. Third, the statute demonstrates how vicarious forms of corporate criminal liability can be fitted with liability based on a theory of organisational or structural fault. Fourth, the statute indicates the role that due diligence should play in different types of corporate offence, and how the burden and standard of proof relating to due diligence can vary depending on which type of offence is charged. Finally, the scope of liability created in the Italian statute is sufficiently encompassing that it can be expected to exert a strong deterrent against corporate criminality.

F.   CONCLUSIONS

It is the failure of a company to practice due diligence that provides the basis for the type of moral accountability that is sometimes claimed to be lacking when a crime is

---

55 Article 7, para 4 DLgs 231/2001.

committed by an inanimate fictional entity such as a company. Like individuals, companies have the power to make choices through their boards of directors and executive officers, and, like individuals, they should be held responsible for the results of their choices. In some ways the failure of a company to practice due diligence is less excusable than individual negligence, recklessness or even gross negligence, as companies are in a better position to analyse the consequences of their policies. Their 'access to practical and theoretical knowledge dwarfs that of individuals' (Donaldson: 1982). Unlike human actors, the company is less likely to be encumbered by the types of emotions and feelings which might cloud accurate risk assessment by a lone individual.

Locating corporate criminal liability in organisational fault offers at the same time a more restrictive and a more expansive model of corporate criminality than vicarious or imputed liability. The American approach to vicarious liability would hold a company liable for the criminal acts of any of its officers, employees or agents committed in connection with a job-related activity, while the English 'identification' variant of vicarious liability would limit the company's liability to crimes committed by individuals in positions of high authority, but regardless of whether the corporate officer was acting in furtherance or against the company's best interests. The proposed approach is more limiting than these models of fault in that it would allow the company to avoid liability for crimes of both employees and officers when it has conducted its affairs with due diligence to prevent criminal activity. Conversely, the proposed model is more expansive than the traditional tests in that it envisages situations where the company can be liable where the resultant crime is committed by a third party who is not an employee or agent of the company, and in situations where no individual can be charged with a corporate crime for, say, lack of mens rea.

Holding companies derivatively liable for the crimes of their employees, staff and officers is unfair to those companies which have made a good faith and reasonable effort to prevent such criminality. Holding companies liable as accessories addresses this unfairness but may encourage a 'see no evil, hear no evil' approach to management, contrary to what should be the law's goal of encouraging diligence. Grounding corporate criminality in organisational fault will direct a company's attention to how its business is organised and will promote systems, procedures and cultures whose aim is to achieve compliance and safety through the practice of due diligence.

CHAPTER 4

Corporate criminality III: Endangerment offences

A. INTRODUCTION

We have now examined two models of corporate criminality: one in which crimes committed by persons working for, or in some significant way connected to, a company are imputed to the company; and the other where the company is held liable for its own culpable failure to prevent a crime which, through the putting into place of effective systems of risk management and control, and the effective monitoring of its workforce, it could have averted. The problem with both models of liability is that neither comes into play until after personal injuries, financial losses and social harm have occurred. This is not uncommon in the criminal law, but given the scale of consequences from corporate malfeasance – 167 workers died when the *Pipa Alpha* oil rig exploded, and nearly 200 passengers and crew were drowned when the *Herald of Free Enterprise* capsized; in the financial sector, thousands lost their life savings because of improprieties at Enron and WorldCom – there is an intuitive case for constructing the criminal justice system so as to allow law enforcement personnel to be able to intervene before, rather than after, the occurrence of serious harm. To a limited extent, the opportunity for such intervention is provided by criminal offences, such as attempt, defined in inchoate mode, and by regulatory laws. However, it is questionable whether either of these approaches is sufficient to cope with incipient *corporate* criminality, and in this chapter we shall examine whether and how a more effective regime of preventative legal control might be constructed.

We shall lay the groundwork for our analysis by first looking at the role of results in criminal law generally, and the arguments for defining crimes without regard to outcomes. Even if one is not persuaded by the case in favour of defining crimes of natural persons without regard to result, arguably the case becomes more compelling in the context of corporate crime because the magnitude and extent of the harm that can be caused by corporate criminality are so much greater. We shall then look at regulatory offences to see if they provide an adequate means for controlling incipient corporate criminality. Concluding that they do not, we consider the alternative of a regime of crimes of endangerment. Endangerment offences would be designed to complement, rather than replace, the substantive offences examined in the preceding chapters.

B.   THE RELEVANCE OF RESULTS IN CRIMINAL LAW

For a criminal justice system to have to wait until a defendant's conduct has caused or is about to cause loss would seem to have several inherent disadvantages. One is that it forces the police to engage in a dangerous game of brinkmanship, where premature intervention can compromise a prosecution (for the defendant will be able to argue that no crime has as yet been committed), while delay may dramatically increase the likelihood of unacceptable injuries and even deaths. Nor is it clear what is to be gained by waiting. Results are not necessarily an accurate measure of culpability and can either exaggerate or understate the extent of an actor's moral blameworthiness. Extremely dangerous acts may not lead to injury but the absence of injury does not detract from the dangerousness of the acts. On the other hand, there are times when the injuries that follow from an act can be grossly disproportionate to the actor's degree of fault. Consequences are often the product of events and fortuities over which the actor has little or no control (Smith: 1971; Ashworth: 1987b, 1988; Gobert: 1993). The problem is one that pervades the criminal law, as we shall argue in this section, but its effects may be exacerbated in the context of corporate criminality, as we shall see in the next.

Many crimes have as part of their definition the requirement that a certain harmful result occur. For a defendant to be convicted of murder or manslaughter, for example, a human being must die. But why should a would-be killer's criminal liability turn on whether a death actually occurs if that was the result the killer intended to bring about by his/her actions? Often what accounts for the difference between an intended death and an actual death is something as criminologically irrelevant as poor aim, a target who moves at the last moment or timely intervention by the police. Sometimes third parties or forces of nature can intervene after a would-be criminal has done all that s/he intended. Consider the case of a wounded victim who is being rushed to a hospital in an ambulance. If the victim dies from his wounds while en route to the hospital, the assailant will be liable for murder. If, on the other hand, the ambulance is struck by lightning and the victim dies, the death will be attributed to an act of providence and the assailant will no longer be liable for murder, even if the victim would have died within the hour from the initial wound. If, rather than being hit by lightning, the ambulance were to be struck by a drunk driver and the victim again were to die, now it would be the drunk driver and not the original assailant who would in law be responsible for the death. In each of these variations, however, the moral blameworthiness of the original assailant will not have changed at all, yet his/her legal liability will have been dramatically altered.

Circumstances peculiar to a victim but unknown to an assailant can also affect the extent of legal liability, as where a haemophiliac bleeds to death from a minor cut or a victim with an eggshell skull dies from a blow which for most ordinary persons would have induced only a headache. The element of chance was endemic to the much-criticised felony-murder rule, which has now been abolished in England but remains in force in many American States. Under this rule, a defendant could be convicted of murder if a death occurred during the perpetration or attempted perpetration of a felony. Whether or not the felony involved risk to life, whether or not it was carried out in a dangerous manner, and even whether or not the defendant could be said to have 'caused' the death under conventional legal doctrines of causation were all irrelevant; all that mattered was that death occurred during the course of the felony. While the rigours of the felony murder rule have been softened in some jurisdictions that continue to adhere to it (usually by limiting its applicability to named felonies or felonies that are dangerous to life or are carried out in a manner that is dangerous to life), there still remains ample opportunity for unforeseen events to lead to an unwanted and unintended death and, as a consequence, to a charge of murder. In England and Wales, the offender cannot be convicted of murder in these situations but can be convicted of what is known as 'unlawful act' or 'constructive' manslaughter.

Third parties over whose actions a defendant may have little or no control may also determine the extent of a defendant's criminal liability. If A urges B to kill C, A is guilty of incitement; if B kills C, then A will also be guilty of murder. But if B decides not to kill C, then A can only be convicted of incitement. Yet A may have no control over B's decision to go ahead with the offence. Similarly, if A loans a gun to B in order to kill C, then A may be convicted of murder if B goes through with the killing under generally accepted principles of accessorial liability, but if B changes his mind, then in all likelihood A is not guilty of any offence (other than one relating to possession of a gun). There would be no crime to which A could be an accessory and his mere loaning of a gun to B would be insufficient to constitute incitement. Moreover, it is not only in crimes involving physical injury or death that the role of others may be critical to a defendant's liability. If charged with obtaining money by fraud or deception, for example, a defendant may not be convicted, despite a clear intent to mislead, if the buyer was not in fact misled.

Few would suggest that the individuals in any of the above examples should escape criminal liability altogether. The issue, however, is whether the extent of liability should turn on results that may have been beyond the defendant's control. Why should a defendant be subjected to greater punishment when, unhappily and unexpectedly, more serious consequences occur than were intended or reasonably could have been anticipated? Conversely, why should a defendant who intends serious injury or loss escape the punishment that would have been his/her due, simply because unforeseen forces over which the defendant had no control led to less serious consequences? Should the law allow a defendant to benefit from his/her 'good luck' if less serious harm results than was intended, but ignore 'bad luck' on the theory that a person who, with a criminal state of mind, sets in motion forces that are likely to result in legally cognisable harm must take the risk that greater harm will occur than was intended or anticipated?

To understand the relationship between consequences and criminal liability requires an examination of the rationales for imposing punishment on those who have been convicted of a criminal offence. The oldest rationale is that of retribution. Under this rationale an offender was punished because s/he had caused harm and deserved to be punished. The harm justified the punishment. In more modern times, retribution theory has been criticised as a primitive and unhealthy from of social revenge and backward- rather than forward-looking. The harm caused by the offender cannot be undone, and punishment of the offender is not designed to prevent future offences. If applied literally, the Biblical formula of 'an eye for an eye' would also seem to divorce punishment from blameworthiness. The person who knocks out the eye of another may do so accidentally, recklessly or purposefully, but, as the outcome would be the same in each instance, the sanction under the Biblical formula would remain the same. Modern developments in the law, especially relating to mens rea, can reduce this problem, but not where criminal liability is strict or absolute.

Results are not as critical to theories of punishment other than retribution. Many penologists (eg Beccaria: 1764; Bentham: 1780) have argued that the primary purpose of criminal sanctions should be to deter future offences rather than to punish past ones. The assumption of a theory of 'general deterrence' is that if other would-be offenders observe a defendant being punished for conduct that they themselves are contemplating, they will refrain from engaging in that conduct. While a retributive punishment might also deter, that is not its primary aim. The severity of a retributive punishment will be determined by the harm caused by the offender, while the severity of a deterrent punishment should be determined by what penalty is necessary to discourage other would-be offenders from committing the same offence. Deterrence theory can also be applied to the convicted offender (known as 'special' deterrence), the idea being that the punishment will deter the offender from repeating his/her crime in the future, as s/he will not want to be subjected to the same punishment again.

Deterrence theory would seem to contain an internal contradiction of sorts as it posits a rational criminal, while ignoring the fact that a rational criminal is unlikely to believe that s/he well ever be caught. Deterrence theory may also not take adequate account of opportunistic or impulsive crimes. The key point for our purposes, however, is that, accepting that there is merit in deterrence theory (either as a stand-alone theory or in conjunction with other theories), society has as much interest in deterring the would-be criminal who may fail as it has in deterring the would-be criminal who may succeed. Regardless of success or failure, what the law wishes to deter are actors who are prepared to violate the law, and actions which are likely to lead to criminal harm.

Punishment of convicted criminals has also been justified on the grounds of restraint and rehabilitation. Members of the public need to be protected from persons who are dangerous, and society achieves this goal by imprisoning and thereby restraining those individuals who have manifested their dangerousness by criminal conduct. However, an offender's dangerousness and consequent need for restraint is determined by the criminal goals that the offender sets for himself/herself and the steps that s/he takes towards achieving these goals. A would-be killer whose victim is, totally unexpectedly, wearing a bulletproof vest is just as dangerous as a would-be killer whose victim has not taken this precaution. While arguably the would-be killer with poor aim is less dangerous than the one whose aim is more accurate, society has little interest in leaving at large persons who are prepared to kill. Regardless of the skill of the murderer or safety consciousness of the victim, those who would kill need to be restrained.

Restraint operates only during the period of a prisoner's confinement, but society's need for protection does not end with the prisoner's release from custody. For this reason, many see an advantage to combining restraint with a programme designed to rehabilitate the offender. If rehabilitation is successful, the offender will not pose a danger to others after release. Restraint and rehabilitation thus can be seen to be opposite sides of the same coin: a dangerous offender needs to be restrained until rehabilitated; once rehabilitated and no longer dangerous, the offender is no longer in need of restraint. But just as the consequences of a crime are a poor indicator of the criminal's need for restraint, so too are they a poor indicator of his/her need for rehabilitation. Whether or not would-be criminals are successful in their enterprise, the fact remains that the social and psychological constraints that inhibit most citizens from committing a crime have not proved effective in their case. If such persons are left to their own devices and are not treated, they may be more successful in their subsequent efforts to break the law.

It is incorrect, of course, to say that the criminal law has ignored the problem of dangerous individuals who have yet to cause harm. Many crimes are defined in terms of conduct and are not dependent on outcome (Ashworth: 1987b). For example, the operator of a motor vehicle who drives dangerously may be convicted of dangerous driving whether or not s/he causes injury to a person or damage to property. Similarly, a lying witness is guilty of perjury whether or not the witness's testimony is believed or affects the verdict; and a defendant may be convicted of forgery even if the forgery is so poor that it does not deceive anybody. Carrying a dangerous weapon or burglary tools is often a crime in and of itself. Indeed, under English law burglary is complete when the offender enters a building as a trespasser with the intent to commit one of a list of enumerated offences, regardless of whether or not s/he actually commits the intended offence. The criminal justice system is not prepared to wait to see if the burglar is successful; the fact that s/he has taken steps towards the commission of the offence is sufficient for its purposes. Likewise, offences against public order often will criminalise conduct that is likely to lead to a disruption of public order, regardless of whether or not any disruption actually takes place, and possession of prohibited drugs is a crime whether or not the drugs are sold or consumed.

In addition to offences defined in terms of conduct, there is the more general offence of criminal attempt. A defendant can be convicted of an attempt to commit a crime (which must be specified; eg attempted murder) based on the defendant's acts and mental state, and regardless of the outcome. The modern law of attempt in England and Wales is codified in the Criminal Attempts Act 1981, and requires that a defendant commit an act that is 'more than merely preparatory to the commission of the offence' with the intent of bringing about consequences, which, if the defendant had been successful, would have rendered the defendant liable for an indictable offence. The fact that the crime attempted is physically or factually impossible to commit is not a defence under the statute. Criminal attempt laws thus implicitly recognise the element of chance in actual outcomes. Those convicted of criminal attempt are punished not because they have caused harm, but in spite of the fact that they have not. They are punished because the attempt itself marks the defendants as dangerous, and in need of restraint and rehabilitation. Their punishment is also designed to deter would-be offenders from embarking on a similar course of action.

If the premise is correct that the defendant whose attempt to commit a crime was foiled by fortuities beyond the defendant's control (as opposed to voluntary withdrawal or abandonment) is as dangerous, as in need of rehabilitation, and as morally blameworthy as the defendant who has committed the substantive offence which was attempted, then it would logically seem to follow that both should be subject to the same penalty.[1] Although equality of sentence is possible in theory under the Criminal Attempts Act 1981, s 4, in practice judges tend to give lesser sentences for defendants convicted of attempt. Perhaps this is testimony to the enduring influence of retribution theory, as the offender convicted of attempt has caused less in the way of social harm. As a practical matter, the absence of an injured victim may reduce the psychological pressure on a judge to impose a severe sentence. However, in some instances the punishment for the substantive offence is beyond a judge's control, and the judge does not have the range of sentencing options that would have been available if the defendant had been convicted of an attempt. Nowhere is this more evident in English law than in regard to a defendant convicted of murder, where the judge must impose a mandatory life sentence, while a defendant convicted of attempted murder may, and usually does, receive a lesser sentence. The potential discrepancy is greater still in those states of the United States which retain the death penalty, which cannot be imposed if the defendant has been convicted only of attempted murder. Yet all that may stand between a conviction for murder and attempted murder may be the defendant's poor aim or a weapon that misfires.

The law of attempt does not solve all of the problems generated by the sometimes random nature of results. To convict a defendant of attempt requires proof of a specific intent to commit the crime intended. One cannot *recklessly* commit an attempt, even where recklessness will suffice for a conviction of the substantive offence. The reckless driver who fatally strikes a pedestrian can be convicted of causing death by dangerous driving, but if the pedestrian were to jump out of harm's way at the last moment, the driver could only be prosecuted for dangerous driving, and not for an attempt to cause death by dangerous driving. In former times the reckless driver who actually caused a death could be prosecuted for what was known as motor manslaughter, but the law was changed to permit a conviction for causing death by reckless (now dangerous) driving because juries would not convict for the more serious manslaughter offence. The jurors, although not the law, recognised that a death could be and often was a matter of chance. A comparable amelioration of the law has not, however, been extended to the assailant who intended to cause grievous bodily harm. Such a defendant may be charged with murder if the victim dies, but not with attempted murder if the victim lives, as attempted murder requires proof of an intent to kill.

One of the effects of defining crimes in terms of results has been that judges have had to manipulate other dimensions of legal liability, and in particular the dimension of legal causation, in order to reach what they think is an appropriate disposition of

---

1   Bentham (1780), however, argued for a lesser sentence for attempt in order to provide an incentive for the offender to abandon the offence.

cases involving morally culpable defendants. One of the elements of the crime of both murder and manslaughter is that the prosecution must prove that the defendant's acts were the legal cause of the death. A defendant sometimes will argue that an intervening force broke the chain of causation, and that his/her acts, although admittedly a 'but for' (or sine qua non) cause of the death, were not its legal cause. When faced with this argument, courts will typically look at whether the intervening acts or events were normal or abnormal, foreseeable or unforeseeable, and whether the actual result was in fact foreseen. If the events were normal, foreseeable or actually foreseen, the defendant will usually remain liable for the offence, even if the result was not intended. While one might expect the logical converse that abnormal, unforeseeable and unforeseen events would break the chain of causation, courts have on occasion held that a defendant remains liable on the rationale that the effects of the defendant's acts were still operative at the time of the death. A well-known but much maligned case in point is *R v Blaue*,[2] where a Jehovah's Witness died of stab wounds after refusing a blood transfusion that would have saved her life. The defendant was convicted of manslaughter, and the Court of Appeal affirmed, rejecting the argument that the defendant was not the cause of the victim's death. The court reasoned that the victim would not have died if the defendant had not inflicted the initial stab wounds. By the same token, however, it could be argued that the victim would not have died if she had consented to the transfusion.

Some would suggest that the actions of the victim in *Blaue* were foreseeable, and therefore insufficient to break the chain of causation. But in what sense could her actions be said to be foreseeable? As a matter of statistical probability, there will be few who will prefer to keep faith with their religion when it will cost them their lives. The decision of Blaue's victim was foreseeable only in the sense that a reasonable person might have been able to conceive of the *possibility,* although surely not the probability, of her refusal to accept the transfusion. The conviction would have been justified if Blaue had been aware of his victim's religiosity, for then her response would have been foreseeable, but there was no evidence to that effect. Hart and Honore (1985) offer, as an alternative rationale for the holding in *Blaue*, the idea that the law should respect a choice made out of conscience not to disregard the dictates of one's religion. It is even questionable, they intimate, whether such a choice should be deemed voluntary, once one has embraced a religion. This analysis would have more merit if an insurance company had refused to pay a death benefit on the victim's life on the ground that she had committed suicide, but it does not explain why Blaue should be held *criminally* responsible for the death.

Nobody would ever suggest that Blaue should have escaped all punishment for his reprehensible acts. He had gone to the victim's home, had demanded she have sex with him, and had savagely attacked her with a knife when she refused. The issue, however, is whether convicting Blaue of manslaughter was the best or even an appropriate way to achieve a result that seemed to fit both the crime and the criminal. The decision in *Blaue* illustrates the tension between a strict application of legal rules of causation and the desire of courts to reach an appropriate disposition in cases involving highly blameworthy and unsympathetic defendants. The reason that the court had to strain the law of causation was that the homicide offence with which Blaue was charged was defined in terms of result and, to convict, the court had

2   (1975) 61 Cr App Rep 271.

to find that Blaue had been the legal cause of the result. To reach this conclusion, the court had to stretch the rules of legal causation. Had the crime been defined in terms of the defendant's acts and mental state but without regard to results, there would have been no need to resort to such mental gymnastics.

The decision in *Blaue* is an atypical example of the rule that 'one must take one's victim as one finds him'. This rule is more commonly invoked where the victim suffers from a physical infirmity, such as haemophilia or an eggshell skull. The rule is so well imbedded in the criminal law that it might seem fatuous to ask why a defendant's liability should be determined, even in part, by the infirmities of the victim. One possible reason is that juries should not be called upon to speculate as to whether a healthier victim might have survived the defendant's attack. As the frailties of the victim pre-exist the defendant's acts, they arguably should be considered as part of the backdrop against which the crime takes place. However, another way of looking at the rule that one must take the victim as s/he finds him is that it reflects the law's unwillingness to allow defendants to escape legal liability because of fortuities relating to the victim's physical health and constitution.

Whatever the merits of a rule that requires a defendant to accept the physical infirmities of the victim, they are less persuasive in a case where the victim's infirmity is not physical but mental or psychological. If the doctors had ignored the protestations of Blaue's victim and had given her a transfusion, and she had subsequently committed suicide because of the perceived offence to her religion, who should be held in law to have caused the result – Blaue, the doctors, or the victim? Or what if the reason for the refusal was the victim's desire to see Blaue convicted of murder – would the victim or Blaue have caused the death; or the doctors who honoured the victim's obstinacy? These are the kinds of pointless inquiries which doctrines of causation engender. They are pointless because the blameworthiness of Blaue's initial actions was in no way altered by subsequent events, and it is on the basis of this blameworthiness that his criminal liability should be judged. After all, had Blaue's victim simply bled to death before her plight had been discovered, or had there been no blood of the appropriate type available for a transfusion, there would have been no question regarding his legal liability for her death. Are not such events equally fortuitous? However, the more appropriate way of dealing with these cases, it is submitted, is not to require that a defendant take the victim as s/he finds him, but to define crimes so that results do not assume critical legal significance. Blaue's attack on his victim was intentional, deliberate and vicious, and his legal liability should reflect these features of the case and not whether his victim was or was not amenable to a blood transfusion.

The medical malpractice cases are also instructive. If a victim of an attack is rushed to the hospital, where a surgeon of exceptional skill manages to save the patient's life, then the assailant will obviously not be guilty of murder or manslaughter, as no victim will have died. On the other hand, if a surgeon of ordinary skill fails to save the patient's life, then the assailant will be convicted of an offence of homicide. But what if the victim's wounds, if treated properly, would not have been life-threatening, but, because of incompetence on the part of the doctor, the wounds were not treated properly and the patient died? Who then should be held legally responsible for the death: the original assailant or the incompetent doctor? The somewhat curious stance of the English courts is to hold that 'ordinary' medical negligence (!) does not break the chain of causation[3] but that gross negligence does.[4] Yet whether a doctor behaves with gross or ordinary negligence, or with ordinary or exemplary skill, is clearly not within the control of the original assailant. The latter should not be treated either more or less leniently by the law because of the competence, or lack thereof, of the attending physician. Arguably, the appropriate way to approach these cases is to focus on the acts, mental state and blameworthiness of the defendant – if a defendant's intentional or reckless acts significantly increase the risk of the victim's death, that should be a sufficient basis for attaching criminal liability. The corollary is that the proper point at which to judge a defendant's criminal liability is at the moment that the defendant commits his/her actus reus.

C. RESULTS AND CORPORATE CRIME

When a Department of Transport inquiry (1987) examined the capsize of the *Herald of Free Enterprise*, it discovered at least six other known instances of open-bow sailings where no adverse consequences had ensued. In the case of the *Herald*, despite calm seas and a clear night, its open bow doors allowed in water which destabilised the ferry and caused it to capsize, with nearly 200 passengers and crew losing their lives. But was there any greater negligence on this instance than there had been on the six identified occasions (and these may have been only the tip of a larger iceberg) of open-bow sailings?

In dismissing the manslaughter charges that were brought against P&O for its role in the *Herald* deaths, Turner J took specific note of the open-bow ferry crossings that had taken place without mishap. Apparently the judge deemed these crossings to be evidence of the fact that P&O executives had not behaved recklessly in not appreciating that there was a serious risk of harm associated with an open-bow sailing. As a matter of logic, this does not follow. Drivers who routinely speed through stop signals without paying attention to whether cars are coming in the opposite direction may never be involved in an accident, but this fact does not detract from the dangerousness of their driving. They have just been lucky. Similarly, the evidence of uneventful open-bow Channel crossings neither proved nor disproved P&O's recklessness. What it did demonstrate, however, is that results can distort the judicial analysis of corporate crime, just as they can distort the analysis of crimes committed by natural persons. By focusing on what had happened on other occasions rather than on what had happened on the fatal night, Turner J may have *underestimated* the risk involved in open-bow sailings. However, had he chosen instead to focus on the terrible consequences on the night in question, the effect would probably have been to *overestimate* the degree of the company's culpability.

The Ladbroke Grove train crash offers another illustration of the same phenomenon. The crash occurred after a driver of a Thames train failed to observe a poorly sited signal light. The signal light was passed at danger (what is known in the rail industry as a SPAD) and the Thames train crashed into a Great Western train coming in the opposite direction. Thirty-two people died as a result of the collision. In the public inquiry which followed, evidence was presented to Lord Cullen that there had been

---

3   See *R v Smith* [1959] 2 QB 35; *R v Malcherek & Steel* (1981) 73 Cr App Rep 173.
4   See eg *R v Jordan* (1956) 40 Cr App Rep 152.

other SPADs involving the same signal. Railtrack, the company responsible for maintaining the signals, was aware of these other incidents, but had failed to convene a meeting of the signal siting committee that could have addressed the problem, a failure that Lord Cullen in his report (2002) characterised as 'incompetent'. But was Lord Cullen's condemnation of Railtrack unduly influenced by the scale of the disaster and the number of deaths? The only difference between the uneventful SPADs and the one that led to the crash was that on the other occasions no comparable calamity had occurred. While the uneventful SPADs may have given the signal sighting committee a false sense of confidence that the situation was not highly dangerous, Lord Cullen's post hoc focus on the SPAD that had resulted in 32 deaths may have caused him to overestimate the a priori degree of danger.

However much results may distort culpability when the defendant is a natural person, the distortion may be exponentially greater when a company is involved because, as the capsize of the *Herald* and the Ladbroke Grove crash illustrate, the injuries, deaths and damage that can follow from a company's failings can far exceed any harm that could conceivably be produced by an individual. At Bhopal, a factory explosion released poisonous gas into the air and caused thousands of deaths and hundreds of thousands of injuries. Comparable numbers may have lost their life savings as a result of the false accounting by Arthur Andersen that led to the collapse of the Enron Corporation in America.

I. The assessment of risk

Recklessness is concerned with risk creation, but not all risk creation is reckless. The risk must be an unreasonable or unjustifiable one for an actor to take under the circumstances. To determine whether this is the case, one must balance the social utility of the actor's conduct against the probability of the risk eventuating, the nature and gravity of the harm that would follow should the risk eventuate, and the cost of neutralising the risk. While it is commonplace to speak of such factors in the abstract, an ever-present problem in risk assessment relates to the fact that the nature of analysis often must be somewhat speculative. Mathematical formulas can give a misleading impression of precision, but they are dependent on the accuracy of the information that serves as the basis of the formula. The provenance of the information may be problematic (after the most recent census in Britain, it was later discovered that a not insignificant number of responses were fabricated by the census takers). Personal opinions that form the basis of a survey questionnaire, that in turn forms the basis of corporate policy decisions, may be distorted by the imprecise, inartful or biased phrasing of the questions asked, or by misunderstandings on the part of the respondents.

If a course of action has no social utility, then exposing others to even a slight risk of harm may be unwarranted. The higher the social utility of the defendant's conduct, on the other hand, the more in the way of risk-creation may be tolerable. To take a simple example, while the dangers involved in driving at 100 mph may be the same if the driver is rushing the victim of a heart attack to a hospital, or attempting to arrive on time for the start of a play, the social utility of the defendant's conduct is quite different in the two cases. It may not be reckless to speed to save the life of the heart attack victim, but there would be little doubt that it would be reckless to speed in order to avoid being late for the theatre.

In addition to the social utility of an actor's conduct, a court must consider the nature of the risk that is threatened. The nature of a risk is a function of the type and magnitude of harm that may occur. How many victims will be harmed if the risk eventuates and what type of harm – death, serious injury, property damage, financial loss or damage to reputation – will they suffer? For example, the likelihood of a rear-end collision if a driver is too close to the vehicle in front may be great, but if the only harm is a dented fender, then the risk assumed is not as significant as it would be if serious injury were likely to follow. The various potential harms can be graded in accord with the value that society attaches to them. Some, such as financial loss, can be quantified numerically.

Risk assessment also requires a calculation of the probability that harm will follow from the creation of a risk. Often only a tentative figure can be put on this dimension of the equation. Situation-specific variables that cannot be factored into the calculus may determine whether a risk actually comes to fruition on a particular occasion. It may be that a concurrence of variables, including a poorly conceived system of risk prevention, human error and the failure of back-up systems, must coalesce for harm to occur. Perhaps all that can be said with certainty is that the more probable the harm and the greater the damage that is posed should the harm come to pass, the more that will be required of the actor in order to neutralise or minimise the risk.

The costs of neutralising a risk cannot be ignored. While it might be reckless to ignore even relatively small risks where the costs of avoidance are minimal, the same might not be said if the costs are prohibitively expensive. In the case of the *Herald of Free Enterprise*, for example, the tragedy might have been averted if the company had accepted the recommendation of the ships' masters to install lights on the bridge that would have indicated when the ferry's bow doors remained open. Given the relatively minimal costs of the indicator lights, at least compared to the risks to the passengers and crew that were threatened, the company's failure to install the lights was arguably negligent or, perhaps, grossly negligent. If the only alternative, on the other hand, would have been a complete re-design of the ferry at a cost which would have undermined P&O's competitive position vis-à-vis the airlines and Eurostar, the refusal to absorb the expense would have been more understandable and would have been entitled to greater consideration in the analysis of the company's legal liability. Yet, in the prosecution of P&O, it did not appear that Turner J considered the costs of eliminating the risk of capsize in his analysis of P&O's alleged recklessness. On the other hand, there may be some risks that are so grave or so probable that the courts may take a doctrinaire stance and rule that it is better that a company should go out of business altogether rather than expose innocent victims to the potential dangers.[5]

Most of our examples so far have dealt with cases of 'corporate violence', but the risk evaluation is also appropriate, perhaps even more so, in the analysis of financial risk. The Financial Services Authority (FSA), which is now in charge of regulating the financial services industry in the UK, has built risk assessment into the definition of its remit. Its starting point is a recognition that the elimination of all risk of business failure is both unrealistic and undesirable. A zero-failure market could stifle innovation and competition, and give investors in the market a false sense of security, intimating that they bore no responsibility for protecting themselves from

---

5 See *R v F Howe & Son (Engineers) Ltd* [1999] 2 All ER 249.

loss. That said, the FSA accepts that it must identify and assess risk in order to establish its priorities and determine the nature and intensity of the relationship it will have with specific companies and specific industries. The FSA employs a conventional but sophisticated approach to risk analysis. First, it seeks to ascertain the risks posed by a company's way of doing business. It then will assess these risks in the light of the likelihood of their coming to fruition and the impact they would have if this were to occur. What the FSA calls firm-specific risks fall into three categories – business risks (risks arising from the nature of an industry, the context in which a firm operates, and the firm's business strategies and decisions), control risks (whether the controls that a firm has in place to prevent risks from materialising are adequate in light of the nature of the risks confronting it), and consumer relationship risks (the risks to consumers from defective products and services, and how many consumers will be affected and to what extent). The FSA also takes account of the fact that the impact of a risk can be affected by the position of a particular firm in the industry, the importance of the firm in the public's mind, the customer base of the firm (its nature and numbers) and the availability of compensation for victims in the event of loss.

Even when the probability of a risk is statistically low, one must balance against that the qualitative nature of the harm that might follow, including its magnitude and extent. Indeed, it is the magnitude and extent of harm that differentiates risk assessment in the corporate context from risk assessment in the context of natural persons. Fifty-one persons were killed when the *Marchioness* was struck on the Thames River by the *Bowbelle*, 32 persons lost their lives in the Ladbroke Grove crash and nearly 200 passengers and crew were drowned when the *Herald of Free Enterprise* capsized. Thousands lost their jobs, their life savings and their hope for a future pension in the Enron collapse. These examples bear witness to the scale of harm that can occur if a company tolerates illegality in its business operation. It is the nature and extent of the potential harm, rather than its statistical probability, that can tilt the risk formula against companies.

The problem with assessing risk against the backdrop of a disaster, such as a train crash, a ferry capsize or a corporate failure on a massive scale, is that, in the wake of the tragedy, emotions will understandably be running high. Achieving a fair and balanced analysis in such circumstances may prove difficult. The obvious source of the difficulty lies in the temporal point at which the issues are considered. Against the backdrop of a disaster, the legislative and judicial response cannot help but be affected by the actual results in the case. Before the incident, on the other hand, there may not even appear to be a problem worthy of consideration. It may or may not have been coincidental that the UK government's consultation paper in which it recommended an offence of corporate killing was published shortly on the heels of the Ladbroke Grove train crash, which itself took place as the inquiry into the Southall train crash was drawing to a close. It is curious, however, that the government's proposals were based on a Law Commission Report that had been in circulation for four years. The two rail crashes, coming so soon after one another, had combined to generate a public outrage, which found support in the media and among politicians, against companies that were perceived to be sacrificing safety to profit. The demand to 'do something' was ringing in the ears of the government. Can one say for sure that these circumstances did not affect at least the *timing* of the release of the government's consultation paper? Equally curious is the fact that, as memories of the crashes faded, as the public's agitation lessened, and as new issues engaged the electorate's mind, the government did not feel under any pressure to include its proposal for a crime of corporate killing in the Queen's speech for the following session of Parliament. It did not do so and, as of the time of this writing, has not done so in the following two sessions of Parliament. It would, indeed, be most unfortunate if the next stage of the government's corporate killing legislation had to await another corporate disaster.

2 A matter of timing

One of the primary purposes of having attempt crimes is to permit law enforcement personnel to intervene to prevent harm before it can occur. While few would oppose providing greater protection to potential victims, the contentious issue with respect to natural persons relates to the point in time at which the police should be able to intervene. An arrest and prosecution will have obvious implications for the defendant's liberty, while the possibility cannot be ignored that the defendant might never have carried through with the substantive offence.

How far must a defendant proceed along the path of criminality before the criminal justice system is justified in intervening? The answer of the Criminal Attempts Act 1981 is that the defendant has to proceed beyond the point of 'mere preparation'. Unfortunately, this answer simply raises another question: at what point can it be said that a defendant has passed the point of mere preparation? There are arguably many factors to be taken into account, including how much the defendant has done towards the commission of the offence (at early common law, the defendant had to have performed the last act before completion of the offence, but this is no longer the general rule), how much remains to be done, how firmly the defendant's resolve to commit the offence has been manifested, does room remain for repentance and a change of mind, and so on.

One factor that tends to be undervalued – or ignored altogether – in the analysis is the seriousness of the harm threatened. Arguably, the more serious the harm threatened, the earlier the point at which the police should be allowed to intervene. Thus, to prevent a murder, the police should be able to intervene at an earlier stage than to prevent a theft, for the loss to society if the offender should succeed will be that much greater. This point has particular salience in a corporate context where the potential harm that can result if a company is allowed to operate its business in a dangerous, reckless or grossly negligent manner is, as we have repeatedly pointed out, on a far greater scale than if an individual were to behave similarly. This consideration supports the case for intervention at an earlier point to prevent corporate crimes than may be warranted in order to prevent comparable crimes by natural persons.

At the same time, some of the factors that weigh against early intervention to prevent the substantive crimes of natural persons are not present in the corporate context. Liberty interests will be implicated when a natural person is arrested and charged with attempt, and it can be argued that when liberty interests are at stake, the criminal justice system should be prepared to give an individual the benefit of the doubt as to whether or not s/he would have carried through with the criminal scheme. In contrast, a company cannot be jailed, and so a similar indulgence is not necessary. Of course, if directors, corporate executives or employees were to face possible confinement, this argument would lose some of its force, but that consideration simply argues for caution in charging natural persons, not caution with respect to early intervention against companies to check their criminogenic practices.

Another factor which argues against early intervention to frustrate crimes by natural persons arises from the fact that, where the charge is attempt, there will be no evidence of actual harm to confirm the defendant's alleged criminal purpose. In such circumstances, a confession can take on critical significance in establishing guilt, and a court needs to be sensitive to the dangers of coerced confessions. Safeguards are needed to protect those subjected to police questioning from unfair tactics and undue pressures to confess. As a company per se cannot be questioned, on the other hand, improper police interrogation practices are less of a worry. To be sure, corporate officials can be questioned, but if the focus of the questioning is on how the business of the company is being conducted, and assuming it is made clear that the investigation is restricted to possible corporate offences and that the individuals being questioned will not be prosecuted based on their statements, then the risk to personal liberty will be largely removed.

Finally, an argument raised against early police intervention against a natural person is that an arrest will deprive the arrestee of the opportunity to abandon his/her criminal scheme. The image seems to be of a would-be criminal engaged in an internal struggle, where the prospective rewards of the criminal enterprise compete against the individual's sense of right and wrong. A case can be made that the law should stay its hand until this struggle has reached its conclusion and the individual has made a firm decision to go ahead with the criminal enterprise. Regardless of the accuracy of this picture, the same type of mental struggle is unlikely to be replicated in a corporate arena. To the extent that corporate crimes are the product of criminogenic and illegal practices that are tolerated by the corporate culture, this culture is not likely to be suddenly changed. It then becomes only a matter of time before an offence involving harm occurs. Indeed, many undetected offences may occur in the interval before overt harm can be detected. This too strengthens the argument for intervention to prevent corporate wrongdoing at an earlier point in time than might be warranted in the case of a natural person.

Accepting, for the sake of argument, the advantages of early intervention to prevent corporate crimes, it is not clear that resort to the law of attempt is the best way to achieve this objective. Proof of mens rea is likely to pose a problem, as the mens rea of attempt is an *intent* to commit a specified crime. Even if the underlying substantive offence can be committed recklessly, a conviction of attempt, as we have noted, requires proof that the defendant intended to commit the offence in question. As has been discussed previously, attributing intent to an inanimate fictional entity such as a company is fraught with difficulties, and commonly the courts have had to resort to imputing the intent of some natural person or persons to the company, at which point the issue becomes whose intent should count as that of the company and whether it is fair to the company to attribute that person's mental state to it. The analysis led to our conclusion in chapter 3 that, with respect to corporate crimes, it would be better to employ a fault element that could be measured by an objective standard such as negligence, objective recklessness, gross negligence or wilful blindness. However, an *objective* fault element would fail to satisfy the *subjective* mens rea requirement of the law of criminal attempt.

Thus, either the mental element of attempt would have to be modified in the case of corporate defendants or an altogether different approach would have to be taken in cases of inchoate offences committed by companies. In Section E we shall propose an approach based on crimes of endangerment, but first we shall take a look at regulatory laws, where there already exists the potential for legal intervention to correct criminogenic corporate conditions before they can ripen into actual harm.

D.   REGULATORY OFFENCES

The argument so far has been that, because of the grave dangers posed when a company is allowed to conduct its business in a dangerous or criminogenic manner, the law should be able to intervene at a point before, rather than after, harm occurs. We have further argued that the point of intervention should be earlier than might be warranted with respect to attempt offences committed by natural persons. We justified this earlier point of intervention by the greater harm that could follow from a company's malfeasance compared to that of an individual, and by the fact that countervailing liberty and personal integrity interests were not present when the object of an investigation was a company. Our conclusion was that what was needed was a regime of corporate criminal offences, defined without regard to the occurrence of harm, where the seriousness of the offence and the range of sanctions were determined by the likelihood, nature, extent and type of harm that was threatened by the way that a company conducted its business. A showing of culpability would, however, still be a prerequisite to a conviction.

In fact, an attempt to define corporate crimes without regard to harm can be found in the regulatory context. Unlike conventional crimes, regulatory offences are often drawn up with companies specifically in mind. Recognising the problems of attributing a mental state to a company, Parliament may impose strict liability; and, recognising the awkward questions involved with respect to whose acts should count as those of a company, it may define the actus reus of the offence in terms of an omission to act or a failure to meet a specified standard. Most significantly for the present purposes, liability will often be independent of actual harm.

The Health and Safety at Work etc Act 1974 provides one of the best-known examples of such a regulatory scheme. At the heart of the Act is a duty on employers to conduct their business in such a way so as to ensure, 'so far as is reasonably practicable', that workers and other persons who may be affected by the operation of the employer's activities are not exposed to risks to their health and safety. Liability is not strict or absolute; a company is only obliged to take such measures as are 'reasonably practicable' to protect health and safety. If it does so, but injury nonetheless occurs, the company will not be liable. The provisions of the Health and Safety at Work etc Act are generally enforced not by the police but by the Health and Safety Executive (HSE). The HSE, whose work will be examined further in chapter 9, carries out its responsibilities through both proactive workplace inspections and reactive investigations following a death or serious injury. Where warranted, the HSE can bring a criminal prosecution either in a magistrates' court or, in more serious cases, in the Crown Court. In the event of a prosecution, liability is not dependent on whether there has been an injury or death.

In practice, health and safety laws have not prevented workplace injuries and deaths to the extent that might have been hoped for or predicted. Many within the HSE would blame inadequate government funding, but external critics are more inclined to fault the HSE for being insufficiently robust and vigorous in its approach to enforcement. With respect to funding, it is probably fair to say that, in an era marked by deregulation, the resources allocated to inspectorates have generally not kept pace with the expansion of business enterprises and their increasing potential to cause serious harm, often on a global scale. The funds available to companies to defend against prosecutions may have induced caution in the less well-funded HSE in initiating potentially expensive criminal cases against corporate violators. Statistics seem to bear this out, as between 1996-1998, only about 11% of major injuries to workers were even investigated by the HSE, and only a shade over 10% of these resulted in a criminal prosecution (CCA: 2001). The HSE is well aware that a company may not readily accept blame, and that a contested trial may place considerable strain on its limited budget.

The alternative to a prosecution-orientated strategy for achieving compliance with the law is one based on negotiating a settlement with offenders in which the goal is to convince companies to voluntarily rectify their dangerous and/or illegal practices. Such a strategy of inducing 'compliance' through persuasion coheres with the HSE's long-term objectives of fostering a culture of safety and reducing workplace deaths and injuries, and may also accord with the self-image of inspectors, who prefer to see themselves as expert advisors rather than as industrial police officers (Carson: 1970). Whether or not a compliance-orientated strategy will be successful will depend both on the willingness of an offender to reform its business operation and the credibility of the HSE's threat to prosecute. To the extent that a company does not believe that the HSE is serious about bringing a prosecution, the company's bargaining position will be strengthened and it may be in a position to drive a 'hard bargain' with HSE inspectors.

A veiled threat to bring a criminal prosecution will also lose much of its force if the sanction that an offender can expect to receive if convicted is minimal. In England and Wales, where health and safety violations are typically heard in a magistrates' court, the maximum fine that can be imposed following a conviction is £20,000 for a criminal offence and £5,000 for breach of a regulation, sums which may not be of a sufficient magnitude to have a meaningful deterrent effect. In the Crown Court, to which an HSE case may be transferred, there are no upper limits on the amount of a fine but there is still no guarantee that a more substantial penalty will be forthcoming. In *R v British Steel Plc*,[6] where a workman was killed when a platform collapsed on top of him, the convicted company was fined only £100, the trial judge apparently viewing the offence as involving only a 'technical' violation. As reflected by the penalty in *British Steel*, the punishment following a conviction for a health and safety violation involving death or serious injury may bear little relationship to the harm caused.

Of course, as we have argued, there are times when results can be fortuitous and the extent of unanticipated injury and damage can distort the analysis of a company's culpability. It would not therefore be wrong for the courts to take this distorting effect into consideration in determining the appropriate sentence in a given case. The problem with regulatory laws is that, rather than taking this factor into account

6   [1995] ICR 586.

in a reasoned manner, it ignores it altogether. Results are simply irrelevant to the determination of whether a company has committed a regulatory offence.

Our point is not that regulatory laws be abolished, for they can serve an important function in the battle against incipient corporate criminality. Regulatory agencies are in a position to set standards for an industry through minimum rules and regulations, and through codes of good or best practice. Many companies will genuinely welcome such guidance, having no desire either to run foul of the law or to conduct their business in a dangerous or crime-conducive manner. Regulatory laws also offer a useful vehicle for dealing with minor offences and inadvertent offenders. They are a suitable first port of call where a company does not have a history of violations or where it is not clear that the company has behaved in a sufficiently blameworthy manner to warrant subjecting it to the expense and stigma of a full-blown criminal prosecution. Although one can legitimately criticise compliance strategies adopted *out of necessity*, such strategies can offer a way of drawing a company's attention to its dangerous and criminogenic practices, which, if uncorrected, could lead to future harm and illegality.

While regulatory laws undoubtedly have their place in a co-ordinated scheme for controlling corporate crime, the problem is that too much has been demanded of regulation, and many of the demands are in conflict, or at least in tension, with each other. For example, in the health and safety field, it is clearly desirable to reduce workplace injuries and deaths. Let us assume, for the sake of argument, that this goal can be most effectively achieved through discussion, education and negotiation. But there is an equally valid goal of holding companies accountable for their culpable violations. A criminal trial may be needed to delineate the limits of proper corporate behaviour, to assuage the anguish of victims and their families, to assure the public that powerful companies are not above the law and to deter other companies contemplating similar courses of action. But a formal criminal trial may work at cross-purposes from the goal of achieving compliance through informal negotiation. The focal point of the two approaches is different – regulation looks primarily to the future, with past events simply being the trigger for discussions, but criminal prosecutions concentrate on what has happened in the past, with future reform being less at the heart of a criminal trial. Whereas the goal of a compliance-orientated strategy is to effectuate change, the main aim of a criminal prosecution is to establish responsibility for and punish past offences. While organisational change may best be realised within a regulatory system, public accountability may best be achieved within the criminal justice system. And while compliance strategies envisage co-operation, criminal prosecutions inevitably engender conflict. Establishing an environment that will facilitate compliance may be frustrated if the parties are, on another front, engaged in an adversarial and antagonistic courtroom struggle.

E. ENDANGERMENT OFFENCES

We have now identified two models that a state might adopt to combat incipient corporate criminality – a compliance-orientated model and a prosecution-orientated model. In a regulatory system, priority is given to compliance; in the criminal justice system, accountability and punishment are the prime objectives. Offenders are publicly 'named and shamed' and sanctions are imposed to deter other would-be violators.

The point of convergence is that each model seeks to prevent future harm, although each goes about it in a different way. Regulators employ compliance strategies to induce voluntary reform of a company's way of doing business, while the criminal justice system endeavours to deter violations by using the punishment of a convicted company to jolt other companies into obeying the law.

Together, regulatory laws and criminal prosecutions offer a stick-and-carrot approach: regulatory laws enforced through compliance strategies are the carrot; while prosecutions followed by criminal sanctions are the stick. The problem with regulatory regimes, as we have observed, is that they are often asked to be both carrot and stick at the same time. Compliance-orientated strategies often founder because agency threats to prosecute lack credibility. Criminal laws, on the other hand, may founder because they require law enforcement personnel to stay their hand until actual harm occurs, and by then it may be too late. What is needed is to combine the best features of the two approaches. What we have in mind is a regime of endangerment offences that, like regulatory laws, would allow for intervention before serious harm can occur but which are backed up by a meaningful arsenal of sanctions.

The main features of the scheme of endangerment offences that we have in mind have been trailed by the discussion to this point. First, the offences would be defined in terms of a culpable failure on the part of a company to identify, assess and guard against serious criminal risks, or to monitor those whom the company has placed in a position to cause harm or violate the law. Second, and what would distinguish the offences that we presently have in mind from those that we discussed in the preceding chapter, the relevant statutes would not require a showing of actual harm. This is in keeping with the themes of this chapter that harm does not necessarily reflect fault, that the extent of injury and particularly death may overstate the degree of fault, and that the absence of harm does not preclude a finding of fault. Third, the 'fault' element in the proposed offences would be defined in 'objective' terms, including negligence, gross negligence, objective recklessness and wilful blindness. These, of course, are the same fault elements as for the substantive offences discussed in the preceding chapter, which should not be surprising, as the major difference between the offences there described and the crimes of endangerment now envisaged is the absence of a requirement of actual harm. The arguments in favour of objective tests of corporate fault were presented in chapter 3 and will not be repeated here. Finally, as the aim of the envisaged endangerment statutes would be to prevent harm before it can occur, among the sanctions following a conviction for an offence of endangerment would normally be a judicial order requiring the offender to rectify the conditions and practices that gave rise to the danger. The penalty would be designed to be more reformative than punitive in nature.

The offences that we have in mind would be specifically directed to corporate entities, and would be based on an a priori calculation of the nature, magnitude and extent of the harm threatened by various types of corporate behaviour. Regulatory laws would be retained, however, to deal with cases where improvements to the way that the company conducts its business operation are advisable but the company has not been at fault, or at least not been seriously at fault, in allowing criminogenic conditions to come into existence or persist, and where the company is amenable to voluntary reform. In cases where a company has made a reasonable and good faith, albeit unsuccessful, effort to eliminate criminogenic conditions, and where what it really needs is counsel and advice, regulators would still have a valuable function to perform.

Endangerment offences are more common in the United States than they are in England (K J M Smith: 1983). However, most of these offences were designed with natural persons and not companies in mind, and the thought that they would be extended to corporate bodies might have given their proponents pause. Both corporate criminality and endangerment offences are on the cutting edge of the criminal law, and in combination might, for some, have constituted a bridge too far. This is not to say that combining the two does not have merit.

While infrequently encountered in English law, several endangerment offences are contained in the Offences against the Person Act 1861 (OAPA). For example:

Section 32 Placing wood, etc, on railway, taking up rails, turning points, showing or hiding signals, etc, with intent to endanger passengers

Whosoever shall unlawfully and maliciously put or throw upon or across any railway any wood, stone, or other matter or thing, or (the statute here goes on to list other types of activity)... or shall unlawfully and maliciously do or cause to be done any other matter or thing, with intent... to *endanger* the safety of any person travelling or being upon such railway, shall be guilty of a felony...(emphasis added)

Section 33 Casting stone, etc, upon a railway carriage, with intent to endanger the safety of any person therein, or in any part of the same train

Whosoever shall unlawfully and maliciously throw, or cause to fall or strike, at, against, into, or upon any engine, tender, carriage, or truck used upon any railway, any wood, stone, or other matter or thing, with intent to injure or *endanger* the safety of any person being in or upon such engine... shall be guilty of a felony...(emphasis added)

A modern illustration of an English statute that combines a substantive offence defined in terms of result (harm to property) with an inchoate offence addressed to the endangering of life can be found in the Criminal Damage Act 1971:

Section 1(2) A person who without lawful excuse destroys or damages any property, whether belonging to himself or another –
(a) intending to destroy or damage any property or being reckless as to whether any property would be destroyed or damaged; and
(b) intending by the destruction or damage to *endanger* the life of another or being reckless as to whether the life of another would be thereby endangered;
shall be guilty of an offence. (emphasis added)

The above examples of endangerment offences are addressed to specific problem areas. There is no general endangerment offence in English law, and the proposal advanced by the Criminal Law Commissioners in 1846 and 1848 to create such a general offence was not incorporated into the Offences Against the Person Act 1861. While it might also seem that the English endangerment statutes contemplate human offenders, because of their subjective mens rea elements, it should be recalled that the House of Lords has in *R v Caldwell*[7] interpreted the reference to recklessness in the Criminal Damage Act 1971 to be satisfied by proof of either objective or subjective recklessness.

---

7   [1982] AC 341.

The English statutes might profitably be compared with the following two American examples of endangerment offences, which are more sweeping in their scope:

Alaska Statutes, s 11.41.250 Reckless Endangerment

(a) A person commits the crime of reckless endangerment if the person recklessly engages in conduct which creates a substantial risk of serious physical injury to another person.

Arizona Revised Statutes, s 13-1201 Endangerment

A. A person commits endangerment by recklessly endangering another person with a substantial risk of imminent death or physical injury.

B. Endangerment involving a substantial risk of imminent death is a … felony. In all other cases, it is a … misdemeanour.

There are several points worth noting about the two statutes. First, both refer to a risk of harm that is 'substantial'. This may be seen as a matter of logic: the less substantial the risk of harm, the more doubt that the defendant was at fault in failing to have foreseen the risk or in failing to have taken precautions against it. Second, in referring to the actus reus of the offence, the Alaska statute speaks of 'conduct', while the Arizona statute speaks more comprehensively of 'recklessly endangering'. The latter phrasing is preferable in order to make clear that the actus reus of the offence can consist of an omission, which is certainly the more common type of endangering that will be encountered in the corporate context. Third, in referring to the risk that must be created by the defendant's conduct, the Arizona statute distinguishes between reckless conduct that poses a risk of death and reckless conduct that poses a risk of serious physical injury, while the Alaska statute refers only to reckless conduct that poses a risk of serious physical injury, which presumably would also include a risk of death. Here the phrasing of the Alaska statute is to be preferred, as whether a death, as opposed to serious physical injury or, indeed, any harm whatsoever, follows from reckless or grossly negligent conduct can depend on circumstances over which a defendant has little or no control. Fourth, while both statutes require proof of recklessness, neither states whether objective or subjective recklessness is contemplated. We have argued that in the corporate context an objective standard is preferable, and this should be made explicit to the extent that the statute is to be applied to companies. Fifth, the Arizona statute's requirement that the death or physical injury be *imminent* may be inadvisable. As we have argued previously, where serious injuries and death are threatened, and particularly in a corporate context where companies are not facing a 'loss of liberty' (as they cannot be imprisoned), a strong case can be made for intervention prior to the point where the danger becomes imminent. To delay up to the point of imminence may be needlessly to put lives and safety at risk. Finally, both statutes are addressed to potential *physical* injuries to the person; neither includes threats to property or financial interests. Yet, as the recent spate of accounting scandals in the United States illustrate, such harm can have a devastating economic and psychological effect on its victims.

Although there would seem to be no reason why the Alaska and Arizona statutes could not be applied to companies, there may be an advantage to constructing a separate regime of endangerment offences that was directed specifically to companies and other organisational entities. We have argued that, because of the scale of harm that is threatened by corporate activity conducted in a risky, dangerous or illegal manner, the point where intervention would be warranted may be earlier in time than in cases involving natural persons, and the statute could make that clear. A company-orientated statute might also adopt a less demanding standard of fault than that of 'recklessness', which is the standard most commonly contained in endangerment statutes. In the corporate context a standard of negligence might, as discussed in chapter 3, not be inappropriate, depending on the harm to be guarded against. Finally, the penalty specified in the statute could be drafted with an eye to the fact that the defendant is a company and that the primary goal is to eliminate criminogenic conditions and to reform criminogenic practices before they can cause harm rather than to 'punish' the company.

The following Oregon statute, even though it speaks in terms of persons, clearly is intended to apply also to companies. In fact, the statute is far more likely to catch companies within its net. Although danger to individuals is a component element of the statute, the title – environmental endangerment – is indicative of the fact that endangerment offences need not be restricted to crimes against the person, as in the previous examples.

Oregon Revised Statutes, s 468.951 Environmental endangerment.
(1) A person commits the crime of environmental endangerment if the person:
(a) Knowingly commits the crime of unlawful disposal, storage or treatment of hazardous waste in the first degree, unlawful transport of hazardous waste in the first degree, unlawful air pollution in the first degree or unlawful water pollution in the first degree; and
(b) As a result, places another person in imminent danger of death or causes serious physical injury.
(2) Environmental endangerment is a felony punishable:
(a) If the defendant is an individual and notwithstanding ORS 161.625, by imprisonment of not more than 15 years, a fine of not more than $1,000,000, or both.
(b) If the defendant is other than an individual and notwithstanding ORS 161.625, by a fine of not more than $2,000,000.
(c) Notwithstanding ORS 161.625, in the case of a second or subsequent conviction under this section, by imprisonment of not more than 30 years, a fine of not more than $5,000,000, or both.

The Oregon statute, s (2)(b) signals the statute's applicability to companies and other organisational entities by specifying that the maximum fine for *non-individuals* is double that for individuals. The maximum amount of these fines – $2,000,000 for a first offence and $5,000,000 for a repeat offence – is a further indication that prosecutions against corporations are envisaged. Penalties of this magnitude may be needed to exert a meaningful deterrent effect on companies and to prevent fines from being 'passed on' to the offender's customers. By setting the fine at a level designed to have a significant impact, the Oregon law makes it difficult for a company to absorb the fine without incurring a major competitive disadvantage.

In sum, where a company conducts its business in a negligent, reckless or grossly negligent manner, or with wilful blindness, the criminal justice system should not have to await the occurrence of actual harm in order to be able to intervene. In the absence of actual harm, the crime charged would reflect the potential risks threatened by the company's way of doing business. In contrast to regulatory laws that may be defined or administered in such a way that actual consequences become irrelevant, and conventional crimes which include results as a definitional element of the offence, which overstate the importance that should be attached to consequences, the endangerment offences we envisage would take into account the *potential* for harm both in respect of the offence and the sanction following a conviction.

In the preceding chapter we argued that a corporate defendant should be able to defend against an alleged corporate crime by showing that it had conducted its business operation with 'due diligence'. In chapter 6 we shall further argue that the burden of proving due diligence should be placed on the corporate defendant, albeit only by a 'balance of probabilities' standard, principally because the relevant records of what the company has done to avert the crime will be in its control and the critical witnesses who can testify as to what actual steps have been taken to prevent crime will be in its employ. In the context of endangerment offences, should due diligence also be a defence?

The answer depends on the goal of the prosecution in bringing its case and the sanction that is likely to be imposed if there is a conviction. If the goal of the prosecution is only to obtain a remedial order that will require the company to reform criminogenic deficiencies in its business operation, then whether or not the company has conducted its affairs with due diligence is largely immaterial. The fact that its operation poses a serious risk of harm to others is sufficient to warrant issuance of the order. On the other hand, if an additional sanction which is 'punitive' in nature (such as a fine, temporary closure or restrictions on the company's activities) is being sought, then the company should be entitled to assert its due diligence in defence. In order to make this system workable, it will be necessary for the prosecutor in the case to set out in advance what penalties the Crown will be seeking in the event of a conviction. It is to this topic that we now turn.

F.   REMEDIAL ORDERS AND OTHER SANCTIONS

Some corporate sanctions are designed to 'punish'; others seek to reform a company's way of doing business in order to prevent future harm. We have already indicated that the issuance of a remedial order will usually be warranted where the charge is an endangerment offence. However, depending on the nature of the company's offence, additional 'punitive' sanctions may be merited as well.

Ashworth (1988: 461–463) distinguishes between two different versions of the crime of 'attempt'. One version is where the defendant has done everything that was intended, but no harm has followed from the defendant's actions, perhaps through sheer good luck. This is a 'complete' attempt. An example is where X shoots at Y, but misses, at which point X is apprehended. The other type of attempt is where the defendant has not completed all the intended steps in the criminal plan. Ashworth refers to this form of attempt as an 'incomplete' attempt. An example would be where X buys a gun to kill Y but has not yet found Y at the point he is apprehended. The rationale for intervention with respect to incomplete attempts is the need to take action to prevent harm before it can materialise. It is already too late to take preventive action with respect to complete attempts, but there is no need to refrain from punishing the attempter simply because s/he was unsuccessful in the attempt.

With respect to endangerment offences, one can envisage comparable instances of 'complete' and 'incomplete' versions of the offence. Say that a lorry company paid its drivers by the mileage they logged and paid all speeding fines incurred by its drivers. Its endangerment offence will be 'complete', as the company will have done everything that it intended to do to bring about the situation of danger (although it was not its intent to cause actual injury). That its drivers were fortunate enough not to be involved in an 'accident' does not detract from its offence. It is every bit as blameworthy as the company which has adopted the same policy but one of whose drivers is involved in a fatal crash attributable to speeding. On the other hand, say that the lorry company fails to inspect the safety of its vehicles before sending them on to the road. One of the drivers refuses to take a lorry on to the road in what the driver judges to be a dangerous condition. When the matter cannot be amicably resolved between driver and company, the driver reports the company to the Health and Safety Executive, and a prosecution is subsequently brought charging an endangerment offence. As the vehicle in question has yet to be driven on the road in its unsafe state, the company's offence is 'incomplete'.

When a company's endangerment offence is 'complete', just as when an individual's criminal attempt is 'complete', but no harm has occurred as a result of fortuitous circumstances over which the defendant had no control, then the offender is no less blameworthy than one whose offence has resulted in harm. In these instances, the penalty should be the same as it would be for the defendant who was not so fortunate as to avoid harm. For companies, this means that the full panoply of sanctions, including fines, community service orders, reputation-orientated sanctions, restraint-orientated sanctions and remedial orders (all of which are discussed in chapter 7) will be appropriate for the offender. In contrast, the case for punitive sanctions is less justified where the endangerment offence is 'incomplete'. The rationale for intervention is to prevent future harmful consequences, and a remedial order will suffice for this purpose. Note that a remedial order will be appropriate for both complete and incomplete endangerment offences, but that punitive sanctions will not be appropriate for incomplete endangerment offences.

A remedial order requires a company to correct the illegal and/or dangerous aspects of its operation that give rise to the offence. This order fits well with the preventative and deterrent nature of endangerment offences. One of the main purposes of having a crime of endangerment is to allow law enforcement personnel to intervene to prevent harm before it can occur, and the penalty for a violation should be designed to remedy the practices and conditions that led the law enforcement personnel (as well as the court) to believe that harm was about to occur. Given the injuries that may occur if dangerous practices and conditions are not corrected, a remedial order should be mandatory unless the defendant can demonstrate that it has already taken or is in the process of taking satisfactory steps to address the problem.

The specifics of a remedial order will depend on the nature of the harm that has been found by the court to be threatened by the company's way of doing business. As the company will be more familiar with its internal structures, operations and organisation than will the sentencing judge, the judge may choose to solicit from the offender its own proposals for rectifying the practices and conditions that gave rise to the offence (Fisse and Braithwaite: 1988). No doubt companies will welcome the opportunity to provide such input for they will not wish to be saddled with an unsuitable or unduly burdensome order. On the other hand, as it is not clear that a corporate offender can be trusted to act in 'good faith' in offering such proposals, as it will have a vested interest in minimising the disruption to its business operation, the prosecutor in the case should also be given the opportunity to make representations and introduce evidence relating to the content of the remedial order. Nor should the sentencing judge be forced to choose between the two sides' positions. If the judge remained dissatisfied, s/he should be able to appoint an independent expert, to be paid for by the convicted company as part of the court costs, to furnish the court with recommendations (Gruner: 1993).

Judges should be encouraged to take a creative and expansive approach to the fashioning of remedial orders. A remedial order may include a reorganisation or restructuring of the company's business operation, the rectification of criminogenic practices and the neutralisation of dangerous conditions, the establishment of additional training programmes as needed, and the appointment of supervisory personnel with responsibility for overseeing compliance not only with the court's order but the law generally. But this may not be enough if those responsible for the culture that tolerated the criminogenic conditions or practices are allowed to remain in a position of authority, for the ethos that lay behind the offence might not be altered even if the specific conditions and practices were to be amended. Thus the reach of the remedial order might extend to the replacement of the executives responsible for that culture.

The issuance of a remedial order would not end the sentencing court's involvement in the case. Regular reports would need to be submitted to it, both by the offender and by a specially appointed external 'probation officer', indicating the progress that the company was making towards fulfilment of the order. If any of the submitted reports indicated that the company was not fulfilling the terms of the remedial order, the court should have several options (Fisse and Braithwaite: 1988), including an amendment of the terms of the order, a suspension of the company's license or authority to engage in its business until such time as it had complied with the order, and, particularly in cases where it did not appear that the company was going about satisfying the court's order in good faith, the appointment of a 'master' to assume control of the company until such time as the company was in compliance.[8] The court-appointed master would displace the company's CEO during the period of his/her appointment, and would have the authority to hire consultants and other necessary personnel, and generally to take whatever steps were judged to be necessary to bring the company into compliance with the law.

G.   ACCESSORIES TO ENDANGERMENT

What of the role of corporate directors, officers and employees in the commission of a company's endangerment offence? In chapter 8 we shall examine generally the relationship between the liability of individuals and the liability of companies for crimes that occur in a business setting, but it might be useful at this point to ask whether an individual might be liable as an accessory to an endangerment offence.

---

8   As is authorised under the US federal sentencing guidelines for organisational offenders under USSG, s 8D1.5.

Our starting point is the general proposition that while it would be wrong to make an individual the scapegoat for a corporate offence, it would also be wrong to make the company a scapegoat for an offence that is the responsibility of an individual. Where corporate criminality is based on imputed fault, by definition an individual will have committed an offence. There will therefore be no problem in independently prosecuting that individual. With respect to corporate crimes defined in terms of organisational fault, on the other hand, no individual offence need precede a charge against the company. The question that must be asked is whether an individual might be an accessory to a corporate offence of endangerment.

It is possible in law for a natural person to be an accessory to an inchoate offence of another natural person.[9] We have argued that if A intends to shoot B, A's liability should not turn on whether his aim is poor, the gun misfires or B moves at the last moment. By the same token, however, if C provides A with the gun to shoot B, C's liability *as an accessory* should not be dependent on whether A decides to go through with the killing. C has already done everything that s/he intended to do to bring about the offence.

Should accessories to a corporate offence of endangerment be treated in the same way? It is easy to envisage situations where directors or officers of a company counsel reckless policies that, if carried to their natural conclusion, would lead to injuries, deaths or significant financial losses. If the police intervene in time to prevent the harm, perhaps as a result of a tip-off by a whistleblower, the company could, under the thesis presented in this chapter, be charged with endangerment. There would also seem to be no reason in theory why the corporate officer could not be tried as an accessory to the company's crime of endangerment. On the other hand, one of the primary rationales for endangerment offences is the need for early intervention to prevent the harm that can follow if a company is allowed to carry on its business in a reckless, grossly negligent or even negligent manner. A conviction allows a court to make a remedial order that will obviate the potential harm.

Early intervention is more troubling if a natural person is to be charged with an offence because the individual's liberty and freedom are at stake. The fact that a company did not face imprisonment to an extent underpinned our argument that the intervention to prevent corporate offences of endangerment could be justified at an earlier point in time than might be appropriate for a natural person suspected of an attempt to commit an offence. When the question is whether to charge an individual as an accessory to an inchoate corporate offence, however, the threat to individual liberty cannot be dismissed. Whether or not the individual is ultimately acquitted, s/he will suffer the inevitable stress and anxiety that accompanies the prosecution. Moreover, co-operation by corporate executives cannot be expected to be forthcoming if they might become subject to criminal prosecution, thus defeating the preventative aims of endangerment offences. The same is true for would-be whistleblowers who only discover their company's criminality after having unwittingly become involved in it. If, by reporting the wrongdoing, they expose themselves to criminal prosecution as an accessory, they are hardly likely to report the company's offence to the authorities.

In short, the analysis becomes more complicated when individuals enter the legal analysis of endangerment offences. With respect to both the corporate offender

9   See eg *R v Dunnington* [1984] QB 472.

charged with endangerment and the natural person charged as an accessory to the endangerment offence, there is a risk of a wrongful conviction stemming from premature intervention by the police, but the consequences to the individual from a wrongful conviction are potentially more far reaching than they are to a company. When a company is wrongfully convicted of an endangerment offence, at worst it will suffer a (presumably constructive) alteration in its business operation following a remedial order. When an individual is convicted of being an accessory to that endangerment offence, s/he will have the stigma of a conviction, a criminal record and a possible prison sentence to serve.

While there is thus a strong case for charging companies with endangerment, the case for charging individuals as accessories is considerably weaker. Where the goal is to allow the correction of dangerous and/or criminogenic conditions in a company's operation before they can cause actual harm, this goal will be achieved by convicting the company of endangerment. There is little more to be gained by prosecuting individuals. While the risk to an innocent company of having a remedial order entered against it may be acceptable in light of the dangers that the law is trying to prevent, the risk of wrongfully imprisoning an innocent individual may not. Even if Machiavellian officers or directors are responsible for the company's deviant policies and practices, the risks of a wrongful conviction caution against charging them as accessories. In some cases, of course, the individual may have committed a substantive offence or an attempt to commit a substantive offence (eg attempted murder) in his/her own right for which s/he can be charged.

The preceding analysis reflects the differing rationale for prosecuting individuals and companies for inchoate offences. In significant part, the rationale for charging an individual with attempt is that by progressing beyond the point of mere preparation, the individual has shown him/herself to be a danger to society. The rationales of restraint and rehabilitation, as well as the need to deter others, justify the consequent punishment. In contrast, the main purpose for having corporate inchoate offences is to allow timely intervention against companies before their criminogenic and dangerous practices can ripen and cause harm to innocent victims. This consideration is not irrelevant to inchoate offences committed by individuals as well, but it is the overriding factor in the case of companies. In order to achieve the preventative goals which underlie corporate offences of endangerment, it may be necessary to forgo the prosecution of individuals who may have counselled, procured, aided, abetted, facilitated or otherwise significantly contributed to the corporate offence.

H.   THE CONTINUING RELEVANCE OF HARM

Crimes of endangerment are defined without regard to actual harm, but this does not mean that the *potential* for harm should be ignored in the formulation and administration of the law. The potential for harm can and should be considered at the legislative stage, on the issue of criminalisation; at the investigative stage, in determining whether an offence has been committed; at the prosecutorial stage, in exercising discretion whether to bring charges and, if so, for what offence; at the trial stage, where the potential for harm will be of evidentiary significance; and at the sentencing stage, where the court will have to consider the harm that might have occurred in shaping its remedial order.

1.   Criminalisation

The criminalisation decision – what to make criminal – is critical to the legislative process. In one sense all criminalisation decisions are made at a point in time before actual harm has occurred; indeed, constitutional provisions against retroactive legislation generally preclude after-the-fact decisions to make conduct criminal. But the decision with respect to endangerment offences is different in kind because the definition of the offence will not incorporate a reference to actual harm, the potential for harm sufficing for a conviction. Parliament therefore must identify what types of potentials for harms need to be guarded against. This requires identification of those social, economic and environmental interests that deserve protection. Inherent in these decisions is a judgment that the potential for harm involved in a course of action is of sufficient gravity that the mere creation of a risk of that harm warrants criminal prosecution. The potential for harm is at the heart of the analysis. Parliament might decide to limit endangerment offences to corporate conduct that posed a substantial risk of death or serious injury, because of the life-threatening implications, but it could go further and criminalise other types of risk-creation.

The potential for harm – its nature, magnitude and extent – will affect the fault element attached to the endangerment offence. We have identified a number of possible fault states which might be appropriate for corporate endangerment offences, including negligence, objective recklessness, gross negligence and wilful blindness. Which of these will be the appropriate fault standard for a particular endangerment offence may depend on the gravity of the harm perceived by the legislature to be threatened. If the legislature's primary aim is preventative, it might deem the least demanding fault standard – negligence – to be appropriate where the dangers were greatest to allow for police intervention at the earliest possible stage. On the other hand, if priority is given to avoiding a possible wrongful conviction of an innocent company, the most demanding fault states – gross negligence or wilful blindness — might be deemed appropriate.

Whether to enact endangerment offences aimed at protecting against financial losses may be a matter of debate. While there will rarely be a legitimate excuse for needlessly endangering lives, investments normally entail risk. Indeed, many investors prefer the opportunity for a substantial return on their investment (especially if the investment involves a relatively modest sum, as in the purchase of a lottery ticket) even if it entails a relatively high risk of losing everything. Virtually all investments carry a risk of failure, and fund managers and their companies should perhaps not have to worry that, if failure is possible, their business judgment will be second-guessed even before they have had the chance to have it vindicated. In the financial arena a more appropriate way forward may be to require companies to inform investors of the full extent of the risks of an investment. In cases of fraud or misleading sales techniques, on the other hand, the endangerment offence might be defined in terms of deception but without regard to actual loss.

2.   Investigations

While the purpose of creating endangerment offences is in part to liberate the law from the fortuity of consequences, it must be acknowledged that, at least as far as investigations are concerned, the practical effect may not be significant. Most criminal investigations are reactive rather than proactive, being triggered by the occurrence of legally cognisant harm being brought to the attention of the proper authorities. When a death or serious injury occurs, for example, an investigation will follow to determine its cause. Negligent, reckless and grossly negligent corporate conduct, or a company's wilful blindness, is unlikely to come to the attention of law enforcement personnel if it does not lead to serious harm, and whether or not crimes are defined without regard to results will not change this realpolitik.

What will change, however, is the nature of the charges if, for example, a routine regulatory inspection were to uncover grossly negligent working conditions or if a whistleblower were to reveal criminogenic practices in a company's operation. Now the fact that the law includes within its arsenal offences of endangerment will allow a criminal prosecution of the company despite the absence of harm. Granted, this can occur under present regulatory legislation, but endangerment offences will permit charges that are perhaps seen to be more commensurate with the egregiousness of the conduct in question. Present regulatory laws, as currently enforced, do not carry the type of censure and stigma we envisage attaching to an endangerment offence, and, as a result, may not deter corporate criminality to the same extent.

3.   Prosecutorial discretion

In most criminal justice systems prosecutors are allowed a degree of discretion in deciding which cases to bring to trial. Discretion is necessary in order that valuable court time will not be taken up with trivial disputes and in order that potential defendants whose deviation from the legal norm is not substantial will not be subjected to the emotional, psychological, and financial costs of a criminal trial. In the case of a company, which is an inanimate lifeless entity, there are no psychological and emotional costs to be considered; and obviously, the absence of actual harm cannot be allowed to deflect a prosecution without undermining the rationale behind endangerment offences. A prosecutor therefore needs to consider the harm threatened, and the reasons why actual harm did not occur. If the absence of harm is attributable to a fortuity not envisaged by the corporate defendant and beyond its control, it should carry little weight.

Conversely, however, if far greater harm has occurred than could ever have been anticipated, a prosecutor might decide to charge the corporate offender with an endangerment offence rather than with a substantive crime. The rationale for this seeming anomaly would be to avoid either a mandatory minimum penalty for the substantive offence or the possibility of an unduly harsh sentence by the court. Particularly where the harm resulting from corporate misconduct has been widely publicised in the media, both judges and juries may be affected, although perhaps only on a subconscious level, by a populist demand for vengeance. If the prosecution was of the opinion that charging an endangerment offence was more reflective of the company's culpability, it should be permitted this option.

The presence or absence of harm may also affect the exercise of prosecutorial discretion in a different and perhaps more subtle way. If no harmful results have occurred, the prosecution's ability to establish criminal liability may be problematic. In choosing among cases meriting prosecution, a prosecutor with limited resources, recognising that bringing every such case to trial may be impossible, will be inclined to select those which are most likely to lead to a conviction. This inclination is reinforced by the guidelines for Crown prosecutors, which advise that a greater than 50% chance of a conviction is needed to warrant a prosecution. Without actual harm to support the prosecutor's characterisation of a company's way of doing business as negligent, reckless or grossly negligent, the case may be too weak to merit taking forward.

4.   Evidence

Results will be relevant at the trial stage, but in an evidentiary rather than a definitional capacity. There is undoubtedly a greater risk of convicting an innocent defendant in a legal system where criminal liability does not require proof of harm. This risk is to some extent ameliorated by the increased practical burden on prosecutors to establish a company's fault when there is no evidence of actual harmful consequences. However, concepts such as negligence, recklessness and gross negligence take their meaning from factual contexts. The result is the 'proof of the pudding', so to speak. When a prosecutor argues that a company has behaved in a reckless manner and there is a victim who has suffered, the victim's testimony will lend colour to the prosecutor's argument.

This is of course not to say that, in the absence of a harmful result, the prosecution will inevitably fail. If this were so, there would be little point in enacting endangerment offences in the first place. The fact-finder may still conclude that the avoidance of harm was attributable to good luck (particularly likely with respect to 'complete' endangerment offences), in which case it would be unlikely to encounter any problem in convicting the company of endangerment. The proper balance, it is submitted, is to allow the trier of fact to draw whatever inferences are appropriate regarding the culpability of a corporate defendant's conduct from the presence or absence of resulting harm.

5.   Sentencing

It is at the sentencing stage that the legal system seeks to distinguish among offenders who may have been convicted of the same offence. By taking account of variables that may not have been relevant to the issue of guilt, judges strive to impose a punishment that fits the offender. Historically, judges have enjoyed considerable discretion in sentencing, although this discretion may need to be circumscribed to some extent or be subject to review in order to promote consistency in sentencing and to avoid sentences that are discriminatory or arbitrary.

We have argued that, following a conviction for an endangerment offence, a judge should normally issue an order that required the defendant to rectify the crime-conducive aspects of its operation. Because the dangers posed by different businesses and their individualistic methods of doing business may vary considerably, however, and because the same generic endangerment offence will bring within its ambit a greater range of illegality than will more narrowly drafted substantive offences, there is a seeming risk of disparity in sentencing. This need not be a concern, for the goal of the remdial order in each case is the same: to rectify the criminogenic conditions. Inevitably the specifics of a remedial order will need to be shaped to take account of the particular risks threatened by a company's way of doing business.

Whether a more drastic sanction than a remedial order will be warranted is likely to depend on the nature, magnitude and extent of harm threatened by the company's conduct and whether the company's offence is 'complete' or 'incomplete'. We have argued that, if the company's endangerment offence is 'complete', then the company should face the full panoply of sanctions that would be authorised if the requisite harm had occurred, but that, in the case of incomplete endangerment offences, the sanction will ordinarily be a remedial order. Examples where a more severe order is warranted, even in the case of an incomplete offence, are not difficult to visualise, however. A company, such as the hopefully fictional 'Murder, Inc', which exists solely for criminal purposes, should clearly be closed down even if it has yet to go beyond the stage of 'mere preparation' on its path to completing a substantive crime. Closure, albeit more likely temporary, may also be warranted when a company demonstrates bad faith in fulfilling the terms of a remedial order and an unwillingness to co-operate with probationary authorities. Although conviction for an endangerment offence will require a showing that the likelihood of a risk's materialising is substantial, within this general category there may be degrees of substantiality. In some cases harmful results may be virtually certain to follow a corporate decision, and may have been prevented only by the timely intervention of the police; in other cases harmful results may have been foreseeable, but less likely. Such nuances can be reflected in the sentence.

We have suggested that in some cases where the charge of a substantive offence may be technically warranted, a prosecutor might none the less decide to charge only the endangerment offence because, in the prosecutor's judgment, such a charge is more reflective of the company's culpability. If the evidence at trial suggests that this exercise of discretion was unwarranted, the deficit may be recaptured at the sentencing stage. The fact that, say, injuries or deaths have actually occurred may lead the sentencing judge to impose a punishment on the high end of the permitted range for the endangerment offence.

I.   CONCLUSIONS

We have seen that the justification for corporate crimes of endangerment is both similar to, yet different from, the case for having inchoate crimes against natural persons. The two situations are similar in that both are underpinned to an extent by a recognition that actual results may be affected by events, circumstances and fortuities beyond a defendant's control and that substantive offences defined in terms of result may distort the extent of a defendant's culpability. On the other hand, the most critical element in the prosecution of a natural person for attempt is proof of an intent to commit a specified crime. It is that intent that marks the human defendant as a danger to society, and which justifies his/her restraint and forced rehabilitation. In contrast, intent is not a particularly meaningful or relevant concept in regard to corporate inchoate offences. The fault element for companies is better captured by an objective test defined in terms of negligence, recklessness, gross negligence or wilful blindness. The purpose of early intervention is to prevent harm and to allow the reformation of business conditions, practices and cultures that pose unacceptable risks to innocent individuals. Indeed, because the dangers threatened by corporate endangerment may be on a far greater scale than that posed by natural persons who commit the same crime, we have argued in favour of earlier intervention that might be warranted in the case of natural persons.

No matter how intellectually satisfying it may be to construct a coherent scheme of criminal law offences, if the scheme fails to strike a chord with those responsible for its implementation and administration, it is likely to meet resistance. Will the proposed regime of endangerment offences be viewed by law enforcement officers as impractical and unrealistic? Will corporate executives see endangerment offences as simply regulatory legislation by another name, in which case the condemnation, censure and stigma normally attached to a criminal conviction may not materialise? Will the public agree? Only time will tell, but regulatory offences may have already lost a significant part of their credibility and value and, concomitantly, their ability to deter. A fresh start may be desirable, and the closer link between endangerment offences and the criminal justice system may cause them to be taken more seriously.

There is a related point, which has to do with the psychological processes whereby crimes come to be perceived as serious. A regime of substantive corporate crimes sends the message that corporate crime is 'real' crime. The creation of a further regime of endangerment offences will signify just how seriously the criminal justice system regards corporate crime. One can argue that the opposite phenomenon occurs with respect to current regulatory legislation, where compliance strategies and derisory penalties following the rare prosecution suggest to both companies and the public alike that these are technical and minor offences. The law on the books and the law as administered in practice can shape public attitudes as much as public attitudes can shape what laws are enacted and how criminal laws are perceived.

CHAPTER 5

Corporate crime in an era of globalisation

A. THE NATURE OF THE PROBLEM

In previous chapters we have examined the doctrinal bases on which companies can or should be held criminally liable for the injuries, damages and harms that they cause. We have looked at theories that would impute crimes of natural persons to companies, theories where the company would be liable as an accessory to an individual's crime, and theories based on a company's organisational fault in failing to prevent an offence that could have been averted had proper attention been paid to the risk. The latter conceptualisation of corporate criminality, which we would maintain offers the most promising means of tackling the problem of corporate crime, finds expression in the UK government's proposal for an offence of 'corporate killing' and in an Italian law addressed to corporate crimes directed at financial and property interests, both of which we examined in chapter 3. More controversially, perhaps, and less conventionally, we advanced in chapter 4 the idea of defining corporate crimes without regard to the occurrence of actual harm.

Any reformulation of the law along the lines suggested could well lead to an increase in the number of prosecutions of companies. No longer in America would the fact that responsibility for a criminal act could not be traced to an identifiable employee within a company potentially frustrate the company's prosecution; nor under English law would the fact that the person to whom responsibility could be traced was not sufficiently senior in the company's hierarchy to be 'identified' with the company be fatal to the prosecution's case. With their burden of proof thus eased, prosecutors might be less reluctant to bring criminal charges against companies, particularly in cases of high-profile 'disasters' where the media and public clamour for a prosecution of the offending company can be intense and sustained.

It is self-evident that the effects of any re-conceptualisation of corporate criminality will be felt only in those states that have chosen to modify their laws in this way. If the government's proposed offence of corporate killing were to be enacted, for example, it would cover corporate killings that occurred in England and Wales but not in other states. The point is trivial, but it does have ramifications. At the very time when Britain is gearing itself up to addressing the problem of companies that cause death within its borders, more and more multinational enterprises (MNEs)[1] are shifting the criminogenic and potentially lethal aspects of their business operation to foreign subsidiaries located in developing states[2] where, for reasons that will be examined subsequently, the criminal law tends not to be as rigorously enforced as it is in Britain.

When an MNE assigns parts of its operation to a foreign subsidiary, it may have more than one goal in mind. Nothing more sinister than the potential for a savings in labour costs may be its primary motivation. Wages in developing states will usually be lower than in industrialised (and probably unionised) states. Why pay the higher wages, reason the MNEs, particularly where the nature of the work does not require skilled labour? Regardless of the skill-level required, an MNE will usually be in a position to offer higher wages than local employers in the state of the subsidiary, while still keeping its own overall labour costs below what they would have been in its home state. Thus the MNE will be able to attract the most able workers in the country of the subsidiary. One benefit of establishing a global network is that, although products may need to be designed, developed and tested in industrialised countries, the products themselves can be manufactured in low-wage markets. By

---

1   The Guidelines of the Organisation for Economic Co-operation and Development (OECD) for Multinational Enterprises (adopted in June 2000) describe multinational enterprises as 'companies or other entities established in more than one country and so linked that they may co-coordinate their operations in various ways'. The Guidelines add that '[w]hile one or more of these entities may be able to exercise a significant influence over the activities of others, their degree of autonomy within the enterprise may vary widely…' Terminology in this area varies and such enterprises are also referred to as transnational companies (TNCs) or multinational companies (MNCs). Just as the government in its consultation paper on corporate killing prefers the term 'undertaking' to company, because of its broader connotations, we prefer 'enterprise' to company for similar reasons.

2   The terminology used to describe these states has changed with the times. Once referred to as 'third world' countries, human rights advocates prefer now to refer to them as 'southern' states. If a generic expression is required to describe these countries, we prefer that of developing states. This avoids the ambiguity of what it means to be a 'southern' state and the pejorative connotations of being a 'third world' country.

doing so, an MNE gains a competitive advantage over rivals who do not have the option of producing their goods in a state where the labour costs are lower.

Another reason why an MNE may decide to locate a subsidiary in a developing country may be a desire to limit its exposure to tort suits. In the United States, where the Alien Tort Claims Act (ATCA) allows for private claims for torts committed abroad by an MNE's subsidiaries, many of the suits have foundered on the plaintiff's inability to show the requisite connection to the US for jurisdictional purposes.[3] In the UK, the *Cape* litigation, with its ongoing lawsuits seeking to establish the appropriate forum for the trial of a British parent company for the tortious acts of its South African subsidiary, gave rise to complex legal questions relating to the proper application of the doctrine of forum non conveniens.[4] These cases illustrate the legal advantages to be gained by operating through a subsidiary in a developing country. In such countries, injured workers are less likely to be aware of their rights, the law of tort may not be as developed, procedural roadblocks may frustrate unrepresented plaintiffs, judges may not be sympathetic, and any damages that might ultimately be awarded may be far lower for both cultural and technical reasons than in the home state of the parent company. Damages may also prove much harder to collect.

A further impetus for locating a subsidiary in a developing country, one even less likely to be admitted although it will be the primary focus of our analysis, may be the perception that the prospect of criminal prosecutions, with their attendant costs and embarrassing potential for unfavourable publicity, is substantially lower in the developing country than it would be in the home state of the MNE. In many developing countries law enforcement is lax and public officials are not above accepting financial inducements (ie bribes) not to prosecute. By assigning to foreign subsidiaries those operational aspects of their business that are most likely to lead to a prosecution, MNEs may hope to put themselves beyond the jurisdiction of the criminal courts in their home states. This trend to shift dangerous and criminogenic aspects of an MNE's business to developing countries can only accelerate as the governments in those home states develop increasingly sophisticated laws for combating corporate criminality.

What is already clear is that modern corporate crime takes place against the backdrop of an increasingly global economy. The UN Committee on Economic, Social and Cultural Rights has identified some of the more important effects of globalisation:

> [G]lobalisation has come to be closely associated with a variety of specific trends and policies including an increasing reliance upon the free market, a significant growth in the influence of international financial markets and institutions in determining the viability of national policy priorities, a diminution in the role of the State and the size of its budget, the privatisation of various functions previously considered to be the exclusive domain of the State, the deregulation of a range of activities with a view to facilitating investments and rewarding individual initiative and corresponding increase in the role and even responsibilities attributed to private actors, both in the corporate sector, in particular to the transnational corporations, and in civil society.[5]

---

3   See eg *Doe v Unocal Corpn* 110 F Supp 2d 1294 (CD Cal 2000).
4   The relevant issues were finally decided by the House of Lords after many years of litigation: *Lubbe v Cape plc* [2000] 1 WLR 1545.
5   Statement on Globalisation and Economic, Social and Cultural Rights (adopted 11/5/98).

The phenomenon of globalisation has implications for social, economic, cultural, political and humanitarian interests. Our more narrow focus is on corporate criminal liability. In a global economy, an MNE will typically be registered or headquartered in one state while its subsidiaries are located throughout the world. When legally cognisant harm occurs at the site of one of these subsidiaries, questions will arise over whom to prosecute, where to prosecute, and for what crime. While the subsidiary at which the harm has occurred might seem the obvious candidate to proceed against, sometimes the harm-causing acts of the subsidiary can be traced to policy decisions of its parent company or a criminogenic culture had been fostered, encouraged or tolerated by the parent. The simple answer might seem to be to prosecute both parent and subsidiary in these circumstances, but jurisdictional hurdles may pose difficulties.

As to where to prosecute, there are three possibilities. The first and most obvious is the host state of the subsidiary. A second possible forum, particularly when the main objective is to address the world-wide, crime-conducive policies and practices of an MNE, is the home state of the MNE. A final possibility is some sort of international tribunal, such as the International Criminal Court, which came into effect on 1 July 2002, but which at present does not have jurisdiction over 'legal persons'.

In certain international and regional courts, such as the European Court of Human Rights, the legal action may proceed against a state, which will have to defend its actions or failure to take action to prevent the offence. States have a duty to protect their citizens against human rights violations by third parties subject to their control, and that includes violations by companies.

Choice of jurisdiction will depend on the nexus between forum and offence, the defendant to be put on trial, and what would have to be proved in order to establish the defendant's liability. The question of 'for what crime to prosecute' will thus have knock-on effects for the questions of whom to prosecute and where.

It is not our contention that MNEs commit more crimes or more serious crimes than do domestic companies. Rather, our point is that, when an MNE does commit a serious crime through a foreign subsidiary, holding it legally accountable poses more complex problems than when the parent company or a domestic subsidiary commits the offence in its home state. The prototypical situation that we shall be addressing in this chapter is that of where a corporate subsidiary located in one state (conventionally referred to as the host state) of an MNE headquartered or registered in another state (conventionally referred to as the home state) *appears to have committed* a criminal offence in the host state. The italicised language is used because, as we shall argue, what might appear to be the crime of the subsidiary may in fact be the crime of the parent company. In these cases the domestic criminal laws of both host and home state need to be considered, as well as applicable international legal standards. Not only may the subsidiary be criminally liable but also the parent company and, in an international forum, a state that may have colluded with or turned a blind eye to the offence.

Much of the 'international' caselaw has developed in the context of 'human rights' abuses, but there is no inconsistency in being the victim of a criminal offence and having one's human rights violated. For example, it would seem clear that if workers were to be randomly shot by members of a state's police, the right to life of the victims will have been infringed by the state. This fact will not preclude – quite the opposite – a prosecution for murder of those who actually killed the workers. The more thorny issue is whether this same analysis holds when it is not the police, but rather members of a company's private security forces, who kill the victims. Human rights law was originally developed to protect individuals against abuses by *states* and *state actors*. Given that a company is not a state, can it be prosecuted for infringing an individual's human rights? The desire to give an affirmative answer stems from the fact that many companies, and in particular MNEs, are economically more powerful and more capable of affecting the lives and the quality of life of those who work for them than are some states (see Rugman: 2001).

Some might see the analogy between multinational enterprises and states, for the purpose of holding MNEs responsible for human rights violations, as being somewhat strained. A more direct path to corporate criminal liability for human rights violations can be found in the law of some states, most notably South Africa. Under the South African Constitution (1996) chapter 2, s 8 natural persons, as well as the state, have an obligation not to violate an individual's human rights. Under South African law, moreover, a company is a juristic person, which simply means that, for the purposes of the criminal law, it can be prosecuted for a criminal offence to the same extent as a natural person. Treating companies as 'persons' for the purpose of the criminal law is not that uncommon, but what separates South Africa from most other countries is the fact that a natural person is subject to criminal liability for a human rights violation. A logical chain of reasoning suggests, therefore, that in South Africa it would also be possible for a company to be prosecuted for a human rights violation. This represents a sharp break from conventional thinking that holds that only states or state actors can commit human rights violations. Further, if parent companies were to be held legally responsible for crimes committed by their subsidiaries, as we shall argue, it should be possible for a parent company to be prosecuted for a human rights violation committed by the subsidiary.

South Africa may be unique in allowing prosecution of companies for human rights violations in their domestic criminal courts. Where this is not possible, resort to an international forum of some description may be required. However, the fact that MNEs operate across state boundaries, whereas jurisdiction for criminal offences is typically territorially based, fuels the case for an international forum in which MNEs can be held to account. In some instances of corporate human rights abuses, moreover, the company will have colluded with the state. It would seem somewhat anomalous, at least as a matter of principle, that the state but not the company can be held accountable for the human rights offence.

B. LIABILITY OF A PARENT COMPANY FOR CRIMES OF ITS SUBSIDIARIES

Whether or not to prosecute a parent company for criminal harm that is caused by or occurs at one of its subsidiaries requires an analysis of both the relationship between parent and subsidiary, and the connection of each to the offence. As a practical matter, the ability of the prosecuting state to acquire jurisdiction over the parent or the subsidiary will affect the decision as to whom to charge. We shall assume that, at a minimum, the host state of the subsidiary has jurisdiction to try the subsidiary and the home state of the parent has jurisdiction to try the parent.

The case for prosecuting the subsidiary is fairly straightforward. It, or its employees, officers or agents, is likely to be the *direct* cause of any criminal harm that occurs in the host state. Should the parent of the subsidiary also be criminally liable, however?

One possibility would be to hold the parent company vicariously liable for the offences of its subsidiary. The parent could also be charged as an accessory if it encouraged, aided, abetted, procured, counselled, facilitated or otherwise contributed in a significant way to the offence in question. Might the parent also be liable if it authorised the subsidiary to engage in activities that it was aware, or should have been aware, posed an unacceptably high risk of illegality, or if it tolerated illegality in its overall operation?

For many reasons parent companies would prefer that any prosecution be restricted to the subsidiary. First, the prosecution would be brought in the host state of the subsidiary, whose laws, procedures and judges might be more favourable to corporate interests than those in the home state of the parent. Second, the prosecutors and investigatory personnel in the host state might be more amenable to persuasion (or even bribes) not to pursue the prosecution than their counterparts in the home state. Third, if the subsidiary were to be convicted, the ensuing punishment would apply only to it. As the typical penalty imposed on a convicted company is a fine, and as the amount of the fine will usually be limited by the assets of the defendant, the far greater assets of the parent company (and other members of the corporate group) could not be looked to in the calculation of the fine or to its satisfaction. Fourth, any remedial order issued by the sentencing court would apply only to the subsidiary and not to all of the other companies affiliated with the MNE. Finally, the parent company would be less likely to find itself the victim of embarrassing publicity, with the concomitant damage to its reputation, when the trial is in the host state of the subsidiary. The media scrum in a developing state will almost certainly be smaller in size and less zealous in its coverage than in the more developed and, in all likelihood, more media conscious home state of the parent. In some developing countries, it is not unknown for reporters to be subjected to government censorship and even intimidation.

I.   Vicarious liability

Whether a parent company should be vicariously liable for the crimes of a subsidiary will depend in part on the view of vicarious liability taken in the jurisdiction. We saw in Chapter 2 that, with respect to a company's criminal responsibility for offences committed by its *employees*, the English courts have not been particularly receptive to the doctrine of vicarious liability.[6] It is even less likely that the courts will be receptive to the doctrine in the more novel context of parent companies and their subsidiaries. However, the policy dynamics of the two situations are different. The practical burden on an MNE of policing its subsidiaries may not be as onerous as that involved in policing its workforce. Subsidiaries also may be less inclined than employees to ignore policies set by parent companies, and the task of supervision will be eased by the fact that subsidiaries can be required to file regular reports with their home office, thereby increasing the transparency of their operations and facilitating the detection of any deviations from policies designed to prevent wrongdoing.

6   See *Seaboard Offshore Ltd v Secretary of State for Transport* [1994] 1 WLR 541. As discussed previously, in the United States vicarious liability is a common basis for holding companies criminally liable.

If a prosecutor claims that a parent company should be vicariously liable for an offence committed by a subsidiary, the parent is likely to counter that it and the alleged subsidiary were separate entities and that therefore it bears no responsibility for the subsidiary's actions or offences. Determining whether a parent company and its subsidiary are in fact separate entities may require a prosecutor to unravel complex inter-firm arrangements, both written and oral, and both explicit and implicit. Familiarity with the world of business, however, cautions against uncritical acceptance of a parent's disavowal of responsibility. In practice, the profits of a subsidiary typically inure to the benefit of the parent and, conversely, the losses of the subsidiary will ultimately be borne by the parent. These considerations suggest that the parent is likely to have reserved to itself a residual power to intervene in the subsidiary's operations.

In the field of competition law, the Euoprean Court of Justice applies an 'economic unit' test. As the court explained in the *Centrafarm* case,[7] the critical issue is whether the undertakings form an 'economic unit' such that the subsidiary 'has no real freedom to determine its course of action on the market, and if the agreements or practices are concerned merely with the internal allocation of tasks as between undertakings'. In *Istituto Chemioterapico Italiano SpA and Commercial Solvents Corpn v Commission*, the presumption that a subsidiary would act in accord with the wishes of its parent was held to be justified on the empirical basis that 'according to common experience they generally do so act'.[8]

The adoption of an 'economic unit' test constitutes a beginning rather than an end to the challenge facing a court. Each case needs to be examined on its individual facts and circumstances in order to determine the degree of control that the parent wields, or, more importantly, has the power to wield, over the subsidiary. The relationship between a parent and its subsidiary, and the degree of integration, can vary considerably, as the OECD Guidelines for Multinational Enterprises make clear (2000: 35):

> [A] foreign subsidiary may be seen as having relatively little autonomy if it belongs to a large multinational group established in many foreign countries; if it manufactures fairly standardised products; if the activities of the members are largely integrated, with important interflows of products between them...; if it has been created to serve a market larger than the country in which it is established; or if the parent company holds a large portion of the equity. On the other hand, a subsidiary may be seen as more autonomous if it was acquired to serve mainly the local market; if it belongs to a small group; if it has interchange of products with the rest of the group and is operating in an activity slightly different from that of other members...; if an important part of its common shares is held by local investors; and if the whole concern pursues a growth strategy.

Muchlinski (2001b: 10) identifies other relevant considerations:

> The nationality and resulting business culture of the parent...; the age of the subsidiary, in that centralisation may decrease over time; the method of entry into the host State, in that a new establishment may be more closely controlled than an acquired local company; the industrial sector in which the firm operates, in that some industries will be more globally integrated and centralised than others; the performance of the subsidiary, in that poor performance increases central control; and the tendency of geographically organised MNEs to be less centralised than functional, product or matrix-organised firms.

7   *Centrafarm BV and Adriaan de Peijper v Sterling Drug Inc* [1974] ECR 1147.
8   [1974] ECR 223 at 264.

The wide range of factors to be considered resists reduction to any formulaic test of a subsidiary's degree of interdependence with its parent. The weaker the operational autonomy and independence of the subsidiary, the stronger the case for holding the parent vicariously liable for its criminal offences.

What should be critical to the analysis should be the reality of the relationship between parent and subsidiary and not the technical legal form that it takes. Instead of focusing on the reality, however, the English courts have allowed legal form to control their decisions. In *Adams v Cape Industries plc*[9] the Court of Appeal refused to lift the 'corporate veil' in order to allow a judgment obtained against an American subsidiary of an English parent company to be enforced against the parent in England. The evidence indicated not only that the subsidiary was wholly owned by the parent, but also that it had been created in part to disguise the role of the parent in the overall operation, and to reduce the parent's exposure to legal liability in tort actions. The Court of Appeal did not dispute this evidence, but rather cited the mantra that each company in a group is presumed to be a separate and independent legal entity. The Court was not prepared to lift the 'corporate veil' in order to discover the reality of the relationship:

> [W]e do not accept as a matter of law that the court is entitled to lift the corporate veil as against a defendant company which is the member of a corporate group merely because the corporate structure has been used so as to ensure that the legal liability (if any) in respect of particular future activities of the group (and correspondingly the risk of enforcement of that liability) will fall on another member of the group rather than the defendant company. Whether or not this is desirable, the right to use a corporate structure in this manner is inherent in our corporate law. Counsel for the plaintiffs urged on us that the purpose of the operation was in substance that Cape would have the practical benefit of the group's asbestos trade in the United States, without the risks of tortious liability. This may be so. However, in our judgment, Cape was in law entitled to organise the group's affairs in that manner and ... to expect that the court would apply the principle of *Salomon v Salomon & Co Ltd* [1897] AC 22 in the ordinary way.[10]

If a parent company can create a subsidiary in order to avoid tort liability, can it create a subsidiary in order to avoid criminal liability? One point repeatedly made by the court in *Cape* was the fact that, while Cape's efforts to avoid tort liability may not have been admirable, they were also not illegal. Obviously, this would not be the case if the subsidiary's acts constituted a crime. Equally obviously, one cannot ordinarily escape criminal liability by ordering another to commit one's offence. While we shall argue in the following section that a parent company should be liable if it is an accessory to the crime of its subsidiary, if a court follows *Cape* and refuses to lift the corporate veil, it may prove difficult to establish the requisite principal-accessory relationship.

2.   Complicity

Neither the mere existence of a parent-subsidiary relationship nor the fact that the parent was responsible for creating the subsidiary should , without more, constitute

---

9 [1990] BCLC 479.
10 [1990] BCLC 479 at 520.

sufficient encouragement or assistance to render the parent liable for an offence of the subsidiary. The 'more' that would need to be shown is that the parent has done something culpable: either it has been at fault in its own right (which will be examined with respect to prosecutions in the parent's home state) or it was an accessory to the subsidiary's offence or it entered into a conspiracy with the subsidiary to commit the offence.

As a general proposition, one who encourages, aids, abets, counsels, procures, facilitates or otherwise significantly contributes to the commission of a criminal offence of another may be liable as an accessory to the offence of the principal.[11] An accessory, as we have noted previously, is generally subject to prosecution and conviction for the same offences as the principal, and to the same potential range of sanctions. Although there is little precedent for applying principles of complicity to corporate parents and their subsidiaries, this is probably attributable to the embryonic state of the law of corporate crime. It makes little sense to inquire into whether one company is an accessory to the crime of another company as long as there is no agreement on what it means to say that a company has committed a crime. If this hurdle were to be surmounted, however, there would seem to be no reason why the law of complicity could not be applied in a parent-subsidiary context. What is critical to complicity is the relationship between the principal and the accessory, not whether the two parties are legal, as opposed to natural, persons.

Cases have recognised that a failure to exercise control, when one has both a right of control and a duty to control, can constitute sufficient aid or encouragement to render a defendant liable as an accessory. In *Du Cros v Lambourne*,[12] for example, the owner of a car was held liable as an accessory when a third party drove his car in a prohibited manner. The fact that the defendant was a passenger at the time was not determinative of his criminal liability, but rather the fact that he had the power *and* the duty to control the actions of the driver. Whether or not a parent company has comparable control over a subsidiary will depend on the relationship between parent and subsidiary, the power that the parent has to direct the subsidiary, and how that power is exercised in practice (both with respect to the setting of general policy and day-to-day operational decisions). Whether or not a parent company actually involves itself in the management of a subsidiary may not be as critical as whether the parent has the authority to involve itself in the subsidiary's management. If it does, and if illegal actions are foreseeable and preventable, and the parent company does nothing to prevent the illegality, it may be liable as an accessory. And of course if the parent actively encourages or assists the violation, or benefits from it, the case for liability is strengthened.

The extent to which a parent will become involved in the subsidiary's operation will to some extent depend on the activity in question. For example, parent companies will routinely determine such matters as the products that a subsidiary manufactures and the means of production. On the other hand, the subsidiary may enjoy considerable autonomy in hiring and firing decisions. In a case where a worker died as a result of the gross negligence of a fellow worker, the parent company might be complicit if the death was attributable to its failure to provide appropriate direction on health and safety matters, but the subsidiary might be solely liable if it was grossly negligent in hiring or supervising the employee who caused the death. Of course, if the system of supervision had been dictated by the parent, and was shown

---

11 See eg in England, Accessories and Abettors Act 1861.
12 [1907] 1 KB 40.

to be grossly deficient, then the parent might be held to be an accessory to the crime of the worker or that of the subsidiary.

In some instances a right of control can give rise to a duty to control (Wilson 1998: 588). Where, for instance, an alleged accessory retains ownership or control of the property used by the principal, it may have a duty to ensure that the property is not used in an illegal manner. In *Tuck v Robson*,[13] a licensee of a public house was held liable when he failed to prevent after-hour's drinking by the pub's customers. A parent company is likely to retain ownership, or at least control, over the property of the subsidiary. Liability as an accessory can also be premised on supplying the means used to perpetrate a crime, such as occurs when one supplies burglary tools to a burglar, knowing of his illegal purpose.[14] Say that a pharmaceutical company supplies its subsidiary with inadequately tested drugs, knowing that the subsidiary will in turn sell the drugs to the public. If the parent fails to provide adequate information regarding the status of the drugs, it might be liable, even if the subsidiary, because of its lack of awareness of any deficiencies, might be able to escape conviction.

3.   Conspiracy

At common law a conspiracy was defined as an agreement between two or more persons to do an unlawful act, or to do a lawful act by unlawful means, although, now, under the Criminal Law Act 1977, the object of the conspiracy must itself be illegal. In respect of the parties to a conspiracy, the key question is whether a parent company can conspire with one of its subsidiaries. We have seen that, when a parent company is sought to be held *vicariously* liable for the offence of its subsidiary, it will frequently argue that it and the subsidiary were separate entities. While acceptance of this argument may defeat vicarious liability, it will have the opposite effect if the parent and subsidiary are also alleged to have entered into a criminal conspiracy. It takes two to conspire, and, under the 'identification' test of corporate liability, which equates a company's directors and officers with the company, it follows that a director or officer cannot conspire with his/her own company.[15] The director/officer and the company are deemed in law to be a single unit. However, in *R v ICR Haulage*[16] the Divisional Court held that a director, or, indeed, a company, could conspire with *another* company. If a parent and its subsidiary were to be deemed separate companies, there would be no legal obstacle to finding that they had entered into a conspiracy.

The actus reus of a conspiracy is an agreement, which need not be explicit but can be inferred. Often an agreement is inferred from a combination of a common purpose, circumstances which indicate an opportunity to agree and subsequent co-ordinated conduct. Applying these factors to a parent and its subsidiary, it is clear that the two will share common goals. Proof that the two companies will have communicated is also not likely to be difficult. As a parent will receive regular reports from the subsidiary, it will be aware of what the subsidiary is doing, or at least be in a position to inform itself of what the subsidiary is doing. On the other hand, proving that the agreement

13 [1970] 1 WLR 741.
14 See eg *R v Bainbridge* [1960] 1 QB 129.
15 *R v McDonnell* [1966] 1 QB 233.
16 [1944] KB 551.

was to commit a criminal offence (or, in the language of the Criminal Law Act 1977, that a 'course of conduct will be pursued which ... will necessarily amount to or involve the commission of any offence or offences') may be more difficult; but if the illegality of the subsidiary was foreseeable, the fact-finder could also infer that the parent knew or was aware of it. As we have argued previously with respect to crimes by a company's workforce, if the company encourages a criminogenic culture or tolerates a criminogenic ethos, it should be liable for the resulting crimes. In the case of a parent or subsidiary, the same is true, but the greater likelihood of formal communication between the two entities, compared to that which typically occurs between a company and its workers, is suggestive of an express or implied agreement and a conspiratorial relationship.

While we have maintained throughout that corporate criminal liability should be based on fault, we have also argued that in giving effect to the fault principle, it would not be violation of a company's rights to allow due diligence as a defence *and* to place the burden of proof with respect to due diligence on the corporate defendant. This defence of due diligence should also be available to a parent company that has been charged as an accessory to the crime of one of its subsidiaries or with having entered into a conspiracy with the subsidiary. If a parent company can demonstrate that it has acted reasonably and responsibly to prevent its subsidiary from committing criminal offences, then it should be entitled to a defence of due diligence.

In summing up this section of the chapter, one can envisage a spectrum of criminal liability with respect to parent companies and their subsidiaries. At one extreme, a subsidiary might be found to have such a degree of autonomy that it will be deemed an independent actor bearing sole responsibility for its criminal offences. In the middle of our spectrum, both subsidiary and parent might be held liable for the *same* offence, the subsidiary as principal and the parent either vicariously, or as an accessory or a co-conspirator. Alternatively, both parent and subsidiary might be criminally liable but for *different* offences, the subsidiary for the substantive offence and the parent for a culpable failure to prevent the substantive offence when it was under a legal obligation to do so. Finally, the parent, but not the subsidiary, might be liable if it could be shown that it used the subsidiary as an innocent agent through which to achieve its criminal objectives.

C.   PROSECUTIONS IN THE HOST STATE OF THE SUBSIDIARY

Once the determination of whom to prosecute (parent or subsidiary) is made, the question of where to bring the prosecution must be faced. The issue is that of jurisdiction. When a crime occurs in the host state of a subsidiary, a court in that state would seem to be the most appropriate forum in which to bring the prosecution. The actus reus of the crime will have been committed in that state (although, as we shall argue in a subsequent section, an actus reus may also have been committed in the home state of the parent) and any resulting harm will most likely have been experienced in the host state. In theory, as it will be its laws that have been violated and its citizens who will have been the victims, the host state should have the strongest interest in seeing that justice is done. Territorial jurisdiction, the most widely accepted and common basis of jurisdiction, will clearly lie in this state, regardless of whether it might lie elsewhere as well.

Practical considerations reinforce this choice of forum. It will be in the host state that victims, witnesses and evidence are most likely to be found. If the criminal trial were to be held in some other state, the inconvenience and expense involved in bringing witnesses to the trial could be prohibitive. Witnesses might decline to attend for legitimate as well as for tactical reasons, and their attendance might not be able to be compelled. Witnesses who did testify might not understand the language of the country of trial, and while interpreters could be employed, they are often an inadequate substitute: literal translations may fail to capture the flavour or subtleties of the points that the witness is trying to convey, while deviations from the literal may put words in the witness's mouth with which the witness would not concur.

I.   Prosecuting a parent company, its directors and its officers in the host state

To prosecute a subsidiary, when a management decision of its parent or a culture tolerant of illegality that has been fostered by the parent has led to the crime in question, may serve only to make the subsidiary the scapegoat for an offence more properly attributed to the parent. However, to prosecute a parent company registered or headquartered in another state will usually require that the host state of the subsidiary acquire jurisdiction over the parent company. The mere presence of the subsidiary in the host state will not give it jurisdiction over a parent that is located in another state. When the parent company is not formally represented in the state, it would have to be extradited, but there is no precedent in international law for extraditing legal, as opposed to natural, persons, and the conceptual basis on which such an extradition could be effected is not at all clear. Whereas extradition normally entails the physical transfer of a natural person from one jurisdiction to another, a company could not be physically transferred from one state to another. However, if the theory of the prosecution is that the parent is liable under an 'identification' test of corporate liability for offences committed by its directors/officers, then by charging these individuals in addition to their company, the individuals in question would be subject to extradition. Inclusion of directors and officers among the defendants would also be tactically advantageous, as it would allow the prosecuting state to take the statements of these individuals. Furthermore, if evidence is contained in documents that are located in the home office of the parent, these defendants might, depending upon the laws of the host and home states, be ordered to produce the documents. In the absence of jurisdiction over the parent company, obtaining discovery of such documents could prove problematic.[17]

Extraditing corporate officers and directors is not without its own difficulties, as Gilbert (1994) makes clear. First, there would have to be an extradition treaty between the host state of the subsidiary and the state in which the directors and officers were to be found. Second, the offence charged would have to be one that was covered by the treaty. Some extradition treaties take an 'enumerative' approach, wherein the treaty lists all offences that are subject to extradition, while others take an 'eliminative' approach, where all crimes whose penalty exceeds a specified minimum are extraditable. In the corporate crime context, where new statutory offences are

---

17 See *Lonrho v Shell Petroleum Co Ltd* [1980] 1 WLR 627.

common, and unlikely to have been included in an extradition treaty of long-standing, the eliminative approach is more likely to result in extradition than the enumerative approach. A third hurdle is that some civil law states will simply refuse to extradite their own nationals.

Perhaps the most difficult obstacle to overcome will be that of 'double criminality'. This principle provides that an individual should not be subject to extradition unless his/her acts are criminal in both the state requesting extradition and the state from which extradition is requested; in other words, there need to be corresponding offences in the two states who are parties in the extradition proceedings. The proper basis for determining whether such correspondence exists has often exercised the courts. Some look to whether or not there are offences in each jurisdiction bearing the same name or definition; others to whether or not there are offences that, although bearing different names, consist of the same elements;[18] and still others to whether there are substantially similar offences in the two jurisdictions. The danger to be avoided is identified by the court in *Riley v Commonwealth of Australia*:[19]

> [T]he utility of the principle of double criminality is... likely to be outweighed by the impediment which it represents to the advancement of criminal justice if its content is defined in over-technical terms which would preclude extradition by reason of technical differences between legal systems, notwithstanding that the acts alleged against the accused involve serious criminality under the laws of both the requesting and the requested states.[20]

The *Riley* court opted for a test of double criminality which turned on whether 'the acts in respect of which extradition is sought are criminal under both systems even if the relevant offences have different names and elements'. This more liberal approach would be especially helpful in an area such as corporate criminality where the law is in a state of evolution and there is no uniform approach among those states that have seen fit to criminalise corporate wrongdoing.

A state that has received an extradition request need not honour the request if it does not recognise the requesting state's basis of jurisdiction. Most states adhere to a 'territorial test', under which jurisdiction is based on the fact that the offence was wholly or partially committed within the boundaries of the state, although some states will claim territorial jurisdiction if the effects of the crime are felt in its territory. Under a strict territorial test, a state will lack jurisdiction when the defendant's alleged actus reus occurred outside of the state. Where a host state seeks to extradite directors and officers of an MNE who may never have set foot within their territory, it will experience obvious difficulty in identifying criminal acts that these individuals have committed within the state.

This issue of where a corporate crime is committed lies at the heart of holding MNEs accountable for criminal harms that occur in the state of a subsidiary. MNEs are able to evade criminal liability by tailoring their argument against jurisdiction to the state which is seeking to assert jurisdiction. When the host state of the subsidiary where the harm occurs claims jurisdiction, the MNE will argue that whatever *criminal acts* may have been committed by it or its officer/directors took place in its home state, not in the host state. On the other hand, when the home state

18 See *The State (Furlong) v Kelly* [1971] IR 132.
19 (1985) 159 CLR 1.
20 (1985) 159 CLR 1.

of the MNE claims jurisdiction, the MNE will argue that the offence took place in the host state where the *resulting harm was experienced*. Taken separately, each of these arguments has a certain plausibility; taken together, they add up to a formula whereby MNEs may be able to escape all legal responsibility for their offences.

Other avenues, however, may be available to a state to secure jurisdiction over an MNE or its directors and officers. Some civil law states claim jurisdiction to try their own nationals, regardless of where their offences are committed. This 'active personality' principle will probably not be of great benefit to a host state, however, as the MNE will typically be registered or have its headquarters elsewhere, and its officers and directors are unlikely to be nationals of the host state. On the other hand, if the home state of the MNE refuses to take action, a host state may claim jurisdiction based on the 'representational principle'. This principle allows one state to assert jurisdiction where another state, which might have a superior claim to jurisdiction, declines to prosecute. It is not clear, however, whether invocation of the 'representational principle' will necessarily advance the cause of a host state, as extradition would still be required, and the home state of the MNE may be no more receptive to a request for extradition than it is to prosecuting the company or the corporate executives whose extradition is sought.

The 'active personality' principle gives states jurisdiction to try their own nationals for crimes that they commit abroad. Some states, however, have adopted a 'passive personality' principle under which claims to jurisdiction are based on the fact that the *victim* is a citizen of the state seeking extradition. While what is critical under the 'active personality' principle is the nationality of the *defendant*, what is critical under the 'passive personality' principle is the nationality of the *victim*. The 'passive personality' principle, however, has generally not been well received in international law. As a state to which an extradition request has been made may refuse the request where it does not recognise the basis of jurisdiction of the requesting state, the fact that a requesting state has adopted the 'passive personality' principle will not be of any advantage to it if the state to which the extradition request has been made does not accept the principle's validity.

A similar rationale to that which underlies the 'passive personality' principle can be found in the 'protective principle', which has found broader acceptance in international law. Under the protective principle a state may claim jurisdiction over defendants whose acts affect or threaten to affect the vital interests of the state. Unlike under the territorial principle, an element of the offence need not have been committed in the state requesting extradition; the requesting state simply has to establish a link between the criminal acts of the persons whom it is seeking to extradite and effects experienced or likely to be experienced in the requesting state.[21] By way of example, consider the case where directors/officers at the head office of an MNE decide to deploy workers at a foreign subsidiary in ultra-hazardous activities without proper safety equipment. The directors/officers are aware that the activities are quite likely to lead to serious injury or loss of life. If these effects were to materialise in the host state of the subsidiary, its claim to jurisdiction could be based on ordinary principles of territoriality. But what if, fortuitously, no worker is injured? The host state might still wish to prosecute the parent company for an endangerment

---

21 See *The Steamship Lotus (France v Turkey)*, PCIJ Rep Series A, No 10, 1927.

offence (see chapter 4) and resort to the protective principle might be necessary in order to acquire jurisdiction over the MNE.

As the preceding discussion indicates, the hurdles facing a state which wishes to extradite an MNE and/or its directors and officers are not inconsiderable. Extradition proceedings can raise arcane points of law, and may be vigorously contested, time-consuming, and expensive. Given these deterrents to pressing a claim of extradition, and with no guarantee of a conviction even if it were to obtain jurisdiction over an MNE or its directors and officers, a host state in which harm has been experienced may decide to vindicate its interests, assuming it were so minded, by prosecuting the subsidiary and its officers, over whom it clearly has jurisdiction.

2   Prosecuting the subsidiary in the host state

In contrast to the case where a host state seeks to put a foreign parent company on trial, there are few problems in asserting territorial jurisdiction over the wrongdoing subsidiary in the state in which it is located. The bigger question is whether there exists the political will to pursue a criminal prosecution. In virtually all states, the decision as to whether or not to bring criminal charges rests with a state official, usually a state prosecutor although sometimes a regulatory agency or the police themselves. Whatever the relevant official decides, his/her discretion is unlikely to be subject to legal challenge. Although some state statutes permit ordinary citizens to bring private prosecutions, the consent of a state official may be a precondition to the filing of the private prosecution. Thus, as a practical matter, if host state officials are not prepared to prosecute the subsidiary, no criminal trial is likely to eventuate.

But why would a host state not want to vindicate the rights of its citizens who have been the victims of a corporate crime? The answer is that in the modern global economy the pursuit of justice often takes a back seat to more parochial economic concerns. MNEs are wealthy, while developing countries are poor, with unemployment often rampant. These countries welcome the employment opportunities that will be created by a decision of an MNE to locate its subsidiary in the state. In addition to reducing unemployment and consequently elevating the standard of living in the host state, both the subsidiary and its employees would be paying taxes in the host state, which would also be of obvious benefit to its economy. Without belabouring the point, it is clear that the advantages of attracting an MNE to locate a subsidiary within a country's territorial borders can be considerable. As a consequence, the competition among developing states to attract MNEs can be intense. One bargaining chip in the negotiations may be the extent to which a prospective host state is prepared to offer the MNE relative impunity from legal liability. Although the state may not be able to prevent civil suits against corporate tortfeasors (although it can place procedural hurdles in the path of such suits or limit the size of damage awards), criminal prosecutions will, as already noted, usually lie within the government's discretion. In its negotiations with an MNE, a developing state may indicate that it will be prepared to exercise this discretion with restraint.[22]

---

22 It might be observed that similar considerations may influence a host state not to initiate extradition proceedings against directors/officers of the MNE, the issue discussed in the previous subsection.

As a formal written agreement to this effect might prove embarrassing if made public, any accord is more likely to take the form of an unwritten understanding.

Sometimes a poor host state will offer an MNE virtual impunity from criminal prosecution to attract its subsidiaries; on other occasions a powerful MNE will exploit its superior bargaining position to extract this concession. Often, however, such an understanding is seen to be mutually advantageous. The host state gains the financial benefits of having the subsidiary in its country, while avoiding the expense of having to police the subsidiary, while the MNE does not have to fear potentially embarrassing criminal prosecutions. The primary victims of this collusive arrangement will be the workforce of the subsidiary and members of the public who may suffer harm as a result of the subsidiary's ability to ignore the criminal laws of the jurisdiction. A practical illustration would occur where an MNE wishes to suppress protests at its subsidiary's plant, but the host state does not wish to commit its limited police force to maintaining order at the plant. Both parties would find it beneficial to agree to allow the MNE to employ its own private security force to police the plants. As they would not be bound by the same professional constraints as the state's police, the private security officers might be prepared to exceed the limits of what would constitute proper police authority. If state officials were to turn a blind eye to these excesses, the security guards could literally get away with murder, as an Amnesty International report (1996) alleges occurred in Nigeria when Royal Dutch Shell was allowed to employ a paramilitary unit to protect its local installations. Conflicts of interest can also arise when MNEs contribute to or pay the salaries of state police, as allegedly did BP in Colombia and the Dabhol Power Company (a joint venture of Enron, General Electric and Bechtel) in India (Kamminga: 1999). It would hardly be surprising if the police were to exercise restraint in enforcing the criminal law against the companies upon whom they were dependent for their wages.

Even in the absence of a formal or informal agreement between a state and an MNE, officials in a host state may be reluctant to enforce the criminal laws of the state against the MNE's subsidiary. The costs in bringing prosecutions aside, state officials will have to weigh the economic loss that could be incurred if an MNE which perceived itself to be the victim of state harassment were to decide to relocate its subsidiary in a less hostile environment.[23] They must also weigh the long-term costs should their state acquire a reputation for being hostile to business interests: might not other MNEs take this into consideration in deciding where to locate their subsidiaries? Thus, both out of fear of provoking relocations and in order not to discourage future investment, a host state may not see it in its self-interest to enforce its criminal laws against subsidiaries of MNEs.

The history of Bhopal makes for interesting reading, revealing the complexities and mixed motives that can affect a state's actions. Following the disaster, surviving victims and the families of those who had died brought suit against both the Indian government and the Union Carbide Corporation (UCC) in a United States federal court. However, it was fairly obvious that the plaintiffs were interested in an out-of-court settlement in order to avoid the delays of litigation that would have meant prolonged waiting for the victims and relatives. In an effort to expedite matters, the Indian government, despite the fact that it was a defendant in the original action, a

---

23 The threat of relocation can often be exaggerated, however, for the costs involved in closing one plant and opening another may be prohibitive. See Robinson (2001).

shareholder in Union Carbide India Limited (UCIL) and in part responsible for the rules of industrial regulation, enacted special legislation appointing itself as the sole representative of the victims. Meanwhile, the United States Court of Appeals held that India was the more appropriate forum to hear the civil claims and dismissed the suits that had been filed in America.[24] At this point the Indian government proceeded to negotiate a settlement with UCC. As part of the settlement, the government agreed to drop all civil *and* criminal actions against the corporation. According to Shrivastava (1987) and Jones (1988), the Indian government simply lacked the fortitude to take on Union Carbide and its army of lawyers in either the civil courts in the United States or in the civil or criminal courts in India (Fortun: 2001). If a country as prominent and powerful as India, which has always taken a strong stand on curbing the powers of MNEs, can find itself so compromised, what must be the position of far less developed countries?

In the final analysis, a host state cannot be compelled to initiate a prosecution against an MNE or its subsidiary. Where a host state indicates – expressly, impliedly, by word or action – that it is not committed to prosecuting companies that break its laws, then MNEs are not going to take the laws of that state seriously. Without the threat of criminal sanction, the incentive to obey a host state's laws will have to be self-generated, and even a company that was so inclined may not see it to be in the company's self-interest to do so if its competitors are flouting the law. Victims' interests, as well as those of the public, will also go unvindicated unless a state's laws are enforced and corporate violators prosecuted. If a host state is unwilling to protect its citizens from corporate abuses, then it is necessary to search either for a means of forcing the state to fulfil its obligations or to find an alternative legal forum in which corporate violators can be brought to justice.

D.   PROSECUTIONS IN AN INTERNATIONAL FORUM

To the extent that modern commerce takes place in a global market, the legal controversies that are an offshoot of globalisation may need to be resolved in an international forum. Increasingly, one sees resort to international tribunals to resolve contractual and other disputes between MNEs. Questions regarding the criminal liability of MNEs likewise have transnational implications. Where the policies of an MNE located in one state give rise to criminal violations by a subsidiary in another, the question of where a prosecution should be brought and whose law should apply may be of critical importance. Where an MNE's policies are replicated throughout the world, a uniform legal approach is desirable. Otherwise, the MNE will simply transfer the criminogenic aspects of their business operation to those states where the prospect of a conviction is perceived to be least likely. That host states may be reluctant to take legal action against MNEs only serves to reinforce the need for an international forum where criminal charges can be brought and common standards applied.

In the first subsection below, we examine the extent to which companies are subject to international law and the prospects for creating an international forum in which companies can be prosecuted for their criminal offences. In the second

---

24 See *Re Union Carbide Corpn Gas Plant Disaster at Bhopal, India in December 1984*, 809 F 2d 195 (2d Cir 1987).

subsection we shall shift our attention to states that have failed to enact or enforce laws that would have prevented corporate criminal violations and ask whether such states can themselves be proceeded against in an international forum. There is in fact, under existing precedent, a greater potential for holding states accountable in an international forum for human rights violations by companies than there is for direct action against the corporate offenders.

1.   Prosecuting an MNE or its subsidiary in an international criminal forum

We have seen that host states are reluctant to prosecute MNEs and their subsidiaries, for fear of undermining their competitive position in preserving existing, and attracting future, commercial investment. One way to counteract the pressures, whether external or self-induced, to which a host state might be subjected to ignore an MNE's criminal violations would be if such offences could be referred to an international tribunal. An internationalised approach also commends itself because of the absence of agreed standards of conduct in the various states in which MNEs operate. In an international forum, internationally accepted norms could be developed and applied, thereby creating a level playing field among countries vying for the patronage of MNEs. In the long term such norms might evolve to form a comprehensive regime of international criminal law applicable to MNEs. Such a development might be welcomed by MNEs prepared to abide by international norms, but only if they could be provided with assurance that their less scrupulous rivals would not take advantage of their commitment to the law.

International laws and international tribunals were created primarily by states for states. The focus on states was understandable, because at the time states were thought to pose the greatest threat to human rights. Although it is obvious that an MNE is not a state, it occupies a position akin to that of a state in its capacity to commit human rights abuses. Today, the ability of MNEs to affect the lives of workers and members of the public is comparable to, and in some instances exceeds, that of many developing states (Rugman: 2001). National courts, the traditional venue for addressing individual wrongdoing, may lack the effective capacity to redress wrongdoing by powerful companies, and, for victims, it hardly matters whether their rights have been violated by a state or an MNE. Admittedly, this is a normative argument for giving international tribunals the responsibility for trying MNEs, but it is an argument that may be fully warranted by the realities of the modern world. The case is well put by Danailov (1998):

> [A]ll social actors have an international legal responsibility to assure the effective protection of human rights, which means that every organisation, every group, every community and *every multinational or national corporation* have human rights duties. The defence of this view is not to be found in technical legal arguments since its purpose is precisely to show how these legal arguments should evolve as to include new developments occurring in the society. The international norms and their dominant interpretations are still reflecting the context which saw their creation. A change in that regard is starting to be perceived as a necessity within different fora dealing with activities of non-State actors that are violating the principles that international human rights law is said to protect.[25] (emphasis added)

25 Danailov at 38.

While international courts have traditionally provided a forum for adjudicating claims against states, in more recent times ad hoc international criminal tribunals have been established to adjudicate criminal charges against *individuals*. Examples include the tribunals established to try cases involving crimes committed in the former Yugoslavia and in Rwanda. While no such tribunal has as yet been created to try companies for their offences, a not uncommon pattern in national law is that courts which were initially established to try *natural* persons will subsequently have their jurisdiction extended to allow them to hear cases against *legal* persons. That same progression may eventually occur with respect to international law tribunals. In principle, there would seem to be no objection to establishing an international criminal court with jurisdiction over companies. While it is true that, unlike in the case of state-created international tribunals, potential corporate defendants will not have been parties to the treaty bringing the tribunal into force, and therefore could argue that they had not consented to its jurisdiction, this conceptual objection has not proved a barrier to the trials of individuals in the ad hoc tribunals.

International law finds its source in treaties, conventions, declarations, internationally approved guidelines and customary practice. The various documents protect economic, social and cultural rights, civil and political rights, and, more generally, human rights. There is a growing consensus that corporations as well as states should promote and uphold these rights. The UN's 1948 'Universal Declaration of Human Rights' applies to 'every organ of society', presumably including corporations. Similarly, the UN Declaration on the Elimination of Violence against Women (1993) applies to non-state as well as state actors. The UN Global Compact (1999) commits corporations who sign up to it to respect nine core principles relating to human rights, labour standards, and protection of the environment. Currently pending consideration is a draft Fundamental Human Rights Principles for Business Enterprises, drawn up by the UN Sub-Commission on the Promotion and Protection of Human Rights, which would impose direct obligations on companies. The ILO (International Labour Organisation) Tripartite Declaration of Principles Concerning Multinational Enterprises and Social Policy (1977, amended in 1987, 1995, 2000) commits governments to working with MNEs to improve labour and employment standards and the OECD (Organisation for Economic Co-operation and Development) Guidelines for Multinational Enterprises (1976, revised in 2000) are not only wide-ranging in their scope (applying to human rights, labour standards, environmental protection and anti-corruption practices), but, significantly, also would commit companies to hold their suppliers and subcontractors accountable to the same standards as themselves.

Comparable developments can be observed on a regional level and in individual states. The European Parliament has passed a resolution calling for a code of conduct for European enterprises operating in developing countries. Individual states that have promulgated standards governing corporate behaviour include the United States, which has adopted 'Model Business Principles' for American corporations conducting business abroad, and England, where the Department for International Development (DFID) has articulated a 'triple-bottom line' that urges companies to be economically viable, environmentally sound and socially responsible. In December, 2000, the UK and US governments, in conjunction with leading extractive and energy companies, released a set of 'Voluntary Principles on Security and Human Rights'.

The problem with all of these initiatives is that compliance is voluntary. Together, the various documents form a body of 'soft law', but with no legal means to compel adherence to their standards, and no means of holding violators to account. As a result, these standards, declarations, and statements of principle amount to little more than a plea for companies to be responsible corporate citizens. Yet those who would wish for a firmer basis for acountability should not despair; often binding international law has evolved from just such hortatory roots.

One situation where a company might be triable in an international forum for criminal or human rights violations is where the company has been allowed by a state to take responsibility for public functions that would normally belong to the state. In this situation the company arguably should be liable to the same extent as would have been the state. A state's liability will be considered in the next subsection, but here it might be noted how this situation might arise. First, a state may decide to 'privatise' a public function for which it was formerly responsible. Such privatisation can increasingly be seen with respect to policing and prisons. In some instances, 'company towns' have been created, with the company assuming all the responsibilities of a government. Alternatively, a state may cede limited authority to a private company on an ad hoc basis. Illustrative is the example, previously referred to, where Royal Dutch Shell was allowed by the Nigerian government to employ its own security forces to protect its installations.

If international laws addressed to corporate criminality were to be devised, where might criminal charges against a company be brought? On 1 July 2002, the International Criminal Court came into existence. At the Rome Conference at which the statutory framework of the court was worked out, France proposed that the court should have jurisdiction to try crimes committed by *legal* as well as by natural persons. Although unsuccessful, the French proposal received considerable support, and most of the objections to it were based not on principle, but on pragmatic considerations. No doubt many of the delegates were of the view that debating whether to extend the jurisdiction of the court to legal persons would distract them from their primary objective of establishing an independent and credible international tribunal in which *natural persons* who had committed internationally condemned offences could be brought to justice. Including companies within the court's jurisdictional remit might have led to corporate lobbying against state ratifications of the proposed statute.

Variations in state practices may also have contributed to the failure of the French proposal to attract more supporters. Several participating states had no provisions in their domestic law for prosecuting companies, and thus were largely unfamiliar, at least on an experiential level, with the concept of corporate criminality. The absence of such provisions would have rested uncomfortably alongside the principle of complementarity embodied in the statute, whereby national courts were to have primary responsibility for prosecutions. If there was no provision in a state's national law respecting corporate criminal liability, it is not easy to see how the principle of complementarity could have been accommodated. Even among the states that did provide for the criminal prosecution of companies, there was lacking a consensus as to the proper test of corporate fault. The French proposal would have allowed a prosecution to be brought against executives of the offending company. Difficult questions regarding sanctions would also have had to be resolved, and it was not clear whether delegates would have been prepared to endorse sanctions other than fines, or whether they would have favoured personal punishment of the executives on trial.

The variation among state practices that may have frustrated acceptance of the French proposal suggests an alternative approach to corporate criminality that is worth considering. The European Union has no authority to enact criminal laws that are binding on member states. However, what the EU has often done through Directives and Conventions is to declare an objective of eliminating an identified evil, while leaving to individual states the responsibility to enact appropriate legislation into their domestic criminal law. It was via this route that laws against insider trading and money laundering came into force in the various EU states.[26] With respect to what is a widely perceived problem area of corporate crime, the OECD Convention on Combating Bribery of Foreign Public Officials in International Business Transactions defines bribery and then advises party states to 'take such measures as may be necessary, in accordance with its legal principles, to establish the liability of legal persons'. The effect of this general approach is to allow for the development of an international consensus on the need to control a particular problem – and corporate crime may well be such a problem – without hamstringing states with laws or enforcement mechanisms that are not compatible with national laws. Although there exists the danger in this approach that the stringency of laws and enforcement mechanisms will vary from state to state, this may be an acceptable price for a global response to problems that are best tackled on a global level. A more serious drawback is that some states will not be prepared to accept the idea that inanimate entities such as companies are capable of committing criminal offences.

While an agreed international approach to corporate crimes committed by MNEs and their subsidiaries may offer the best long-term solution, it is probably fair to say that such a solution is unlikely to be realised in the near future. The subject of international criminal jurisdiction is itself controversial, and it is understandable that the even more controversial problems that would be presented in prosecuting MNEs have been put on hold for the present. After the International Criminal Court has become firmly established, and after more states have had the opportunity to develop their national law of corporate criminal liability, it may be that the issue of the court's jurisdiction over legal persons will be revisited. Even now, however, it might be noted that companies can be implicated in a case before the court because the statute envisages prosecutions where an individual may be liable for a crime committed 'through another person, regardless of whether that other person is criminally responsible'.[27] There would seem no reason why that 'other person' could not be a legal person (Clapham: 2000).

2. Holding states accountable for human rights abuses perpetrated by MNEs

Historically, states have been responsible for protecting the human rights of their citizenry. It is now accepted that a state which violates the rights of its citizens may

---

26 See Council Directive of 13 November 1989 Coordinating Regulations on Insider Dealing (89/591/EEC); Council Directive of 10 June 1991 on Prevention of the Use of the Financial System for the Purpose of Money Laundering (91/308/EEC).

27 Article 25(3).

be held to account in an international forum. The more complicated issue is the responsibility of a state to protect its citizens from human rights violations by third parties, and in particular by private companies. A state may be faulted for not enacting laws that would have criminalised corporate misconduct, for not enforcing what laws and regulations were on its books, and for not prosecuting companies that it is aware have violated state laws. The state is not vicariously liable for the company's offences but it is responsible for allowing the offences to go unregulated, unchecked, undiscovered, untried and unpunished. Nor can a state absolve itself of its obligation to protect the rights of its citizens by delegating this responsibility to a private third party. In *Costello-Roberts v United Kingdom*, the European Court of Human Rights held that a state could not avoid its legal responsibilities by such delegation.[28]

A state has an obligation not only not to violate the rights of its own citizens, but also to prevent violations by third parties. Further, the UN Covenant on Civil and Political Rights requires states to ensure an effective remedy to any person whose rights or freedoms are violated, whether or not by persons acting in an official capacity.[29] Similarly, the Maastricht Guidelines on Violations of Economic, Social and Cultural Rights refer to the '[S]tate's responsibility to ensure that private entities..., *including transnational corporations over which they exercise jurisdiction*, do not deprive individuals of their economic, social and cultural rights'.[30] The OECD Convention on Combating Bribery of Foreign Public Officials in International Business Transactions commits party states to prosecute domestic corporations which have bribed a public official in a foreign state.[31] The problem with these various treaties, covenants, conventions and guidelines, however, is that there often is no mechanism for forcing a state to honour its commitments and no sanction for a state's failure to do so. Observance of the relevant standards is voluntary rather than mandatory, and many states that sign up to a treaty or convention fail to enact the necessary domestic legislation to bring the treaty or convention into force.

International legal precedent can be found for requiring states to protect their citizens against violations of their rights by third parties. In the *Velasquez Rodriguez* case, the Inter-American Court of Human Rights stated that:

> [a]n illegal act which violates human rights and which is initially not directly imputable to a state... can lead to international responsibility of the state, not because of the act itself, but because of the lack of due diligence to prevent the violation or to respond to it as required by the Convention.[32]

In the jurisprudence of both the European Court of Justice and the European Court of Human Rights can also be found precedents for requiring states to prevent offences by third parties. In the *Spanish Strawberries* case, France was held to account by the European Court of Justice for not stopping French farmers from interfering with the

---

28 *Costello-Roberts v United Kingdom* (1993) 19 EHRR 112, ECtHR.
29 Article 2(3a).
30 Para 18 (emphasis added).
31 Adopted 23 May 1997. See also Council of Europe, Criminal Law Convention on Corruption, adopted 27 January 1999; OAS Inter-American Convention against Corruption, adopted 29 March 1996.
32 *Velasquez Rodriguez* case, Inter-American Court of Human Rights, Decisions and Judgments (1988:151).

free movement of Spanish strawberries.[33] In *X and Y v Netherlands*, the European Court of Human Rights held that the Dutch government had violated the right of privacy of a mentally handicapped girl who had been sexually abused in a private nursing home. The Netherlands' fault lay in its failure to provide the victim with a criminal remedy that would have allowed for the prosecution of her assailant.[34]

The above cases involved the state's failure to prevent or redress violations committed by individuals, but in *Guerra v Italy* the European Court of Human Rights held Italy liable for not protecting the right of privacy of its citizens against toxic fumes released by a fertiliser plant.[35] The company was not a party to the case, only sovereign states being subject to the court's jurisdiction. However, if one were to examine the company's liability from a national criminal law perspective, it was arguably guilty of assault. In human rights terms, the company had violated not only the victims' right of privacy, but also the right to life of those workers who had died of cancer as a result of having been exposed to the poisonous fumes. Because the company was not a defendant in the case before the European Court of Human Rights, however, these violations had to be approached indirectly by holding Italy, the state in which the company's plant was located, responsible for not protecting the victims from the company's offences.

The legal position that seems to be emerging is that states have a duty to enact and enforce laws that will protect against corporate violations, and to establish legal remedies to vindicate any infringements that do occur. The failure to do so can lead to sanctions against the state in an international or regional forum. However, bringing an action against a state should not be seen as a panacea. At best it provides an indirect method for controlling corporate wrongdoing. Furthermore, if a state has not signed up to the instrument that created the relevant tribunal, it will usually not be subject to its jurisdiction. An even more serious problem may be the lack of an effective remedy. An international court cannot directly punish the corporate violator, because it will not be a party in the case, or even order a state to prosecute the offender in its national courts, because such an order would conflict with accepted notions of state sovereignty. Thus the typical remedy is financial in nature – either the state is fined, or damages are awarded against the state in favour of the victims of the state's inaction.

The problem with monetary sanctions is that they may not be sufficient to offset the economic benefit that a state derives from the presence within its jurisdiction of a corporate offender. If a state perceives itself to be better off financially absorbing the penalties imposed by an international court than it would be in alienating the MNE and losing the tax and other revenue that is generated from having the MNE or its subsidiary within its territory, it may choose not to take remedial action to curb the corporate wrongdoing. While some states may wish to avoid the embarrassment that could result from the publicising of their refusal to enforce their own laws, others, perversely, may see such publicity as advancing their efforts to attract future investment by other MNEs. There is simply no guarantee that international sanctions will prompt a state to crack down on companies that violate the rights of their citizens.

---

33 Case C-265/95, *Spanish Strawberries*, ECJ (December 1997).
34 *X and Y v Netherlands* (1985) 8 EHRR 235, ECtHR.
35 *Guerra v Italy* (1998) 26 EHRR 357, ECtHR. See also *Lopez Ostra v* Spain (1994) 20 EHRR 277, ECtHR.

This and the preceding subsection envisage the basis of a two-pronged attack in an international forum on wrongdoing by multinational enterprises. One prong would consist of legal actions against a state that had failed to protect its citizens against human rights violations by MNEs. However, the underlying assumption that a state that has been found to be in violation of this duty will take steps to prevent corporate abuses in the future may be naïve, failing to take account of the economic pressures to tolerate criminal and human rights violations by MNEs and their subsidiaries. The second prong would entail prosecutions of the MNEs themselves in an international forum. An obligation on the part of companies to refrain from human rights violations has been recognised in treaties, conventions, multi-party state declarations, internationally endorsed guidelines and customary practice, with the challenge now being to convert this body of 'soft law' into binding obligations that can be vindicated in an international court.

E.   PROSECUTING A PARENT COMPANY IN ITS HOME STATE

The previous sections have highlighted the problems in prosecuting an MNE in either the host state of a subsidiary or in an international forum. The most promising avenue for holding MNEs accountable for the offences of their subsidiaries, at least for the present, may lie in a prosecution of the MNE in its home state. An additional advantage of proceeding against the MNE in its home state would be that any sentence following a successful prosecution would have a more far-reaching impact than if the prosecution had been brought against the MNE's subsidiary in the host state. A conviction of the subsidiary would lead only to a change in its practices; a conviction of the parent may lead to changes in its policies and the practices of all of its subsidiaries throughout the world. When harm has been experienced in the host state of a subsidiary, however, there are two hurdles to be overcome in order to prosecute the parent company in its home state. The first is the territorial bias of jurisdiction, and the second is the articulation of a viable theory for holding the parent company liable.

1.   Jurisdiction

When criminally cognisant harm occurs, caused in part by a subsidiary of an MNE but also in part by the organisational fault or management failure of the MNE, the first hurdle in prosecuting the MNE in its home state will be that of establishing jurisdiction in the home state. The problem is that territorial principles of jurisdiction seem to dictate that the prosecution should be brought in the state where the harm was incurred. Or do they?

a.   The 'active personality' principle

We have discussed previously the problems in extraditing an MNE which is registered in another state. The conceptual difficulty of physically removing a company from one jurisdiction to another might frustrate the proceeding before the merits of the case could be reached, and extradition of the MNE's officers/directors might not be possible unless it could be shown that these individuals were themselves responsible for the offence or were complicit in the company's offence. A state might also decline to extradite on the basis of the principle of 'double criminality' if its own law of corporate crime was grounded in a different concept of 'corporate fault' than that of the state seeking extradition.

Basing jurisdiction on the 'active personality' principle would allow the home state of the parent company to bring it, and its officers and directors, to trial. The 'active personality' principle allows a state to try its own nationals for crimes committed abroad. It is the defendant's links to the state of trial and not the state's links to the crime that are critical. The 'active personality' principle is particularly useful in those states, mostly civil law jurisdictions, that are not prepared to extradite their nationals for trial in another country. If a state is not prepared to extradite its nationals, then it needs a basis for proceeding against them within its own criminal justice system or else they will end up being able to commit, with impunity, crimes anywhere in the world save in their home state. While primarily of benefit in civil law countries, common law countries also have provisions for applying the 'active personality' principle, at least with respect to very serious crimes. For instance, the Offences Against the Person Act 1861, s 9 empowers a court in England or Wales to try a British subject who commits murder or manslaughter, regardless or where in the world the killing is committed.

Although it has primarily been applied to *natural* persons, there would seem no reason in theory why the 'active personality' principle could not be applied to *legal* persons. The lack of precedent is more likely attributable to the absence of cases that raise the issue than to a rejection of its theoretical merit. Given the conceptual difficulty of extraditing a company and the practical problems of extraditing its officers/directors, there may indeed be a more compelling case for founding jurisdiction on the 'active personality' principle with respect to companies than there is with respect to natural persons. However, invocation of the 'active personality' principle in order to try an MNE in its home state for a crime that was committed by its foreign subsidiary would not solve all of the prosecutor's problems. Unless mutual co-operation treaties or agreements had been entered into, police from the home state of the MNE could encounter difficulties in conducting an effective investigation in the host state of the subsidiary. They would lack the authority to interrogate witnesses, seize physical and documentary evidence, and generally carry out their inquiries. Compelling witnesses from a foreign state to testify at a trial in the home state might also prove problematic. If a witness refused to attend, and if there was no inter-state compact that compelled attendance, or allowed the witness's statement to be taken or received indirectly (eg by means of an audio or video link-up), the prosecution could find itself with a critical hole in its case.

b.   Universal jurisdiction

The principle of 'universal jurisdiction' allows, and in some instances requires, a state to prosecute persons who have committed crimes that are universally condemned. Jurisdiction is not dependent on where the crime was committed, as under the territoriality principle, or on the nationality of the perpetrators, as under the 'active personality' principle, but is rather based on the nature of the offence. Universal jurisdiction is reserved for those offences that are so heinous and reprehensible that they are, as the term implies, universally condemned. Internationally accepted principles of justice demand that perpetrators of such crimes be brought to justice, and the state in which a perpetrator is found is under an obligation either to prosecute or to extradite the offender to a state that is willing to prosecute. The idea is that those who commit the condemned offences should not be allowed to find sanctuary anywhere in the world. It is also believed, although not always borne out in practice, that the availability of universal jurisdiction will have a strong deterrent effect against the commission of the condemned offences.

To what crimes does universal jurisdiction apply? The International Law Commission's 'Draft Code of Crimes against the Peace and Security of Mankind' (1996) would limit the exercise of such jurisdiction to genocide, war crimes, crimes against humanity, and comparably abhorrent offences. Although the Draft Code lacks precision in its definition of these crimes, this shortcoming has been rectified in the statute that creates the International Criminal Court.[36] Torture too is subject to universal jurisdiction under the UN Convention against Torture. However, as that convention is limited to offences committed by *state officials*, a prosecutor would probably have to establish that a corporate defendant was acting as a state agent when it committed its offence.

While universal jurisdiction has so far largely been invoked in prosecutions of natural persons, there would appear in principle no reason why it could not also be applied to legal persons. The precedent for invoking universal jurisdiction against companies, as opposed to individuals, is weak but not totally lacking. The Nuremberg trials were limited to prosecutions of individuals, but in some cases, although individuals were nominally on trial, the focus of a trial was clearly on the role of a corporation (Clapham: 2000). In the trial of the directors of the Farben Corporation, for instance, the Nuremberg tribunal was not in any doubt about the company's responsibility:

> The result was the enrichment of Farben and the building of its greater chemical empire through the medium of occupancy at the expense of the former owners. Such action on the part of Farben constituted a violation of the Hague Regulations. It was in violation of the rights of private property, protected by the Laws and Customs of War.[37]

The tribunal's opinion indicates its view that companies can violate international laws, including those that are subject to universal jurisdiction. However, the opinion was delivered at a time when the law regarding war crimes and crimes against humanity, as well as the law on corporate criminality, were both in an embryonic state of development. With precedents now available on both fronts, it may be possible in an appropriate case to marry the two concepts. In *Farben*, the directors may have committed their offences using the corporate form, but the tribunal's comments seemed to indicate that it would have been prepared to convict the company as well had its jurisdiction not been limited to individuals.

While most corporate offences in developing countries relate to violations of either labour or health and safety laws, and are therefore unlikely to be found to be of sufficient seriousness to warrant the invocation of universal jurisdiction, it is not

36 See Articles 6-8.
37 *I G Farben Trial*, US Military Tribunal Nuremberg, 14 August 1947-29 July 1948, Law Reports of Trials of War Criminals, Vol X, p 1 at 50.

inconceivable that this could occur. In modern times companies can play a major role in the development of biological, chemical and nuclear weapons. If these weapons are used, say, for the purposes of genocide, and if the company is aware of the intended use, it too may be guilty of genocide. In *Wiwa v Royal Dutch Petroleum Co*,[38] a civil case, the plaintiffs alleged that Royal Dutch Shell had paid the Nigerian military to arrest, jail, torture and, following fabricated murder charges, hang Ken Saro-Wiwa and John Kpuinen for their opposition to the company's oil exploration activities in Nigeria's Ogoni region. If these allegations could be proved, they would arguably constitute the type of offences that would warrant the invocation of universal jurisdiction.

In the final analysis, although the exercise of universal jurisdiction would avoid the conceptual conundrum of how physically to extradite a company, while obviating any reservations that a state might have about extraditing officers and directors of the company, universal jurisdiction may not have much practical impact on MNEs because of the limited number of crimes to which the principle applies. Moreover, before universal jurisdiction can be invoked, a state will need to have enacted implementing legislation. Many states, perhaps wary of being accused of jurisdictional imperialism, have not done so (Kamminga: 1999). National courts too have proceeded cautiously in order not to be seen to be meddling in the internal affairs of another state. Given the demonstrable judicial preference for clear-cut cases before allowing universal jurisdiction to be invoked, it is predictable that courts will be even less inclined to allow its invocation in an area that is as fraught with ambiguity as is corporate crime.

2.   A violation of home state law?[39]

Under the active personality principle the claim of a home state to jurisdiction over an MNE is based on the fact that the MNE is registered or located within the state. Under the principle of universal jurisdiction the claim is based on the presence of the MNE within the jurisdiction, coupled with the universally condemned nature of the crime charged. Under neither of these approaches is it necessary to determine where the crime was committed, whether in the home state of the parent or in the host state of the subsidiary. The locus of the crime is irrelevant. The argument in this section brings the locus back into the picture. While the home state of the parent would be asserting jurisdiction, the basis of its claim would be the well-accepted principle of territoriality. The argument is that the crime, whose effects in terms of harm and injuries may have been experienced in the host state of a subsidiary, was in fact committed in the home state of the parent. On what basis might this argument proceed?

The answer to this question requires us to return to the question of the nature of corporate fault. In chapter 3 we argued that corporate fault inheres in a company's failure to properly assess and evaluate the criminological risks in its business operation, its failure to devise and implement systems for preventing such risks from materialising, and its tolerance of a culture that accepts the commission of criminal offences by its personnel. If one accepts the view that a company has a legal duty not

---

38   226 F 3d 88 (2d Cir 2000).
39   The analysis in this section was first presented in Gobert (2002).

only not to commit crimes, but also to prevent crimes, then arguably the duty of prevention extends beyond its workforce to its subsidiaries. If so, then the failure which forms the actus reus of an offence will have taken place at the headquarters of the parent company *regardless of where the eventual harm is experienced*. Accordingly, jurisdiction for a criminal prosecution of an MNE will lie in *its* home state.

The logic of this position was accepted in the Italian statute on corporate criminality that we looked at in chapter 3. Article 4 of the statute would allow the prosecution in Italy of a company, headquartered in Italy, whose overseas subsidiary had committed an offence under the Italian law, as long as a prosecution had not been initiated in the host state of the subsidiary. This enlightened provision arguably reconciles the realities of a modern global economy and traditional territorial concepts of criminal jurisdiction. It would prevent companies from exporting the criminogenic aspects of their business to foreign subsidiaries.

On the other hand, the British government in its consultation paper (Home Office: 2000) on the creation of a crime of corporate killing did not accept the logic of the argument. Under the government's proposal, it will be recalled, an undertaking would commit a corporate killing when a management failure, which fell 'far below' what reasonably could have been expected of the undertaking in the circumstances, was one of the causes of a death. Liability would be grounded not in the vicarious attribution to the undertaking of the offence but in its own organisational failure to prevent the offence. In the case of an MNE, the failure would arguably consist of not exercising the requisite degree of control over a subsidiary to ensure that the latter did not cause a death. Although the acts of the subsidiary would be one of the causes of the death, so too would the failures of the parent. The actus reus of subsidiary and parent, however, would take place in a different location and at a different point in time – the parent's actus reus would have occurred in its home state when it failed to consider the implications of its policies, and the subsidiary's actus reus will have occurred in its host state when the actual death occurred.

Under the government's proposals, when an English parent company causes a death in England or Wales, a prosecution could be brought against the parent company if its management failure was *one of the causes* of the death. Not only would the government's proposals allow for the prosecution of an English parent company for a corporate killing committed by one of its subsidiaries in England and Wales, it would also allow for the prosecution of a *foreign* parent company for a killing by one of its subsidiaries in England or Wales. While the government thus seems to accept a principle that would permit a prosecution of an MNE in a country other than that in which it was registered or its headquarters located, it declined to extend that principle to an English parent company for a corporate killing committed by one of its subsidiaries in a foreign country. As a result we are left with the seeming anomaly that a foreign parent company can be held liable for a death caused by its subsidiary in England; but an English parent company cannot be held liable for a death caused by one of its foreign subsidiaries, at least not in the English courts.

The government seeks to explain this anomaly by the demands of a territorial conception of jurisdiction. The deaths resulting from a corporate killing by an English subsidiary of a foreign parent company will occur in England, while any deaths resulting from a corporate killing by a foreign subsidiary of an English parent company will occur in the foreign country. The underlying assumption seems to be that jurisdiction will lie where the death occurs. In the case of an individual, the assumption is logical – the actus reus of a homicide will almost certainly take place in the same jurisdiction as where the victim dies. This is not so, however, with respect to a corporate killing where the actus reus is a management failure. The management failure will typically occur at the board meeting of the directors of the company. If the directors of an MNE, meeting in the home state of the MNE, ignore the dangerous practices of a foreign subsidiary, the management failure that will be one of the causes of any resulting death will have occurred in the home state of the MNE.

When the actus reus of an offence occurs in one state and its effects are experienced in another, which state's courts have jurisdiction to hear the case? In answering this question, a distinction is often drawn between 'conduct' crimes and 'result' crimes (Hirst: 1981). A conduct crime is one whose actus reus consists of an act or an omission of the defendant without regard to the consequences. The endangerment offences discussed in the preceding chapter are prototypical examples of conduct crimes. In contrast, a result crime requires that the offender's act or omission produce a specified outcome. Before the crime of 'dangerous driving' (a 'conduct' crime) is converted into the crime of 'causing death by dangerous driving' (a 'result' crime), a person must be killed. Similarly, the offence of criminal damage requires that property be damaged, whether or not the defendant intended to cause damage or was reckless with respect to whether damage occurred. Jurisdiction for conduct crimes is generally held to lie where the actus reus is committed;[40] for 'result crimes' where the harm is incurred.[41]

Although it might seem that an offence of homicide, such as murder, manslaughter or corporate killing, would be a classic example of a result crime, the decision of the Queen's Bench Divisional Court in *Re Reyat's Application for a writ of Habeas Corpus*[42] indicates that the analysis can be rather complicated. The case arose as a result of a request by the Canadian government to extradite the (habeas corpus) applicant in order that he might stand trial in Canada for manslaughter. The applicant was alleged to have planted a bomb on an airplane in Canada, which exploded over Japan, killing a number of victims. One of the issues before the Divisional Court related to where the crime was committed – in Canada, where the bomb was planted, or in Japan, where the victims had died. If manslaughter was indeed a 'result' crime, then the offence was committed where the victims died, and jurisdiction would lie in Japan (with whom England at the time did not have an extradition treaty). On the other hand, if manslaughter was deemed a 'conduct' crime, as argued by the Canadian government, then the actus reus took place in Canada and its courts would have jurisdiction. The Divisional Court held that, as a significant portion of the actus reus had occurred in Canada, then, under Canadian law, Canada had jurisdiction to try the case. The court went on to consider whether the defendant could be tried in England. It concluded that under the Offences Against the Person Act 1861, s 9 (see below) he could, but also, more presumptively, that the same result could be reached on the basis that manslaughter was a 'conduct' crime.

If the reasoning of *Re Reyat* were to be applied to the proposed offence of corporate killing, the management failure that would constitute one of the causes of a death would take place in the home state of the parent company whose directors and officers had failed properly to superintend the operation of the company's subsidiary. If this

---

40 See eg *Treacy v DPP* [1971] AC 537.
41 See eg *DPP v Stonehouse* [1978] AC 55; *Secretary of State for Trade v Markus* [1976] AC 35.
42 CO/1157/88 (unreported).

analysis is correct, then the position taken by the government in its consultation paper is the logical antithesis of what one would expect. In the case of the foreign parent whose subsidiary causes a death in England, the actus reus is committed in the foreign state where that parent is located, and jurisdiction should lie in that state, not England. Yet in this situation the government would claim jurisdiction. On the other hand, the actus reus of an English parent whose subsidiary commits a corporate killing in a foreign country occurs in England, and jurisdiction should lie with the English courts. Yet here the government would disclaim jurisdiction.

The government's disinclination to try an English parent company in England for a corporate killing committed abroad stands in stark contrast to its position in cases where a British subject commits a homicide in a foreign country. The Offences Against the Person Act 1861, s 9 provides:

> Where any Murder or Manslaughter shall be committed on land out of the United Kingdom, whether within the Queen's Dominions or without, and whether the person killed were a Subject of her Majesty or not, every Offence committed by any Subject of Her Majesty, in respect of any such Case, whether the same shall amount to the Offence of Murder or of Manslaughter... may be dealt with, inquired of, tried, determined and punished... in England... provided that nothing herein contained shall prevent any Person from being tried in any Place out of England ... for an Murder or Manslaughter committed out of England....

The government does not propose to relinquish this jurisdictional claim with respect to the individual homicide offences of reckless killing, and killing by gross carelessness, that are contained in its consultation paper. As a company is a *legal* person and as it would also seem, if registered in England, to be a 'Subject of Her Majesty' (a phrase which has not been defined in the caselaw), in the sense that it would be obligated to obey the laws of England, it should be treated similarly. However, the government's proposals, somewhat curiously, exclude the prosecution of English companies in England for corporate killings which occur in the home state of an overseas subsidiary.

This juxtaposition of the individual and corporate defendant becomes all the more puzzling the closer one compares the situation of the two. An individual will usually commit the act or omission that causes a death in the country where the victim dies. Under the general rule of territorial jurisdiction, the trial should be held in the courts of that country. For an English court to assert concurrent jurisdiction would appear extraordinary, but under the Offences Against the Person Act 1861, s 9 it does. In contrast, the actus reus of the proposed corporate killing offence would consist of a management failure that could be expected to occur where the parent's head office was located. In the case of an English MNE, this would be England.

On what basis, then, does the government purport to justify the differential treatment not only of individuals and companies, but also of parent companies registered abroad but doing business through a subsidiary in England and parent companies registered in England but doing business through a subsidiary abroad? The government cites the practical difficulties involved in gathering evidence in countries where English police have no jurisdiction (or, more accurately, where the Health and Safety Executive has no jurisdiction, for the government proposes that it, rather than the police, should bear the primary responsibility for investigating corporate killings[43]). The government

---

43 Home Office (2000) *Reforming the Law of Involuntary Manslaughter: The Government's Proposals* para 3.3.5.

also refers to the double criminality problem, which we have examined previously, and concludes that extra-territorial jurisdiction is appropriate only where the wrongful behaviour in question constitutes an offence both under English law and under the law of the host state of the subsidiary.[44] It supports its position by citing a desire not be accused of exporting English laws to other countries.

The government's reasoning is not persuasive. The general principle that one state should not impose its laws on another is well-accepted and non-controversial, but if an English parent company were to be tried in England for a crime whose actus reus occurred in England, England would not be exporting its laws. No foreign state would be required or even asked to adopt the government's definition of corporate killing. The offence would be confined to the English legal system and any trial would be held in England or Wales. If the parent company were to be convicted, the Crown would have to prove that the actus reus of the offence – the management failure – had occurred in England or Wales.

The government's argument that prosecutions of a parent company in England would be handicapped by the difficulties of conducting an investigation in a foreign country may have greater force, but the government seems to have ignored the fact that the same practical problems would exist with respect to killings committed abroad by natural persons, where the government is not prepared to relinquish its claim to try the offender. Indeed, the government's point would seem to have more salience with respect to natural persons, as witnesses and evidence relating to the killing would likely be found in the jurisdiction where the death takes place. In contrast, evidence relating to the management failure that constitutes the actus reus of a corporate killing would be more likely to be found in the home state of the parent; ie England. A similar point regarding the problems of conducting an investigation could be made with respect to parent companies registered in foreign countries whose subsidiaries commit a corporate killing in England. Here the government proposes to assert jurisdiction over the foreign parent, but ignores the fact that the practical difficulties in investigating the management practices of a foreign parent will be far greater than would be involved in investigating the management practices of an English parent whose subsidiary commits a corporate killing in a foreign country. Again, the government's arguments regarding the practicability of investigations should seemingly have led it to the opposite conclusions of those it actually reached.

In a final attempt to justify its position with respect to domestic parent companies, the government refers to England's tradition of 'oral evidence and cross-examination'.[45] It is hard to see the relevance of this factor, as the contemplated trial of the parent for corporate killing would be held in England, where the trial court would be able to adhere to English traditions of oral evidence and cross-examination. Many of the critical witnesses at the trial of an English MNE would be executives of the parent company, or persons associated with the company. These witnesses likely would be found in England and the Crown would not encounter untoward difficulty in securing their testimony. Securing the testimony of witnesses from the foreign country might be more problematic, especially if the witnesses declined (perhaps at the instigation of

---

44 Home Office (2000) *Reforming the Law of Involuntary Manslaughter: The Government's Proposals* para 3.7.3.

45 Home Office (2000) *Reforming the Law of Involuntary Manslaughter: The Government's Proposals* para 3.7.3.

the MNE) to attend the trial in England. However, the comparable problem exists with respect to securing the testimony of executives of a foreign parent company prosecuted for an alleged corporate killing by its subsidiary in England, yet here the practical problem of obtaining witness testimony did not deflect the government from asserting jurisdiction to try the foreign parent.

What explains the logical inconsistencies in the government's position? To seek the answer in pure logic may be to ignore the dialectic at work between the forces of capital and the forces representing the public interest. While the government is sensitive to the public's resentment of companies that appear to be putting profits before safety, it is at the same time not insensitive to the risks involved in reining in big business. If MNEs, alienated by what they perceived to be an anti-business animus on the part of the government, were to relocate their headquarters to countries which were perceived to offer a more corporate-friendly environment, the damage to the state's economy from lost taxes and increased unemployment could be enormous. The government, therefore, is understandably reluctant to advocate an interpretation of its proposed legislation that might precipitate the flight of MNEs currently registered in England but which, because of the global nature of their operations, have the flexibility to relocate in any number of jurisdictions. Nor does the government wish to discourage MNEs from locating in the UK.

Holding foreign parent companies liable for the corporate killings of their subsidiaries in England would not have the same adverse effect. Under the government's proposals, there would be no advantage to being registered outside of England as long as an MNE intended to continue to do business in England through a subsidiary. If its subsidiary in England were to commit a corporate killing, the MNE could not escape liability. Thus an MNE would not gain any advantage by locating its headquarters abroad if its goal were to avoid a criminal trial. This could only be achieved by not doing business in England at all, and the loss of the English market might be too steep a price to pay.

The situation where a foreign subsidiary of an English MNE commits a corporate killing abroad is an altogether different matter. Had the government left open the possibility of a criminal prosecution in England against the English parent for such deaths, MNEs would have faced a potential liability that arose by mere virtue of the fact that they happened to be registered in England. Now the potential downside of locating one's corporate headquarters in England would have been immense. First, the parent could face an embarrassing prosecution in England when such a prosecution would not have been possible if the company had been registered elsewhere. Second, if there were to be a conviction, the full extent of the parent's financial resources could be looked to by the court for any fine that might be imposed as a sentence. Although the parameters for determining the amount of a fine following a conviction for a corporate killing have yet to be formulated, it would not be surprising if courts were to take into account the financial resources of the defendant corporation. Finally, the possibility could not be ignored that a sentencing court might issue a remedial order which would have ramifications for the way that the MNE conducted its business not only in England but throughout the world.

We have focused on the jurisdictional authority of England to try an English MNE for a corporate killing where the death occurs in the host state of a foreign subsidiary for two reasons. First, this issue, and the converse issue of whether a foreign parent can be tried for a corporate killing where the death occurs in England or Wales, are specifically addressed in the government's consultation paper. Second, these cases involve what can be argued to be 'result' crimes, where the claim for jurisdiction in the state of the subsidiary where the death occurs, rather than in the home state of the MNE, is strongest. In cases involving conduct crimes, locating jurisdiction in the home state of the MNE would be less contentious. In *R v Hornett*,[46] the charge consisted of uttering a forged instrument in England that was intended to defraud a victim in a foreign country, but the court had no difficulty in holding that the English courts had jurisdiction to try the defendant. If the defendant had been an MNE that had similarly forged documents to be disseminated by its overseas subsidiaries, the result on the jurisdictional issue would presumably have been the same. To the extent that MNEs are able to control their subsidiaries, have a duty to do so, and fail to do so, the home state of the MNE should have jurisdiction to try the MNE for any resulting offences. As Lord Diplock explained in *Treacy v DPP*:[47]

> There is no rule of comity to prevent Parliament from prohibiting under pain of punishment persons who are present in the United Kingdom, and so owe legal obedience to our law, from doing physical acts in England, notwithstanding that the consequences of those acts take effect outside the United Kingdom . . . In my view where the definition of any such offence contains a requirement that the described conduct of the accused should be followed by described consequences the implied exclusion (of jurisdiction of an English court) is limited to cases where *neither* the conduct *nor* its harmful consequences took place in England or Wales.[48]

F.   CONCLUSIONS

In an era of global commerce marked by a growing trend towards deregulation, MNEs increasingly seem to be able to place themselves beyond effective legal control. There is a clear mismatch between traditional territorial bases of criminal court jurisdiction and the transnational repercussions of forces set in motion by MNEs and their subsidiaries. While host states are unwilling to prosecute for economic reasons and home states are claimed to lack jurisdiction, international criminal forums tend to restrict themselves to human rights violations committed by states or individuals.

While, perhaps, in the long term the criminality of MNEs would best be addressed in an international forum, the most effective short-term approach to the problem may lie in home state prosecutions of parent MNEs. Even if an international court with jurisdiction to prosecute MNEs were to be established, it would not eliminate the need for effective national remedies, as international law recognises that states bear the primary responsibility for prosecuting offences that occur within their territory. International legal tribunals offer a forum in which to achieve accountability, but only when a state is unable or unwilling to undertake a domestic prosecution. Conceiving of corporate criminality in terms of organisational fault provides a logical basis for the prosecution by a home state of an MNE for an offence that occurs in a host state of an overseas subsidiary. Britain would be well advised to follow the lead of Italy and allow such a prosecution.

46   [1975] RTR 256.
47   [1971] AC 537
48   [1971] AC 537 at 561-562, 564.

CHAPTER 6

When a company is on trial: Rules of evidence and procedure

A. INTRODUCTION

Previous chapters have looked at both the traditional substantive law for holding companies criminally liable and possible reform of that law. In the present chapter we examine what rules of evidence and procedure should apply when a company is on trial. The creation of a viable procedural system that can effectively deal with companies on trial, like the construction of a viable substantive test of corporate criminal liability, has been hampered by the judicial tendency to equate the situation of corporate defendants with that of human defendants. This linkage is neither inevitable nor desirable. It has served to saddle the trial with procedures that may not make particularly good sense for corporate defendants. Once the link between substantive corporate liability for humans and companies is broken, however, it becomes possible to envisage and consider new rules of evidence and procedure that can be utilised in the trial of a company that are both more efficient and fairer.

In the Anglo-American criminal justice system, trials are, for the most part, 'adversarial' in nature: the state, represented by a prosecutor, and the defendant present their evidence and arguments to a fact-finder for a decision. In England, the Magna Carta guaranteed to a person accused of a crime the right to a 'jury of his peers'. Although the term 'peers' should not be taken literally (a female defendant, for example, does not have the right to an all-woman jury and a member of a racial minority cannot demand that the jury be composed of others of his race), the fact that a defendant could not be convicted of a serious crime except by a verdict of ordinary members of the community has long been regarded as an inestimable safeguard of individual liberty in both England and the United States.

Although the adversarial model is probably sufficiently well entrenched to resist any proposals to replace it with an inquisitorial model of trial along the lines followed in much of continental Europe,[1] it is worth noting that over the years many inroads have been made on a 'pure' version of the model. In England, many cases formerly tried by juries are now heard and decided in jury-less magistrates' courts. Also, while the presumption of innocence and its corollary that the state prove the defendant's guilt by proof 'beyond reasonable doubt' (described by Viscount Sankey in *Woolmington v DPP*[2] as the 'golden thread' running through the English criminal law) have long been lionised, it is in fact not uncommon for Parliament to create a defence in favour of an accused and require the accused to prove the defence by a 'balance of probabilities'. Ashworth and Blake (1996) found 219 instances, out of 540 serious offences examined, which involved such a shifting of the burden of proof. Interestingly, at the time of Magna Carta, the procedural rules governing trial before a jury were not particularly favourable to the accused – there was no right to be legally represented, no right to compel favourable witnesses and no right to speak on one's own behalf, all of which are now taken for granted and protected by human rights jurisprudence.

The fact that traditional rules governing criminal procedure and evidence in English law have proved not to be as immutable as might have once been thought indicates that it would not be inappropriate to analyse how these rules might be modified in criminal trials involving companies. The keystone for trials of both companies and individuals is that the trial must take place within a criminal justice system that is fair and just, and is seen to be fair and just. But what does fairness and justice mean with respect to a company on trial? If what is to be established is not human blameworthiness but organisational fault, and given that a company does not face the prospect of imprisonment if convicted, then procedures and rules of evidence developed in order to safeguard human liberty might not be as necessary. The issues at least deserve to be considered on their merits. Inside this Pandora's

---

1   All the latest official studies on the criminal justice system agree that 'there is no persuasive case for a general move away from our adversarial process': *Review of the Criminal Courts of England and Wales by the Right Honourable Lord Justice Auld* (London: The Stationery Office, 2001) para 28, p 16, referring to the Reports of the Philips Commission *Report of the Royal Commission on Criminal Procedure* (London: HMSO, 1981) para 1.8 and the Runciman Commission *Report of the Royal Commission on Criminal Justice* (London: HMSO, 1993) paras 11–14. The two Commissions, however, inspired very different legislation. Whereas the Philips Commission led to the passage of the Police and Criminal Evidence Act 1984 (PACE 1984), which laid out a detailed legislative framework for the operation of police powers and suspects' rights, the Runciman Commission favoured, overall, the interests of the police and prosecutor more than those of the suspects. Legislation implemented after the Runciman Report (Criminal Justice and Public Order Act 1994, the Criminal Appeal Act 1995, the Criminal Procedure and Investigations Act 1996, the Police Act 1997, the Crime and Disorder Act 1998 and the Criminal Justice (Terrorism and Conspiracy) Act 1998) may have combined to significantly reduce the rights of suspects (Sanders and Young: 2000: 17–21).

2   *Woolmington v DPP* [1935] AC 462 at 481.

Box lie such fundamental questions as who should serve as the trier of fact when a company is on trial – a lay jury, a professional judge or some hybrid panel which includes a judge and business professionals; whether the traditional burden of proof (which is on the prosecution) and standard of proof ('beyond reasonable doubt') applicable to criminal cases might be modified; and, in light of the practical fact that the trial of a company is likely to turn on documentary evidence, whether rules relating to the admission of documentary evidence should be relaxed.

Many rules of evidence trace their origin to the fact that a jury composed of ordinary citizens, untrained in the law, served as the principal decision-maker. The fear was that these jurors might give undeserved weight to certain types of evidence, such as hearsay, or be confused by other types of evidence, such as documents. There were other reasons for the restrictions on hearsay and documentary evidence, but a solicitude to the perceived limitations of jurors was undoubtedly a factor. The English tradition of oral evidence stemmed from the conviction that it was unrealistic to expect jurors to understand technical and complex written materials. Indeed, at the time of the jury's development, few jurors could read. Thus, if it were to be decided that juries should be dispensed with in trials of companies, then these rules of evidence, fashioned with the jury in mind, might also be rethought, as they have been in civil cases in England, where juries feature infrequently. Since the Civil Evidence Act 1968, most evidence is admissible if the judge deems it to be relevant.

We can glimpse what types of modifications might be made by examining proposals relating to serious fraud trials that have been advanced in England by prestigious committees. In addition to looking at these, we propose to examine other legal systems to see how the trials of companies have been dealt with there. The United States provides a natural point of comparison, finding the roots of its criminal law in English common law decisions; using, like England, an adversarial system of trial; and, in addition, having a long tradition of putting corporations on trial. Interesting insights can also be gleaned from civil law jurisdictions. As discussed in chapter 3, Italy has recently enacted a comprehensive statute on the criminal liability of corporations based on concepts of organisational fault not dissimilar to proposals contained in this book. As Italian criminal procedure is now structured along the lines of an adversarial system of trials, it would be useful to compare how the Italian legislature has handled the procedural hurdles of a criminal trial where the defendant is a company.

In an accusatorial system of criminal justice, a balance needs to be struck between the needs of the prosecution, the search for the truth and the protection of the rights of the accused. In common law jurisdictions, the rights of privacy and to be free from governmental interference have played a prominent role in the effort to regulate the state-individual relationship, and the powers of the prosecution have often been restricted even at the expense of the search for the truth. Today, many of these same interests are protected by the Human Rights Act 1998 and, in the larger world of Europe, by the European Convention of Human Rights (in the United States, similar protections are guaranteed by the US Constitution). Under the relevant constitutional provisions, conventions and caselaw, a defendant in a criminal trial retains certain fundamental rights that cannot be abridged by the state without good cause. Of course, as Judge Sir Nicholas Bratza has observed (2000: 2), one must still determine whether a convention which was drawn up 'to protect the fundamental rights of individuals to life, liberty, fair trial, privacy, freedom of thought, expression and association [has] any relevance in what may be loosely described as a commercial context'. Stated another way, do companies have 'human' rights?

B. THE CHOICE OF TRIER OF FACT: ARE JURIES APPROPRIATE?

Litigation where the defendant is a company can entail lengthy trials, complex documentary evidence and highly technical issues that call into question the effectiveness of using a jury as the trier of fact. Jurors may not understand the critical business issues raised by a corporate case and, because of the need to tailor presentation of the evidence to facilitate the jurors' comprehension, the trial may last longer than if a judge were the adjudicator. Technical objections stemming from the need to keep certain evidence from the jury, because it might be given disproportionate weight, can distort or skew the proceedings. If relevant but potentially prejudicial evidence is withheld, the jury may be left with an incomplete picture of the extent of the defendant's misconduct. Also, as a practical matter, evidence may be voluntarily withheld from the jury by the prosecution in order to speed up the trial, as some prosecutors believe that jurors have a tendency to forget the evidence presented at the beginning of a lengthy trial. Finally, the prospect of lengthy jury service may induce many who are summoned for jury duty to find excuses to avoid serving, leaving unrepresentative juries, composed of the unemployed, the unemployable, the very old and the very young, to decide the case.

There are two ways of meeting these various objections. One would be to substitute some decision-maker other than a jury when a company is on trial. The other would be to reform the jury system so that jurors would be better able to understand the evidence in complicated business cases. To illustrate the lack of consensus as to how best to proceed generally, there have been proposals to broaden the composition of the jury by expanding the range of backgrounds of the persons who serve on juries, as well as proposals to restrict jury service in certain cases to a limited class of persons with a background in business and financial matters.

1. The Roskill Report

In 1986, a committee under the chairmanship of Lord Roskill was asked to analyse criminal procedures in cases involving serious frauds. A serious fraud case for the purposes of the committee was one:

> ... in which dishonesty is buried in a series of inter-related transactions, most frequently in a market offering highly-specialised services, or in areas of high-finance involving (for example) manipulation of the ownership of the companies. The complexity lies in the fact that the markets, or areas of business, operate according to concepts which bear no obvious similarity to anything in the general experience of most members of the public, and are governed by rules, and conducted in a language, learned only after prolonged study by those involved' (Roskill: 1986: 153).

Although the committee's proposals were developed for one fairly specific category of property offence and were not designed with the trial of companies particularly in mind, they none the less provide a useful starting point for considering changes that might be made in the trial of complicated cases involving a company.

Roskill argued for a specialised panel, the Fraud Trials Tribunal (FTT), as the trier of fact in cases involving serious fraud that were marked by a high degree of complexity. The FTT, which would replace the jury, was to be composed of a High Court or circuit judge and two lay members selected from a panel of persons with skills and expertise in business generally and experience in complex business transactions (Roskill: 1986: 149). Because the lay members of the panel would be capable of understanding and reading through complicated documents, trials could be expected to be more efficient. Complex documentary evidence that might mislead or confuse jurors could be admitted without qualms, and lengthy explanations by counsel of the significance of the documents would become unnecessary. The judge would be responsible for dealing with questions of law and evidence, but in other respects the lay members would be allowed to participate fully, including being entitled to ask questions of witnesses and counsel (Roskill: 1986: 150–51).

The committee's recommendation for the use of a specialised tribunal in serious fraud trials was based on its belief that the complexity and length of such trials set them apart from most other criminal cases. It was not uncommon for thousands of pages of documentary evidence to be introduced at the trial. The view of the committee was that ordinary jurors would encounter difficulty in absorbing this evidence and in assessing it accurately. Even though jurors are allowed to take notes, they receive no training on how to do so efficiently; and even though they may pose questions to the judge when they are confused, few are inclined to do so unless they receive the appropriate judicial encouragement, which is rarely forthcoming. The ultimate fear of the Roskill committee was that a jury's verdict in a serious fraud case could be based upon an overall subjective impression of guilt or innocence that might not be reliable or be supported by the evidence.[3] It might be observed, however, that there is in fact little empirical evidence as to whether or not jury verdicts are reliable in serious fraud, or, for that matter, any other trials, as, under the Contempt of Court Act 1981, jurors are forbidden from discussing their deliberations with researchers or other outsiders.

The Roskill Committee had received evidence that the average serious fraud prosecution between 1979 and 1983 lasted longer than 20 working days. The committee thought that many prospective jurors would not be willing to give up such an amount of time and would seek to be excused. If their requests were to be granted, the case would be heard by a jury composed of persons who were either not gainfully employed or who were prepared to sacrifice other engagements because of an undisclosed 'axe to grind'. Where gainfully employed persons are excused because to serve would cause financial hardship, the resulting jury can hardly be said to be representative of a cross-section of the community. A further concern with respect to lengthy trials was that ordinary jurors might not be capable of maintaining the required level of attention and concentration for the required periods.

The Roskill Committee addressed and rejected a number of counter-arguments that had been advanced in favour of retaining jury trials. The first argument related to public confidence in the verdict. Normally, the fact that juries are composed of

---

3   Roskill (1986) Fraud Trials Committee Report: paras 8.25-8.30, pp 139–141.

members of the community like themselves will give the public a confidence in their verdicts. This confidence might not be present if the decision-maker were to be a judge sitting alone or with business professionals. Indeed, if such a jury were to acquit a corporate executive, it might popularly be viewed as a 'stitch-up'. The Roskill Committee was of the opinion, however, that the ordinary man and woman's confidence in jury verdicts might well be misplaced, as it was not clear that the public appreciated either the extent of the complexities in serious fraud trials or the consequences of such complexities (Roskill: 1986: 135–36). In some cases, the difficulty of presenting evidence in a comprehensible form to lay jurors was seen to be one of the contributing factors that could lead to a decision not to bring a case to trial or to charge a less serious offence (Roskill: 1986: 142–143).

A common argument in favour of jury trial generally is that juries serve as a safeguard against the operation of unjust and oppressive laws. The case of Clive Ponting is often given as an example.[4] Ponting was charged with violating the Official Secrets Act 1911 for having disclosed to Parliament sensitive information regarding an incident that had occurred during the Falklands War. Although it seemed clear that Ponting had violated the Act as a factual matter, the jury returned an acquittal. Such examples of 'jury nullification', mostly in cases involving issues of free speech, are, however, far removed from cases of serious fraud, and even the most ardent advocate of free speech would be hard-pressed to argue that freedom of speech includes the right to defraud others through word or deed.

There is also the 'thin end of the wedge' argument that, once an alternative to traditional jury trial has been established in cases of serious fraud, it might lead to the elimination of juries in other serious crimes – including murder, battery, rape and robbery – that should remain the province of jury trial. Tellingly, the Roskill Committee pointed out that the vast majority of criminal cases in England and Wales were already tried before non-jury specialist tribunals composed of lay magistrates. If the assumption is correct that trial by jury is the fairest form of trial, it asked, then why was jury trial not used in the over 90% of cases where the defendant could face imprisonment in a summary trial?[5] Using a specialist decision-maker rather than a jury should not concern society at large, reasoned the committee, because it is in society's interest that verdicts be delivered by the persons best qualified by training and experience to do so (Roskill: 1986: 139).

Another argument advanced in favour of jury trial in serious fraud cases is that the main issue in such cases is nothing more complicated than honesty, and that randomly selected jurors can assess honesty as well, if not better, than a specialist tribunal. The committee opined that 'society seems to have an attachment for jury trials which is emotional or sentimental rather than logical' (Roskill: 1986: 139) and this point may have particular salience for a jury's alleged ability to distinguish between honest and dishonest defendants. The mannerisms that lay persons associate with honesty and dishonesty have little empirical basis and may not be reliable.

---

4 *R v Ponting* [1985] Crim LR 318.
5 Some would argue, however, that the decision to allow verdicts in serious cases to be returned by magistrates rather than juries is itself questionable (eg Gobert: 1997).

A final issue had to do with the Magna Carta's guarantee of a 'jury of one's peers'. The scope of this 'right' and what exactly it entailed has always been somewhat unclear. The Roskill Committee offered two possible interpretations: one was that it guaranteed a citizen the right to be tried by a group of other citizens, randomly selected; the second was that a defendant had the right to be tried by those having a background, experience etc similar to his/her own (Roskill: 1986: 137). The first position reflected prevailing practice. The second would suggest that the jury in a serious fraud case involving a business professional should consist of other businessmen and businesswomen. Yet these are the persons most likely to seek and be granted relief from jury service, as their business interests would suffer (particularly when the juror is a sole proprietor of a business) if they were required to spend an undue length of time on jury duty.

One member of the Committee, Mr Merricks, dissenting from the proposal to use specialised tribunals in serious fraud cases, pointed out that that it was the lawyer's responsibility to present complicated technical information in a way that could be understood by a jury. Merricks argued that the public explanation of the charges 'performs a vital function – that of ensuring that members of the public and the press are also informed of the nature of the case'. Not only does the jury represent the public's interest at the trial, but also its presence ensures a public exposition of the case. There is the danger in a trial before an expert panel that this public dimension would be lost: 'I do not think that the public would or should be satisfied with a criminal justice system where citizens stand at risk of imprisonment for lengthy periods following trials where the state admits that it cannot explain its evidence in terms commonly comprehensible.'[6] Furthermore, an acquittal delivered by a judge sitting alone or with a panel of expert assessors is in danger of being perceived as a case of the establishment looking after its own. The desire to avoid such public criticism might even produce undue pressures to return a conviction in a marginal case.

It remains only to observe that many of the objections to jury trial referred to in the Roskill Report would seem equally applicable when a company is charged with serious fraud (Levi: 1991). If a specialised tribunal or jury were to be employed in such cases, not only would the tribunal be able to understand the financial dimensions of the case, but also it would be able critically to evaluate the internal command structures of the corporate organisation. Further, the tribunal would be capable of drawing the correct inferences from the financial records and other documentary evidence that often are the lynchpin of the prosecutor's case. Traditional rules of evidence restricting the admission of documents could then be relaxed, allowing for a more complete picture of events to emerge than would have been the case in a jury trial where such evidence was excluded.

Many of the recommendations proposed by the Roskill Committee were put into effect by the Criminal Justice Act 1987. These included, most importantly, the establishment of a Serious Fraud Office (discussed in chapter 9) and the streamlining of pre-trial procedures. Of the recommendations that were not accepted, the most significant was the proposal for non-jury trials. This did not end the matter, however, as a series of post-1987 cases continued to raise questions regarding whether juries might be experiencing difficulty in comprehending the evidence in serious fraud

---

6   Roskill (1986) Fraud Trials Committee Report: paras C19, C20 (Note of Dissent by Mr Merricks), pp 195, 196.

trials. Whenever corporate defendants were acquitted, critics of the jury system were quick to assert, with little or no empirical basis, that the reason for the acquittal lay in the jury's inability to understand the prosecution case. The government too remained sceptical about what it deemed to be an unduly high rate of acquittals by juries, although these did not necessarily occur to a disproportionate extent in cases of serious fraud. None the less, the government in 1998 decided yet again to issue a consultation document on the use of jury trials in serious fraud cases.[7] The resulting report was in turn superseded by the broader review by Lord Auld of the criminal justice system.

2. The Auld Report

The 2001 Review of the Criminal Courts of England and Wales by Lord Auld accepted the premise that the resolution of issues of fact should in the main continue to be the responsibility of the jury (and, in a magistrates' court, lay magistrates). Rather than discarding the jury system, Lord Auld recommended that it be reformed and streamlined (Auld: 2001: chapter 11). With the aim of empanelling juries that were more representative of the diversity and range of experiences found in the community, he recommended expanding the categories of persons eligible for jury service and narrowing the scope for excusals from service, particularly in the case of professional persons. Similarly, he recommended the vigorous and well-publicised enforcement of the obligation to undertake jury service, going so far as to favour a system of fixed penalties for those who deliberately evaded service. When it came to serious fraud cases, however, Lord Auld seemed to retreat from his more expansive vision of the jury. Echoing the Roskill Report and the 1998 consultation paper, and accepting the complications posed by serious fraud cases, he supported substituting some other form of decision-maker in these cases. He also noted that the procedural and evidential reforms of the Criminal Justice Act 1987 had not reduced the problems that had been identified as being associated with jury trial in serious fraud cases.

The two main factors that most influenced Lord Auld's analysis were the burdensome length of serious fraud trials and the increasing specialty and complexity of the cases. His report quoted the Director of the Serious Fraud Office to the effect that the average trial prosecuted by the Serious Fraud Office lasted for six months and that in such cases the juries tended to be composed of the 'unemployed or unemployable' (Auld: 2001: 204). It also accepted that fraud and other long and specialised cases demanded more, rather than less, in the way of skills and knowledge than the traditional English jury was able to provide. Lord Auld recommended that, as a preliminary matter, serious fraud cases should be assigned to a High Court or circuit judge experienced in trying such cases to decide, after hearing from the parties, whether the case should be heard by a traditional jury or by the judge sitting with a panel of persons with experience in complex financial matters. Lord Auld also was of the opinion that, if the defendant desired, the case should be able to be heard by a trial judge sitting alone (Auld: 2001: 208).

---

7 'Juries in Serious Fraud Cases: A Consultation Document' (London: Home Office, 1998) paras 2.4–2.8.

Lord Auld saw scope for the referral of other complex cases to the envisaged tribunal. He recognised, however, that sole reliance on the criteria of 'complexity' to justify a non-jury trial could give rise to claims of disparities of treatment between cases tried by a jury and cases tried by some other form of tribunal. He therefore considered adoption of criteria similar to those for determining whether there should be trial by jury in civil cases of fraud, libel, slander, malicious prosecution and false imprisonment. These cases will be heard by a jury 'unless the court is of the opinion that the trial requires any prolonged examination of documents or accounts or any scientific or local investigation which cannot conveniently be made with a jury'.[8] In determining what can be 'conveniently' investigated by a jury, civil courts have looked at several factors: the physical problem of handling the documentation, the prolongation of the trial (jury trials tending to last longer than trials before a judge sitting alone), the cost (jury trials being more expensive than trials before a judge sitting alone) and the possibility that the jury might not understand the case.[9] A further consideration is that a judge, sitting alone or with an expert panel, can be required to give a reasoned judgment, thereby facilitating appellate court review, whereas juries have never been required and, realistically, given their composition, probably never could be required to give reasons for their verdicts. However, in the final analysis, Lord Auld decided that it would make for a more orderly starting point to change the tribunal of decision only in those cases that involved frauds of such seriousness and complexity to fall within the Criminal Justice Act 1987, ss 4 and 7 (Auld: 2001: 211). He left open the option for a future broadening of this category as 'the overriding criterion in each case should be the *interests of justice* (Auld: 2001: 211–212; emphasis added).

3. 'Justice for All'

In July 2002 the government brought forward a White Paper, *Justice for All* (Home Office: 2002). The aim of the White Paper was to reform the criminal justice system so as to better protect the interests of victims and the community, to make prosecutions more effective and efficient and, ultimately, to reduce the incidence of crime. Following in the steps of the Roskill and Auld Reports, the White Paper accepted the by now familiar litany of difficulties in trying cases of serious fraud and other complex 'white-collar' crime cases. The solution proposed, however, was different than that of Auld or Roskill. Commenting on the concept of a judge sitting with a panel of financial experts, the government offered its opinion that 'identifying and recruiting suitable people raises considerable difficulties, not least because this would represent a substantial commitment over a long period of time' (Home Office: 2002: 4.30). The preferred solution of the government was for a trial by a judge sitting alone.

The White Paper did not stop there, however. It also considered the suitability of judge-only trials for other complex and lengthy cases, giving as an example those cases involving 'organised crime…. where there are similar complex financial

---

8　Supreme Court Act 1981, s 69.
9　See *Beta Construction Ltd v Channel 4 TV Ltd* [1990] 1 WLR 1042.

and commercial agreements' (Home Office: 2002: 4.31). The restriction to 'organised crime' cases seems somewhat puzzling, as the point about the length and complexity of such trials would appear to be more germane to the question of whether or not to dispense with a conventional jury. If length and complexity are, indeed, the critical considerations, it is not difficult to envisage the use of judge-only trials being extended to cases where a company is the defendant. These cases, by their very nature, tend to be more complex and lengthy than trials of natural persons.

The merits of entrusting serious fraud trials, and possibly lengthy trials involving complex financial issues, to a single judge, as opposed to a judge sitting with persons with experience in complex business and financial affairs, as recommended by both Roskill and Auld, are questionable. First, it may be naïve to assume that any judge will be as knowledgeable of the intricacies of the world of finance as those involved in that world on a daily basis. Lord Lawton once commented about a complex fraud case that there were only three people in the courtroom who truly understood the case, and that these did not include the prosecuting counsel, the defence counsel (Lord Lawton) and the judge (Harman and Griffith: 1979: 19). Second, even assuming a class of specialist judges with a general knowledge of commercial and financial matters, the judge selected for a particular trial may lack the expertise needed to evaluate what has occurred in the case. For example, a judge knowledgeable about business affairs generally may not have the technical computer skills to understand a fraud perpetrated through use of the Internet. The desired expertise would be more likely to be found in a specialist panel with a more diverse range of backgrounds and experiences. Third, there is the ever-present difficulty posed whenever a single person decides a case: no matter how strenuously the decision-maker strives to be fair, unconscious biases may compromise his/her objectivity. One of the strengths of the jury system is that on a panel of 12 (or whatever number), a particular juror's biases will be exposed, challenged and refuted by other members of the panel who do not share the speaker's prejudices (Gobert: 1997). Finally, it might be noted that a primary function of jury trial is to incorporate the views of the community into the decision-making process. Granted that it would be the business community whose views would be incorporated into the decision-making process under the specialist tribunal envisaged by both Auld and Roskill, at least their perspective would be closer 'to the ground' than would be the perspective of a perhaps long-sitting judge with a great deal of judicial experience but less in the way of practical experience in the world of business.

It is no doubt true, as the government maintains in the White Paper, that serving as a member of an expert financial tribunal, along with a judge, could represent a substantial investment of time over an extended period. However, by its own reckoning, the government anticipates only about 15–20 serious fraud trials each year. Thus, it would be unlikely that any given individual would be called upon to sit on a panel more than once in his/her lifetime. The persons who would sit on the panel, moreover, would presumably be both prestigious and financially secure, so that the burden on them from sitting would not be as great as it might be on ordinary jurors. Finally, as the business community should have a strong interest in eliminating fraudsters who damage the reputation of respectable companies, it would be in its self-interest to become involved in the decision-making process in these cases.

4. Crimes of corporate violence

Both the Roskill and Auld Reports highlighted the problems of jury trials in cases involving serious fraud, where the trial tends to be long and the evidence complex. However, even assuming that the recommendations of these reports were to be adopted and applied to crimes by companies involving serious fraud, they would touch only one dimension of corporate crime. Many would maintain a more critical dimension relates to cases involving 'corporate violence', and especially cases of corporate manslaughter. While the government has proposed the creation of an offence of corporate killing, it did not address the issue of who should sit in judgment of the corporate defendant. Presumably it would continue to be the jury.

In support of jury trial in cases involving corporate violence, it might be argued that the issues in these cases do not differ significantly from those in homicide or assault cases involving natural persons. Indeed, under tests where the company's liability is vicarious or based on the liability of a person 'identified' with the company, it would have to be proved at trial that an individual for whose offence the company could be held responsible had committed a homicide or assault. This would seem to suggest that these cases would be no more complicated and roughly equal in length to cases where only the individual alone was charged. Moreover, it is in cases involving homicides and serious physical injury that public confidence in the resulting verdict is a particularly compelling consideration. While the public might be prepared to defer to the views of a specialist tribunal where the charge is one involving the loss of property (especially when the victim is another company or an amorphous entity such as the stock exchange), it is less likely to grant such deference when a human being has been killed or seriously injured. The victim and his/her family are also likely to take a stronger interest in such cases and may be seeking either accountability or some form of cathartic vindication.

With respect to cases tried under an 'identification' test of corporate criminal liability, however, this analysis overlooks the requirement of proof that the individual who is alleged to have committed the crime in question can be identified with the company. As noted by Steyn LJ (as he then was) in *R v British Steel Plc*,[10] proof of this issue can occupy the bulk of a trial. Establishing the requisite 'identification' status may require a close examination and interpretation of complex documents, including the company's constitution, its articles of association and its contractual arrangements with the relevant officer or director. Even under the more expansive American approach to vicarious liability, comparable documents may have to be introduced and examined to exclude the possibility that the employee who perpetrated the offence was not 'on a frolic of his own'. This proof might depend on the employee's contract of employment, terms of reference, job description and directives issued by the company, all of which evidence could be expected to prolong and complicate the trial, making it resemble in character more that of a serious fraud case than a case of homicide.

If instead of a derivative test of liability, the courts were to adopt a test of organisational fault, then documentary evidence would likely become even more critical. Board minutes might have to be examined to determine what the directors knew with respect to the risk of criminality, when they had acquired their knowledge

10 [1995] ICR 586.

(before or after the offence) and what steps they had taken to prevent criminality of the sort that had occurred. To determine a company's ethos, culture or attitude towards criminality might require an examination of the history of the company over an extended period of time. Introduction of such evidence would inevitably prolong and complicate a trial, and would demand a degree of interpretive ability that might well be unfamiliar to even the more sophisticated jurors.

Juries are prized for their alleged impartiality, but one can question how impartial jurors will be in cases involving companies. As discussed in chapter 3, the test of mens rea in cases of involuntary manslaughter in England and Wales is that of gross negligence. The leading authority is *R v Adomako*.[11] However, the concept of gross negligence as set out in *Adomako* was somewhat circular, leaving open the question of how negligent must a defendant's negligence be before it can be characterised as 'gross'. In addressing this issue, Lord Mckay stated:

> It is true that to a certain extent [gross negligence] involves an element of circularity, but in this branch of the law I do not believe that is fatal to its being correct as a test of how far conduct must depart from accepted standards to be characterised as criminal. This is necessarily a question of degree and an attempt to specify that degree more closely is I think likely to achieve only a spurious precision. The essence of the matter which is supremely a jury question is whether having regard to the risk of death involved, the conduct of the defendant was so bad in all the circumstances as to amount in their judgment to a criminal act or omission.[12]

Lord McKay puts the onus on the jury to determine whether a defendant's conduct has reached the requisite level of negligence to be characterised as gross. In the case of a natural person, there will usually be little danger of a wrongful *conviction* if the issue of gross negligence is left to a jury. The natural empathy of jurors will lie with the fellow human being on trial. This empathy helps to ameliorate any potential harshness that might be implicit in the controlling law. While there may be a risk of an erroneous *acquittal* in such circumstances, such a risk is already implicit in the law's requirement of proof 'beyond reasonable doubt' and is generally not viewed with as much concern as the possibility of the conviction of an innocent individual. In the case of a corporate defendant, on the other hand, the jury's natural sympathy is not likely to lie with the defendant. On the contrary, the greater risk is that jurors who may have had an unsatisfactory experience with an insurance company, lending institution, bank, department store or any large 'impersonal' organisation may choose the trial on which they are serving to vent their frustration. There is for this reason a greater risk of an erroneous conviction in the trial of a company than in the trial of a natural person. The risk is especially great in cases where a victim has died or been seriously injured for the jurors' natural sympathies are likely to lie with the deceased worker and his/her family. As the jurors may be aware that their verdict may have ramifications for a subsequent civil suit by the victim or his/her family (even if neither counsel nor the judge allude to this point), they may convict despite 'reasonable doubt' regarding the guilt of the corporate defendant.

There is also the question of a jury's competence to determine when a company has been at fault. In cases where an ordinary person is charged with a crime of gross

11 [1995] 1 AC 171.
12 [1995] 1 AC 171 at 187.

negligence, the jurors, by virtue of their collective experience, are usually able to discern what would have been a reasonable course of action for the defendant to have followed in the circumstances. 'Would we have acted as did the defendant?' is the type of question that jurors will ask themselves, whether the question relates to the legal test of culpability or their evaluation of the credibility of the defendant's denial of liability. The question may become somewhat more complicated when a defendant with a specialist background and skills, such as Dr Adomako, is on trial. Few jurors will be sufficiently knowledgeable to be able to judge whether Dr Adomako had behaved as would a reasonable anaesthetist under the circumstances, because few jurors will know what a reasonable anaesthetist would have done. But often, as arguably occurred in Dr Adomako's case, the defendant's misconduct will be of so egregious a nature as to virtually speak for itself, or expert witnesses will be able to provide testimony that will simplify the jury's task.

When the question is whether a company has conducted its affairs in a reasonable manner, on the other hand, the jurors will rarely be able to use their collective personal experiences or the intrinsic nature of the company's course of conduct to guide them. And while expert witnesses may be called to testify, in all likelihood, the Crown and the defence will each call their own experts whose testimony will be in conflict because of the experts' social and economic philosophy. A difference in philosophy is less likely to affect expert testimony in, say, a case of alleged medical misconduct that resulted in death or serious injury. Who is competent to say what a *reasonable company* would have done under the circumstances of the case or, indeed, what constitutes a 'reasonable company'? Few, if any, jurors would be qualified to answer such questions. While there might possibly be a juror with experience in the industry, there then would be the danger that that one juror's opinion would carry disproportionate weight in the deliberations.

C.   RULES OF EVIDENCE

The strong oral tradition in English trials is due not only to the widespread illiteracy of the original jurors, but also to the belief that seeing and hearing the evidence of a witness with personal knowledge of the events under consideration is the best way of learning the truth. The psychological assumption is that a witness is most likely to be truthful when testifying under oath, in the witness box, in public, and subject to cross-examination.

1.   The hearsay rule and documentary evidence

Generally speaking, the hearsay rule excludes testimony that is not based on the first-hand knowledge of a witness. However, there are numerous exceptions to the hearsay rule and whether documentary evidence falls within the rule or within an exception to the rule has often been a bone of contention.

Although the distrust of documentary evidence and its exclusion under the hearsay rule originally had been a by-product of having as the trier of fact a jury of lay citizens, many of whom were illiterate, this does not explain the continuation of the practice in an era of mass literacy. Some have attributed the distrust of documentary evidence to the nature of an adversarial system of trial that relies on cross-examination to expose inconsistencies, misperceptions and outright falsehoods on the part of a witness (Morgan: 1957). A document obviously cannot be cross-examined, although its maker can. Research seems to support the view that in an adversarial system, where witnesses often are closely identified with the interests of one party or the other, and where judges are not directly involved in the fact-finding, secondary sources of information can be difficult for a jury to understand and evaluate (McEwan: 1998). In any event, whether it is due to the jury system or to the nature of an adversarial mode of trial, common law systems retain a distrust for documentary evidence that is not shared by civil law systems in continental Europe that do not employ juries and that take a more inquisitorial approach to fact-finding. In continental jurisdictions there is often a preference in favour of documentary evidence because it is regarded as less prone to distortion or manipulation in cross-examination than is oral testimony.

Irrespective of the mode of trial, in certain cases documents are more reliable evidence than oral testimony. Cases involving complex transactions that have taken place over a lengthy period of time can usually be more easily proved through documentary evidence than through oral testimony. In addition, much relevant evidence occurs naturally in documentary form, making it somewhat artificial and inefficient to deal with the matter through oral testimony. *Myers v DPP*[13] is often cited as an illustration of the problem. In this case, records compiled in the process of manufacturing cars were excluded on the basis of the hearsay rule. The workers who had compiled the records could not be identified but, even if they could have been identified, their testimony probably would have added little. Their cross-examination would not have established anything other than the fact that they had no interest in making false records and that the records were truthful to the best of their knowledge. As a consequence of the problems exposed by *Myers*, the Criminal Evidence Act 1965 changed the law so that documents of the sort that were involved in *Myers* became admissible.

The Roskill Committee was sensitive to how the hearsay rule could hamper the prosecution of complicated fraud cases and offered a framework that could also be useful in other prosecutions of companies in which documentary evidence rated to figure prominently. The report, noting that evidential rules that were devised to protect the innocent should not become a shield for the guilty, observed:

> These rules were all clearly designed for an era when most of the population could be presumed to be illiterate. While their strict application has caused few difficulties in the general run of criminal cases, they seem increasingly inappropriate and burdensome in cases of fraud and dishonesty which themselves arise from business transactions which are the subject of written records (Roskill: 1986: 65).

The report recommended giving to the judge an 'inclusionary' (as opposed to an 'exclusionary') discretion. The judge would decide *before* trial whether a document should be admitted into evidence. The party seeking to have the document admitted without calling its maker or some other appropriate witness would have to give an indication of its nature and source. Similarly, the report advocated giving judges the authority to admit into evidence experts' reports, schedules and charts.

13 *Myers v DPP* [1965] AC 1001.

Roskill favoured a system in which documents could be admitted at the discretion of the judge over one consisting of a basic hearsay rule with structured exceptions to deal with particular situations. The latter approach had been taken in the Police and Criminal Evidence Act 1984 (PACE 1984). PACE 1984 had acknowledged the general preference for oral evidence subject to a set of exceptions where oral testimony was not available: where the relevant witness was either dead, ill or could not be found; where the witness was outside the United Kingdom and could not attend the trial; and where the witness could not be expected to have any recollection of the matter at trial in the light of the circumstances and the time that had elapsed.

The Criminal Justice Act 1988 also addressed the admissibility of documentary evidence. The Bill originally presented to Parliament was far reaching in its scope and purported to render first-hand documentary evidence, which would otherwise be excluded as hearsay, admissible without the need to satisfy the strict requirements of admissibility of both statutory and common law exceptions to the hearsay rule. Under the original Bill the control over hearsay evidence was to be exercised through the discretionary power of the judge to exclude evidence which it was not in the interest of justice to admit. In this respect the Bill went beyond the Roskill recommendation that the trial judge be given an inclusionary discretion with regard to otherwise inadmissible documentary evidence. However, opponents in Parliament pointed to the safeguards for the defendant that were built into the adversarial system of trial and argued that these could only work within the framework of oral testimony and the possibility for meaningful cross-examination of witnesses. Lord Hutchinson summed up their thinking:

> [I]t is the reaction and the demeanour of the witness when tested which may cause doubts in the jury's mind as to his reliability. It is not the material which happens to be in the advocate's hand which is going to make any difference.[14]

As a consequence of such criticisms, the resulting Act was restructured in a similar way to PACE 1984, s 68, with strict conditions that needed to be satisfied in order to overcome the hearsay rule.

Documentary hearsay is now controlled by the Criminal Justice Act 1988, ss 23 and 24. These sections allow for the introduction of otherwise inadmissible evidence. The first step for the court in applying these sections is to determine whether or not the evidence in question is hearsay. Only if it is, and only if there is no common law exception that would allow for the evidence to be admitted, do ss 23 and 24 come into play. Under s 23, documentary evidence can be admitted provided that the maker is unavailable for one of the reasons identified in sub-ss (2) and (3). Sub-section (2) requires that:

(a) the person who made the statement is dead or unfit to attend as a witness by reason of his bodily or mental condition;
(b) The person who made the statement is outside the United Kingdom and it is not reasonably practical to secure his attendance;
(c) all reasonable steps have been taken to find the person who made the statement but he cannot be found.

14 Lord Hutchinson in 489 HL Official Report (5th series) col 77, 20 October 1987 (quoted in Birch: 1989: 17).

and sub-s (3) that:

(a) the statement was made to a police officer or some other person charged with the duty of investigating offences or charging offenders; and
(b) the person who made the statement does not give oral evidence through fear or because he is kept out of the way.

Under both subsections the burden of proof is on the party seeking to introduce the evidence to convince the judge, in the absence of the jury, of the maker's unavailability. If it is the prosecution that is seeking to introduce the evidence, the standard of proof is that of 'beyond reasonable doubt'. If it is the defence, it is only required to meet a 'balance of probabilities' standard.[15]

The Criminal Justice Act 1988, s 24 allows into evidence documents 'created or received by a person in the course of a trade, business, profession or other occupation, or as the holder of a paid or unpaid office'. The information may be supplied directly or indirectly, and does not need to be first-hand, provided that the person supplying the information 'had, or may reasonably be supposed to have had, the personal knowledge of the matters dealt with'.

There is a greater willingness on the part of the courts to admit business documents than other forms of written hearsay because of the greater reliability attached to these documents. Business documents are more likely to be reliable because it can be expected that, for reasons of professional pride and to avoid adverse repercussions in their employment, persons who are responsible for keeping records will strive to do so accurately. Furthermore, the regularity of business procedures itself arguably promotes accuracy. The same considerations apply even when the information has been passed through several individuals before being written down, as long as all of the persons in the chain passed on the information in the course of business. None the less, there can be confusion as to what falls within the category of 'business' documents and the words 'received by' also can cause problems of interpretation (Ockleton: 1992). If taken literally they would seem to render admissible, as a business document, any document which at some point had been physically passed to a person in the course of that person's employment, such as, for example, a letter to the editor of a newspaper, as the editor would have received the letter in a professional capacity.

Under the Criminal Justice Act 1988, ss 25 and 26, judges retain an 'exclusionary' discretion. Section 25 permits a judge to exclude a document that would otherwise be admissible under s 23 or s 24 if the judge deems that it is not 'in the interests of justice' to admit the document. In considering this question, the judge is to be guided by the factors identified in s 25(2): the nature, source and likely authenticity of the document; the extent to which the document appears to supply evidence not otherwise readily available; the relevance of the evidence; and any risk of unfairness to the defendant from its admission or exclusion (in particular, whether it is going to be possible to controvert the statement if the person making it does not attend to give oral testimony). Section 25 generally has been construed to create a presumption in favour of admitting the evidence, the section serving primarily to mitigate against an overly literal reading of the requirements of s 24. In its consultation paper on evidence (Law Com Report: 1997), the Law Commission observed that the considerations to be taken into account by courts in deciding whether to admit evidence under s 25 tended to cancel each

15 *R v Mattey and Queeley* [1995] 2 Cr App Rep 409.

other out, so that judges could be left without clear guidance. As a result, cases often turned on their own facts, with the concomitant risk of unpredictability and inconsistent rulings. In some cases courts have seemed to strain to admit documents that form the main body of the case against a defendant.[16]

The Law Commission's report sought greater consistency in the application of the hearsay rule. The issue that the Commission had to decide was whether such consistency could better be achieved by a discretionary approach or by a rule-based approach to the law of evidence. The Commission favoured the latter, as it believed that the discretionary power granted to courts under the Criminal Justice Act 1988 had led to significant inconsistencies in the law (Law Com Report: 1997: 4.28–4.31). It proposed a general 'exclusionary' hearsay rule with specified exceptions and a limited 'inclusionary' discretion. In respect to business documents, the Commission recommended that statements falling within the business documents exceptions should be admitted, but that the court should retain the power to decide that a certain document should not be admissible as a business document if it had doubts regarding its reliability (Law Com Report: 1997: 8.71–8.83).

It is arguably useful to distinguish between jury trials and trials before a judge, although the Commission's proposed reforms were intended for all criminal proceedings in which the strict rules of evidence apply. It is submitted that more leeway with respect to the admission of documentary evidence can be allowed when a judge, rather than a jury, is the trier of fact, as the judge is less likely to be misled by such evidence or give it inappropriate weight. The Commission's proposals seem to rely on the exercise of a judicial inclusionary discretion to admit into evidence documents whose probative value is such that they should be admitted in the interests of justice. Although the Commission purported to forsake a discretionary approach to exceptions, its recommendation of an inclusionary discretion would seem to bring discretion in by the back door.

With respect to the future direction of the law, the 2002 White Paper, *Justice for All*, endorses comprehensive reform of evidentiary and procedural rules, and the enactment of both a criminal evidence code and a criminal procedure code (Home Office: 2002: 4.51). The government states that 'it is important that when witnesses are testifying, rules of evidence do not artificially prevent the true and full story from being presented to the court' (Home Office: 2002: 4.62). Referring specifically to hearsay evidence, the government states:

> We believe that the right approach [to hearsay evidence] is that, if there is a good reason for the original maker not to be able to give the evidence personally (for example, through illness or death) or *when records have been properly compiled by businesses*, then the evidence should automatically go in, rather than its admissibility being judged. Judges should also have discretion to decide that other evidence *of this sort* can be given. (Home Office: 2002: 4.61; emphasis added.)

The vague reference to other evidence 'of this sort', which judges would have the discretion to admit, suggests that the entire topic of business documents and their admissibility may be open to review. Further, the White Paper's emphasis on the rights of victims and communities may portend a greater willingness to admit such evidence when companies are on trial for offences in which victims or the community have suffered grievous harm.

16 *R v Dragic* [1996] 2 Cr App Rep 232.

2. The privilege against self-incrimination/right to silence

Most rules of criminal procedure and evidence that apply to a criminal trial of an individual can be adapted to the trial of a company. However, a few raise more problems than others. One feature that might merit modification when a company is on trial relates to the privilege against self-incrimination or, as it is commonly referred to in Britain, the right to silence.[17] Generally speaking, the idea is to protect a person from having to answer questions or producing documents if to do so would expose the individual to a possible criminal charge. A defendant also cannot be compelled to testify in his/her own trial.

Does the right of silence or privilege against self-incrimination apply to an organisational entity such as a company? The courts in England have recognised that a company can claim the right of silence,[18] but the position in the United States regarding a company's ability to invoke the privilege against self-incrimination has proved more controversial. However, the right of silence in Britain has now been significantly watered down as a result of the Criminal Justice and Public Order Act 1994, and adverse inferences may be drawn by the fact-finder from its invocation (s 34) or from the failure to give evidence at trial (s 35). As a result, the right of silence now plays a reduced role in the English criminal justice system. Because of this feature, and because the courts in the United States have explored more fully the reasons for and against allowing a corporation to invoke the privilege of self-incrimination, it is to the better developed jurisprudence of the US Supreme Court that we shall turn in our exploration of the issues.

The Fifth Amendment of the US Constitution protects against an individual's being 'compelled in any criminal case to be a witness against himself'.[19] In *Boyd v United States*,[20] the US Supreme Court recognised that the government could not compel a person to produce documents which could be used against him/her, because the Fifth Amendment prohibited 'any forcible and compulsory extortion of a man's.... private papers to be used as evidence to convict him of a crime or to forfeit his goods'.[21] Subsequent to this decision, Congress and state legislatures enacted numerous regulatory statutes, with criminal sanctions attached to them, aimed at controlling corporate misconduct.[22] These statutes required a reconsideration of *Boyd*'s broad protection and, in a series of cases, the Supreme Court held that the privilege did not extend to artificial persons and other 'collective entities'.[23] In addition, the court assimilated the position of corporate officials to that of the company they represented.

Although the practice of allowing law enforcement personnel to obtain corporate documents now seems to be fairly firmly established, the Supreme Court has not

---

17 The two rights are not identical, and their reach has been interpreted differently by the courts, but, for the purposes of delineating their applicability in the corporate context, it is useful to concentrate on their similarities rather than their differences.

18 See *Triplex Safety Glass Co Ltd v Lancegaye Safety Glass Ltd* [1939] 2 KB 395.

19 United States Constitution, Amendment Five.

20 116 US 616 (1886).

21 116 US 616 (1886) at 630.

22 See eg Elkins Act 1903; Sherman Act 1890; Interstate Commerce Act 1887.

23 See eg *Bellis v United States* 417 US 85 (1974) (three-member partnership); *Wilson v United States* 221 US 361 (1911) (corporation).

been particularly enlightening with respect to the rationale for this development in the law. The problem may be that the court has been less than clear generally on the underlying interests protected by the privilege against self-incrimination itself. One of the more succinct, but embracing, articulations of these interests was offered by Justice Goldberg in *Murphy v Waterfront Commission*:

> The privilege against self-incrimination.... reflects many of our fundamental values and most noble aspirations: our unwillingness to subject those suspected of crime to the cruel trilemma of self-accusation, perjury or contempt; our preference for an accusatorial rather than an inquisitorial system of criminal justice; our fear that self-incrimination statements will be elicited by inhumane treatment and abuses; our sense of fair play which dictates 'a fair state-individual balance by requiring the government to leave the individual alone until good cause is shown for disturbing him and by requiring the government in its contest with the individual to shoulder the entire load'; our respect for the inviolability of the human personality and of the right of each individual 'to a private enclave where he may lead a private life'; our distrust of self-deprecatory statements; and our realization that the privilege, while sometimes a 'shelter to the guilty' is often 'a protection of the innocent'.[24]

It can readily be seen that some of the values identified by Justice Goldberg as lying behind the Fifth Amendment privilege have applicability to companies while others do not. If the purpose of the privilege is to protect the inviolability of the human personality, for example, then it is questionable whether the privilege has any relevance to a company. On the other hand, if the purpose is to embody an adversarial approach to criminal justice wherein the prosecutor is required to shoulder the burden of proving guilt without the accused having to assist the state in any manner whatsoever, then the case for applying the privilege to companies is every bit as compelling as it is with respect to individuals.

In some of its early decisions, the Court seemed to be making a distinction between individuals, who were protected by the Fifth Amendment privilege, and 'collective entities', which were not. Unfortunately, the Court did not supply a definition of what constituted a collective entity. In *Hale v Henkel*,[25] the Court held that documentary evidence did not fall under the Fifth Amendment when held by a corporation, even though similar evidence would have been privileged if in possession of an individual.[26] The Court reasoned that the privilege could not be invoked to shield a third party, and that the corporate agent was not acting to protect him/herself, but rather the corporation.[27] A few years later, the Supreme Court reached the same conclusion but on a different line of reasoning, holding in *Wilson v United States* that corporations were a creation of the state and only enjoyed such rights as the state of incorporation was prepared to grant, and that the privilege against self-incrimination was not one of these rights.[28]

In 1944 the Court reaffirmed that the privilege was not available to a collective entity in a case involving a labour union. The Court stated that the union was too 'impersonal' in nature to invoke the privilege.[29] However, rather than identifying

---

24 *Murphy v Waterfront Commission* 378 US 52 (1964) at 55 (citations omitted).
25 *Hale v Henkel* 201 US 43 (1906).
26 *Hale v Henkel* 201 US 43 (1906) at 69–70, 74–75.
27 *Hale v Henkel* 201 US 43 (1906) at 69, 70.
28 *Wilson v United States* 221 US 361 (1911) at 385.
29 *United States v White* 322 US 694 (1944) at 698–702.

explicitly the 'personal' interests protected by the privilege, the Court chose to emphasise the needs of law enforcement:

> The greater portion of the evidence of wrongdoing by an organization or its representatives is usually to be found in the official records and documents of that organization. Were the cloak of privilege to be thrown around these impersonal records and documents, effective enforcement of many federal and state laws would be impossible.[30]

The analysis that the Supreme Court has applied to collective entities has also influenced its approach to individuals closely associated with a collective entity. Basically, such individuals stand on the same footing as the collective entity. Although a rule allowing individuals to assert the privilege over business documents had been established in *Boyd* (see above), the Court in *Hale* held that a corporation president could not invoke the Fifth Amendment to avoid producing documents owned by the corporation (but in his possession) even if they might serve to incriminate him.[31] Similarly, the Court has held that a corporation's secretary who was ordered to produce potentially self-incriminating records, the subpoena in this case being addressed to him personally and not to the corporation, could not invoke the privilege.[32] The crucial point seems to be that the corporation owns the documents, no matter who has created or signed them, and regardless of who is asked to produce them. Summing up, the Court in *United States v White* stated that when individuals represent a collective group, they 'cannot be said to be exercising their personal rights', and therefore were not entitled to 'their purely personal privileges'.[33]

One might question whether the Supreme Court in these cases has taken sufficient account of the fact that the individual required to produce corporate records can suffer the humiliation and mistreatment that is protected against by the Fifth Amendment. It would arguably have advanced the analysis had the Court been more careful to distinguish between the type of evidence which was being sought and the characteristics of the person who was being asked to produce the evidence. When the state is seeking documents, the probative value of the documents is likely to be high, while the risk that the person being asked to produce the documents will suffer intimidation, humiliation or mistreatment is low. The interest in effective law enforcement will also support requiring the evidence to be produced. In *Braswell v United States*[34] the Court seemed to endorse this position. After reviewing the 'collective entity' doctrine and rejecting arguments that it had been superseded by later decisions, the Court held that 'without regard to whether the subpoena is addressed to the corporation, or as here, to the individual in his capacity as a custodian.... a corporate custodian.... may not resist a subpoena for corporate records on Fifth Amendment grounds'.[35]

An analysis of Fifth Amendment jurisprudence, as it relates, not to collective entities, but to individuals, supports the conclusion that business documents should

---

30 *United States v White* 322 US 694 (1944) at 700.
31 *Hale v Henkel* 201 US 43 (1906).
32 *Dreier v United States* 221 US 394 (1911).
33 *United States v White* 322 US 694 (1944) at 699.
34 *Braswell v United States* 487 US 99 (1988).
35 *Braswell v United States* 487 US 99 (1988) at 108–109.

be regarded as non-privileged no matter who is being asked to produce them. The amendment protects an individual from being 'compelled' to be a 'witness against himself'. The two elements – compulsion and being a witness – must both be present together. Supreme Court decisions take the view that 'witness' should be read narrowly to embrace only communications that relate to information that has been processed in the mind of the witness. Accordingly, samples of blood,[36] voice[37] and handwriting[38] have been held not to be protected by the Fifth Amendment because there is no mental processing of information involved. Information contained in pre-existing documents that simply need to be produced in court without any 'processing' on the part of the witness can likewise be regarded as unprivileged information, irrespective of whether it is an individual or a collective entity that is being asked to produce the information. Thus the Supreme Court has held that a potential witness served with a document request must meet three conditions in order to raise the privilege against self-incrimination successfully: first, the witness must demonstrate that the request implies compulsion in preparing the document and not just producing it;[39] second, the witness must prove that the information is testimonial in nature;[40] and, finally, the witness must show that the act of production is self-incriminating.[41] A witness who has been granted immunity cannot claim a violation of the Fifth Amendment, no matter how humiliating, damaging or invasive of privacy the information in question will be to the witness.[42]

Although the Supreme Court has tried to find historical precedent in the common law rule of 'visitation' that would allow a state to investigate the affairs of corporations because corporations have only the rights that are given to them in the state charters that authorise their creation,[43] this does not seem to be the real reason behind the Court's more recent decisions. Rather, the Court seems to be increasingly worried that the effectiveness of law enforcement investigations of companies might be compromised if prosecutors were denied access to business documents and records. In *Braswell v United States*,[44] the Court noted that white-collar crimes were more complex and harder to prosecute than other criminal offences, and refused to impose any broad restrictions on the power of prosecutors to gain access to documents and to gather information in the course of their investigation. The Court stated that to allow the custodians of records to raise the Fifth Amendment privilege 'would have a detrimental impact on the Government's efforts to prosecute "white-collar crime", one of the most serious problems confronting law enforcement authorities'.[45] Lower courts also have accepted that the judiciary should not hinder the investigation of complex business and white-collar crimes by imposing broad, restrictive limitations. On the contrary, Henning (1993) discerns a continuing judicial trend in favour of allowing the government ever greater leeway to investigate in this area.

---

36 *Schmerber v California* 384 US 757 (1966).
37 *United States v Wade* 388 US 218 (1967).
38 *Gilbert v California* 388 US 263 (1967).
39 *United States v Doe* 465 US 605 (1984) at 610.
40 *Fisher v United States* 425 US 391 (1976) at 411.
41 *Fisher v United States* 425 US 391 (1976) at 408.
42 *Zicarelli v New Jersey* 406 US 472 (1972).
43 See eg *Hale v Henkel* 201 US 43 (1906) at 74–75.
44 *Braswell v United States* 487 US 99 (1988).
45 *Braswell v United States* 487 US 99 (1988) at 115.

D. THE BURDEN AND STANDARD OF PROOF

Generally, every contested issue of fact in a criminal case needs to be proved in court. As a consequence, three questions arise: first, which party has the *evidential burden* of introducing evidence as to an issue in question; second, which party bears the *burden of proof* – of persuading the trier of fact that, between the competing positions being asserted, his/hers is the correct one; and third, to what extent must the party having the burden of proof persuade the trier of fact of his/her position – by a 'balance of probabilities', by proof 'beyond reasonable doubt' or in accord with some intermediary standard such as by 'clear and convincing evidence'. The terminology relating to these respective burdens can be confusing, as the term 'burden of proof' has at times been used indiscriminately to refer to each of these separate burdens. In Britain the term 'burden of proof' properly refers to the party which bears the burden of persuasion, and the term 'standard of proof' refers to the weight by which that party must convince the trier of fact of his/her position.

In civil law litigation, the issue of which party bears the evidential burden may be resolved by reference to either statute or caselaw. In the absence of a statutory provision or precedent, the general principle, however tenuous, is that the evidential burden should be borne by the party that affirms a proposition rather than by the party who denies it.[46] However, this general principle is qualified in that 'the burden of proof in any particular case depends on the circumstances under which the claim arises'.[47] Courts have avoided a mechanical approach to the affirmation/denial test, and the issue will not be determined by the choice of words used in stating the case.[48] Courts in civil cases seem comfortable in admitting that 'where the burden of proof should rest is merely a question of policy and fairness based on experience in the different situations'.[49] Questions of fairness may be resolved by looking at which party will find it easier to discharge a burden of proof,[50] even when it will imply proving the negative.[51]

When deciding an issue in a civil case, the trier of fact (in England, virtually always the court) must be convinced on a 'balance of probabilities' or, in the United States, the equivalent standard of a 'preponderance of the evidence'. What this means in practical terms is that the party carrying the burden must prove that his/her version of the facts is more likely than not to be the correct version. In contrast, in a criminal case the burden of proving that an offence has been committed by the defendant rests on the prosecution and a more stringent standard of proof is applied, usually that of 'beyond reasonable doubt'.

The difference in the standard of proof in civil and criminal cases reflects the harm that society attaches to the risk of error. In a criminal case, avoiding the conviction of an innocent defendant takes precedence over the possible acquittal of a guilty defendant. When the burden of proof is 'beyond reasonable doubt', the likelihood of an innocent individual being convicted is low although, concomitantly,

---

46 *Constantine (Joseph) Steamship Line Ltd v Imperial Smelting Corpn Ltd* [1942] AC 154 at 174.
47 *Constantine (Joseph) Steamship Line Ltd v Imperial Smelting Corpn Ltd* [1942] AC 154 at 174.
48 See eg, *Soward v Leggatt* (1836) 7 C & P 613.
49 *Rustad v Great Northern Rly Co* 122 Minn 453, 142 NW 727 (1913).
50 See *Constantine (Joseph) Steamship Line Ltd v Imperial Smelting Corpn Ltd* [1942] AC 154; *Levison v Patent Steam Carpet Cleaning Co* [1978] QB 69.
51 *Pickford v Imperial Chemical Industries plc* [1998] 3 All ER 462.

there is a much greater risk that a guilty defendant may go free. If a 'balance of probabilities' test were to be used, the risks would be reversed, and an innocent person would be in greater danger of being wrongfully convicted. Because an accused in a criminal trial is seen as having more at stake (an erroneous conviction can lead to imprisonment and deprivation of the defendant's liberty) than a defendant in a civil case (where usually all that is at stake is money), the more demanding 'beyond reasonable doubt' standard applies in criminal trials. As a general proposition, it is the responsibility of the prosecutor in a criminal trial to establish each and every element of the offence charged by proof 'beyond reasonable doubt'. A defendant, on the other hand, typically only needs to raise a reasonable doubt about any element of the offence in order to be entitled to an acquittal. In *Woolmington v DPP*[52] the House of Lords further held that when a defendant has introduced some evidence with respect to a defence, then the burden of proof is on the prosecution to negate the defence by proof 'beyond reasonable doubt'.

There are various reasons why the burden of proof is normally placed on the prosecution. First, as Roberts (1995: 285) points out: 'The burden of proof checks and constrains the power of the state to intervene in the lives of individuals and their families in the far-reaching and sometimes catastrophic ways sanctioned by the machinery of criminal law.' Placing the burden of proof on the prosecution is also justified on the ground that to hold otherwise would in effect make defendants presumptively guilty with the onus on them to prove their innocence. A further reason for placing the burden of proof on the prosecution is that it is able to determine the charges that will be brought against the defendant and can decline to bring those with respect to which the evidence is weak. Finally, it has been noted that there is a 'resource imbalance' in that in most criminal cases the prosecution has access to superior investigative resources (in the form of the state's police, its laboratories and its forensic and other services) than are available to the defendant.[53]

Is there a case for reversing the burden of proof when a company is on trial, at least after the prosecution has introduced evidence that the company has committed a criminal offence? Considering the applicability of the justifications for the normal allocation of the burden of proof to the prosecution identified above, the first sets of concern relate to which party should bear the risk of an erroneous verdict. Historically, the criminal justice system and the guarantees of the law of evidence evolved against a backdrop where the death penalty, corporal punishment, deportation and life imprisonment were common sanctions. None of these punishments can be imposed on a company (although closure of a company might be argued to be the equivalent of a death penalty for the company). Nor can a company be sentenced to prison. The most probable penalty that will be imposed following the conviction of a company will be economic in character (a fine). This sanction resembles more that which follows a civil judgment (although the fine following a criminal conviction goes to the state rather than to the plaintiff/victim) than that which typically follows from a criminal conviction.

We noted that in civil cases policy considerations are more likely to be considered in allocating the burden of proof, but many of those same policy considerations

52 *Woolmington v DPP* [1935] AC 462.
53 There are, of course, some exceptional cases, such as that of O J Simpson, where the defendant has access to equal, if not superior, resources.

come into play when a company is on trial for a criminal offence. It will be the company which has primary access to the relevant records, and it will be the company's employees who are a principal source of information. Further, where large corporate entities are on trial, it can be extremely difficult for a state investigative body to pierce the veil that masks the company's criminal activity. Also, while there can be a resource imbalance between the state and a defendant who is a natural person, that imbalance is less likely to be present when the defendant is a company. Many wealthy corporations, and in particular multinational enterprises, have more financial resources than the entire governments of some developing countries (Rugman: 2001).

There are in fact numerous exceptions to the rule that places the burden of proof on the prosecution. In *Woolmington*, Viscount Sankey noted that, under the decision in *R v McNaghten*,[54] the burden of proving the common law defence of insanity was on the defendant. Apart from insanity, many statutes allocate the burden of proof to the defendant on a particular issue or with respect to a defence established by the statute.[55] In *R v DPP, ex p Kebilene*,[56] the House of Lords upheld these burden-shifting provisions in response to a challenge that they violated the Human Rights Act 1998. However, it should be noted that in cases where the burden of proof has been placed on a defendant, the burden relates to a benefit that has been afforded to an accused; it does not relate to proof of the elements of the crime. Also, the standard of proof, as already noted, is only that of a 'balance of probabilities'.

When the allocation of the burden of proof in a statute is not explicit, it will be the responsibility of the courts to interpret the statute to determine which side should bear the burden of proof. To promote judicial consistency in this interpretative exercise, Parliament enacted the Magistrates' Courts Act 1980, s 101:

> Where the defendant to an information or complaint relies for his defence on any exception, exemption, proviso, excuse or qualification, whether or not it accompanies the description of the offence or matter of complaint in the enactment creating the offence or on which the complaint is founded, the burden of proving the exception, exemption, proviso, excuse or qualification shall be on him; and this notwithstanding that the information or complaint contains an allegation negativing the exception, exemption, proviso, excuse or qualification.

The problem that can arise is that a statute may not be framed so as to clearly differentiate the affirmative elements of the offence from the 'exceptions, exemptions, provisos, excuses and qualifications'. Sometimes what may appear, for example, to be an 'exception' is, in reality, just an alternative way of expressing an element of the offence. In *R v Hunt*,[57] the House of Lords held that s 101 applied not only to provisions which could be brought within the linguistic boundaries of exceptions, but also to provisions that created exceptions even if otherwise characterised. As a general test, if it is possible to state an offence sensibly without making any reference to the

---

54 (1843) 1 Car & Kir 130n, sub nom *M'Naghten's Case* 10 Cl & Fin 200.
55 See eg, Sexual Offences Act 1956, s 30(2); Obscene Publications Act 1959, s 2(5); Obscene Publications Act 1964, s 1(3); Public Order Act 1986, ss 18(4), 19(2), 20(2), 21(3), 22(3)–(5) and 23(3); Criminal Justice Act 1988, s 93D(6); Official Secrets Act 1989, ss 1(5), 2(3), 3(4) and 4(4)–(5); Drug Trafficking Act 1994, ss 53(6) and 58(2)(a).
56 [2000] 2 AC 326.
57 [1987] AC 352.

'exception, exemption, proviso, excuse or qualification", then it is a 'genuine' exception, etc (Williams: 1988). In *Hunt* the House stated that judges should not restrict themselves to a literal construction of the statute at issue, but should also consider such factors as 'the mischief at which the Act was aimed and the practical considerations affecting the burden of proof and, in particular, the ease or difficulty that the respective parties would encounter in discharging the burden'.[58] The decision in *Hunt*, however, addressed only statutory offences, leaving common law defences to the general *Woolmington* rule that the burden of proof rests on the prosecution to rebut a defence by proof 'beyond reasonable doubt'. In respect of common law cases, the defendant thus bears only the evidential burden.

Once the question of 'who' bears the burden of proof is resolved, it must be resolved by 'what' standard of proof the bearer of the burden must persuade the fact-finder of his/her position. As a general rule, when the burden of proof is on the prosecution, the standard is proof 'beyond reasonable doubt'; when the burden is on the defendant, he/she will usually only have to convince the trier of fact by a 'balance of probabilities'. A more searching inquiry, however, reveals that more than these two points of reference have been applied in practice. In the United States, three standards appear to be recognised: proof 'beyond reasonable doubt', proof by a preponderance of the evidence and an intermediate standard of 'proof by clear and convincing evidence'. England too appears to recognise standards other than proof 'beyond reasonable doubt' and proof by a 'balance of probabilities', but it does not seem to have created an explicit intermediate standard. Rather, the English courts take a flexible approach to the 'balance of probabilities' standard. In *Re H*, the House of Lords stated that 'the more serious the allegation the less likely it is that the event occurred and, hence, the stronger should be the evidence before the court concludes that the allegation is established on the balance of probabilities'.[59] Although the House disclaimed that it was imposing a higher standard of proof, it conceded that the effect would be the same. It based its holding on the fact that the 'inherent probability or improbability of an event is itself a matter to be taken into account when weighing the probabilities and deciding whether, on balance, the event occurred'.[60]

Who, then, should bear the burden of proof in a criminal prosecution of a company and by what standard should it have to be discharged? While we noted previously that, when charged with a crime, a company is in a significantly less disadvantageous position than a natural person, particularly in that it does not face possible imprisonment, it can still suffer the same type of censure, stigma and damage to its reputation as a natural person who is convicted of a crime. Indeed, reputation may be an even more valuable commodity to a company than it is to an individual. Moreover, the conviction of a company may tarnish not only its reputation, but also that of innocent persons who are employed by or are affiliated with the company. Whether these reputational interests qualify as liberty interests is not altogether clear but, in any event, they should not be lightly dismissed. When a heavy fine is imposed on a company, there can also be ancillary effects on innocent workers, who may be made redundant in order to generate the money to pay the fine.

---

58 See also *Nimmo v Alexander Cowan & Sons Ltd* [1968] AC 107.
59 *Re H* [1996] AC 563 at 586. See also *Hornal v Neuberger Products Ltd* [1957] 1 QB 247.
60 *Re H* [1996] AC 563 at 586.

In light of these considerations, placing the burden of proof on a corporate defendant, even by only a 'balance of probabilities' standard, arguably would fail to protect the legitimate and important interests that could be adversely affected by a conviction of the company. A company, no less than a natural person, should not have to prove its innocence. Just as a human defendant, a company finds itself in criminal court not of its own volition but by virtue of charges brought by the state. The state should bear the burden of proving those charges. However, the traditional criminal standard of proof – 'beyond reasonable doubt' – may be unfair to the prosecution in cases where the bulk of the incriminating evidence is likely to be under the control of the corporate defendant and not readily available to law enforcement officers. The alternative of proof by a 'balance of probabilities', on the other hand, may be unfair to the company on trial for reasons already identified. Nor may the use of a standard of proof normally associated with civil cases convey to the public the gravity of the company's wrongdoing.

In the context of corporate crime, an intermediate standard of proof such as 'clear and convincing evidence' recommends itself. However, some degree of flexibility is also desirable. The more serious the charge, the greater the consequences to a company's reputation and financial well-being from a conviction, and the more demanding should be the standard of proof.[61] Thus, one can envisage a sliding scale, comparable to that which has been developed in England with respect to the 'balance of probabilities', which might begin at 'clear and convincing evidence', appropriate, perhaps, where the charge is that of an endangerment offence (see chapter 5), but which would become progressively more onerous as the charge gained in gravity. For a crime such as corporate killing, the standard of proof would be that of 'beyond reasonable doubt'.

E.   DUE DILIGENCE

If companies are to be criminally liable for offences that occur in the course of their business operation, and if that liability is not to be strict, then the corporate defendant must be allowed to show that it has not been at fault. Such traditional common law defences as automatism, self-defence, duress, insanity and provocation make little sense in the context of corporate entities. We have argued that corporate fault is to be found in crime-conducive policies, in corporate cultures that tolerate illegality and where there is a culpable failure to devise, implement and enforce systems that would prevent harm. When charged with an offence defined in 'organisational fault' terms, the corporate defendant should be allowed to show that it has not been at fault in carrying out its responsibilities. As we argued in chapter 3, a company should be able to defend by showing that it has conducted its business affairs with 'due diligence'. In this section we shall elaborate on the nature of due diligence and examine whether the company on trial should bear the burden of proving its due diligence or whether it should be the burden of the prosecution to rebut the defence, once some evidence of due diligence has been introduced by the defendant, by proof 'beyond reasonable doubt'.

---

61 See *Hornal v Neuberger Products* [1957] 1 QB 247; *Re H* [1996] AC 563 at 586.

I.   The due diligence defence under English law

The defence of due diligence is not unknown in English law and can be found in numerous statutes. Examples include the Weights and Measures Act 1985,[62] the Trade Descriptions Act 1968,[63] and the Food Safety Act 1990.[64] Under the current statutory framework for consumer protection, a defence of due diligence is available to a defendant who 'took all reasonable precautions and exercised due diligence to avoid the commission of the offence'. Provisions such as these are usually part of a larger regulatory scheme imposing strict liability and are limited in their scope. What we have in mind, in contrast, is a more broadly conceived, across-the-board due diligence defence within a fault-based scheme of criminal justice. Given corporate and legal familiarity with the statutory concept of due diligence, however, an expanded, more general obligation to practice due diligence in order to avoid criminal liability would probably not impose a novel burden on companies.

In *Tesco Supermarkets Ltd v Nattrass*,[65] best known for the House of Lords' articulation of an 'identification' test of corporate criminal liability, an issue of due diligence provided the context for the decision. The defendant had argued that the offence of which it was charged had been committed by 'another person' and that it had conducted its business operation with the 'due diligence' that the controlling statute recognised as a defence. In interpreting the statute, Lord Diplock stated that due diligence was the converse of negligence and that to establish its due diligence, a company had to show that it had in place 'a reasonably effective system' for preventing the offence and that the system 'was being observed' in practice.[66] Viscount Dilhorne cautioned that the defence of due diligence:

> .... could not be established merely by showing that a good system had been devised and a person thought to be competent put in charge of it. It would still be necessary to show due diligence on the part of the accused in seeing that the system was in fact operated and the person put in charge of it doing what he was supposed to do.[67]

Although the defence itself is referred to as 'due diligence', there are in fact two related, but distinct, component elements – 'reasonable precautions' and 'due diligence'. 'Reasonable precautions' consists of the establishment of a safe system of operation that will prevent offences from occurring. The system must be tailored specifically to the dangers that it aims at preventing. To satisfy the requirement of 'reasonable precautions', a corporate defendant would have to show the steps that it had taken before, during and after the event to ensure compliance with the law, including the kinds of actions that were taken when breaches of the system were discovered. In contrast to 'reasonable precautions', the 'due diligence' dimension of

---

62 S 34.
63 S 24(1).
64 S 21. See also Consumer Protection Act 1987, s 39; Sale of Food (Weights and Measures) Act 1926, s 12(5).
65 *Tesco Supermarkets Ltd v Nattrass* [1972] AC 153.
66 *Tesco Supermarkets Ltd v Nattrass* [1972] AC 153 at 197-199.
67 *Tesco Supermarkets Ltd v Nattrass* [1972] AC 153 at 186.

the defence relates to the implementation of the system, and to ensuring that it works effectively and as intended. To have a well-conceived system of checks and controls in place would accomplish little if they were not effective in practice. A defendant will also have to show that the risk-prevention system was operating at the time the offence was committed, and that the offence occurred despite its safeguards.

The distinction between 'reasonable precautions' and 'due diligence' was highlighted in *Rotherham Metropolitan Borough Council v Raysun (UK) Ltd.*[68] The defendant, an importer of pencils, had specified in its contract with its supplier that the pencils had to conform to relevant UK standards. A system of control was put in place, according to which an agent submitted regular samples from the factory to the local government chemist for analysis. Had any contraventions of UK standards emerged, the results of the analysis were to be sent to Raysun. In the event, Raysun did not receive any negative reports. Once the pencils entered the United Kingdom, Raysun sent one set of 12 pencils (out of the yearly 10,000 12-pencil sets) to the Public Analyst for chemical analysis, the results of which were reported to the company. Again, there were no reports which were negative. However, after the pencils came onto the market, they were found to be in contravention of the relevant UK legislation.

In its analysis of the case, the High Court stated that there were two distinct reference points that required scrutiny. First, it looked at Raysun's control system in the country of manufacturing and found that it satisfied the requirements of 'reasonable precautions'. However, the reporting system was held to be inadequate. Raysun had assumed that when it had not received any negative report, it meant that all was well. The court did not find this assumption to be reasonable, as the absence of violations did not necessarily equate with a legally compliant process; it was just lack of evidence that anything was wrong with respect to the samples. As a consequence, the court concluded that the requirements of 'due diligence' had not been met. Once the pencils reached the United Kingdom, on the other hand, the position was reversed. Now the reporting system was deemed to be sufficient, as all the analysis results were fully reported to Raysun. Thus the demands of 'due diligence' were satisfied. However, the court found that the analysis of just one set of pencils was not sufficiently representative to meet the requirements of 'reasonable precautions'.

In *Garrett v Boots Cash Chemists Ltd,*[69] the court recognised that what was needed to be done to satisfy the requirements of 'due diligence' and 'reasonable precautions' could vary depending on the situation of the company and the circumstances of the case: 'what might be reasonable for a large retailer might not be reasonable for the village shop'. In *Wright v Smith,*[70] a licensee had hired an experienced manager to run his bar. The rest of the staff employed was equally experienced, so no additional formal training was provided. The licensee was prosecuted because one member of staff had served a 'short measure' to a client. The court was satisfied that by appointing experienced bar staff the defendant had met the requirements of both reasonable precautions and due diligence.

---

68 *Rotherham Metropolitan Borough Council v Raysun (UK) Ltd* [1988] BTLC 292.
69 1980, unreported, QB.
70 [1986] BTLC 180.

In sum, to raise a successful due diligence defence, a company would have to show that:

- a well-conceived system for preventing criminal violations was in place;
- the system was appropriate for preventing the type of offence that occurred;
- the system was operative at the time of the offence and funtioning properly; and
- the offence occurred despite its preventative safeguards.

Should a corporate defendant bear the burden of having to prove its due diligence, and, if so, what should be the standard of proof? Alternatively, should it fall to the prosecution, after a corporate defendant has introduced some evidence of its due diligence, to have to rebut the defence by proof 'beyond reasonable doubt'? In statutes which grant a defence of due diligence, the burden of proving due diligence is typically placed on the defendant, but only by proof that meets a 'balance of probabilities' test. Should this same allocation of the burden of proof, and by the same standard of a 'balance of probabilities', be applied to the general due diligence defence that we have proposed?

In *Constantine (Joseph) Steamship Line Ltd v Imperial Smelting Corpn Ltd*,[71] it was observed by the court that proving a negative will inevitably be more difficult than proving an affirmative. It will virtually always be easier for a company to show what steps it has taken to avert illegality than it will be for the prosecution to show what the company has failed to do. The company will know what directives have been issued to its workforce and what resolutions have been adopted by its governing board. Relevant documents and memoranda will lie within the company's files. Critical witnesses who can testify to these matters will include the company's directors, executive officers and managers. They will be able to offer first-hand testimony as to what systems have been implemented to prevent crime, and what alternative systems were rejected and why. These are also the witnesses who can best speak to the company's culture and ethos.

If, conversely, the burden were to be placed on the prosecution to disprove a company's claim of due diligence, and by proof 'beyond reasonable doubt', it would find itself in an extremely precarious position. State investigators would be most unlikely to uncover a written order or a formal company policy that explicitly authorised, allowed or even admitted the company's tolerance of illegal behaviour. Far more likely to be discovered would be pro forma pronouncements that forbade employees and staff from violating the law. And this assumes that law enforcement personnel will have access to a company's files. Access would not be automatic, and, while a search warrant might be obtainable, the applicant would probably have to identify, with some degree of specificity, which files among potentially hundreds of thousands were being sought. Decisions of the European Court of Human Rights have recognised that companies have a privacy interest in the protection of their files.[72]

Even if all of a company's files were required to be produced, the task of sifting through them for incriminating evidence might be akin to searching for the proverbial needle in the haystack. A further complicating factor pointed out by Fisse and Braithwaite (1993) is that it is not uncommon for companies to keep two sets of records, a full and candid set for internal use and a truncated, anodyne version for public consumption. It is not difficult to guess which set of records would be produced

---

71 [1942] AC 154.
72 *Niemietz v Germany* (1992) 16 EHRR 97.

if required by a court order. Nor can police expect co-operation from corporate officers and managers if it might lead to the individual's being charged with an offence. Employees subjected to police questioning are often instructed by their superiors to restrict their answers to the questions asked, and not to volunteer information.

An additional factor, to which attention has already been drawn, is that, if convicted, a company, unlike a natural person, does not face the possibility of incarceration. The most likely penalty will be an economic sanction, probably a fine. The case for allocating to the prosecution the burden of proving all elements of a crime, as well as disproving defences on which the defendant has introduced evidence, by proof 'beyond reasonable doubt', is based in part on the fact that a human defendant faces a potential loss of liberty if convicted. Because the company's 'liberty' is not under threat, there need be less concern in shifting to it the burden of proof of due diligence.

2.   Due diligence in Italy and the United States

In the United States, the Model Penal Code, s 1.12 recognises that in some cases the burden of persuasion on an issue can be placed on a defendant. Most of these cases involve situations where the prosecution would have difficulty in obtaining evidence. The Code gives as a specific example the situation where a corporation is allowed the defence (under s 2.07(5)) that the managerial staff having supervisory responsibility over the subject matter of the offence had exercised 'due diligence' to prevent its commission. In this situation the corporate defendant must prove 'due diligence' by a preponderance of the evidence. The purpose of the defence is to encourage diligent supervision of corporate personnel.

As we shall discuss more fully in chapter 7, an attempt to give content to the concept of due diligence can be seen in the United States in the federal guidelines for sentencing organisational offenders. Under the guidelines, the fine that might otherwise be imposed on a convicted company can be significantly reduced if the company has in place an effective compliance programme and reports its offence to the authorities. The establishment of a compliance department is strong evidence of due diligence, as are the adoption of codes of good practice and mechanisms for the prompt discovery of any crime that should occur. The other major factor specifically mentioned in the federal guidelines, the self-reporting of the company's crime before it is discovered by the relevant authorities, is another indication that due diligence is practiced by a company.

Italian law also allows the burden of proof of due diligence to be placed on a corporate defendant. As discussed in chapter 3, Italy has enacted a statute imposing broad criminal liability on corporations for financial crimes. The key concept in the Italian statute is 'structural negligence'. However, what constitutes structural negligence will vary depending on whether the crime is committed by the head or director of the corporation, on the one hand, or by a subordinate member of staff, on the other. In either case, however, the corporation needs to have established guidelines and control systems that take into account the risk of offences being committed. If it has not, then it will be found to be 'structurally negligent'. The control system, moreover, needs to be tailored to specific risks, and it is not enough that the corporation has set up a generic control system. The details and specifics of the control system are left for companies to work out for themselves, taking into account their individual needs and circumstances, or possibly to develop within a group such as a trade association involving companies engaged in the same business.

With respect to heads, directors and managers, the burden of proving a control system sufficient to defeat liability rests on the corporation. Article 6 reverses the usual burden of proof, providing that 'the corporation will not be liable if *it proves*' (emphasis added) that an efficient and suitable control system has been put in place.[73] The presumption is that if a crime has been committed by a top-level officer, such as the head of a corporation, then the corporation is liable because normally the officer would be representing the corporation and there would be a coincidence of criminal 'intent' between the officer and the corporation. If the presumption is inaccurate in a given case, then it is up to the corporation to prove that to be so. If it fails to do so or if it has not put into place a system of control, then the corporation will in effect be strictly liable for the offence of its officer, providing that the offence was committed to benefit the corporation or to advance its interests.

Under Article 6, a defendant corporation will have to prove that it had created guidelines suitable to prevent offences such as the one that had occurred and that the guidelines were in place before the crime was committed. It will further have to prove that there has been a system of effective control and supervision of the system (usually through an independent body internal to the corporation), and that the head or manager who committed the offence did so with an intent to evade the system. Thus a corporation will need to identify the various risks associated with its business and its way of carrying out its activities, and then it will have to establish generally effective guidelines, policies, procedures and systems for avoiding these risks.

The burden and standard of proof relating to due diligence changes with respect to crimes committed by subordinate personnel. Most significantly, Article 7 does not reverse the normal burden of proof. As in the case involving a head of the corporation, the 'subjective element' of the crime will be found in the form of a 'structural negligence'. In this instance the corporation will be negligent if it has failed to set up an effective system of control and supervision over its employees. However, the components of such a system need not be as stringent as those required to prevent crimes by a head or manager of the corporation. Taking into account the nature and size of the organisation and the type of activities in which it is engaged, Article 7, para 3 states that the system should be appropriate to guarantee that the corporation acts in accord with the law and that situations that can lead to a criminal offence can be timely discovered and eliminated. Under Article 7, para 4(a), the system has to be reviewed periodically and modified when significant violations have occurred or where there have been changes in the structure or the activities of the corporation. Under para 4(b), the corporation must establish an internal disciplinary system suitable to punish any violation. If the corporation introduces evidence that an appropriate system of control and supervision has been put in place, the burden will be on the prosecution to prove that it was either inadequate or ineffective to prevent offences of the kind that occurred. Thus, while a company has the evidential burden of introducing evidence of its due diligence, the prosecution will still have to prove the requisite degree of negligence on the part of the corporation by proof 'beyond reasonable doubt'.

---

73 DLgs 231/2001, Art 6, para 1.

The examples of Italy and the United States show that it is feasible to shift the burden of proof to a corporate defendant even when the company is on trial for a serious crime, and particularly when liability is based on organisational fault. Such liability, as in the Italian statute, can be structured within a system of nominal strict liability but with the corporate defendant being allowed to raise a defence of due diligence. The role of fault in the law of corporate crime is thus preserved, albeit in the form of allowing the company to prove that it has not been at fault. Where policy considerations dictate, it is not inappropriate to place the burden of proof of due diligence on the company, but in these situations the standard of proof should be that of a 'balance of probabilities'.

F.   THE IMPACT OF THE HUMAN RIGHTS ACT 1998

Would shifting the burden of proof on the issue of due diligence, as well as the other changes in the rules of evidence that have been broached in this chapter, violate a company's rights under the Human Rights Act 1998 (HRA 1998), the European Convention on Human Rights, or the jurisprudence of the European Court of Human Rights? The question is in one sense a 'loaded' one, for it assumes that a company has 'human' rights.

HRA 1998, s 7 applies to persons who would qualify as a victim under the European Convention on Human Rights, Article 34, which provides:

> The Court may receive applications from any person, non-governmental organisation or group of individuals claiming to be the victim of a violation [....] of the rights set forth in the Convention or protocols thereto.

The term 'person' has been interpreted to include corporate and unincorporated bodies, such as companies, trade unions, churches, political parties and other bodies.[74] That said, it has also been held that a corporate body is entitled to some, but not necessarily all, of the rights to which an individual would be entitled.[75] However, the right to a fair trial under Article 6, the provision most relevant to the present discussion, is among those rights that have been held to be applicable to companies. While the text of Article 6 implies that its protections are absolute, the European Court of Human Rights has, in practice, taken a more flexible approach in interpreting its provisions. This approach was endorsed by the House of Lords in *Brown v Stott*[76] with respect to the admissibility of evidence under Article 6. The House indicated its view that evidentiary issues were a matter for national courts, and that, depending

---

74 See eg *Niemietz v Germany* (1992) 16 EHRR 97; *Sunday Times v United Kingdom* (1979) 2 EHRR 245. Where the interests of a company are affected, it is in principle the company that will have the status of 'victim' under the European Convention. Shareholders have been recognised as victims under Art 6 of the Convention: see eg, *Neves e Silva v Portugal* (1989) 13 EHRR 535. However, it has been held that a claim under Art 1, Protocol 1 can only be brought by shareholders after it has been established that it was impossible for the company itself to bring the claim: see *Agrotexim v Greece* (1996) 21 EHRR 250.

75 Arts 6, 8, 10 and Art 1, Protocol 1 (which expressly provides that it applies to both legal and natural persons), eg, have been recognised as protecting rights of corporations.

76 *Brown v Stott (Procurator Fiscal, Dunfermline)* [2001] 2 All ER 97.

on the circumstances, unlawfully obtained evidence could be admitted into evidence without compromising the overall fairness of the trial.[77]

Although the right to silence, as such, is not expressly mentioned in HRA 1998, it has been held to be part of the presumption of innocence protected by Article 6(2) of the European Convention. In *Saunders v United Kingdom*,[78] the European Court of Human Rights held that the right to a fair trial of the former director of Guinness had been breached when statements that he had given to inspectors appointed by the Department of Trade and Industry (DTI) under the Companies Act 1985 were later introduced in evidence against him at his trial. The court ruled that this use of the statements breached the applicant's right not to incriminate himself, which was inherent in the notion of fair procedure and the presumption of innocence protected by Article 6.

It is worth noting that in *Saunders*, the European Court focused on the *use* of the statements independent of their *content*. Even apparently 'neutral' statements may infringe Article 6 when introduced to support the case of the prosecution. Of further note is the fact that the European Court stated that the public interest in combating fraud was not sufficient to outweigh the right to a fair trial. However, for there to be a violation of Article 6, the statements have to be used in an incriminatory way. In May 2000, the European Court declared inadmissible the case of *Staines v United Kingdom*,[79] in which the applicant claimed, under *Saunders*, that her Article 6 rights had been breached because the prosecution had relied on statements that she had made to DTI inspectors under the Financial Services Act 1986, s 177. The court found that the prosecution had not relied on the statements 'in a manner calculated to incriminate her'. On the contrary, it found that her statements, which had been volunteered in written and oral form to the inspectors, constituted an integral part of the case that the prosecution had to discredit to prevail.

Hearsay testimony might also give rise to challenges under the Convention and HRA 1998. Article 6(3)(d) protects a defendant's right in a criminal trial 'to examine or have examined witnesses against him and to obtain the attendance and examination of witnesses on his behalf under the same conditions as witnesses against him'. The European Court's jurisprudence on Article 6(3)(d) has emanated largely from jurisdictions that rely heavily on the use of dossiers and untested evidence and where previous interrogations of a witness have been treated as admissible evidence.[80] The European Court's position seems to be that the defence should be allowed a chance to confront all evidence on which the prosecution relies (whether pre-trial or during trial), unless it is genuinely impossible for the evidence to be tested in court (because, for instance, the source is dead or if testifying would put the witness in real danger). However, the applicability of these decisions to the English hearsay rule and its many exceptions is far from clear. Although it has been argued that the narrowing of the hearsay exceptions has evolved in a way which, at least in particular cases if not generally in spirit, contravenes the values of Article 6(3)(d) (Spencer: 1999), this criticism seems directed more at protecting individuals against testimony from

---

77 *Brown v Stott (Procurator Fiscal, Dunfermline)* [2001] 2 All ER 97 at 107–108.
78 *Saunders v United Kingdom* (1996) 23 EHRR 313.
79 *Staines v United Kingdom*, App No 41552/98, Decision of 16/05/2000.
80 See eg *Unterpertinger v Austria* (1986) 13 EHRR 175; *Kostovski v Netherlands* (1989) 12 EHRR 434; *Van Mechelen v Netherlands* (1997) 25 EHRR 647.

witnesses who are not present in court to be cross-examined than at the introduction of business records and other documents against a company on trial. In any event, hearsay and other untested evidence is, under Strasbourg rulings, acceptable as long as the final judgment is not based on it alone.

The European Convention on Human Rights, Article 6(2) provides that 'everyone charged with a criminal offence shall be presumed innocent until proved guilty according to law'. The hidden question raised by this provision is whether imposing the burden of proving due diligence on a corporate defendant, as has been proposed, would impermissibly infringe upon the presumption of innocence. After HRA 1998 came into force, challenges were made to statutes which imposed a burden of proof on the accused with respect to a defence. In *R v DPP, ex p Kebilene*,[81] the House of Lords, interpreting the jurisprudence of the European Court, held that Article 6(2) did not preclude the burden-shifting provision at issue.[82] Lord Hope stated that the principles embodied in the Convention had to be applied taking into account and balancing the different interests protected by the Convention: those of the individual and those of society.[83] In this balancing exercise, consideration should be given to the real nature of the burden on the defendant, how easy it would be for the defendant to discharge the burden (for example, does the burden relate to something which is likely to be within his/her knowledge), what is the threat faced by society that the provision in question is designed to combat, and so on.[84]

Kebilene was followed in *R v Lambert*,[85] which brought together three consolidated appeals. The first involved a defendant charged with possession of drugs, where the statute provided that once the prosecution had established that the defendant knowingly had a packet in his possession which contained controlled drugs, the burden was upon the defendant to show that he neither suspected nor had reason to suspect the substance in question was a controlled drug. In the second and third cases, the defendants challenged the requirement in a murder prosecution that placed the burden of proving diminished responsibility as a defence to murder upon them. The three cases all raised the generic issue of whether Article 6(2) was violated by statutory provisions that conferred on a defendant a benefit but required the defendant to prove certain facts to be entitled to the benefit. It should be noted, however, that in each instance the defendant had only to establish the required facts by a 'balance of probabilities'. The Court of Appeal held that, where Parliament had created a special defence in favour of an accused but had also required that the accused prove the facts to establish the defence by a 'balance of probabilities', this shift in the burden of proof did not violate Article 6(2).

In his opinion in *Lambert*, Lord Woolf observed that the *Woolmington* view that the burden of proof should not be placed on the defendant had been significantly eroded by numerous statutory exceptions, of which the provisions at issue were examples. He also took specific note of the fact that the defendants were not being

81 [2000] 2 AC 326.
82 Quoting *Salabiaku v France* (1988) 13 EHRR 379 at 388: 'Presumptions of fact or of law operate in every legal system. Clearly, the Convention does not prohibit such presumptions in principle. It does, however, require the contracting states to remain within certain limits in this respect as regards criminal law.'
83 See also *Sporrong and Lonroth v Sweden* (1982) 5 EHRR 35 at 52.
84 *R v DPP, ex p Kebilene* [2000] 2 AC 326, per Lord Hope.
85 [2002] QB 1112.

asked to disprove an element of an offence but rather to prove a defence that had been extended to them as a benefit by a democratically elected Parliament. He continued that the courts, when considering alleged violations of an individual's rights under the Convention and in interpreting HRA 1998, should pay a degree of deference to Parliament's view of what was in the public's interest. His conclusion was that the burden-shifting provisions did not violate Article 6.

In light of the decisions in *Kebilene* and *Lambert*, it is most unlikely that shifting to a corporate defendant the burden of proof of due diligence would run foul of HRA 1998. HRA 1998 and the Convention protect not only the interests of a company on trial, but also those of the public at large. The public interest in curbing corporate crime is obviously great, given the vast extent of the harm that can be caused by corporate misconduct. Further, as we have argued, it is most likely that the corporation will be in possession of the relevant evidence or have access to it, and thus discharging the burden of proving due diligence should not be unduly onerous. Under the proposals discussed in this chapter, the standard of proof would only be that of a 'balance of probabilities', the same standard that was upheld in *Kebilene* and *Lambert*. Taking this lesser standard of proof into account and balancing the relevant policy interests, it would appear doubtful that requiring a company to prove its due diligence by a 'balance of probabilities' would be found to contravene either the European Convention or HRA 1998.

G. CONCLUSION

A change in procedural and evidence law with respect to the trial of companies is appropriate and opportune. If the new model of corporate criminal fault proposed in this book were to be accepted, the case for revising outmoded rules of evidence and procedures designed for human defendants would be strengthened. However, even in the absence of such reform, there is a formidable case for reconsidering the evidentiary and procedural rules applicable in trials of companies. Decisions interpreting the European Convention on Human Rights and HRA 1998 suggest that 'human rights' challenges to such reform would not succeed.

Sentencing and sanctions

A. INTRODUCTION

In a criminal trial the sentencing decision is, perforce, the last to be taken. However, from the outset the issue of sanctions needs to be borne in mind by the prosecution, as it should have some idea of what objectives are to be achieved by a bringing a case to trial. Moreover, in the corporate context, to answer such questions as whom to charge (employees, supervisory personnel, directors, corporate officers and/or the company itself), for what crimes to charge (regulatory or substantive offences) and in what court to file charges (magistrates' court or Crown Court) will require the prosecutor to think seriously in advance about the penalties that will follow a conviction.

It is a mistake – common to legislators, lawyers and the general public – to assume that changes in the law of corporate crime will lead to changes in corporate behaviour. From a company's perspective, there may be little point in altering an illegal but profitable way of doing business until it is demonstrably shown not to be in the company's financial interest to continue its unlawful practices. If there are no meaningful sanctions for wrongdoing, companies may see little to be gained by being a good corporate citizen, and much to be lost if less scrupulous rivals exploit their commitment to the law.

Oliver Wendell Holmes (1897) advised law students that if they wished to understand how the law worked, they should see it through the eyes of the 'bad man'. The 'good man' needs no reason to obey the law other than the fact that it is the law, but the 'bad man' – or perhaps, more accurately, the amoral man – obeys the law because of the consequences that he envisages will befall him if he does not. A company may, in a sense, be the epitome of the 'bad man'. Its prime, although by no means sole, preoccupation is with profits, and the question it will ask itself is whether profits will increase or decrease by virtue of having followed a particular course of action. When the course of action entails a decision as to whether or not to break the law, the economic calculation is whether the profits from pursuing the illegal course of action, less the costs incurred in the defence of a criminal prosecution and the sanctions following a conviction, discounted by the estimated probability of detection, prosecution and conviction, are greater than the profits to be achieved through a law-abiding approach to the company's business.

Holmes' 'bad man' metaphor helps to explain how judges and legislators have traditionally approached the sentencing of companies. The thinking appears to be that corporate crimes are committed because they benefit the company financially. To eliminate corporate crime, therefore, one must take the profit out of such criminality. The way to do so is to impose on a convicted offender a fine that outweighs the financial gain from the offence. Once criminality becomes unprofitable, rational companies will refrain from engaging in it.

In England and Wales the practical problem has been that fines have traditionally been so low that they are unlikely to have the hoped-for effect. Jurisdictional limits restricting the maximum fine that a court can impose combine with a judicial mentality that may fail to take corporate crime sufficiently seriously to produce fines that often can only be described as derisory. Part of the problem is that, until fairly recently, sentencing courts have received little in the way of guidance from appellate courts as to how to calculate the appropriate fine in a given case.

On a more basic level, one can question the economic model that sees corporate crime as the product of a rational cost-benefit calculation. In some cases this may be so, but in others, as we tried to demonstrate in chapter 1, corporate crimes are attributable to organisational and structural flaws within an organisation. If so, it is not simply a question of taking the profit out of the offence, even assuming this could be done. Rather, what may be needed is reform of the offender's structures, policies, practices and ways of doing business. What may also be needed is a shift in priorities, fundamental change in the ethos and culture of the company and improved systems of risk management and crime prevention.

In this book we have advanced a theory of corporate criminality grounded in a concept of organisational fault. To correct organisational faults may require structural reforms and systemic change, and not just a re-calibration of the cost-benefit calculus. To achieve reform, courts will need to add to their sentencing arsenal innovative penalties such as remedial orders, corporate probation, restraint-orientated sanctions and community service. With events of the past several decades throwing a spotlight on corporate criminal liability, and with the emergence of new and more sophisticated conceptions of corporate fault such as we have advocated, the courts can expect an increase in the number of prosecutions and convictions of companies, making the time ripe to reconsider the topic of sanctions.

In developing the recommended wider range of sanctions, Parliament and the courts need to be aware of and sensitive to the ancillary consequences of sanctions as well as the conviction itself. On the 'negative' side, sanctions can have undesirable spill-over effects. A fine may be 'passed on' to consumers in the form of a price rise in the company's products or workers may be made redundant to generate the savings to pay off a fine. Why should the public or the company's employees bear the burden of the company's criminality? Is spill-over inevitable? Conversely, a conviction can stigmatise a company and cause consumers to boycott its products. In some instances a boycott can have a potentially far greater financial impact on the company than any fine allowable under the law, but the effects are unpredictable. After Arthur Andersen's role in the Enron collapse was revealed, the accounting firm began to lose both clients and key staff at such an alarming rate that its continued viability was threatened, and this was even before it had been prosecuted, convicted and sentenced for obstruction of justice. Such 'informal sanctions' imposed by the public may be as punitive and as much a deterrent to corporate criminality as the formal penalties imposed by the sentencing judge.

B.   THEORY

In the largely virgin territory of corporate sentencing, it is necessary to return to first principles and to identify the penological objectives to be achieved by imposing sanctions on a company. A principled approach to sentencing must be grounded in a sound understanding of the goals of punishment, and we begin our inquiry by examining commonly advanced and long-accepted rationales for punishment in cases of human offenders. We then ask whether, and in what ways, these rationales have relevance to companies convicted of a crime.

I.   Theories of punishment

Over the years various theories of punishment have been advanced, the oldest of which is retribution. A retributive punishment is imposed because the offender has caused harm. Through formal punishment the offender atones for his/her offence. The Biblical principle of lex talionis determined the type and severity of the sanction – 'an eye for an eye, and a tooth for a tooth'. In modern times, where punishment more typically takes the form of imprisonment, the application of lex talionis would indicate that the length of the sentence should be proportionate to the harm caused. While retribution theory has fallen somewhat out of favour, perhaps because it fails to address itself to the protection of society from future crimes, there has been a recent revival of interest in the retributive concept of 'just deserts'. Many modern theorists would maintain that the primary reason for punishing offenders is because, quite simply, they deserve to be punished.

Whereas retribution looks backwards to the offender's crime, other rationales are more orientated to the future. The theory of restraint, sometimes referred to as isolation or incapacitation, justifies the imprisonment of offenders by the need to prevent their causing harm to other members of society. The assumption is that, by virtue of having committed a criminal offence, an offender has manifested his/her dangerousness to society. In theory, criminals need to be restrained only until they are no longer dangerous. To reach that point, many penologists have advocated combining restraint with rehabilitation. If successful, rehabilitation programmes have the advantage of saving the government the expense of continued incarceration and the costs of future criminality by the offender.

At one time hailed as the way forward in penology (Allen: 1959), the 'rehabilitative ideal' has lost some of its lustre as a result of not being able to follow through on its theoretical promise (Allen: 1981). The sticking point, often hard to accept because it concedes the limits of human knowledge, is that the complex constellation of factors – biological, physical, psychological, social and economic – that underlie the decision to commit a crime are not well understood, and even less may be known about how to go about 'curing' criminality.[1] Criminologists teach that most persons who commit crimes are never caught, let alone convicted, and that the majority desist from the criminal activity after their teens or early twenties; only a small proportion go on to a life of 'professional' crime (Canter and Alison: 2000). The maturational processes that naturally wean delinquents from a criminal career have nothing to do with formal rehabilitative programmes. One intriguing aspect of recidivism statistics, moreover, is that many recidivists have served a prison sentence. For them prison may have been little more than a 'school for crime', a school where minor offenders who may not have been particularly criminally inclined or dangerous to begin with are exposed to hardened criminals and toughened by the rigours of prison life.

The logic of restraint and rehabilitation theory suggests that courts should impose indeterminate sentences – an offender needs to be restrained until rehabilitated. The problem with indeterminate sentences, however, is that they can easily lead to sentences that are disproportionate to the harm caused by the offender, and thus offend the principle of 'just deserts'. Protesters who 'trash' a military installation because of their opposition to war could wind up serving a life sentence if they refused to abandon their pacifist convictions. Such a sentence might well seem unjust not only to the protesters' peer group, but also to the general public. It may also be doubted whether rehabilitation can ever be achieved in the coercive environment of a prison. Even when a regime of rehabilitation appears to be effective within a prison setting, there remains the question of whether it will continue to be effective after the offender is released into the community. In the community offenders will again be exposed to the temptations that got them into trouble in the first place, including alcohol, drugs and an undesirable peer group, and from which prison had separated them.

Whereas retribution, restraint and rehabilitation are directed towards the individual offender, the aim of general deterrence is to discourage others from committing similar offences. The theory is that would-be criminals will observe the punishment of the offender, will not want to suffer a similar fate, and therefore will reject any thoughts that they might have had to commit the crime in question, or, indeed, any crime. There is a second branch of deterrence, known as special deterrence, which focuses on the effect of a punishment on the individual subjected to it. Here the

---

1   Disagreement even exists as to such fundamental matters as what constitutes rehabilitation. Some see the goal as nothing less than the moral reformation of the offender, while others are content to teach the offender skills which would render resort to crime after release unnecessary.

thinking is that, having been exposed to the rigours of imprisonment, the defendant will have no desire to re-offend and risk being returned to prison. According to deterrence theory, the sanction imposed needs to be sufficient, but no greater than, what is necessary to deter the offender and other would-be offenders from committing the offence in question. Determining the specific punishment that will suffice to achieve this end is obviously going to present difficulties, as the threshold at which would-be criminals will be deterred will vary with different individuals.

Moralists criticise deterrence theory because punishment of one offender is being used to serve as an example to other would-be offenders. The individual, in Kantian terms, is being used as a means to an end rather than being treated as an individual in his/her own right. In theory, a deterrence-oriented sentence could result in greater punishment than is warranted by the intrinsic wrongfulness of the offence, which would be the case, for example, if a severe punishment were deemed to be necessary to achieve deterrence of an offence that was widespread, but not particularly threatening (eg failure to obtain a TV licence). In any event, criminal sanctions may not deter offenders who do not expect to be caught or convicted. General deterrence theory may also have little applicability to crimes whose commission is not carefully plotted in advance and, in particular, to the many crimes which are impulsive or opportunistic (and the available evidence suggests that many conventional crimes are of this nature, including some rather serious ones: Katz: 1988; Canter and Alison: 2000).

Retribution, restraint, rehabilitation, special deterrence and general deterrence comprise the primary rationales for punishment, but other theories have also been advanced. In some instances, criminal sanctions can serve an educative function, indicating to the public that certain conduct is not only illegal (a message conveyed by the trial and conviction), but is also deemed sufficiently serious to warrant punishment. Education may be particularly important where doubt as to the moral culpability and criminality of the conduct in question may exist in the community. Somewhat similarly, punishment can also serve a denunciatory function, but whereas the educational dimension of punishment aims at informing the public of the seriousness of an *offence*, denunciation serves to alert the public to the *offenders* who are deserving of their censure. If members of the public then decide that they do not wish to associate with the offender, they are in a position to do so. Both education and denunciation have symbolic as well as practical significance.

In recent times legislatures have also conceived of the criminal trial as a forum in which compensation might be awarded to the victims of a criminal offence or restitution ordered. Unlike a fine, which goes to the state, compensation is paid to the victim and restitution is used to repair the harm caused by the offence. The ability of a court to impose a compensatory sentence or to order restitution will usually depend on specific statutory authority. In many instances the opportunity to receive compensation and restitution will be welcomed by victims who cannot afford a lawyer, and who would otherwise find it difficult to bring a civil suit against a powerful company. On the other hand, criminal compensation schemes usually offer more limited recompense than that potentially available in a civil suit, with the effect that some victims will prefer to pursue their civil remedies.

The various justifications for punishment that have been discussed are not mutually exclusive. Often, more than one theory will support a given sanction. So, for example, *imprisonment* of a convicted defendant may be justified on the grounds of retribution (because of the harm the offender has caused), restraint (because the offender is dangerous), rehabilitation (to prevent further offending by aiming to change the offender's attitudes and behaviour while s/he is incarcerated), general deterrence (to discourage others from committing the same offence), special deterrence (to discourage the offender from re-offending following release) and denunciation (to express society's outrage and censure). If the sentence is for an activity not generally regarded as criminal, imprisonment may also serve an educational function. Sometimes a package of sanctions will be imposed, each designed to achieve a different purpose. If, in addition to a brief prison term, an offender were to be ordered to undergo counselling, the latter would be designed to promote more strongly the goal of rehabilitation.

2. The applicability of the theories to companies

To what extent are the various theories of punishment that have been discussed, developed largely in cases involving natural persons convicted of common law crimes, relevant to companies convicted of a criminal offence? In some instances the theories seem almost irrelevant or inappropriate; in others their weight may need to be adjusted to take account of the corporate context; and in still others they can play a far more central role than they do in respect to human offenders.

In chapter 4 we argued that the extent of a company's culpability could be distorted because of the catastrophic harm that follows from corporate negligence, gross negligence or recklessness. We gave as an example the nearly 200 passengers and crew who lost their lives when the *Herald of Free Enterprise* capsized. Even conceding that P&O should have been held criminally liable (it was not) for these deaths, one could in good faith question whether the number of deaths reflected the degree of the company's culpability. The eye-for-an eye model of retribution would exaggerate even further this distortion. Conversely, a company can be highly culpable but, through good fortune, escape harmful consequences. The *Herald* capsized because its bow doors had been left open, but other ships had previously sailed with open bow doors without mishap. It was because of considerations such as these that we advocated establishing a regime of corporate crimes defined without regard to harm. If so defined, however, retribution theory loses its ability to provide a compass in sentencing, although the case can still be made that a company that has caused or threatened to cause social harm on so great a scale should be punished simply because it 'deserves' to be punished.

Consider the converse problem. When harm is minimal or non-existent (as it is with respect to endangerment offences), sanctions linked to harm may not be sufficient to deter profitable but illegal practices. To deter these, punishment that greatly exceeds harm may be required. The point was recognised by the Court of Appeal in *R v F Howe & Son (Engineers) Ltd*,[2] when, in the context of a health and safety case, it stated that a fine should be large enough to bring home the importance of safety to the company, its managers and its shareholders. Companies may be the prime example of the rational cost-benefit calculators which those who champion deterrence theory had in mind, even if the theory was not conceived with any thought

---

2   [1999] 2 All ER 249.

of companies. Deterrence may be especially important in the corporate context because of the vast potential for harm when a company conducts its operation in a negligent, reckless or grossly negligent manner, even if the first offender to be tried has caused minimal harm. The next may not be as fortunate.

Turning to theories of restraint and rehabilitation, it is obvious that courts will need to rethink what constitutes a restraint in respect of a company. Companies obviously cannot be imprisoned. Although corporate directors and officers can be imprisoned, they do not pose the same type of danger to the public as do hardened criminals who inflict violent injuries on their victims, an issue we will examine further in the next chapter. Restraint, however, may be achieved by limiting the types of activities in which a convicted company can engage, and rehabilitation by changing the criminogenic practices that led to the crime in question. Furthermore, while rehabilitation with respect to natural persons is often limited by our lack of knowledge as to why individuals commit crimes and how to convert those who do commit crimes into law-abiding citizens, such ignorance is less likely to be a problem with respect to offending companies. Expert consultants can be enlisted to advise on health and safety matters. At the same time, it may be much easier to reform the way that a company conducts its business than it is to change the character of a natural person who offends. Reformation is crucial, moreover, for, unlike the case with rebellious youths, coporate criminality cannot be expected to decline with the maturational process. Indeed, to the contrary, uncorrected crime-conducive conditions will continue to cause future harm and a failure to address the problem may reinforce the company's criminal tendencies. If practices cannot be changed, then the sentencing court may wish to consider the restraint option of closing down altogether the particular sphere of the company's operation that gave way to the offence, and perhaps even the company itself.

Finally, two theories of punishment – education and denunciation – often accorded lesser weight in discussions of punishment, may have greater salience in the corporate context. As we have observed previously, members of the public do not view many forms of corporate crime as 'real crime'. While murder and manslaughter are universally regarded as serious offences, how many people – and how many companies – would put an inattention to safety issues in the same category, even if in the back of their minds they were aware that neglect of safety could lead to serious injuries and death? A hefty fine of a company for its health and safety violations will serve to impress on the offender and other companies, as well as the public, the importance which the law attaches to safety. Forcing the company to change its way of doing business may have an even greater impact.

The denunciatory function of sentencing is achieved by the 'naming and shaming' of the particular corporate offender. This can lead to a ripple effect, as consumers may not wish to give their patronage to companies who flout the law. Organised boycotts can have a potentially far greater public relations and financial impact, and consequently exert a much greater deterrent effect, than any fine that a court is realistically likely to impose. Companies also typically place a high value on their reputation, as do corporate executives; in certain industries, such as finance and retail merchandising, trust and image are considered essential. Being labelled and punished as a criminal offender can damage a company's reputation, and the threat of such denunciation may prove a powerful lever for affecting a company's behaviour, as well as that of its directors and officers.

C.   AN ARSENAL OF SANCTIONS

In *R v ICR Haulage*, Stable J made the point that a court should not 'stultify itself by embarking on a trial in which, if a verdict of guilty is returned, no effective order by way of sentence can be made'.[3] The logic of this position would seem to lead to perverse results: the more serious a corporate offence, the less likely would be a prosecution, for the more difficult would it be for a court to devise a penalty commensurate with the gravity of the crime. Yet, obviously, the more serious the corporate offence, the greater the public's need to protection. This dilemma makes it all the more imperative that Parliament and the courts think seriously about the types and range of sanctions that can be applied to companies convicted of criminal offences, but in an area which cries out for creative thinking, little seems to be forthcoming.

I.   Fines and monetary sanctions

Historically, the penalties imposed on *individuals* convicted of serious criminal offences have included death, corporal punishment and imprisonment. Corporal punishment and the death penalty have now been abolished, and putting a company in jail would appear to be a physical impossibility. Fines have become the sanction of default for convicted companies.

For regulatory offences, the fine may have seemed a fitting penalty, a monetary sanction for an offence typically precipitated by the desire to increase a company's profits. However, now that the English judges have recognised that companies can be guilty of manslaughter and the government has proposed an offence of corporate killing, the question that must be addressed is whether a fine is an appropriate punishment for a company that has caused death or serious injury. In its 1996 report, the Law Commission did not appear to be troubled by the prospect of a monetary penalty for a corporate killing, but if a social scientist were to suggest that offenders who committed a homicide should merely be fined, the political and public outcry would likely be deafening.

a.   The case for monetary sanctions

Monetary sanctions are not without their advantages. One advantage of a fine is that it is a relatively cost-free sanction to administer. When offenders are sentenced to imprisonment, the state must construct secure facilities, provide the inmates with food and sustenance, employ guards to maintain order and prevent escapes, and generally administer to prisoner needs. Recent figures have put the cost of maintaining an inmate in prison in excess of £25,000 per year per prisoner. In contrast, the expense involved in collecting a fine will be minimal and whatever administrative costs are incurred can be charged to the offender. Where the offender is a company, it will normally continue in business and be able to apply its income to the payment of the fine.

3   [1944] KB 551 at 554.

Another advantage to monetary sanctions is that they can be used to compensate victims or provide restitution.[4] In the absence of a statutory directive, the government is not usually under any obligation to use fines for either of these purposes. In England, there is statutory authority that allows a criminal court to award compensation to the victim of a criminal offence,[5] and comparable provisions are included in the United States Sentencing Guidelines (USSG) for organisational offenders.[6] Compensating victims makes particularly good sense in a corporate context, as companies will ordinarily be better placed to pay compensation than individual offenders. If left to their civil remedies, the victims of corporate offences might discover that their ability to pursue their claims was no match for the financial resources which the corporate defendant could bring to bear in defending against their suits. The prosecution may be better placed, because of its superior investigative resources, to establish the extent of corporate misconduct and victim damages. Considerations of efficiency also support adjudicating both civil and criminal liability in a single proceeding, even if it might mean prolonging the proceedings to receive evidence (such as that pertaining to the amount of the loss) that might not otherwise be admissible in a criminal trial. The benefits of compensation and restitution orders are so great that there should be a strong presumption in their favour in all cases involving corporate defendants, and Gruner (1993) suggests that a sentencing court might even be required to give reasons for not making such an order. Under the USSG, restitution orders are not only mandatory, but take priority over any fine due to the state.[7] However, the federal guidelines do not preclude a victim who so wishes from pursuing a civil remedy in a separate proceeding, a valuable option where either the compensation that can be awarded by a sentencing court is capped by statute, or a victim envisages a more sympathetic response from a jury (in the United States, tort suits are heard by juries).

In a sense, compensation and restitution are consistent with retribution theory, as the sanction against the defendant will be determined by the harm incurred by the victim – an application of the principle of lex talionis. However, as it is arguable that a corporate offender should not be in the position where, at worst, it breaks even financially when convicted, while coming out ahead if it escapes detection or prosecution, compensation and restitution orders should not preclude additional sanctions designed to achieve other penological goals, such as deterrence. A more onerous sanction may be needed to persuade other would-be offenders that it is not in their interest to break the law.

---

4   Whereas compensation seeks to provide victims with money damages for the harm incurred as a result of a defendant's crime, restitution, more ambitiously, seeks to restore the status quo ante, either by undoing the harm done or placing the victim in the same position that s/he would have been had the crime not occurred. However, under English law, restitution is largely limited to the restoration of stolen goods: see Powers of Criminal Courts (Sentencing) Act 2000, s 148.

5   Power of Criminal Courts (Sentencing) Act 2000, s 130.

6   USSG, s 8B1.1. A court may decide to forego restitution if it determines that the process of fashioning a restitution order would unduly complicate and prolong the sentencing process. USSG, s 8B1.1(b) This might be the case where the victims are unknown or the amount of the damage will not be clear until some future point in time (often the case with respect to environmental offences).

7   See USSG, s 8D1.4(b)(4).

In the case of natural persons, the cost-benefit calculation that is claimed to underlie deterrence theory is complicated by the fact that the would-be offender is not comparing like with like – the individual may have to weigh the psychological satisfaction of assaulting an enemy against the prospect of five years in prison. In contrast, where corporate crimes are motivated by financial gain, a would-be corporate offender can directly compare the profit it expects to gain from violating the law with the loss it can expect to incur if its offence is discovered and it is prosecuted, convicted and fined. Thus, to the extent that a company is a rational cost-benefit calculator, it can be expected to be responsive to financial penalties. Because loss of profitability strikes at one of the essential purposes of the company, a fine does hold the potential to be an effective deterrent.

As noted, the above-hypothesised calculation assumes detection, prosecution, conviction and imposition of a sanction. Based on past experience, or the perception that the government will not be aggressive in investigating corporate wrongdoing, corporate officials may be inclined to discount the likelihood of this parlay. If a prosecution is perceived as unlikely, the deterrent effect of sanctions that presume both a prosecution and a conviction may not weigh heavily in corporate planning decisions. To provide a counterweight to such thinking, fines may need to exceed the intrinsic 'wrongfulness' of an offence in order to achieve the desired deterrent effect. Say that a company's illegal practices earn it an extra £500,000 per year and that the company puts the chances of its criminality being discovered and its being prosecuted and convicted at 10% (which may well be a generous figure). Given these assumptions, it would then be in the company's financial interest to continue in its illegal but profitable course of conduct as long as it calculated that the odds of investigation, prosecution and conviction remained below 10%. In order to achieve deterrence, the fine would in theory have to be set at a level ten times greater (or £5,000,000 in our example) than would be necessary if detection and conviction was a certainty. But a court might well be reluctant to impose so heavy a fine because it could easily drive the convicted company out of business. This is what Coffee (1981) has referred to as the 'deterrence trap'. Further, in industries where a particular type of violation is widespread, a fine that is grossly in excess of culpability could place the company singled out for prosecution at a significant competitive disadvantage vis-à-vis its competitors. While such a fine may be consistent with deterrence theory, it may conflict with the principle of 'just deserts'.

This theoretical analysis notwithstanding, the more common criticism of the English courts is not that they impose excessive fines on convicted companies, but rather that the fines they impose are so low that they are unlikely to exert any deterrent effect whatsoever. If it is cheaper for a company to commit an offence and pay the fine than to operate its business in a lawful manner, why would a rational company choose to obey the law?; or, as Braithwaite (1985: 7) puts it, 'why do so many business people adopt the "economically irrational" course of obeying the law?' The fines imposed by the English judges sometimes verge on the derisory – in *Tesco Supermarkets Ltd v Nattrass*,[8] better known for its articulation of the 'identification' test of corporate criminal liability, the corporate defendant was fined

8   [1972] AC 153.

£25. And in *Alphacell Ltd v Woodward*[9] the defendant was fined £24 for polluting a river. Even by the 1972 standards of when *Alphacell* was decided, this was a grossly insufficient amount to repair the damage caused by the pollution, deter other companies from similar environmental offences or even cover the costs of the investigation. Fines have also been astonishingly low in cases where a death has occurred. In *R v British Steel Plc*,[10] where a worker died as a result of a health and safety violation, the offending company was fined £100. Even more astonishingly, the company saw fit to argue on appeal that the fine was excessive.

The above examples may admittedly be extreme, but they form part of a disturbing pattern. According to the Health and Safety Executive (2001), the average fine for a health and safety violation in 1999/2000 (excluding the exceptional case where the fine exceeded £100,000 and would therefore distort the average), was slightly under £5,000. For a violation resulting in death, the average fine in 1998/99 was £6,062 in cases brought in a magistrates' court, and £32,632 in Crown Court, where the maximum fine is in theory unlimited (HSE: 2001). However, there are winds of change: between 1996/97 and 1998/99, the average fine in cases of worker death more than doubled (Unison and the Centre for Corporate Accountability: 2002). Still, even double the level of fine may represent 'small change' to a multimillion pound corporation. Rather than being a deterrent, such penalties may embolden companies not to take the law seriously (Box: 1983). A company may, of course, decide to comply with the law because it does not wish the distraction of a criminal prosecution, or because it is concerned that criminal charges will tarnish its reputation, or because it simply believes that it is the right thing to do. For companies that think in this way, large fines may not be needed to deter illegality. For companies more preoccupied with profit and loss, the level of fines needs to be pegged at a level to discourage, not encourage, law-breaking.

Part of the explanation for the historically low fines in England has to do with the jurisdictional limits of a magistrates' court, where most corporate prosecutions are brought. As of the year 2002, the maximum fine that a magistrates' court could impose was £20,000 for a criminal offence and £5,000 for breach of a health and safety regulation (these limits are raised periodically to keep pace with inflation and Parliament has under consideration a Bill that would expand the range of offences that currently attract the £5,000 maximum). For an individual offender, a £20,000 fine is likely to constitute a substantial penalty. For a company, it may be a barely discernible blip on the company's financial radar. The obvious reason is that the net worth of most companies will far exceed the net worth of most individuals, and a fine that might be oppressive for an individual will impose little hardship on a successful company, even assuming that the fine cannot be passed on to the company's customers. While in a Crown Court there are no upper limits on the amount of the fine that a judge can impose, HSE statistics none the less indicate that the fines imposed by the judges are not significantly higher than those imposed by the magistrates. The explanation is not altogether clear, but one possibility may be that the judges are not thinking about the functions that the fine is designed to serve. A fine sufficient to deter individuals from future criminality may not have the same effect on a company. The English approach might be compared with that taken in

9   [1972] 2 All ER 475.
10 [1995] ICR 586.

Australia, where the Australian Commonwealth Crimes Act 1914, s 3 authorises a fine for a company that is five times the amount that could be imposed on a natural person who committed the same offence.

b. Determining the amount of a fine – the Howe criteria

What factors should a court consider in determining the amount of the fine to be imposed on a company convicted of a criminal offence? The obvious starting point is for the court to ensure itself that the company does not profit from its offence. At a minimum, the fine should be sufficiently high to remove any advantage that the company might have achieved by its illegality. However, simply to confiscate any unlawfully acquired advantage is not enough, or else companies will come to see violating the law as a break-even, no-risk proposition.

In England and Wales, guidance regarding the appropriate level of fines was largely lacking until the 1999 decision of the Court of Appeal in *R v F Howe & Son (Engineers) Ltd*.[11] The case involved a worker who was electrocuted while cleaning the company's factory. It was the company's responsibility to ensure that the equipment was in good working order, and it had failed to do so. The company pleaded guilty to a number of health and safety-related violations and was fined £48,000, with an additional £7,500 being assessed in costs. The company appealed on the ground that the sentence was excessive.

In its decision the Court of Appeal identified various factors that a judge should bear in mind in sentencing a company. In general terms, the court advised judges to look to the gravity of the offence and the means of the offender. The court downgraded the precedential significance of sentences handed down in other cases because, in the court's opinion, the fines previously imposed were too low and 'not an appropriate yardstick for determining the level of fine in the present case'.[12] The court was correct to draw attention to the inadequacy of the fines historically imposed for health and safety offences, for fines that are inadequate to exert a meaningful deterrent effect are unlikely to foster compliance with health and safety regulations. On the other hand, while precedent might not be a useful guide for determining the *absolute* amount of a fine, it might still be relevant to the determination of the *relative* seriousness of an offence.

Beyond the general admonition to consider the gravity of the offence and the means of the offender, the Court of Appeal in *Howe* identified several specific factors that should be taken into account in sentencing:
- the extent of the violation;
- how far short of the appropriate standard the company had fallen;
- the degree of risk and the extent of the danger that had been created;
- whether the violation was deliberate;
- whether the violation was an isolated lapse or a continuing breach;
- the defendant's resources; and
- the effect of a fine on the defendant's business.

11 [1999] 2 All ER 249.
12 *R v F Howe & Son (Engineers) Ltd* [1999] 2 All ER 249 at 253.

Most of these factors would appear uncontroversial, with the possible exception of the financial resources of the convicted company and the effect of a fine on the company's business, about which more will be said later. There are, however, a number of omissions from the list, some of which might perhaps have appeared so self-evident that the Court of Appeal thought it unnecessary to mention them. These would include such matters as the defendant's awareness of the dangers it had created, its general attitude towards risk, its understanding of whether or not it was operating within the law, its attitude to the victims (has it paid compensation?), the extent of its co-operation with investigating authorities (including whether it promptly notified the authorities of the offence or tried to cover it up) and any record of previous convictions and how the company had responded to them. Where the actions or inactions of multiple parties (whether human or corporate) had combined to bring about an offence, did the corporate defendant play a major or minor role? Presumably the *Howe* court's identification of specific sentencing factors was not intended to preclude consideration of others.

The Court of Appeal in *Howe* also identified aggravating and mitigating factors that a sentencing court might consider. Among the primary aggravating factors were:
- the fact that a death resulted from the violation;
- a failure to heed past warnings; and
- a deliberate breach with a view to profits.

These three aggravating factors address themselves to concerns of a different order. The failure to heed past warnings, a category that could be expanded to include a failure to act in response to warnings from regulatory agencies, employees and others, is indicative of bad faith. The fact of previous warnings would also preclude a claim that the company was not aware of a risk, and a failure to heed such warnings might reflect a cavalier attitude to both safety and the requirements of the law that would arguably be appropriate for a sentencing court to take into account. It would seem to fall into the same category as a failure to reform the criminogenic aspects of one's business practices following a previous conviction, and would clearly constitute an aggravating factor.

In contrast to a failure to heed past warnings, the *Howe* court's reference to the fact that a corporate violation is deliberately committed with a view to increasing profits seems odd. Companies are in business to make a profit, and most corporate decisions are made with an eye to reducing costs and increasing profits. This realpolitik of the business world would not seem to put this dimension of corporate decision-making within the category of, in the words of the court, a 'seriously aggravating feature'.

Also questionable as an aggravating factor is the fact that a death has occurred. In chapter 4 we made the point that whether or not a death occurs as a result of a company's illegal practices is often a matter of chance beyond the company's control. A company's recklessness in tolerating slipshod workplace practices is neither increased nor decreased by the incidence of a death. If so, its sentence likewise should not be affected by the death. To include death not only as a relevant, but as an aggravating, factor in sentencing would appear to pander unduly to the 'eye-for-an-eye' concept of retribution.

The mitigating factors identified by the *Howe* court included:
- a prompt admission of responsibility;
- a timely plea of guilty;
- remedial measures taken after the deficiencies were drawn to the company's attention; and
- a good safety record.

While for a court to take into account a company's previous good record in determining the appropriate sentence would seem sensible, the other mitigating factors identified by the Court of Appeal are more questionable. A plea of guilty, although traditionally considered in mitigation, may indicate nothing more than the self-evident nature of a company's offence. The company's lawyers may have made a strategic decision that it would be futile to dispute the charges, and that the best hope for a lenient sentence lay in pleading guilty. While a plea of guilty by a natural person may be viewed as an expression of contrition, a metaphysical entity such as a company is incapable of such emotions. On the other hand, it can be argued that a plea represents an acceptance of responsibility, and this consideration applies to both corporate and human defendants. In any event, a plea of guilty saves the state the costs of a trial, and spares witnesses from having to relive traumatic events and having to testify in open court. Whether a company should be treated more severely because it insists on a trial, however, is another matter. Where fault is a matter of dispute or where a company believes that it has acted in good faith or has a viable defence, it may well decide not to enter a plea of guilty. To receive a more severe sentence if its denials are not accepted or its defence fails would seem to penalise it for exercising its right to trial; and also put it in an invidious position vis-a-vis more egregious offenders who plead guilty because of the self-evident nature of their offence.

Another of the mitigating factors identified in *Howe* with which one might take issue is the fact that remedial measures were taken after a company's wrongdoing was brought to its attention. Fisse and Braithwaite (1993) promote a somewhat similar concept which they refer to as 'reactive fault'. They would judge a company's culpability in part by the corrective measures that the company takes after having become aware of wrongful acts committed by personnel acting on its behalf. Either building reactive fault into the concept of corporate criminality, as do Fisse and Braithwaite, or allowing consideration of post-offence remedial measures in mitigation of sentence, as the *Howe* court suggests, could be argued to provide an incentive to companies to take the initiative in correcting dangerous, unlawful and crime-conducive conditions. A cynic might counter, however, that such an approach allows a company to conduct its business in an illegal manner until such time as it is caught, at which point it can put right the practices in question and receive a legal 'benefit' from having done so. In some of the environmental cases in the United States, companies have been cited for literally hundreds of violations. Following a chemical leak at the Union Carbide complex in Institute, West Virginia, for instance, the company was fined $1.4m for 221 violations of 55 federal health and safety laws. Labor Secretary Brock commented: 'We were just surprised to find constant, wilful, overt violations on such a widespread basis.' In March 1986, the company negotiated a settlement with OSHA, agreeing to pay $408,000 for 'five serious violations' in return for an agreement to correct the violations immediately (Fortun: 2001: 60–61).

In the sentencing of a thief or burglar, the sanction imposed is not likely to be affected by return of the stolen goods, especially if it seems to have been prompted by fear of an imminent arrest. In the case of an offending company, it also may not change its business operation until it becomes obvious that the authorities have detected, and intend to take action to curb, its illegal practices. Meanwhile, the wrongdoer will have profited at the expense of its less unscrupulous rivals during the period before its illegal practices are detected, and, indeed, may have driven some or all of its competitors out of business. Furthermore, as was pointed out with respect to guilty pleas in mitigation, the companies that may wind up losing out are not the egregious violators but those which believe in good faith that they have not broken the law, and therefore have nothing to correct. Such a company may be reluctant to change its operating procedures lest it be construed as an admission of wrongdoing.

Although one can take issue with specific aspects of the *Howe* guidelines, none the less the decision of the court represents a commendable effort to provide direction to English judges in the sentencing of convicted companies. Although issued in the context of a health and safety offence, there would seem no reason why the guidelines could not be applied to all cases of corporate criminality. It would be better still if they were to become part of a more comprehensive and integrated approach to the sentencing of companies, as exemplified by the United States Sentencing Guidelines for organisational offenders, which we shall examine in a subsequent section.

c.   *Differential fines*

The straightforward way to address the problem of fines that are too low to have the hoped-for deterrent effect would seem to be for the courts to increase the fines that they impose on convicted companies. Where an artificial ceiling is set by statute, as it is in the case of fines in a magistrates' court, Parliament or the government might raise the maximum fine which the court would have the authority to impose on an offender. But are higher fines truly the answer? For a company operating in the red or on the margin of profitability, a steep fine may simply drive it into liquidation, in which case the fine becomes the virtual equivalent of a death sentence for the company. For multi-million pound corporations, on the other hand, higher fines may have only a minimal impact. In the year that British Petroleum (BP) was fined the seemingly impressive amount of £750,000 for safety violations, it reported an even more impressive profit of £1,391,000,000 (Slapper: 1993: 429–430). The fine represented a little more than one-half of one percent of the company's after-tax profit. Large companies often have a contingency reserve for such 'emergencies', and, although it is generally deemed to be against public policy to allow companies to insure against criminal fines, a company may be able to obtain insurance to cushion itself against the ancillary financial effects of a conviction.

The criminal justice system needs to be sensitive to the problem of the disparate treatment of similarly situated offenders, a problem that could be exacerbated if the ceiling on fines were to be raised. In industries where violations of a particular law are commonplace, prosecutors may be unable, because of budgetary constraints, to prosecute every violator. Prosecuting one company in the industry would seem to be sufficient to achieve the goal of deterrence, for the conviction of the target defendant should cause similarly situated companies to reform their unlawful practices, but the effect on the company that has been singled out for prosecution can be devastating. Despite not having behaved any differently from its rivals, it may emerge from the trial with its reputation damaged, its finances depleted from the costs of its defence and having to find the money to pay a fine imposed by the court. The higher the fine, the more of a disadvantage will the company find itself at in comparison with its equally culpable competitors which are not selected for prosecution.

To treat similarly situated corporate offenders similarly may call for a sentencing court to impose differential fines. Say that Company A, a small family-owned business with an annual profit of £25,000, commits an offence, and Company B, a multinational enterprise (MNE) with profits in the millions, commits the identical offence. If a court were to fine the two companies the same absolute amount, the fine clearly would have a more damaging impact on the small family business than on the MNE. An equal sanction for two offenders is arguably one that has an equal impact on the offenders. In terms of criminological theory, differential fines for identical offences can be justified on the grounds of special deterrence. In each case the monetary penalty will be of an amount that will deter the particular offender from future violations. Such a fine, moreover, would not necessarily detract from the general deterrent effect of the sanction as long as larger companies appreciated that the fine that could be imposed on them would not be bound by the precedent of the fine imposed on the small company. On the other hand, differential fines do run the risk of offending the principle of 'just deserts', being too little in the case of small companies and too much in the case of MNEs. To some they might even appear to penalise successful companies for their efficiency and profitability.

The Court of Appeal in *Howe* sent mixed messages on this issue. On the one hand, the court indicated that the size of a company should not affect the relevant standard of care. The court pointed out that the goal was to ensure a safe working environment for employees and members of the public and that this goal did not change depending on the size of the company. This consideration would suggest that fines should be independent of a company's size and resources. On the other hand, in reducing the fine imposed in the case by the trial judge, the Court of Appeal referred to the company's precarious financial situation. It also listed a defendant's resources and the effect of the fine on the defendant's business as among the criteria to be taken into account in sentencing. Finally, the court stated that a fine should be sufficiently onerous to bring home the importance of safety to the company, its managers and its shareholders (and, presumably, to similarly situated companies and their managers and shareholders). These sorts of considerations suggest that it would not be inappropriate for fines to take account of the size and profitability of the offender.

Precedent for differential fines can be found in the Criminal Justice Act 1991.[13] Under the provisions of the Act, after the seriousness of the offence was fixed according to a pre-set sliding scale, the fine in an individual case was calculated on the basis of the offender's 'disposable weekly income'. Offenders with different 'disposable weekly incomes' could therefore receive different fines for the same offence, the idea being to make the penalty comparably burdensome for rich and poor. This aim may have been laudable, but in practice 'unit fines' on occasion produced ridiculous results in the form of exorbitant penalties for trivial offences. In one case, an offender was fined in excess of £1,000 for littering. When a sanction bears so little relationship to the crime, it threatens to overshadow the offence in the minds of both the public and the defendant, thereby diverting attention from the crime committed by the offender to the injustice of the penalty inflicted on him/her. Rather than receiving society's condemnation, the offender becomes the beneficiary of its sympathy; and rather than reflecting on the wrongdoing that had given rise to the sanction, the offender may focus on and be resentful of the treatment that s/he received vis-à-vis others who had committed the identical offence.[14] After a two-

13 Criminal Justice Act 1991, s 18, repealed by Criminal Justice Act 1993, s 65.
14 See General Note to Criminal Justice Act 1993, Pt VI.

year period of experimentation, the unit fine provisions were repealed,[15] although the means of an offender remains a legitimate consideration for a sentencing judge to take into account.

Although conceived of with individuals and not companies in mind, the unit fine may have more merit in a corporate context. When a natural person is convicted of a serious offence, s/he can be sentenced to prison, a fine being reserved for less serious violations. In the case of companies, a fine has to serve as the sanction for both minor and serious offences, as imprisonment is not a viable alternative. The level of fine that is needed to signify that an offence is serious will vary depending on the company's financial situation. It may be pointless to impose a million pound fine on a company with an annual turnover of one-tenth that amount, for a far smaller fine would have the same impact on it. Conversely, a million pound fine for a multinational corporation whose annual profits are measured in billions of pounds may have little effect. To impress on the MNE the seriousness of its offence may require a fine that is disproportionate to its actual culpability or the harm it has caused. Moreoever, there is unlikely to be the same sympathetic backlash in favour of a corporate offender in such circumstances as there would be for an individual who received a fine disproportionate to culpability or harm caused.

Accepting the principle of differential fines is only a first step. A court would still need to determine the amount of the fine in a given case. What exactly is it that a proportionate fine should be proportionate to? European Union competition law allows for fines of up to 10% of an offending company's previous year's global turnover.[16] But is global turnover the appropriate yardstick for calculating a fine? A company might have a substantial turnover, but be operating at a loss. The same point could be made about liquidity and 'cash flow', other possible gauges of a company's financial worth. Perhaps a court should look at the offender's profits, either for the previous year or for a specified number of preceding years. But on what basis does a court determine a company's profits? Tax returns may not provide a reliable guide as there are many tax avoidance schemes which can affect the amount of tax a company pays.

One of the more intriguing questions is what fine should be imposed on a company that is less profitable than it might be because it is poorly run. Some companies almost never make a profit (Meyer and Zucker: 1989 observe that some media enterprises are run virtually as a private hobby by the wealthy). In the field of family law, a court, for the purpose of preventing a vindictive partner from deliberately lowering his/her income (by, perhaps, refusing a promotion or quitting a well-paying position) in order to decrease the financial support that might be awarded to a child or ex-partner, is allowed to calculate an award on the *earning capacity* of the parties, as opposed to their actual income.[17] A comparable approach in the corporate field would allow a sentencing judge to determine a company's profitability by looking to the profits of similarly situated companies in the industry. However, this approach could unfairly penalise a company that might consciously have chosen to sacrifice maximum profits in favour of, for example, a less stressful working environment for

---

15 Criminal Justice Act 1993, s 65.
16 Regulation 17, Art 15(2). Daily fines may also be imposed under Art 16. For similar provisions in England and Wales, see Competition Act 1998, s 36(8).
17 See Matrimonial Causes Act 1973, s 25(1)(a).

its employees. In the final analysis, each case will have to be addressed on its individual merits, and no single criterion is likely to provide a reliable benchmark in all situations.

d.   Are fines really the answer?

For a court or legislature to debate whether fines should be absolute, limited or unlimited, or proportional to a company's profits or potential profitability may be to deflect itself from the more fundamental question of whether a fine is a useful or desirable sanction against a convicted company. The problem with fines is that they can have a spill-over effect. The fine may be passed on to consumers of the company's products in the form of increased prices or, if that is not possible, may be borne by workers who are made redundant or forced to take a reduction in salary.

The sentencing of British Rail for its role in the Clapham Junction train crash is illustrative of the difficulties facing a court. In the case, the company was fined £250,000 for its safety violations. The judge, however, acknowledged that British Rail would in all likelihood have to raise its fares to pay the fine. Even if fare increases had been precluded by the court (assuming a court had the power to do so), ordinary citizens could still have wound up paying, as British Rail's funding came from the government. If its budget had been frozen and a fare increase proscribed, British Rail may have had to reduce its wage bill by laying off staff in order to pay the fine. Either way, innocent persons would have borne the brunt of the fine.

Although at the time British Rail was publicly funded, the same effects could be envisaged in the case of a private company which enjoyed a monopolistic position and the demand for whose product was relatively inelastic. Discounting customer loyalty, the only time a company might not be able to pass on a fine to consumers would be in a highly competitive, price-sensitive market involving products which were largely interchangeable, where an increase in the cost of a product might drive consumers to the company's competitors. Setting fines at a level where they could not easily be passed on without the company losing a significant share of its market would minimise the pass-on effect, but at the same time would increase the chances that workers would need to be made redundant in order to pay off the fine. If the fine were so high that the company was driven out of business, those most affected would be the innocent workers who would have lost their jobs. The state may find itself saddled with paying benefits to the unemployed workers at a time when it will have lost the benefit of not only their taxes, but also those of the company that has been forced into liquidation.

One could argue that all convictions have ancillary consequences, and that a court should not concern itself with spill-over in determining whether and how much to fine a company. In the cases of human offenders sentenced to prison, friends and family may suffer and hardship will be experienced by persons who themselves have committed no crime. Might not a court view employees who are made redundant by a convicted company to pay off its fine in the same light? The difference is that in the corporate context the spill-over effect on employees is in danger of displacing the punishment intended for the company. If laying off employees allows a company to maintain its former level of profitability, the company will experience less adverse effects from the fine than will the employees made redundant. This is quite different from the situation of an offender who is sentenced to prison, where the offender will have to endure incarceration and his/her family, although doubtless disadvantaged, will not suffer any loss of liberty.

Spill-over effects might be less troublesome if their burden fell on the persons responsible for the company's criminal predicament. Under the currently prevailing test of corporate criminality in England, companies are liable when a person of sufficiently high standing within a company to be 'identified' with it commits an offence.[18] However, these executives are probably the last who will lose their posts if the company is forced to retrench in order to pay an onerous fine. Much more likely is that innocent members of the company's workforce would be made redundant. Such employees are expendable and easier to replace in better times than those who constitute the 'directing mind' of the company.[19]

In theory, a fine ought to accomplish three objectives: first, it should effect a confiscation of any and all illegal profits generated by the offence; second, it should include an amount to provide compensation to identifiable victims and to repair the damage attributable to the offence; and, third, it should be sufficient to punish and to deter future violations by the offender and similarly situated other companies. The challenge is to achieve these objectives, but not at the expense of innocent members of the company's workforce or the general public. An ingenious solution to this challenge has been proposed by Coffee (1981), who advances the concept of what he calls an 'equity fine'. The convicted company would be ordered to issue new shares of stock equal in value to the fine which the court would wish to impose. These shares would then be sold on the open market, with the revenues being used, among other purposes, to make restitution or compensate the victims of the company's offence.[20] Equity fines are attractive because they take into account a company's future as well as its current assets and thereby effectively raise the limit of the pecuniary penalty which can be assessed against the company. Because an 'equity fine' would precipitate no immediate need for cash, it would not be necessary for the company to raise the price of its products or services; and, because the company's operating capital would not be reduced, the company should not have to lay off any workers. However, equity fines would not be available in the case of a partnership, co-operative, private company or company whose shares were not traded on the stock market.

The group that might suffer most from the imposition of an equity fine would be the company's shareholders, the value of whose stock would be reduced, sometimes dramatically. With more shares on the market, moreover, their company would also become more vulnerable to a hostile takeover. These disadvantages need not cause undue concern, however, for several reasons. First, the shareholders presumably

---

18 See *Tesco Supermarkets Ltd v Nattrass* [1972] AC 153.

19 The Law Commission in its original discussion of corporate manslaughter did not agree. It stated: 'We are confident that no respectable company or organisation would leave in place.... the people responsible for the operation of systems which had been condemned by a jury....' (*Criminal Law: Involuntary Manslaughter: A Consultation Paper* (Law Com no 135) para 5.92). The authors of the report, however, supplied no reasons for their optimism, and empirical evidence would seem to contradict their assertion. In many instances corporate officials who have been convicted of crime have suffered no loss of position or salary, and have even been rewarded: see Box (1983: 53).

20 An alternative would be to present the equity shares directly to the victims, which would allow them the choice of either retaining the shares (possibly to be in a position to influence future corporate policy) or selling them.

benefited from the profits generated by the company's illegality, and have no more entitlement to such illegal profits than does the company. Second, it is the shareholders' responsibility to exercise supervisory control over management. Although, traditionally, few shareholders seek to become involved in the company's management, one salutary effect of the prospect of an equity fine might be to spur shareholders to play a more active role in corporate governance. It might finally be observed that if an equity fine were to be imposed on a convicted company the shareholders would not necessarily be without recourse, as they might be able to bring an action against the officers and directors of the company for breach of their fiduciary duties in exposing the company to criminal liability.

In the final analysis, however, fines – whether they be large, small, differential or equitable – may send the wrong message, encouraging companies to see compliance with the law in crude cost-benefit terms. Like wages and advertising, the fine becomes another entry on the corporate ledger book, somewhat akin to the payment of a license fee to be allowed to carry on the company's business in a particular, albeit unlawful, manner. Although a fine might prompt a company to bring its operation into conformity with the law, the company is under no obligation to do so, and in theory can continue to operate illegally as long as it is prepared to pay whatever fine is imposed on it from time to time.[21] If continuation of a company's illegal practices, burdened by the occasional fine, will yield a net be profit, a company might decide it would be irrational for it to change its way of doing business. In short, fines convert corporate criminality from a wrong against society to a cost of doing business.

2.   Community service orders

One of the more significant developments in the sentencing of individuals over the past half-century has been a shift away from imprisonment in favour of the greater use of community service sentences. The concept of community service can also be advantageously applied to companies convicted of crime. A community service order of a convicted company would require it to undertake a specified project in the community. Such an order is particularly attractive because it avoids the spill-over effects of a fine and can be imposed in cases where an equity fine is not feasible because the offender is a partnership, co-operative or company whose shares are not traded on the stock market.

A community service order would be entered against the company itself and not against designated individuals. The company, with its already established organisational framework, would be expected to redeploy its workforce to engage in the assigned undertaking. Urban renewal projects and environmental clean-up programmes offer examples of the type of sentence that might be appropriate (Fisse: 1981). The order could and should be shaped to take into account the company's particular expertise, and it would not be unreasonable for a court, without binding itself, to solicit proposals from the corporate offender as to the type of projects that would be best suited to its capabilities.

In the first instance, and if feasible, a community service order should seek to achieve restitution. It should be designed to repair the damage or undo the harm that

---

21 As, arguably, do prostitutes and illegal street traders.

the company had caused, an obvious example being an order that required an industrial polluter to clean up the air, land or river that it had contaminated. In the event that an envisaged project was beyond the company's capabilities, it could be ordered to provide the backup support, as well as the financing, for others who were qualified to perform the tasks required. Financial underwriting of a project that would be undertaken by a third party, however, is less attractive than a sentence which directly engages the company in community service, for it might come to be regarded as a fine by another name. To the extent that community service is seen as a means for a corporate offender's atoning or making amends to the community for its crime, this dimension would be lacking if the convicted company could simply write a cheque in satisfaction of its punishment.

Compulsory research into the causes of an offence provides another avenue for an order wherein community service can be linked to the offender's crime. Although a court could order a corporate offender convicted of a health and safety violation to introduce state-of-the-art safety equipment, sometimes the 'state of the art' is severely deficient (perhaps because no company in the industry sees it in its economic interest to have a well-financed Research and Development department). In such cases the offender might be ordered to undertake the necessary research. Assume, for instance, that P&O Ferries had been convicted of manslaughter for its role in the deaths that occurred following the capsize of the *Herald of Free Enterprise*. As part of a package of sanctions, a sentencing judge might have ordered P&O to undertake research into the stability of 'roll-on, roll-off' ferries (if further study was needed), which many analysts had suggested were inherently unstable and partly responsible for the capsize. Similarly, had Railtrack been prosecuted and convicted for its role in the Ladbroke Grove crash, it could have been ordered to develop a more effective signalling system for its drivers, as that was clearly one of the causes of the disaster. As it was, in both of these cases the responsibility for making recommendations for future improvements was relegated to a public inquiry. At the very least, it would seem that the cost of such inquiries should be charged to the company found to have been at fault.

The provision of assistance to the underprivileged offers another model for a community service order. In *United States v Danilow Pastry Corpn*,[22] a New York judge ordered convicted bakeries to supply fresh baked goods without charge to needy organisations for a 12-month period. Such sentences suggest that companies have obligations to the community and to society that transcend, or at least are not incompatible with, the duty to maximise the financial return to investors/ shareholders. Although it is true that the order in that case would not have been imposed had a crime not been committed, none the less a community service sentence such as that in *Danilow Pastry* might provide a springboard for discussion of corporate social responsibility generally. Community service orders directed for the benefit of society would not necessarily result in compensation or restitution to the victims of the offence, however, and should not preclude compensation and restitution orders. In some instances, community service could be targeted to help the 'community' that was most directly disadvantaged by the company's offence. The required training or re-training of workers who were made redundant as a result

---

22 563 F Supp 1159 (SDNY 1983).

of a company's need to downsize in order to generate the savings to pay off a fine would be an example.

One major advantage to community service orders is that they are likely to avoid spill-over effects. Indeed, whereas a heavy fine can lead to redundancies, a community service order may have the opposite effect, as a company may have to take on additional staff to help fulfil the terms of the order. Workers, on the other hand, may be called upon to undertake jobs other than those for which they were hired, but job reassignments in industry are not uncommon and, like others who are reassigned under less exceptional circumstances, the workers would be free to seek alternative employment. Workers may also, with more justification, resent having to perform community service of a type normally associated with those convicted of serious crimes, and may see such service as constituting a stigma and a stain on their reputations. These are legitimate concerns, but the damage to an individual worker's reputation will be diluted by the fact that the sentence will be entered against the company and not its individual employees, and the fact that numerous people, ranging from directors and senior executives down to on-line workers, would be involved in the community service.

In imposing a community service order, a court must take care to ensure that the directors, officers and senior managers are not able to delegate to the company's workforce the responsibility for satisfying the order, and thereby avoid all personal involvement. Ironically, under an 'identification' test of corporate criminal liability, it will have been the offence of one of these executives that led to the prosecution of the company in the first place. Even if the prosecution were to be restricted to the company and not include the individual whose offence precipitated the charge, to allow that individual to escape all participation in the community service would be paradoxical, to say the least. Indeed, the education, training, skills and experience of persons such as directors, officers and senior managers may be essential to the successful fulfilment of the community service.

Community service orders of companies hold a greater potential for abuse than when such orders are imposed on natural persons. There are undoubtedly numerous meritorious candidates that might be suitable for a community service order, and it would be undesirable if the choice of project were to become intertwined with political considerations. In *United States v Missouri Valley Construction Co*,[23] the trial judge ordered a convicted corporation to endow a chair of ethics at the state university. Although there was no indication that the judge had acted improperly or had any ulterior motive, one can imagine the outrage if it was revealed that the judge was a graduate of the university, or if he were subsequently to be appointed as its Chancellor or President. In fact, the judge's order in the case was reversed on appeal.[24] A similar danger is that the government might come to regard community service orders as a means for co-opting private industry into undertaking projects for which it was reluctant or unwilling to pay. Why build a library or hospital at public expense when one can order a convicted company to do the job for free (criminal defendants on community service orders not normally receiving compensation for their service)?

23 741 F 2d 1542 (8th Cir 1984).
24 741 F 2d 1542 (8th Cir 1984) at 1550.

In making decisions as to where to concentrate their limited resources, prosecutors must guard against charging companies because of the potential community service that they envisage the defendant might be able to perform if it were to be convicted. In picking and choosing among cases that merit prosecution when, because of limited resources, a prosecutor's office is unable to pursue all cases, the potential community service that could be provided by an offender should not be a factor. For their part, courts must be wary of community service orders whose costs to perform would substantially exceed the amount of the fine that would have been imposed if community service had not been an option. One way to avoid this trap is for the sentencing court first to determine the appropriate level of a fine, and then 'cap' the cost of the community service at this amount. However, it would make little sense if a community service project had to be halted mid-stream because the 'cap' had been reached, particularly if the company's inefficiency had caused it to be reached prematurely. The amount of a putative fine, therefore, should serve only as a rough guide to a court contemplating a community service order and not as a terminal point of the assigned project. In determining the cost of a project, a budget could be prepared by an independent consultant appointed by the court, with the consultant's fee being charged to the offender as part of the court costs. The ultimate cost of any project is of course difficult to predict, as overruns in business are not uncommon. Perhaps the safety net lies in a reviewing appellate court satisfying itself that the sentence is appropriate for the offender, not unreasonable in its projected cost, and not disproportionate to the offence.

We have noted that criminal sanctions have a denunciatory dimension, signalling the censure that should be attached to the offender. A subtle danger of a community service order is that, rather than resulting in stigma to a corporate offender, it may enhance the offender's reputation. Consider again the case where the convicted corporation was ordered to endow a university chair in ethics. Long after the illegal activity that gave rise to the order would have been forgotten, the chair would presumably remain in existence. If designated by the name of the company (not uncommon with respect to endowed chairs), this involuntary established linkage would provide the company with considerable free publicity, and, ironically, associate it with the highest of ethical standards. Likewise, if a library or hospital were to be named after the company which constructed it (again, not uncommon), the offender might gain an undeserved reputation for public-spiritedness, when in fact it should be branded as a law-breaker. It would be unfortunate if criminal sentences designed to impose a stigma were to boost a corporate offender's public image, thereby overshadowing the illegal acts that gave rise to the sentence. As discussed in the next section, this danger might to some extent be avoided by joining to a community service sentence an adverse publicity order.

3.   Reputation-orientated sanctions

One of the purposes of punishment is to denounce both offender and offence. No denunciatory effect will be achieved, however, if the public (or that segment of the public which has dealings with the offender) remains ignorant of the conviction and sanction. In an earlier age, when prisoners were placed in the stocks or hanged in a public place, the visibility of the sanction brought the identity of the offender to the public's attention and reinforced the condemnation of the conviction. It also served as a clear and observable warning to other would-be offenders. Denunciation, education and general deterrence all were achieved in the public sentence. With the termination of corporal punishment and the virtual abolition of the death penalty, there is less likelihood that the public will become aware of the identity of those convicted of crimes. This is especially true in the case of companies, whose crimes, save for those emanating from widely reported 'disasters' (for example, the capsize of the *Herald* or the Southall train crash) and high-profile cases (for example, the Enron scandal in the United States and the Guinness affair in the United Kingdom) are less likely to be noted in the media.

If a denunciatory effect is deemed desirable and is to be achieved, therefore, the sentencing court will have to take the initiative in seeing to it that the company's wrongdoing is publicised. It can do so by entering an 'adverse publicity order' against the company (Fisse and Braithwaite: 1983). Such an order requires the offender to inform others of its crime. The offender, for instance, might be ordered to place an advertisement in the newspapers at its own expense. A somewhat melodramatic example is the advertisement reported by Clinard (1990: 180) that was placed by the American Caster Corporation in the Los Angeles Times newspaper pursuant to a court order:

> Warning. The illegal disposal of toxic waste will result in jail. We should know. We got caught!… We are paying the price. Today, while you read this ad, our president and vice president are serving time in jail and we were forced to place this ad.

Alternatively or in addition, a target audience might be specifically selected, as would occur if the corporate offender were ordered to send a letter to its shareholders or relevant members of the public (such as purchasers of its products) informing them of its offence. Such a letter would not only be appropriate, but necessary where the company's offence involved the sale of defective and potentially dangerous products. An adverse publicity order would be in addition to, rather than in replacement of, any other sanctions that a sentencing court might be minded to impose.

The idea of providing public notice of an offender's conviction is not new. Fisse (1991) notes that under the nineteenth-century Bread Acts, magistrates were authorised to order the publication of the names of those found guilty of adulterating bread. Recently, the Health and Safety Executive (HSE) has begun to publish on its website and in its reports the names of companies that have been convicted of health and safety violations. According to the HSE (2001), the goal is 'to help everyone with an interest in an organisation's performance, in particular, would-be customers, investors, employees or insurers, to find out about convictions and to create pressure for health and safety improvements'.

The premise behind adverse publicity orders is that a company's reputation is one of its most valuable and valued assets. Support for this premise can be found in the great lengths to which companies go in order to cultivate their public image through advertisements in radio, television, newspapers and the media generally. While the ultimate goal of advertising is to persuade consumers to buy the company's product, creating a favourable impression of the company in the public's mind may be an important ingredient in the overall strategy. Once lost, a company's reputation may take years to recoup. Thus, if the company's 'good name' were to be threatened by a conviction and sanctions, a powerful incentive might be created for companies to obey the law. While an actual adverse publicity order serves to denounce the convicted offender, the very possibility of such an order may exert a considerable deterrent effect on others.

For companies which sell to the public, adverse publicity orders can have economic ramifications beyond those of the typical fine. If consumers were to choose to boycott a company's products, the loss of revenue might far exceed the maximum fine that a court could have imposed. Adverse publicity orders in effect give members of the public, through their purchasing power, a voice in determining the ultimate sanction incurred by a corporate offender. This voice, however, is indirect and somewhat unpredictable, and will depend for its effect on social reactions rather than on formal legal processes. In practice, the effect is difficult to gauge in advance.

One clear class of beneficiary from an adverse publicity order would be the victims of the company's crime, who might have been unaware of their victimisation or its cause. An example would be workers who were suffering from the effects of exposure to a dangerous chemical present in their employer's plant who did not know the source of their ill health. Thus alerted, these workers might then be able to pursue their civil remedies. An adverse publicity order would also provide notice to those contemplating entering into a contractual arrangement with the offender, including other companies and consumers, with a possible outcome being a decision to take their business elsewhere or at least to proceed with caution in dealing with the offender.

To ensure that a company's offence is brought to public attention, but at the same time is not misrepresented, it is advisable that the sentencing court remains involved in the information dissemination process. There is a danger, where a company has been ordered to publicise both the harm that it has caused and the remedial steps it plans to take to repair that harm, that a clever advertising agency will skew the publicity to emphasise the company's 'public spiritedness' in remedying deleterious social or environment conditions, while glossing over the company's role in creating the conditions in the first place. As it would clearly be undesirable for adverse publicity orders to be used to boost an offender's public persona, a sentencing court should arguably screen *all* proposed pronouncements by the company designed to satisfy an adverse publicity order. Often, moreover, companies damaged by adverse publicity will take countermeasures by placing, at their own expense and initiative, advertisements aimed at restoring their tarnished image.

The above examples suggest that in some cases an even more powerful sanction than an adverse publicity order may be a ban on all advertising by the offender for the duration of a probationary period. Especially in markets where advertising is seen as critical to sales, such as the automobile and drinks industries, the lost revenues could be far greater than the loss from a fine. The very threat to a company's sales from such a ban could have a considerable deterrent effect as well. On the other hand, a ban on advertising, in an advertising-sensitive industry, may lead to the offender suffering harm (being driven out of business) that is grossly disproportionate to the seriousness of its offence.

Both adverse publicity orders and bans on advertising will have the greatest impact on companies in a highly competitive market who sell directly to the public. Neither is likely to have much of an effect on a company that enjoys a monopolistic position in the market, or which obtains contracts pursuant to public tender (where the lowest bidder is awarded the contract) or whose products are sold to entities, such as foreign governments, which are not troubled by the company's reputation. Nor is it likely to influence the purchasing habits of customers who are more interested in a company's reputation for producing a quality product at a reasonable price than in whether the company is a law-abiding citizen; nor consumers who, for whatever reason, never had bought, and never would contemplate buying, the company's product in the first place.

Like fines, adverse publicity orders and bans on advertisements can have undesirable spill-over effects. Indeed, the more effective these sanctions, the greater the potential for spill-over. An adverse publicity order or advertisement ban that led to a total consumer boycott of a company's products might, in penological terms, be judged a success, but, if the resulting loss of sales forced the company out of business, the real losers would be the employees who lost their jobs. Those responsible for the critical decisions that led to the offence would doubtless be better able to cushion themselves from the financial hardships that might result.

4.   Restraint-orientated sanctions

One of the primary goals of punishment is to prevent future wrongdoing by convicted offenders. In the case of individuals, restraint is achieved through sentencing offenders to prison. Imprisonment protects the general public from the offender for the duration of the prisoner's term of confinement. The death penalty, of course, was the ultimate restraint, but for all practical purposes it has now been abolished in England. Restraint, however, need not necessarily be equated with physical confinement. It can take the form of restricting the offender from engaging in the type of activity that led to the offence. Examples include where a driver's licence is suspended or revoked because of motor vehicle offences and where a grossly negligent doctor is removed from the medical rolls. Might it be possible to devise a comparable regime of activity-related restraints for convicted companies?

In chapter 3 we examined the Italian legislation designed to reform the law of corporate criminal liability (DLgs (Legislative Decree) of 8 June 2001), primarily as it pertains to financial and property offences. The statute includes a number of monetary sanctions (fines, the confiscation of profits and compensation orders), but also contains restraint-orientated or what it terms 'interdictory' sanctions, which are designed to restrict the activities in which the offender would be allowed to engage following a conviction (Article 9). Whereas pecuniary sanctions will always be ordered and as such are unavoidable once responsibility has been established (Article 10), interdictory sanctions are generally not mandatory and will be invoked only with respect to serious offences. Article 13 provides that interdictory sanctions may be imposed when at least one the following conditions is present:

- the corporation has conspicuously benefited financially from the crime and the crime has been committed by a director or officer of the corporation;
- the crime has been committed by a subordinate employee, but the offence was made possible or aided by serious organisational deficiencies; and
- the crime has been committed repeatedly.

Article 13 does not permit the use of interdictory sanctions when an offence has been committed by a human perpetrator for his/her personal benefit, with the corporation not gaining any or only minimal financial advantage.

Article 13, para 2 lists the possible interdictory sanctions available to the judge:

(a) the corporation will be forbidden from carrying out its activities;
(b) the suspension or revocation of authorisations, licenses or concessions that were functional to the crime;
(c) prohibition from entering into contracts with the public administration;
(d) the exclusion from state financial benefits or the possible removal of benefits previously granted; and
(e) prohibition from advertising goods and services.

The Italian legislature considered interdictory sanctions to be necessary because fines were deemed insuffient to address financial crimes that might depend on a certain organisational pattern of the corporation. The government's notes accompanying the statute recognise the danger that we alluded to previously – that the fine might come to be regarded by a company as one of the costs of doing business in a particular, albeit illegal, way.

Article 14 of the Italian statute addresses when an interdictory sanction is appropriate, and what form it might take. Article 14, para 1 sets out the principle that '[I]nterdictory sanctions are to be targeted towards the specific activity in relation to which the crime has been committed'. This admonition is a reminder to courts that interdictory sanctions should be limited to the branch of the company or the specific activity that gave rise to the offence; they are not the occasion for a judge to reform a company to fit the judge's preferred image. The judge, then, has both to identify the causes of an offence and select a sanction that would reform, punish and prevent future offences. Article 14, para 1 states that it is the judge's responsibility to determine the type and duration of an interdictory sanction, taking into account the ability of the sanction to prevent other crimes of the general type committed. More than one interdictory sanction may be imposed in a given case.

Interdictory sanctions are, as a rule, temporary. Article 13, para 2 indicates that minimum period for an interdictory sanction is three months, while the maximum period is two years. But what is to be done about incorrigible offenders who fail to amend their criminogenic practices in response to an interdictory order? In such cases, the Italian statute *permits* a court to impose *permanent* sanctions on the offender on the rationale that the company's continued serious violations leave the court with no other effective means to curb the company's criminality. Article 16, para 1 allows a judge to order the permanent prohibition of the activity that has generated the offence if the corporation has achieved a substantial economic gain from the offence and if the corporation has already been sentenced at least three times in the previous seven years to the same, but temporary, sanction. Permanent sanctions include a prohibition from entering into contracts with the public administration and a prohibition from advertising goods and services. Again, these measures are available when the same sanctions have been ordered on a temporary basis at least three times in a seven-year period (Article 16, para 2). While temporary interdictory sanctions are mandatory if the conditions specified in Article 13 have been satisfied, permanent sanctions generally lie within the judge's discretion. Given that permanent sanctions are a last resort, it is left to the judge to decide when the point has been reached where there is no other realistic way of 'rehabilitating' the offender.

There is, however, one exception to the permissive nature of permanent sanctions. Under Article 16, para 3, when a company or a productive unit has been consistently used for the sole or primary aim of committing criminal offences or aiding and abetting in their commission, a permanent prohibition from activities should *always* be ordered. When a company is intrinsically criminal (for example, the apocryphal (?) 'Murder Inc'), or is set up with the sole or primary aim of being a conduit for illegal activities (for example, a bank whose sole function is to 'launder' money for organised crime), then there is little point in trying to restructure it to prevent future offences from being committed.

The aim of interdictory sanctions is a combination of reform, deterrence, prevention and punishment. Given their potential intrusiveness, however, and given the consequences they can have for a company and its workforce, these sanctions will be ordered, as we have noted, only when the special circumstances identified in Article 13 are present. Article 17 further provides that a convicted company can avoid an interdictory sanction if it:

- makes full reparation for any losses that it has caused (if full reparation is not possible, it may be sufficient that the offender has done as much as is possible to that effect (Article 17, para 1(a));
- eliminates the organisational faults that have produced the offence by setting up structures appropriate to prevent the commission of future offences of the same kind (Article 17, para 1(b)); and
- makes available the profits of its crime for confiscation (Article 17, para 1(c)).

Critically, however, the defendant must take all of these measures *before* the trial officially begins (Article 17, para 1), although if they are taken at a later point in time, the interdictory sanctions can be converted into a fine by an order of the judge (Article 78). While the reparatory measures will not save the company from a monetary penalty, they will allow the company to avoid temporary interdictory sanctions. Thus, they give convicted companies an incentive to reform themselves.

The ultimate restraint for a natural person convicted of a heinous crime is the death penalty, which, whatever its theoretical shortcomings, undeniably prevents future law-breaking by the executed offender. The analogue to the death penalty for a company is the required liquidation or forced closure of the company. Closure is included among the sanctions against enterprises identified in the recommendations of the Council of Europe (to be discussed in a subsequent section). In *R v F Howe & Son (Engineers) Ltd* the Court of Appeal also recognised that 'there may be cases where the offences are so serious that the defendant ought not to be in business'.[25] In state courts of the United States, legal actions have been instituted to revoke the charters of flagrant corporate offenders.

The challenge lies in determining when the point has been reached that liquidation or closure is appropriate. Restraint theory envisages a degree of restriction commensurate with the offender's dangerousness; the more serious the offence, the harsher the punishment. As recognised by the Italian legislation, repeat offenders also should be dealt with more severely than first offenders. Both of these principles have salience in determining whether a company should involuntarily be required to wind up its business. Offences such as corporate manslaughter might in and of themselves be deemed sufficiently serious to give rise to closure, even for a first offence, although the submission of mitigating circumstances should not be precluded. A continuing series of violations, although of a lesser order than

25 [1999] 2 All ER 249 at 255.

manslaughter, might also lead a court to order closure, at least for a limited period. Not all corporate offences are of equal gravity, of course, and a legislature might choose to construct a points system for offences. Each corporate offence would be assigned a number of points based on its potential to cause social harm. After the accumulation of a specified number of points, the company would be required to close (Gobert: 1998). Drivers of motor vehicles will be familiar with the concept, and its potential deterrent and restraining effects. As in the case of motor vehicle offences, each of the crimes that contributed to the company's points total would carry an independent penalty as well.

Restraint orientated sanctions, irrespective of their efficacy in preventing future violations by a corporate wrongdoer, are not without their downside. One problem which we have alluded to previously is that of spill-over. Closure of a company would have an obviously disastrous impact on employees, who would lose their jobs. Penalties such as precluding a convicted company from bidding on government contracts, or temporarily suspending a company's licence to engage in certain activities, could have a similar, although less drastic, effect. Lost contracts can lead to lost jobs, and suspension of a company's licence may result in temporary layoffs for the duration of the suspension. In both cases it will be the employees who will suffer. While loss of a company's profitability will also adversely affect shareholders, these individuals, as observed previously, presumably benefited from the profits generated by the company's crime, and should not be insulated from its losses after the company has been convicted of a criminal offence.

One particular problem to which a court needs to be sensitive in making a closure order is that of the 'phoenix' company. It is not unknown for a company that has been forced out of business to regroup and rise from its ashes under a different name and in a slightly altered form. One way to combat the phoenix phenomenon would be to combine an order of closure with an order for the disqualification of the convicted company's directors and officers under the Company Directors Disqualification Act 1986 (to be discussed further in chapter 8). Under the current version of the Act, a corporate executive may be precluded from serving as a director or officer in another company for a maximum period of 15 years. A true 'death penalty' analogue, designed to match the seriousness of the offence(s) that led to the closure order, would be a life ban on its directors and officers. Personal sanctions against directors, combined with a vigilant screening of charter and licence applications, may be the best counterweight to phoenix companies and those who would form them.

5.   Remedial orders

In our initial discussion of the various theories of punishment, we observed the relationship between restraint and rehabilitation – offenders need only be restrained so long as they are dangerous; they cease to be dangerous at the point when they have been rehabilitated. We also noted, however, the practical difficulties in achieving rehabilitation of individuals. Social scientists and others have yet to reach the point where they understand the human psyche sufficiently to know with any degree of assurance how to divert offenders from a life of crime and induce them to become 'law-abiding' citizens.

Although efforts to rehabilitate human offenders have not been as successful as proponents of the 'rehabilitative ideal' might have hoped, these disappointments should not cause one to despair of devising rehabilitative measures for convicted companies. To the contrary, there are sound reasons to believe that reformation of a company may be more feasible than rehabilitation of an individual. Whereas crimes by individuals are frequently committed on impulse, or for less than rational reasons, many, although certainly not all, corporate crimes are the result of policy decisions whose ramifications have been carefully considered by a committee or board of directors. If it could be demonstrated that engaging in criminal activity was not in the company's best interests, then the company should be amenable to reform of its criminogenic practices. Furthermore, while the rehabilitation of human offenders may require a psychological understanding of the offender, the reformation of a company can concentrate on the way that the company's business is structured without having to examine the minds or personalities of those responsible for establishing that structure. Indeed, those responsible for dangerous practices or a criminogenic culture may be long deceased or no longer active in the company's affairs. This fact too may be an advantage, as their successors in the company may not have the same vested interest in the preservation of the way that the company was conducting its business. In short, the rehabilitation of a convicted company can focus on corporate behaviour, irrespective of its psychological underpinnings.

The objectives of a remedial order are to eliminate illegal practices, amend criminogenic policies, improve dangerous conditions, foster the necessary systemic changes to avoid future offences and reform a culture that has been tolerant of (or is perceived by workers to be tolerant of) illegality. Following a conviction, the company would be placed on 'probation'. As a term of probation, the sentencing court would enter an order that would require the company to reform the way it conducted its business in order to prevent future criminality. Given the ongoing harm that is threatened by the continuation of crime-conducive policies, practices, conditions and cultures, remedial orders should be mandatory unless the defendant can show that it is already taking or has taken satisfactory steps to address the problems. To concentrate the company's attention on the remedial order, the sentencing court should have the power to suspend the company's licence to engage in its business until such time as it had complied with the order, thereby combining restraint with enforced rehabilitation, a similar approach to that which we saw was embodied in the Italian statute. Nor should a company be allowed to reject a remedial order, as is sometimes permitted when an individual offender is offered a probationary sentence that the individual finds oppressive for, unlike in the case of a human offender, a sentence of imprisonment is not a feasible alternative for a convicted company.

In England and Wales, remedial orders are authorised under the Health and Safety at Work Act etc 1974.[26] In its consultation paper on corporate killing, the government envisaged the possibility of remedial orders for companies found guilty of a corporate killing. Although the proposal is restricted to this particular offence, this limitation probably reflects nothing more than the scope of the consultation paper. In the United States, remedial orders may be issued under the federal sentencing guidelines for organisational offenders (discussed in the following section).

26 S 42(1).

In shaping a remedial order, a court may wish to take account of the fact that it will be the defendant which is most familiar with its internal structures and organisation, and therefore in the best position to identify the deficiencies that gave rise to the offence. Certainly, it is more competent to do this than the Health and Safety Executive or the Crown Prosecution Office on whom, under the government's corporate killing proposals, the responsibility for drawing up a remedial order would be placed.[27] A court accordingly should be prepared to entertain an offender's own proposals for remedying the criminogenic aspects of its business operation. The prosecution should, of course, be able to comment on any proposed package of reforms, and the sentencing court should not be bound by the company's proposals. If dissatisfied, the court might appoint its own independent experts, to be paid for by the convicted company as part of the court costs, to conduct an independent examination and furnish it with recommendations (Gruner: 1993). Having received and considered the views of the prosecution, the defence and any court-appointed experts, the court could then prepare its order.

The scope of a remedial order should look beyond the particular offence to the prevention of future offences of a similar type, or future offences more generally. To achieve the latter goal, for example, the court's order might require the promulgation of a code of ethics and detailed operating procedures designed to avoid violations of the law. These may include improved screening procedures for prospective employees, better training programmes for the company's workforce and the establishment of effective monitoring systems (Stone: 1975). Sometimes channels of communication need to be established. Employees who are aware of dangerous or criminogenic conditions on an operational level often have no way of bringing their concerns to the attention of management. Prevention of crime also needs to be given a status commensurate with profitability, which perhaps could be achieved by the establishment of a career ladder that rewarded employees not only for their productivity, but also for their initiative in combating dangerous and illegal conditions and practices. The mandatory creation of a compliance department with extensive powers to ensure that a company adhered to the law in the future might also be part of a remedial order. Alternatively, the court might order the company to appoint staff who would be responsible for seeing that the company's practices and policies were in conformity with legal standards and safety requirements. While the most difficult remedial goal to achieve would be reformation of a company's culture or ethos, because these are so intangible and difficult to measure, none the less a change in policies, practices and procedures would signal a change in priorities which might in turn lead to the more intangible effect of a change in the corporate culture.

In some cases, a remedial order might extend beyond systemic changes to the replacement of those persons who were directly responsible for illegal policies, even if their involvement might not have reached the point of warranting criminal charges against them. If responsibility for a company's offences were to be traced to the company's CEO, the court might appoint a master to assume control of the company's operation. The master would have the authority to take whatever steps were deemed necessary, including the employment of consultants and the hiring of new staff, to ensure that other aspects of the remedial order were satisfied. In the

---

27 Home Office (2000) *Reforming the Law of Involuntary Manslaughter: The Government's Proposals* para 3.6.2.

United States, appointment of masters is authorised under the federal sentencing guidelines for organisational offenders.[28] A court-appointed master would replace the company's CEO during the period of appointment, and the CEO's powers would be suspended. The very threat of a court-appointed master might itself be a spur to reform, as few companies will want to see their business operations under the control of a chief executive not of their own choosing. This is not to say that the company's officers and managers will not co-operate with a court-appointed master. Apart from any legal obligation to do so, they will want to hasten the day when they are able to resume control of their business.

During the period of the company's probation, unannounced inspections by regulatory officers would be permitted. The company would also have to submit periodic self-evaluative progress reports to the court. These would be in addition to the more formal reports of a 'probation officer'. As the court would retain jurisdiction of the case, if the report of the offender or that of the probation officer suggested that the company was not making adequate progress towards fulfilling the terms of the remedial order, it could alter the terms of the order. It might decide, for example, to suspend the company's licence to engage in certain aspects of its business operation until such time as it had complied with the order as it related to those aspects of the business (assuming that such a condition had not been imposed as part of the court's original package of sanctions). In even more extreme cases, the court might want to consider closing down the company until such time as it complied with the remedial order. At some point the temporary closure might even be made permanent. Unlike a closure order that was imposed because of the seriousness of the company's offence (for example, manslaughter) or a pattern of recidivism, the permanent closure in this instance would be because the unwillingness to make even a good faith effort at reformation was indicative of a company that was not prepared to obey the law or to reform itself.

D.   AN INCLUSIVE PACKAGE OF SANCTIONS

So far, we have examined a number of possible sanctions individually. These would need to be graded within an integrated scheme so that a court could decide which sanction or combination of sanctions to impose in a given case. In this section we examine two such schemes. The first is based on recommendations advanced by the Council of Europe. In contrast to the Council of Europe's recommendations, which are not binding and have yet to be adopted wholesale by any country, the United States Sentencing Guidelines for organisational offenders have been in effect in United States federal courts since the early 1990s.

I.   The Council of Europe recommendations

In 1988, the Committee of Ministers of the Council of Europe (1990) made a number of non-binding recommendations for penalties in the case of companies. The recommendations are designed in particular with an eye to preventing future offences

---

28 USSG, s 8D1.5.

and to providing reparation to the victims of a corporate offence. Underpinning the recommendations were a number of considerations, including:

- the increasing number of offences committed in the exercise of the activities of business enterprises;
- the extent of harm to both individuals and the community from these offences;
- the desirability of attaching responsibility for offences to those enterprises that derived the primary benefit from the illegal activity;
- the difficulty, due to the often complex management structure in an enterprise, of identifying the particular individuals responsible for the commission of an offence;
- the difficulty, rooted in the legal traditions of many European states, of rendering enterprises which are corporate bodies criminally liable; and
- the desire to overcome these difficulties, with a view to making enterprises as such answerable, without necessarily exonerating from liability natural persons implicated in an offence.

The goal was to offer, for consideration by the legislatures of the various states, a range of possible sanctions and measures that were suitable for corporate enterprises convicted of a criminal offence.

The Council's proposed range of penalties is sweeping in its scope:

- a warning, reprimand, recognisance;
- a decision declaratory of responsibility, but no sanction;
- a fine or other pecuniary sanction;
- confiscation of property which was used in the commission of the offence or represents the gains derived from the illegal activity;
- a prohibition on certain activities, in particular exclusion from doing business with public authorities;
- an exclusion from fiscal advantages and subsidies;
- a prohibition upon advertising goods or services;
- an annulment of licenses;
- removal of managers;
- appointment of a provisional caretaker management by the judicial authority;
- closure of the enterprise;
- winding-up of the enterprise;
- compensation and/or restitution to the victim;
- restoration of the former state; and
- publication of the decision imposing a sanction or measure.

Although comprehensive, the Council's inventory of options does not give priority to particular sanctions. Perhaps this is appropriate, as the nature of different organisations may warrant different sanctions even with respect to the same offence. Nevertheless, one can envisage an escalating series of sanctions that could be fashioned from this list.

A first, inadvertent or minor offence by a company might lead only to a warning, reprimand or judicial declaration of responsibility. For subsequent or more serious violations, the company could be temporarily prohibited from engaging in activities associated with the offence or activities that the court envisaged might lead to future offences. The period of prohibition should equal in length the term of imprisonment that the court would have imposed had the offender been a natural person. During this period, the company might be precluded from bidding on government contracts or be denied tax allowances, government subsidies or other financial benefits that lay within the prerogative of the government. Progressing still further up the ladder of restraint-orientated sanctions, the company's licence to engage in certain activities associated with its crime could be first temporarily and then permanently suspended. The effectiveness of such orders would be reinforced if the court were also to order the confiscation of equipment used in the perpetration of the offence.

Beyond restraint-orientated or interdictory sanctions, the Council was also concerned with the victims of the company's offence. In addition to fines, therefore, a court would be able to order compensation or restitution to a victim, and the restoration of a former state of affairs. Given the importance that the Council attaches to reparation in its general introductory comments, perhaps a court should have to give reasons for *not* ordering compensation or reparation.

When a natural person is convicted of a crime, it is normal that a record of the conviction be kept. This record allows those who would deal with an offender to learn about his/her criminal past. The Council of Europe envisages a comparable record for companies convicted of criminal offences. It would be contained in a register in which all convictions and sanctions were recorded, which would be available not only to the government and to the courts, but also to private companies who might be contemplating doing business with a particular company. To the same end, the Council's recommendations would empower a court to order the publication of its decision to impose a sanction.

2.   The federal guidelines for organisational offenders

The United States Sentencing Guidelines for organisational offenders (USSG) came into effect on 1 November 1991. Four assumptions underpin the guidelines: first, that an offender should have to remedy the harm caused by its offence; second, that companies that are operated for criminal purposes should be divested of all their assets; third, that companies that are not operated for criminal purposes should be fined according to the seriousness of the offence and the culpability of the offender; and, fourth, that probation may be appropriate if needed to ensure that other sanctions are followed or that the convicted organisation reduces the likelihood of future violations. Although perhaps best known for their sophisticated approach to the setting of fines, the guidelines also allow for a range of non-traditional sanctions and remedies. Together, the guidelines probably form the most ambitious effort yet undertaken by a state to address the problem of corporate sanctions.

One striking feature of the guidelines is their concern for victims. The Sentencing Reform Act 1984 had emphasised the importance of restitution and remedies, and the guidelines give concrete expression to these concerns. Whenever practicable, a sentencing court *must* order a corporate offender to remedy the harm caused by the offence, and to eliminate the threat of future harm. Sometimes this may best be achieved through imposition of a community service order,[29] which will be appropriate when the offender possesses the 'knowledge, facilities, or skills that uniquely qualify it to repair damage caused by the offense'.[30] The sentencing court *must* also enter an

29 USSG, s 8B1.3.
30 See comment to USSG, s 8B1.3.

order allowing for full compensation to be paid to known victims. Such an order can extend to competitors whose market position may have been damaged as a result of the offender's illegal practices. Because the order can be included as a condition of probation, the failure to make payments to the victim will constitute a violation of the terms of probation and lead to harsher consequences than would normally be associated with the failure to pay a civil damage award.

While a sentencing court can order an offender to give reasonable notice to the victims of its offence, in some cases the identity of the victims may not be known. One way of surmounting this problem is for the court to issue an order requiring the offender to publicise its crime[31]. Such publicity orders will serve not only to alert victims who may not be aware of the source of their injuries, but also those who might not even be aware that they have been injured (for example, by exposure to chemicals whose effects may not be felt until some years in the future). Publicising the offender's crime also serves to notify the public of companies which they then can then decide are not deserving of their custom although, as we noted previously, this information may not always have the desired effect. The publicity order can include a requirement that the offender indicate the remedial steps it plans to avoid future violations, which should have the salutary effect of forcing the offender to think more carefully about the nature of its business operation and the potential for illegality.

The chief punitive sanction envisaged by the guidelines is a fine. In practice these have proved to be quite severe in some cases, often running into the millions and even hundreds of millions of dollars (which stand in stark contrast to the far lower level of fines imposed by the English judiciary). Where a company has been operated primarily for criminal purposes or by criminal means, the guidelines advise that the fine should be set sufficiently high to divest the company of *all* of its net assets. In other cases, the fine is supposed to reflect the seriousness of the offence and the culpability of the offender. The guidelines indicate how this calculation is to be made, setting out a three-stage process through which a court should proceed in determining the appropriate amount of the fine.

First, the court sets a base fine that reflects the seriousness of the company's offence.[32] Seriousness is measured by the greater of the pecuniary gain to the offender, the pecuniary loss to the victim (to the extent that the loss was caused intentionally, knowingly or recklessly) and the intrinsic wrongfulness of the offence as established by a statutory table.[33] Second, the court multiplies this base fine by a numerical factor that reflects the culpability of the offender.[34] The determination of this 'culpability score' is probably the most critical stage of the process. The convicted company begins with a score of five, which may then be adjusted upwards to ten or downwards to zero to reflect the presence or absence of aggravating and mitigating factors.[35] Among the more egregious aggravating factors identified in the guidelines are past misconduct of a similar nature and the involvement of high-level corporate personnel in the offence. The most significant mitigating factors are the establishment

---

31 USSG, s 8D1.4(a).
32 USSG, s 8C2.4.
33 USSG, s 8C2.4(a) and (d).
34 USSG, s 8C2.5.
35 USSG, s 8C2.5(a).

of a generally effective compliance programme to prevent and detect criminal violations and the self-reporting of the offence by the company to the appropriate authorities before the latter learn of it from an independent source. Mitigation points are also awarded for co-operating with official investigations and for accepting responsibility for the offence. The product yielded by multiplying the base fine by the company's culpability score provides the court with a recommended fine range. The final stage of the sentencing process is for the court to select an appropriate fine from the recommended range. This allows for a fine-tuning that can take account, for instance, of a company's role in the offence (organiser or 'bit player'), and other factors which might not have entered into the court's consideration in the somewhat more prescribed technical calculation of the recommended range of fine.

For a compliance programme to be deemed effective, it will usually have to involve the formulation and communication of rules, regulations and standards to the company's employees, effective monitoring of employees and auditing of the company's financial systems, reporting mechanisms which include safeguards for whistleblowers, the attachment of high-level personnel to the compliance department, consistent enforcement and appropriate internal responses in cases of violations. By placing heavy reliance on internal policing, compliance departments, and the self-reporting of offences, the guidelines in effect put the onus on companies to police themselves. If compliance departments are adequately funded, staffed by respected and competent personnel and taken seriously by those in the organisation, they can play a critical role in the prevention of corporate crime. As such, they are a critical feature of the corporate enterprise, but, in truth, a feature that one might have expected companies to see as being in their own self-interest and have developed on their own. Many large corporations had in fact done so prior to the promulgation of the guidelines. None the less, the extra impetus provided by the guidelines is not to be decried. The guidelines go further, moreover, as, under ss 8D1.1(a)(3) and 8D1.4(c), a court can effectively order the establishment of a compliance programme if the offender has 50 or more employees and has not established its own programme before sentencing.

Unlike creation of compliance departments, which, as noted, were already becoming increasingly prevalent even before enactment of the guidelines, self-reporting of the company's crimes is probably not a step that would normally have occurred to a company in the absence of the guidelines. Few criminals turn themselves in to the police, and those that do are typically driven by an unbearable sense of guilt. Guilt is not the type of emotion that an inanimate entity such as a company is likely to experience. By encouraging and rewarding the self-reporting of offences, the guidelines seek to promote good 'corporate citizenship'.

Finally, the guidelines view probation as a punishment and authorise probation orders in appropriate cases. A court is instructed to order probation:
- if necessary to secure restitution or the payment of a monetary penalty;
- if the organisation has over 50 employees but does not have an effective programme to detect and prevent offences;
- if the organisation has engaged in similar misconduct in the previous five years;
- if high-level personnel were involved in the offence and had been involved in similar misconduct within the previous five years;
- if needed to ensure organisational changes to reduce the likelihood of future offences;

- if the sentence imposed does not include a fine; or
- if necessary, to accomplish one of the purposes of sentencing (which seems somewhat of 'catch-all' provision).[36]

There are both required and recommended probation conditions. Required conditions include a prohibition on committing future offences, and, in the case of conviction for a felony, one of the following: restitution; notice to victims; or an order requiring the organisation to reside, or refrain from residing, in a specified place or area unless 'extraordinary circumstances' render such a condition unreasonable.[37] Recommended probation conditions include publicising of the offence and the steps the company plans to take to avoid a recurrence; submission to unannounced entries for the purpose of examination of the offender's books, records and premises; notification of the court of material changes in the company's financial position or prospects; and the development of a compliance programme to prevent and detect violations of the law, including a schedule for implementation; and the submission of periodic reports to the court.[38] Probation may last for up to a maximum of five years.

E.   PROCEDURES IN SENTENCING

After an individual has been convicted of a serious crime, it is common for a pre-sentence report to be prepared. Pre-sentence reports in the cases of convicted companies, on the other hand, are a rarity. Yet a sentencing judge will need to know not only about such traditional issues as the company's record of previous violations, but also about such matters as the defendant's economic position (if the court accepted the propriety of differential fines based on the company's financial situation); what systemic deficiencies may have caused the offence to occur and what the defendant had done post-offence to rectify the criminogenic conditions (if the court were minded to impose a remedial order); what type of community service is most suited to the company's expertise (if the court proposed to issue a community service order); what the company had done to redress the harm it had caused (if the court proposed to order restitution or compensation); and many other variables that would not likely be as relevant in the sentencing of an individual.

If a court were to order the preparation of a pre-sentence report in the case of a convicted company, who would prepare it and what would it contain? Normally, a pre-sentence report will be prepared by a probation officer, typically with a background in the social sciences or social work. Such a background will give the probation officer insight into the character and psychological make-up of the human defendant. In preparing a report on a convicted company, in contrast, an understanding of business economics and the ability to analyse a company's management structures is likely to prove more valuable. To unravel a company's financial situation may require the skills of a professional accountant. A systems analyst may be needed to discover the deficiencies in the company's methods of operation. Although the preparation of a pre-sentence report on a company may

36 USSG, s 8D1.1.
37 USSG, s 8D1.3.
38 USSG, s 8D1.4.

require several consultants with different skills, and may take time and be expensive, the financial costs could be charged to the offender as part of the court costs.

In determining the appropriate sentence, the sentencing court might seek to enlist the assistance of counsel for both sides to a greater extent than is customary. In *R v Friskies Petcare Ltd*,[39] where the defendant pleaded guilty to a health and safety violation, the Court of Appeal advocated that the Health and Safety Executive (which prosecuted the case) should identify in writing the aggravating features of the case which should be taken into account in sentencing. The court similarly advocated that the defendant should identify any mitigating factors that it wished to have considered. While the court favoured a common submission by the two sides, it recognised that the trial judge might have to hold a hearing if the two sides could not agree on a common submission.

The Court of Appeal's recommendations raise important questions about the role of counsel in the sentencing process. Traditionally, defence lawyers have been permitted to make partisan representations, while the prosecutor's role has been restricted to correcting false submissions (for example, where the company misrepresents the number of its past convictions) and possibly misleading statements (for example, if the company maintains that it has a 'clean' safety record, because it has no prior criminal convictions, when it in fact has received several cautions and/ or warnings from regulators). Even in such circumstances, it has been the practice of prosecutors not to intervene. The Bar's Code of Conduct counsels that prosecutors 'should not attempt by advocacy to influence a court in regard to sentence'. However, a more activist role may be warranted in cases of corporate crime, because the sentencing judge is likely to have less experience in sentencing companies, and because the factors relevant to sentencing are less likely to be self-evident. This is particularly true if a pre-sentence report has not been prepared. The more complex the case and the greater the offender's systemic deficiencies, the more the court will be in need of specialised assistance.

Where the fine that the prosecution would wish to see imposed on a company following a conviction exceeds the authority of a magistrates' court to impose, the prosecution should seek to have the trial transferred to Crown Court, where the fine would not be restricted by the statutory limits which constrain magistrates in sentencing. Factors which might be pointed to by the prosecution would include the seriousness of the offence, the financial situation of the offender, and any aggravating circumstances of the case. Similarly, where a corporate defendant has opted to enter a guilty plea, the prosecutor might argue in favour of transferring the case to Crown Court for sentencing to allow for a fine that is in excess of the magistrates' court's jurisdictional ceiling. One effect of enacting an offence of corporate killing would presumably be to make unmistakably clear to the magistrates the seriousness of the company's violation.

In *R v F Howe & Son (Engineers) Ltd*,[40] discussed previously, the Court of Appeal stated that a company which failed to supply information about its financial affairs should be presumed to be able to pay any fine that the court was minded to impose. The court proffered this observation with respect to accounts and other financial information that the convicted company might desire the sentencing judge to

39 [2000] 2 Cr App Rep (S) 401.
40 [1999] 2 All ER 249.

consider. However, one could look upon the court's admonition as a harbinger of a broader duty of a convicted company to co-operate in the preparation of a pre-sentence report. The failure to do so could constitute an independent offence of contempt or obstruction, or perhaps just increase the burden on the corporate defendant if it sought to contest the sentence imposed by the trial judge.

F. CONCLUSIONS

A broadened basis of corporate criminal liability will inevitably lead to an increased number of prosecutions and convictions of companies. The subject of sentencing will concomitantly take on greater significance and, with it, the permissible range of sanctions for convicted companies. Historically, the philosophy of corporate sentencing has been driven by two models – an 'economic model' and a 'structural reform' model (Note: 1992). The economic model, which viewed companies as rational cost-benefit calculators and saw fines as the best way of influencing corporate behaviour, has traditionally held sway, especially in England and Wales. In more recent years, and with the growing recognition that companies can commit crimes as serious as manslaughter, the structural reform model may be in the ascendancy. Proponents of this model argue that the best way to prevent corporate crimes lies in changing the policies, practices, procedures, culture and ethos that gave rise to the offence in question. However, fashioning orders that will achieve the goal of 'structural reform' will be more challenging, and more fraught with ambiguity and difficulties, than is present in what may now seem, in the light of the United States Sentencing Guidelines and the decision in England of the Court of Appeal in *Howe*,[42] the relatively straightforward calculation of a fine.

What is needed from courts and legislatures is more imaginative thinking than has been brought to bear on the topic of corporate sentencing in the past. In this chapter we have looked at a number of possible sanctions, including traditional and not-so-traditional fines, compensation and restitution orders, community service orders, remedial orders, adverse publicity orders and restraint-orientated sanctions. These various punishments should not be regarded as mutually exclusive, and should be imposed in whatever combination is warranted by the nature of the offence and the circumstances of the offender. At the same time, we have observed that courts need to be sensitive to spill-over effects that can adversely affect innocent individuals. In particular, fines, adverse publicity orders and interdictory sanctions may all wind up costing workers their jobs, or be passed on to the public in the form of higher prices for a company's goods and services. This is not to suggest that these sanctions are in any way inappropriate, but rather that, in imposing them, courts should be aware of the dangers of spill-over, and, to the extent that they can, take independent measures to eliminate, or at least minimise, such effects. An 'equity fine', for example, may provide a means of imposing a monetary penalty while avoiding spill-over; and community service orders are not only relatively spill-over free, but may force an offender to take on additional personnel to satisfy the terms of the order.

---

42 *R v F Howe & Son (Engineers) Ltd* [1999] 2 All ER 249.

CHAPTER 8

Individual liability

A. INTRODUCTION: STRUCTURAL COMPLEXITY

In focusing on *corporate* criminal liability, there is the danger of overlooking *individual* fault and responsibility. Where criminal liability is imputed to a company on the basis of a crime committed by an individual working for or associated with the company, as it is under the vicarious liability and 'identification' tests of corporate criminality, then by definition there will be an individual who will have committed an offence. Likewise, when a company is charged as an accessory to an individual's offence, there will, again by definition, be an individual who in law will be the principal who will have committed an offence. And in cases where the company's fault lies in not preventing an offence by one of its members of staff, there will also be an individual who will have committed a crime that the company should have prevented. Indeed, the issue of individual liability does not disappear even if the theory of the prosecution is that the company should be criminally liable for its organisational fault. It simply appears in a different guise, the question becoming whether the company's directors, officers, managers or employees might be chargeable as accessories to the corporate offence.

In all of the above situations, the issue that arises is whether individual offenders should be prosecuted along with their company. Readers might be struck by the juxtaposition of the phrasing – the traditional question, and one that is only infrequently asked at that, has been whether a company should be prosecuted in addition to the individual, not whether an individual should be prosecuted in addition to the company. We have reversed the order to indicate the priority we believe the criminal justice system should give to the role of the organisation in corporate crime and the secondary, although not unimportant, role of the individual.

There are several categories of individuals whose criminal liability merits examination: ordinary employees, supervisory personnel, middle-level managers and corporate officers and directors. Within these categories there are many finer levels and gradations of appointment, as well as individual variations among companies. It is primarily to facilitate the analysis that we have chosen to focus on these broad groupings. Our model, for the purposes of discussion, is that of a fairly conventional, vertically structured, largely hierarchical company with clear lines of authority (often expressed in an organisational chart), which is engaged in business activities entailing risks to the public and/or the company's employees. Such conditions are often found in companies engaged in manufacturing, production or transport. The potential for a different type of risk, to financial interests, characterises the 'service industries'. While the 'modern' corporation may be quite unlike the 'command-and-control' monolith that Albert Sloan set up at General Motors, and that for a long time served as the model for large, conventional organisations, to a large extent both academic and legal thinking still appears to be mired in this conception of the company. Legal doctrines and judicial analyses continue to reflect this old-fashioned view of companies.

Even within the broad category of 'command and control' companies, however, one can find considerable variation in organisational form, ranging from the relatively uncomplicated small company to the opaquely intricate multinational enterprise. On the one hand, there is the 'one-man band' (for example, the lorry driver, with but a single vehicle, but who is registered as a company); on the other, there are global conglomerates with a web of subsidiaries. Personnel may be full-time, part-time, hired to do piecemeal work, or take the form of consultants and independent contractors employed on an ad hoc basis for a limited period and for a limited assignment. In contrast, in the 'service industry' many companies now have relatively 'flat' organisational structures, with multiple business units, a significant degree of devolved responsibility, and 'flexible' and 'loosely coupled' partner companies located in dispersed geographical locations throughout the world and linked by information and communication technology, and by computer networks. Many major corporations, moreover, have experienced considerable change within the last 20 years with reorganisations – including mergers and acquisitions, diversification and internationalisation – altering structures, cultures and long-accepted certainties; indeed, a pundit might say that the only certainty is constant change. These developments may increase flexibility and fluidity, but they can also cause conflict and turbulence within business organisations and management.

The implications of a judicial failure to grasp the new realities of organisational structures can be seen in the example of P&O Ferries. We have discussed the capsize of the *Herald of Free Enterprise* on several occasions in different contexts, but here we wish to look at how management structures contributed to the tragedy. At the time of the capsize, P&O was a large, diversified multinational enterprise. Townsend Thoresen, which operated the *Herald of Free Enterprise* and other ferries, was one of its subsidiaries. Townsend Thoresen had its own managing board, answerable in turn to the board of P&O. Below the respective boards of directors there were upper-level managers responsible for so-called 'functional' areas such as finance, marketing and personnel. Each ship had its own on-board hierarchy, with the captain or master at the pinnacle, but on shore a layer of middle-managers had responsibility for ensuring the smooth operation of the ships and adherence to schedules. At the top were situated corporate executives and directors with overall responsibility for setting organisational targets, priorities and policies. Thus, although a ship's master may have been in charge of the ship while it was at sea, it is clear that there existed several higher layers of bureaucracy, wherein resided decision-making authority that would impact greatly on what happened aboard the ship.

The tragedy of the *Herald* took place against a backdrop of deregulation that characterised the 1980s. The idea was that companies should be freed as much as possible from government regulation in order to allow their executive officers to follow their entrepreneurial instincts. The expectation was that the result would be greater productivity and, in turn, profits. Townsend Thoresen, with its reputation for being cost-conscious, production-orientated and driven by profits, was reflective of the climate of the times. The very names it chose for its ships – such as *The Herald of Free Enterprise* – signified its ethos. Its parent company, P&O, was a major contributor to the Conservative Party and a supporter of the then government's neo-liberal economic policies. It was against this political and economic background that the requests from the ships' masters for a warning light on the bridge that would tell them if the bow doors of a ferry were open or closed was curtly rejected on grounds of cost. The view of the company's executives and directors was not so much that the lights would not have added to the safety of the ship, but rather that, if all the crew tended to their assignments, there should have been no risk of an open-bow sailing. The executives and directors could see all too clearly how the requested expenditure would eat into profits, but failed to appreciate the risk of human error and the potential catastrophic consequences that could follow.

In the manslaughter prosecution of P&O, Turner J was faced with the consequences of a tragic 'accident', but unclear legal liability. The decisions taken by the directors did not breach any regulatory guidelines on ship safety. While several of the directors and executives on trial had relatively little first-hand experience or knowledge of what went on aboard the company's ships, this too was not a crime. Turner J's conclusion that the executives were not aware of an obvious and serious risk of harm from an open-bow sailing may have been factually correct but, arguably, the more pertinent legal question was whether the directors had a responsibility to make themselves aware of the risks that were associated with the business they were running, especially where those risks posed such a danger to human life. The judge also failed to consider whether the culture that the directors had created, which prized profitability and keeping to schedule over safety, might have contributed to the capsize. For their part, the master and crew had to cope, as best they could, with working conditions which they were powerless to change, seemingly contradictory standing orders, and a de facto system of negative reporting ('if one does not hear of anything that is wrong, then everything is alright'). The seat of decision-making authority regarding the perils of the business was far removed from the locus of the dangers, and those with authority had little sense of what was at stake in terms of human lives. According to the Sheen Committee, which investigated the tragedy:

> At first sight the faults which led to this disaster were the.... errors of omission on the part of the Master, the Chief Officer and the assistant bosun, and also the failure by Captain Kirby to issue and enforce clear orders. But a full investigation into the circumstances of the disaster leads inexorably to the conclusion that the underlying or cardinal faults lay higher up in the Company. The Board of Directors did not appreciate their responsibility for the safe

management of their ships. They did not apply their minds to the question: What orders should be given for the safety of our ships? The directors did not have any proper comprehension of what their duties were. There appears to have been a lack of thought about the way in which the HERALD ought to have been organised for the Dover/Zeebrugge run. All concerned in management, from the members of the Board of Directors down to the junior superintendents, were guilty of fault in that all must be regarded as sharing responsibility for the failure of management (Department of Transport: 1987: para 14.1).

The committee's telling conclusion was that 'from top to bottom, the company was infected with the disease of sloppiness' (Department of Transport: 1987: para 14.1). This finding and the trial court's dismissal of the manslaughter charges against the directors and the company seem hard to reconcile, and may serve to illustrate both the blinkered approach of the law and the difficulties in allocating blame between organisation and individuals.

Of the three layers that we have chosen to focus on, employees present the 'softest' target for a prosecution. Their acts will usually be the direct cause of whatever injury or damage has occurred; and these acts normally will have been committed 'intentionally', even if the harmful result was not intended. Often, in retrospect, it will emerge clearly from the evidence that a 'reasonable person' in the employee's position would – and should – have foreseen the danger. However, while proof of the elements of a crime may be the most straightforward when a prosecution is brought against an ordinary employee, the policy issues relating to whether or not to charge the employee may be the most complex. Should an employee be prosecuted for a crime that was made possible, if not probable, by the fact that s/he was required to work in criminogenic conditions created by the employer? What of the fact that the employee, like the crew members of the *Herald*, was unable to alter these conditions and, at least in their minds, would have risked dismissal by even raising the issue?

The second class of individuals whose criminal liability merits attention consists of intermediate-level 'supervisory' personnel. These middle-level managers do not fit easily within the 'hands-brains' metaphor that underpins the 'identification' test of corporate criminality. Unlike ordinary workers, who may in conventional settings be expected to perform assigned tasks unquestioningly, supervisors will often be accorded some discretion in how they carry out their responsibilities. To some, a disaster like that of the *Herald* points up the need for giving middle-level managers greater discretion, but others reach the opposite conclusion and argue for reduced discretion and ever more detailed operational rules and procedures. Irrespective of the merits of the two positions (it may depend on the sector of the industry that is in issue), what does seem clear is that the choice between these alternatives is not likely to be made by those who will be charged with direct supervisory responsibility. Such individuals clearly do not form part of 'the directing mind' of the company, and will not have the authority to reject outright the policies whose implementation they oversee. On the other hand, compared with directors and corporate officers, supervisors will doubtless have more influence over events 'on the ground', and will be able to exercise a degree of control over workers that is not realistically available to more senior members of the corporate hierarchy. Part of the supervisor's responsibility will be to identify potentially unsafe and dangerous conditions in the company's business operation, as well as criminogenic flashpoints. A supervisor has also to be alert to incipient illegality by workers and prevent it before harm ensues.

The question we will have to examine is whether the failure to do so should lead to formal legal liability for resulting criminal offences.

The final class of persons whose criminal liability needs to be considered consists of a company's directors and officers. In contrast to ordinary workers, who may be the direct perpetrators of harm-causing acts, and supervisors, who often are in a position to prevent those acts from occurring, corporate executives will usually be further removed from the 'scene of the crime', or at least the scene of the harm. Their role – and fault – will consist of authorising or approving the harm-causing policy, or encouraging or tolerating a criminogenic culture. Directors and officers are responsible for giving 'moral' direction to their company and for setting an example to employees. Under the Health and Safety at Work etc Act 1974, they have a duty to prepare a general policy with respect to health and safety (s 2(3)) and, if requested by worker safety representatives, to establish a safety committee (s 2(7)). When a company's workforce carries out its assignments in a dangerous or unlawful manner, part of the blame may rest with the indifference to such behaviour that is manifested or conveyed by corporate officials. Of course, if the directors and corporate executives actively *encourage* such behaviour, there is all the more reason to hold them responsible for the resulting crimes.

Ever since Sutherland's ground-breaking research (1949), criminologists have tended to lump together offences committed by directors, officers and senior managers under the banner of 'white-collar' crime, the metaphor serving to identify the status of the perpetrator within the organisation (persons who wear a 'white collar' as opposed to a 'blue collar'). While in the beginning no doubt valuable in drawing attention to a class of 'hidden' wrongdoing (many of the 'crimes' which Sutherland had in mind were not in fact criminal under the existing law), the distinction between white and blue-collar crime has frequently been attacked for its lack of precision (Nelken: 1997: 896). Middle-level managers in particular may resist ready classification. However, the more significant problem with placing one's emphasis on the status of the offender is that it serves to obscure the arguably more significant point that business crimes take place in a business setting and are made possible by virtue of the offender's position within the organisation. Legally, the distinction between white and blue-collar workers only assumes importance for a company's criminal liability under an 'identification' test of corporate criminality, blue-collar workers virtually never having the requisite status. Under a test of vicarious liability as implemented in the US courts, or if companies were to be held liable as accessories to an individual's offence, or liable in their own right for failing to prevent crimes by their staff, it would not matter whether the staff member who committed the underlying crime wore a white or blue collar – or, for that matter, brightly coloured braces.

Although the categories may lack precision, given the variety and complexity of contemporary business life, it will serve the purposes of our analysis to draw a rough distinction between ordinary employees, supervisors and middle-level managers, and corporate executives and directors. The characteristics of the offender aside, it is also important to distinguish between crimes that are committed for personal gain, unmindful of the company's interests, and perhaps even contrary to the company's interests, and crimes that are committed to further the company's interests. A clear example of the former category would be where an employee or officer embezzles money from the company, the company being in effect the victim of the offence. While we would argue that this feature of the crime should not necessarily preclude a prosecution of the company (for example, for the absence of systems that would have prevented the offence or for allowing a criminogenic culture to flourish), it will rarely be the case that the individual offender should not also be prosecuted. We do not propose to address such cases in detail, as they fall under conventional criminal law analysis, the only difference being that the victim is a company and not a natural person. More complex issues are raised by cases where an individual commits an offence to advance corporate interests, even if the individual also benefits. Say that an insurance salesman makes fraudulent representations to prospective customers in response to internal pressures to increase sales. There will be an upsurge in corporate profits, but the seller's commissions will also rise. Where offences are committed by directors or other corporate executives and officers, the predominant motive is more likely to be a desire to boost the fortunes of the company, even though a more profitable company may also work to their personal advantage by enhancing their reputation (and, concomitantly, their chances for promotion and bonuses). While the motive for a criminal offence is technically irrelevant to guilt, it may be relevant to the decision to charge, to proof and to any sentence following a conviction.

Where a company has gone out of existence, the liability of directors may take on especial import. In this situation, the prosecution of the company may seem little more than a ritualistic denunciation of an entity that no longer existed. Moreover, if the company were to be convicted, on whom might sanctions be visited? One plausible answer is the company's former directors. Under an 'identification' test, the company's liability will often be based on the crime of a director or officer, and there would seem to be nothing inappropriate in prosecuting and punishing the relevant individual. On the other hand, holding all of a company's directors liable as a proxy for the company may be terribly unfair to those directors who had tried to run the business in a lawful manner.

B. LIABILITY OF ORDINARY EMPLOYEES

In cases where corporate mismanagement combines with employee gross negligence to produce a result that warrants criminal charges, who should be prosecuted? Typically it will be the actions or inactions of an employee which will form the most immediate causal link to any resulting harm and, indeed, under the Health and Safety at Work etc Act 1974, s 7, employees have a duty to take reasonable care for their own health and safety and that of others who may be affected by their acts or omissions. But if an employee was forced to work in an environment, or under conditions, that were highly conducive to the commission of the offence, is s/he solely at fault? In such circumstances, would a prosecution of the employee be regarded as just or fair, and would any sense of unfairness be exacerbated if the company were to escape criminal liability altogether?

We have seen that even prosecutors are not immune from thinking along such lines. Following the Southall train crash, in which seven persons died, both the driver of the train and the company, Great Western Railway, were indicted for manslaughter: the driver for his alleged gross negligence in failing to observe several warning signals and a stop signal (by his own admission, he was 'packing his bags' at the critical juncture); and Great Western for its alleged gross negligence in allowing its train to proceed without the benefit of two warning/protection systems that were in place on the train but not operational. Adhering to a traditional 'identification' test of corporate liability for common law crimes, the Court of Appeal dismissed the manslaughter charges against the company. Following this dismissal, however, the prosecution decided not to proceed with its prosecution of the driver. As a matter of logic, this decision made no sense. Whether or not the driver had been grossly negligent was not altered by the liability of the company.

A similar sequence of events had occurred with respect to the manslaughter prosecution of P&O following the capsize of the *Herald of Free Enterprise*. Charges were initially brought against both the company and members of the crew, as well as against several of the company's directors. The charges against the latter were dismissed when Turner J ruled that they had not been reckless (as required under the then prevailing standard of reckless manslaughter) in failing to appreciate the dangers of a ferry sailing with its bow doors open. As a result of this ruling, the case against the company also had to fail, as there was no longer any individual who could be 'identified' with the company who was guilty of manslaughter. Interestingly, however, the charges against the crew members were also dropped. Again, strictly as a matter of logic, the recklessness of the crew was independent of any recklessness on the part of the company or its directors. One might have thought that at the very least the prosecution of the assistant bosun, who was asleep at the time he should have been closing the bow doors, or that of the Chief Officer, whose job responsibilities included ensuring himself that the bow doors were in fact closed, might have been continued.

Perhaps the prospect of an adverse public reaction played a role in the decisions to discontinue the cases against the Great Western driver and the crew of the *Herald*. Even if technically defensible legally, there is something unseemly in singling out the 'small fry' for prosecution while allowing the 'big fish' off the hooks. The more telling point, however, perhaps grasped by the prosecutor in each case, is that where a company has organised its business operation in such a way as to effectively 'force' its employees to work in conditions where there is an unacceptably high risk of a crime being committed, the worker who displays normal human frailty and unintentionally (even if grossly negligently) commits a crime should not be held solely responsible for the offence. Although it could be argued that an individual is always able to exercise choice, and remains ultimately responsible for his/her choices and actions, countless accounts of people in work organisations repeatedly reveal that employees feel that they are under constant pressure to break rules and that they see little alternative but to do so if they are not to lose their jobs. Another factor in these situations is that often the ordinary employees will suffer from the consequences of their acts to such a degree that they virtually become additional 'victims' of the crime. It was apparent to all who saw the Great Western driver on television that he was emotionally shattered as a result of events. As for the indicted crew-members of the *Herald*, not only had they lost valued friends and co-workers, but several had also distinguished themselves in attempting to rescue passengers.

These cases highlight the 'accountability gap' that can arise when those responsible for formulating crime-conducive policies are not involved in their implementation, while those required to carry out such policies have no voice in their development. A closer look at the Great Western and P&O cases reveals this accountability gap in practice. The crew of the *Herald of Free Enterprise* worked 24-hour shifts at a stretch. The bosun responsible for closing the bow doors was asleep at the time when he should have been attending to the doors. The Chief Officer of the *Herald*, responsible for ensuring that the bow doors had in fact been closed, was virtually required by company standing orders to be in two places at the same time. Meanwhile, as we noted previously, the directors of the company had rejected, on grounds of cost, a request from ferry captains for warning lights on the bridge that would indicate whether the ship's bow doors were open or closed. The directors' short-sightedness meant that human error would go undetected, with potentially catastrophic consequences. The same short-sightedness was evident in the Southall crash, where the driver was similarly deprived of technological backup that would have protected him against human error, in that case his own. The driver may have had nobody to blame but himself for packing his bags when he should have been watching the signals on the line, but the tragic consequences that were to follow were also in part attributable to a number of ill-judged operational decisions that reflected corporate priorities, policies and practices.

In recommending the creation of an offence of corporate killing, the Law Commission (1996) took the view that individuals should not be chargeable with the corporate offence either directly or as secondary parties. It reasoned that to allow individuals to be charged with corporate killing would be at odds with the concept of organisational fault that underlay the corporate offence. However, it was not the intent of the Commission to rule out individual liability altogether and it specifically observed that individuals could still be prosecuted for reckless killing or killing by gross carelessness (two other offences which it recommended in its Report) in an appropriate case. Some might have preferred that the Commission had gone further and excluded this latter possibility as well, at least for ordinary workers. It is often the case that in tragic 'accidents' – and, again, we are referring primarily to industrial and transport accidents – it will be an ordinary worker whose acts are the direct cause of injury. However, when that employee has not been properly trained, has been forced to work in crime-conducive conditions and has not been given adequate direction, supervision or back-up, it is apparent that management failures have contributed significantly to the result.

That the bosun on the *Herald of Free Enterprise* was asleep at the time that he was supposed to be closing the bow doors was hardly surprising given the fact that he was required to work a 24-hour shift. Even if this were standard operating practice in the industry, it would raise issues of exhaustion and lack of attention related to tiredness (on which there is a fair amount of research data indicating indisputably the vulnerabilities of working long hours). Likewise, it is hard to fault the Chief Officer who failed to observe that the bosun had not closed the doors when he was under company orders that seemed to require him to be somewhere else at the time that he was supposed to be carrying out this check. Referring to the bosun and the Chief Officer, Bergman (2000) comments:

> It is certainly arguable whether these two men ought to have been charged with manslaughter. It is inappropriate for junior members of a company to be prosecuted when their actions only had the results they did because of very poor management. When workers are put in a

position where an easily made mistake could lead to death or injury, prosecutors ought to think twice before taking legal action against them (Bergman: 2000: 27).

Bergman concludes that '[a] worker should not be prosecuted when the only reason he acted in the manner in which he did, or the only reason it had the particular consequences, was due to a serious failure on the part of the company' (Bergman: 2000: 79; see also Wells: 2001).

To give workers virtual blanket impunity from criminal prosecution for all harm that they might cause while engaged in a company's business is not wise, however. When crime-conducive working conditions form but a backdrop to a worker's irresponsible acts, prosecuting the worker may be justified. If, for example, the assistant bosun on the *Herald* or the driver of the Great Western train had been drunk at the critical juncture, there would have been far fewer who would have opposed a prosecution, even if there were evidence to the effect that their drinking had been induced by the pressures of work. From a policy perspective, impunity from prosecution could produce an undesirable complacency or carelessness on the part of a company's workforce. The possibility of criminal liability is also needed to strengthen worker resistance to corporate orders that the workers, from their first-hand experience and on-the-ground perspective, can foresee are likely to lead to harm. While some might argue that employees who perform tasks that they know or believe could lead to harm should bear the consequences of their decision, this would place the employee in an invidious position: on the one hand, the worker would face criminal liability if s/he complied with a work-related order and criminally cognisant harm followed; on the other, the employee would risk internal disciplinary sanctions or even dismissal for insubordination if s/he refused to carry out a job assignment. If the employee were to refuse to carry out an assignment that s/he perceived to be dangerous, moreover, there would not even be the evidence of harm that would confirm the employee's assessment of the situation. That the refusal might be protected by labour laws, and ultimately be upheld in a tribunal, is not likely to be relevant except to those sufficiently hardy to endure the psychological pressures and uncertainties of pursuing legal remedies following suspension from their job. If the employee loses at the tribunal stage, s/he will not only be out of a job, but may find it difficult to secure future employment. If the employee prevails, it may turn out to be a pyrrhic victory, as challenging the orders of a superior, even successfully, is not the normally recommended route to rapid advancement within an organisation.

A possible compromise position between prosecuting employees and giving them impunity from prosecution would be to create a legal defence in favour of a defendant whose offence was directly attributable to the conditions in which s/he was compelled to work. Interestingly, we have already seen examples of statutes that provide a *company* with a defence based on an employee's fault. In *Tesco Supermarkets Ltd v Nattrass*,[1] for instance, where the corporate defendant was charged with having violated the Trade Descriptions Act 1968, it was able to raise a statutory defence that it had taken 'all reasonable precautions', and had exercised 'due diligence', to avoid the default of 'another person' (the other person in the case being the branch manager of one of its local supermarkets). In the present context,

---

1 [1972] AC 153.

the converse is proposed: the employee's offence would be excused by the greater fault of the company in creating a working environment that was conducive to the commission of the offence. The argument is that where a company forces its staff to work in conditions that pose a high risk of a crime being committed while corporate assignments are being carried out, an employee should not be liable for showing 'normal' human frailty and thereby contributing to the realisation of the risk.

This is a difficult position to maintain under traditional principles of English law. The *economic* pressure created by the fear of losing one's job does not rise to the level of a threat of death or serious bodily injury required for a defence of duress, necessity or duress of circumstances.[2] Nor is the fact that one is acting pursuant to the orders of a superior a valid defence. The courts reason that one can always quit one's job, or refuse to carry out an illegal order, apparently oblivious to the consequences of a suspension, or even dismissal, that can follow from the refusal to obey the command of a superior. And then, of course, the employee (not being a lawyer) often will not be aware that the order entails the commission of a criminal offence. Should not employees be able to rely on the presumed superior legal knowledge of the officials who formulated the relevant policies? Unfortunately for the employee, neither ignorance of the law nor good-faith reliance on the legal advice of another (even if that other is law-trained) is generally recognised as a defence under English law.[3] This is not to say that a jury may not be sympathetic, however.[4] A Vanderbilt Law Review Note (1978) probes the thinking of jurors in such cases:

> [J]uries have frequently found corporate defendants criminally culpable while acquitting agents who clearly committed the criminal acts. The phenomenon perhaps reflects an intuitive feeling by jurors that individuals acting within the pressures of a bureaucratic and sometimes highly diffuse corporate structure are often unwitting or even unwilling participants in an illegal transaction, and that a criminal conviction is too harsh a sanction for business misconduct that is not of a highly immoral or detestable character (Note: 1978: 268).

If the courts are not prepared to recognise a defence of 'economic necessity', or 'reasonable reliance on the superior knowledge of those in higher authority' or 'greater corporate responsibility', and if the prosecution is not dissuaded from bringing charges against an employee because of such considerations, a judge might nevertheless consider the company's role in the offence in determining the appropriate sentence of the convicted employee. Arguably, the dilemma in which the employee had been placed – having to perform an illegal act or risk losing his/her job – should count in mitigation of sentence. Another mitigating factor would be if organisational fault or a management failure were shown to be a significant contributing factor in the offence, even if it were not deemed sufficient to warrant a conviction of the company. For the most part, employees will not be inherently dangerous, in the sense of being likely to commit further crimes, having in effect

---

2 See *DPP for Northern Ireland v Lynch* [1975] AC 653.
3 See *R v Bailey* (1800) Russ & Ry 1.
4 American courts have expressed their incredulity when a jury has managed to convict a company while acquitting the individuals whose fault formed the basis of the conviction of the company. See eg *US v General Motors Corpn* 121 F 2d 376, 411 (7th Cir); *cert denied* 314 US 613 (1941).

only become 'dangerous' by virtue of working in a crime-conducive environment. Restraint could be achieved by removing them from that environment or, better still, requiring the company to take remedial measures to correct the criminogenic conditions. No general deterrence would likely be achieved by sentencing the employee to prison if other workers who found themselves in a similar dilemma preferred not to put their jobs in jeopardy by refusing a direct order of a superior. Nor do employees have the power to change corporate policy. Finally, it is questionable whether the general public or the workers' peers would regard a custodial sentence to be the 'just desert' for an employee who obeyed an illegal order of a superior.

C. LIABILITY OF SENIOR SUPERVISORY PERSONNEL

In chapter 3 we argued that organisational fault could consist of a company's failure adequately to monitor its workforce and to prevent it from engaging in activities that were illegal or unduly dangerous to the public. But let us posit that a company takes this responsibility seriously and appoints managers or compliance officers to supervise the actions of its employees and agents. Now, if a crime were to occur, the responsibility would seem to rest either directly with the individual who commits the actus reus of the offence and/or with the supervisory personnel whose job it was to oversee the actions of that individual and prevent any crimes from occurring. Both may bear some, albeit perhaps different degrees of, responsibility for any resulting harm. Having examined the worker's potential criminal liability in the previous section, we now turn our attention to what liability should attach to the supervisor.

Supervisors hold an intermediate, middle-management, but none the less crucial, position in the corporate hierarchy. They typically will be allotted more in the way of discretion than ordinary workers, but will lack the authority to formulate policy that is reserved to the company's directors and officers. On the other hand, they will have a degree of hands-on control over what transpires in the workplace that cannot be exercised from the boardroom. The supervisor's role will usually include responsibility for identifying risks, taking steps to prevent these risks from materialising and ensuring that those workers subject to their control do not engage in illegality while on the job. If workers can be said to be a company's 'hands' and directors its 'brains',[5] then supervisors are the company's 'eyes' and 'ears'. They are the 'on-the-beat constables' for what passes as a private police force. Like constables, they will have to react to wide-ranging, unforeseen and sometimes unforeseeable, situations laden with criminal potential. To do so effectively, they will need proper training, sound judgment and a large degree of discretion to respond to novel circumstances.

When a supervisor fails to identify criminogenic risk, or fails to take steps to prevent harm, s/he bears some moral responsibility for any resulting offence. But what is the supervisor's legal position? There would be no question of the supervisor's liability if s/he were to order the employee to commit a crime; one who counsels another to commit a crime is in law an accessory and can be tried, indicted and punished to the same extent as the principal.[6] Likewise, a supervisor who threatens

---

5   See *H L Bolton Co Ltd v T J Graham & Sons Ltd* [1957] 1 QB 159 at 172.
6   Accessories and Abettors Act 1861, s 8.

an employee with the loss of his/her job if the employee does not obey an order to commit an offence would be liable as an accessory. Indeed, in such circumstances the employee may be found to be an innocent agent of the supervisor.

More troublesome from a legal perspective are those cases where a supervisor simply ignores offences which the supervisor is aware are being committed by those under his/her command. The common law offence of misprision of felony, under which the failure to inform the police of a criminal offence of another was itself an offence,[7] has now been altered by Parliament such that it is now only an offence to receive remuneration for not reporting the crime.[8] While a prosecutor might argue that a supervisor is under a *legal duty* to report the crimes of those subject to his/her control and thus is liable for omitting to do so, a court might find that the duty, assuming it existed, was *contractual* in nature and was owed to the employer and not to the police. Nor in this situation is it clear that the supervisor would be an accessory to the employee's offence, as the relevant English statute speaks of aiding, abetting, counselling or procuring of an offence,[9] all of which seem to envisage affirmative acts.

Nevertheless, caselaw can be found where the failure to exercise a right of control has been found to constitute sufficient encouragement to render a defendant liable as an accessory. In *Du Cros v Lambourne*,[10] the defendant was found guilty of aiding and abetting when he allowed a third party, while he was present, to drive his automobile in a dangerous and illegal manner. Similarly, a supervisor has both the right and arguably the duty to control the actions of employees over whom the supervisor exercises authority. In order that a supervisor be held liable as an accessory, however, the prosecutor would also have to prove that the supervisor shared an *intent* with the worker to commit the substantive offence or, at the very least, that s/he provided assistance to the worker *knowing* of the criminal consequences.[11] As a general proposition, it is questionable whether one can be an accessory to a crime of which one is not aware. However, in the case of supervisors, it could be argued that the deliberate failure of a supervisor to inform him/herself of illegal acts by those whom the supervisor was responsible for overseeing constituted wilful blindness, which in law is the equivalent of knowledge. Wilful blindness exists where an individual shuts his/her eyes to an obvious danger or refrains from making inquiries because s/he suspects the true state of affairs but does not wish to have those suspicions confirmed.[12]

Where an employee's offence is committed with what seems to be the acquiescence of a supervisor, might it be said that the employee and supervisor have entered into a conspiracy? The problem with charging conspiracy is that the prosecution would have to show that there existed an agreement between the employee and the supervisor.[13] An agreement need not be explicit, and can be inferred, but there would probably have to be shown that a common purpose existed between the employee and supervisor that would warrant such an inference being drawn.[14] Where

---

7   See *Sykes v DPP* [1962] AC 528.
8   See Criminal Law Act 1967, s 5(1).
9   Accessories and Abettors Act 1861, s 8.
10 [1907] 1 KB 40.
11 See *National Coal Board v Gamble* [1959] 1 QB 11.
12 *Westminster City Council v Croyalgrange Ltd* [1986] 2 All ER 353 at 359.
13 Criminal Law Act 1977, s 1.
14 See *R v Brisac* (1803) 4 East 164.

there is a common purpose, the supervisor's liability would be unproblematic, but where this could not be proved, it would seem that a charge of conspiracy would fail.

Neither liability as an accessory nor liability as a conspirator quite fits the situation of the supervisor who ignores or fails to prevent criminal activity by an employee under his/her charge. Yet it is clear that society has an interest in encouraging vigilant supervision, and perhaps also in bringing grossly negligent supervisors within the compass of the criminal law. In order to do so, while at the same time avoiding the awkward legal issues of actus reus, causation and mens rea that would arise if supervisors were to be charged as accessories or conspirators to an employee's offence, a Harvard Law Review Note (1979) proposes an offence of 'reckless supervision'. For the purposes of this offence, recklessness would be defined in objective terms – the disregard or the failure to make oneself aware of criminological risks that a reasonable supervisor in the same or similar circumstances would have been aware. Recklessness would also include wilful blindness and gross negligence. The actus reus of reckless supervision would consist of either a failure to identify a criminologically significant risk, or a failure to take appropriate steps to eliminate the risk. It would be a defence for the supervisor to show either a reasonable and actual unawareness of the danger, or a good faith and reasonable effort to neutralise it.

Some supervisors may fail to take their duties seriously because they are lazy or incompetent; others, because they do not wish to antagonise those who work under them; and, still others, because they perceive that the illegal methods adopted by their supervisees are efficient or profitable. For the lazy or incompetent supervisor, the creation of an offence of reckless supervision would provide an incentive to become more conscientious. For supervisors who tolerate illegality because they do not wish to upset their supervisees, the offence would provide a counterweight to the loyalty that might be felt to those who work under one's charge. For those supervisors who see illegal methods as efficient or profitable, the offence would bring home the higher duty to obey the law. The creation of the offence of reckless supervision could also be expected to have a salutary ripple effect on employees, for they would know that they were subject to increased scrutiny and that the chances of their illegal activity escaping detection will have been drastically reduced. In service industries the public would be better protected from financial crimes; and in industries such as transport and manufacturing, the workplace would become a safer place to work. The criminalisation of reckless supervision could also spur the development of more effective monitoring systems, if supervisors began to lobby for technologies that would assist them in their task (for example, CCTV cameras), thereby reducing their own exposure to criminal liability.

An offence of reckless supervision need not be limited to on-site supervisors. In recent years, several financial collapses of highly-regarded corporations have focused attention on the critical supervisory role played by auditors and accountants. In the United States, in the wake of the collapse of the Enron Corporation, it was revealed that the accountancy firm Arthur Andersen had signed off on books which gave a false picture of Enron's financial situation. That the oversight was not inadvertent was suggested by Andersen's shredding of potentially incriminating documents. The firm was subsequently indicted, convicted of obstruction of justice and fined $500,000. As a by-product of the Enron and other accounting scandals, CEOs of American companies, as well as companies which are registered in foreign countries but are 'listed' in the United States, now must affirm that their annual financial reports are not false or misleading. The CEO seems in effect to have been co-opted into becoming a guarantor of the firm's accounting integrity, subject to sanction for 'dereliction of duty' if a false report is issued. The maximum penalty for this offence is a $5,000,000 fine and a somewhat draconian 20-year term of imprisonment.

In contrast, similar accounting scandals in England have not led to a criminal prosecution. No charges were brought, for instance, against Coopers and Lybrand with respect to the collapse of Barings Bank, even though the firm's auditors failed to uncover (or at least failed to report) the false accounts that had been constructed by Nick Leeson, the bank's head Singapore trader, in order to cover up his unauthorised and illegal dealings. Allegedly, the fictitious nature of Leeson's accounts was not only fairly transparent, but also well-known to the staff in the Singapore office (according to interviews that Leeson gave after his release from prison; cf Rawnsley: 1996). The failure of auditors to detect or reveal the transgressions of the Bank of Credit and Commerce International (BCCI) was the subject of reproach by a special committee of inquiry that had been set up by the House of Commons to inquire into the causes of BCCI's collapse. The auditing profession claimed in response that the duty of auditors extended only to the companies that hired them, a view that ignored any possible professional obligation owed to the Bank of England, which had overall responsibility for banking supervision, and to the investing public, which relied on auditors to provide independent verification of a company's financial health. An offence of 'reckless supervision', if applied to accountants and auditors, would encourage these professionals to see their supervisory responsibilities in a broader light.

In examining the liability of ordinary workers who committed criminal offences while engaged in job-related assignments, we suggested that the inability of a worker to refuse to carry out such an assignment without putting his/her job in jeopardy might form the basis of a legal defence, or at least serve as a mitigating factor in sentencing. Can the same be said of supervisors who receive direction from officers at a higher level of the corporate hierarchy, or independent accountants and auditors who fear that their contract with the company will not be renewed if they report 'bad news'? The difference between these professionals, on the one hand, and ordinary workers, on the other, is that the supervisor, accountant and auditor will be expected to report operational irregularities that they discover as part of their contractual obligation. After all, for them to fail to do so may expose the company, and its officers and directors, to legal liability. Even if their advice is not heeded, it is less likely to lead to recriminations or charges of insubordination than it might in the case of an employee who refused to carry out a direct command of a superior or a work-related assignment.

We shall discuss in the next section the possibility of imprisoning a corporate director or officer convicted of a criminal offence. However, in the present context it might be observed that the same types of factors that mitigate against a prison sentence of a corporate executive – an exemplary employment history, the absence of a criminal record, the improbability of recidivism and strong community and family ties – are also likely to argue against the need to imprison a person convicted of 'reckless supervision'. On the other hand, a realistic prospect of a prison sentence may need to exist if accountants, auditors, supervisors and middle-level managers are to be deterred from 'reckless supervision'. Otherwise, internal reward structures for performance may overwhelm reservations of conscience, particularly given the long odds of detection, prosecution and conviction.

D.   LIABILITY OF DIRECTORS AND OFFICERS

Of the various categories of persons who might be involved in a company's criminality, the role of the directors and corporate officers is probably one of the most difficult to assess. These are the persons who are responsible for giving direction to and managing the company. Included in their oversight responsibilities is a duty to satisfy themselves that the company is not being operated in a dangerous or illegal manner. 'Employers' have a duty under the Health and Safety at Work Act etc 1974 to ensure, so far as is reasonably practicable, the health and safety of both employees and others who may be affected by their workplace practices (ss 2 and 3). Yet directors are typically far removed from operational activities and may encounter obstacles in obtaining reliable information from subordinates. Anthony Downs claimed that there is a 'Law of diminishing control' at work whereby 'the larger any organisation becomes, the weaker is the control over its actions exercised by those at the top' (Downs: 1966: 143). Large firms may be able to take advantage of economies of scale, but they may encounter greater obstacles than smaller firms in maintaining adequate internal communications and in securing compliance (Coffee: 1977: 1139). The law, on the other hand, may give undue and unrealistic weight to the theoretical role of a board of directors.

None the less, directors in large, successful companies are often handsomely rewarded for what might appear to be relatively little work in terms of demands on their time. The directors of the failed Enron Corporation received cash payments and stock options estimated to have been worth $300,000 per year. Yet in the wake of Enron's collapse, a catalogue of director errors came to light. The board had approved many of the questionable partnerships that concealed the true state of the company's finances from its shareholders and creditors. After the frauds were exposed, several directors claimed not to have understood the nature of the policies that they had been asked to approve, although one must wonder why they voted for policies that they did not understand. The directors also seemed to have ignored ethical constraints and the demands of good practice; several were paid consultancy fees from the corporation (in one case, close to $900,000), without due regard to the potential conflict of interest.

Board-level errors, which may be attributable to something in between laziness, incompetence and criminal negligence, are not restricted to the United States. In England, Barings Bank collapsed after Nick Leeson made a number of unauthorised, high-risk and ultimately disastrous investments and dealings on the Singapore Stock Exchange. The bank's senior management in London, however, played a major role in the collapse. Directors failed to keep themselves informed on Leeson's activities, going so far as to discontinue the previous practice of receiving regular reports from him (which is not to deny that 'information overload' can be a serious problem in large companies). Many of the directors did not even understand the nature of the 'derivatives' trading in which Leeson was engaged. Management uncritically accepted reports of 'too-good-to-be true' profits in areas of activity noted for generating small but steady gains, and paid generous bonuses to Leeson without questioning how someone who was so relatively young and inexperienced had been able to achieve such uncharacteristic profitability. Fatally, corporate executives continued to honour Leeson's requests for large infusions of cash despite the fact that the requests themselves seemed to signal that the financial state of the Singapore office might be in a critical state. Finally, Leeson was allowed to be in charge of both the 'front' and 'back' offices in Singapore, a highly irregular and dubious practice that meant that there was no independent review of his trading. The infamous 88888 'error account', in which Leeson concealed his losses, was not discovered until too late, despite the fact that the account was apparently known to a large number of persons who worked in the Singapore office.

Should corporate directors and officers be held criminally liable when misjudged polices, lax oversight and the failure to devise and implement effective control systems lead to the commission of offences by the company's personnel? Rhetoric in cases that support an 'identification' test of corporate criminality refers to directors and corporate officers as constituting the 'directing mind and will' of the company. While we have been critical of 'identification' as a legal test of corporate criminality, this does not mean that the judicial rhetoric is off the mark. Whatever difficulties may be encountered in separating out the diverse strands that lead to the formulation and execution of a criminogenic policy, what is indisputable is that the ultimate power to approve or disapprove the policy resides in the company's board of directors. Directors may be at fault in adopting policies likely to cause harm or lead to illegality, or they may be grossly negligent, wilfully blind or objectively reckless in failing to consider or accurately assess the criminal implications of the policies they adopt. Studies have highlighted the major role that directors and corporate executives play in setting the 'moral' tone for the company (Brenner and Molander: 1977; Clinard: 1983). A criminogenic culture is reflected in the tolerance of deviance, the absence of codes of good practice, the lack of ethical constraints, inadequate monitoring and control systems, a 'paper' internal disciplinary system that is not taken seriously by employees and the bare-bones funding of compliance departments and safety divisions. The responsibility for correcting these deficiencies ultimately rests with a company's board of directors and its executive officers; they may be the only persons with the authority to order change.

As we noted at the outset of this chapter, one downside of focusing on a company's criminal liability is that the misconduct of directors and officers is in danger of being overlooked. Yet a company should not be made the scapegoat for the crimes of its officers and directors any more than officers and directors should be made the scapegoat for crimes that are properly attributable to the company. When directors and corporate officers deliberately take their company in criminal directions, they should not escape personal liability. When they create or encourage an ethos or culture that is conducive to or tolerant of illegality, or deliberately turn a blind eye to practices of dubious legality, they should be held to legal account. In the absence of a legal incentive to change such a culture, directors may become desensitised to their responsibility to their employees, to the public and to the state.

1. Legal responsibility

If corporate directors and officers are to be held accountable in the criminal courts, with what crimes might they be charged? If a director or officer were to order the commission of an offence by a member of staff, s/he would be liable as an accessory to the offence. But sophisticated corporate executives are generally too astute to command that an offence be committed. They have learned that their objectives can be achieved simply by offering suitable incentives for employees to take illegal shortcuts. Career ladders can be established where results are all that count and the means used to attain the results are given at most a cursory glance (Jackall: 1988). Lucrative bonus systems based on commissions may tempt poorly paid sales personnel to cross the legal divide. Dangerous and criminogenic aspects of a company's business operation may be subcontracted out to firms with a dubious reputation or subsidiaries located in foreign countries where the criminal laws may not be rigorously enforced (see chapter 5). By allocating inadequate resources to departments responsible for safety and for ensuring that the company is in compliance with the law, directors may signal their priorities as clearly as if they had announced them in a mission statement. Meanwhile, the company's formal mission statements will typically declare its opposition to illegality in any form. In a subsequent prosecution, the latter pro forma pronouncements will be wheeled out and introduced as evidence of the directors' good faith and lack of mens rea.

Linking directors and corporate officers to an offence by a member of staff will often be problematic. As we have noted previously, the actual harm-causing act will almost certainly have been committed by the staff member. The case against the directors and officers will be based on their failure to anticipate an offence and to take appropriate measures to prevent it. But a failure to act will not normally give rise to criminal liability in the absence of a legal duty to act, and it is not clear that duties of directors and officers of a company extend beyond the fiduciary obligations that they owe to the company's shareholders. Even if a legal duty were to be found, the individual defendant could argue that the subsequent acts of the employee, or even the failures of a supervisor, broke the legal chain of causation.

Proof of mens rea could also be problematic. By remaining ignorant of the illegal actions within the organisation, directors could cite their lack of knowledge with respect to crimes defined in terms of intentionality, knowledge or subjective recklessness. Often, moreover, their ignorance is not a matter of choice, but comes about by virtue of the fact that managers are reluctant to bring their own errors, or 'bad news' generally, to the board's attention. Even without a conscious design to withhold such information from the board, reports are often 'sanitised' as they wend their way up an hierarchical path. A CEO may choose not to present disturbing problems to the board, especially if the CEO believes that the conditions giving rise to the problem are temporary and correctible. If the board is to discover misconduct, it may have to go around the CEO and order an independent outside investigation. One might argue that this should be part of a board's oversight responsibilities, but it is hard to fault directors for trusting a CEO whom they may have appointed or in showing faith in the company's highest executive officer.

If directors were to be charged with a crime of objective recklessness, they might be able to point to the fact that similarly situated directors in other companies would have behaved no differently. A comparable argument, it might be recalled, succeeded in the manslaughter prosecutions of the directors of P&O Ferries. Liability based on a theory that the directors had been 'wilfully blind' might not so easily be parried, but the determination of 'wilfulness' often will turn on credibility. It is not difficult to envisage a director testifying that, in concentrating on long-term corporate goals and strategy, s/he may have paid insufficient attention to the minutiae of the day-to-day activities of the company's workforce but did not do so 'wilfully'. In summary, conventional criminal law doctrines do not easily lend themselves to the prosecution of directors.

If not directly liable, might a director or officer be charged as an accessory, either to an offence committed by an employee or one committed by the company? The prosecution would have to show that the defendant had encouraged, incited, aided, abetted, facilitated, counselled, procured or otherwise significantly contributed to the offence. Proving such an actus reus might be less challenging than establishing that the defendant had personally ordered the offence to be committed, but it would still be difficult for the reasons identified above. Establishing mens rea might be more difficult still. In *Gillick v West Norfolk and Wisbech Area Health Authority*,[15] it was held that a doctor who prescribed contraceptive devices to a minor below the age of consent did not become an accessory to the crime of unlawful sexual intercourse with a girl under the age of consent unless the doctor intended to encourage the intercourse. By analogy, corporate directors or officers could claim that their objective in formulating corporate policy was to promote profitability and benefit shareholders, and not to encourage the commission of crimes by the company's employees. Although the Court of Appeal in *National Coal Board v Gamble*[16] held that knowledge that one's acts would assist the commission of an offence constituted prima facie evidence of an intent to assist, this holding would not necessarily rescue the prosecution. The corporate directors would presumably argue that they had no *knowledge* that their policies would cause an employee to commit a crime.

In the United States, under what is known as the 'responsible corporate officer' doctrine, a corporate official who holds a position of 'responsibility and authority' within a company can be held criminally liable for not exercising the 'highest standard of foresight and vigilance' to prevent a crime from occurring in the sphere of the company's operation for which the officer had responsibility.[17] The quoted language of the US Supreme Court indicates the heavy burden that has to be met if the officer is to avoid criminal liability. The officer's defence will fail if s/he was aware of potentially criminogenic conditions and failed to correct them, or if s/he delegated this responsibility to another without checking that the necessary remedial measures were in fact carried out. The 'responsible corporate officer' doctrine removes the need for the prosecution to prove mens rea on the part of the officer, but, by allowing the defendant to escape liability by showing that s/he was 'powerless' to prevent or correct the violation, at least pays lip service to the role of fault. None the less, it sets a difficult target. Perhaps because of the difficulties in meeting the standard's proof requirements, its application has been limited to areas, such as food and drugs, which demand exceptional vigilance because of the direct risks to public health and safety.

In England the Health and Safety Commission has proposed a variant of the 'responsible corporate officer' doctrine, under which companies would be required to appoint a 'health and safety director' (Health and Safety Commission: 2001; the proposal was initially contained in a consultation document, 'Revitalising Health and Safety', issued by the Department of Environment, Transport and the Regions in 1999). Such a proposal would address the stumbling block in cases such as P&O Ferries, where the absence of a designated safety officer allowed the company to escape liability because no person 'identified' with it could be shown to have been

15 [1986] AC 112.
16 [1959] 1 QB 11.
17 *United States v Park* 421 US 658 (1975). See also *United States v Dotterweich* 320 US 277 (1943).

aware of the risks of open-bow sailings. Presumably, a health and safety director would have the responsibility of making him/herself aware of such risks. As this individual would have director status, there would be no question but that s/he was 'identified' with the company. The designated director would be responsible for ensuring that the company's business operation was conducted in a safe, compliant and non-negligent manner. While the required appointment of a health and safety director would serve to highlight the importance that the government attached to issues of health and safety, the post itself could easily prove to be a poisoned chalice. If a board of directors were to decline to heed the director's recommendations or the finance director declined to allocate the requested funding for safety improvements, the director would seemingly none the less be liable for any ensuing violations. Similarly, with respect to the American 'responsible corporate officer' doctrine, unless the board of directors were prepared to underwrite the costs of rectifying dangerous or crime-conducive conditions, the 'responsible corporate officer' could wind up being made the sacrificial lamb for the board's intransigence. Yet to forego prosecuting 'responsible corporate officers' or 'health and safety directors' would be a recipe for encouraging boards of directors not to take their recommendations seriously.

To protect the 'responsible corporate officer' or the health and safety director from unwarranted criminal liability, the courts might fashion a formal legal defence when their recommendations had been rejected by higher authorities within their company. But this alone would not solve the problem of how to induce companies to take safety seriously. Perhaps, where a board of directors has refused to heed the recommendations of a health and safety director, the board should be held 'collectively' liable for any resulting offence, just as if the board had approved a clearly crime-conducive policy. But what of board members who favour a recommendation of a health and safety director but who are outvoted? Should only those who spoke against the recommendation be held liable? If so, the effect might be to inhibit candour at board meetings. Furthermore, good faith differences of opinion are not uncommon on boards, and the mere fact that subsequent events showed that one faction was mistaken in its assessment of a policy's criminogenic potential would not necessarily prove that those who took this position had acted in bad faith or unreasonably. Even unanimous board actions cannot be taken at face value. On occasion, members of a board, like members of a government's Cabinet, may see value in speaking with a single voice. Dissenters may choose to support colleagues in order not to call their judgment into question. If the colleague was, for instance, the company's CEO (or, in the case of the government, the Prime Minister), disagreement could spark a vote of confidence that was not desired by any of the parties. The collective decisions of a group may thus at times be more a function of psychological, social and political dynamics than a reflection of individual states of mind.

Another approach to hold directors accountable would be to extend to them the 'reckless supervision' offence that we examined in relation to supervisory personnel. Like middle-level managers and supervisors, directors have an obligation to make themselves aware of the potentially dangerous and criminogenic aspects of the company's business operation and to take steps to prevent illegality from occurring. However, the directors' obligation in this respect would extend to the entirety of the company's operation, whereas the remit of a supervisor would ordinarily be more limited. Another difference between directors and ordinary supervisors is that directors have a far greater power to effect change; indeed, they possess the ultimate authority for ordering changes in the way that the company's business is conducted. Proof of recklessness, however, may be problematic. Where information is deliberately withheld from directors by executive management, can the directors be faulted for their lack of knowledge? Their fault, if any, would consist of failing to investigate the situation more closely. But, in the absence of warning signals, is there a duty to investigate? Moreover, presuming that recklessness would be defined in objective terms, and that the standard of comparison would be that which a reasonable director would have been aware of in the same or similar circumstances, the prosecution would encounter the 'modern' problem that directors are increasingly chosen for their general business acumen, and not for their knowledge of the industry in which the company is engaged. As other directors with a general business background could be expected to testify that they too would not have been aware of the faults in the system, the prosecution's assertion of recklessness may be stymied. However, the company itself may be found to be (grossly) negligent for not having on its board of directors persons conversant with all of the various aspects of the company's business and the attendant risks.

Although directors are generally much further removed from the daily actions of employees than are supervisors, the directors are in a position to inform themselves of what is going on 'in the field', and thereby put themselves in a position to promulgate policies that would frustrate any incipient illegality that might be discerned. 'Suggestion boxes' would allow workers to communicate to corporate officers and directors on-line risks of which they were aware or about which they were concerned. A corporate compliance department could also be established with responsibility to discover illegality that arose in the company's operation and report it to the board. Receiving and acting on these reports would demonstrate the directors' good faith, while the failure to take these reports seriously or to act upon them would be evidence of wilful blindness.

One final scenario that bears examination is where a company has gone out of business after it has committed a serious offence, but before it can be prosecuted. In such circumstances proceeding against the company's directors and officers might seem to be the only remaining option. Where criminality was to have been imputed to the company because of the crime of an executive officer or director, as it is under an 'identification' test, it would obviously not be inappropriate to proceed with the prosecution of the relevant individual. More troubling are prosecutions based on organisational fault. Now, if the company were to go out of business, there would cease to be a defendant against which the prosecution could be brought. In such cases, the temptation may be to charge its former directors and executive officers in order to ensure that there is some legal accountability. The problem is that the directors and officers may not have been at fault, or in any way involved in the company's crime, and, indeed, may have tried to prevent the crime. The mere fact of holding an executive position in a company that has committed a criminal offence should not, by itself, be an offence. On the other hand, if it can be shown that the directors and officers had made a tactical decision to go out of business in order to frustrate the prosecution, or to evade criminal sanctions, then charging them with an offence along the lines of 'attempting to pervert the course of justice' would not be inappropriate.

2. Sanctions

In the consultation paper in which it proposed an offence of corporate killing (Home Office: 2000), the government invited comments on whether directors and officers who 'contributed' or 'substantially contributed' to a corporate management failure that resulted in a death should be subject to criminal sanction.[18] Presumably, what the government had in mind were actions or inactions that did not rise to the level that would warrant a prosecution for one of the personal homicide offences also proposed in its consultation paper. The 'contributing' offences were thus a way to extend the potential liability of directors. According to the government's proposal, the sanction for 'contributing' to the corporate offence would be disqualification. For 'substantially contributing' to the corporate offence, the government indicated that it was prepared to entertain the prospect of a more serious penal sanction, including imprisonment.

Contributing to a corporate killing addresses one small, albeit clearly important, aspect of a much wider field of possible criminal offences that might be committed by or attributed to a company's directors and officers. Much of the legal liability for corporate misconduct is governed by regulatory laws, and these too contain provisions for the individual liability of corporate executives. Under the Health and Safety at Work Act 1974, s 37, a company's directors, managers, corporate secretaries and other officers can be held liable for an offence committed by the body corporate if the HSE can prove consent, connivance or neglect on the part of the individual charged.

The usual penalty, at least in England and Wales, for an officer convicted under the health and safety laws is a fine. The maximum fine that can be imposed in a magistrates' court (where most cases are brought) is £20,000 for a criminal offence and £5,000 for the breach of a regulation, the same as it is for a company. Even the maximum fine may not be overly burdensome to a well-paid executive or director, but the real problem is that there is nothing that would preclude the company from paying the fine on the convicted defendant's behalf. Even if there were a law prohibiting reimbursement of a fine to a convicted officer, it would be extremely difficult, if not impossible, to enforce. How could the law prevent the company from awarding bonuses or salary increases in future years that were designed to compensate for a past fine (and it goes without saying that such a purpose would never be admitted)? A judicial order suspending a convicted executive's pay for a set period might be a feasible alternative or, even more draconian, disqualification of the convicted director/executive from holding corporate office. Even then, the former employer might, in a parting ceremony, provide the disqualified officer with a 'golden parachute' in acknowledgment of his/ her contributions to the organisation. The 'realpolitik' is that no company is likely to allow a director or officer who took a legal 'hit' on behalf of the company to suffer financially, especially where the offence was committed for the good of the company. If it were to do otherwise, it would find itself in difficulty recruiting future executives, having to build into all of their contracts 'golden parachutes' to assure the recruits that they will not be left unprotected if they were to commit an offence while trying to better the company's position.

---

18 Home Office (2000) *Reforming the Law of Involuntary Manslaughter: The Government's Proposals* paras 3.4.7–3.4.11.

It might be noted that the sentence imposed by a court does not exhaust the range of adverse consequences that may be visited on a convicted director or officer. Self-regulatory organisations governing companies in a particular industry or field (discussed in chapter 10) may restrict the convicted individual's privilege to engage in certain types of activities. Thus, for example, the London Stock Exchange may suspend an offender's right to trade on the Exchange. However, representatives on such bodies may be inclined to be indulgent to offenders who have been convicted of activities in which they themselves have engaged in the past, or which they do not believe should ever have been made criminal in the first place.

A similar problem can arise with respect to internal sanctions by the offender's company. While some would argue that a conviction of a company should logically lead to internal sanctioning of the individual responsible for the offence, a board of directors may not be that enthusiastic about disciplining a respected colleague, especially where they are of the opinion that the individual has suffered sufficiently already by being 'named and shamed' as a result of the criminal prosecution. In the discussion of its recommended offence of 'corporate killing', the Law Commission stated that it was 'confident that no respectable company or organisation would leave in place.... the people responsible for the operation of systems which had been condemned by a jury....'[19], but supplied no reasons for such confidence. The limited, largely anecdotal, evidence would seem to suggest the opposite. Box (1983) discovered that corporate officials who had been convicted of a criminal offence frequently suffered no loss of position or diminution of salary, and in some cases were even promoted. This finding should hardly be surprising when an offence has inured to the company's financial benefit, or when the offence was tolerated or even encouraged by the company's board of directors. On the other hand, where the prosecution of corporate officers has received widespread coverage in the media, the pressure of public opinion may force the company to sever its ties with the convicted executives. An example can be found in Guinness' decision to dismiss its then CEO, Ernest Saunders, after he and various associates, whose links to the company were also severed, were convicted of offences arising from an illegal share-support scheme.

a.   Imprisonment

Under the Accessories and Abettors Act 1861, s 8, an accessory to an indictable offence can receive the same penalty as the principal. The drafters of the 1861 Act, however, had in mind accessories and principals who were both natural persons, and probably never considered the situation of a natural person, such as a director or officer, who was convicted of being an accessory to the offence of a company. Historically, the penalty imposed on a convicted company has been a fine. As we have argued in the preceding chapter, a fine of a company, to be meaningful, would have to be set at a level that, were the same fine to be imposed on an individual, would be oppressive. In such a case, the fine for the accessory would have to be a proportion of the company's fine. Of course, if in England the case were to be tried in a magistrates' court, the £20,000 ceiling on fines would not have much of an impact on either company or director.

---

19 *Criminal Law: Involuntary Manslaughter: A Consultation Paper* (Law Com no 135, 1994) para 5.92.

Often no sanction other than a fine will be mentioned in the statute that creates corporate liability. Presumably, the reason has to do with Parliament's understandable inability to conceive of putting a company in jail. That, however, is not an obstacle in the case of a director or corporate officer. Such individuals can be imprisoned. This raises the question of whether an accessory can be subjected to a mode of punishment that is not authorised for the principal. There would seem to be no reason why not, although precedents are hard to find. The American Law Institute's Model Penal Code solves the problem by providing that an individual should be accountable 'to the same extent as if [his conduct] were performed in his own name or behalf' and 'is subject to the sentence authorised by law when a natural person is convicted of an offence of the grade and the degree involved'.[20] An alternative approach would be to create a specific offence of contributing to a company's crime, with a separate regime of sanctions, including imprisonment, for those directors and corporate officers who were convicted of the offence.

The symbolic value of imprisoning a corporate executive should not be underestimated. The message to other directors and corporate executives, as well as to the public, is that corporate offences are taken seriously by the courts, and that corporate officers are not above the law and will be subject to the same type of punishment which the criminal justice system reserves for serious offenders. Likely media coverage would add to the denunciatory effect of the sentence, and presumably to the embarrassment, shame and guilt experienced by the convicted executive. The processing through the criminal justice system – the pro forma photographing and fingerprinting, the confinement to a holding cell during remand, the fact of having to share that cell with a common criminal – are all likely to prove highly disconcerting to a corporate executive who has never previously come into contact with the criminal justice system other than, perhaps, as the victim of a crime. Even though the court may eventually sentence the executive to a low-security prison (the so-called 'country club' jail), the mere fact of confinement may be humiliating. The executive will have to go through the depersonalising rigours of being processed as an ordinary prisoner, while unruly fellow prisoners and guards, who may be jealous of the offender's wealth and fame, often will add to the executive's state of acute discomfort. The routine and tediousness of prison life may also prove frustrating to one accustomed to the freedom of being able to do whatever s/he wants whenever s/he so wants.

Less clear is what penological functions will be served by imprisoning a convicted corporate executive or director. Such persons may be aggressive in their working style, and may be responsible for causing harm through their policies, but they rarely inflict direct physical injury on others. They are not prone to physical aggression and, left free in the community, they are not likely to pose a danger. Indeed, deprived of their corporate position (as can be achieved through a disqualification order), they will be unlikely again to cause the type of harm that led to their conviction in the first place. Imprisonment is therefore not needed for restraint purposes. As for rehabilitation, it is not clear what type of programme would be suitable for a convicted director or corporate executive. Unlike common criminals who may turn to crime because they are unable otherwise to make a living, and for whom rehabilitation may consist in learning a trade, corporate

20 American Law Institute, Model Penal Code, s 2.07(6).

executives are hardly likely to be in need of education or job training. Their values may have gone astray, but this may have been due to the pressures of their corporate position, or an uncontrolled desire to see their company succeed at any cost. The prosecution, trial and conviction will have already brought home the point that the means that they chose to attain corporate success were not acceptable.

Probably the primary aim of imprisoning a convicted director or corporate executive would be to serve as a deterrent to other corporate directors and executives, who too need to be aware that business crimes are taken seriously by the criminal justice system. If one of their colleagues were to be convicted, but then were to receive a nominal fine, the message would be seriously diluted. However, in theory it should not require an onerous sentence to deter corporate executives from criminal behaviour. Directors have much to lose in terms of status and reputation if convicted of a criminal offence, and also presumably have less to gain, as they will usually already be in possession of a substantial income. Logic therefore suggests that it may not take a lengthy term of imprisonment to achieve the hoped-for deterrent effect. To the contrary, too lengthy a prison term may deter entrepreneurial and innovative strategies whose legality has yet to be tested and is unclear (what some, for example, would contend was an apt description of the share-support scheme for which the Guinness defendants were convicted; see chapter 1). In any event, criminology teaches that the effectiveness of a deterrent sentence may depend less on its length and more on the perceived likelihood of its being imposed. The threat of prison, although in theory capable of exerting a considerable deterrent effect on corporate directors and officers, will not do so if prosecution, conviction and imprisonment are seen as a remote and improbable parlay. Statistically, they are no doubt correct in this perception.

If sentencing courts were seriously to entertain the idea of imprisoning convicted directors and corporate officers, they would need to rethink the types of factors that are relevant to the decision as to whether to send an offender to jail. The two primary considerations that courts have traditionally taken into account are the seriousness of the offence and the character of the offender. Where the company's offence is one of risk creation, with no harm having occurred, and the executive's role consists of not thinking sufficiently critically about the potential dangers inherent in a particular policy, a sentencing judge may not view the aiding and abetting as being particularly serious. Even where harm has occurred, negligent actions of employees may also have contributed to the result, thus diluting the role of the corporate officer. Any harmful consequence will typically be remote from the executive's act or omission. All these factors may serve to diminish the gravity of the executive's crime in the eyes of the judge.

In addition to the nature of the offence, a sentencing judge will normally take into account the character of the defendant. It is exceedingly improbable that a corporate executive will have a criminal record. In mitigation of sentence, on the other hand, the executive will likely be able to point to a distinguished employment record (or else s/he would never have achieved his/her position in the company). Furthermore, the executive is likely to have strong community and family ties and a lengthy track record of public service. Many companies actively encourage their officers to engage in charity work and in projects for the disadvantaged (Useem: 1984), no doubt in part for the perceived public relations value. Because they are in a position to take time from work without significant financial disadvantage, and because the publicity may advance their careers, executives will often seize these opportunities. Whether or not such civic virtue is prompted by a genuine sense of altruism or by a cynical desire to bolster a public image is a question that a court is unlikely to speculate about. The public service will be taken at face value (Doig: 2000: 120). Moreover, as a result of the contacts developed through such activities, local and national dignitaries may come forward to testify to the executive's good character. In making a personal statement to the court, the officer also is likely to make a favourable impression. It should come as no surprise if an executive accustomed to persuading large audiences and high-powered boards of directors were to be able to convince a sentencing judge of his/her contrition and willingness to learn from past mistakes. The judge will no doubt also be impressed by the defendant's articulateness and seeming self-awareness.

The weight that a judge may give to the personal characteristics of a convicted corporate executive may depend more on the judge and his/her philosophy of sentencing than on the defendants or their crimes. In the sentencing of Terry Ramsden, who had pleaded guilty to a fraud amounting to £90m, the sentencing judge praised the defendant for having built up 'an honest, impressive and phenomenally successful business' of which he could justifiably be proud. The judge stated that Ramsden's character stood him in good stead and that, while offences of the sort he had committed would normally warrant a sentence of imprisonment, a suspended sentence in his case would satisfy the demands of justice. In contrast, Henry J imposed lengthy prison sentences on the 'Guinness' defendants (by the then standards for white-collar crimes), defendants who had been comparably successful in their business careers, including two who were the CEOs of their company and another who had been knighted by the Queen. None of the defendants had a previous criminal record and all were actively involved in community projects. These contrasting judicial approaches serve to highlight the disparity in sentences that can follow when different judges have different sentencing philosophies and sentencing guidelines are largely absent. One feature that apparently influenced Henry J was the need to send a clear signal to those in the business community. He spoke caustically of an attack on the integrity of the market and of the need for a deterrent sentence ('the sentence I pass must send a clear message that persons who seek commercial advantage by acting dishonestly can expect little mercy from the courts': *The Times*, 29 August 1990). While these comments do fit comfortably into a deterrence rationale, they also appear to give the media an undue and unwarranted voice in sentencing – the Guinness case had attracted considerable media attention; Terry Ramsden's case had not.

There may be a conscious or subconscious psychological identification between a sentencing judge and a convicted corporate executive to which the judge must try to be sensitive. It would not be surprising if the two shared a similar upbringing, university education at an elite university and a middle or upper-class life style. They may have friends in common or even know each other, at least by reputation. These traits in common are far less likely to be present when a judge is called upon to sentence a defendant from the 'underclass'. How this sense of identification will actually affect a judge's sentencing decision is, of course, difficult to predict. It is possible that the judge, as Henry J in the Guinness case, may be more critical of the offender for having abused a position of trust. The judge in Terry Ramsden's case, on the other hand, seemed more impressed with Ramsden's success in the business world rather than the fact that it may have been achieved through illegal means.

Often, in cases involving more conventional criminals – thieves and burglars, for example – the defence will argue that the fact that the defendant suffered from economic and social deprivation should be a mitigating factor in sentencing. In a case involving a director or corporate executive, the prosecutor might attempt to turn this argument around by asserting that the high social status and privileged position of the corporate executive should be considered as an *aggravating* factor. Whereas the crime of a thief may be prompted by economic necessity, that of a corporate director or officer is more likely to be the product of unbridled ambition or greed, even if the defendant tries to rationalise the offence by seeking to attribute it to a desire to advance shareholders' or the company's best interests. Still, arguments along this line may not influence the sentencing decision as much as the defendant's lack of previous convictions and strong record of community and public service.

b. Disqualification

While one purpose of punishment is to restrain potentially dangerous individuals, imprisonment is not the only means of achieving restraint. The state restrains dangerous drivers by taking away their licence to drive, and it restrains doctors who are guilty of malpractice by removing them from the medical rolls. A comparable approach to corporate directors and officers convicted of a crime may have merit. Their 'dangerousness' arguably is a product of their being in a position to cause harm through the promulgation of criminogenic corporate policies and practices. If removed from that position and disqualified from holding comparable positions in the future, they should in theory cease to pose a danger.

Disqualification can be achieved through an order entered pursuant to the Company Directors Disqualification Act 1986 (CDDA 1986). Although the primary purpose of disqualification would be to prevent convicted directors and officers from being in a position where they could again cause damage and injury, one should not discount the deterrent effect that the threat of such an order might have. Few directors will wish to see their career paths so rudely short-circuited or their reputation tarnished in this manner.

CDDA 1986 subjects to potential disqualification any person who has been convicted of an 'indictable offence' concerned with the 'promotion, formation, management, or liquidation of a company'. While CDDA 1986 is primarily concerned with corporate officers whose fiscal judgment has been called into serious question, there would seem to be no reason why a disqualification order could not be entered against directors and corporate executives who have been convicted of being an accessory to a company's crime. In its consultation paper on corporate killing, the government suggested that disqualification would be an appropriate punishment for officers and executives who had contributed to a management failure that caused a death.[21]

Under CDDA 1986, a disqualification order can extend up to 15 years, and precludes the person subject to it from serving as a company director or being concerned in the promotion, formation or management of a company. However, CDDA 1986's penalty structure was conceived with financial crimes primarily in mind, and the law might be amended to allow for a longer period of disqualification in the case of directors and officers who have contributed to a crime of violence, such as corporate killing. But is disqualification a sufficiently severe sanction, and

---

21 Home Office (2000) *Reforming the Law of Involuntary Manslaughter: the Government's Proposals* paras 3.4.7–3.4.11.

will it be seen as such by the public, in a case involving death? A natural person found guilty of aiding and abetting a homicide would be likely to receive a lengthy prison sentence, possibly even life imprisonment. Might not disqualification be viewed as a slap on the wrist for the director or corporate officer who has contributed to a corporate killing? Will this differential treatment not add fuel to the already existing perception that there is one law for the rich and another for the poor? Add to that the fact that some convicted corporate executives may be approaching retirement age, with the effect that any disqualification order will entail only a few years of lost income and pension benefits, the fact that the company may provide a 'golden parachute' as parting remuneration and the fact that a director's reputation may be relatively secure, and the bottom line is that the disqualification order may have relatively little practical impact on the offender. In any event, the likelihood of a disqualification order may be perceived as extremely remote. A recent HSE report (2001) notes that, although directors who have been found guilty of health and safety violations are subject to disqualification, since passage of CDDA 1986, only eight directors have been disqualified for health and safety offences, and none in 1999/2000, the last year covered by the report.

The effectiveness of a disqualification order as a restraint is also unclear. It is not unheard of, following the entry of a disqualification order against a director, for the director's spouse to be appointed to fill the vacancy on the board. If so, the income of the disqualified director's household may not be affected. The perspectives aired at board meetings may not be affected either, as it would come as no surprise if the views expressed by the spouse were to prove remarkably similar to those of his/her partner. Although disqualification orders would in theory prevent the ex-director from becoming a de facto or 'shadow' director of a company, demonstrating that this has occurred may be less easy. The effectiveness of disqualification orders is further weakened by the fact that the order does not preclude an ex-director from serving as a paid consultant, joining a partnership or working as an ordinary, although no doubt highly-paid, employee. Michael Milken, the United States 'junk-bond' king, who pleaded guilty to a number of financial crimes, was able to subsequently reinvent himself as a 'consultant', and in the United Kingdom several of the Guinness defendants took a similar path in re-establishing themselves in the world of business after serving their sentence. Often the notoriety of a conviction, coupled with a professed contrition and new insights on corporate ethics, have allowed convicted corporate executives to become highly sought (and highly paid) after-dinner speakers. Thus the practical effect of a disqualification order on a director may not be as far-reaching as, say, the practical effect on a doctor who has been struck from the medical rolls or a lawyer who has been disbarred. Both the doctor and the lawyer will be unable to practice the one profession for which they have been trained and will suffer financially. Disqualified directors and corporate officers may find many other ways of putting their experience and expertise to profitable use.

When a corporate officer has been convicted over time for a series of criminal offences, even if none are particularly serious (or at least, not as serious as manslaughter), disqualification might also be appropriate. The fact that the illegal violations were repeated would suggest that the executive in question either had not learned from the previous convictions or was not prepared to reform his/her behaviour despite the previous convictions. As we suggested in the previous chapter with respect to the sentencing of companies, a penalty points system might be devised, whereby after the accumulation of a certain number of points, a disqualification order would be entered.

Offences would be accorded a point range based on the gravity of the offence and offenders would be accorded points within that range based on their degree of culpability.

c.   Community service

Even conceding that a disqualification order will have a restraining effect, the order will also have the effect of depriving the business world of the contributions that the disqualified ex-director is capable of making. From a utilitarian perspective, it would be more valuable to channel the talents of such individuals into more socially useful directions. The way to achieve this would be by imposing a community service order on the offender. These non-custodial sentences, which have become increasingly common in the case of ordinary defendants convicted of less serious offences, require the offender to engage in socially constructive work assignments.[22] A community service order offers a means for an offender to atone for his/her offence by providing service to the community.

Because many ordinary criminals will have at best a secondary school education, few if any qualifications and no formal skills training, the type of community project to which they can be assigned will be limited. In contrast, corporate executives are likely to be university graduates with the specialist expertise and talent that allowed them to rise to the top of their profession. Over their working lives they will have acquired a variety of skills. They would bring to a community service project not only their aptitude, but also their experience in running a successful business. As a result, the projects to which they can be assigned can be far more ambitious than those reserved for offenders whose background may render them unsuitable for anything other than unskilled manual labour. In one US case, for instance, a convicted corporate officer was ordered to help design a rehabilitation programme for ex-offenders.[23] Not only does this example illustrate the type of sophisticated and challenging undertaking that may be suitable for an ex-director or corporate officer, but it also demonstrates how a community service order might be shaped to aid the socially disadvantaged. In the case of ex-directors and officers where fines of their companies led to unskilled employees being made redundant to allow the fine to be paid off, the community sentence could be targeted to assist the former employees. It might, for example, take the form of tuition in literacy or numeracy skills, where needed, or perhaps the teaching of new job skills.

The range of contributions that corporate executives are able to make to a community opens a potential for abuse that is less likely to be present when a community service order is entered in cases involving more typical offenders. As the executive is likely to be competent to take on many different and challenging projects, a judge might be tempted to assign him/her to a personal favourite. Even if the specific community assignment is made by a government agency, there is still the danger that the government will view the corporate executive as a source of cheap labour, as offenders on community service are not usually entitled to receive financial compensation. If an ex-director were available to head up a complex and ambitious project for free, why would the government want to pay a fair market wage to an

---

22 See Powers of Criminal Courts (Sentencing) Act 2000, ss 46–50.
23 *United States v Mitsubishi Intl Corpn* 677 F 2d 785 (9th Cir 1982).

individual whose qualifications were comparable? Furthermore, the time required to complete such a project might lead to pressures on a sentencing judge to enter a community service order whose length might be proportionate to the time required to complete the project but disproportionate to the seriousness of the executive's offence.

An objection of a different kind is that the public may not view a community service order as sufficiently punitive. The public's perception may be that whereas ordinary criminals are sent to jail or assigned to community projects involving hard manual labour, convicted corporate officers are presented with challenging new opportunities in a comfortable office setting. Although the convicted executive would no doubt suffer a greater loss of income than a blue-collar criminal, the impact may not be as great on his/her family as, in all probability, the executive will have already reaped the financial rewards of a successful business career, and may even have received a generous 'golden parachute' from his/her former company. Furthermore, success in the assigned community service may enhance the executive's reputation, negate any censure or stigma that would otherwise attach to the conviction and lead to future well-paying job offers following the completion of the community service. In short, unlike many ordinary criminals, convicted executives may be able to turn their community service sentence to their long-term advantage. The challenges of the project may even cause the offender to lose sight of the fact that s/he is supposed to be atoning for a criminal offence. Of course, if community service orders were to become standard for all but the most dangerous of offenders, and if more meaningful types of community service were to be made available to all convicted defendants, then the perception that corporate officers were being treated unduly leniently might disappear.

d. Combinative sanctions

The types of sanctions that have been examined for directors and corporate officers convicted of a criminal offence should not be viewed as mutually exclusive. It may well be, on balance, that the most appropriate sentence in a given case consists of a combination of penalties:

*   a monetary penalty sufficient to remove the profit from the crime;
*   the 'short, sharp shock' of a brief term of imprisonment;
*   a term of community service following release from prison; and
*   the entry of a disqualification order for its restraining effect.

Such a combination of sanctions would be designed to cause directors and corporate officers to recognise that their company's success cannot be allowed to take precedence over their obligation to be a law-abiding citizen. The two must be made compatible.

E. CONCLUSIONS: INDIVIDUAL AND ORGANISATION

This chapter has been designed with the aim of redressing in part what some might have seen as an imbalance in the text between corporate criminal liability and individual liability. Its placement after several chapters discussing corporate liability reflects both the relative neglect of the latter topic in traditional scholarship and our belief that concentrating on the criminal liability of individuals may do little to address society's interest in eliminating dangerous and criminogenic corporate practices. Workers are expendable, and even the most highly respected directors can be replaced, even if not so easily. If a company's ethos is such that it is prepared to tolerate illegality that is profitable, the conviction of the company's directors, officers, managers and employees may have little impact on the approach it takes to its business. Offered a sufficiently attractive compensation package, others will be found to replace the convicted directors and officers. Furthermore, if the empirical sociological research is correct which suggests that individuals are subsumed within their working groups, and as a result rapidly conform to organisational norms and values, then the law may be relatively powerless to affect the behaviour of corporate directors and executives. Once having absorbed the prevailing corporate ethos of a criminogenic organisation, they are not likely to become champions of reform. It is the culture and ethos of the organisation that must be reformed, but changing the nameplates of the individuals sitting around the table at a board of directors meeting is unlikely to achieve that end. None the less, one should not generalise too much in this area, as the variations among organisations is almost endless.

If we could sum up in a sentence the point of the present chapter, it is simply that in analysing corporate crimes, the role of the individual should not be ignored. In Western society we continue to hold individuals responsible, both morally and legally, for their choices and for their actions. Where an individual has used the corporate form to perpetrate a criminal offence, the prosecution should be brought against the individual and not the company, especially where the individual has pursued personal ends which have no ancillary benefit for the company, and has deliberately evaded reasonable systems of control put in place by the company to prevent illegality. A company should not be liable simply by virtue of the fact that a person who has committed a crime happened to work for it (unless, of course, it was at fault in employing the individual, in inadequately supervising him/her or in failing to have in place systems that would have averted the offence) any more than an employee, director or corporate officer should be subject to criminal liability simply by virtue of the fact that s/he happened to work for or represent a company that has violated the law. Companies perforce act through individuals, but individuals also act through companies, and the criminal liability of the one should not preclude, or require, a prosecution of the other.

CHAPTER 9

'Policing' companies: Dilemmas of regulation

A.　INTRODUCTION AND HISTORICAL BACKGROUND

If companies break the law, and the available evidence suggests that they do, and in ways that can cause considerable injury, damage and financial loss, then one must consider how they can best be policed. Or is it naïve to think that large companies can be induced to obey the law? Might multinational enterprises already be effectively beyond government control? The answer may depend on modes and styles of regulation, and how companies respond and adapt to external regulation.

Historically, the primary focus of the police has been on solving crimes committed by natural persons. Historically – and institutionally – the police have had little experience in tackling corporate crime. The task of policing companies has been entrusted to regulatory agencies, sometimes aided by the police and sometimes with the support of local authorities. Whether regulatory agencies are up to the challenge is a matter of debate. There are three main views.

Many sceptics see the battle between regulators and corporations as a gross mismatch. A poorly funded agency cannot be expected to rein in powerful corporate monoliths with their financial and political muscle. The cynic would add that this state of affairs is no coincidence but only what is to be expected in a capitalist system. Indeed, many of the cases cited in this book are examples of regulatory failure – for example, BCCI, *Herald of Free Enterprise*, Maxwell and Guinness

(Clarke: 2000) – and the same can be said of the large American corporations that have been exposed for running rough-shod over accounting and reporting rules (Elliot and Scroth: 2002). Idealists, at the other end of the spectrum, would like to think that companies are prepared to 'do good', but offer few reasons for a confidence that seems to be born of wishful thinking. None the less, the idealist's views should not be dismissed too lightly – part of the challenge in controlling corporate crime lies in marshalling those social forces committed to seeing companies become good corporate citizens and in examining how they can bring pressure to bear on companies to obey the law. In between the cynics and the idealists are the realists who believe that, given the proper incentives and disincentives, companies are amenable to obeying the law. After all, most companies would prefer to pursue their quest for profit and prestige without the distraction of a criminal prosecution. On the other hand, devising suitable incentives and disincentives for companies ranging from small one-person firms to large multinationals, and doing business in such diverse areas as manufacturing, transport and financial services, may not be that simple.

One's personal position on this scepticism-realism-idealism spectrum may be a function of ideology or philosophical values; but what needs to be appreciated is that the issue of how best to regulate companies inevitably draws one into the political arena and into debates on corporate power, the philosophy of regulation, the goals to be achieved through regulation, the strategies most likely to achieve these goals, the resources needed to implement these strategies and the nature of the relationship between regulators and regulated in a particular industry. These debates are ongoing and unresolved. Social movements such as consumerism, feminism and environmentalism have managed to place a spotlight on corporate social responsibility and accountability, but translating their agenda into law has proved to be more of an obstacle.

But should the law even attempt to regulate companies? Some free-market economists would maintain that market forces are more than adequate to the task, and that the government should refrain from interfering. In Britain, views such as these have led at various periods to 'regulation' that has consisted of the government's handing over to a trade or professional association the right to set standards for their members and to police themselves. In the Middle Ages, the craft guilds were allowed to establish their own standards of quality, to determine what constituted a substandard product and to exercise the necessary control to prevent anti-competitive practices. In 1540, the Royal College of Physicians was allowed to inspect 'local apothecaries' shops for 'faulty wares' (Abraham: 1995: 38).

Colonisation abroad, and the rapid expansion of foreign trade in the sixteenth and seventeenth centuries, prompted legislation to curb the excesses of non-chartered companies in the South Sea Act 1720 (the so-called 'Bubble Act' enacted in response to the massive speculation – or 'bubble' – and subsequent collapse of the South Sea Company). A reluctant government was being drawn into setting conditions, however rudimentary, for regulating commerce. Then the economic and social changes ushered in by the 'industrial revolution' accelerated the movement to greater government involvement in the regulation of business. Beginning in the early nineteenth century, critical voices were increasingly heard to rail against corporate excesses and the dangers of the factory. Marx, Engels and other social reformers, as well as government reports, set out in graphic detail the appalling conditions in mines, iron mills, railway and canal construction, potteries and textile factories where workers, including women and very young children, laboured long hours in unwholesome, unsanitary and often hazardous working conditions.

The first legislation designed to reform working conditions in factories was the Health and Morals of Apprentices Act 1802. Further Acts passed in 1819, 1825, 1831 and 1833 addressed various aspects of child and female labour, including hours of work, night work, sleeping arrangements and the right to education for the young. The 'Ten Hour Movement' in 1847 led to an Act which limited working hours for women and children under 18 years of age to ten hours per day (Carson: 1980). Still, however, commentators complained that these laws did not go far enough to end abuses and that many people continued to work inordinately long hours in dreadful conditions. It was only at the beginning of the twentieth century that governments began consciously, if perhaps in fits and starts, to inject themselves in a more meaningful way into such areas as health and safety at work, the quality of medicines, pensions and education. The period immediately after the Second Word War, when Attlee's Labour government was in power, was marked by increased government intervention into the workplace. A second wave of intervention occurred in the 1970s.

By the 1980s, however, a reaction against excessive government interference had set in and that decade was characterised by the retreat of government from overt involvement in regulation, not just as rule-maker, but also as referee of last resort. Under the political leadership and neo-liberal economic philosophies of Ronald Reagan in the United States and Margaret Thatcher in the United Kingdom, an era of 'deregulation', designed to stimulate entrepreneurship and competition in business and privatisation in government, was begun. One of the spurs to deregulation was a growing appreciation that government regulation had often not fulfilled its objectives. Indeed, in many instances, regulation was seen as an impediment to successful business performance. From the earliest attempts under the Factory Acts to exact conformity to government-set standards to the modern inspectorate charged with controlling multinational enterprises, the evidence appeared to suggest the futility of attempting to regulate businesses through legislation enforced by regulatory agencies. Initially, the responsibility for inspecting factories fell to justices of the peace, who were plainly reluctant to press for the prosecution, let alone for the conviction, of business leaders whom they regarded as their peers. From the early nineteenth century onwards, both official and unofficial reports lamented the fact that too few inspectors had to cope with too many, too powerful and too antagonistic factory owners, scores of whom were quite content to violate the law, pay the relatively modest fines imposed following a conviction, and get on with their illegal methods of operation (Carson: 1979).

This sombre portrait of early regulation reflects what has proved to be ongoing dilemmas that characterise the attempt to control business and industrial organisations through regulatory agencies or inspectorates. These agencies, it has been claimed with some justification, are all too often not given adequate resources to do their jobs properly. At the same time they find themselves confronted by powerful business interests that are not hesitant to contest both legislation and enforcement. In extreme instances this opposition can take the form of concerted resistance to all proposals, regardless of their reasonableness, emanating from a disfavoured agency (Braithwaite: 1989: 127). Even assuming this resistance is somehow overcome, sanctions following a hard-won court case and conviction are often feeble and disappointing. This realpolitik has, according to some, induced a guarded and cautionary approach to enforcement on the part of regulatory agencies. Other critics are more biting, suggesting that all too often regulators are co-opted by big business and succumb to the blandishments of the companies they are supposed to be controlling. They point to supine and even 'moribund' agencies which almost never issue a warning or citation – Gunningham (1987) provides an illustration of this from the Australian asbestos industry – while Ayres and Braithwaite (1992: 40) refer to regulation by 'raised eyebrows'. The regulation of business, the critics claim, amounts in reality to a form of collusion with business.

B.   REGULATORY AGENCIES

While the judges were wrestling with the question of how to impute the criminal acts and mental states of individuals to companies, Parliament decided to approach the problem of corporate criminality from a different direction by enacting laws that were specifically designed with companies, rather than with natural persons, in mind. The initial laws imposed sanctions on a company for *failing* to perform a legal duty. Issues of corporate actus reus were thus avoided, for the offence was defined in terms of an omission, of not doing something that the company was under a legal obligation to do; and the problem of where to find a company's mind for purposes of mens rea was skirted by the imposition of strict liability. The mere fact that the corporate defendant had failed to satisfy its legal obligation was sufficient, in and of itself, to warrant the imposition of criminal liability.

Although several points of substantive and procedural concurrence suggest that regulatory laws are not that dissimilar from criminal laws, the differences become more pronounced when issues of enforcement are considered. Most criminal offences are investigated by the police; regulatory offences, in contrast, are investigated by an agency or inspectorate. Whether inspectors are as skilled, as well-trained and as searching in their inquiries with regard to criminal culpability and evidence as the police may be questioned (Bergman: 2000). Certainly, they do not have the breadth of experience in investigating serious crimes of violence as do the police.

The nature of corporate crime is such that it usually takes place during the course of a company's pursuit of its legitimate business. As a result, the crime is often first discovered by an *internal* agent of the company. At this point, the question arises of how to proceed and, in particular, whether the police should be informed. Companies are reluctant to report financial offences to the police, even when the company has itself been the victim of the offence. Understandably, a company wants to avoid the unfavourable publicity that can follow from an admission that it has been duped by its own employees or, worse, its officers. No company wishes to raise doubts in the minds of its customers, its business partners and associates, and past and future investors regarding its own competency to control the actions of its staff.

By definition, external agencies will be unable to investigate offences of which they are unaware and they will normally be unaware of offences that are not reported to them. This is a quite different situation from that which occurs with respect to 'street crime', where victims will either report an offence (rape being a notable exception) or visible harm will signify that an offence has occurred. Companies are under a legal duty to report certain types of incidents, primarily those involving death, serious injury or other dangerous occurrence, to the local authority or the HSE (HSE: 1995). On the other hand, to unearth an offence that is not required to be reported and that is committed on corporate premises may require a proactive approach in which the investigator first has to conduct an intensive investigation just to discover whether an offence has been committed. Unlike the police, regulatory agencies may not be able to employ forms of surveillance such as CCTV. Inspectors may also have entered into implicit arrangements with companies whereby they have agreed to provide advance notice to a company before entering on to its premises (perhaps to maintain a viable working relationship). The investigative powers of an agency may be extensive in theory (see, eg, Health and Safety at Work etc Act 1974, s 20), but too often in practice, inspectors are reserved in asserting their authority.

The picture of weak and under-funded agencies is widespread, but not universally accurate – there are some fairly well-resourced regulatory agencies. Of course, to some extent this depends on how one defines being 'well-resourced'. Regulatory agencies are, because of competing demands on the revenue from health, education etc, unlikely ever to be allocated the physical, human and logistical support that they need in order to inspect, test, certify, evaluate and oversee all the companies for which they are given responsibility. The dependence on self-reporting of crimes by companies and the difficulties of gaining access to private premises render regulators highly reliant on the companies they 'police' for co-operation, and regulators are often forced to 'negotiate' access with these companies in order even to begin their inquiries.

It might seem that the solution would be to give agencies greater political independence, more funds, more and better qualified staff, and greater power to intervene when faced with recalcitrant companies. For many reasons this 'wish list' is unlikely to be forthcoming. The competing demands on government funds are not going to disappear. Inevitably, there will be strong lobbying pressures from business interests, as well as from champions of the 'free market', opposed to greater intervention by the government in the affairs of the market-place. And the public may only lend their support to government regulatory initiatives after a tragic 'accident' causes multiple deaths or the media manages to incite a 'moral panic'. Radical critics would argue the roots of the difficulties lie deeper, in the nature of a capitalist society where regulation is made subordinate to the primacy of commerce and industry (Slapper and Tombs: 1999; Pearce and Tombs: 2000). While governments tend to intervene robustly when markets are threatened by business deviance – because the fundamental workings of the economy represent both powerful institutional interests and can affect their own future political prospects – they are noticeably more reticent when it comes to deaths and injuries in the workplace (Snider: 1991). But critics who assume that the government is capable of galvanising regulatory agencies into vigorous enforcement may be taking insufficient account of the long-entrenched culture of these agencies. The overwhelming evidence is that the predominant style of most regulatory agencies is co-operative rather than adversarial; and Rock argues that this mode of regulation has become so pervasive that it 'deserves to be taken as the major pattern or archetype of formal social control in western society' (quoted in Hutter: 1997: 242).

1.   Public, private and self-appointed regulators: an overview

In general, when researchers refer to regulatory agencies they mean the public 'inspectorates' which enforce standards and licensing in companies, primarily through audits and inspections. Probably the best known of these inspectorates is the Health and Safety Executive (HSE), and we shall examine this agency in more detail in a subsequent section. However, looking more broadly, one can see a whole range of firms, organisations and institutions that perform some type of regulatory function in business and industry. These agencies may be formal or informal, public or private (or some mix), and international, regional, national or local in their field of operation.

The source of many domestic regulations can be traced to decisions of international bodies. In the field of banking, for example, the central banks of the industrialised nations have promulgated accords, such as the Basel I Concordat of 1988 and Basel II, currently under consideration, that can then be formally incorporated into national legislation in order to be made binding on banks and other financial institutions in a state. United Nations treaties and conventions similarly require ratification by individual states to become operative. On a regional level, the European Union will adopt Directives, and has done so in regard to such topics as fraud, money laundering and insider dealing, that have no direct effect but which rather require member states to take the necessary measures to bring the state into compliance with the Directive. Different countries are left to decide for themselves how they will implement the Directive in the context of their national legal system (Savona: 1999).

On a national level, one can find numerous government departments assigned the task of overseeing, regulating, licensing and auditing companies engaged in trade and industry. Among the foremost examples in Britain are the Department of Trade and Industry, the Office of Fair Trading, Customs and Excise and the Inland Revenue. These agencies may also be assigned a policing function, and be able to mount investigations by their specialist units into serious crimes that relate to their mandate. Some will also be able to bring their own criminal prosecutions, although others may have to refer cases to the Crown Prosecution Service (CPS). Specialist agencies, such as the Serious Fraud Office (SFO), may be accorded powers not available to other law-enforcement agencies (see, for example, the Criminal Justice Act 1987 for the specialist powers of the SFO). Finally, some agencies may be able to resolve cases in innovative ways not generally available to Crown prosecutors; so, for instance, the Inland Revenue can engage in bargaining (the technical term is 'compounding') to recover unpaid taxes in exchange for not pursuing a prosecution.

Government agencies often have a fairly narrow remit. The general responsibility for investigating criminal offences, including most serious crimes of violence, belongs to the police. In the corporate context, a 'Protocol of Liaison on Work-Related Deaths' between the HSE and the police has been in force since 1998 which envisages a joint initial investigation when there has been a work-related death in order to determine whether a manslaughter charge might be warranted. In addition, if, during the course of an HSE investigation, evidence of manslaughter comes to light, then again under the terms of the Protocol the case is supposed to be referred to the police. However, the responsibility for referral falls to the HSE inspector, who may not have a clear conception of the difference between a case of manslaughter and an unfortunate workplace 'accident'. In its consultation paper on corporate killing, the government would further undermine the Protocol by its recommendation that the HSE be primarily responsible for investigating instances of corporate killings.[1] Apart from cases of workplace deaths, the police may assist regulatory agencies by co-ordinating raids on corporate premises for evidence and by making formal arrests of suspects charged with commercial crimes. Almost all police forces in Britain have now established their own 'fraud squads', with responsibility for investigating serious cases involving fraud, but there remain considerable differences between them in capacity, task-definition and implementation of policies (Doig, Johnson and Levi: 2000: 13).

In some fields one finds a long tradition of self-regulation. Professional bodies, such as the Law Society, the Bar Council, the British Medical Association and the British Association of Registered Accountants, have historically regulated the profession, deciding whom to admit to practice, what rules govern practitioners and what sanctions should be imposed for violations of these rules. While professional associations may be created with the dual function of controlling access to the profession and enforcing professional discipline in mind, they often will, because of their professional status, subsequently be able to take on the responsibility for lobbying on behalf of the profession (for example, the British Medical Association on behalf of doctors).

Self-regulatory organisations (SROs) are not limited to the professions. For many years the financial services industry was allowed to engage in self-regulation (although more recently this responsibility has been shifted to the Financial Services Authority (FSA), a powerful umbrella regulatory agency). In some fields, SROs have been imposed by statute, while in others they have been created by the companies in a particular industry. Industry associations will typically issue codes of conduct, and endeavour to pressurise deviant members to comply with these codes, but at the same time they will also be active in promoting their industry (particularly when it has been under sustained scrutiny). Examples include the British Council of Mortgage Lenders, the Building Societies Association and the Association of British Travel Agents.

Finally, there are a significant number of private companies and organisations which can perform a valuable monitoring function. Investigative journalism by the press often can lead to the discovery and publicising of corporate wrongdoing. The Sunday Times Insight Team, for example, was responsible for exposing the Thalidomide scandal, in which an inadequately tested sedative drug prescribed to pregnant women was shown to cause deformities in their embryos. Public interest groups and non-governmental organisations (NGOs), such as Transparency International, Amnesty International and Greenpeace, are examples of a new breed of self-appointed watchdog organisation. Many of the NGOs have chosen to concentrate on exposing the corrupt and criminal practices of multinational enterprises which through their subsidiaries commit human rights violations and criminal offences in developing countries. Their lack of a statutory mandate is an advantage, as their remit is self-determined and unrestricted. Thus they may be able to investigate transnational crimes that would be beyond the jurisdiction of the police. NGOs are also unfettered by legislatively imposed regulations and constraints. While they and the media may lack formal sanctioning powers, their

---

1   Home Office (2000) *Reforming the Law of Involuntary Manslaughter: The Government's Proposals* paras 3.3.1–3.3.5.

informal power, including their ability to galvanise public support in favour of a boycott of an 'offender's' products, may allow them to exert considerable influence (Schwartz and Gibb: 1999).

The point is that, in relation to standard setting, performance monitoring and evaluation and the policing and control of companies, one should think expansively and look beyond the conventional government inspectorate. There is an increasing range of organisations and institutions – public, private, public-private partnerships and NGOs – that function both formally and informally, and at different levels, to cajole, steer or pressurise companies into compliance with the law and the demands of good practice. In subsequent sections we will look more closely at two of the major public agencies. First, we will examine the HSE, which may be considered to be the prototypical and conventional model of a government inspectorate; but it is of especial interest because of its role in investigating and prosecuting industrial injuries and deaths (perhaps the most unappreciated examples of corporate crimes). Second, we will look at the SFO, which at the time of its formation represented a new breed of specialist, interdisciplinary agency established to tackle a specific problem, in its case that of serious fraud. Before looking at the functioning of these two agencies, however, we first propose to examine the role of government in setting strategy and parameters, as well as in allocating powers and resources, for regulation.

2.   The role of the government

Governments have the primary responsibility for initiating the *public* control of business and industry and do so through legislation, regulatory agencies, public inquiries, where appropriate, and, often as a last resort, criminal prosecutions. From the earliest days of regulation it has been clear that the government has had to balance diverse and competing interests. In the nineteenth century, the balance tilted in favour of businesses, as the government had no desire to put a brake on the industrial revolution or to damage the burgeoning economy. Even legislation with humanitarian overtones often could be seen to have mixed motives: laws on child labour ostensibly designed to protect the welfare of children also benefited business by producing a more healthy, literate and disciplined workforce (Carson: 1979).

It is not unusual for a government to experience a conflict of interest when dealing with the control of questionable business practices. For instance, while, on the one hand, the government may genuinely desire to improve working conditions and the health and safety of workers, on the other, it may be dependent on corporate taxes to be able to fund the social programmes that it has in mind. A concrete example is provided by Carson (1982), whose research on the North Sea oil and gas industry demonstrated how production pressures led to a neglect of safety (with a high level of avoidable deaths and injuries compared with other high-risk industries). In this instance it was not only industry-induced pressure, but also the government's own desire to exploit a new and profitable fuel industry for its own economic and political benefit, which fostered a culture that was unduly tolerant of regulatory violations. One significant element in the government's willingness to bend to the industry's lobbying efforts was its decision to allocate responsibility for monitoring the off-shore oil and gas industry to the Department of Energy, which was thought to be less aggressive in enforcing safety standards than the HSE. Likewise, the Department of

Health can often find itself on both sides of the public-private divide, being both a prime sponsor of medical and drugs-related research *and* the regulator of the pharmaceutical industry (Abraham: 1995: 246).

Against this background, the establishment and funding of regulatory agencies can be seen as the product of an extended and contested bargaining process involving government, big business and representatives of the public interest (Snider: 1991). The nature of regulation – its philosophy, mandate and implementation – is responsive to political and ideological winds that alter the tone and thrust of the debate. Shifts in government priorities and policies are not uncommon. The most recent major shift occurred with the 'deregulation' movement which was ushered in during the 1980s. Where an industry has been deregulated, there often will follow a concomitant reduction in the budget of the regulatory agency that is responsible for overseeing the industry. In the health and safety field, however, a reduced budget may translate into fewer inspections and less intense investigations. In other areas, computerisation may be a compensating factor, allowing the agency to be able to retain (or even improve upon) its former efficiency. But there can be no doubt that agencies have been subjected to downsizing in both the United States and Britain.[2] Slapper and Tombs (1999) sum up the situation generally:

> [I]n the last two decades there has been a general, but by no means universal, push towards deregulation or (ever) more conciliatory regulatory strategies, towards the (selective) limiting of state control, and towards the freeing of business from the meddlesome interventions of bureaucrats (that is, inspectors). As Snider has put it, during this period 'nation after nation has unmade corporate crime by repealing regulatory statutes, firing staff, dismantling monitoring and data gathering machinery' (1997: 6); and it is important to emphasise that these trends have been particularly marked in Britain, which is a state with a long (perhaps the longest) history of highly conciliatory regulatory approaches across a whole range of areas of regulatory enforcement (Slapper and Tombs: 1999: 178).

The tug-of-war between representatives of the public interest and capitalist forces is ongoing and played out on many levels. Politicians are understandably reluctant to risk the wrath of the electorate whose support they need to remain in office. Particularly when an election looms, the government will respond, or at least try to give the appearance of responding, to matters of strong public concern. It is at times like this that one hears talk of the 're-regulation' of once national industries (transport and public utilities in particular). Highly-publicised disasters can fuel the public's disillusionment with privatisation, and lead to a cynical view of companies that are characterised as putting profit ahead of safety. Protest demonstrations may be staged which the government finds difficult to ignore. For example, after improprieties in the retail financial services industry, relating primarily to pensions and mortgages, were exposed, the government was forced to 're-regulate' the industry (Clarke: 2000). At the same time, however, the government remains sensitive to the risks involved in tightening regulatory controls. If large numbers of companies, and, in particular, multinational enterprises, alienated by what they perceived to be an anti-business animus on the part of the government, were to relocate to countries which were deemed

---

2   Under Margaret Thatcher's government there was a deregulation unit within the Cabinet Office, whose logo was a scissors cutting through red tape (Clarke: 2000: 29).

to offer a more corporate-friendly environment, then the damage to the state's economy from lost corporate taxes and increased unemployment could be crippling.

But are corporate threats to relocate to be taken at face value or are they really just part of an elaborate charade in which companies threaten and the government pretends to take seriously their threats, when all concerned know that few companies would seriously contemplate shifting their headquarters to France, Germany or Thailand? Most pharmaceutical companies, for example, are located in the south-east of England because of the economic infrastructure, the proximity of major airports and easy access to the City of London. Robinson (2001: 183) quotes a representative of the industry who observes that, because of these considerations, pharmaceutical companies are not very likely to shift the base of their operations, and especially not to a non-English-speaking country. However, whether the government can afford to call what may be an elaborate bluff on the part of the industry is another matter. When clinical trials of new medicines became subject to more stringent testing requirements in the United Kingdom, some British companies did indeed transfer the departments responsible for product testing to foreign countries (Abraham: 1995: 74). In the United States, one can cite numerous examples of companies that relocated from northern to southern states to escape the tighter regulation and tougher unions of the northern states (Miles: 1987).

C. COMPLIANCE AND DETERRENCE STRATEGIES

A number of themes appear over and over again in discussions of regulatory agencies: agencies tend to be small and under-resourced, both absolutely and relative to the industries they are charged with regulating; inspectors are dependent on the firms in the industry for co-operation and access to their premises and information; the powers of an inspectorate to intervene at a company's place of business may be circumscribed; a tradition of pre-announced inspections hinders the discovery of deviant practices; violations can often be disguised or suspended for the duration of a site visit, only to be resumed when the visit is completed; and regulatory agencies display a marked reluctance to initiate prosecutions, perhaps because of the perceived superior financial and legal resources of their corporate opponents. Even if a prosecution is undertaken and proves successful, an agency may be disappointed in the relatively weak sanctions that are imposed following a conviction (see generally chapter 7), a sentencing pattern criticised by the Court of Appeal in *R v F Howe & Son (Engineers) Ltd*.[3] On the other side of the ledger, powerful industries are able to mount sophisticated lobbying campaigns and are thereby able to play a major role in preventing, delaying or shaping regulatory and criminal legislation (Shover: 1980). A company may also be able indirectly to influence agency policies by pressurising a member of Parliament who may, in turn, be in a position to pressurise the agency.

The confluence of these factors has led to a relationship between regulators and regulated that has sometimes been described in terms of co-optation and even 'capture' (Bernstein: 1955; cf Pontell and Calavita: 1993: 228 on 'capture' of the Federal Home Loan Bank Board in respect of the Savings and Loan scandal). One feature of this relationship is the 'revolving-door' of personnel moving between an industry and the

---

3   [1999] 2 All ER 249.

governmental agency responsible for regulating the industry or, indeed, the government itself. Regulators may have been trained by the industry, and corporate executives may have begun their careers working for a regulatory agency before joining the board of a company which the executive was formerly responsible for regulating. Following retirement, many former regulators have become consultants to the industry. Conversely, corporate executives in an industry may be appointed to sit on relevant regulatory commissions or may decide to enter politics or run for Parliament. Abraham (1995: 72) describes the situation in the pharmaceutical industry:

> [A]ll the major elements of the regulatory organizations concerned with drug safety and efficacy have exhibited a close relationship with the pharmaceutical industry via direct representation, consultancies or prior and/or subsequent employment.

All this may seem to paint a rather gloomy picture, making of regulation at best a ritual or at worst a sham. However, some would maintain that institutionally weak agencies are not necessarily a bad thing. Supporters of this position would argue that for an agency to take an adversarial and aggressive stance can be time-consuming, expensive and counter-productive, and that more can be achieved through education, negotiation and conciliation based on persuasive bargaining (with the implicit or perhaps explicit threat of prosecution to follow if an agreement is not reached). Clarke (1990: 224) asserts that a great deal of prevention already takes place within business without the need for prosecutions and supports his assertion with a body of evidence that suggests that external control agencies are able to achieve more through non-confrontational techniques than through aggressive confrontation. The culture and relationship of agencies with companies in the industry, and not necessarily limited resources, are, according to Clarke, what incline regulators to turn to 'compliance' strategies as the means of fulfilling the agency's mandate. Agencies that adopt a compliance strategy tend to be reactive, to focus on incentives, to utilise persuasive techniques and to promote self-regulation in companies. Deterrence-oriented regulators, in contrast, are more likely to be proactive, to believe in coercive techniques and the imposition of penalties, and to take an adversarial approach to enforcement.

The choice between compliance and deterrence may be reflective of philosophical and ideological differences (Reiss: 1983, 1984; Hawkins: 1984). Both deterrence and compliance aim to induce conformity to the law, but go about achieving this end in different ways. While deterrence seeks to make an example of an offender to dissuade the offender and other would-be offenders from committing crimes in the future, compliance seeks to work with individual offenders and, in the case of a company, to persuade it to change its behaviour. Deterrence strategies assume that the decision to commit a criminal offence is a matter of rational and conscious choice; compliance strategies are prepared to accept that many infractions are unintended or the product of ignorance. Proponents of compliance strategies argue that in such circumstances what is needed is to educate the offender and show it ways of reforming its business operation to allow it to avoid future violations.

The theoretical merits of the debate aside, surveys in a number of societies have shown compliance strategies to be statistically the most common approach taken to enforcement by regulatory agencies. But are compliance strategies chosen because regulators genuinely deem them to offer the best hope for obtaining adherence to the law? Or are they chosen as a pragmatic adaptation to the problems created by inadequate staffing and funding? Stated in a different way, is 'compliance' a rational response to corporate crime or a rationalisation for an inability to pursue criminal prosecutions?

The premise behind compliance strategies is that it is more important that a company redress dangerous and criminogenic conditions than it is that the company be punished for past offences. In line with this priority, a regulatory agency, rather than threatening a criminal prosecution, typically will seek a settlement with the offender. It may offer not to prosecute in exchange for the company's commitment to address deficiencies in its operation (Hutter: 1988). The processes of a compliance strategy entail dialogue between regulators and regulated, a dialogue that both sides may find to their advantage. Businesses benefit, not only because they may be able to deflect a potential prosecution, but also because, looking to the longer term, they gain the opportunity to provide direct input into the development of government standards. For their part, regulators see compliance strategies as an efficient and cost-effective way to induce companies to correct criminogenic conditions and practices. Sometimes a regulator may even be able to persuade a company voluntarily to make changes to its operating procedures that have yet to be legally mandated, but which the regulator believes will reduce, for example, workplace injuries and deaths or will improve the safety of products and medicines (Abraham: 1995: 35).

Although compliance-oriented regulation may appeal to both regulators and regulated, it is less clear that it is in the interest of either victims or the general public. The public may never learn of corporate transgressions, as they would if there had been a public trial, and may continue to give their custom to companies whose products they might have boycotted had they been aware of the company's unlawful practices. Similarly, other companies need not fear any secondary damage to their reputation by continuing to do business with the offender. Victims and their families will be deprived of the accountability and explanations that they may have been seeking and which could have emerged in a criminal trial. In jurisdictions where criminal courts are empowered to make compensatory awards, victims will lose this avenue for obtaining damages. In jurisdictions where criminal courts cannot order compensation, victims will lose the benefit of being able to introduce the criminal judgment into evidence in a subsequent civil suit, and will not receive the cathartic vindication that can come from a conviction.

If a compliance strategy is adopted because a regulatory agency envisages that it offers the best opportunity for inducing reform, one may question the agency's judgment, but not its good faith. More worrying is when questionable motivations lie behind compliance strategies. Regulators and regulated are involved in a symbiotic relationship where both sides may prefer a 'comfortable' and non-antagonistic working relationship to one that is adversarial and combative. A more insidious danger is that a regulator's integrity may be compromised by the prospect of future employment within the industry. It is not unknown for retired regulators to go to work for companies which they were previously responsible for overseeing,[4] or for talented young regulators to be lured to the world of business by higher salaries. Whether such a prospect might affect the zeal that a regulator brings to an inspection or investigation is difficult to gauge, for any such effect is likely to be experienced on a subconscious rather than on a conscious level. It

---

4   The desire of companies to employ such persons is understandable given their experience, expertise and general insight into the regulatory mind-set.

is also not clear what effect the hospitality typically extended to regulators prior to the commencement of a site visit may have on a regulator's mind-set (in some instances they have been invited to confer with corporate officials in resort locations, with all expenses paid by the company). Finally, there is the self-image of regulators to take into account. Carson (1970) suggests that regulators prefer to see themselves as 'expert advisers' rather than as industrial police officers. They define their role in terms of bringing problematic areas of a company's operation to its attention and advising how to remedy the problems that have been identified. Seen in this context, having to initiate a prosecution may be viewed as tantamount to an admission of failure.

Compliance strategies work best when regulators have something to offer companies on ways to address the dangerous and crime-conducive aspects of their business, and where companies are prepared to listen (or regulators have the clout to force them to listen). However, where compliance strategies are perceived as a sign of weakness, they can be counter-productive. If companies believe that they need have no fear of legal repercussions following from their deviancy, a compliance approach to regulation can foster a crime-conducive environment. At best, a compliance strategy may elicit a surface conformity designed to deflect regulators, but with very little real change underneath (Braithwaite: 1993). Companies trade on the weaknesses of regulatory agencies to perpetuate criminogenic cultures and persist in their illegal ways. Part of the challenge is to disentangle legitimate arguments in favour of compliance strategies from those which are little more than self-serving rationalisations. If an agency has inadequate resources to do anything other than adopt a compliance strategy, its options are to lobby, probably unsuccessfully, for more funds or to invent arguments to justify its approach. As observed previously, arguments to the effect that an aggressive enforcement policy will cause companies to relocate in more corporate-friendly countries may in reality be little more than a bluff, but one that an under-funded agency may be all too ready to believe to legitimise its compliance orientation.

A final but important point to make before leaving this discussion is that compliance and deterrence are not incompatible, and that a strategy based primarily on one need not preclude the other. The idea that a regulatory agency has to choose between compliance and deterrence is a false dichotomy. An agency may adopt one or the other strategy according to the circumstances – a compliance approach with co-operative firms and a more hard-line approach in regard to chronic offenders. Or it may have an integrated strategy that incorporates both approaches. Fisse and Braithwaite (1993) offer a 'pyramid' model of enforcement, which starts with gentle prodding and warnings at the base and escalates to criminal prosecution at the top. They argue that companies and corporate officials are acutely sensitive to the consequences of being branded a 'criminal' and the concomitant stigma for themselves and their firms; but that the option of prosecution should not be too quickly invoked or it will lose its in terrorem effect. Often, in fact, prosecutions will only be brought when an agency can discern a persistent pattern of resistance and recalcitrance. Hawkins (1984: 205), speaking of environmental offences, avers that criminal prosecutions have less to do with the pollution offences themselves and more to do with 'deliberate or negligent law breaking that symbolically assaults the legitimacy of regulatory authority'. We shall return to these themes, particularly with respect to what is appropriate in fostering compliance and to the important ideas of Braithwaite and his colleagues in respect of self-regulation, in the final chapter.

Clearly, this is a complex area and the quality and nature of regulation depends on many variables – the political will of governments, the resources and powers of agencies, the appropriateness of the rules governing a regulated industry, the credibility of the agency in the eyes of the industry (is the agency seen to be prepared to move forcefully against violators?), the operational style adopted by the agency and even the working personalities of individual inspectors. What emerges is an intricate matrix of variables that can influence the nature of the interaction both at agency level and also at the face-to-face level of inspectors entering premises to enforce rules and regulations. But what is patently clear is that in practice most agencies adopt a strategy based on inducing compliance through persuasion. This strategy may be a product of institutional weakness, but it may also be based on a conviction that 'bargain and bluff', as Hawkins (1984) puts it, is the most effective style for eliciting compliance. Behind this conviction lies an assumption that management is genuinely concerned with compliance, a view that finds some support among researchers (for example, Ayres and Braithwaite: 1992). Theory reinforces practice, and more so when compliance can be shown to 'work', which is more likely to be the case when a lack of co-operation or repeated recalcitrance is treated quite harshly (Clarke: 2000).

One important factor to be taken into account, and especially in relation to the discussion in the sections to follow, is how the number and type of companies to be regulated can have an influence on an agency's effectiveness. A 'general' agency with relatively complex rules, which have to be applied across a very wide range of firms and industries (such as in health and safety), has a more arduous task facing it than an agency with a more tightly defined mandate, responsible for a smaller number of firms within one industry and with specific industry-related rules (as in pharmaceuticals). There is evidence, for instance, that having to regulate many firms, with a low frequency of interaction, leads to a more strained relationship than develops when inspectors are able to spend more time with fewer firms, enforcing rules that are generally perceived to be legitimate (Ayres and Braithwaite: 1992; Hutter: 1988; Clarke: 2000). The predicament of the former is often found in conventional 'inspectorates' and we shall now turn to examining these with specific reference to the HSE.

D.   INSPECTORATES AND SPECIAL INVESTIGATORY AGENCIES

Having examined the theoretical dimensions of compliance and deterrent strategies, it behoves us to look at how these strategies are implemented in practice. We will examine a conventional inspectorate, the Health and Safety Executive (HSE), and one of the new breed of specialist, interdisciplinary agencies, the Serious Fraud Office (SFO).

I.   A conventional inspectorate: the Health and Safety Executive

In selecting the HSE for attention we are mindful of three points in particular. First, the HSE represents a classical, conventional inspectorate beset by most of the familiar and well-chronicled dilemmas of regulatory agencies. Second, the HSE plays a central role in cases of corporate violence, and, under the government's proposals, would be the primary investigator in cases of corporate killing. Third, the costs of regulatory failure are enormous; according to the HSE itself (2001), the total economic cost to Britain in failing to manage health and safety can be as much as £18bn a year.

The pioneering work of Carson (1970) established, and subsequent studies have confirmed (for example, Mokhiber: 1988; Slapper and Tombs: 1999), that the workplace can be quite dangerous, and that many of the injuries that occur in the workplace are attributable not to worker carelessness, as was long maintained, but to corporate and managerial fault. Research on deaths at work in the United Kingdom has been carried out in particular by Bergman (1991; 1994) and by the Centre for Corporate Accountability (CCA, which was founded by Bergman and is located in London). Various public interest groups, such as Disaster Action, have also concerned themselves with issues of health and safety at work, particularly as they relate to serious injuries and deaths.

The argument, put persuasively by Bergman (2000), is that the way that deaths and injuries at work are treated reveals structural weaknesses in the investigation of work-related crimes and a confusion concerning the roles of the police and the HSE. With respect to the investigation of workplace injuries, the police tend rarely to become involved and then only if there is a strong reason to believe that a crime has been committed (for example, when a worker has fallen from a height as a result of having been pushed by a co-worker). Otherwise, the attitude of the police seems to be that they do not possess the technical knowledge necessary to understand the context of workplace injuries and that such cases are more properly investigated by the HSE. For its part, the HSE may be too short-handed to conduct anything more than a perfunctory investigation unless the case is seen as sufficiently serious that prosecution is the only proportionate response. Generally, however, in line with the self-image of HSE inspectors as expert advisers, they are inclined to adopt a compliance strategy in dealing with the putative offender, offering information, advice and guidance as needed to secure future compliance with the law. Historically, neither the HSE nor the police have paid much attention to the potential criminal liability of senior management or directors. At a coroner's inquest, the lack of investigatory zeal by the police and the HSE can manifest itself in a somewhat perfunctory hearing, a lack of thrust in questioning witnesses and company representatives, and a hasty verdict of 'accidental death'. Local authorities may also be reluctant to probe health and safety violations so as not to expose their own role in their commission. The net result of this web of factors is that criminal prosecutions are rarely brought in cases of workplace 'assaults'. Crime in the workplace is thus effectively *decriminalised* (Bergman: 2000).

Among its enforcement powers, the HSE may issue cautions and improvement and prohibition notices, and initiate prosecutions. Despite its avowed policy that 'when inspectors find serious breaches, prosecution is often the only proportionate response' (HSE: 2001), of the workplace deaths recorded in 1988/99, only about a third led to a criminal prosecution (Unison and the Centre for Corporate Accountability: 2002). The number of prosecutions in cases of serious injuries was only 11%. Furthermore, although there is a great deal of evidence – including material from HSE reports – that management decisions often play an important role in occupational fatalities, it is even more rare to find a prosecution being brought against a director or corporate executive. Yet the HSE itself recognises that '[s]uccessful prosecution, coupled with penalties that properly reflect the gravity of health and safety offences, is an important lever in helping to achieve the Government's and the Health and Safety Commission's targets for reducing the toll of work-related injury and ill health....' (HSE: 2001).

The paucity of criminal prosecutions for health and safety violations is somewhat surprising for the relevant legislation is drafted in a way that should facilitate prosecutions. The Health and Safety at Work etc Act 1974 imposes on employers a duty to 'ensure' 'so far as is reasonably practicable' the health and safety of both employees and other persons who may be affected by their business operation. This duty, as it has been interpreted by the courts, imposes an *absolute* prohibition.[5] The company's obligation is to 'ensure' safety, with only a narrow statutory defence ('so far as is reasonably practicable') being available to the corporate defendant. The burden is on the company to establish this defence (Health and Safety at Work etc Act 1974, s 40). The HSE, furthermore, is under obligation to prove that any individual has acted intentionally or with mens rea. Nor is it necessary to attribute any particular state of mind to the company. The low rate of prosecutions is even more surprising given that HSE statistics (2001) claim to have achieved a success rate of over 80% in its prosecutions in 1999/2000.

Why, then, is the HSE seemingly so reluctant to take corporate violators to court? Like many regulatory agencies, the HSE claims not to have the resources to prosecute all violations (although its claim may have more validity to it than most). The agency is aware that companies are not likely to concede liability readily. If a company is accused of a health or safety offence, its quasi-instinctive reaction, like that of most individuals, will be to deny culpability. Once having done so, the company may become committed to contesting the charges, and the financial resources of the company may allow it to withstand what could prove to be a lengthy and expensive legal battle. If the case proceeds to trial, the company can be expected to secure impressive expert witnesses, sometimes drawn from across the world, and employ skilled counsel, who will not be constrained by resources from devoting whatever time it takes to prepare the company's defence thoroughly.

Delaying tactics are a not uncommon strategy for companies charged with crimes, for a wealthy company may be in a better position to wage a war of attrition than an agency, and has more to gain by doing so. If it refuses to consider a civil settlement with victims until after all criminal charges are resolved, then the civil claimants may in turn press the government to drop the charges or accept a plea to a lesser charge so that they can obtain compensation. Such pressures from the parents of children who were born deformed as a result of their mothers having taken the drug Thalidomide during pregnancy, proved instrumental in the settlement of outstanding criminal charges against Chemie Grunenthal in Germany (recounted by the Sunday Times Insight Team in Knightley et al: 1980); and likewise in the decisions to drop criminal charges against Union Carbide in India with respect to Bhopal (Shrivastava: 1987). Delaying tactics may work in a company's favour for a different reason. Agency staff who are committed to a prosecution may retire or be replaced by less zealous personnel, and key witnesses may die or leave the jurisdiction. Government priorities have also been known to change, especially before an election (where the political parties are keen to attract corporate donations to their election campaign) and afterwards, if a new government takes office.

5   *R v British Steel Plc* [1995] ICR 586.

It may be that it is in part the weak prospects for a successful prosecution that have led the HSE to prefer education, negotiation, persuasion and cautionary warnings to criminal prosecutions. The trend away from enforcement and prosecution to persuasion and co-operation seems to have accelerated in recent years; following an HSE policy statement of 1995, inspections fell by 41% over a five-year period (HSE: 2002: 3). Prosecutions, as we have noted, can lead to protracted litigation which works against the HSE's interest in having dangerous workplace conditions rectified as soon as possible. Lawyers representing a company that has been formally charged may advise that any changes to the way that the company organises its business may be construed as an admission of fault. Delay is not in the HSE's interest, however, because further injuries may be incurred while dangerous and criminogenic conditions are allowed to fester. As the HSE's main aim is to promote safety and reduce workplace deaths and injuries, it will therefore refrain from a criminal prosecution except in egregious cases.

There is another possibility to be considered, which is that criticisms of the HSE for failing to press criminal prosecutions are based on a misconception of the reason why health and safety legislation was enacted in the first place. Writing on the legislative control of bribery in the United States, Reisman (1979) introduced the concept of 'lex imperfecta' to refer to laws that are not really expected to have much practical impact, but are enacted more for their symbolic value. Perhaps health and safety legislation falls into this category. The Health and Safety at Work etc Act 1974 may have served its purpose simply by drawing the attention of companies to workplace safety issues, even if it has not generated a plethora of prosecutions. The same may be said of the government's more recent proposal for a crime of corporate killing (Home Office: 2000). Although the government's consultation paper was issued in 2000, it was based on a report of the Law Commission that had been published four years previously; over three years have now elapsed since the issuance of the consultation paper and still the government has not introduced a formal Bill. Nor does one detect any great urgency on the government's part to do so. While perhaps this is an inevitable facet of the consultation process in a controversial area, perhaps the government believes that the consultation paper, which received considerable publicity and media attention, has already achieved a large part of its intended objective merely by virtue of its publication. Just as the health and safety laws focused corporate minds on safety in the workplace, the consultation paper's concept of a 'management failure' drew attention to the role of management structures and policies in work-related deaths.

While the institutional dilemmas facing the HSE may reflect deeper conflicts about the goals of health and safety legislation, they also illustrate the difficulties of making general regulation across industries work in practice. Approximately 400–500 HSE inspectors are responsible for inspecting some 736,000 premises 'concerned with construction, agriculture, general manufacturing, quarries, entertainment, education, health services, local government, Crown bodies and the police',[6] with the result that a registered premise may receive an inspection 'once every 20 years' (see HSE: 2002: 3). The responsibility of directors and senior

---

6   Local authorities are responsible for a further one million premises including, shops, offices, nursing homes and hotels.

management is an issue which is rarely examined. Even in cases of major disasters – with high loss of life – there have been no criminal prosecutions. This was true of the *Piper Alpha* oil-rig explosion and the Kings Cross underground fire. The investigation of P&O for the deaths that followed the capsize of the *Herald of Free Enterprise* was not begun until eight months after the disaster; and then only as a result of persistent pressure from friends and relatives of the victims; the HSE had declined to investigate further despite a highly critical report on P&O. Similarly, despite a verdict of unlawful killing by an inquest jury (some six years after the event) there still was not an investigation of the suspicious circumstances surrounding the deaths that resulted when the *Bowbelle* collided with the *Marchioness* on the Thames.

However, there is evidence that the picture may be slowly changing. The debate on corporate manslaughter seems to have stimulated the number of prosecutions in recent years. In 1999/2000, there was an increase of 9% in the number of prosecutions, 28% of which were initiated by the HSE (HSE: 2001). There was also an increase in the number of improvement and prohibition notices issued (HSE: 2001). And in 2002, the Health and Safety Commission published a new Enforcement Policy Statement containing clearer guidelines as to when investigations and prosecutions would be warranted. Among the factors that would 'normally' lead to a prosecution are the occurrence of a death, the gravity of the offence, a reckless disregard of health and safety requirements, the absence of a licence or serious disregard of its requirements, a failure that falls 'far below what is required', repeated breaches despite formal cautions, and the intentional obstruction or deception of a regulator's investigation (HSC: 2002: para 39). While resources may affect the decision to investigate, they are to have no effect on the decision whether to prosecute. Although these developments are encouraging, and suggest a re-awakened interest in and commitment to enforcement, it is too early to determine whether they harbinger a long-term trend. At present the evidence remains that deaths and serious injuries at work, involving employees but also members of the public, do not always attract the HSE investigation that is envisaged by health and safety legislation. Furthermore, there exist strong regional differences in enforcement as well as between industries; in some HSE areas prosecution is 'almost non-existent', while rarely does an investigation of a death lead to the prosecution of a manager or company director (Unison and the Centre for Corporate Accountability: 2002; 11).

It is scarcely surprising, then, that despite the winds of change, critics, looking at the overall record of the HSE, continue to assert that the agency is characterised by an institutional disinclination to treat injuries and deaths at work as 'real' crime. The *decriminalisation* of health and safety offences persists, and one still can discern a clear discrepancy between how traditional homicides – and even road deaths – are treated compared with deaths at work. While many, including front-line inspectors, would maintain that the answer lies in increasing the resources allotted to the HSE, what may really be needed is a change in philosophy and approach and, in particular, a rethinking of the role of compliance strategies. Certainly, the thrust of the CCA, working closely with the unions, is to argue for more resources, more inspections, more thorough investigations, less haphazard enforcement across the regions and more prosecutions (particularly of senior managers). Perhaps it was in response to such criticisms that the HSE in 2002 issued new guidelines that sought to replace the discretionary standards of the past with clearer directions as to when a prosecution should be brought in the case of a workplace death. But while prosecution is an indispensable tool in the HSE's armoury, a knee-jerk filing of criminal charges in every case may not be advisable. Rather, a forceful mix of compliance and deterrence, judiciously administered, may be needed if health and safety laws are to be taken seriously.

2. A special inter-disciplinary, investigatory agency: the Serious Fraud Office

If the HSE represents a classic inspectorate with a broad remit touching potentially hundreds of thousands of firms, then the SFO is a quite different creature. It is a specialised agency with a limited remit, a narrow and specific focus, and a well-qualified and inter-disciplinary staff. Of particular significance is the clear vision of the SFO that it is an integral part of the criminal justice system. Thus, unlike the HSE and other inspectorates, the SFO dispenses with warnings, notices and cautions and proceeds directly to prosecutions in the Crown Court. Unlike some other special investigatory agencies, notably the Internal Revenue Service and Customs and Excise, the SFO is not inclined to negotiate settlements or 'plea bargain' with offenders (Clarke: 1990).

The founding of the SFO had its roots both in world financial developments and in scandals that occurred in the City of London in the 1980s. This decade was marked by a rapidly globalising economy. The role of the City was correspondingly changing; London had become the second leading financial centre in the world after Wall Street and a motor of commercial expansion, employment and a new share-holding public. Under the leadership of Margaret Thatcher, deregulation was being actively promoted by the Conservative government. However, this period in time was also characterised by a number of financial scandals related to frauds, mismanagement and bankruptcies – including Johnson Matthey, Barlow Clowes, Morgan Grenfell, Polly Peck and Norton Warburg. These scandals threatened to damage the reputation of the City for probity and formed a potential embarrassment for a government that was seen as strongly pro-City (Levi: 1987; Clarke: 1986, 1990). To cope with the situation, Parliament passed a spate of legislation and regulatory reform in relation to the banks, Lloyds, the Stock Exchange and the financial services industry generally. While powerful financial interests opposed the creation of an English version of the SEC (Securities and Exchange Commission), the government felt that it had to be seen to be 'cleaning up' the City. The compromise solution was twofold: the creation of the Serious Fraud Office (SFO), designed to be a highly aggressive body with the authority to prosecute; and the formal establishment by statute of a number of self-regulatory bodies (SROs), with a co-ordinating and supervisory agency to oversee these bodies – the Securities and Investments Board (SIB).

The SFO was set up following the Criminal Justice Act 1987. Its remit was to investigate and prosecute complex cases of 'serious' fraud by which was understood those cases meeting specified criteria:
- sums of money above £1m were involved;
- the nature of the case or the legal issues were particularly complex;
- the case aroused considerable public interest; or there had been some especially novel feature to the fraud (SFO: 1989).

The filter for selecting cases may in fact be even more stringent than the criteria suggest. Since the SFO's inception, the monetary amount at stake has been regularly raised and as of 2002 was said to stand at £6m, although the formal criterion is still listed as £1m (SFO: 2002). Cases also now seem to have to have an international dimension to them to merit prosecution. In addition, the traditional criterion relating to the decision to initiate a prosecution – that there has to be greater than a 50% chance of conviction – has been retained.

In practice, these prosecution criteria have allowed the SFO to be highly selective in its caseload, which has vacillated between 40–80 cases per year, with as much as £5bn being at stake at any one time. With about 230 permanent staff and a relatively modest budget, there is a gaping disparity between the institutional capacity of the SFO and the financial resources of the companies it investigates. Defendants in contested cases often are able to outspend the SFO many times over, although whether this factor or the complexity of the cases accounts for the SFO's initial mixed record of success is hard to know. None the less, in its early days the SFO was heavily criticised, with some pundits going so far as to refer to it as the 'not so serious' fraud office or the 'seriously flawed' office.

In evaluating the performance of the SFO, one has to take into account the fact that large-scale frauds are often highly complex and require time – and therefore money – to investigate and prepare for trial properly. Documents need to be discovered and payments traced, but sometimes the money trail is blocked by banking secrecy laws in 'tax havens'. Foreign witnesses may decline to co-operate or appear in an English court. Traditional jury trials, as discussed in chapter 6, may not be well-suited to fraud cases because of their length and complexity, and many (including the government in its most recent proposals for reform of the criminal justice system) have recommended that fraud cases be tried before a judge sitting alone or with a panel of financial experts.

The SFO's first major prosecution was against Ernest Saunders and others for their role in the Guinness illegal share-support scheme, which was discussed in chapter 1. The case was complex and, for a number of reasons, the prosecutions were brought in stages. In the first of a series of prosecutions the SFO claimed a success when a jury returned guilty verdicts against the defendants and the court imposed relatively heavy sentences (five years for Saunders). However, subsequently three more Guinness trials were brought with none leading to a conviction. Guinness II folded when the judge dismissed the jury when one of the defendants became seriously ill (in large part due to the strain induced by the defendant's decision to represent himself); Guinness III collapsed before trial when the prosecution offered no evidence; and in Guinness IV the defendant was acquitted (*Observer*, 16 February 1992, p 31). After its initial success, the SFO's Guinness campaign seemed simply to run out of steam (Punch: 1996: 177).

But should the outcomes of the Guinness cases serve as the benchmark against which the success of the SFO is evaluated? Attempting to determine whether any regulatory agency has been 'successful' is always complicated by the difficulty of knowing what constitutes 'success' and, in particular, the extent to which the agency's mere presence elicits compliance and induces deterrence. Its supporters would argue that the very existence of the SFO has had a significant symbolic impact. The SFO may not need to take on a wide range of cases to be effective if the cases that it does prosecute have the desired deterrent effect. All that may matter is that *some* cases are pursued and prosecuted, thereby conveying the message that companies that do not put their own house in order risk a prosecution. To the extent that these companies make rational decisions, and this is more likely to be true of the types of financial houses that are likely to be the target of an SFO investigation and prosecution, then they are going to be amenable to deterrence. Although the statements might be self-serving, several spokespersons in financial markets in London have admitted that SFO crackdowns have been effective in inducing large firms to look at their own operation and to 'clean up their act'. Whether the house-cleaning is only cosmetic or temporary is more difficult to gauge, but prosecutions do seem to have had at least a short-term effect.

Since its early days, the prosecution record of the SFO has in fact improved significantly, and it now boasts a considerably higher rate of convictions. Overall, the SFO has dealt with 237 cases, involving 516 defendants, and has achieved a 71% conviction rate. However, in the last five years it has prosecuted 69 cases, involving 134 defendants, while obtaining convictions in 86% of the cases (SFO: 2002). Whether the SFO is simply being more selective nowadays in its choice of cases or has learned how better to present its evidence (in some instances making use of advanced computer graphics and other technological advances) is in a sense irrelevant. The critical point is that the SFO has demonstrated that it is prepared to pursue, to investigate and to prosecute major cases of fraud. That it has also been able to secure convictions in the vast majority of the cases it brings to court cannot help but further increase the deterrent effect on would-be fraudsters, whether they be individuals or companies.

Can it be said that the SFO has succeeded where the HSE has failed? It may not be a fair comparison, as the SFO appears to be better funded and staffed, and has a more focused and narrower remit. Whereas the HSE's target group consists of all businesses, whether or not their aim is to break the law, the SFO is only concerned with those whom it has reason to believe are engaged in serious fraud. The SFO does not conduct 'random' investigations of companies, as does the HSE, and is therefore able to conserve its resources and apply them to cases where serious fraud is suspected. On the other hand, what the perceived success of the SFO demonstrates to critics of the HSE is that an aggressive, well-staffed, multi-disciplinary agency, which is not reluctant to prosecute, can be effective in a British culture that has traditionally preferred a more low-key and 'keep it in house' approach to regulation. The success of the SFO casts doubt on the claim that compliance strategies are the most effective means of controlling and deterring corporate criminality.

E.   THE ROLE OF THE POLICE

Police form the front-loading component in a criminal justice system whose goal is the detection, prosecution, conviction and punishment of offenders. Police investigations are primarily reactive, and are typically initiated as a result of reports from victims or members of the public, or offences discovered by the police themselves while on patrol. The majority of the offenders are young and male, and primarily but not exclusively from the socially disadvantaged classes of society. Offenders are 'processed' through the criminal justice system, passing from arrest and custody by the police, to trial in criminal court, to a term of imprisonment or community service in the event of a conviction. On the other hand, the police have never, historically or institutionally, been involved in a significant way in the investigation of offences that occur on private business premises. In general, they possess little expertise in the technical aspects of safety, 'accidents' at work or high finance.

While fraud investigation units are now prevalent, there are only a few, such as the joint Metropolitan and City Police Company Fraud Department in London, which are sizeable and which treat serious commercial and company fraud as a specialty. Several factors, moreover, limit the effectiveness of fraud squads. Most police forces do not have fraud as a priority, and the number of detectives assigned to these squads may be relatively small compared with more high-profile crime areas. Nor is assignment to a fraud squad especially coveted by officers. Cases can be long, complex and require wading through dense financial records. Outcomes are uncertain and sometimes ambiguous. Even in the event of a conviction, there is not the same satisfaction that comes from removing from society persons who pose a serious danger to the community. Many of the victims of fraud are either financial institutions, which are seen to be able to protect themselves, or ordinary persons who have only their own greed to blame for a decision to invest their savings in a fraudulent 'get-rich-quick' scheme.

Fraud squad detectives are themselves rarely knowledgeable in matters relating to finance and may require 18 months or more of training to familiarise themselves with the work. Despite this lengthy training period, their tenure on a fraud squad may be relatively short, not longer than three to four years – either because the officer requests a transfer or because department policies require periodic job rotation. In any event, without a substantial re-conceptualisation of fraud squads, the police may not be the right agency to investigate business fraud. In conducting the research for his treatise on fraud, Levi (1987) was told by corporate executives that they would be extremely reluctant to call in the police when faced with a case of fraud. The executives were not only sceptical of the competence of the police, but also feared that, because officers would not know where to look for evidence, they might stumble upon other practices that the company would prefer to be kept private.

In the health and safety area, the police are also not geared to investigating workplace 'accidents' involving serious injuries, and rarely will do so. The police presume that health and safety inspectors will have a more intimate knowledge of the relevant standards in the industry, and will be more familiar with the workplace environment in which the injury has occurred. Inspectors are also presumed to be more aware of what technical measures were feasible and what safeguards could have been put in place to avoid the incident. The police appreciate that they are less likely to understand how workplace practices and conditions can contribute to employee injuries. The police also appreciate that inspectors have had more experience in interviewing managers and corporate executives, who for their part may feel more comfortable in talking to inspectors than in answering the questions of the police. Employees who might be able to testify about a possible corporate crime may be reluctant to confide in the police because they fear that co-operation may have repercussions for them at work, and the police may not be in a position to allay their concerns. Inspectors may be able to 'negotiate' co-operation with the employees' managers.

When it is a case of a worker's death, however, the picture changes. Now it is the police who are most likely to have the relevant background and expertise to conduct an effective investigation. The officers assigned to the case will usually be experienced in the investigation of suspicious deaths. They will usually have received some tuition in the elements of gross negligence manslaughter and murder, and will therefore know what evidence they should be looking for in their investigations. They will have well-developed routines for examining the crime scene and preserving evidence to be sent to forensic laboratories for analysis. Their questioning of witnesses is also likely to be more incisive and more rigorous, and they will be able to hold open the prospect of an interrogation at police headquarters, rather than on company premises, if co-operation is not forthcoming. At the same time, the police will be aware of when a suspect will need to be 'cautioned'.

Apart from the technical advantages of having the police in charge of the investigation of a workplace death, there is a considerable symbolic value as well. The involvement of the police in a case signifies that the death in question may involve a possibly serious criminal offence. This symbolism may not be lost on employees who , as a result, may be more willing to co-operate with the police than they are with respect to a health and safety matter.

The optimal approach, however, may be one that entails co-operation between the HSA and the police. Each can then take advantage of the experience and expertise of the other (assuming that professional jealousies do not impinge). As noted previously, in 1998 a Protocol was entered into between the Association of Chief Police Officers (ACPO), the Health and Safety Executive and the Crown Prosecution Service, which agreed a procedure for liaison between the three signatories in the event of a work-related death. The Protocol allows for a joint initial investigation by the police and the HSE in cases of workplace deaths, with the police making an initial assessment of whether 'the circumstances might justify a charge of manslaughter'. But whether a *brief* initial investigation is sufficient for this purpose may be doubted. Also, under the Protocol a case is to be referred to the police if, during the course of an HSE investigation, evidence of manslaughter comes to light. However, it is not clear that this always occurs, as inspectors' knowledge of the legal dimensions of manslaughter may be lacking in sophistication. There is also evidence that the effectiveness of the Protocol has been patchy due to differences between forces and districts with regard to their understanding of the Protocol, and how it is to be implemented.

The ideal of police-HSE co-operation would seem to make particularly good sense in cases of possible 'corporate killings'. While the police may have the technical expertise to conduct the investigation of a suspicious death, they are less likely to understand the concept of a 'management failure' which lies at the heart of the government's proposal. Regulators, more familiar with the standards of an industry and with what can be reasonably expected of 'management', could play an invaluable advisory role in these cases. These considerations make even more puzzling the government's insistence on placing the HSE in charge of the investigation of a corporate killing (Home Office: 2000, para 3.3.5).

F.   REGULATION IN THE UNITED STATES

It is difficult to know just how large and powerful a regulatory agency needs to be in order to be effective. In England, each health and safety inspector is responsible for approximately 700 premises subject to inspection; in the construction industry there is one inspector per 5,000 building sites. The HSE data for 2000/2001 revealed that across the board 'only one in 20 premises throughout Britain had been inspected in that year (HSE: 2002). On the other hand, to have some kind of ubiquitous presence with large numbers of personnel available randomly to inspect companies would require an enormous administrative apparatus with far-reaching and intrusive powers, which no democratic government would be likely to permit – and no business community would long tolerate.

It is also difficult to know what to make of claims that agencies are under-funded and under-staffed. Most agencies, even if they are reasonably well staffed and resourced, will plead poverty in order to attract additional funding and/or to set up an advance excuse in the event of failure. Numbers of staff and resources are, in point of fact, relatively arbitrary and usually are historically set with expansions in periods of 'moral panic' about corporate crime and reductions during deregulatory cycles. In any event, inadequate staffing and resources are no response to the criticism that the real problem with regulatory agencies is that they are insufficiently robust and aggressive in their approach to law enforcement.

Critics of English inspectorates tend to point to American agencies, such as the Food and Drug Administration (FDA) and the Securities and Exchange Commission (SEC), both of which enjoy a reputation for being forceful, proactive and effective, as possible role models for Britain. In this section we take a look at these American agencies to see if in fact there is something to be learned from the way that they go about carrying out their remit. Inter-country comparisons are inevitably tricky, as there are many cultural factors that may affect the analysis. The United States, for instance, has traditionally been a more litigious society than Britain, and, as a consequence, a greater willingness to resort to criminal prosecutions is not surprising. None the less, in law enforcement generally and in regulation in particular, one can discern in the United States a more creative range of incentives to compliance and a greater willingness to adopt 'innovative' enforcement strategies than can be found in Britain (Braithwaite: 1989: 171; Punch: 1991; Clarke: 1990).

Cultural variations to one side, the FDA and SEC are generally credited with having achieved a measure of 'ascendancy' over the industries that they are responsible for regulating (Clarke: 2000: 117). They are held up as models of success, to be contrasted with 'captured' British agencies. Interestingly, the SEC for many years was regarded by the financial community in Britain as almost the antithesis of what it wanted in a regulatory agency, but it now appears to have served as a model for the FSA, which we shall look at in a subsequent section. This feature gives an analysis of the SEC's approach to regulation a particular poignancy. Despite the long-sustained opposition to an English version of the SEC, the City of London now appears to have a powerful watchdog – and one with an American pedigree.

1.   The Food and Drug Administration

The FDA has a broad mandate to regulate the safety of food, drugs, medical devices, biological products, animal feeds and some aspects of consumer products. Like most agencies, it has had a mixed history, with many shifts and turns. At one time it was regarded as far too pro-industry, but industry forces have felt it has at times been overly aggressive. In recent years the FDA has emerged as a respected and credible partner for the industries it regulates. This partnership relation is particularly evident in the area that receives the most attention and where the FDA has had to fight its hardest battles – namely, the control over the testing, manufacturing and monitoring of drugs.

It is clear from even a cursory examination of the FDA that it possesses a number of advantages over many other regulatory agencies. First, the number of companies in the pharmaceutical industry is limited, which in turn means that the number of companies which the FDA is responsible for monitoring is limited (Robinson: 2001). Thus, in 2001, it was able to conduct some 16,000 site visits to laboratories and premises (FDA: 2002). Second, issues of health and medicine will receive high media and public priority because they relate to products which people ingest and which can directly affect their well-being in fairly obvious ways (and which impact particularly on the vulnerable in society, including infants, the elderly and pregnant women; Peppin: 1995). Third, the FDA is well-funded and well-staffed, with a total staff of 9,000 spread throughout the country. Finally, the FDA has been granted broad administrative powers in a series of Congressional enactments over the years, not only for inspecting the industry, but also for licensing medical and other health products. In part, these powers were granted after a series of scandals had revealed that leading companies were falsifying laboratory test results and bribing the responsible supervisory officials; findings that were confirmed in Braithwaite's (1984) path-breaking study on deviance in the drug industry. These scandals strengthened the position and the backbone of an agency that was initially criticised for being too close to the drug industry.

American agencies have been rightly praised for their willingness to be innovative when conventional regulatory methods have not proved to be feasible or effective. The FDA, for example, has responsibility for testing and ensuring that drugs are safe before allowing them to come on to the market. The burden of testing can put strains on the agency's resources. Recognising that the pharmaceutical industry has a vast research capacity of its own, and also that it frequently sponsors academic research, the FDA decided to shift a large portion of the burden for research and development to the industry itself, even though it was aware that the industry had a record for dubious practices in other areas (particularly in relation to cartel-forming and price-fixing; Elliot and Scroth: 2002: 60). With respect to testing, the FDA appreciated that the industry could boast of world-class scientists. Although the presence of such scientists did not preclude the possibility of misconduct, it did provide a powerful impetus towards quality control, maintenance of scientific standards and openness through publication. Capitalising on these features, the FDA developed a Code of Good Laboratory Practices, but then required firms in the industry to establish their own 'Quality Control Units' to monitor compliance with the Code. In a relatively short period, the FDA was able to achieve very high levels of compliance (Fisse and Braithwaite: 1993: 135).

The establishment of this type of partnership arrangement between agency and firms in the industry has not prevented the FDA from challenging drug companies when merited. The example of Thalidomide is a well-known case in point that contributed greatly to the FDA's reputation for toughness when called for. In that instance, an FDA medical officer, Dr Frances Kelsey, was successful in keeping the tranquilliser Thalidomide, subsequently shown to be the cause of severe deformities in embryos during pregnancy, out of the American market. In contrast, both Germany and Britain appeared to have succumbed to the blandishments, pressures and misinformation generated by the manufacturer, Chemie Grunenthal, and its licensed distributors. The FDA has also not shirked from issuing recalls when manufacturing defects are discovered after a drug has been released on to the market. Overall, the agency has managed to get across the message that any company that appears indisposed to co-operate with it, or which seems to be behaving suspiciously, can expect 'a blitz of inspections, complaints, citations and requirements to improve' (Clarke: 1990: 216). The resulting image of the FDA is that of an agency which is prepared to use its authority to extract a high level of compliance from the pharmaceutical industry and from other food and health producers.

Over time, the drug companies have learned that meeting FDA standards and maintaining high levels of quality can be turned to their advantage. 'FDA approval' is now regularly used as a marketing tool. It can also play a significant role in a company's defence in a product liability suit, and can be introduced as evidence of a company's 'due diligence' (see chapter 3). In the pharmaceutical industry, the FDA has a powerful adversary, but also one with a strong self-interest in the quality of products. The FDA has been able to turn this self-interest to its advantage. The industry appreciates that it is dependent on the FDA for 'pre-marketing clearance of new drugs, approval of in-process quality controls, approval of drug testing protocols' and also at other crucial stages in bringing its products to market (Braithwaite: 1989: 136). Just as the drug companies have learned that it can be to their interest to co-operate with the FDA, so too has the FDA learned that overly aggressive measures to secure compliance can backfire and lead to counter-measures by the industry to evade controls and to continue legally questionable practices. Although the FDA has now established that it is prepared to take on large companies when required, it also appreciates that there are times when a less confrontational approach can be more effective. In summary, the FDA exemplifies a 'mature' regulatory agency which has arrived at what has been called a form of 'ascendancy' through the judicious combination of compliance and deterrence strategies.

Nevertheless, tensions remain. The industry has a strong interest in being able rapidly to bring new medicines on the market (the development of a new drug is estimated to cost $800m and to take on average more than ten years from laboratory to market; Elliot and Scroth: 2002: 59). Many of the more commercial interests in the pharmaceutical industry see the FDA as bureaucratic and its processes of approval as drawn-out and overly protracted. It holds the FDA responsible for delays in bringing new products, which promise to reduce suffering and enhance well-being (for instance, with regard to anti-AIDS drugs), on to the market. The industry is rich and powerful, possessing a substantial in-house research capacity costing $44bn in 2001, as well as playing a major role in funding academic research at prestigious institutions. It constantly lobbies the FDA to enhance the chances of approval of its products, and on occasion companies have even sought to have removed from the approval process medical officers who are seen by them to be too painstaking and 'conscientious' in their approach. The industry also uses its considerable clout to fight for its interests in the legislative and political arenas (Abraham: 1995). When these counter-offensives have failed, companies have transferred the questionable aspects of their business abroad, often to developing states which have less stringent laws and regulatory controls.

2.   The Securities and Exchange Commission

The American political and economic system has been characterised by cycles of scandal and reform. The government generally takes a laissez-faire, hands-off approach, but seems also periodically to indulge in reforming 'crusades' (Reisman: 1979). That regulatory agencies are stiffened – but also pushed into action – by such campaigns was evidenced in the 1980s and at the beginning of this century. In both instances, a pro-business administration was forced by events, public opinion and political self-interest to respond to major financial scandals. The large American corporations and globally operating banks, the financial lawyers and experts of Wall Street, the exchanges and the accountancy firms are all powerful players, politically and economically. However, when damaging excesses are exposed, there can be a coalition formed among an outraged media, congressional and house committees (which, on other occasions, can be equally astute at blocking reform), and a raft of regulators and agencies, which is capable of taking on the deviant firms.

The effects of a reformist crusade are not always as the reformists visualised and sometimes reforms can be subverted by political agendas (Reisman: 1979). For example, although the outcry against the 'robber-barons' at the end of the nineteenth century led to the passage of the Sherman Anti-Trust Act 1901, the Act was at first used to bust unions rather than to break up monopolies. It was not until the traumatic stock market crash of 1929 and the impact of the Great Depression that the belief in self-regulation in banking, investments and securities was severely shaken, leading to a conviction that reform had to be genuine and not cosmetic. The SEC was created in 1934; and with President Franklin Roosevelt's 'New Deal', a period of enhanced government interference in economic life was ushered in.

Initially, the SEC was responsible for overseeing a number of self-regulating agencies, and, as a result, was heavily dependent on the financial services industry. Perhaps for this reason, it was not particularly adversarial in its approach. In the 1970s, however, there were further financial scandals, followed by congressional hearings and a strengthening of the relevant legislation (the Securities Act 1975). From being a small and reactive agency, the SEC became, according to Shapiro (1984: 140) who documented these developments, a 'large, specialised, proactive, self-initiating office, constantly expanding the boundaries of enforcement policy and serving as a leader and model for the regions'.

Nevertheless, the resources of the SEC remained quite limited compared with those of many of the large investment firms that it had to regulate. With 3,000 personnel, the SEC is relatively small for a government agency. As a consequence, it has been forced to find creative ways of achieving its goals. Its approach to the challenge of discovering the extent of illegal kickbacks and bribes, after the scandal revealing such practices in the 1970s had broken, is illustrative. Rather than attempting to investigate and prosecute all potential cases of wrongdoing, it induced companies to investigate themselves and to make voluntary statements of disclosure and 'declarations of cessation' by offering, in exchange, its forbearance from formal enforcement actions. The strategy proved an immense success when more than 300 companies voluntarily came forward and disclosed over $300,000,000 of illegal payments.

Often the SEC will call in firms which it suspects of rule-breaking, confront them with the evidence and seek to negotiate a settlement. The deal it typically offers is to allow the firm not to have to admit or deny the offence, but simply to promise not to do it again and pay an agreed sum in settlement (Vise and Coll: 1990: 133). Although the SEC can only bring civil actions against firms (roughly 400–500 a year comprising in the fiscal year 2001 some 205 civil injunctions and 248 administrative proceedings: SEC *Annual Report* (2001) Enforcement, p 1), it can and often has co-operated with prosecutors through its Enforcement Division in preparing and taking cases to the criminal courts. Among those with whom the SEC has enjoyed a fruitful collaboration are state regulators and prosecutors (such as the Attorney-General of New York and the US Attorney for the Southern District of New York, whose Manhattan office has jurisdiction over Wall Street) and the Justice Department (which possesses a task force dedicated to the prosecution of corporate fraud).

In common with other regulatory agencies, the SEC has frequently been a target of the deregulation lobby. However, it showed its backbone following the Wall Street scandals of the 1980s (which some argued were the direct result of the new opportunities for illicit gain created by deregulation). In the 1980s, the revival of the American economy and a spate of corporate mergers and acquisitions put a premium on information in forecasting and anticipating developments in the market. Corporate raiders, investment analysts and financial consultants profited, but in some instances by misusing insider information. The sanctions against insider trading had been sharpened by the Insider Trading Sanctions Act 1984 (Reichman: 1993), while in 1988 Congress responded to the scandals by passing the Insider Trading and Securities Fraud Enforcement Act, which required firms to adopt and enforce policies designed to prevent the use of insider information. The responsibility for enforcement of the Act fell to the SEC. While before this time some had accused the SEC of 'cherry picking' small firms, a charge supported by the research of Shapiro (1984), the insider trading scandals forced the Commission to sharpen its focus. Prominent Wall Street figures, including Ivan Boesky, Dennis Levine and Michael Milken (all of whom were associated with the Wall Street firm Drexel Burnham Lambert) were exposed for profiting personally, and on a large scale, from insider information. Although the Chairman at the time was himself from Wall Street and a presidential appointee, the SEC took an aggressive stance, finding an ally in the then US Attorney for Manhattan, Rudy Giuliani. An early breakthough that identified Levine, the willingness of suspects to inform on their colleagues and to co-operate in the investigation, and astute plea-bargaining with the readiness of the key players to negotiate with the authorities, all aided in bringing the cases to a successful conclusion. A number of high-profile prosecutions followed and many of the key individuals either pleaded guilty or were convicted. Leading figures on Wall Street and in the aggressive mergers and acquisitions market were among those who were heavily sanctioned: Boesky was sentenced to three years' imprisonment, while a prison sentence of ten years was meted out to Milken along with a hitherto inconceivable fine for a natural person of $600m. Drexel Burnham and Lambert, the firm at the centre of the scandal, entered a guilty plea and was fined $650m (Vise and Coll: 1991: 343f).

To all appearances, the SEC had achieved success in a difficult and complex area and had signalled to the business community that it was to be taken seriously. However, a closer look reveals that several behind-the-scenes factors worked in the SEC's favour and contributed to its success. Rather like the pharmaceutical industry, the core of the financial services industry was composed of a small number of key firms which were concentrated in a relatively few cities. Therefore, the burden of keeping tabs on all of them did not stretch the limited resources of the SEC. Also, when illegal practices were exposed, forces within the financial industry generated their own pressure for companies in the sector to disassociate themselves from the illegality. Financial markets are dependent on investor and consumer confidence and, to bolster that confidence, a robust, even if ritual, condemnation of illegal practices is essential. The SEC could therefore count on the support and co-operation, however reluctant and grudging, of the firms in the industry when it ordered a change in their practices. Of importance too is the political will which emerges when markets are seriously threatened; some commentators went so far as to claim that capitalism itself was put at risk by Milken and his co-conspirators and that confidence in the markets had to be dramatically restored (Fisse and Braithwaite: 1993: 142). Additionally, legislation had given the SEC the power to demand disclosure of financial data from firms (to the extent that companies use the SEC data base for research in preparing investment decisions), to scrutinise internal compliance structures and to push for standards in financial services, accounting and the exchanges.

Currently, the SEC again finds itself under attack as a result of its failure to prevent the fraudulent accounting scandals that led to the collapse of some of the top firms in the corporate United States. These cases differ from the Wall Street scandals of the 1980s. There, the improprieties were committed by a few key individuals associated with a company, Drexel Burnham Lambert, which was a relative newcomer to the market. In the current (mid-2002) crisis, the scandal has engulfed established companies, reputable banks, respected accounting firms and seemingly highly successful ICT (Information, Communication and Technology) firms. Enron, Xerox, General Electric, Arthur Andersen, Tyco, WorldCom, Adelphia, Salomon Smith Barney (a subsidiary of the Citigroup), J P Morgan Chase, Lehman and Goldman Sachs have, among others, attracted regulatory, prosecutorial and congressional scrutiny – and even presidential condemnation. Substantial abuses at the highest levels have been exposed in relation to a series of questionable practices ranging from excessive remuneration packages to 'innovative' financial constructions such as 'SPES' (special-purpose entities), and including equity research, premature 'IPOs' (Initial Public Offerings), conflicts of interest, mergers and acquisitions and, above all, 'creative' accounting. So many CEOs, CFOs and prestigious companies now find themselves in the dock that some commentators have concluded that the deviance is endemic and *the system* itself has failed (Useem: 2002: 63–72; Elliot and Scroth: 2002). When the CEO of Goldman Sachs spoke to the National Press Club, he said:

> In my life-time, American business had never been under such scrutiny. To be blunt, much of it is deserved (Gimein: 2002: 84).

In response to the current crisis of confidence, the SEC has proposed new accountancy standards, rules of disclosure and revised corporate governance structures for companies (and also for the exchanges). The role of the SEC was strengthened by the Sarbanes-Oxley Act 2002 on reporting standards. It has displayed assertiveness in collaboration with the Attorney-General for New York State, Eliot Spitzer (who came to a $100m settlement with Goldman Sachs) and the US Attorney for the Southern District of New York, James Comey (who has a securities fraud unit, specialised on corporate crime cases, among his 230 prosecutors; *The Economist*, 6 July 2002; 14 September 2002). In reaching a settlement with Arthur Andersen, which had issued 'clean' opinions on financial statements that 'overstated Waste Management's pre-tax profits by $1 billion', the SEC achieved the first anti-fraud injunction in 20 years and the largest civil penalty, $7m, against one of the 'Big Five' accounting firms (SEC *Annual Report* (2001) Enforcement, p 2). After a slow beginning, the SEC was booking success against the elite firms.

From a historical perspective, the SEC has established and re-established itself as an agency which may not be exactly liked by the financial industry, but which is respected. Firms have become reliant on the valuable information which the SEC accumulates. They value the agency's expertise. As a result, the SEC has been able, and has not been afraid, to take the lead in setting standards for the industry. At the same time, the SEC has shown that it can be creative and work with firms which are prepared to co-operate with it. In times of scandal many firms appreciate that rigorous house-cleaning is essential to restore the trust which is fundamental to the financial services industry. The SEC's 'ascendancy' may fluctuate and its authority may be continually contested, but it cannot be ignored or taken for granted – companies simply have to take the SEC into account when conducting their business.

To repeat a point made at the outset of this section, our examination of the SEC and the FDA has been prompted not so much because they are representative of American regulatory agencies – they are not[7] – but rather because these agencies are frequently cited as models for Britain. The FDA and SEC face many of the dilemmas common to all inspectorates, but they have seem to have had more success than their British counterparts in resolving them. Structurally, the FDA and SEC illustrate the advantage of having only a relatively small number of companies to monitor. Further, they demonstrate that, despite a firm approach, which includes a preparedness to be tough when the occasion demands, the respect of the industries they regulate can be earned and the support and co-operation (albeit sometimes grudging) of firms in the industry can be obtained. Unlike the perception of some British regulatory agencies, the perception of the FDA and SEC is that they will not be intimidated by large and powerful firms, and that Congress, more so than Parliament, will support their efforts with the necessary legislation, resources and psychological support. Finally, the FDA and SEC have displayed a flexibility, innovativeness and ability to combine compliance and deterrent-oriented strategies as appropriate that often seems to be missing in Britain.

G.   THE FINANCIAL SERVICES AUTHORITY

For many years, whenever the topic of how the financial services industry was to be policed was broached, the City of London rejected the solution of establishing an English equivalent of the SEC. The SEC was seen as too formal, too impersonal and

---

7   As in Britain, there are weak and 'captured' agencies in the United States, and not just exemplary ones. Some agencies are so unpopular because of their complex rules, intrusiveness and 'citation mentality' that they have elicited a culture of resistance. OSHA (Occupational Safety and Health Administration) and the EPA (Environmental Protection Agency) are two that are often put in this category. It has been alleged that at the height of its unpopularity some companies responded by automatically objecting to every OSHA injunction, thereby bogging the agency down in excessive red tape to achieve even the most minimal and uncontroversial changes (Braithwaite: 1989: 127; Clarke: 2000: 148, 162).

too rule-bound. It seemed ill-matched to the more 'clubbish' world of the City, where 'everybody knew everybody' and a 'gentleman's word was his bond'. Self-regulation seemed to offer an approach that was more consonant with how business was conducted in the City. However, the emergence of a class of entrepreneurs who were less committed to the traditions of the City and perhaps less to be trusted, along with some structural weaknesses in the self-regulatory systems that were set up (and which will be discussed in the next chapter), led to disillusionment with self-regulation on the part of both the government and companies subject to self-regulatory organisation (SRO) control. In place of SROs was substituted the Financial Services Authority (FSA), a powerful umbrella agency which came into being with the new millennium. The move from self-regulation to more intrusive external regulation reflects a concession that the SROs were inadequate to cope with the power of the financial services industry.

The statutory objectives of the FSA are fourfold: to maintain market confidence, to promote public awareness, to protect consumers and to reduce the incidence of financial crime. To achieve these ends, the FSA has indicated its intention to promulgate rules, prepare codes, give advice and determine general policies and principles. While the FSA's goals include a reduction in the incidence of failures among regulated firms as a means of preserving market confidence, it at the same time recognises that some failures are not only inevitable, but healthy. A goal of zero-failure would not only be unrealistic, but could lead to over-regulation or induce an undesirable complacency among investors and remove any sense of responsibility for protecting their own investments. To help protect the public, the FSA aims to improve both transparency, by making more and better information available, and the general level of 'financial literacy' through programmes designed to help individuals acquire the knowledge and skills needed to make financial decisions. To protect consumers specifically, the FSA seeks to ensure that they have a better understanding of prudential risk (the risk of an investment's failure because of bad management or financial collapse), bad faith risk (the risk from fraud, misrepresentation and the like), complexity/unsuitability risk (the risk of an investor making an investment that was unsuitable in light of his/ her needs and circumstances) and performance risks (the risk that an investment would not produce the hoped-for return).

With respect to its goal of preventing financial crime, the FSA more resembles a traditional agency, with both monitoring and policing functions. The three main types of financial crime which the FSA has set as its objective to prevent are money laundering, fraud and dishonesty, and criminal market misconduct, including insider dealing. It plans to meet the challenge by assessing the effectiveness of a company's internal controls, in particular with respect to money laundering. With respect to other types of crimes, the FSA envisages more of a secondary role for itself, one in which it co-operates with other agencies, including the police and the SFO, much as does the SEC with various prosecutorial authorities. The type and intensity of the FSA's regulation of individual firms is to be determined based on a complex matrix of risk assessment and prioritisation that we examined in chapter 4.

It is far too early to assess whether the FSA will succeed where other regulatory agencies have failed. At present, the FSA enjoys strong backing, but so probably did most regulatory agencies when they first came into being. None the less, the government at least appears to be committed to funding the FSA sufficiently to allow it to carry out its ambitious programme. However, the role that the FSA sees for itself is perhaps less clear. It does not appear to relish a prosecutorial role, but at the same time seems to relish a more aggressive and interventionist role than that which has been associated with the HSE. Whether or not this constitutes the right mix remains to be seen but, in any event, the experience of the FSA should add to our understanding of the effectiveness of different types of regulation.

H.   CONCLUSIONS

The topic of regulation is complex and confusing. There are innumerable cultural, political, economic and ideological variables that have to be taken into account in explaining what works and what does not. It is difficult to gauge how much prevention is achieved by the often limited successes of an agency. Different agencies face different challenges and dilemmas brought on by the practical and legal interpretation of their powers, levels of funding and staffing, inter-agency conflict, and the combativeness or co-operativeness of the industry they have been established to control. If the variables were not already sufficiently complex, ideas about the best way to police companies are constantly evolving, as actions by regulators produce reactions by companies. An excessively rule-bound system of adversarial policing by external regulators may be too inflexible, but compliance-orientated strategies may cause companies not to take an agency seriously. The evidence, including a survey of 96 agencies in Australia, indicates that most agencies cope with the dilemmas they face by adopting a pragmatic, adaptive and persuasive approach to compliance (Grabosky and Braithwaite: 1994). It has been argued, however, that this style of regulation is more symbolic than effective, potentially permitting a great deal of deviance to go undetected, and thus unregulated, and, in extreme circumstances, even acting as a stimulant to corporate crime when regulation fails too dramatically (as in the BCCI case; Clarke: 2000: 196–200).

The way forward, we believe, lies in corporate self-regulation. The United States has led the way by encouraging the creation of corporate compliance departments, but primarily through the negative reinforcements provided by federal sentencing laws. In contrast, Britain remains steeped in traditions that favour non-confrontational, non-interventionist and often non-legal solutions to the problem of corporate misconduct. The creation of the SFO and, more recently, the FSA, may signal a long overdue re-evaluation of compliance-orientated strategies. However, both the SFO and the FSA maintain the tradition of external control. While external agencies may be able to 'coerce' compliance, they may do little to change the overall philosophy of companies towards law obedience. In the next chapter we consider a fresh approach, designed to change the 'soul' as well as the conduct of a company, based on self-regulation.

CHAPTER 10

Self-regulation and the socially responsible company

A. INTRODUCTION

From Sutherland's pioneering work onwards, academics have maintained that a great deal of law-breaking takes place within companies; they draw on legal and other cases, media exposures, public inquiries, surveys and assumptions about the 'dark' number of crimes for and by corporations (Slapper and Tombs: 1999). A separate body of evidence indicates that external public agencies are not as effective as society might hope for in regulating and controlling corporate misconduct (Clarke: 2000). The reasons are complex, but include the fact that governments are often reluctant to alienate business interests; that the use of criminal law is cumbersome, costly and risky in respect to outcomes (and can sometimes even be counter-productive); and that external agencies predominantly prefer a more pragmatic approach to compliance in order to make their relationship with companies more 'manageable' (Ayres and Braithwaite: 1992).

   If regulatory agencies are not particularly effective in policing companies, as we saw in the previous chapter, then society may be forced to rely on companies to police themselves. But can companies be entrusted with this responsibility, given that the core of business activity involves the search for profits in a competitive market where, according to many (for example, Friedman: 1970), social responsibility is at best a secondary consideration? Cases where the causes of corporate wrongdoing are examined after-the-fact often reveal that both external and internal control mechanisms have failed dismally. To learn from these cases, and to prevent a repeat of these failures, may require a reconsideration of whether or not companies have, or should have, an obligation to act in socially responsible ways, which in turn may lead to a re-examination of the nature of corporate governance.

There are two main models of self-regulation that merit consideration. In the first, an industry is policed by a professional or industry-wide regulatory body. The self-regulatory body may be imposed or mandated by statute or be established voluntarily by firms in an industry who agree to be subject to its control. We shall refer to this model of regulation as *collective self-regulation*. The second approach involves each individual company taking the responsibility for monitoring itself. This model of regulation we shall call *individualised self-regulation*. The two models are not incompatible.

B. COLLECTIVE SELF-REGULATION

Collective self-regulation in industry and the professions has become increasingly commonplace. Doctors, lawyers, accountants, the press, financial institutions, sporting associations and various trades and industries are now frequently governed by self-regulatory bodies. Some of these self-regulatory organisations (SROs) are established by the firms in an industry, and have no links to the government whatsoever. Other SROs are formed as a result of a delegation by the government to the industry of the authority to regulate itself. The delegation may be total, in which case the SRO will be independent of government control; or partial, in which case all or some of the SRO's actions and decisions will be subject to monitoring or auditing by an external government oversight body, an appointed 'super-regulator' or perhaps an ombudsman. Sometimes, the formation of an SRO may be mandated or encouraged by statute; other times a veiled threat from the government that it will otherwise enact a statute is sufficient to prod firms in an industry 'voluntarily' to establish their own SRO. While the government may define the remit of an SRO, and set general rules and policies for it, the SRO will typically be left to enforce these rules and regulate its members, with the government maintaining at most a supervisory or oversight function. The government does not, however, forefeit its right to prosecute if a criminal offence has been committed.

When a government requires, encourages or allows an industry to establish an SRO, it may have different objectives in mind than when the industry sets up the SRO on its own initiative. Priest (1997/98) points out the advantages to the government:

> Self-regulation permits government to influence behaviour without becoming intimately involved in an industry. It allows for regulation that would not otherwise be possible in practical terms due to restraints on resources, whether financial, personnel or expertise. The regulator leverages its regulatory power and resources by using the resources of the regulated industry.

SROs in effect allow the government to transfer much of the costs of regulation from the public to the private sector, reserving for itself only the residual expense of auditing or monitoring the SRO. The government is spared from having to employ an army of regulators to enforce its rules and standards, as the SRO becomes responsible for ensuring that its members are compliant with the law. Furthermore, if violations should occur, the government can deflect any criticism from itself to the SRO. Thus, SROs allow governments to obtain the benefits of regulation without its costs, while at the same time allowing them to assure the public that they are not leaving the industry unchecked and to avoid blame when corporate misconduct none the less occurs.

For firms in an industry, SROs may also be attractive, but for different reasons. Priest again outlines the benefits. SROs provide companies with a forum through which they can explore common problems, share information and formulate a collective response to external threats. SROs thus facilitate co-operation and, perhaps, instil a sense of 'community' in the industry. At the same time, SROs are cost-efficient, for, by pooling their expertise, member firms are able to reduce the expense of regulation. Because the standards of the SRO will be drafted by representatives of the industry, who presumably will have extensive knowledge of, and experience in, the industry, the resultant policies can be expected to be sensitive to conditions in the industry and to the industry's real needs. SROs are also better positioned than regulatory agencies to respond to changing market conditions and crises in the industry, as they are able to change their rules without having to go through the often long and cumbersome process which is attendant to amending legislation. From a public relations vantage point, SROs can give 'legitimacy' to, or enhance the status of, an industry, and thereby increase consumer confidence in the products or services of the industry. For individual firms, the SRO may provide a 'seal of approval'. And in the legislative arena, the SRO can function as the lobbying arm of the industry, thereby allowing companies to stay above the fray. The very establishment of an SRO may help to convince the government of the industry's good faith and thereby deflect plans to set up an external regulatory agency or enact formal (and usually more stringent) rules of regulation.

Among the functions that may be allotted to an SRO are the responsibility for establishing rules and codes of conduct; for keeping members informed of these rules and codes, as well as of changes in government policies; for inspecting, monitoring and auditing the firms in the industry; for enforcing both its own rules and those imposed by the legislature or the government; and for disciplining members which violate these rules. When disputes arise between firms in an industry, the SRO may be able to serve as a mediator, or as the designated arbitrator in a scheme of binding or non-binding arbitration. Furthermore, the SRO can represent the 'public face' of an industry to the community; while, behind the scenes, serving as a buffer to protect the industry from government interference. Thus the SRO occupies an intermediary position between the government and the society at large.

In the 'professions' can be found a long tradition of self-regulation. Doctors, dentists, nurses, solicitors, barristers, psychologists, architects and accountants are but a few of the professional groups that regulate themselves through what are known as RPBs, or recognised professional bodies (a sub-category of SROs). Unlike SROs that are created by statute, RPBs are typically not subject to the supervision of an oversight agency or 'super-regulator'. Perhaps the greatest power that an RPB has is that of being able to control entry into the profession. The SRO may be delegated the authority to issue a licence, without which an individual cannot practice in the profession. This licensure power is a two-edged sword, for while it serves to assure the public that practitioners have been carefully vetted, it also has the potential to allow the RPB to create a monopoly within the profession by excluding new, perhaps non-conformist, applicants for entry. For this reason, some RPBs are restricted to 'certifying' its members. Certification is not required to engage in the occupation, but those who have received certification are able to hold themselves out as 'certified' members of the profession or use a particular title.

RPBs are allowed to formulate rules and standards of conduct for their members, and to determine when there has been a violation of these rules, and with what consequences. Disciplinary sanctions may include withdrawal of the licence or certification status of the offender, or a temporary (or permanent) suspension of the offender's ability to practice in the profession. The fact that an RPB may have the authority to discipline its members, however, will not preclude a criminal prosecution in an appropriate case – a lawyer who steals a client's funds, for example, can still be prosecuted for theft. This is a necessary reservation, for, although an RPB may be able to discipline its members, it may not be empowered to impose a purely 'penal' sanction such as imprisonment, which is reserved to the courts. None the less, in some instances RPB sanctions can be extremely onerous to the individual concerned. If a doctor or lawyer is suspended from practice, or the right to trade on the Stock Exchange is withdrawn from a stockbroker, the financial repercussions may far eclipse any fine that might have realistically been imposed by a court of law. In one case reported by Levi (1987: 240–246), a Lloyds' broker was expelled from Lloyds, fined £1m and ordered to pay 'substantial' costs; the expulsion may have been the most expensive part of the sanction.

Leniency, however, more often seems to characterises RPB disciplinary measures. Clarke (1990) reported that in the financial services sector the penalty most likely to be imposed by an SRO was a reprimand, at least if the offence was not seen as wilful or particularly egregious, and the offender was sufficiently perceptive to appreciate the need to co-operate with the investigation and display suitable contrition. As an SRO may not publish a report of its disciplinary hearings or the reasons for its decision, it may be impossible to ascertain whether an SRO has been lenient or strict in a particular case; or, indeed, whether, across the board, it has acted in a consistent and non-discriminatory manner.

While the RPBs generally have been deemed to be a success, SROs in the financial services industry have had a more chequered history, at least in England. In the 1980s, when the financial services industry accepted the need for regulation but resisted the creation of an English version of the SEC (discussed in chapter 9), SROs were seen as a viable alternative. By the 1990s, however, disillusionment had set in, and, in 2000, most of the SROs were replaced by the Financial Services Authority (FSA), a powerful umbrella regulatory agency established by Parliament. A few SROs remain, but they are subject to the close supervision of the FSA. The experiences that led to the replacement of SROs with the FSA offer a cautionary tale of the dangers of SROs. The rules of the SROs had become increasingly elaborate and technical, and lacking in overall coherence, so much so that the SROs lost the confidence of firms that had supported their creation (Clarke: 1998). Some firms, particularly those which had diversified and had a wide range of business interests, found themselves subject to the jurisdiction of multiple SROs whose rules and regulations imposed contradictory obligations.

Even where SROs are not required by statute, or created in response to a veiled threat by the government to enact a statute imposing a more formal regime of regulation, companies in an industry may nevertheless see benefits in establishing their own 'private' SRO. We have already discussed some of the perceived benefits to an industry. SROs are a vehicle through which firms can pool knowledge, facilitate co-operation and deflect government intervention. Sometimes SROs are a defensive measure that comes into being when firms in an industry do not trust their competitors to monitor themselves; by 'buying in' to an SRO, these competitors become bound to abide by its rules.

A private SRO may be established through informal agreement or formal contract among firms in an industry, with the authority of the SRO shaped by the terms of the agreement or contract. A minimalist role might simply entail promulgation of 'codes of (good/best) practice' for the industry. The SRO may also be charged with keeping firms abreast of developments relating to the industry and for providing training to member companies. There has now developed an entire industry, typically consisting of private security companies, but with some universities and accountants' firms entering the market, which provide instruction in fraud prevention, risk assessment, physical security of premises and computer systems, screening of personnel and the development of corporate codes of conduct. A more extensive role for a private SRO would entail some or all of the following: rule-making, inspections, monitoring, enforcement, adjudication and sanctioning of non-compliant members. The SRO may be authorised to undertake independent investigations of member firms without seeking advance permission from the firm being investigated. In cases where there is a question of whether a breach of the SRO's rules has occurred, the SRO may act as a quasi-judicial tribunal for determining the truth of an accusation. If it finds a violation, it may be empowered to impose a sanction on the offender.

In theory, SROs should create a 'level playing field' for all firms in a given industry. In practice, uniform and consistent treatment may depend on who is responsible for drafting and enforcing the codes, rules and standards of the SRO and, perhaps even more importantly, on who was in charge of determining whether there had been a violation and with what sanctions attached to the violation. The 'big players' in an industry can sometimes wield disproportionate influence, especially when they underwrite the lion's share of the costs of the SRO, or 'volunteer' their executives to serve on the SRO's governing body (neither of which smaller firms may be in a position to do). These representatives may have a vested interest in preserving the established ways of doing business of their own firms, and may undermine proposals for reform. Indeed, all of the member firms in an SRO may recognise that it is in their collective interest to allow each other the maximum latitude short of the point where the government feels that it must intervene and impose external regulation. Thus, an SRO may proceed cautiously where bold reform measures are called for. Members of the SRO's disciplinary committee may also proceed cautiously in imposing sanctions on other members, recognising that at some future stage the 'shoe may be on the other foot'.

These 'problems' raise the basic issue of whether members of an industry can be trusted to deal fairly and objectively with themselves or their colleagues. Without public accountability, and without judicial review of SRO disciplinary decisions (discussed below), it is hard to know the answer. Although the various financial services SROs in place in England failed to prevent a series of major scandals in the City of London during the 1980s and 1990s, it is difficult to know whether any other system would have been more effective. One is hard-pressed to believe that the threat of even a criminal prosecution would have had much effect on a Robert Maxwell or Ernest Saunders. Their example highlights the difficulties in controlling the misconduct of shrewd, prestigious and powerful business leaders who dominate their organisation, engage in sophisticated deviance, and camouflage that deviance with legal and accountancy devices that are virtually impervious to detection.

Another danger arises when an SRO defines its mission in terms of serving the interests of their members, in which case the public interest may be given too short shrift. This danger can be avoided in the case of statutory SROs if the government directs that there be lay members or public interest representatives on the governing board of the SRO; or if an appointed external monitoring body or 'super-regulator' is assigned the specific task of ensuring that the public interest has been taken into account in SRO proceedings. A private SRO can similarly decide to include public interest representatives on its governing board, but it is under no obligation to do so. None the less, it may see a benefit in recruiting such representatives in order to promote public confidence in the SRO.

Private SROs may be particularly valuable with respect to international disputes and alleged misconduct. Public investigative bodies, such as the police or customs, may be frustrated by jurisdictional barriers, corrupt or intransigent foreign officials and unco-operative local witnesses. As an SRO will not be bound by inter-state agreements and compacts, or by multilateral treaties, it may be less hampered by such obstacles. In response to the growing problem of maritime fraud, for example, the International Chamber of Commerce set up the International Maritime Bureau (IMB) in 1980. The IMB's remit ranges from providing information on trends and developments in the industry, to investigating and preparing criminal and civil cases (sometimes in co-operation with legal authorities). When prosecution seems remote or for some reason inappropriate, the IMB is empowered to 'negotiate' a settlement with the suspected offender. (Conway: 1981; Ellen and Campbell: 1982). Clarke (2000: 203–221) takes the position that to expect the IMB to be able to eliminate international maritime crime may be unrealistic, but, this fact notwithstanding, asserts that the IMB has helped 'honest' shippers to protect themselves, while making life difficult for many of the dishonest shippers. Clarke sees the IMB as a significant complement to the weaknesses of the main regulatory regime administered through the International Maritime Organisation.

If an SRO has the authority to enact rules for its members and to discipline those who violate these rules, and if a company which has been subjected to sanctions by the SRO believes that the rules are unfair or that it has not been treated fairly by the disciplinary committee, what recourse, if any, does it have? The traditional method for reviewing the allegedly improper or unlawful exercise of government power is through judicial review, but the amenability of SROs to judicial review remains a matter of controversy (Black: 1996). As a general proposition, if an SRO is established by statute, or by the executive by exercise of the prerogative, it is a 'public' body, and its 'public' decisions will be subject to judicial review.[1] However, in the leading decision of *R v Panel on Take-overs and Mergers, ex p Datafin plc*,[2] the Court of Appeal made clear that it was not only the *source* of a decision-making body's powers and duties that count, but also their *nature*; and that, if the powers that were exercised were of a 'public' nature and the body was exercising essentially 'public law' functions, a court could entertain an application for judicial review even though the decision-making body had not been created by statute or by exercise of the

---

1 See *R v Criminal Injuries Compensation Board, ex p Lain* [1967] 2 All ER 770.
2 See *R v Panel on Take-overs and Mergers, ex p Datafin plc* [1987] 1 All ER 564.

prerogative. On the other hand, the holding in *Datafin* has been held not to disturb the orthodox view that, where an SRO has been created by contract and is engaged in purely 'private' functions, its decisions are not amenable to judicial review.[3] Although the distinction between 'public' and 'private' bodies and functions may sound fairly straightforward, in practice it may be difficult to fit an SRO neatly into one of these pigeonholes. Some SROs exercise both public and private functions, in which case its public but not its private functions may be the subject of judicial review.[4] There is also a line of argument that would make the decisions of a *private* SRO amenable to judicial review, if, in the SRO's absence, the government would have had to establish a comparable *public* regulatory body.[5] In the final analysis there is no clear litmus test for when an SRO's decisions are amenable to judicial review, and courts will need to consider a wide range of factors, as well as the situational context.

The availability of judicial review is one aspect of a larger issue that relates to the transparency and accountability of SROs. SROs that are created by statute may be required to include lay members or representatives of the public interest on their governing board, or they may be subject to monitoring by a government-appointed regulatory body or 'super-regulator'. Annual reports may also be mandated and published. In theory, all of these mechanisms would seem to promote transparency and accountability. Unfortunately, much of the work of an SRO may take place 'behind the scenes', and the ordinary citizens on its governing board may not realise the self-centred motivations that gave rise to proposed policies, rules and regulations. The public reports of an SRO can be rather opaque, consisting of a mass of statistics, but providing no real insight into the workings of the SRO. In respect to both statutory and private SROs, there may be no published record of the SRO's disciplinary proceedings or decisions. Unlike criminal trials, which are open to the public, whether or not a disciplinary hearing is open to the public may depend on the SRO's internal rules of procedure (or those imposed by the government), and there will not necessarily be a formal opinion issued by the fact-finder. As a consequence, it may be difficult to determine whether the SRO has applied its own rules correctly or whether its decision is consistent with existing 'precedent' or supported by the evidence. The problems of transparency and accountability may be exacerbated in respect to private SROs, which may not include members of the public on their decision-making bodies, and may not even publish statistical reports. If, further, private SROs are not subject to government oversight, if their decisions are not amenable to judicial review by the courts, and if their publications are mere public relations exercises, they are in danger of becoming a law unto themselves.

In short, there is much about SROs, especially private SROs, that we do not know. Little research has been undertaken, or perhaps even could be undertaken. Whether or not collective self-regulation is an improvement on government regulation depends on so many variables that it is difficult to reach any definitive conclusions. Priest (1997/98) maintains that SROs are most likely to be effective where the number of firms in the industry is limited, where there is a history of effective co-operation

---

3   See *R v Football Association, ex p Football League Ltd* [1993] 2 All ER 833; *R v Disciplinary Committee of the Jockey Club, ex p Aga Khan* [1993] 2 All ER 853.

4   See *R v Jockey Club, ex p RAM Racecourses Ltd* [1993] 2 All ER 225.

5   See *Poplar Housing and Regeneration Community Association Ltd v Donoghue* [2002] QB 48.

among these firms, where there is adequate expertise and resources to support the SRO, where peer pressure can be garnered to support compliance with SRO standards and codes, where consumers value compliance and non-compliance is 'punished', where the SRO has created fair and respected dispute mechanisms, where the exit costs from the industry are high and where there is opportunity for public participation. None the less, she favours a residual auditing or monitoring role for the government, for the risk of failure is often too great for the government to be allowed to abdicate its responsibilities to the public. According to Priest, SROs may work best when they function in the 'shadow' of government regulation. SROs, and particularly private SROs, can consciously or unconsciously promote anti-competitive behaviour, and can contribute to the creation of monopolies by unreasonably excluding new entrants to an industry, thereby stifling innovation and increasing the costs to the consumer. If firms in an industry have the sense that they have been coerced into joining an SRO, or if they believe that that the standards set by the SRO are designed to advance the interests of the 'big players' and are inappropriate for smaller firms, they may simply refuse to comply with its dictates. To make SRO codes, enforcement mechanisms and disciplinary processes effective, the government and the courts may have no choice but to exercise a monitoring function.

C. INDIVIDUALISED SELF-REGULATION

To return to basics, the goal is an effective system of policing companies that overcomes the practical limitations that hinder traditional inspectorates and the problems of accountability that are associated with collective self-regulatory bodies. The police do not have the time, expertise or inclination to ferret out corporate wrongdoing. Government agencies may have the expertise, but too often lack the resources, and sometimes the will, to do the job properly. The lack of accountability of SROs, and the concomitant sense that SROs are akin to a 'private club' and are overly indulgent to the transgressions of their members, raises questions about their credibility and legitimacy.

At a time when the public's demand for corporate accountability seems to be growing, the government increasingly appears to want to transfer the responsibility (and cost) of regulating companies from the public to the private sector. The confluence of these forces gives rise to the question of whether the way forward might be to allow – or require – companies to regulate themselves. Undoubtedly, the entity that has the competency and resources to investigate a company, which is in the best position to conduct such an investigation, and which is able to effect meaningful changes in the company's practices, methods of operation and ways of doing business, if they are found to be deficient, is the company itself. All that may seem to be missing is the motivation, which, as we shall see, can be supplied through various elements of the criminal justice system.

1. Advantages

The advantages of individualised self-regulation are catalogued by Ayres and Braithwaite (1992), who have done much of the groundwork in this area. In general terms, they point out that individualised self-regulation permits a company to establish rules and regulations that are specifically tailored to the risks associated with the company's particular way of doing business. State laws are unavoidably general because corporate legislation must be sufficiently encompassing to take account of a large number of companies doing business in a wide variety of ways. In a regime of individualised self-regulation, the excess baggage can be shed.

From the perspective of the state, individual self-regulation shifts the costs of regulation from the state to the companies who are entrusted with regulating themselves. However, because a company would only be responsible for itself (or in the case of parent companies and multinationals, itself and its subsidiaries), the expense would not be exorbitant. Nor, indeed, is it unreasonable that companies should bear the costs of monitoring themselves. In any event, the overall cost of a regime of individualised self-regulation can be expected to be less than the cost of a regime of external regulation, as efficiency gains can be expected. Because external regulators may not know where to focus their attention, their inspection is often of a hit-or-miss variety. In contrast, an internal self-regulatory unit will be aware of the criminogenic fault lines within the organisation and can direct its investigations with greater precision.

The felt 'presence' of a company's self-regulatory body will be both immediate and pervasive, much more so than that of an external agency. While external agencies may be able to inspect a company only infrequently because of resource and personnel constraints, an internal body can engage in regular surveillance, and will have access to corporate files at all times. Unlike an external agency, the internal body will be intimately familiar with the company's culture and ethos, and with its decision-making processes and structures, both formal and informal. Finally, while an external agency may lack the authority to tell a company how it should be conducting its business and may only be able to negotiate compliance with its standards, an internal body, being an arm of the company, will be in a position to mandate (or recommend to the board of directors that it should mandate) needed changes in the company's business operation.

The potential of individualised self-regulation to generate creative solutions to problematic areas of corporate activity, and at relatively little risk should the solutions fail, should not be discounted. If a company chooses an innovative approach to self-regulation that proves ineffective, the consequences will largely be confined to that company and those with whom it has dealt. In contrast, if the state were to adopt the same innovative approach to an entire industry and that were to fail, a far greater number of victims would be affected. This consideration may provide a partial explanation as to why governments are generally inclined to proceed cautiously. The governmental body charged with reviewing and approving corporate submissions (see below) should, therefore, be receptive to experimental proposals. If they succeed, they will provide a model of best practice for other companies, and if they fail, other companies will at least learn from the experience of the innovator.

Ayres and Braithwaite point out that while individualised self-regulation can foster experimentation, innovation and, ultimately, progress, external regulation that is perceived as meddlesome and nit-picking tends to breed a culture of resistance (1992: 20). External regulation can degenerate into a cat-and-mouse game in which regulators write rules, companies search out the loopholes in the rules and regulators are forced to respond with more and more rules in an attempt to close the loopholes.

When companies write their own rules, on the other hand, there should be a commitment to them that is lacking when the rules are imposed upon them from 'on high'. The company which writes its own regulations obviously cannot be heard to complain that the 'regulator' does not understand its situation or that of the industry, or that the regulator's rules are not relevant to the way that the company conducts its business.

Most corporate executives will instinctively favour individualised self-regulation, seeing it as less bureaucratic and less distortive of the free market than state regulation. They too envisage that self-regulation will foster experimentation and entrepreneurial initiatives. But what assurance is there that companies will take seriously the obligation to regulate themselves? Managers have often been criticised for being insufficiently risk-aversive (Coffee: 1977). Can such impulses be checked in a system of self-regulation? What incentives can be created for a company to invest the time, personnel and resources needed to make a programme of self-regulation effective? We shall return to the issue of incentives in a subsequent section, but first it behoves us look at how a programme of individualised self-regulation might be brought into being.[6]

2. A model

The goal is to persuade companies to adapt management systems designed to identify and avert criminologically significant risks before they can ripen and lead to illegality and/or social harm. Too often such systems are first considered only after an unfortunate 'accident' has revealed deficiencies in the company's business operation. But often these so-called 'accidents' are avoidable, and often the failure to reflect on how to avoid them constitutes, in legal terms, wilful blindness, objective recklessness or, at the very least, negligence.

Traditional law enforcement, as we have seen, is primarily reactive; it is only after a victim has died or been injured, investors have suffered financial loss or property damage has occurred that the authorities are called in to investigate. It would be far better for companies to have in place systems that would prevent these consequences from occurring in the first place. Companies need to focus their attention on better risk management and the monitoring of persons whom the company has put in a position to cause harm or commit criminal offences.

The first step is for each company to construct a set of rules, regulations, policies and procedures that are designed to achieve corporate objectives while avoiding unduly dangerous and/or illegal practices. Because the resulting codes of conduct would have to be sufficiently broad to encompass all aspects of the company's business, including some which were unique to the particular company, they might well include proscriptions that one would not encounter in more general legislation. In addition to codes of conduct, which would set minimum standards, companies should also be encouraged to promulgate codes of ethics and good (or best) practice, which would embody the company's aspirations. Whereas employee misconduct might lead to an internal disciplinary proceeding, meeting the standards of a code of good practice might be recognised affirmatively, say by a bonus or promotion. Together, the company's rules, regulations, policies and procedures and its codes of

---

6   The scheme which is presented below draws heavily on the work of Ayres and Braithwaite (1992), while also differing from their analysis in significant respects.

conduct, ethics and good practice would comprise the heart of a system of self-regulation, establishing what conduct is acceptable, unacceptable and commendable in the company's business operation (Clarke: 1991).

Once constructed, a company's proposed system of self-regulation would have to be submitted for approval to a reviewing body, which would ensure itself that the company's self-regulatory system was adequate to meet government objectives, which are more likely to be couched in general terms (such as environmental protection, non-discrimination and worker safety). The challenge to companies would be to put flesh on the bare-bones objectives, but in a way that suited the particular situation of the company. In the first instance, and for practical reasons (to avoid placing too great a burden on small companies), such submissions might be limited to companies above a certain size. The current regulatory agencies would, given their expertise in the field, be well suited to reviewing these submissions. Given their self-image of expert advisors (Carson: 1970), inspectors might well welcome this responsibility. If the reviewing body found that the company's proposals were in some respect inadequate or ambiguous, it might then enter into negotiations with the company to resolve outstanding issues of concern. The body might offer its own recommendations as to how deficiencies might be overcome.

The reviewing body would also be charged with devising model rules and codes of good practice for the general guidance of companies in an industry. These would not be binding, but would provide a useful starting point for a company constructing its own system of self-regulation, providing it with guidance and benchmarks against which it could compare its own proposals. The model rules would also help to guard against insularity and oversights. If a company did choose to adopt the model rules, it would create a prima facie case for their being approved, unless there was some specific feature of the company's business operation to indicate their inappropriateness or unsuitability. Once established and published, the model rules would allow the approval process, discussed above, to be extended to smaller firms that might otherwise have found it overly burdensome to create a system of self-regulation. The model rules, as well as approved company-specific self-regulatory systems, would become a matter of public record, and their publication would assist smallish companies in the task of generating their own individualised self-regulatory systems.

The model of individualised self-regulation envisages not only that companies create self-regulatory systems, but also that they take responsibility for their enforcement. After its self-regulatory scheme was approved, a company would next need to communicate to its workforce what was expected of each individual under the scheme, preferably in writing to guard against poor memories and potential misunderstandings, and provide any necessary retraining. The scheme will likely have to be amended from time to time in light of changed circumstances, technological advances and newly discovered risks, and periodic review should be an integral component of all self-regulatory systems. In this connection it might be noted that one of the strengths of self-regulation is that internal rules and procedures are far easier to amend than is legislation. As amendments to a company's regulatory system are made, they too will need to be communicated to the company's workforce, which might be achieved through email updates, newsletters and/or regular information/training sessions.

After a self-regulatory system has been devised, approved and explained to a company's workforce, the focus shifts to implementation and enforcement. Again, a scheme of individualised self-regulation envisages companies taking the primary responsibility. Every company would have to put into place a monitoring system that was adapted to the regulatory scheme that it had adopted and was appropriate to the risks that were presented by its way of doing business. Like the self-regulation schemes themselves, monitoring mechanisms may vary from company to company, and no prescribed approach will necessarily fit all. In the United States, the trend has been to delegate the task of monitoring to 'corporate compliance' departments, but there will still be variations in how each of these functions. Generally speaking, a corporate compliance department will investigate improper practices reported to it and carry out independent investigations on its own initiative. Its task, as the name suggests, will be to induce compliance both with internal company rules and the law. A corporate compliance department fosters communication within an organisation by providing whistleblowers, including employees, corporate officers and members of the public, with an identifiable body to which they can convey their concerns regarding practices that may be dangerous, illegal or in violation of the company's policies. The compliance department will be responsible for investigating the reported infractions. As a matter of good practice, it should keep its informant abreast of the progress of its investigation, as well as its conclusions and actions. To the extent practicable, it should strive to preserve confidentiality[7] and to protect the informant from suffering any adverse repercussions as a result of the report.

In addition to investigating improprieties that are reported to it, a compliance department should have the authority, and be encouraged, to undertake proactive investigations on its own initiative. In conducting such investigations, it would enjoy several advantages over a regulatory agency. Unlike an agency, it could institute an investigation at a time of its choosing. Further, it would be in a position to make unannounced 'raids' and even 'sting' operations, which, had they been conducted by the police, might have raised thorny legal issues of entrapment. Because the compliance department would be an integral organ of the company, the 'us against them' mentality that often frustrates the investigations of the police and external agencies is less likely to be present,[8] particularly where the company's board of directors has formally endorsed the work of the compliance department and insisted on employee co-operation with its investigations. To be effective, a compliance system needs to have the backing of senior management and an informational flow system that brings incidences of non-compliance to the attention of managers who have the authority to take the necessary remedial actions; in other words, there must be 'focused accountability' (Priest: 1997/98).

3.   In the event of a violation

When a compliance department discovers that a criminal offence has been committed by an employee or by the company, how should it proceed? There are two main schools of thought. One holds that the offence should be reported to the appropriate

---

7   At some point, considerations of natural justice may require disclosure of the whistleblower to the member of staff accused of wrongdoing.
8   However, if employees come to view compliance officers as the enemy prepared to turn them in to their employer or the police, they may stop co-operating with it.

legal authorities; the other favours handling the matter internally. Most companies would probably prefer to deal with *minor* transgressions internally and not have to report them to law enforcement agencies. In this 'private justice' system (Tonry and Reiss: 1993), an offender may be reprimanded, demoted or dismissed, depending on the egregiousness of his/her violation. In the event of a dismissal, the company will have to decide whether to give a positive reference to future employers. In order to maintain good employee relations, some companies will routinely provide a positive reference. However, in doing so the company may not only be 'passing on' its problem to some other company but may also be exposing itself to at least civil liability if the former employee commits a similar offence in the new working environment. However, the company is in a difficult position, for it may also be sued for giving a poor reference that it cannot justify in court. Accordingly, a company may prefer to transfer an employee suspected of an offence to another assignment where there is less opportunity for wrongdoing rather than instituting a formal proceeding where charges would have to be proved (and where the company's failure to provide proper training or supervision might also come to light). In cases of offenders who may be approaching retirement age, early retirement with full pension rights and the honorific trappings of a retirement ceremony become an option. All of these responses have a long pedigree and which a company chooses may depend on the status of the offender, the nature of the offence and the culture of the organisation. Whichever option is chosen, it is a fair assumption that the goal is less the best interests of the individual and more the desire of the company to avoid bad publicity, with the attendant damage to the company's reputation. However, if it is to deter future rule violations, a company must be careful that the sanctions of its 'private justice' system are not perceived as a reward for deviance, as they might be if, for example, a promotion were to accompany the re-assignment of a known violator or overly generous pension benefits were to be offered for 'early retirement'.

While 'private justice' systems and internal dispositions may commend themselves in cases of minor breaches of a company's self-regulatory system, they are problematic when serious wrongdoing has occurred. Numerous issues would arise with respect to an internal proceeding where the charge is, in effect, the commission of a crime, including: the procedural and evidentiary rules that should govern; whether the employee should be entitled to assistance of counsel (and if s/he cannot afford a lawyer, whether one would be provided free of cost, and by whom – if the company, there is a potential for a conflict of interest); the defences that would be available to the employee charged; whether there would be a right to call and cross-examine witnesses; the standard of proof by which the company would have to prove its case (proof 'beyond reasonable doubt'?); the types of sanctions that might be imposed following a finding that the charges have been proved; and so on. Further, should an employee dissatisfied with the results of the internal proceeding be entitled to seek judicial review or appeal as of right, either with respect to process or sanction, to a court of law? While there are in law procedural protections which govern an unfair dismissal, these are not necessarily co-terminus with the rights of an accused in a criminal trial, and it would have to be determined how the two sets of rules might mesh in a system of self-regulation. Because the internal disciplinary proceeding would, in effect, be displacing the formal criminal processes of the state, a strong argument could be made that principles of natural justice, as well as the provisions of the Human Rights Act 1998, should apply to it and that the process should be subject to judicial review.

Even assuming internal procedures that were adequate to safeguard the rights of an 'accused'employee, there are other worrying dimensions to internal disciplinary proceedings. Consider the case of an employee charged with an offence for which the company might bear some degree of responsibility: for instance, a lorry driver is brought before an internal tribunal for driving in a reckless and dangerous manner. Will the internal tribunal be prepared to entertain the argument that the company's system of compensating its drivers by the number of deliveries they make promotes irresponsible driving habits? Who will ensure that the person subjected to the disciplinary proceeding, although perhaps guilty in his/her own mind and perhaps even in law, is not simply a sacrificial lamb for policies formulated at a higher level? When fault may rest with corporate policies, can the company be trusted to determine objectively an individual's guilt? Obtaining uniform treatment of offenders in an industry can also be a problem when corporate private justice systems are in force. Dispositions of similar cases may vary from company to company. A worker in one company may only be reprimanded in an internal proceeding whereas in another company the identical offence could lead to dismissal. Where the 'accused' is a corporate officer, the internal proceeding may be a collusive sham, with the officer 'accepting' responsibility for an offence for which the company bears the blame in exchange for some, perhaps unspecified, future benefit. In the absence of the spotlight of a public trial, such a pact may never be revealed.

Nor should the educative and deterrent functions of a public trial be lightly dismissed. Public trials inform other companies of the limits of the law. Particularly in areas where the line between permissible and impermissible business practices may be hazy or in the process of changing, it is important that companies be aware of the extent of their legal obligations. Companies will learn little, if anything, from an unreported internal disciplinary proceeding in another company to which they were not privy (unless information on it reaches them through the grapevine). In any event, an internal disciplinary decision would have no precedential effect, and its deterrent effect would depend on others in the industry becoming aware of the internal proceedings and consequences. But most companies will be reluctant to air their 'dirty linen'. Even the company's own workforce may not learn of the outcome of an internal hearing if the company is not minded to reveal the outcome, and it would be under no legal obligation to do so. One of the most serious drawbacks to private justice systems is the very fact that they do take place in private, with the result that other companies, the company's own employees, and the general public may never learn of the disposition (or even the existence) of an offence. Nor will the public learn of companies in which law-breaking is chronic and/or tolerated. Private justice systems, in short, allow companies to insulate themselves from public scrutiny.

The main alternative to internal disciplinary proceedings is to require a compliance department to report criminal violations to the appropriate legal authorities. One might go so far as to maintain that there is a duty to do so that is more far-reaching than that imposed on ordinary citizens. Although misprision of felony (the failure to report a felony) was at one time a crime under English law, it is no longer, at least so long as one's silence is not improperly compensated or rewarded.[9] The more far-reaching duty of reporting envisaged for companies can be justified by the fact that, under regimes of individualised self-regulation, the state in effect

9   See Criminal Law Act 1967, s 5(1).

cedes to companies investigative powers that would normally belong to the police. It follows that the company's compliance department should be under no less a duty to report violations than would be a constable who uncovered a crime while on patrol. Placing compliance officers under a duty to report crimes of which they are aware would allow these officers to justify actions that might otherwise be misconstrued as disloyalty to the organisation. Ayres and Braithwaite (1992) go so far as to advocate that the failure to report a corporate offence of which a compliance officer was aware *should itself be criminal.*

One of the drawbacks to compliance departments is the friction that can be created between members of the compliance department and employees of the company, especially if the department is required to report employee criminal offences to outside authorities. Indeed, such an obligation raises the question of whether compliance officers should have to 'caution' employees suspected of having committed a crime. In any event, if compliance officers are seen as little more than 'snitches', employees will be understandably loathe to co-operate in their investigations. The intangible and elusive dimension of corporate morale – what motivates employees to work over-and-above the minimal demands of the job – will be placed in jeopardy. A mandatory duty to report criminal activity thus does not come without cost to employer-employee relations. On the other hand, knowledge that a compliance department will be obliged to report violations to the authorities should strengthen the department's effectiveness in preventing illegality, as both employees and the company's board of directors and officers will be under no illusions that the matter can be swept under a corporate rug.

4. Pitfalls

While we have attempted to show how a system of self-regulation might be constructed in theory, the more critical question is whether it would be effective in practice. If a twenty-first century researcher interested in self-regulation were to pay a visit to a modern company, it would not be unusual for him/her to be shown corporate mission statements pronouncing the importance of integrity, codes of conduct for managers and employees, internal and external auditing systems which were in place, screening and training programmes for both new and senior employees, fraud prevention units, risk assessment specialists, an in-house legal department and a compliance department. These features have all become part of the corporate landscape, and yet, the evidence is that, despite these safeguards, dangerous practices and illegality persist. Why?

There are several reasons why self-regulation may not function as intended or envisaged. First, and probably foremost, the effectiveness of any system of self-regulation will depend on the commitment of the company's executive officers and directors to the system. A compliance programme may be undermined by the unwillingness of a board of directors to provide adequate resources for it to carry out its job properly or, more subtly, by assigning junior staff to the programme who will not command the respect of the company's workforce. There is evidence, moreover, that some compliance units see their remit in terms of protecting the company against external probes and instructing employees in how to cope with questions from police or outside investigators (Bosworth-Davies: 1992: 40). Other compliance departments seem to be created for their symbolic effect and to provide support for a 'due diligence' defence if subsequently needed.

Whether a board of directors and corporate executive officers take a compliance department seriously can be seen in their reaction when confronted with damaging reports. In a tough, 'bottom-line' company, compliance department reports of dangerous or illegal practices that will be costly to rectify may simply be ignored by the board of directors. Indeed, if it is the board which is alleged to be at fault by the compliance officers, there may not be much enthusiasm for approving an internal investigation or the institutuion of disciplinary proceedings (let alone the reporting of the offence to the police).

As well as being taken on board by directors and executives, the success of a self-regulatory system will depend on whether the relevant rules and regulations are accepted by the employees who will be expected to abide by them. Compliance systems can founder simply because those engaged in wrongdoing are unwilling to give up their illegal approach to carrying out work assignments. It has to be recognised that many illegal shortcuts in companies are adopted simply because they make the job of the workforce easier. To increase the likelihood of acceptance of a company's scheme of self-regulation, workers or their representatives should be consulted and involved in the process of formulating the relevant rules and regulations. The rationale for the rules adopted needs in any event to be explained to employees, and compliance must be 'sold' to those on the front-line if it is not to be resisted. Any compliance programme can be breached by those with the determination to do so and sufficiently sophisticated to understand how to get around the controls in place. The higher the offender is on the corporate ladder, the greater the danger of evasion. A high-ranking corporate executive may not only enjoy considerable autonomy and freedom from scrutiny, but may also be able to intimidate compliance officers, either formally or informally. It is doubtful, for example, that any compliance officer would have been able to stand up to Robert Maxwell.

This raises the more general question of whether compliance officers may be subject to the same sort of 'capture' that is alleged to occur with respect to government regulators currently. Indeed, as employees of the company, compliance officers would seem to have less independence and be in an even more vulnerable position than external regulators; at least a regulator cannot be fired by the company to which it reports its bad news. It would be naïve for compliance officers not to expect to encounter resistance and hostility from superiors whose own actions were being called into question, especially if the latter could envisage themselves as potential defendants in a criminal prosecution. The compliance officer may also face a measure of social isolation from immediate colleagues in the workplace. A central unit in a large company may develop an élan and social life of its own, but a sole local compliance officer in a branch office may feel lonely and exposed (and choose the path of socialising with colleagues rather than becoming a corporate pariah). In order to ensure the independence and integrity of compliance officers, and to attract qualified individuals to take on this 'thankless task', American companies have had to make compliance officers among the highest paid employees in the company. It is important that compliance officers be respected, or at least be taken seriously, by other employees in the company, and a high salary and commensurate status help to ensure that this respect will be forthcoming.

There are other ways of strengthening the position of compliance officers. One that we have already noted is for Parliament to enact laws that would subject them to personal criminal liability for failing to report a corporate offence of which they were aware. This potential liability could, of course, make the post of compliance officer even more unattractive than it already is, but it would allow compliance officers to rationalise their decision to inform the police of corporate wrongdoing if their commitment to the company was queried by the board of directors or fellow employees. Another way of strengthening the hand of a compliance department would be by including on the investigatory team representatives of non-governmental organisations (NGOs), public interest groups, worker associations and other 'stakeholders'. Members of such constituencies can be expected to be more resistant to 'capture' than compliance officers, who are dependent on the company for their pay-cheques. If corporate wrongdoing were uncovered, one would expect that the NGO and 'public interest' representatives would not be amenable to a cover-up.

A more subtle reason why self-regulatory systems may fail despite a commitment to them on the part of management is because of fragmentation and a lack of co-ordination between the legal and accounting departments, as well as others, and the formal compliance department. Each of these departments has a responsibility for various components of compliance. However, the focus of accountants may be on financial figures, and that of lawyers on the firm's exposure to legal liability, while a corporate communications department might be obsessed with the need to avoid or counter unfavourable publicity. As a result, warning signals received by one of these departments could be ignored as irrelevant to it and not passed on to another department for whom the signals would be more meaningful. 'Chinese walls', erected to protect against potential conflicts of interest where the same firm represents clients with antagonistic interests, may in fact bar two units of a company from communicating with one another. When each unit develops tunnel vision, the 'big picture' may not be seen or appreciated.

Corporate audits, both financial and social, often form an integral part of self-regulation. However, financial auditors have not always seen it as their responsibility to report criminal offences. They would claim that they were not police officers; that they were not trained or skilled in the detection of crime; that they were not employed to seek out criminal violations; and that for them to report such violations to the authorities would violate client confidentiality. In a number of the major scandals (for example, BCCI and Barings) auditors kept their silence in the face of strong evidence of illegality (which later formed the basis of civil suits against the accounting firms). The dynamics of the profession contribute to the problem, as relatively few large firms are in fierce competition for contracts from large companies and multinational enterprises. This argues for a legal obligation being imposed on auditors, as now exists in England, to report illegality that they discover in the course of an audit to the proper authorities. This move has been reinforced by European directives and national legislation on money laundering, which has had an impact on the reporting of suspicious transactions by accountants, lawyers and those in the financial services industry (Savona: 1999).

Compliance departments represent an advance in corporate self-governance, but the nagging question that remains is 'who will police the policemen?' Having in place a government-approved system of self-regulation is a fine starting point, but if the company's compliance department fails to ensure that the scheme is adhered to in practice, the whole structure will collapse. Who is to hold the compliance departments to account? Will an external regulatory agency have to be established for this purpose? If so, it would bring us full circle, again beset with the challenge of making external regulation effective. Going down this road would defeat the purpose of moving towards a system of individualised self-regulation in the first place, which was to eliminate the need for external regulatory bodies, which historically had not proved effective.

There may, however, be several ways of strengthening the role of compliance departments, short of re-establishing a system of external monitoring. One way would be to impose heavy sanctions on a company that was convicted of a crime where it could be shown at the trial that the company did not have in place an effective compliance department. This is the approach, it will be recalled, that has been adopted in the United States under the federal sentencing guidelines for organisational offenders. Another approach, which we have already suggested, would be to include on the compliance 'team' representatives of NGOs and public interest groups. These representatives would not have any vested interest in hushing up a company's illegality, and could be expected to resist any suggestions to do so. Finally, to be discussed in the final section of this chapter, are the psychological developments that we envisage emerging from individualised self-regulation, including the internalisation of a commitment to compliance with the law, the development of a 'corporate conscience', and the acceptance by companies that, as corporate citizens of the state, they have an obligation to act in socially responsible ways.

5.   Legal and other effects

If individualised self-regulation is to be effective in practice, and assuming it is not mandated by law (which might prove disruptive, at least initially), it would be desirable to create legal incentives to encourage the voluntary adoption of self-regulatory systems. Of course, one can argue that the establishment of an effective system of self-regulation is its own reward, as it would likely lead to fewer torts and fewer civil suits, as well as fewer criminal violations and fewer prosecutions. However, some companies might be disinclined to spend the money, time and energy required to establish and enforce such a scheme unless the benefits were more tangible. The failure of the criminal justice system formally to acknowledge a company's efforts at self-regulation would also erase the criminological distinction between companies which make a good faith, albeit unsuccessful, attempt at self-regulation and those which cannot be bothered even to try. What *legal* effect, then, might be given to a company's efforts at self-regulation?

As a starting point, it needs to be made clear that the mere adoption of a system of self-regulation is not some sort of magic wand that will make all possibility of a criminal prosecution disappear. A self-regulatory scheme is relatively simple to construct, especially where model rules are available, and would no doubt become pro forma if it could insulate a company from prosecution. A prosecutor might argue that the very fact that a crime has occurred was prima facie evidence that the company's self-regulatory system was deficient or that the company had not taken its enforcement responsibilities sufficiently seriously. Regardless of the merit of this somewhat circular line of reasoning, we have maintained that a company should not be subject to criminal sanction unless it can be proved that it has been at fault and that it should be able to avoid liability if it can show that it has devised, implemented and enforced systems that would generally prevent the commission of crime. We have advocated that 'due diligence' should be a defence to a criminal charge against a company (see chapters 3 and 6). In this context, the defendant's system of self-regulation would be evidence of its 'due diligence', as well as of its good faith (Walsh and Pyrich: 1995). This is, in fact, the effect of such a system under the Italian corporate crime statute discussed in chapters 3 and 6.

The fact-finder, however, would need to be satisfied that the scheme of self-regulation was well-conceived and effectively enforced. Approval of the scheme by a state reviewing board set up for this purpose would create a presumption that the system was well-conceived, but if the system met only the bare minimum standards of the reviewing body, the presumption would not be as strong as if the system were more demanding than the minimum required to meet the law. Nor would a finding that the system was well-conceived resolve the issue of whether it was effectively enforced. With respect to this issue, the fact-finder will want to focus particular attention on what purports to be the compliance department (or its equivalent) in the company. How long has it been in operation and with what degree of success? What sort of budget is allocated to it? Does it have a multi-disciplinary composition of staff with the appropriate skills (say with forensic accountants, former police officers with investigatory and interrogation experience and behavioural scientists for management development programmes on integrity)? Are senior management involved in its operation or is the burden entrusted to low-status employees whose advice is likely to be ignored by employees? Do compliance officers take their responsibilities seriously and do they robustly investigate reported violations? What action is taken against violators – are internal disciplinary proceedings held, and, if so, what sanctions follow if the charges are proved? Disciplinary proceedings, sanctions and the publicising of the facts of the case and the outcome of the proceedings are all important, for they send a message to the company's workforce about how seriously the company takes its own rules and regulations. This message helps to shape the corporate culture. If a company ignores violations which are profitable, other employees will be left in little doubt about the company's priorities.

A company that has made a good faith effort at self-regulation that falls short of the relevant standard required to establish 'due diligence' would still be entitled to have its regulatory efforts considered at sentencing. This, indeed, is the primary effect given to corporate compliance departments under the sentencing guidelines for organisational offenders promulgated by the US Sentencing Commission.[10] As we have discussed previously, the monetary sanction in a particular case is determined by a point system. The sentencing court first calculates a 'base fine' that reflects the seriousness of the company's offence,[11] and then multiplies this figure by a numerical factor that reflects the 'culpability' of the offender.[12] A convicted company begins with a putative culpability score of five, which can be adjusted upwards to ten or

---

10 United States Sentencing Guidelines, ch 8 (USSG). The Commission was established following passage of the Sentencing Reform Act 1984 to develop specific policies for the benefit of judges required to implement the mandates of the Act.
11 USSG, s 8C2.4.
12 USSG, s 8C2.7.

downwards to zero to reflect the presence of aggravating or mitigating factors.[13] The most significant mitigating factors are the establishment of a 'generally effective' compliance programme and the reporting of the offence by the company to the appropriate authorities before the latter learn of it from an independent source. The compliance programme does not have to be foolproof, but it does have to be 'generally effective'.

The fact that a company's efforts at self-regulation will be taken into account in sentencing may not be a sufficient incentive to induce some companies to adopt a self-regulatory system. The federal guidelines seem to invite a cost-benefit analysis in which a company must calculate the point at which the cost of compliance is less than the fine that would follow a conviction. Of course, under the sentencing guidelines, fines can range up to seven figures. None the less, a cynic might observe that a company which had established a compliance department would be more likely to uncover its own offences and thereby become obligated to report these to the authorities under the federal guidelines. Although self-reporting may mitigate the severity of the company's sentence, the company may judge that it is better off not to establish a compliance department in the first place and therefore not risk discovering crimes committed by its staff and officers, trusting that they will not otherwise come to light. While the federal sentencing guidelines may reduce the severity of the punishment of companies that have adopted compliance programmes and self-report their crimes, such companies still will suffer the stigma of a criminal conviction. Moreover, a company that has been driven into a non-competitive position or, worse still, liquidation by a multi-million dollar fine is not going to derive much consolation from the fact that the fine could have been two or even ten times the amount had the company not put into place a compliance department and self-reported its offence.

What might prove a stronger inducement for a company to adopt a meaningful scheme of self-regulation and an effective compliance programme would be the opportunity to avoid a prosecution altogether (Gobert: 1998; Walsh and Pyrich: 1995). Whatever the test of corporate criminal liability, a prosecutor will normally be able to exercise discretion as to whether to bring a formal prosecution. In exercising this discretion, the prosecutor should arguably look favourably on companies that have made a good-faith effort at self-regulation, even if their efforts have not proved altogether successful. Setting up and operating a programme of self-regulation entails considerable administrative costs, and compliance departments can place a strain on employer-employee relationships. Given the downside, companies need a strong incentive to self-regulate. More to the point, a company that has taken its self-regulation responsibilities seriously has behaved in the way that the state expects of its corporate citizens and should be treated accordingly (Gobert: 1998).

Of course, a prosecutor would have to be satisfied that a company's programme of self-regulation was not merely cosmetic. If in doubt, the prosecutor should proceed with the case, allowing the company to raise a 'due diligence' defence at trial. Accordingly, a company that wished to avoid the negative publicity, litigation costs, and uncertainty of a criminal trial will want to install and enforce a system of self-regulation that not only meets, but *exceeds*, the bare minimum standards that the law demands. In other words, the company would be guided by the spirit of the law and not just its letter, while progressive companies might even anticipate

---

13 USSG, s 8C2.5.

legislation and implement regulation before it was required (Punch: 1992). The scheme will have to be one that is transparently likely to be effective, and has been shown to be generally effective in practice. Adequate resources will need to have been allocated to the compliance department, as well as up-to-date technologies. The commitment of the board of directors, corporate executives and senior management to the compliance programme will need to be demonstrated. Compliance programmes thrive best in an open culture where mistakes are admitted and lessons learned from them, where personnel are encouraged to report shortcomings and suspicions without fear of reprisal, and where there is a willingness to work with external authorities. This is the evidence that a prosecutor should be looking for in order to be persuaded to refrain from bringing criminal charges.

The self-regulatory obligations of multinational enterprises (MNEs) should extend beyond the headquarter offices of the parent company. An MNE should have an obligation to ensure the safe, humane and legally compliant operation of its foreign subsidiaries as well. If, as advocated in chapter 5, parent companies were to be held legally responsible for crimes committed by their overseas subsidiaries where the parent had failed properly to superintend the subsidiary's operation, then the absence of a programme of individualised self-regulation in the subsidiary should have the same effect as its absence in the parent's company's own headquarters. Already, one can find compliance departments not only in the foreign branches of many American MNEs, but also in companies with whom the MNE does significant business. Whether in response to an overt threat by the MNE to sever relations with the foreign partner or simply informal advice that was heeded, foreign companies with whom American MNEs do business have begun to install compliance departments of their own. Thus, compliance departments have sprouted even in the barren landscapes of countries where the law of corporate crime is not terribly well-developed, where the legal system does not encourage self-regulation, and where no promise of a 'reward' for the establishment of a compliance department is on offer. Of course, what constitutes 'compliance' may vary from one country to another.

To summarise, a company's regime of individualised self-regulation should be relevant at three distinct junctures in a criminal prosecution. First, it should be relevant in the exercise of prosecutorial discretion in deciding whether to bring a criminal charge and for what offences; second, it should be relevant to the establishment of a 'due diligence' defence at trial; and, finally, it should be a factor to be taken into account in sentencing should the company be found guilty. Giving legal recognition and effect to a company's efforts at self-regulation will encourage companies to take seriously their responsibility for self-regulation. Where a company has not made a good faith effort to regulate itself, and a criminal offence occurs for which the company is legally accountable, punishment will reflect *both* the company's failure to prevent the resulting offence *and* its failure to undertake the responsibility of self-regulation. It might seem that a breach of a duty to obey the law is present with respect to all criminal offences, but it is deserving of special emphasis in a scheme of legal control where companies are allowed to formulate their own rules and enforce a private system of justice. The failure to take this responsibility seriously amounts to a breach of the trust placed in the company by the government in allowing self-regulation in the first place. For a system of individualised self-regulation to be effective, there should be not only the carrot of being able to avoid prosecutions and minimise penalties in the case of a conviction, but also the stick of meaningful sanctions for a company's failure to follow through on its self-regulatory responsibilities ('the benign big gun' in the terms of Ayres and Braithwaite (1992: 19), which is to be used sparingly as a measure of last resort at the apex of the enforcement pyramid).

D.   CORPORATE GOVERNANCE AND SELF-REGULATION

The argument so far is that the best way to combat corporate crime is to prevent it before it can occur, and that the best way to prevent it before it can occur is through a regime of individualised self-regulation in which every company takes responsibility for policing itself. In the preceding section we examined how the criminal justice system might be structured to promote such self-regulation. There is a danger, however, that, even though self-regulation may instinctively accord with the philosophical predilections of corporate directors and executives, if it is seen as a method of control foisted upon companies by the state, it will either be resisted or else not implemented with any vigour or enthusiasm. The fact is, however, that an effective system of self-regulation is in a company's best interest, and that the opportunity to create such a system should be embraced rather than resisted. Having a functioning and effective system of risk management and control is part of being a well-run company. In this section we look at how constituencies within the company, or aligned to it, might be marshalled to persuade companies to support self-regulation.

In a well-known article, Milton Friedman (1970), the Nobel prize-winning economist, wrote that the 'social responsibility of business is to increase its profits'. The corollary would seem to be that it is socially *irresponsible* for management to do anything that would detract from profitability. While Friedman and his ideological cohorts would presumably not condone outright illegality, even if it would be profitable, it is easy to see how their economic philosophy could engender corner-cutting and shoddy workplace practices that in turn could lead to law-breaking. Today, however, most corporate executives are sufficiently astute to appreciate that blunt sentiments such as those expressed by Friedman are best kept to oneself. In public at least, 'corporate outreach' efforts tend to stress concepts such as sustainable development, environmental concerns, human rights and social welfare. Recent advertisements by Royal Dutch Shell, for example, purport to welcome the monitoring of their exploration sites by public interest groups, claiming to see this process as an 'important investment in our goal of sustainable development, balancing economic progress with environmental care and social responsibility'. Progressive companies speak publicly of the importance of being virtuous citizens and good neighbours, and providing 'moral leadership' (Carroll: 2001: 145); but, in private, it is less clear how many corporate executives or institutional shareholders would subscribe to these larger social goals, or how many would be prepared to sacrifice profitability to achieve them.

In a sense, the challenge is to convince companies to take seriously their own rhetoric. The very fact that companies feel impelled to make corporate outreach pronouncements indicates the value that is attached to reputation, image and identity. A good reputation can be a fragile commodity, a point that we made in chapter 7 with respect to reputation-orientated sanctions, and one that is appreciated by those who would seek to influence corporate decision-making. Internal pressure to change a company's policies may be brought by those already associated with the company in some formal capacity, such as the company's employees, creditors, suppliers and investors, as well as its lawyers, accountants and, not least, its shareholders. From outside the company, the pressure may come from consumers, trade unions, potential business partners, public interest groups and NGOs.

The various persons and constituencies to which modern companies either have to respond or choose to respond are sometimes lumped together under the label of 'stakeholders'. Broadly speaking, stakeholders include those who either contribute to the attainment of a company's goals or whose lives, well-being or property may be threatened by a company's activities. Stakeholder theory envisages a role in corporate governance for such persons and constituencies, perhaps represented through organisations. In bringing them into the corporate/government (regulatory agency) equation, Ayres and Braithwaite (1992) speak of 'tri-partism'.

But who are these 'stakeholders'? It is undoubtedly easier to speak of stakeholders in the abstract than to identify all persons and constituencies who should be included in this elusive category. Blair (1995: 239) defines stakeholders as 'all parties who have contributed inputs to the enterprise and who, as a result, have at risk investments that are highly specialised to the enterprise'. Others, with a broader perspective, would include organisations and individuals who see the company as having a responsibility to promote social justice, the environment and sustainable development. Still others would include representatives of the local and, perhaps, national community within the category of stakeholders. These broader conceptions of stakeholders seem to assume that companies have an obligation to contribute to the greater good of society. From where this obligation might be derived will be explored in the next section, but here it might just be noted that this view of the company stands in stark contrast to Friedman's more narrow, profit-driven vision. Clashes between these competing images of the company will be inevitable, for what may be in the best interests of society or the environment will not always be in the best economic interests of a company (Useem: 1993).

Leader (1999) draws a potentially useful distinction between sovereign stakeholders, who have the responsibility for setting a company's agenda, and a class of secondary stakeholders who would have a right to be heard, but not a definitive voice, on *strategic* decisions affecting their interests. Both sovereign and secondary stakeholders would be involved in corporate governance, but at different levels of decision-making. While sovereign stakeholders would be able to establish corporate objectives and priorities, secondary stakeholders would be able to exert more of a constraining influence. They would be entitled to be consulted, to have their concerns taken into account and to have their interests protected (although perhaps sometimes only by compensation in the event of damage). Both constituencies would presumably be supportive of effective individualised self-regulation, whether for ideological or financial reasons.

Stakeholders represent a vehicle for bringing to bear pressure on companies to devise and implement effective systems of self-regulation, and, for this purpose, we take an expansive, rather than a narrow, view of who should be included within the category of stakeholders – basically, any persons or groups who can have a legitimate influence on corporate policies. Different categories of stakeholders, however, may be able to influence corporate policies in different ways, some directly and some indirectly. Employees, for example, operate from inside the company and may have a direct input on corporate decision-making. The influence of consumers, in contrast, is indirect, but, this fact notwithstanding, the consuming public represents a potentially powerful constitutency (although whether 'the public' can be aptly characterised as a stakeholder is debatable, for to do so may broaden the term beyond the point that it has any real meaning). Even in – or especially in – Friedman's paradigm of the company, consumer views need to be taken into account, as indifference to a company's products will adversely affect corporate earnings. A successful consumer boycott, such as occurred with respect to companies doing business in South Africa during the era of apartheid, can irredeemably damage a company's reputation and profitability and even drive it out of business altogether. The idea behind the boycott of companies doing business in South Africa was to persuade such companies that it was in their economic interest either to divest themselves of their South African holdings or, at the very least, to use their position to lobby the government of South Africa for fundamental change in its political structures and social policies.

Consumer boycotts can succeed, but their limitations should be recognised. Sometimes a company's products are sold not to members of the general public, but to other companies or to foreign governments whose decisions may not be affected by the company's reputation. Even where a company is dependent on sales to the public, consumers may not be prepared to purchase inferior goods or pay uncompetitive prices in order to punish a company for its lack of commitment to social and environmental justice. A further problem with boycotts, and 'name and shame' campaigns as well, is that of sustaining momentum. The media quickly tire of well-rehearsed stories and, for an adverse publicity campaign or boycott to succeed, either an organisation will need the financial resources to persevere over a sustained period of time (as did Greenpeace in its battle against Royal Dutch Shell with respect to the dismantling of the Brent Spar oil storage tank) or powerful social and political allies will need to be found who can take up the cause (as did churches in the boycott of Nestlé's Infant Formula; Schwartz and Gibb: 1999).

Consumer boycotts are most effective where the differences in the price and quality of the competing products in the market are not significant. It is in such markets that consumers can indulge a preference for companies that they perceive to be socially responsible. The critical word in the preceding sentence, however, is 'perceive'. Perceptions can be misleading. Adverse publicity campaigns against a company are often countered with sophisticated promotional advertising by the company under attack. These latter advertisements, coupled with denials of whatever charges are being lodged against the company, may leave the consumer at a loss as to whom to believe, especially if the charges against the company have not been established in a court of law. Where there has been no judicial declaration of illegality, moreover, those alleging corporate impropriety cannot lightly dismiss the possibility of a libel suit that may prove far more expensive for the corporate critics to defend than they are for companies, with their greater financial reserves, to pursue.

In contrast to the consuming public, employees constitute a class of stakeholder that operates from inside the company, whether or not with the backing of a trade union. The claim of employees to be involved in corporate decision-making is based on the investment of their 'human capital' in the company. Whether their claim is weaker or stronger than that of shareholders who invest their 'financial capital' in the company depends on what value one places on these respective 'capital' interests. If European Union directives are any indication, it would appear that the employees claim is the weaker of the two. Various directives give employees a right to be heard in the corporate decision-making process, but not a right to vote on actual decisions. The European Works Council Directive,[14] for example, requires that companies consult with employee representatives on issues relating to, inter alia, redundancies and corporate restructuring.

Directives such as the European Works Council Directive set a floor for worker participation in corporate decision-making processes and do not preclude individual states from granting employees a more meaningful role. In some European countries, such as Germany, worker representatives are accorded a seat on corporate boards of directors. British companies, as well as the government, on the other hand, have historically been less enamoured with this concept of 'co-determination'. Nor do employees always welcome the opportunity to sit on a board of directors, as it may put them in the awkward position of having to choose between policies that are in their own and their co-workers best financial interests and policies that are in the best interest of the company. For instance, where a proposed investment in technology might lead to workers being made redundant, employee directors might find it difficult to wear both their 'worker representative hat' and their 'director hat' at the same time.

None the less, even in the absence of a formal legal mandate, it will usually make sense for companies to consult with their employees. While some see such consultation as part of a grander ideological movement towards 'industrial democracy', on a more pragmatic level, front-line workers can offer invaluable input, based on first-hand experience, on the types of risks that they regularly encounter in carrying out the company's business. If management fails to listen to worker concerns, workers may devise their own ways of dealing with the risks, which can sometimes bring the company into conflict with the law. With respect to the development of schemes of self-regulation, it similarly makes sense for companies to consult their employees, if for no other reason than that employees are more likely to be committed to a scheme of self-regulation that they had a hand in developing. Conversely, the failure to involve workers in the decision-making process may be damaging to labour-management relations; where workers are disgruntled, a rise in absenteeism and turnover often follow. Worse, from the company's point of view, is the possibility of work stoppages, slow-downs, industrial sabotage and strikes. Even if these are averted, there is a critical link between morale and productivity that should not be ignored: increasingly, one finds workers who are not prepared to extend themselves on behalf of companies whose commitment to social and environmental issues does not measure up to their own.

Like employees, prospective employees are in a position to affect corporate policies, albeit indirectly. Although it might seem that the position of prospective employees should be considerably weaker than that of employees who already work for a company, in practice it may be stronger. The next generation of management and executives is typically recruited from an elite core of business schools, with the major corporations chasing the same top band of graduates. As most large companies will offer roughly comparable salary and benefit packages (in order to remain competitive with each other), the critical factor in the decision of these graduates as to which firm to join may turn on non-economic considerations. Recruiters increasingly encounter job applicants with a strong sense of idealism, perhaps nurtured

14 Directive 94/95/EC on European Works Councils (EWCs) (OJ 1994 L254/64) as amended by Directive 97/74/EC (OJ 1998 L10/22).

by the trend in some of the leading business schools to teach corporate ethics and champion corporate social responsibility. Appreciating their bargaining position, these graduates may question the recruiter about a company's ethics, and may even choose not to interview with those companies that have acquired a reputation for engaging in dubious practices. Still, it would be naïve not to acknowledge that many business school graduates will prize a high salary and attractive benefits over a company's record of social and environmental responsibility.

Another broad constituency that often vies for stakeholder status consists of non-governmental organisations (NGOs) and public interest groups. While some of these organisations prefer the independence of being able to challenge companies from without, others see an advantage in being able to try to influence corporate policies from within. Pursuit of an 'internal' strategy may entail the purchase of shares in a company, not as an investment, as would be the case for traditional shareholders, but to obtain a platform from which they may affect, or at least draw attention to, the company's policies. Shareholders will be kept informed of corporate activities and will be entitled to attend and speak at the company's annual general meeting (AGM) and, possibly, at 'open' committee meetings. What effect these activists will have on more profit-driven shareholders is speculative, but they may be able to raise the social consciousness of the occasion (often, NGOs will organise a high-visibility protest demonstration to coincide with an AGM). The target company may even make concessions to the activists in order to be able to focus the AGM on the company's achievements, as well as to avoid embarrassing publicity. If pressed to a vote, however, resolutions advanced by public interest activists rarely succeed. One difficulty is that institutional investors, such as pension funds, may hold the largest numbers of shares in the company. At the AGM, the institutional investor may be represented by a single delegate who is pledged to vote the shares of the fund in a pre-determined manner. These blocs of shares may be so large that they could not be defeated even if all of the other shareholders who were present were prepared to unite and vote against the institutional investor. Pension funds, with a fiduciary obligation to their membership to consider, may not be persuaded by the arguments of public interest representatives in favour of social and environmental goals, as opposed to more commercial, profit-driven policies (Useem: 1993).

While sovereign stakeholders will usually prefer to deal *internally* with a company's alleged improprieties and deficiencies, NGOs often relish public exposure of what they see as the company's failings – its unconscionable labour practices, its human rights violations and its environmental record – both at home and particularly at its overseas subsidiaries. These 'name and shame' campaigns are nominally designed to inform the public of a company's practices, thereby allowing for more informed decision-making by consumers or those considering doing business with the company, but are really aimed at persuading the target company to reform its business operation. A well-known example of such a 'name and shame' campaign was that pressed by Greenpeace against Royal Dutch Shell in relation to its plans to dispose of the oil storage tank Brent Spar. Not only did Shell lose the ensuing media battle, but the company was also forced to rethink its obligation to take the public interest into account in its decision-making processes; as a result, it ended up rewriting its mission statements to make clear its commitment to social and environmental justice (Schwartz and Gibb: 1999).

With respect to MNEs, the target of a 'name and shame' campaign is more likely to be the parent company than the subsidiary at whose site a violation has occurred because of the, probably correct, assumption that a parent company has the power to change the practices and policies of its subsidiaries. Although, as discussed in chapter 5, an MNE may gain an advantage in not exercising this power in order to put itself in a position to argue that any unlawful activities by the subsidiary were the responsibility of the subsidiary and the subsidiary alone, if adverse publicity threatened to undermine the reputation of the parent, then it might well decide to assert more control over the subsidiary (or else sever its ties with the subsidiary). No company will wish to sacrifice a reputation which it has been at pains to establish over a long period of time in order to preserve its ability to engage in illegal practices at what might be the margins of a global empire.

However, there are drawbacks to relying on NGOs to promote corporate social responsibility and self-regulation. Because of both financial constraints and ideological agendas, there is no guarantee that an NGO will take up a particular cause, even if it accepts that it has merit. There is also a serious problem of NGO accountability, as NGOs may not be formally answerable to either the state or to the public for their actions (indeed, it is not at all clear to whom they are answerable, except perhaps their membership). Driven by an ideological agenda, an NGO may take liberties with the truth. With respect to its campaign against the disposal by Royal Dutch Shell of its Brent Spar oil platform, referred to earlier, Greenpeace in fact eventually had to concede that the scientific basis of its analysis was in error and that parts of its campaign against Shell had been misleading. By that time, however, the media publicity had achieved the desired effect, and for Shell to have sued Greenpeace for libel would only have served to keep in the spotlight an issue that the company wanted to see laid to rest.

Creditors, contractors, insurers and investors comprise another group of stakeholders who are able to influence corporate policies. Contractors will want to know the compliance record of firms to whom they are considering submitting tenders, and may choose not to do business with firms with a poor record of compliance lest they be implicated in the company's illegality. Insurers will similarly wish to know of the health and safety record of a firm before determining the premiums to charge it for a policy of insurance. Lending institutions are in a position to lay down the terms on which they are prepared to loan money to a company, and may insist that the borrower have in place an effective system of self-regulation, not so much out of an altruistic concern for society, but because an effective self-regulatory system serves to increase the likelihood that a loan will not be misspent or diverted to pay a fine imposed following a criminal conviction. Investors have a comparable power as they can sell their shares in a company whose policies do not conform to their own views of what the company should be doing. During the era of apartheid, progressive American universities were instrumental in causing MNEs to divest themselves of their business holdings in South Africa by threatening to sell their endowment shares in the MNE; and, more recently, the refusal of leading American universities to do business with corporations that co-operated with the repressive regime in Burma caused several companies to reconsider their Burmese ventures.[15] These universities may be examples of a new breed of investors who are prepared to evaluate companies not only on their profitability, but also on their commitment to a high standard of corporate ethics, social justice, the environment and human rights.

15 See eg S Wollenberg 'PepsiCo Pulls Out of Burma' Associated Press, 27 January 1997.

Stock markets are becoming increasingly aware of the 'socially responsible investor' and have begun to develop indices that attempt to quantify a company's record on social and environmental issues.[16]

The trend of stakeholders to involve themselves in corporate decision-making can ratchet the pressure on companies to devise and implement effective systems of self-regulation beyond whatever encouragement is provided by the law. However, as the class of stakeholders expands and stakeholders are given an increasing voice in corporate decision-making, the effectiveness of corporate governance may suffer. Stakeholder interests often can clash, and what may be seen as being in the best interests of employees, for example, may conflict with what an environmental NGO sees as the best interest of the environment or a community sees as being in its best interest. The result may be increasing paralysis at board level and the transfer of real decision-making power to executive management. Pressures from stakeholders may cause companies to review their practices and policies, but the result of such a review is often difficult to predict. Despite being the target of a 'name and shame' campaign for its dealings with the Burmese government, Unocal did not pull out of Burma and even began negotiations with the then Taliban regime about an oil pipe-line in Afghanistan (Schwartz and Gibb: 1999: 37). A company may embrace only those measures that are seen to be in its self-interest and, in any event, uniformity in practices among companies in an industry is less likely to result as compared with when standards are set down in law or by a collective self-regulatory body. Such standards provide benchmarks both for companies and groups that would seek to monitor companies, as well as giving legitimacy to the claims of those companies which exceed the minimum to be regarded as 'good corporate citizens'. It is for these reasons that we would maintain that the pressures generated from stakeholders should be seen as a means of reinforcing the legal structures that we have advocated and not as a substitute for them.

E.   BEYOND COMPLIANCE: THE SOCIALLY RESPONSIBLE COMPANY

Claims for broadening the class of stakeholders and, in particular, for including members of the local and national community within this category, are based in part on the effects that companies can have on these communities and in part on the relationship between companies and the state. Companies owe their very existence to the state, which issues them a charter or licence to operate. In addition, the state often grants companies various 'concessions', including the right to trade using the corporate form, to operate their business within a regime of limited liability, and to use the state's court system to obtain relief against the unfair practices of competitors and to secure outstanding debts owed to the company. The 'concessions' expand if companies are allowed to police themselves and to write their own rules with legal effect. In exchange for being allowed to undertake self-regulation, as well as being able to operate under the umbrella of the state's legal system, with all of the concessions that entails, companies arguably should incur, as a quid pro quo, an obligation to obey the state's laws and to carry on their business in a socially responsible manner. Furthermore, in a regime of individualised self-regulation, where the company replaces

16 See eg FTSE4Good series.

the state as the body responsible for protecting the public from the dangers of corporate crime, companies should also incur a duty to respect citizen rights to the same extent as would the state when it is responsible for law enforcement.

In the twenty-first century, it is not difficult to find companies which are prepared, at least in public, to commit themselves in principle to the concept of corporate social responsibility. But many see such proclamations as little more than a form of astute marketing whereby companies seek to bolster their public image and, in turn, their sales. Moreover, there are wide variations in corporate conduct and, within the business community, genuine differences of opinion as to the bounds of a company's social responsibility and as to what counts as proper and improper practices.

A focus on media-publicised corporate crimes can leave an impression that deviance is more widespread than it actually is. There are in fact companies with deserved excellent reputations – which strive to comply with the law and to prevent illegality by their workforce, which are progressive in their employment practices and generous to the communities in which they are located, and which are sensitive to issues of equal opportunities, the environment, human rights and sustainable development. There are companies which encourage frankness and openness by their employees, which are amenable to reform when improper or unsafe practices are pointed out to them, and which take the concerns of public interest groups and other stakeholders seriously. Examples are not hard to find. The Body Shop endorses ethical practices and supports Third-World causes; The Gap has adopted guidelines to ensure that its products are produced in an ethical manner; the Co-operative Bank in the United Kingdom not only fosters a 'social auditing' model which prizes 'value deliverance, social responsibility and ecological sustainability', but also demands personal responsibility from managers for achieving performance in these areas (Gao and Zhang: 2001). Recently, the Dutch RABO Bank – a bank with a triple AAA rating – went so far as to refuse a loan to a company producing paté de fois gras because of its concern for 'animal welfare' (*De Volkskrant*, 26 June 2002).

The motivation for corporate commitment to social justice and environmental integrity – whether it be a matter of principle, a public relations ploy, or a recognition that it is in the company's self-interest to pursue its goals without the expense, distraction and adverse publicity that accompany a legal prosecution – may, in the final analysis, not matter. What is of importance is that firms conduct their business in socially responsible and ethical ways. Interestingly, companies which do so tend to be admired (and therefore able to attract talented managers and employees). The firms which have consistently headed the *Financial Times* 'most respected companies' list also topped its list of companies perceived by other CEOs as having the most 'integrity' (*Financial Times*, 30 January 2003). Even more interestingly, perhaps, these firms also tend to perform well, proof that corporate social responsibility and profits are not incompatible. Such companies enjoy both good relations with their employees and the support of their local community, wherein they are held in high regard.

But why is it that some companies take corporate ethics and social responsibility seriously while others do not? The answer may lie with the directors, senior managers and executives, and most particularly, the CEO of a company (Fleming: 2002). These are the individuals who have the most influence in setting their companies on an ethical and responsible course, and who are best positioned to shape the corporate culture and ethos. A notable example was Jack Welch at General Electric, whose 'pep talks' to staff on the topic of corporate ethics have been compared with 'revivalist meetings' (*The Economist*, 27 July 2002). Until his retirement, Welch also ranked as the world's 'most respected business leader', as judged by his fellow CEOs (*Financial Times*, 30 January 2003). Braithwaite and his colleagues (1989, 1995; Ayres and Braithwaite: 1992: 22–23) have documented in their fieldwork, in several different countries and in various industries, that many managers are sensitive to their company's image and reputation, and will not shirk from taking decisions which may detract from profitability in order to provide a public service.

It is not enough, however, to simply want to be a good corporate citizen. To translate hopes into reality requires companies to engage in risk assessment, to devise management structures and self-regulatory systems to avert risks, to enforce these systems with due diligence, to monitor their workforce with care and to establish a corporate culture that will not tolerate misconduct or illegality. History teaches that criminogenic corporate cultures are not immutable and that compliant cultures can be brought into being if a company's directors and executive officers are prepared to invest in codes of conduct, training and education, a well-resourced compliance department and the rewarding of good practice (Andriof and McIntosh: 2001).

What, then, will be the effect of a company's acceptance of the importance of corporate social responsibility and the creation of the types of self-regulatory systems outlined above? On a rudimentary level, one would expect a reduction in the incidence of corporate crime, with concomitantly less harm to employees, the public, the markets, the environment and society. But there may be deeper, more subtle transformations that will be brought about. In respect of natural persons, the criminal law helps to shape an individual's sense of right and wrong. When conduct is made illegal, we refrain from engaging in that conduct, not necessarily because the conduct suddenly is seen as immoral when previously it had no moral content, but because it is illegal and therefore wrong. We become conditioned to believe, and internalise the belief to the point that it is no longer even thought about consciously, that conduct proscribed by law is simply not to be engaged in. This leads to a habit of law-abiding conduct. Engaging in such habits produces a sense of virtuousness, which in turn reinforces the psychological commitment not to engage in the proscribed conduct.

It may well be that similar processes occur with respect to companies. In industries where there is a high potential for personal injury or property damage, such as manufacturing, it has been found that where safety is taken seriously by top management, there can develop a 'virtuous circle' with high reporting of mistakes, scrupulous monitoring of workers and the judging of managerial performance by how high a level of compliance has been attained (Ayres and Braithwaite: 1992: 82; Clarke: 2000: 119). Committing itself, and adhering to, a system of self-regulation will imbue a company with an ethos of compliance. This ethos will be internalised and become part of the company's 'personality', and the company will have developed the corporate equivalent of a 'conscience'. At this point, one can anticipate a heightened sense of civic responsibility, along with a commitment not simply to the letter of the law, but also to its spirit. Rather than being a 'negative externality' that must be achieved in order not to incur the wrath of external regulatory agencies, compliance will become part and parcel of the corporate culture.

A change in the corporate culture and ethos will have knock-on effects for the conception of directors' duties. The benchmarks by which corporate officers will be judged will no longer be limited to their skill in generating profits, but will extend to how effectively they are able to manage risk, to ensure compliance and to fulfil the company's obligations of corporate citizenship. Already, one can see the harbingers of change in the conception of directors' duties: in a Delaware case, *Re Caremark International Inc Derivative Litigation*,[17] the court held that corporate directors had a duty to exercise an oversight function, which included seeing to it that adequate information and reporting systems existed within the company; in *McCall v Scott*,[18] a US federal appeals court held that directors breach their fiduciary duty when they recklessly disregard 'red flags' that should alert them to fraudulent practices within the organisation; and, in England, directors of Barings Bank were found unfit and disqualified from holding similar offices in the future because of their failure adequately to control the activities of Nick Leeson and to ensure that he complied with both internal and external regulations.[19]

In a world where self-regulation reigns, directors would be held to account by 'stakeholders', who either would be accorded a place on the company's board of directors or who would be able to institute legal proceedings as representatives of the public interest to hold directors to their fiduciary obligations, including those owed to society. The 'bottom line' as we see it, to use a phrase that is commonplace in business, would be a more 'inclusive' version of the company, an increased commitment by firms to corporate social responsibility and a readiness on the part of companies to assume the mantle of corporate citizenship, with all the responsibilities which that entails.

---

17 698 A 2d 959 (Del Ch 1996).
18 239 F 3d 808 (6th Cir 2001).
19 *Re Barings plc, Secretary of State for Trade and Industry v Baker (No 5)* [2000] 1 BCLC 523.

Bibliography

Abraham, J, (1995) *Science, politics and the pharmaceutical industry: Controversy and bias in drug regulation*

Adams, J R, (1990) *The Big Fix: Inside the S & L Scandal*

Adams, S, (1984) *Roche versus Adams*

Addo, M K, (ed) (1999) *Human Rights Standards and the Responsibility of Transnational Corporations*

Allen, F, (1959) 'Legal Values and the Rehabilitative Ideal' 50 J Crim L, Criminology and Police Science 226

—(1981) *The Decline of the Rehabilitative Idea*

American Law Institute, (1962) *Model Penal Code*

Amnesty International, (1996) *Nigeria: Time to End Contempt for Human Rights*

Andrews, J, (1973) 'Reform in the Law of Corporate Liability' [1973] Crim LR 91

Andrews, J, and Hirst, M, (1997) *Andrews & Hirst on Evidence*

Andriof, J, and McIntosh, M, (eds) (2001) *Perspectives on Corporate Citizenship*

Arlen, J, (1994) 'The Potentially Perverse Effects of Corporate Criminal Liability' 23 JLS 833

Arlen, J, and Kraakman, R, (1997) 'Controlling Corporate Misconduct: An Analysis of Corporate Liability Regimes' 72 NYU LR 687

Ashworth, A, (1987a) 'Belief, Intent, and Criminal Liability' in J Ekelaar and J Bell (eds) *Oxford Essays in Jurisprudence*

—(1987b) 'Defining criminal offences without harm' in P F Smith (ed) *Criminal Law: Essays in Honour of J C Smith*

—(1988) 'Criminal Attempts and the Role of Resulting Harm under the Code, and in the Common Law' 19 Rutgers LJ 725

—(1999) *Principles of Criminal Law* (3rd edn)

—(1999) 'The Human Rights Act 1998 – Article 6 and the Fairness of Trials' [1999] Crim LR 261

—(2000) *Sentencing and Criminal Justice* (3rd edn)

Ashworth, A, and Blake, M, (1996) 'The Presumption of Innocence in English Criminal Law' [1996] Crim LR 306

Auld, (2001) *Review of the Criminal Courts of England and Wales*

Avery, C, (1999) 'Business and Human Rights in a Time of Change' (unpublished report prepared for Amnesty International)

Ayres, I, and Braithwaite, J, (1992) *Responsive Regulation: Transcending the Deregulation Debate*

Bakker, M, (1985) 'Scheepsfraude: het onbekende "zwarte gat"' FEM Supp 23, 15 June, 47

Baldwin, R. (1985) *Regulating the Airlines*

Barings Report, (1995) *Report of the Board of Banking Supervision: Inquiry into the Circumstances of the Collapse of Barings*

Barnard, J, (1999) 'Reintegrative Shaming in Corporate Sentencing' 72 SCal LR 959

Bassouini, C, (1999) *Crimes Against Humanity in International Criminal Law* (2nd edn)

Beccaria, C, (1764) *Dei Delitti e Delle Pene*

Bennis, W, (1976) *The Unconscious Conspiracy: Why Leaders Can't Lead*

Bentham, J, (1780) *Introduction to the Principles of Legislation*

Bergman, D, (1990) 'Recklessness in the Boardroom' 26 NLJ 1496

—(1991) *Deaths at Work: Accidents or Corporate Crime?*

—(1992) 'Corporate Sanctions and Corporate Probation' 144 NLJ 1312

—(1994) *The Perfect Crime*

—(2000) *The Case for Corporate Responsibility*

Bernstein, M A, (1955) *Regulating Business by Independent Commission*

Bingham, (1992) *Inquiry into the supervision of the Bank of Credit and Commerce International*

Birch, D, (1987) 'Hearsay-Logic and Hearsay-Fiddles: *Blastland* revisited' in P Smith (ed) *Criminal Law: Essays in Honour of J C Smith*

—(1989) 'The Evidence Provisions – Documentary Evidence' [1989] Crim LR 15

Birks, P, (ed) (1995) *Criminal Justice and Human Rights: Pressing Problems in the Law* vol 1

Black, J, (1996) 'Constitutionalising Self-Regulation' 59 MLR 24

Blair, M, (1995) *Ownership and Control*

Boisjoly, R, Foster Curtis, E, and Mellican, M, (1996) 'The Challenger Disaster: Organizational Demands' in M D Ermann and R J Lundman (eds) *Corporate and Governmental Deviance* (3rd edn)

Bologna, J, (1984) *Corporate Fraud: The Basics of Prevention and Detection*

Bosworth-Davies, R, (1988) *Fraud in the City: Too Good to be True*

—(1992) 'Practical Training for Compliance Officers' 1 Int'l J Reg L and Practice 42

Bower, T, (1989) *Maxwell: The Outsider*

Bowles, M L, (1991) 'The organization shadow' 12 Organization Studies 387

Box, S, (1983) *Power, Crime and Mystification* (2nd edn)

Braithwaite, J, (1982) 'Challenging Just Deserts: Punishing White Collar Criminals' 73 J Crim L & Criminology 723

—(1984) *Corporate Crime in the Pharmaceutical Industry*

—(1985) 'White collar crime' 11 Ann Rev Sociology 1

—(1989) *Crime, Shame and Reintegration*

—(1993) 'The nursing home industry' in M Tonry and A J Reiss Jr (eds) *Beyond the Law*

—(1997) 'On Speaking Softly and Carrying Big Sticks: Neglected Dimensions of a Republican Separation of Powers' 47 U Toronto LJ 305

Braithwaite, J, and Drahos, P, (2000) *Global Business Regulation*

Braithwaite, J, and Fisse, B, (1987) 'Self-Regulation and the Control of Corporate Crime' in C Shearing and P Stenning (eds) *Private Policing*

Braithwaite, J, and Geis, G, (1982) 'On Theory and Action for Corporate Crime Control' 28 Crime and Delinquency 292

Braithwaite, J, and Pettit, P, (1990) *Not Just Deserts: A Republican Theory of Criminal Justice*

Bratza, N, (2000) 'The Implications of the Human Rights Act 1998 for Commercial Practice' 1 E Human Rights LR 1

Brenner, S N, and Molander, E A, (1977) 'Is the ethics of business changing?' 55 Harv Bus Rev 57

Brickey, K, (1981) 'Corporate Criminal Accountability: A Brief History and an Observation' 60 Wash ULQ 393

—(1988) 'Rethinking Corporate Liability under the Model Penal Code' 19 Rutgers LJ 593

Brown, B, (1989) 'Culpable Homicide, Endangerment and Aggravated Violence' [1989] NZLR 299

Brown, D, (2001) 'Street Crime, Corporate Crime, and the Contingency of Criminal Liability' 149 UPaLR 1295

Brown, M, (1994) *Richard Branson: The Inside Story* (3rd edn)

Bucy, P, (1991) 'Corporate Ethos: A Standard for Imposing Corporate Criminal Liability' 75 Minn LR 1095

—(1992) 'Organizational Sentencing Guidelines: The Cart Before the Horse' 71 Wash ULQ 329

Burrell, G. (1997) *Pandemonium: Towards a Retro-Organization Theory*

Business Week, 13 December 1993, 'Freedom is no picnic for Mike Milken'

Calavita, K, and Pontell, H N, (1990) '"Heads I win, tails you lose": deregulation, crime and crisis in the savings & loan industry' 36 Crime & Delinquency 309

—(1991) '"Other people's money": collective embezzlement in the savings and loans insurance industries' 38 Social Problems 94

—(1993) 'Savings and loan fraud as organized crime: towards a conceptual typology of corporate illegality' 31 Criminology 519

—(1995) 'Saving the Savings and Loans? US Government Response to Financial Crime' in F Pearce and L Snider (eds) *Corporate Crime: Contemporary Debates*

Cannon, T, (1992) *Corporate Responsibility*

Canter, D, (2000) 'Destructive Organisational Psychology' in D Canter and L Alison (eds) *The Social Psychology of Crime*

Canter, D, and Alison, L, (eds) (2000a) *The Social Psychology of Crime*

Canter D, and Alison, L, (2000b) 'The Social Psychology of Crime: Groups, Teams and Networks' in D Canter and L Alison (eds) *The Social Psychology of Crime*

Carroll, A, (2001) 'The moral leader: essential for successful corporate citizenship' in J Andriof and M McIntosh (eds) *Perspectives on Corporate Citizenship*

Carson, W G, (1970) 'White-collar Crime and the Enforcement of Factory Legislation' 10 BrJ Crim 383

—(1979) 'The Conventionalization of Early Factory Crime' 7 IJ Sociology of Law 37

—(1980) 'The Institutionalization of Ambiguity: Early British Factory Acts' in G Geis and E Stotland (eds) *White-collar Crime: Theory and Research*

—(1982) *The Other Price of Britain's Oil*

Centre for Corporate Accountability, (1999) Evidence to the Environment Sub-committee on the Health and Safety Executive (unpublished)

—(2001) Conference briefing material: Law Enforcement and Coporate Accountability

Cho, K, (1999) 'Reconstruction of the English Criminal Justice System and its Reinvigorated Exclusionary Rules' 21 Loyola I & CLJ 259

Clapham, A, (2000) 'The Question of Jurisdiction under International Criminal Law over Legal Persons: Lessons from the Rome Conference on an International Criminal Court' in M Kamminga and S Zia-Zarifi (eds) (2001) *Liability of Corporations Under International Law*

Clarke, M, (1981) *Fallen Idols: Elites and the Search for the Acceptable Face of Capitalism*

—(ed) (1983) *Corruption: Causes, Consequences and Control*

—(1986) *Regulating the City: Competition, Scandal and Reform*

—(1990) *Business Crime: its Nature and Control*

—(1991) *Mortgage Fraud*

—(1998) *Citizens' Financial Futures: The Regulation of Retail Financial Investment in Britain*

—(2000) *Regulation: the Social Control of Business between Law and Politics*

Clarke, M, Smith, D, and McConville, M, (1994) *Slippery Customers: Estate Agents, the Public and Regulation*

Clarkson, C M V, (1996) 'Kicking Corporate Bodies and Damning their Souls' 59 MLR 557

—(1998) 'Corporate Culpability' 2 Web JCLI, webjcli.ncl.ac.uk/1998/issue2/clarkson2/html

Clegg, S R, (1990) *Modern Organizations: Organization Studies in the Post-modern World*

Clinard, M B, (1952) *The Black Market: A Study of White-collar Crime*

—(1983) *Corporate Ethics and Crime*

—(1990) *Corporate Corruption: The Abuse of Power*

Clinard, M B, and Yeager, P C, (1980) *Corporate Crime*

Coffee, J, (1977) 'Beyond the Shut-Eyed Sentry: Toward a Theoretical View of Corporate Misconduct and the Effective legal Response' 63 Va LR 1099

—(1981) '"No Soul to Damn: No Body to Kick": An Unscandalized Inquiry into the Problem of Corporate Punishment' 79 Mich LR 386

Coleman, J W, (1985) *The Criminal Elite: the Sociology of White Collar Crime*

—(1989) *The Criminal Elite: The Sociology of White Collar Crime* (2nd edn)

Colvin, E, (1995) 'Corporate Personality and Criminal Liability' 6 CrimL Forum 1

Comment, (1961) 'Increasing Community Control over Corporate Crime – A Problem in the Law of Sanctions' 71 Yale LJ 280

Conklin, J E, (1977) *Illegal but not Criminal: Business Crime in America*

Conway, B, (1981) *The Piracy Business*

Cornwell, R, (1984) *God's Banker*

Council of Europe, (1990) *Recommendation No R(88) of the Committee of Ministers to Member States concerning Liability of Enterprises having Legal Personality for offences committed in the Exercise of their Activities*

Cowles, W, (1945) 'Universal Jurisdiction over War Crimes' 33 Calif LR 177

Cressey, D R, (1953) *Other People's Money*

—(1969) *Theft of the Nation*

Croall, H, (1992) *White Collar Crime: Criminal Justice and Criminology*

Cullen, E T, Maakestad, W J, and Cavender G, (1984) 'The Ford Pinto case and beyond' in E Hochstedler (ed) *Corporations as Criminals*

Cullen Report, (1990) *The Public Inquiry into the Piper Alpha Disaster*

Cullen Report, (2002) *Ladbroke Grove Rail Inquiry*

Dalton, M, (1959) *Men Who Manage*

Damarska, M, (1973) 'Evidentiary Barriers to Conviction and Two Models of Criminal Procedure: A Comparative Study' 121 UPaLR 506

Danailov, S, (1998) 'The Accountability of Non-State Actors for Human Rights Violations: the Special Case of Transnational Corporations' www.humanrights.ch/dokumentationen/000218danailov.pdf

Day, K, (1993) *S & L Hell: The People and the Politics Behind $1 Trillion Savings & Loan Scandal*

Department of Transport, (1987) 'm.v. Herald of Free Enterprise', Report of Court No 8074

Dimento, F, Geis, G, and Gelfand, J, (2000/2001) 'Corporate Criminal Liability: A Bibliography' 28 W State ULR 1

Ditton, J, (1977) *Part-time Crime*

Dixon, N F, (1979) *On the Psychology of Military Incompetence*

—(1994) 'Disastrous decisions' 7 The Psychologist 303

Doig, A, (1984) *Corruption and Misconduct in Contemporary British Politics*

—(2000) 'Investigating Fraud' in D Cantor and L Alison (eds) *The Social Psychology of Crime*

Doig, A, Johnson, S, and Levi, M, (2000) *Policing Fraud in the UK*

Donaldson, T, (1982) *Corporations and Morality*

Douglas, J D, and Johnson, J M, (eds) (1977) *Official Deviance*

Dowie, M, (1977) 'Pinto madness' Mother Jones 17 (September/October)

Dowie, M, and Marshall, C, (1982) 'The Bendectin cover-up' in M D Ermann and R J Lundman (eds) *Corporate and Governmental Deviance* (2nd edn)

Downs, A, (1966) *Inside Bureaucracy*

Duff, A, (1990) *Intention, Agency and Criminal Liability*

Dunford, L, and Ridley, A, (1996) '"No Soul to be Damned, No Body to be Kicked": Responsibility, Blame and Corporate Punishment' 24 IJ Sociology of Law 1

Dworkin, R, (1986) *Law's Empire*

Easton, S, (1998) *The Case for the Right to Silence* (2nd edn)

Economist, The, (2002) 15 June 'Special report: corporate governance' 75

—(2002) 6 July 'Accounting Scandals and SEC: Harvey Pitt fights back' 73

—(2002) 27 July, 'Corporate Culture' 57

—(2002) 14 September 'White-collar crime in America: Out to catch the big fish' 61

Eddy, E, Potter, E, and Page, B, (1976) *Destination Disaster*

Eggleston, R, (1983) *Evidence, Proof and Probability* (2nd edn)

Ehrenfeld, R, (1992) *Evil Money: Encounters along the Money Trail*

Elkins, J, (1976) 'Corporations and Criminal Law' 65 Ky LJ 73

Ellen, E, Campbell, D, (1981) *International Maritime Fraud*

Elliot, A L, and Scroth, R J, (2002) *How Companies Lie*

Emmerson, B, and Ashworth, A, (2001) *Human Rights and Criminal Justice*

Ermann, M D, and Lundman, R J, (eds) (1978) *Corporate and Governmental Deviance*

—(1982) *Corporate and Governmental Deviance* (2nd edn)

—(1996) *Corporate and Governmental Deviance* (3rd edn)

Ernst and Young, (2000) *Fraud: The Unmanaged Risk*

Etzioni, A, (1993) 'The US Sentencing Commission on Corporate Crime: A Critique' in G Geis and P Jesilow (eds) *White-Collar Crime*

Faberman, H A, (1975) 'A Criminogenic Market Structure: the Automobile Industry' 16(4) Sociological Q

Fennell Report, (1988) *Investigation into the King's Cross Underground Fire*

Fidler, D G, (1998) 'The Due Diligence Defence' 148 NLJ 328 at 379

Field, S, and Jorg, N, (1991) 'Corporate Liability and Manslaughter: should we be going Dutch' [1991] Crim LR 156

Financial Times, 30 September 1994, 'Ferries in six "near accidents"'

—19 July 1995, 'Controls failure sank Barings'; 'The Barings Report'; 'Barings and the Bank'

—4 December 1995, 'Singapore may prosecute former Barings executives'; 'Leeson Trial'; 'Singapore moves to defend reputation'

—30 January 2003 'World's most respected companies'

Fisse, B, (1981) 'Community Service as a Sanction against Corporations' [1981] Wis LR 970

—(1983) 'Reconstructing Corporate Criminal Law: Deterrence, Retribution, Fault, and Sanctions' 56 SCal LR 1141

—(1990) 'Sentencing Options against Criminals' 1 CrimL Forum 211

—(1991) 'The Attribution of Criminal Liability to Corporations: A Statutory Model' 13 Syd LR 277

Fisse, B, and Braithwaite, J, (1983) *The Impact of Publicity on Corporate Offenders*

—(1988) 'The Allocation of Responsibility for Corporate Crime: Individualism, Collectivism and Accountability' 11 Syd LR 469

—(1993) *Corporations, Crime and Accountability*

Fisse, B, and French, P, (eds) (1985) *Corrigible Corporations and Unruly Law*

Fitzgerald, A E, (1989) *The Pentagonists: an Insider's View of Waste, Mismanagement and Fraud in Defense Spending*

Fleming, J E, (2002) 'Integrating Ethics Programs' 31 Acad Management News 19

Foerschler, A, (1990) 'Corporate Criminal Intent: Toward a Better Understanding of Corporate Misconduct' 78 Calif LR 1286

Fombrun, C, (1996) *Reputation: Realizing Value from the Corporate Image*

Food and Drug Administration, (2002) *FDA Annual Report 2001*

Fortun, K, (2001) *Advocacy after Bhopal: Environmentalism, Disaster, New Global Orders*

Franklin, P, (1990) *Profits of Deceit: Dispatches from the Front Lines of Fraud*

Frantz, D, (1987) *Levine and Co: Wall Street's Insider Trading Scandal*

Frederick, W C, Davis, K, and Post, J E, (1988) *Business and Society: Corporate Strategy, Public Policy* (6th edn)

French, P, (1984) *Collective and Corporate Responsibility*

Friedland, M, (ed) (1990) *Securing Compliance: Seven Case Studies*

Friedman, L, (2000) 'Essay: In Defense of Corporate Criminal Liability' 33 Harv J Law & Public Policy 833

Friedman, M, (1970) 'The Social Responsibility of Business is to Increase its Profits' New York Times Magazine, 13 September, 32

Friedmann, W, (1964) *The Changing Structure of International Law*

Friedrichs, D O, (1996) *Trusted Criminals: White Collar Crime in Contemporary Society*

Fusaro, P C, and Miller, R M, (2002) *What Went Wrong at Enron*

Gao, S S, and Zhang, J J, (2001) ' A comparative study of stakeholder engagement approaches on social auditing' in J Andriof and M McIntosh (eds) *Perspectives on Corporate Citizenship*

Geis, G, (1962) 'Toward a delineation of white-collar offences' 32 Sociological Inquiry 160

—(1967) 'White collar crime: the heavy electrical equipment antitrust cases of 1961' in M B Clinard and R Quinney (eds) *Criminal Behavior Systems*

—(ed) (1968) *White Collar Criminal*

—(1982) 'White collar crime: the heavy electrical equipment antitrust cases of 1961' in M D Ermann and R J Lundman (eds) *Corporate and Governmental Deviance* (2nd edn)

Geis, G, and DiMento, J F, (1995) 'Should We Prosecute Corporations and/or Individuals?' in F Pearce and L Snider (eds) *Corporate Crime: Contemporary Debates*

Geis, G, and Goff, G, (1983) 'Introduction' in E H Sutherland *White Collar Crime*

Geis, G, and Meier, F R, (eds) (1977) W*hite Collar Crime: Offences in Business, Politics and the Professions*

Geis, G, Pontell, H N, and Jesilow, P D, (1988) 'Medicaid fraud' in J E Scott and T Hirschi (eds) *Controversial Issues in Crime and Justice*

Geis, G, and Stotland, E, (eds) (1980) *White-collar Crime: Theory and Research*

Gilbert, G, (1992) 'Crimes *Sans Frontieres*: Jurisdictional Problems in English Law' LXIII BYIL 415

—(1994) 'Multinational Corporations and Extradition' (unpublished, paper prepared for The Permanent Peoples' Tribunal)

Gimein, M, (2002) 16 September 'Eliot Spitzer: The Enforcer' Fortune

Gioia, D A, (1996) 'Why I Didn't Recognize Pinto Fire Hazards: How Organizational Scripts Channel Managers' Thoughts and Actions' in M D Ermann and R J Lundman (eds) *Corporate and Governmental Deviance* (3rd edn)

Gobert, J, (1993) 'The Fortuity of Consequence' 4 CrimL Forum 1

—(1994a) 'Corporate Criminality: Four Models of Fault' 14 LS 393

—(1994b) 'Corporate Criminality: New Crimes for the Times' [1994] Crim LR 722

—(1997) *Justice, Democracy and the Jury*

—(1998) 'Controlling Corporate Criminality: Penal Sanctions and Beyond' 2 Web JCLI, webjcli.ncl.ac.uk/1998/issue2/gobert2/html

—(2002) 'Corporate Killings at Home and Abroad – Reflections on the Government's Proposals' 118 LQR 72

Gobert, J, and Mugnai, E, (2002) 'Coping with Corporate Criminality – Some Lessons from Italy' [2002] Crim LR 619

Gottfredson, M, and Hirschi, T, (1990) *A General Theory of Crime*

Grabosky, P, and Braithwaite, J, (1986) *Of Manners Gentle: Enforcement Strategies of Australian Business Regulatory Agencies*

—(1994) *Business Regulation and Australia's Future*

Greenslade, R, (1992) *Maxwell's Fall*

Gregory, M, (1994) *Dirty Tricks*

Gross, E, (1980) 'Organization structure and organizational crime' in G Geis and E Stotland (eds) *White-collar Crime*

Gruner, R, (1988) 'To Let the Punishment Fit the Organization: Sanctioning Corporate Offenders Through Corporate Probation' 16 Am J CrimL 1

—(1993) 'Beyond Fines: Innovative Corporate Sentences under Federal Sentencing Guidelines' 71 Wash ULQ 261

—(1994a) *Corporate Crime and Sentencing*

—(1994b) 'Towards an Organizational Jurisprudence: Transforming Corporate Criminal Law Through Federal Sentencing Reform' 36 ArizLR 407

Guardian, 28 August 1990, 'The Guinness trial' (four-page report); 'Guinness Four guilty'

—9 March 1992, 'Maxwell pensions: angry reactions'

—1 February 1994, 'Crime without punishment'

—21 October 1994, 'How store saga engulfed stiff-necked accountant and ambitious right-winger'; 'Tories on ropes over "sleaze"'

—19 July 1995, 'Leeson to carry can over Barings fiasco'; 'The mugging of an old lady'; 'Freewheeling into the Wimbledon abyss'; 'Brown savages the old boys' network'

Gunningham, M. (1987) 'Negotiated Non-Compliance: A Case-Study of Regulatory Failure' 9 Law and Policy 69

Gurwin, L, (1984) *The Calvi Affair: Death of a Banker*

Hagan, F, and Benekos, P J, (1990) 'The biggest white-collar crime in history: the great Savings & Loans scandal' (Paper presented at Annual Meeting of American Society of Criminology, Baltimore, 1990)

Haines, J, (1988) *Maxwell*

Halperin, M H, (1977) *The Lawless State*

Handy, C, (1990) *The Age of Unreason*

Harman, H and Griffiths, J, (1979) *Justice Deserted*

Hart, H, (1958) 'The Aims of the Criminal Law' [1958] Law and Contemporary Problems 401

Hart, H L A, (1968) *Punishment and Responsibility*

Hart, H L A, and Honore, T, (1985) *Causation and the Law* (2nd edn)

Hartley, R F, (1993) *Business Ethics: Violations of the Public Trust*

—(1994) *Management Mistakes and Successes* (4th edn)

Hartung, R E, (1950) 'White-collar offences in the wholesale meat industry in Detroit' 56 Am J Sociology 25

Harvard Business School, Case 383-129, (1983) 'Managing product safety: the Ford Pinto'

—Case 9-383-128, (1984) 'Managing product safety: the case of the McDonnell Douglas DC 10'

Harvey, J B, (1988) 'The Abilene paradox: the management of agreement' 17 Organizational Dynamics 17

Hawkins, K, (1983) 'Bargain and Bluff: Compliance Strategy and Deterrence in the Enforcement of Regulation' 5 Law & Pol Q 35

—(1984) *Environment and Enforcement*

—(1990) 'Compliance Strategy, Prosecution Policy and Aunt Sally: A Comment on Pearce and Tombs' 30 BrJ Crim 444

Hawkins, K, and Thomas, J M, (eds) (1984) *Enforcing Regulation*

Hay, G, and Kelly, D, (1974) 'An empirical survey of price-fixing conspiracies' 17 JL & Econ 13

Hayes, M, and Pearce, R, (1976) *Crime, Law and the State*

Health and Safety Commission, (2002) *Health and Safety Responsibilities of Directors*

—(2002) *Enforcement Policy Statement*

Health and Safety Executive, (1995) *Reporting of Injuries, Diseases and Dangerous Occurrences* (RIDDOR)

—(2002) *Health and Safety Offences and Penalties*

Helmer, C. (1999) 'De neutralisatie theorie van Sykes en Matza toegepast op witte boorden criminaliteit' thesis, Department of Law, University of Utrecht

Henning, P J, (1993) 'Testing the limits of investigating and prosecuting white collar crime: how far will courts allow prosecutors to go?' 54 U Pitt LR 405

—(1998) 'Finding what was lost: sorting out the custodian's privilege against self-incrimination from the compelled production of records' 77 Nebraska LR 34

—(1999) 'Defence Discovery in White Collar Criminal Prosecutions' 15 Georgia State ULR 601

Henry, S, (1978) *The Hidden Economy*

Herlihy, E D, and Levine, T A, (1980) 'Corporate crisis: The overseas payment problem' in E Bittner and S L Messinger (eds) *Criminology Review Yearbook*

Herling, J, (1962) *The Great Price Conspiracy: The Story of Anti-Trust Violations in the Electrical Industry*

Hidden Report, (1989) *Investigation into the Clapham Junction Railway Accident*

Hirst, M, (1981) 'Jurisdiction over Cross-Frontier Offences' 97 LQR 80

Hochstedler, E, (ed) (1984) *Corporations as Criminals*

Hodgson, G, (1986) *Lloyds of London*

Holmes, O W, (1897) 'The Path of the Law' 10 Harv LR 457

Home Office, (1988) *Juries in Serious Fraud Trials: A Consultation Document*

—(2000) *Reforming the law of Involuntary Manslaughter: the Government's Proposals*

—(2002) *Justice for All*

Honess, T M, Levi, M, and Charman, E A, (1998) 'Juror Competence in Processing Complex Information: Implications from a Simulation of the Maxwell Trial' [1998] Crim LR 763

Honore, T, (1988) 'Responsibility and Luck' 104 LQR 530

Hopkins, A, (1994) 'Compliance with What? The fundamental regulatory question' 34 BrJ Crim 431

Howard, M, Crane, P, and Hochberg, D, (1990) *Phipson on Evidence* (14th edn)

Huff, K, (1996) 'The Role of Corporate Compliance Programs in Determining Corporate Criminal Liability: A Suggested Approach' 96 Col LR 1252

Hughes, E C, (1963) 'Good people and dirty work' in H S Becker (ed) *The Other Side*

Huisman, W, (2001) *Tussen winst en moraal*

Huisman, W, and Niemeijer, E, (1998) *Zicht op organisatie criminaliteit*

Human Rights Watch, (1999a) *The Enron Corporation: Complicity in Human Rights Violations*

—(1999b) *The Price of Oil: Corporate Responsibility and Human Rights Violations in Nigeria's Oil Producing Communities*

Hutter, B, (1988) *The Reasonable Arm of the Law? The Law Enforcement Procedures of Environmental Health Officers*

—(1993) 'Regulating Employers and Employees: health and safety in the workplace' 20 J Law & Soc 452

—(1997) *Compliance: Regulation and Enforcement*

Independent, 4 March 1995, 'Fraud office goes into Barings'

—19 July 1995, 'Barings Report'; 'Bank of England offloads blame for Barings collapse'; 'Three strikes and you're out'; 'Barings makes case for break-up of Bank'

Ives, J H, (ed) (1985) *The Export of Hazard: Transnational Corporations and Environmental Control Issues*

Jack, I, (2001) *The Crash that Stopped Britain*

Jackall, R, (1988) *Moral Mazes: The World of Corporate Managers*

James, B G, (1985) *Business War Games*

Jamieson, K M, (1994) *The Organization of Corporate Crime*

Janis, I L, (1972) *Victims of Groupthink*

Jennings, A, Ashworth, A, and Emmerson, B, (2000) 'Silence and Safety: The Impact of Human Rights Law' [2000] Crim LR 879

Johnson, J M, and Douglas, J D, (eds) (1978) *Crime at the Top: Deviance in Business and the Professions*

Johnston, L, (1992) *The Rebirth of Private Policing*

Jones, T, (1988) *Corporate Killing: Bhopals Will Happen*

Kagan, R A, and Scholz, J T, (1984) 'The criminology of the corporation and regulatory enforcement strategies' in K Hawkins and J Thomas (eds) *Enforcing Regulation*

Kamminga, M, (1999) 'Holding Corporations Accountable for Human Rights Abuses: A Challenge for the European Community' in P Alston (ed) *The European Union and Human Rights*

Kamminga, M, and Zia-Zarifi, S, (eds) (2000) *Liability of Multinational Corporations under International Law*

Kapur, R, (1990) 'From Human Tragedy to Human Right: The Accountability of Multinational Corporations for Human Rights Violations' 10 Boston College Third World LJ 1

Katz, J, (1980) 'The social movement against white-collar crime' in E Bittner and S Messinger (eds) *Criminology Review Yearbook: Volume 2*

—(1988) *The Seductions of Crime*

Keane, A, (ed) (1989) *The Modern Law of Evidence* (2nd edn)

Khanna, V, (1996) 'Corporate Criminal Liability: What Purpose Does It Serve?' 109 Harv LR 1477

—(1999) 'Is the Notion of Corporate Fault a Faulty Notion?: The Case of Corporate *Mens Rea*' 79 Boston ULR 355

Kim, S M, (2000) 'Characteristics of Soulless Persons: the Applicability of the Character Evidence Rule to Corporations' [2000] Ill ULR 763

Kirk, D N, and Woodcock, A J J, (1997) *Serious Fraud – Investigations and Trial* (2nd edn)

Knightley, P, Evans, H, Potter, E, and Wallace, M, (1980) *Suffer the Children: the Story of Thalidomide*

Kochan, N, and Pym, H, (1987) *The Guinness Affair*

Kochan, N, and Whittington, R, (1991) *Bankrupt: the BCCI Fraud*

Kochan, T A, and Useem, M, (eds) (1992) *Transforming Organizations*

Koffer, T J, (2001) 'All quiet on the paper front: asserting a fifth amendment privilege to avoid production of corporate documents *in re* three grand jury subpoenas *duces tecum* dated January 29, 1999' 46 Vill LR 547

Kornbluth, J, (1992) *Highly Confident: the Crime and Punishment of Michael Milken*

KPMG, (2001) Report of KPMG Forensic Accounting Amstelveen, The Netherlands

Kramer, R C, (1984) 'Corporate criminality: the development of an idea' in E Hochstedler (ed) *Corporations as Criminals*

Kreisberg, S, (1976) 'Decision-Making Models and the Control of Corporate Crime' 85 Yale LJ 1091

Krisberg, B, (1975) *Crime and Privilege: Toward a New Criminology*

Langbein, J H, (1994) 'The Historical Origins of The Privilege Against Self-Incrimination at Common Law' 92 Mich LR 1047

Laufer, W, (1994) 'Corporate Bodies and Guilty Minds' 43 Emory LJ 647

—(1999) 'Corporate Liability, Risk Shifting, and the Paradox of Compliance' 52 Vand LR 1343

Law Commission, (1989) *A Criminal Code for England and Wales*

—(1996) *Legislating the Criminal Code: Involuntary Manslaughter*

Leader, S, (1999) 'Participation and Property Rights' 21 J Bus Ethics 97

Lederman, E, (2000) 'Models for Imposing Corporate Criminal Liability: From Adaptation and Imitation Toward Aggregation and the Search for Self-Identity' 4 Buffalo Crim LR 641

Leigh, L, (1969) *The Criminal Liability of Corporations in English Law*

—(1977) 'The Criminal Liability of Corporations and Other Groups' 9 Ottawa LR 247

—(1982) 'The Criminal Liability of Corporations and Other Groups: A Comparative View' 80 Mich LR 1508

Leonard, W M, and Weber, M G, (1970) 'Auto Makers and Dealers: a Study of Criminogenic Market Forces' 4 L & Society Rev 4

Lester, A, and Pannick, D, (1999) *Human Rights Law and Practice*

Levi, M, (1981) *The Phantom Capitalists*

—(1987) *Regulating Fraud: White-Collar Crime and the Criminal Process*

—(1991) 'Sentencing White-Collar Crime in the Dark: Reflections on the Guinness Four' 30 How J Crim Justice 257

—(1992) 'Policing the Upper World: Towards the Global Village' in D J Evans, N R Fyfe and D T Herbert (eds) *Crime, Policing and Place: Essays in Environmental Criminology*

—(2001) 'Risky money: regulating financial crime' in N Gray, J Laing and L Noaks (eds) *Criminal Justice, Mental Health and the Politics of Risk*

—(2002) 'Suite Justice or Sweet Charity?: Some Explorations of Shaming and Incapacitating Business Faudsters' 4 Punishment and Society 147

Levine, D B, (1991) *Inside Out: a True Story of Greed, Scandal and Redemption*

Lofquist, W, Cohen, M, and Rabe, G, (eds) (1997) *Debating Corporate Crime*

Maguire, M, (1997) 'Crime Statistics, Patterns, and Trends: Changing Perceptions and their Implications' in M Maguire, R Morgan and R Reiner (eds) *The Oxford Handbook of Criminology* (2nd edn)

Makkai, T, and Braithwaite, J, (1994) 'Reintegrative shaming and compliance with regulatory standards' 32 Criminology 361

March, J G, and Simon, H A, (1958) *Organizations*

Margolis, D R, (1979) *The Managers: Corporate Life in America*

Mars, G, (1982) *Cheats at Work*

—(2000) 'Culture and Crime' in D Canter and L Alison (eds) *The Social Psychology of Crime*

Martin, J M, and Romano, A T, (1992) *Multinational Crime: Terrorism, Espionage. Drug and Arms Trafficking*

Mayer, M, (1990) *The Greatest Ever Bank Robbery: The Collapse of the Savings & Loan Industry*

Mays, R, (1998) 'Towards Corporate Fault as the Basis of Criminal Liability of Corporations' 2 Mountbatten JLS 31

McBarnet, D, and Whelan, C, (1999) *Creative Accounting and the Cross-Eyed Javelin Thrower*

McEwan, J, (1998) *Evidence and the Adversarial Process – The Modern Law* (2nd edn)

McIntosh, M, (1975) *The Organization of Crime*

Meron, T, (1998) 'Is International Law Moving Towards Criminalization?' 9 EJIL 18

Meyer, M A, and Zucker, L G (1988) *Permanently Failing Organizations*

Miles, R H, (1987) *Managing the Corporate Social Environment*

Mills, C W, (1940) 'Situated actions and vocabularies of motive' 5 Am Soc Rev 904

Mintz, M, (1985) *At Any Cost: Corporate Greed, Women and the Dalkon Shield*

Mintzberg, H, (1973) *The Nature of Managerial Work*

Moesteller, R P, (1987) 'Simplifying subpoena law: taking the fifth amendment seriously' 73 Vill LR 1

Mokhiber, R, (1988) *Corporate Crime and Violence*

Monahan, J, and Novaco, R W, (1980) 'Corporate violence: a psychological analysis' in P D Lipsitt and B D Sales (eds) *New Directions in Psychological Research*

Morgan, E M, (1957) *Some Problems of Proof under the Anglo-American System of Litigation*

Morton, J, (1994) *A Guide to the Criminal Justice and Public Order Act 1994*

Muchlinski, P, (1999) *Multinational Enterprises and the Law*

—(2001a) 'Human rights and multinationals: is there a problem?' 77 Int Affairs 31

—(2001b) 'Corporations in International Litigation: Problems of Jurisdiction and the United Kingdom Asbestos Cases' 50 ICLQ 1

Mueller, G, (1983) '*Mens Rea* and the Corporation' 19 U Pitt LR 21

Murphy, P, (1997) *Murphy on Evidence* (6th edn)

Nader, R, (1965) *Unsafe at Any Speed*

Needleman, N, and Needleman, C, (1979) 'Organizational crime: two models of criminogenesis' Sociological Q 517

Nelken, D, (ed) (1994) *White-Collar Crime*

—(1997) 'White-Collar Crime' in M Maguire, R Morgan and R Reiner (eds) *Oxford Handbook of Criminology* (2nd edn)

Norrie, A, (1991) 'A Critique of Criminal Causation' 54 MLR 685

—(1997) *Crime, Reason and History* (2nd edn)

Note, (1961) 'Increasing Community Control over Corporate Crime – A Problem of Sanctions' 71 Yale LJ 280

Note, (1978) 'Individual Liability of Agents for Corporate Crimes under the Proposed Federal Criminal Code' 31 Vand LR 965

Note, (1979a) 'Developments in the Law – Corporate Crime: Regulating Corporate Behavior Through Criminal Sanctions' 92 Harv LR 1227

Note, (1979b) 'Structural Crime and Institutional Rehabilitation: A New Approach to Corporate Sentencing' 89 Yale LJ 353

Note, (1992) 'Corporate Probation Under the New Organizational Sentencing Guidelines' 101 Yale LJ 2017

O'Reilly, G, (1994) 'England Limits the Right to Silence and Moves Towards an Inquisitorial System of Justice' 85 J Crim L & Criminology 402

Observer, 2 September 1990, 'A creed of greed'

—16 February 1992, 'Guinness: Seelig speaks'

—4 October 1992, 'How BCCI hoodwinked the Bank'

—25 October 1992, 'Bingham blames the Bank'

Ockelton, M, (1992) 'Documentary Hearsay in Criminal Cases' [1992] Crim LR 15

Orland, L, (1980) 'Reflections on Corporate Crime: Law in Search of Theory and Scholarship' 17 Am Crim LR 501

—(1993) 'Beyond Organizational Guidelines: Toward a Model Federal Corporate Criminal Code' 71 Wash ULQ 397

Parker, J, (1989) 'Criminal Sentencing Policy for Organizations: The Unifying Approach of Optimal Penalties' 26 Am Crim LR 513

Parliamentary Inquiry Bilmer Disaster, (1999) *De Bijlmerramp: rampenbstrijding en crisis management in Amsterdam* Stadsdrukkerij

Parliamentary Inquiry Construction Industy, (2002) *Parlementaire Enquête Bouwnijhverheid*

Pearce, F, (1976) *Crimes of the Powerful*

Pearce, F, and Snider, L, (eds) (1995) *Corporate Crime: Contemporary Debates*

Pearce, F, and Tombs, S, (1998) *Toxic Capitalism: Corporate Crime and the Chemical Industry*

—(2000) 'States, Corporations and the "New" World order' in G Potter (ed) *Controversies in White-Collar Crime*

Pearce, F, and Woodiwiss, M, (1993) *Global Crime Connections: Dynamics and Control*

Peppin, P, (1995) 'Feminism, Law, and the Pharmaceutical Industry' in F Pearce and L Snider (eds) *Corporate Crime*

Perrow, C, (1984) *Normal Accidents*

Pilzer, P Z, and Deitz, R, (1989) *Other People's Money: The Inside Story of the S & L Mess*

Pitt, H, and Groskaufmanis, K, (1990) 'Minimizing Corporate Civil and Criminal Liability: A Second Look at Corporate Codes of Conduct' 78 Geo LJ 1559

Pizzo, S, Fricker, M, and Muolo, P, (1989) *Inside Job: The Looting of America's Savings & Loans*

Pontell, H N, and Calavita, H N, (1993) 'The savings and loan industry' in M Tonry and A J Reiss (eds) *Beyond the Law*

Posner, R, (1986) *Economic Analysis of Law* (3rd edn)

Potts, M, Kochan, N, and Whittington, R, (1992) *Dirty Money: BCCI: The Inside Story of the World's Sleaziest Bank*

Priest, M, (1997/98) 'The Privatization of Regulation: Five Models of Self-Regulation' 29 Ottawa LR 233.

Punch, M, (1991) 'Tough or Tame?: The Contextuality of Tackling Business Crime in Three Societies' 6 Corruption and Reform 211

—(1992) Address at Honorary Degree Ceremony: Opening Academic Year 1992/93, Nyenrode University, Breukelen, The Netherlands

—(1993) 'Bandit banks: financial services and organized crime' 9 J Contemporary Crim Justice 175

—(1996) *Dirty Business*

—(1999) 'Tackling Business Crime Within Companies' 12 Security J 39

—(2000) 'Suite violence: why managers murder and corporations kill' 33 Crime, Law & Social Change 243

Quaid, J A, (1998) 'The Assessment of Corporate Criminal Liability on the Basis of Corporate Identity: An Analysis' 43 McGill LJ 67

Quinney, R. (1977) *Class, State and Crime: On the Theory and Practice of Criminal Justice*

Rakoff, J, Blumkin, L, and Sauber, R, (1996) *Corporate Sentencing Guidelines: Compliance and Mitigation*

Ramsey, D K, (1987) *The Corporate Warriors: The Battle of the Boardrooms*

Raw, C, (1992) *The Money Changers*

Rawnsley, J, (1996) *Going for Broke: Nick Leeson and the Collapse of Barings Bank*

Reed, M, (1989) *The Sociology of Management*

Reed, M, and Hughes, M, (eds) (1992) *Rethinking Organization*

Reichman, N, (1993) 'Insider trading' in M Tonry and A J Reiss Jr (eds) *Beyond the Law*

Reiman, J, (1990) *The Rich Get Richer and the Poor Get Prison*

Reiner, R, (1997) 'Policing and the Police' in M Maguire, R Morgan and R Reiner (eds) *The Oxford Handbook of Criminology* (2nd edn)

Reisman, M, (1979) *Folded Lies*

Reiss, A J, Jr, (1983) 'The policing of organizational life' in M Punch (ed) *Control in the Police Organization*

—(1984) 'Selecting Strategies of Social Control over Organizational Life' in K Hawkins and J Thomas (eds) *Enforcing Regulation*

Reiss, A J, Jr, and Biderman, A, (1980) *Data Sources on White-collar Lawbreaking*

Reuter, P, (1993) 'The cartage industry in New York' in M Tonry and A J Reiss Jr (eds) *Beyond the Law*

Richardson, G, Ogus, A, and Burrows, P, (1982) *Policing Pollution: A Study of Regulation and Enforcement*

Roberts, J, (1995) 'Some procedural problems in criminal fraud cases' in P Birks (ed) *Pressing Problems in the Law, Volume 1, Criminal Justice and Human Rights*

Roberts, P, (1995) 'Taking the Burden of Proof Seriously' [1995] Crim LR 783

Robinson, J, (1985) *The Risk Takers: Portraits of Money, Ego and Power*

—(1990) *The Risk Takers: Five Years On*

—(2001) *Prescription Games: Money, Ego and Power inside the Global Pharmaceutical Industry*

Roskill, (1986) *Fraud Trials Committee Report*

Rosoff, S M, Pontell, H N, and Tillman, R, (1998) *Profit Without Honor: White-Collar Crime and the Looting of America*

Ross, I, (1992) *Shady Business: Confronting Corporate Corruption.*

Ruggiero, V, (1996) *Organized and Corporate Crime in Europe*

Rugman, A, (2001) *The End of Globalization*

Sanders, A, and Young, R, (2000) *Criminal Justice* (2nd edn)

Savona, E U, (1999) *European Money Trails*

Schlegel, K, (1990) *Just Deserts for Corporate Criminals*

Schrager, L S, and Short, J E, (1980) 'How serious a crime?: perceptions of organizational and common crimes' in G Geis and E Stotland (eds) *White-Collar Crime*

Schulhofer, S, (1974) 'Harm and Punishment: A Critique of Emphasis on the Results of Conduct in the Criminal Law' 122 UPa LR 1497

Schwartz, P, and Gibb, B, (1999) *When good Companies Do Bad Things: Responsibility and Risk in an Age of Globalization*

Seabrooke, S, and Sprack, J, (1996) *Criminal Evidence and Procedure – The Statutory Framework*

Securities and Exchange Commission (2001) *SEC Annual Report: Enforcement Section*

Serious Fraud Office, (1989) SFO First Annual Report

—(2002) *SFO Annual Report 2001/02*

Shapiro, M, (1974) 'Legislating the Control of Behavior Control: Autonomy and the Coercive Use of Organic Therapies' 47 SCal LR 237

Shapiro, S P, (1984) *Wayward Capitalists: Targets of the Securities and Exchange Commission*

Sharpe, S, (1999) 'The Human Rights Act 1998 – Article 6 and the Disclosure of Evidence in Criminal Trials' [1999] Crim LR 273

Shover, N, (1980) 'The criminalization of corporate behaviour: federal surface coal mining' in G Geis and E Stotland (eds) *White-Collar Crime*

Shover, N, and Wright, J P, (2001) *Crimes of Privilege: Readings in White-Collar Crime*

Shrivastava, P, (1987) *Bhopal: Anatomy of a Crisis*

Slapper, G, (1993) 'Corporate Manslaughter: An Examination of the Determinants of Prosecutorial Policy' 2 Social & Legal Studies 423

—(1999) *Blood in the Bank: Social and Legal Aspects of Death at Work*

Slapper, G, and Tombs, S, (1999) *Corporate Crime*

Smith, A T H, (1995) 'The right to silence in cases of serious fraud' in P Birks (ed) *Pressing Problems in the Law, Volume 1: Criminal Justice and Human Rights*

Smith, D, and Tombs, S, (1995) 'Beyond Self-Regulation: towards a critique of self-regulation as a control strategy for hazardous activities' 32 J Management Studies 619

Smith, J C, (1971) 'The Element of Chance in Criminal Liability' [1971] Crim LR 63

—(1989) *Justification and Excuse in the Criminal Law*

Smith, K J M, (1983) 'Liability for Endangerment: English Ad Hoc Pragmatism and American Innovation' [1983] Crim LR 127

Smyth, M, (1998) 'The United Kingdom's Incorporation of the European Convention and Its Implications for Business' 3 E Human Rights LR 273

Snider, L, (1990) 'Cooperative Models and Corporate Crime: Panacea or Cop-out' 36 Crime and Delinquency 373

—(1991) 'The Regulatory Dance: Understanding Reform Processes in Corporate Crime' 19 IJ Sociology of Law 209

—(1993) *Bad Business: Corporate Crime in Canada*

—(1997) 'Downsizing, Deregulation and Corporate Crime' paper presented at Annual Meeting of American Society of Criminology, San Diego

Spencer, J R, (1999) 'European Convention and Rules of Criminal Procedure and Evidence in England' in J Beatson (ed) *The Human Rights Act and the Criminal Justice Process*

Starmer, K, (1999) *European Human Rights Law*

Stavros, S, (1993) *The Guarantees for Accused Persons under Article 6 of the European Convention of Human Rights*

Stein, J, (1992) *A License to Steal: The Untold Story of Michael Milken and the Conspiracy to Bilk the Nation*

Stein, P, (1984) *Legal Institutions – The development of dispute settlements*

Stern, Y, (1987) 'Corporate Criminal Personal Responsibility: Who is the Corporation?' 13 J Corporation L 125

Stessons, G, (1994) 'Corporate Criminal Liability: A Comparative Perspective' 43 ICLQ 493

Stewart, J B, (1991) *Den of Thieves*

Stone, C, (1975) *Where the Law Ends: The Social Control of Corporate Behavior*

Stone, D G, (1990) *April Fools: An Insider's Account of the Rise and Fall of Drexel Burnham*

Stotland, E, and Geis, G, (eds) (1980) *White-collar Crime*

Streeck, W, and Schmitter, P, (1985) *Private Interest Government: Beyond Market and State*

Sullivan, G, (1995) 'Expressing Corporate Guilt' 15 OJLS 281

—(1996) 'The Attribution of Culpability to Limited Companies' 56 CLJ 515

Sunday Telegraph, 2 October 1994, 'Why these ferries are still not safe'

—12 March 1995, 'Barings knew of Leeson ban'; 'Leeson trial "to be in UK"'; 'Cazenove merger plan fuelled Barings' gambles'

Sunday Times, The, 8 March 1987, 'Guinness roll out the barrel'

—2 September 1990, 'Guinnesty: an everyday odyssey of brewing folk'; 'Guinness: the clan keeps its head'; 'Saunders, a man convinced he could do no wrong'

—5 March 1995, 'Meltdown: how an entire financial system failed to stop a trader's mad gamble that flushed Barings bank into oblivion'

Sutherland, E H, (1940) 'White-collar criminality' 5 Am Soc Rev 1

—(1945) 'Is 'white-collar crime' crime?' 10 Am Soc Rev 132

—(1949) *White-collar Crime*

—(1982) 'White-collar crime is organized crime' in M D Ermann and R L Lundman (eds) *Corporate and Governmental Deviance* (2nd edn)

—(1983) *White-collar Crime: The Uncut Version*

Swigert, V L, and Farrell, R A, (1980/81) 'Corporate homicide: definitional processes in the creation of deviance' 15 Law & Society Rev 161

Sykes, G, and Matza, D, (1957) 'Techniques of neutralization: a theory of delinquency' 22 Am Soc Rev 664

Tappan, P W, (1947) 'Who is the criminal?' 12 Am Soc Rev 96

Tapper, C, (1995) 'Trends and techniques in the law of evidence' in P Birks (ed) *Pressing Problems in the Law, Volume 1, Criminal Justice and Human Rights*

—(1997) 'Hearsay in Criminal Cases: An Overview of Law Commission Report No 245' [1997] Crim LR 771

—(1999) *Cross and Tapper on Evidence* (9th edn)

Taylor, I, (1997) 'The Political Economy of Crime' in M Maguire, R Morgan and R Reiner (eds) *Oxford Handbook of Criminology* (2nd edn)

Taylor, R, (1993) *Going for Broke*

Taylor Report, (1990) *Hillsborough Stadium Disaster*

Thompson, P, and Delano, A, (1989) *Maxwell: A Portrait of Power*

Tigar, M, (1990) 'It Does the Crime But Not the Time: Corporate Criminal Liability in Federal Law' 17 Am J CrimL 211

Time, 2 February 1987, 'Fearing that "muck" will stick'

—23 February 1987, 'A raid on Wall Street'

—2 March 1987, 'From pinstripes to prison stripes'

—9 March 1987, 'The Vatican: behind the walls'

—30 March 1987, 'Serving his clients all too well'; 'Wall Street: more suspects held'

—28 December 1987, 'Boesky gets an inside trip'

Times, The, 29 August 1990, 'Guinness three are jailed after Parnes collapse'; 'Judge's tough sentencing receives widespread support'

—20 February 1995, 'Problems for Ward in fight with Guinness'

—19 July 1995, 'Calling into question the Bank's role as regulator'; 'Clarke attacks blunders that sunk Barings'; 'Barings Report'; 'Lost Barings'; 'City welcomes reforms in Barings Report'

Timmer, D A, and Eitzen, S, (1989) *Crime in the Streets and in the Suites*

Tombs, S, (1995) 'Corporate Crime and New Organisational Forms' in F Pearce and L Snider (eds) *Corporate Crime: Contemporary Debates*

Tonry, M T, and Reiss, A J, Jr, (eds) (1993) *Beyond the Law: Crime in Complex Organizations*

Transparency International, (2001) *Global Corruption Report 2001*

Truell, P, and Gurwin, L, (1993) *False Profits: The Inside Story of BCCI, the World's Most Corrupt Financial Empire*

Tuleja, T, (1987) *Beyond the Bottom-Line*

Twining, W, and Stein, A, (eds) (1992) *Evidence and Proof*

Uff Report (2001) *The Southall Rail Accident Report*

Unison and the Centre for Corporate Accountability (2002) 'Safety Last'

Useem, M, (1984) *The Inner Circle: Large Corporations and the Rise of Business Political Activity in the US and UK*

—(1993) *Executive Defense: Shareholder Power and Corporate Reorganization*

—18 November 2002 'From Heroes to Goats . . . And Back Again? How corporate leaders lost our trust' Fortune 40

Vagts, D, (1970) 'The Multinational Enterprise: A New Challenge for Transnational Law' 83 Harv LR 739

Vandivier, K, (1982) 'Why should my conscience bother me?' in M D Ermann and R J Lundman (eds) *Corporate and Governmental Deviance* (2nd edn)

Vaughan, D, (1980) 'Crime between organizations: implications for criminology' in G Geis and E Stotland (eds) *White Collar Crime: Theory and Research*

—(1983) *Controlling Unlawful Organizational Behavior: Social Structure and Corporate Misconduct*

—(1996) *The Challenger Launch Decision: Risky Technology, Culture and Deviance at NASA*

Vise, D A, and Coll, S, (1991) *Eagle on the Street*

Volkskrant, de, 22 November 2001, 'Hoge boetes voor kartelvorming'

—26 June 2002, 'Banken willen "gezond" krediet geven'

Walsh, C, and Pyrich, A, (1995) 'Corporate Compliance Programs as a Defense to Criminal Liability: Can a Corporation Save its Soul?' 47 Rutgers LR 605

Walton, C C, (1988) *The Moral Manager*

Warbrick, C, (1995) 'Self-incrimination and the European Convention on Human Rights' in P Birks (ed) *Pressing Problems in the Law, Volume 1, Criminal Justice and Human Rights*

Ward, R, (1991) 'The black market in body parts' 7 Int Criminal Justice Newsletter 1

Weeramantry, C, (1999) 'Human Rights and the Global Marketplace' 25 Brook JIL 49

Weick, K E, (1979) *The Social Psychology of Organizing*

Wells, C, (1988) 'The Decline and Rise of English Murder: Corporate Crime and Individual Responsibility' [1988] Crim LR 788

—(1993) 'Corporations, Culture, Risk and Criminal Liability' [1993] Crim LR 551

—(1995) 'Corporate Manslaughter: A Cultural and Legal Forum' [1995] Crim LR 45

—(1996) 'The Corporate Manslaughter Proposals: Pragmatism, Paradox and Peninsularity' [1996] Crim LR 545

—(2001) *Corporations and Criminal Responsibility* (2nd edn)

Welsh, R, (1946) 'The Criminal Liability of Corporations' 62 LQR 345

White, L J, (1991) *The S & L Debacle: Public Policy Lessons for Bank and Thrift Regulation*

Whyte, W H, (1956) *The Organization Man*

Wigmore, J, (1981) *Wigmore on Evidence*

Williams, G, (1988) 'The Logic of "Exceptions"' 47 CU 261

Wilson, W, (1998) *Criminal Law: Doctrine and Theory*

Wolf, S, (1985) 'The Legal and Moral Responsibility of Organisations' in J Pennock and J Chapman (eds) *Criminal Justice*

Wolfgang, M, Figlio, R, Tracy, P, and Singer, S, (1985) *The National Survey of Crime Severity*

Wollenberg, S, Associated Press (27 January 1997) 'Pepsi Pulls out of Burma'

Wyngaert, C V D, (ed) (1993) *Criminal Procedure Systems in the European Community*

Yeager, P C, (1993) 'Industrial water pollution' in M Tonry and A J Reiss Jr (eds) *Beyond the Law*

Yoder, A, (1978) 'Criminal Sanctions for Corporate Illegality' 69 J Crim L & Criminology 40

Zander, M, (1995) *The Police and Criminal Evidence Act*

Zedner, L, (1997) 'Victims' in M Maguire, R Morgan and R Reiner (eds) *The Oxford Handbook of Criminology*

Zey, M, (1993) *Banking on Fraud: Drexel, Junk Bond and Buyouts*

Zimring, F E, and Hawkins, G, (1993) 'Crime and justice and the Savings and Loan crisis' in M Tonry and A J Reiss Jr (eds) *Beyond the Law*

Zuckerman, A, (1989) *The Principles of Criminal Evidence*

Index